Spain

Spain

A Phaidon Cultural Guide

With over 650 colour illustrations
and 12 pages of maps

Phaidon

Editor: Franz N. Mehling

Contributors: Arantza Blanco Ganuza, Dr Rosabella Eisig-Ritter, Joachim Hertlein, Dr Karl Kern, Dr Marianne Mehling, José Miranda, Dr José Maria Moran, Dr Eva Rapsilber, Dr Brigitte Regler-Bellinger

Photographs: Editorial Everest, S.A., León; Staatliches Spanisches Fremdenverkehrsamt, Munich; Walter Blau; Joachim Hertlein; Franz N. Mehling; Dr Albin Rohrmoser

Phaidon Press Limited, Littlegate House, St Ebbe's Street, Oxford, OX1 1SQ

First published in English 1985

Second impression 1986

Originally published as *Knaurs Kulturführer in Farbe: Spanien*
©Droemersche Verlagsanstalt Th. Knaur Nachf. Munich/Zurich 1981
Translation ©Phaidon Press Limited 1985.

British Library Cataloguing in Publication Data

Spain. — (A Phaidon cultural guide)
  1. Spain — Description and travel — 1981-
  — Guide-books
  914.6'0483   DP14

  ISBN 0-7148-2352-X

Translated and edited by Babel Translations, London
Typeset by Electronic Village Limited, Richmond, Surrey
Printed in Spain by H. Fournier, S.A.-Vitoria

Cover illustration: Abd-ar-Rahman I aisle in the Mosque (*Mezquita*), Córdoba
(Joseph P. Ziolo, Paris — photo: Oromoz)

Preface

In the twentieth century, Spain has become an extremely popular tourist country. It offers a great variety of scenery – wide plains and craggy mountains, torrid tracts and great rivers, wilderness and luxurious vegetation – and is bounded by the Atlantic on the north and by the Mediterranean with its sandy beaches on the south and east. It is a land of great natural charm and countless, sometimes primeval, cultural treasures. The monuments of Spanish culture may at first glance appear peculiarly foreign to central and northern Europeans, since the Moorish influence from North Africa is unmistakable everywhere, but particularly in the south. The centuries-long struggle between Christians and Moors for dominion over the country has had a decisive effect on its art.

But Spain has also retained a particularly rich ancient heritage. The cave paintings of the late Palaeolithic age are of great interest, especially the superb animal paintings in northern Spain. In early historic times Iberians and Celts left clear traces here. But there are also more and more remains of Phoenician, Punic, Greek and, above all, Roman art being discovered through excavations. Especially fine are the architectural monuments dating from the Visigoth kingdom of the ninth and tenth centuries in northern Spain.

A native Spanish art developed under the influence of the Arabs and their Byzantine-Muslim wealth of forms, frequently blended with Romanesque and later with Gothic elements. Various architectural peculiarities arose — such as the *coro* (choir) moved to the nave of some churches – and an incredible variety of ornamentation, which resulted in works of strange beauty, despite the often apparently cold severity of the Spanish Renaissance and Early Baroque. The Baroque, Rococo, Neoclassical and Modern periods, though sharing the traits typical of middle-European styles, also possess a gravity and gloom suffused with a luminosity and passion that distinguish Spanish art from Italian, for example. Even in the twentieth century, the famous Spanish painters,

Picasso, Gris, Moró and Dalí have not lost this typical Spanish touch, which combines an astonishing inventiveness with marked elements of the macabre.

As with other guides in this series, the entries are arranged in alphabetical order for easy reference. There are over 650 illustrations in colour, of churches, castles, theatres, museums and works of art and including many ground-plans of famous buildings.

The heading to each entry gives the town in bold type, followed by the province and region and a reference to the map section (pp. 386-97), giving page number and grid reference. (Since each map covers two pages and the system of grid squares runs across both pages, only even-numbered page numbers are given.)

Within each entry the sights are generally given in the following order: sacred buildings, secular buildings, particularly significant objects of interest, theatres, museums, less significant objects of interest (under the heading **Also worth seeing**) and places of interest in the immediate vicinity (**Environs**). The appendices consist of a glossary of technical terms, an index of major artists whose works are mentioned, and a list of places cross-referred to the entries under which they are discussed.

The Publishers would be grateful for notification of any errors or omissions.

Abadía
Cáceres/Estremadura   p.392☐D 6

This town, about 40 km. N. of Plasencia, derives its name (abadia:abbey) from a Gothic Cistercian abbey, built within a former Templar castle. Gothic arches lead to the inner courtyard, where the cloisters date from the 13C; an upper gallery was added in the 16C. Horseshoe arches rest on short pillars. The building was later converted into a palace for the Dukes of Alba. The palace and its parklands were designed by Italian and Flemish artists in the 16C. Of the palace gardens, whose praises were sung by Lope de Vega, there remain but a few marble busts (satyrs, bacchantes, dolphins) to recall their former glory.

Adra
Almería/Andalusia   p.394☐H 11

The Phoenician colony of *Abdera*. Formerly a port, it was occupied in turn by Romans and Arabs. Historical traces of its changing population are to be found in the ruins, among which are old Arab *fortifications* with two great towers.

Environs: Berja (13 km. NE): Ruins of the *town fortifications* and remains of Arab *reservoirs*.

Agramunt
Lérida/Catalonia   p.390☐M 3

Armengol IV, Count of Urgel, seized the town from the Arabs in 1070. In 1163 Armengol V granted the town municipal rights, which led to an increase in its size and importance.

Santa María: Consecrated in 1163, this church is a good example of the Lérida school of architecture, which displays Western influences, but is rendered freer and richer by its Islamic elements. The church is a Romanesque building, with a nave and two aisles, ogives and three apses, the central one of which is larger than the outer ones. Nave and aisles are separated from each other by reinforced arches resting on double columns with embellished capitals. In the outer part of the smaller apses there are blind arches. The larger apse is decorated with columns against the wall and the capitals are decorated with simple plant motifs. The *bell tower* is Gothic from the 15C. Most impressive is the *portal* with archivolts supported by 18 columns on each side. The gateway is formed by two square pillars with small columns at the corners; the decoration on the arch shows praying figures integrated with plant motifs. According to an inscription, the figures on the middle of the arch were donated by the Guild of Weavers in 1283. They represent a seated Madonna and Child flanked by the Three Kings to the left and the Annunciation to the right. The capitals of the pillars and columns are embellished by plant and animal motifs and display great technical expertise. In the archivolts the motifs are mainly geometrical. The side portal, far simpler in design than the main one, also has archivolts, which are supported on six pillars with decorated capitals with geometrical motifs.

Ágreda
Soria/Old Castile   p.389☐I 3

Situated on a cliff, the village is dominated by the ruined castle of *La Muela*. This was once encircled by walls, the ruins of which show evidence of a Roman and, more importantly, an Arab past.

Nuestra Señora de la Peña: A Romanesque church with twin aisles. Consecrated in 1193 by Bishop Juan Frontin. Of particular interest are the 15C paintings, especially the altarpiece of St.John the Evangelist.

San Miguel: A mixture of Gothic and Plateresque with a pinnacled Romanesque tower. The church contains outstanding Renaissance paintings; there are several Gothic and Plateresque retables in the chapels.

Nuestra Señora de los Milagros: This church possesses two 15C retables, one Castilian, the other of the Aragonese school, as well as a 14C polychrome Madonna.

Convento de la Concepción: The mortal remains of María de Agreda (nun and adviser to Philip IV) lie here. 17C retable.

Also worth seeing: The church of *San Juan* with a 12C Romanesque portal and 15C Gothic nave; the church of *Nuestra Señora de Magaña* with several 15C Gothic and Plateresque retables from the Aragonese school; medieval *watchtower* and the 12C *Palacio de los Castejones*.

Environs: In **Muro de Ágreda** (*c.* 15 km. SW) there are remains of the old Romanesque *Augustóbriga* and a single-aisled Romanesque church, which has a portal with five archivolts.

Agüero
Huesca/Aragon   p.389☐K 3

Church of San Jaime: Built in the 12C with three apses. Numerous sculptures make the building interesting. The beautiful portal is striking, framed by columns with interesting capitals, which include finely carved scenes from the life of Christ and the Virgin Mary, as well as representations of fabulous beasts and dancing women.

Aguilar de Campóo
Palencia/Old Castile   p.388☐F 2

The town is first documented at the founding of the Benedictine (later Premonstratensian) monastery in 822, but Iberian, Roman and Visigoth finds suggest a much longer history. The town's strategic importance during the Middle Ages is shown by the remains of walls and six surviving gates (of which the *Reinosa* bears a 14C Hebrew inscription), and the ruins of a 12C castle.

Aguilar de Campóo, Santa Cecilia and castle

Monastery of Santa María la Real (Outside the town): This monastery and national monument is the town's most important ancient building. It was founded in 822 and is now in a bad state of repair because it has been uninhabited since the middle of the last century. Some of the most beautiful capitals from the monastery may be admired in the National Museum in Madrid. The Premonstratensians are now trying to restore and renovate it. The Gothic church, with nave, two aisles and 13C polygonal apse, Romanesque cloister, chapterhouse and some other rooms are open to view.

Collegiate church of San Miguel: A Gothic church towering above the main square. The Romanesque main portal originates from an earlier building of the 11C, which was itself built upon the foundations of a Visigoth church. It contains tombs from the 13–17C, the most remarkable being the tomb of the Counts of Aguilar, which is adorned with praying figures; there is also a 12C sculpture.

Also worth seeing: The Romanesque church of *Santa Cecilia* with a tower which has two upper storeys and arched windows; the Gothic *Santa Clara* dates from the 15C; and *San Andrés*, whose Romanesque portal and Gothic-Romanesque arches were set up in the graveyard to prevent their complete destruction. There are many interesting *mansions* from the 13–17C, which display family coats-of-arms; these include the three-storeyed house of the Velardes with its beautiful façade, the houses of the Villalobos, the Solórzanos, the Siete Linajes and in particular the 15C Gothic Casa Rectoral (rectory).

Environs: Some 3 km. N. lies **Corvio**, whose 13C single-aisled Romanesque-Gothic parish church, *Santa Juliana*, has two beautiful 14C sculptures on the high altar. The Romanesque *church* in **Cabria** (4 km. NE), built in 1222, has a portal with fine decorated capitals. **Villavega** (*c.* 6 km. N.): Romanesque parish church with barrel vaults and interesting buttresses in the apse. **Revilla de Santullán** (*c.* 2 km. N.): The church is one of the finest Romanesque buildings in Palencia. **Mave** (*c.* 3 km. S.): Remains of the old monastery, *Santa María la Real*, consist of the 13C church (nave and two aisles, barrel vaults, dome over the transept and archivolts over the portal) and 17C cloister. **Lomilla** (4 km. S.): Single-aisled Romanesque church with beautiful capitals and a Gothic cloister. **Pozancos** (*c.* 5 km. S.): 13C church built in classic Romanesque style and restored in the 16C. **Gama** (*c.* 6 km. S.): 12C Romanesque church with one of the most

beautiful portals in Palencia and very interesting capitals. **Frontada** (7 km. W.) with the 12C single-aisled church of *San Andrés*.

Aguilar de la Frontera
Córdoba/Andalusia   p.394☐ F 9

Santa María de Soterraño has a beautiful altar.

Nuestra Señora del Carmen: This 16C church contains a statue, *Jesus falling beneath the cross,* attributed to Montañés.

Convento de las Carmelitas Descalzas: The chapel interior has sumptuous baroque decoration.

Ruins of Castle Poley: The *Torre del Reloj,* the former clock tower, rises out of the ruins of this Arab castle.

Plaza de San José: An attractive hill-top plaza, particularly remarkable for its oc-

Aguilar de la Frontera, Plaza de San José

tagonal shape; four gateways open into the plaza.

Aguilas
Murcia/Murcia   p.396☐ I 10

Aguilas has a population of about 18,000 and as well as being a holiday resort it is an important trading centre and fishing port.

The town is reputed to be the ancient town of Urci which, as legend has it, was founded in 1200 BC by fleeing Trojans. Up to the 18C there were ruins of extensive Roman thermal baths, but these fell victim to the redevelopment of the town. After an eventful history and repeated devastation, the town was re-established by Charles III in the 18C. The church, with a *Mater Dolorosa* by the sculptor Salzillo, is of particular interest.

Also worth seeing: The *Castle of Juan de Aguilas* on a hill and (12 km. E.) the *Torre de Cope*.

Aibar
Navarra/Navarra   p.388☐ I 2

A hillside town of arcaded streets and old houses with interesting doors; it has preserved its medieval character right up to the present day.

San Pedro: According to records, in 1146 work had already begun on a Romanesque church. Originally designed to have just a nave and two aisles, it gained a Renaissance transept and choir in the 16C. The aisles are topped by half-barrel vaults supported by transverse arches. Decoration on the capitals is splendid, with plant and animal motifs, the most striking of which are the beautifully carved birds. The large late 16C Renaissance high altar is reputed to be the work of Juan de Berrueta; the high altar also has a painting of Christ dating from the time of the Crusades.

Also worth seeing: The *church of Abajo*, is also 12C, but less important than San Pedro. There are ruins of a *castle*, in which

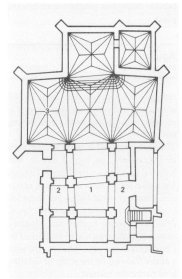

Aibar, San Pedro **1** nave **2** aisle with half-barrel vaulting **3** 16C transept

Aguilar de la Frontera, Santa María

King García Iñiguez was killed in 855 whilst repelling a Moorish attack, and which later served to defend the Prince of Viana from attacks by his father, Don Juan. The town also has many mansions with beautiful Gothic halls and richly decorated armorial bearings on the façades.

Ainsa
Huesca/Aragon   p.389☐L 3

The former capital of the medieval kingdom of Sobrarbe, which extended over the valleys of Bielsa, Broto, Gistain and Puértolas. The town is surrounded by defensive walls and today is a protected monument.

Collegiate church: Romanesque, built in

the 12C, extended several times subsequently. The church has many interesting capitals at its entrance, in the crypt and in the cloister.

Castle ruins: The Moorish system of fortifications was seized by Sancho el Mayor de Navarra in the 11C. The castle was the residence of the Aragonese court in the early days of the Reconquista. A square courtyard is surrounded by high arcades. A five-sided tower has survived. There is a passage from the underground vaults to the Plaza Mayor.

Also worth seeing: Ruins of the 9C monastery, *San Victorián.* The nearby *church* dates from the 18C and contains tombs and altarpieces from the 16C, as well as sculptures and reliquaries. The church of *Santa*

María has a tall Romanesque tower. The town still has many old buildings with Gothic and Plateresque windows.

Environs: Outside Ainsa, a monument dedicated to the 'Cruz de Sobrarbe'.

Alanís
Seville/Andalusia   p.394☐E 9

Nuestra Señora de las Nieves: A 14C Gothic church, altered in the 18C in classical style. The tower dates from the 15C. Inside, the 16C high altar has survived, while the frescos on the vault of the *Capilla Mayor* are classical and 18C. The Mudéjar azulejos in the *Capilla de los Melgarejo* are of particular interest.

Vera Cruz: Apart from a beautiful portal, this church has good Baroque paintings from the 17&18C.

Ermita de Nuestra Señora de las Angustias: A 15C Gothic hermitage, originally built as a memorial to a victory over the Arabs. In the 18C the sanctuary dome, among other things, was restored. Inside there is a 16C painting of Mary Magdalene.

Castle: Built in 1376 and enclosed by a wall. It was involved in the constant feuds between the Trastamara family and the Portuguese, as well as in the feuds between the Dukes of Arcos and Medina Sidonia.

Casa de Doña Matilde Guitart: Interesting inner courtyard with two-storeyed arcades: the lower arches have elements of the Mudéjar style, while the upper ones are baroque and date from the 18C.

Also worth seeing: *Ermita de San Juan Evangelista:* The 14C church of the hermitage has a baptismal font in Mudéjar

style. Outside the town there are ruins of a monastery, the *Basilios de San Miguel de Breña,* and near this there is a hermitage (dome and altar in neoclassical style), which must once have been part of the monastery. The *Casa Cuartel* has a finely worked portal. The *mill* is notable for its 15C tiled portal. *Fuente de Santa María*: A spring, with a Renaissance gable and an 18C ceramic effigy of the Virgin Mary.

Environs: Guadalcanal (*c.* 17 km. NW): Mudéjar church of *La Asunción* with 16–18C alterations (near Arab fortifications). Church of *San Sebastián*: beautiful Mudéjar design; 18C portal. Church of *Santa Ana*: Mudéjar style, though much-altered; 16C tomb decorated with azulejos. Two 18C churches, *La Concepción* and *San Vicente.* Hermitage of *San Benito*: baroque with small Mudéjar portal. Hermitage of *Nuestra Señora de Guaditoca* is also baroque. Nearby are the ruins of the *Castillo de la Ventosilla.*

Alarcón
Cuenca/New Castile   p.396☐I 7

The town was once surrounded by thick walls, some of which have survived, as have the gateways.

Santa María has a façade which looks very like a Roman triumphal arch. The arch over the portal is decorated with reliefs and framed by two pillars. The high altar and the various parts of the altarpiece are the work of the Berruguete school.

Castillo: An imposing castle of Moorish origin, which was rebuilt under Christian rule. Now a Parador hotel.

Also worth seeing: The churches of *Santiago* and *Santo Domingo*, in a style transitional between Romanesque and Gothic.

Environs: Valeria is some 40 km. N. A Roman town and castle were discovered nearby.

Albacete
Albacete/Murcia   p.396□l 7

A town on the plain of La Mancha founded by the Arabs. Today it has a population of about 92,000. Its name comes from the Moorish *Al Basiti*. Before being granted municipal rights by Don Alfonso, Count of Villena, Albacete was merely a large village dependent upon Chinchilla. In 1833 it became provincial capital. In the upper part of the town, *(El Alto de la Villa)*, there are still some remains of the Arab town walls, as well as a few 15–17C mansions, such as the *Casa de los Picos* and the *Casa de la Maternidad*.

San Juan Bautista: Work on this parish church began in the early 16C to the design of the great architect, Diego de Siloé; it was finished in the baroque style. Inside: nave and two aisles with Tuscan columns and a Churrigueresque high altarpiece (1726); in the apse on the right there is a 17C *crucifixion*. The chapels have several Plateresque altarpieces by Juan Muñoz and in the sacristy there are some grisaille paintings (1550).

Museo Arqueológico Provincial: The Archaeological Museum is housed in the modern provincial assembly building (*Diputatión provincial*). The valuable collections consist mainly of objects found in the province: Iberian sculptures from the *Cerro de los Santos*, Bronze Age objects, ceramics, amber and ivory figures from the *Necropolis of Ontur*, as well as Gothic

◁ *Alarcón, Castillo*

Albacete, Lady from Cerro de los Santos (Madrid Archaeological Museum)

Museo Arqueológico, amber figure

sculptures and paintings from the former Museo de la Trinidad in Madrid.

Also worth seeing: The *Ermita de San Antonio* (16C), with Gothic apse and classical interior decoration. High altar with paintings from *c*.1600.

Environs: Hellín (*c*. 60 km. S.): The 16C *parish church* combines elements of Gothic and Renaissance styles. The church of the *Convento de los Franciscanos* was built in the transitional style of the 15–16C. The *Camarín* has rococo decoration with ceramic tiles from Valencia. The town stretches to the foot of a hill upon which lie the ruins of the *Castillo*. Nearby, the *Cueva de Minateda* has rock-paintings of men and beasts.

Alba de Tormes

Salamanca / León   p.386 □ E 5

This little town, lying about 920 ft. above

Albacete, Museo Arqueológico, cross

sea level, and with around 4,000 inhabitants, is one of the most popular places of pilgrimage in Spain. St.Theresa of Ávila (born 1515), mystic and patron saint of Spain, died here on 4 October 1582.

Convento de Carmelitas Descalzas/Convent of Discalced Carmelite Nuns: The convent was founded in 1571 by St.Theresa and added to in the 17C. Interesting Renaissance-Mudéjar portal. Main altar in the style of Alonso Cano and Herrera Barnuevo. Beneath the altar lie the saint's relics in a coffer, which originally belonged to Isabella Clara Eugenia, daughter of Philip II. Fine pictures include: a Mater Dolorosa by Pedro de Mena and paintings by Luis de Morales (Madonna and Child), the Italian Marco Palmezzani de Forlí (Christ on the Cross), Francisco Rizi, González de la Vega and Felipart.

San Juan: Built in the 12C in a mixture of Romanesque and Mudéjar styles. Nave and two aisles. Retable 1771, 14C crucifix, 16C tomb, 14C Madonna and Child, 15C painting of the Adoration of the Magi and an Ecce Homo, painted in the style of Luis de Morales.

Also worth seeing: 12C church of *Santiago*, a mixture of Romanesque and Mudéjar with 15C tombs and 16C retable. 13C *San Miguel* is Mudéjar with Romanesque influence and tombs from 13–16C. 17C *San Pedro* has an early 16C portal and 16&17C sculptures. The *Convento de Santa Isabel* (1481) has a Renaissance chapel, 13C crucifixion and 16C sculptures and paintings. The 13C *Convento de Santa María de las Dueñas/Convento de las Benitas* was restored in the 18C; 16C portal, 15&16C tombs, and baroque altars. A sturdy tower from the 16C palace of the Duke of Alba still stands.

Albarracín
Teruel/Aragon   p.388☐ I 5

A small medieval town on a hill above the river Guadalaviar in the Montes Universales, about 37 km. from Teruel. Its alleys, streets, plazas and palaces have kept their medieval character and the town is so typical of its kind that it has been listed as a national monument. During Visigoth rule, Albarracín was known as *Santa María de Oriente*. In the 11C it was the seat of an Arab ruler, who owed feudal duties to El Cid Campeador. The town gained independence under the rule of the Azagras, who called themselves 'Vassals of the Virgin Mary and Lords of Albarracín'. The town has fortifications dating from two different periods. The oldest part was probably built before 1000 and stretches from the church of Santa María and the Alcázar across the *Portal del Agua* to the town hall. The later part, with nine square towers and the *Torre del Andador*, was built in the 11C. The defences as a whole exemplify the military architectural style of the Caliphs.

Santa María: Santa Maria is the town's oldest church and was begun by the Mozarabs (although it is impossible to tell the exact date of construction). The church was given its present form in the 16C by the architect Quinto Pierres Vedel. It consists of a single aisle to which several chapels were added. The chapel of St.Francis has a Plateresque vault. The main altar, which is not of particular artistic interest, is decorated with 16C paintings of the mysteries of the rosary. In 1599 the church was affiliated to a Dominican monastery. Of this building there remains only the *Torre de Doña Blanca*. Its origins go back to the Middle Ages.

El Salvador, the cathedral: Built around 1200 by Bishop Don Martín as a modest church. It was rebuilt towards the end of the 14C and again in 1532. The tower was built on Romanesque foundations towards the end of the 16C. The main chapel and

Albarracín, view with city walls

altar date from 1533. The chapel of Mary Magdalene has a Renaissance altar consecrated to St. Peter. There is a cathedral museum in the chapterhouse and the collection of 16C Flemish tapestries is worth seeing. The treasury contains a processional cross of the 11–12C and other fine things.

Also worth seeing: The *Bishop's Palace* has a beautiful Baroque façade. The monasteries *San Bruno* and *San Esteban*, both baroque, contain many 17C paintings.

Environs: Numerous caves nearby contain fascinating prehistoric rock paintings, in particular the caves of *Navazo* and *Callejón*.

Albocácer
Castellón de la Plana/Valencia   p.389□L 5

Albocácer is about 55 km. N. of Castellón de la Plana in the Maestrazgo hills, an area held by the Knights of Montesa in the 14&15C. Their castle is still to be found in Albocácer. There are interesting architectural features throughout the Maestrazgos, e.g. the beautiful church doorways or fine paintings, but usually the tourist who comes to Albocácer chooses the town as a starting point from which to visit the Stone Age caves in the area.

Environs: The farmstead *Masía de Montalbana* (12 km. outside Albocácer and not easy to find without a guide, which is available at the town hall): A path leads for two miles from the farmstead to the **Barranco de la Gazulla**, a cave with pictures of a wild boar hunt. The rock paintings here and round about are some 10,000 years old. In the **Cueva Remigia**, only 220 yards away, there is a group of faded rockpaintings and a charming picture of an animal, possibly a roe-deer, which is only 1.7

in. high. The *Barranco de la Valltorta* ravine contains the **Cueva del Civil**, whose rock paintings depict both hunting and battle scenes. **San Mateo** (Catalan Sant Mateu) is 20 km. NE of Albocácer. The village has numerous remains from the Middle Ages, when the Grand Master of the Order of Montesa lived in San Mateo. At that time San Mateo was also the main town of the Maestrazgo area. On the arcaded Plaza Mayor is the Romanesque façade of the parish church, dating from the 13C. The round arches and the portals' capitals are in rather bad condition. The superb Gothic nave and apse (1350–60) have survived. In the sacristy there is an interesting 15C processional cross. The *Town Hall* (near the Plaza Mayor) and the *House of the Borull family* are Gothic; the *Palace of the Count of Villores* was built during the Renaissance. **Catí** is about 25 km. N. of Albocácer. The village has remained true to its medieval appearance and some inhabitants still live in 15C houses. The *Town Hall* with its interesting Lonja (market), mighty pointed arches and Gothic windows makes a severe impression. However, round and pointed arches, as well as the numerous coats-of-arms on the houses, attest to the erstwhile importance of Catí. The *parish church* has a fine altarpiece by Jacomart, dated 1460.

Alburquerque
Badajoz/Estremadura   p.392□C 7

On the Portuguese border, *c.* 44 km. N. of Badajoz, Alburquerque is a picturesque little town, with remains of medieval town walls. It was the birthplace of Juan Ruiz de Arce, the historian of the conquest of Peru. There are the ruins of a *castillo* built in 1276 by Alonso Sánchez, an illegitimate son of the King of Portugal.

Santa María del Mercado: Gothic

Alburquerque, Castillo

church with fortified belfry within the town walls. Inside, a 16C Renaissance altar.

San Mateo (outside the town walls): 16C church with groin vaults. Principally Renaissance, it was renovated in Herrera style in the 17C.

Also worth seeing: Various Gothic houses.

Environs: The **Castillo Azagala** is on a steep hill 14 km. towards Cáceres. It was built in the 13C. The 13C *castle* of **Valencia de Alcántara** (about 42 km. N.) was fiercely fought over during the wars between Castile and Portugal; the *Iglesia de Roquemador* has a 17C baroque high altar and a painting by Morales on the altar in the sacristy; 16C Town Hall in the Plaza Mayor; Gothic-Renaissance *Iglesia de l'Encarnación.*

Alcalá de Chivert
Castellón de la Plana / Valencia   p.389 □ L 6

Alcalá de Chivert, to the N. of Castellón, is probably of Moorish foundation. A ruined castle stands high above the town.

Parish church: Baroque, built in the middle of the 18C. It has a three-storeyed classical façade with sculptures by José Tomás. The tapering, polygonal tower is the work of the architect Barceló. Inside the church there is an interesting retable with paintings attributed to Jerónimo Jacinto Espinosa.

Alcalá de Chivert, Castillo

Alcalá de Guadaira
Seville/Andalusia   p.394 □ E 10

Arab Castle: This fortress, high above the Rio Guadaira, may date back to Roman fortifications. It is a most impressive sight as the walls are defended by many towers. Ferdinand III stayed here in 1248, before moving into Seville (16 km. away). In the 14C the castle was used as a prison for the enemies of Pedro the Cruel. The church of *San Miguel* (on whose day Ferdinand took Seville) can still be recognized as the mosque it once was. The belfry replaces the former minaret.

Mills: Roman and Arab mills stand at the foot of the hills and as a result the town was known as 'Alcalá de los Panaderos' (Bakers'

castle). Nothing remains of the castle's once-famous underground granaries. For many years the town provided Seville with bread.

Also worth seeing: The parish church of *San Sebastián*, in Mudéjar style, with a 16C picture in azulejos above the portal. The parish church of *Santiago* dates from the 15&16C. The *Convento de Santa Clara* has reliefs by Juan Martinez Montañés.

Environs: **Oromana** is a short distance SE and has the remains of foundations of the *Caños de Carmona* (12C), a six mile long aqueduct, which started here and carried water to Seville. The **Castillo de Marchenilla** (5 km. SE) is a beautiful fortress built upon Roman foundations; the *Torre del Homenaje* is 14C.

Alcalá de Chivert, parish church

Alcalá de Henares, Colegio de Málaga

Alcalá de Henares
Madrid/New Castile   p.393☐G 5

The Roman name for the town was *Com-plutum*. When it fell into Arab hands it became *Al-Kala-en-Nahr*, from which derives its present name. The royal seat of many Spanish kings, it later fell to the archbishopric of Toledo. In 1498 Cardinal Cisneros laid the foundation stone of the 'Universitas Complutensis', the great university which was to achieve international fame through the first polyglot bible, the 'Complutensian'. In 1836 the university was transferred to Madrid and the town consequently declined in importance. Alcalá was the home town of Miguel de Cervantes Saavedra, who was born here in 1547.

Colegio de San Ildefonso: The university was founded in 1498 by Cardinal Cisneros and its construction, directed by Pedro Gumiel, was completed in 1508. Of the original building there remains only the Great Hall, which is decorated with lavish panelling and a Plateresque gallery. In 1543 the university's Plateresque façade (one of the most beautiful in Spain) was built under the direction of Rodrigo Gil de Hontañón. The main portal, as well as the windows and balconies are richly carved with Renaissance decoration. The first of the inner courtyards, the baroque main court, was built in 1662 by José Sopeña. The other is by José de la Cótera (1551).

The Church of San Ildefonso: Houses the tomb of Cardinal Cisneros, which was begun by Domenico Fancelli and continued by Bartolomé Ordóñez; it is one of the finest pieces of early 16C Spanish sculpture.

Iglesia Magistral/Los Santos Justo y Pastor: Similar in design to Toledo Cathedral. Gothic portal. A slender 16C tower stands next to it.

Las Bernardas Monastery: Founded in 1618. Brick façade; niche in portal has a statue of St.Bernard. The building is oval with chapels, and is probably the work of the architect Juan Bautista Monegro. The main chapel, decorated with the work of the painter Angelo Nardi, has a tiny sanctuary with four altars.

Jesuit Church: Built 1602–25, to the designs of Juan Gómez de Mora. The façade is framed by large Corinthian columns and crowned by a triangular gabled roof. Four figures by Manuel Pereira stand in rounded niches.

Oratorio de San Felipe Neri, also known as *de los Filipenses*: Houses an interesting collection of 17&18C paintings and a statue of *St.Theresa of Ávila*, variously attributed to Gregorio Fernandez or Manuel Pereira.

Archbishop's Palace: The building originally dates from the 13C, but was altered and added to in the 14–16C. The palace is surrounded by walls and towers, which have battlements and embrasures. Its three façades are of different styles, the two side ones are Gothic-Mudéjar and the main façade is Plateresque and decorated with superb coats-of-arms.

Hospital de Antezana: Founded in 1483 by Luis de Antezana. Originally Gothic, it was greatly altered in 1702.

Casa de Cervantes: House of the author of 'Don Quixote'. The original building is no longer standing; in its place there is a building imitating the style of the town's 16C houses.

Hotel Laredo: Built at the beginning of

Alcalá de Henares, university, tomb of Cardinal Cisneros

this century, using parts of older buildings.

Colegios: In the 16C Cardinal Cisneros had various colleges built. These were extended in the 17C. Among them is the *Colegio de Málaga*, presumably designed by Sebastián de la Plata. Some of these buildings are to be found in the Calle de los Colegios.

Town walls: Only ten bartizans remain of the original 14C defensive walls, which have been continually altered since that time. The Madrid Gate was not built until the 18C. The St.Bernard Gate is 17C.

Castle: The old castle stands outside the town and is of Arab origin; only ruins remain.

Environs: About 15 km. SE of Alcalá de Henares lies **Nuevo Baztán:** This town was founded at the beginning of the 18C by Juan de Goyeneche in order to create a local ceramics and decorative glass industry. In 1709 José de Churriguera was commissioned to draw up the plans. The town is one of the most interesting settlements in the whole of Spain, and was probably built in 1709–13. *Castle:* Two-storeyed with two towers and a bartizan. The design for the courtyard shows the influence of the Herrera school and indeed the staircase is reminiscent of Herrera's own work. *Parade Ground:* This is surrounded by stands with iron railings and stone pillars. *Market Square:* Here there is a somewhat dilapidated fountain, which may have been designed by Churriguera. *Parish church of San Francisco Javier:* The church façade is decorated with towers with slate capitals, which are linked by windows and a stone balustrade. The marble altarpiece within is by Churriguera and depicts St.Francis Xavier. **Loeches** (*c.* 15 km. S.): The parish church, *La Asunción*, is Renaissance. One portal has Gothic features, another is Renaissance and the third is 17C. Inside: nave and two aisles with beautiful cross-arches and a Renaissance dome. The *Dominican Monastery* (1640) serves as a pantheon for the Dukes of Alba. It consists

Alcalá de Henares, façade of the university

Alcalá de Henares, university, Patio de los Filósofos

of a single nave with chapels and a large dome. The interior decoration is typically 17C baroque. The front façade is probably the work of the architect Juan Gómez de Mora. The *Convent of the Discalced Carmelite nuns* is single-aisled.

Alcañiz
Teruel/Aragon   p.389☐L 5

A little town of about 10,000 inhabitants on the banks of the river Guadalupe. The Iberians called the town *Anitorgis*. In 1119 Alfonso I regained the town from the Moors and had a castle built in Pui Pinos. It was Jaime I's favourite residence.

Santa María la Mayor: A baroque col-

legiate church built by Miguel de Aguas in 1736. This huge and impressive church is as large as a cathedral. It has a nave and two aisles divided by pillars. A colossal portal is in keeping with the size of the church. The spacious interior contains numerous sculptures. The high altar is in proportion to the size of the building. There are numerous chapels, which are crowned with cupolas. The *Capilla de la Soledad* has barrel vaults; its shape is modelled on the main church. The *Capilla del Corazón de Jesús* has a pulpit, from which St.Vincent Ferrer used to preach. On the tabernacle is a copy of the *Salvator Mundi* by Juan de Juanes. The baptistery has a copy of the *Baptism of Christ* by Tintoretto. In the *sacristy* there are various Gothic paintings. The main tower is all that remains of an earlier Gothic church.

Alcalá d.H., seat of Cardinal Cisneros

Monastery of Dominicos or Santa Lucía: No longer a religious building. Built towards the end of the 14C and added to in the 17C.

Castillo de los Calatravos: Large parts of this fortress date from the 12C. It was once a seat of the military order of Calatrava in the Aragon area and it is typical of palaces in the region. There are square towers at the sides. The façade dates from the first half of the 18C. The late 12C Romanesque chapel is adorned with numerous wall-paintings. The tomb of the Viceroy of Aragon, Don Juan de Lanuza, on the Gospel side is in a bad state of repair. It was built in Plateresque style by Damián Forment in 1537. Romanesque wall-paintings, primarily of chivalrous themes, are also to be found in the tower.

During the War of Independence of 1809 and the Carlist Wars there were bloody battles in the castle.

Ayuntamiento/Town Hall (Plaza de España): The town hall was built in the 16C in classical style. Façade windows are gabled and in the middle of the façade is the town's coat of arms, which is finely carved. The main building has an arcaded gallery, which is typically Aragonese.

Lonja: Connected to the Town Hall you find the Exchange, built in the 14C. Its façade is reminiscent of that of an Italian Quattrocento building. Above the three arcades there is an earlier gallery.

Also worth seeing: *Dominican Convent*, with a pretty 17C portal; the church of *Los Escolapios*, built towards the end of the 18C; *Franciscan Monastery*, founded in the 16C; the 17C *Carmelite Convent*, with colonnaded portal.

Environs: Cueva del Charco, with cave paintings.

Alcántara
Cáceres/Estremadura   p.392 ☐ D 6

This little town is situated on a cliff on the left bank of the Tagus. It is surrounded by a 20 ft. wall.

History: Called *Norba Caesarea* by the Romans, the town was seized from the Moors by Alfonso IX in 1213 and given to the Portuguese Knightly Order of Pereiro, which was founded in 1170. They settled here in 1218, since when the town has been known as Alcántara.

Bridge: The town takes its name from the bridge over the Tagus (Arabic 'Al Kantara'), which was built in AD 98–103 under Tra-

jan. The bridge is 26 ft. wide, nearly 200 ft. long and is composed of 6 arches. It is constructed of granite blocks without mortar and has been frequently rebuilt as a result of damage inflicted by the Moors e.g. during the reign of Charles V in 1543. In the middle there is a 45 ft. high gate tower in the form of a triumphal arch; it is dedicated to Trajan and on it appear the coats-of-arms of the Habsburgs and the Bourbons. At the bridgehead stands a small Roman temple, 20 ft. high, with the tombstone of Gaius Julius Lacer, the builder of the bridge. On the right bank there is a Gothic fort, dating from the time of Charles V.

Monastery of San Benito: Impressive ruins of the former seat of the Knights of Alcántara, which was built in 1505–76. The façade has coats-of-arms. There is a Gothic tower with Renaissance embellishments. Inside: the nave and two aisles are decorated with carved garlands; the *Capilla Mayor* and the *Capilla de Bravo de Jerez* (on the right) were built by Pedro de Ibarra (1550). At the top of the choir steps there is Renaissance portal which opens to the two-storeyed *cloister*, whose Gothic style shows Renaissance influence. The refectory dates from the 16C.

Santa María de Almocóbar: Extended in Gothic style in the 13C. The Romanesque portal, which stands at the top of a flight of steps, has triple archivolts of the same date. The façade was altered in the 16C. Of interest inside are the 16C winged altar, paintings by Morales, and, in the sacristy, a Plateresque marble tomb of Bravo de Jerez, commander of the order.

Also worth seeing: Ruins of the *castle*, in which the Knightly Order of Alcántara was founded in 1218; the *palaces* of the Marquis de Torre Orgaz, the Counts of

◁ *Alcañiz, Santa María la Mayor*

Alcántara, coat-of-arms

Camilleros, the Viscounts de la Torre, as well as the *Casa de las Animas*.

Alcaraz
Albacete/Murcia   p.396□H 8

A town with 7,000 inhabitants, *c.* 81 km. SW of Albacete, at the southern source of the river Guadelmena, in the Sierra of the same name. Dominated by the ruins of a famous Moorish fortress, it has remained medieval in character. The lower town is most interesting, with the *Plaza Mayor*, a protected monument, in the centre. The steep, narrow streets have many beautiful mansions, whose lavish 15&16C façades are decorated with coats-of-arms.

History: An old Iberian-Celtic settlement,

it was mentioned by Ptolemy as *Urcesa* and called *El Carrash* by the Arabs. Repossessed under Alfonso VIII of Castile. In 1265 Alfonso X (the Wise) and James I (the Conqueror), King of Aragon, met here to sign a treaty uniting against the Moors.

La Trinidad: 15C church on the Plaza Mayor with a splendid Gothic S. portal and interesting tower. Inside there are 15C tombs, painted wooden statues by Salzillo and Roque López and, 17C panelling (in the sacristy); the Plateresque monstrance is by Pedro González (1574).

Also worth seeing: The *Casa Consistorial*, also to be found in the Plaza Mayor (entered through the *Aduana Gate*), with Plateresque reliefs. The *Town Hall* has a beautiful classical portal, dated 1588, and a façade, which is splendidly decorated in Italian style (1530). The *Lonja del Corregidor* (altered in 1718), has Plateresque embellishments and a large upper gallery (1518). The *Torre del Tardón* (clock tower) dates from 1568. The *Lonja de Santo Domingo* (exchange). The 16C church of *San Miguel* as well as the ruins of a medieval *aqueduct*.

Environs: Nuestra Señora de Cortes (Santuario de Cortes), a place of pilgrimage, about 4 km. NW of Alcaraz, in the Sierra de Alcaraz. **Segura de la Sierra** (*c.* 60 km. S. in the mountains) has mansions with coats-of-arms and an Arab castle with a mighty battlemented tower.

Alcázar de San Juan
Ciudad Real/New Castile   p.393□ G 7

Santa María la Mayor: The exact date of construction of the parish church is unknown, but there are good reasons to suppose that in 1226 it was already a parish church. Owing to numerous restorations the original, simple character of the church has been lost, although there are still Romanesque and Arab features inside. The church, as was customary at that time, was built from the ruins of a Roman temple (in

Alcántara, Monastery of San Benito

this case consecrated to Hercules). In the 18C the holy shrine of the Virgin of the Rosary (Camarín de la Virgen) was added. The interior decoration of the church consists mainly of plaster ornaments, mirrors and tiles.

San Francisco: Built in 1532 on a cliff, it is a monumental church, in Gothic transitional style. Consecrated to St.Francis (according to the inscription above the portal) it was built by the entire population. Civil wars have robbed the church of its valuable paintings and works of art.

Santa Quitería: Built by Sebastian de Argüello in the late 16 or early 17C to the designs of Herrera, the architect of the Escorial.

Torreón de Don Juan de Austria: A tower belonging to the old fortified castle, from which the town takes its name. During the Spanish Reconquista many battles between the Spanish and the Arabs took place here. In the 13C the tower had to be restored; another storey was added in the 17C and the upper part of the building altered. It now houses an interesting heraldry museum.

Fray Juan Cobo Archaeological Museum: This building was once the palace chapel and now houses a valuable collection of Roman mosaics of the 1&2C, which came from a nearby Roman villa. The museum displays further objects from the villa and there are also finds from other archaeological sites, e.g. the large stone mortars, which were used to make gunpowder in the 15&16C.

Environs: Campo de Criptana (*c.* 8 km. E.): The supposed site of Don Quixote's battle with the windmills. The *Capilla de la Paz* from the 16C only survives as a ruin. It is partly Byzantine in style. The window spaces resemble embrasures and give the whole building a military air. The image

of the patron saint dates from the 14C or 15C. In **La Hidalga**, near the hill of Criptana, where numerous examples of Iberian pottery with geometrical patterns have been found, there are also traces of an Iberian-Celtic settlement with tombs, weapons and remains of pillars.

Alcocer
Guadalajara/New Castile   p.388☐H 5

Alcocer originally belonged to Doña Guillén de Guzmán, Alfonso X's mistress. It was later owned by the Dukes of Infantado. Some houses decorated with coats of arms date from this time as do the impressive town walls, which have survived.

Santa María: Building of the parish church began in the 13C in a style transitional between Romanesque and Gothic; extended in the late 15C. These different building styles are most apparent in the various doors; the first is Romanesque, the second Romanesque-Gothic and the third

Campo de Criptana, windmills

Gothic. The delightful *tower* consists of two parts: the lower part is square and made of solid stone, the upper part is octagonal with large Gothic windows and dates from the 15C.

Environs: Escamilla is *c.* 10 km. N. of Alcocer. The 16C *parish church* has two beautiful Renaissance portals and an 18C baroque tower topped by 'La Giralda', a weather vane in the form of a woman carrying a flag. In the main chapel there are a few interesting paintings, one of which is baroque. The medieval *castle* is almost totally ruined.

Alcoy
Alicante/Valencia   p.396☐K 8

Alcoy, on the river of the same name, is about 50 km. from the sea. This picturesque medium-sized town lies off the beaten track, surrounded by the *mountains* of the Sierra de Montcabrer (4,550 ft.). With its cold winters and hot summers the region is agriculturally rather unproductive. Today it is an area of industrial development.

In Alcoy, the last ten days of April are a time of religious celebrations, including the staging of a medieval game 'Moors and Christians', in which victory over Islam is celebrated. Such battle games take place in other towns as well, but in Alcoy the 'Fiesta de moros y cristianos' is particularly impressive.

Environs: 3 km. away **La Serreta**, an *Iberian town* of the 4C BC has yielded interesting finds, which are now in Alcoy's archaeological museum. Driving N. from Alcoy, a few kilometres away, is **Cocentaina**, important in the Middle Ages. It is now both an agricultural and industrial town. On the steep hill above the town lie

the ruins of an Arab *Alcázar*, dominated by three well-preserved towers. In the town itself the 15C *Palace of the Dukes of Medinaceli* is of interest. A well-preserved chapel, richly decorated rooms and parts of a Renaissance patio testify to the former importance of the palace and its owners. The church of *Santa María*, built upon the site of an earlier mosque, dates from the 17C and contains notable paintings. Trips to the *Ermita San Cristóbal* and other hermitages of the Sierra are worthwhile, as is climbing Montcabrer (4,550 ft.). **Guadalest,** *c.* 35 km. E. of Alcoy, on a massive, precipitous cliff is dominated by a flat-roofed church tower. It is a real eyrie, in which Moors driven from the Levant in 1609 were able to hold out for a short time. The town comprises barely more than a street, a mansion, a village hall and a church. It is reached via a tunnel through the cliff.

Alfaro
Logroño/Old Castile   p.389☐I 3

San Miguel Arcángel: A 16C church whose façade has two towers. The interior consists of a nave, two aisles and a choir. Numerous 17C sculptures and a Plateresque iron reja are worth seeing. The Capilla de San Ildefonso has a Renaissance altarpiece with a Mater Dolorosa statue.

Also worth seeing: Numerous mansions, such as the *Houses of the Frías, the Echagüe, the Orovio and the Saenz de Heredia*, and the old *Palacio Abacial*.

Algeciras
Cádiz/Andalusia   p.394☐E 11

The original Roman settlement was called *Al Djasiras* by the Moors and belonged to the Kingdom of Granada. Because of its important link with North Africa, Alfonso XI of Castile and León took the town as early as 1344. The Treaty of Algeciras was signed at the Moroccan Conference in 1906 in the *Casa Consistorial*.

Nuestra Señora de la Palma (Plaza del Generalísimo Franco): 18C church in classical style. Inside, nave and four aisles with interesting statues.

Also worth seeing: Remains of an Arab *aqueduct*.

Alicante
Alicante/Valencia   p.396☐K 8

The city of Alicante lies in the middle of the Costa Blanca. From an early date, Mediterranean peoples were attracted by the favourable location and the pleasant climate of the region. Phoenicians, Greeks, Carthaginians and Romans succeeded each other. The Carthaginian general Hamilcar Barca had a fortified camp on the hill where the Castillo Santa Bárbara now stands. In the 2C BC the Romans founded *Lucentum* 3 km. from the town's present position. After the barbarian invasions, the Moors arrived in the 8C. They named the town *Al Lucant*. Repossessed by the Christians in the 13C, Alicante was annexed by the Kingdom of Aragon. For a long time during the Spanish Civil War (1936–39) the town was in the hands of the Republican government.

Today Alicante is bright and pleasing, with its white houses and flat roofs. In recent years streets and boulevards have been widened and parks laid out. The palm-lined Esplanada de España runs along the coast and extends into the Parque Canalejas. The high-rise buildings and many new hotels make Alicante a thoroughly modern city. Of the old Alicante there remains only the *Santa Cruz* quarter—with steep, narrow streets and alleys—where the Moors once lived.

Alcoy, view

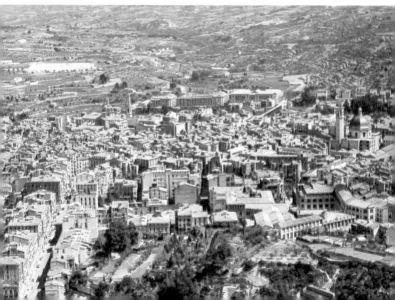

Alicante has little to offer those interested in art, but there are some buildings worth mentioning.

San Nicolás: This church is the city's most important historical monument. Built 1612–62 in honour of the patron saint of the city, Nicholas of Bari, the single-aisled church typifies the austere Herrera style. At the beginning of the Civil War it was gutted and has since been faithfully restored. Inside there are beautiful carved gilded altars (particularly the high altar), as well as fine rejas. A richly carved portal leads to the cloister, which has Churrigueresque decoration.

Santa María: Built by Ferdinand and Isabella in the late 15C, on the site of a mosque. Originally Gothic, later baroque. The very ornate, almost cluttered portal with various pillars, pilasters, pinnacles and cherubs, as well as other decoration, is in stark contrast to the massive unadorned tower. Inside there are beautiful altars, fine paintings and a marble font.

Ayuntamiento/Town Hall: Built 1696–1760, this is the most important secular building in Alicante. The broad façade with two superb portals is flanked by two square towers; a balcony runs along the main floor. There is a balustrade across the top of the building, decorated with guttering and pinnacles. Inside, the *Salón Azul* (Blue Room) with its mirrored gallery is worth visiting.

Castillo Santa Bárbara: The castle is the highest point in the city. The bare 650 ft. cliff rises out of the sea and is visible for miles. As mentioned above, the Carthaginians had a base here and the Romans and the Arabs were later to make use of this strategic position. After the Reconquista the Spanish Kings added to, and greatly restored, the fortress. The castle affords a superb view of the city.
Enthroned upon the smaller hill to the NW is the *Fortress of San Fernando*.

Archaeological Museum: The museum is to be found in the Diputación Provin-

Alicante, Museo Arqueológico

cial building and has finds from Iberian, Greek and Roman times.

Environs: About 20 km. S. of Alicante lies **Santa Pola**, a picturesque fishing village. This pretty little harbour is built upon the ruins of the ancient *Portus Ilicitanus*, which served as a port for Greeks and Romans stationed in nearby Elche. In the middle of the village there is a 16C *Castillo*.

Almadén
Ciudad Real / New Castile   p.393 ☐ F 8

Parish church with a painting of *Nuestra Señora de la Estrella*, dating from the late 15C or early 16C.

Castle of Retamar: In the old part of the town and in a very bad state of repair.

Environs: A few km. NW of Almadén is **Chillón**, which has a late Gothic *church*. The nave has a panelled ceiling and two aisles. *Parish Museum:* Many pieces of religious art.

Almagro
Ciudad Real / New Castile   p.393 ☐ G 8

Almagro, of Roman origin, in the great plain of La Mancha, is the headquarters of the Order of Calatrava, the oldest and most important Spanish Knightly Order. Almagro is also famous for its lace. After the Moors invaded, it was a border town, alternately in the hands of the Arabs and the Christians. In 1214 the Archbishop of Toledo, Don Rodrigo Jiménez de Rada, settled the old Roman *Castrum miraculum* with seventy old noble Christian families. Two years later building began on the Fortress of Calatrava la Nueva, the fortified headquarters of the Order.

Dominican Monastery: Built between 1524–44. The most important architectural monument in the province, with interest-

Alicante, Museo Arqueológico

Alicante, Castillo Santa Barbara

ing cloisters in Ionic and Doric style. Pillars were cut from a single piece of Carrara marble. The rooms have beautiful panelling and carving. The Gothic church has a very fine transept and tombs of the priors. Elements of Renaissance, as well as Graeco-Roman styles, can be seen on the portals.

Madre de Dios: Majestic church with stone pillars by the architects Enríquez (1546). In 1797 the architect Toraya made some alterations.

San Agustín: Former Augustinian house (1635–1821) with fine paintings of the Zurbarán school on the ceilings and walls.

Capilla del Salvador: Built for the famous Augsburg banker Jakob Fugger (1459 – 1525), who had warehouses in Almagro for the mercury and silver mined in Almadén. His coat-of-arms is to be found inside and on the portals. The building is single-aisled with ribbing and beautiful rose-windows.

Former University of Santo Domingo: Begun in 1534. Degrees were conferred between 1597 and 1824. The stone figures in the *Capilla del Rosario* are of interest, as are the shields of the founder, Fernando Fernández de Córdoba, the Order's Master of the Keys, and the coats-of-arms of the Counts of Cabra and the Dukes of Infantado, as well as of the Emperor Charles V.

Town Hall: The beautiful stone staircase and the assembly hall are worth seeing. Inside there is a splendid chest, which is said to have held Fugger's money.

Quarter of the Nobility: The original atmosphere of this quarter has been perfectly preserved in its streets, squares, coats-of-arms and courtyards. Outstanding is the *Palacio Maestral*, in which Alfonso X, the Wise, allowed the Cortes to hold an assembly in 1273.

Corral de Comedias: A 16C theatre, which is a protected monument and one of the town's most important art treasures.

Calzada de Calatrava (Almagro), Castillo de Calatrava la Nueva

Regular productions were mounted here once Spanish classical theatre began to develop. With its decorated wooden galleries, stage and dressing rooms, the theatre is a memorial to the golden age of Spanish theatre. On the Feast of St.Bartholomew (end of August) classical plays are still performed.

Plaza Mayor: An elongated plaza in front of the Town Hall (1372); it is surrounded by stone arcades and small wooden balconies.

Environs: Bolaños de Calatrava to the NE of Almagro. The castle is of Arab origin and the towers, walls and the most important rooms have survived. **Calzada de Calatrava** is 21 km. S. of Almagro. The *parish church* was consecrated in 1526. It has Plateresque portals with Gothic pointed arches on pillars with Renaissance embellishments on the inside. The *Castillo de Calatrava la Nueva*, near the town, was founded in 1217 by the Grand Master Martín Fernández de Quintana. The *de la Es-trella* doorway with its enormous rose-window is striking. The castle chapel has been restored but the rest of the colossal building is in a dilapidated condition. The castle is of enormous proportions and even has two parade grounds. Walls rise vertically from mighty cliffs and the tower continues to defy the passing of centuries. The *Castle of Salvatierra* is, in fact, an extension of a Roman town, started by the Arabs and completed by Christians. In 1198 knights of the Calatrava Order seized the castle. Only the tower, the foundations and part of the underground passages remain. **Moral de Calatrava** is 18 km. SE. The Gothic *parish church* probably dates from the 13C. It was renovated several times, during the Renaissance and in the 18C.

Almansa
Albacete/Murcia   p.396□K 8

A town of 17,000 inhabitants. It lies at the

Almagro, Corral de Comedias

Almagro, university, coat-of-arms

foot of Mugrón, a limestone hill, which rises to about 4,000 ft. and upon which a Moorish fortress still stands. The modern name of this supposed Iberian settlement comes from the Arabs. After the Reconquista it was in the possession of the Knights Templar and from 1312 belonged to the Kingdom of Castile. In 1707, during the War of the Spanish Succession, the Austrians were defeated here by the troops of the Bourbon Philip V; there is a memorial 7 km. outside the town.

In the town itself old Gothic and baroque houses can still be seen. Especially fine are a house with a beautiful façade of 1704 in the *Plaza de las Monjas* and the *Mansion of the Marquis of Montortal.*

Santa María a la Asunción: Gothic parish church with a 15C Renaissance portal (two groups of double pillars supporting an arcade). On either side of the vestibule there is a fine Annunciation; next to the vestibule is a tall clock tower.

Also worth seeing: The 16/17C *Augustinian Convent* has a baroque portal (1704). The *Franciscan Monastery* is 17C. The *Palace of the Condes de Cirat,* also known as the *Casa Grande,* has a striking portal in Italian baroque style.

Environs: The remains of a 4C BC Iberian settlement have been found some 24 km. SW at **Montealegre del Castillo,** also called **Monte Arabi,** at the foot of the Cerro de los Santos. Finds are displayed in the archaeological museums of Madrid, Albacete and Murcia. **Santuario de Belén** (*c.* 14 km. W.) has Arab waterworks.

Almansa, Castillo

Alpera (*c.* 20 km. NW of Almansa): 5 km. from the town are prehistoric caves, the *Cuevas de la Vieja*, and *del Queso*, which have early Stone Age paintings. There are hunting and battle scenes of different dates, which are often painted in layers, one on top of the other. Most striking is a straddle-legged figure standing above four horned animals and wearing feathers. **Yecla** (*c.* 30 km. S.): The *Iglesia de la Asunción*, built in 1512, is essentially Gothic with some Renaissance features. The tower has a frieze with symbolic heads. The *Iglesia del Colegio de San Francisco* (also known as *de los Escolapios*) houses a *Virgen de las Angustias* by Salzillo. The 17C *Iglesia de la Purísima* is almost classical in style. The dome is decorated with glazed tiles. The *Ermita de San Roque* has a Renaissance artesonado ceiling. The *Ayuntamiento/Town*

Hall, a baroque building of 1687, stands next to a 16C tower. Inside there are oil paintings by Andrés Ginés de Aguirre, a native of the town. In the *Casa de la Cultura* there is an interesting archaeological collection. The caves of *Los Cantos de la Visera* on Monte Arabí contain schematic Mesolithic paintings.

Almazán

Soria/Old Castile   p.388☐H 4

Almazán was one of the best fortified towns of Antiquity. Parts of the Roman walls and gateways have survived.

San Miguel: 12C Romanesque church with a two-storeyed portico from the 18C. Inside: fine Mudéjar vaults and, in front of the altar and in the left aisle, 13C stone reliefs (the martyrdom of St.Thomas Becket).

Other interesting churches: A Romanesque church, *Nuestra Señora del Campanario,* has the tombs of some of the town's important families. *San Vicente* has an apse supported by consoles. The *Mercedarian Monastery* has the tomb of Tirso de Molina (1648). *Santa María de Calatañazor* has a beautiful altarpiece and two iron pulpits.

Palacio Hurtado de Mendoza: The rear of the palace has two-storeyed galleries, which were built in the 15C in a style transitional between Gothic and Plateresque. In front, facing on to the Plaza Mayor, there is a Renaissance façade, dating from the 16C; it has a tower at each corner and a beautiful coat-of-arms in the middle.

Environs: Morón de Almazán is *c.* 10 km. SE and has a 16C Gothic parish church, *Iglesia de la Asunción,* which has a beautiful tower and Plateresque façade (1540) with the escutcheon of Charles I. The interior is single-aisled, has stellar vaults, several interesting Gothic and baroque altarpieces, a Romanesque Madonna, a Gothic crucifix of the 14–16C, as well as a tomb of 1516, with the escutcheon of the Mendoza family. The *Town Hall* is a Renaissance building with two-storeyed arcades. The palace next to it has a beautiful late Gothic façade. **Andaluz** (*c.* 20 km. W.): *San Miguel,* dating from 1144, is one of the oldest Romanesque buildings in the province. **Caracena** (*c.* 25 km. S.): The Romanesque church of *San Pedro* has a gallery with seven arches and fine capitals. It is one of the most beautiful in the region.

Almendralejo

Badajoz / Estremadura   p.392☐D 8

A fair-sized town set in fertile countryside between high hills.

Parish church of the Purification: Built in Renaissance style in 1539 with a beautiful bell tower, which can be seen for miles.

Palacio del Marqués de Monsalud: An 18C palace with a splendid collection of Roman antiquities.

Environs: Villafranca de los Barros (*c.* 15 km. S.): The church of *Santa María del Valle* is mainly Renaissance with a 17C high altar. **Ribera del Fresno** (*c.* 9 km. from Villafranca), has various old mansions, including the *Casa de Grajera,* with a Renaissance portal. In **Hornachos** (8 km. from Ribera) there is a 16C municipal granary (pósito), the *Church of the Concepción,* rebuilt in the 16C, and ruins of an Arab *fortress.*

Almería

Almería/Andalusia   p.396☐H 10

A provincial capital, cathedral city and port, Almería lies on the broad Gulf of Almería, enclosed by the mountains of the Sierra de Gádor, the Sierra Almahilla and the Sierra de Gata. The original Phoenician settlement was known in Roman times as *Portus Magnus* and was called *Mirror of the sea* by the Arabs. Almería achieved great importance in the 10C as an independent Emirate, but this position was eroded by repeated sieges. In 1489 Ferdinand and Isabella seized the town and in 1522 it was destroyed by an earthquake.

Cathedral: Shortly after the destruction of the mosque by the earthquake of 1522 work on the fortress-like church began. It was built in accordance with a design of Diego de Siloé and had four corner-towers and battlements. The beautiful N-facing *Renaissance portal,* designed by Juan de

Orea, is adorned with Ionic and Corinthian pillars. Credited to the same artist are the portal in the Calle de Perdones and the carved walnut choir stalls. The cathedral has a nave, two aisles and rib vaults. In the *Capilla del Cristo de la Escucha* the sarcophagus of the church's founder, Bishop Villalán, can be seen. Ventura Rodríguez created the *Trascoro* (18C).

Church of Santiago (Calle de las Tiendas): Remarkable Renaissance portal by Juan de Orea. The church was destroyed in the Civil War.

Alcazaba: Mighty Moorish castle, with multiple fortifications, stepped battlements and defensive towers; frequently restored. Of the original Moorish palace buildings only the ruins of the foundation walls remain. The fortress originates from the 8C. Of particular interest is the massive *Torre del Homenaje* (keep), whose Gothic gateway is embellished with the arms of the Ferdinand and Isabella. The ruins of the Mozarabic Chapel of San Juan

date from the same time. To the N. a rampart links the hill of San Cristóbal with the ruins of a castle, which formerly belonged to the Knights Templar. Looking E. one gets a good impression of the course of the Arab town walls with their towers.

Archaeological Museum (Calle de Javier Sanz): A remarkable collection of prehistoric objects, including local Stone Age finds; Greek and Punic items, good medieval reliefs and a collection of coins.

Also worth seeing: The 18C *church of Santa Clara* (Calle de las Tiendas). The 17C *church of Santo Domingo* (Plaza de la Virgen del Mar): baroque altar; painting of the town's patron saint *Nuestra Señora del Mar*; and altarpieces by Perceval. The *church of San Pedro* (Glorieta de Sartorius): converted from a mosque in the 15C and restored in the 18C. The *church of San Sebastián* (Plaza San Sebastián): classical interior. The 18C *Convento de las Puras* (Calle de Bailén): chapel with baroque portal. The *Ayuntamiento/Town Hall* is in the

Almazán, town gate

Almendralejo, Palacio del Marqués de Monsalud

Almería, cathedral, detail of main portal

Almería, Alcazaba

charming *Plaza Vieja* and has a rather austere façade.

Environs: Gador is 12 km. N. and has a 17C *parish church*, a Moorish *fort* and prehistoric evidence, which includes *megaliths and burial grounds*. **Gergal** is 40 km. N. and has a castle, which has survived quite well. **Tabernas**, 32 km. N., is an interesting old Roman town with Moorish *castle ruins*. **Sorbas** is 55 km. NE with Arab *fortress ruins*.

Almodóvar del Campo
Ciudad Real/New Castile   p.392□F 8

The 13C *parish church* has been restored several times. 14C ceiling; 16C main chapel and tower. Some *castle* ruins.

Almuñécar
Granada/Andalusia   p.394□G 11

Castillo de San Miguel: A Moorish *alcazaba* on a hill, it was restored under Charles V in the 16C; now in ruins. Corners were fortified with round towers. There are some remains dating from the time of Carthaginian and Roman occupation.

Cuevas de Siete Palacios: 'Cave of the seven palaces', a subterranean structure, the purpose of which has not yet become fully clear.

Torre del Monje: To the N., on the Río Verde lies the 'Monk's Tower', which has underground chambers and served as a burial place.

Almería, cathedral, treasury ▷

ON CARLOS

por la diuina clemencia empera
dos semper augusto Rey de alemania
doña juana su madre y el mismo do
Carlos por la gracia de dios Reyes
de Castilla de leon de aragon delas
dos secilias de hierusalem de nauar
ra de granada de toledo de valecia
de gallisia de mallorcas de seuilla
de cerdeña de cordoua de corçega
de murcia de jahen delos algarbes de
algesira de gibraltar delas yslas de
canaria delas yndias yslas z tierra
firme del mar oceano condes de barcelona señores de bizcaya z
de molina duques de atenas z de neo patria Condes de Ruysello
z de cerdania marqueses de oastan z de gociano Archiduques
de austria duques de borgoña z de brauante Condes de flandes
z de tirol zc. Al nuestro justicia mayor y a los del nuestro conse
jo presidentes y oydores delas nras audiencias alcaldes algua
ziles dela nuestra casa y corte z chancillerias y a todos los corre
gidores assistentes gouernadores alcaldes y otros jueses z justi
cias qualesquier ansi dela ciudad z obispado de almeria como
de todas las otras cuidades villas z lugares delos nuestros Rey
nos z señorios que agora son o seran de aqui adelante z a cada uno
z qualquier de vos en vuestros lugares y jurisdiciones a quien z
esta nuestra carta executoria fuere mostrada o su traslado signa
do de escriuano publico sacado con autoridad de juez o de alcal
de. Salud z gracia sepades que pleyto pendio y se trato ante los
del nuestro consejo en grado de segunda suplicacion con la pena y
fiança delas mjll z quinientas doblas que la ley de segouia dispone
entre el obispo dean z cabildo fabricas beneficiados y hospitales
dela yglesia y obispado dela dicha ciudad de almeria dela una par
te z don pedro faxardo marques delos veles dela otra z la qual pri
meramente se començo ante el presidente z oydores dela nra audi
encia y chancilleria que esta y Reside enla ciudad de granada y vino
ante mi el Rey enel dicho grado de segunda suplicacion con la oba
pena y fiança z ciertas sentencias que enel dieron y pronunciaron
y fue sobre Razon que enla dicha ciudad de granada a veinte dia

Almería, cathedral, façade

Also worth seeing: The remains of a Roman *aqueduct* on the Río Seco Bajo, in the upper town.

Environs: Salobreña (15 km. E.): Ruins of a Moorish *alcázar* with remains of a medieval defensive wall. **Motril** (23 km. E.): *Collegiate church of La Encarnación* (16–17C) with fine paintings and a reliquary. The *church of Nuestra Señora de la Caeza* stands on the site of a former Moorish palace. **Castell de Ferro** (46 km. E.) is a ruined Arab *castle*.

Alquézar

Huesca/Aragon   p.388 ☐ L 3

Collegiate church of Santa María:

Built by King Sancho Ramírez and consecrated in 1099 on a site next to his castle. Of the Romanesque predecessor of the present collegiate church only the foundations of the cloister remain. Santa María is Gothic, single-aisled and was built by Juan Segura in 1525–32. The interior is decorated with frescos and has a 17C organ. Juan de Moreto designed the Renaissance high altar and the work, along with the choir stalls, was undertaken by Miguel de Peñaranda and Pedro de Lasaosa. In the Capilla del Santo Cristo there is a beautiful 13C *Christ on the Cross*. The Capilla del Santísimo contains the *Holy Family* by Murillo. The church treasure can be admired in the sacristy. Apart from fine goldsmith's work it includes two 15C altars. One comes from the workshop of the so-called Master of Argüis, the other

Almería, cathedral, detail of choir stall

is a work by Juan de la Abadía. During the building of the cloister in the 16C arcades from the atrium of the old church were used, with the result that Romanesque and Mudéjar elements appear side by side. The capitals of the columns are decorated with ornate carving.

Also worth seeing: The *castle* above the town. In the 11C King Sancho Ramírez took over the Moorish castle, had it rebuilt and added a palace and cloister. The picturesque *Plaza Mayor* is also worth a visit.

Altamira
Santander/Old Castile   p.388 □ G 1

Altamira Caves (open all year, limited numbers on guided tours): The rock paintings in this cave are considered to be the most impressive evidence of prehistoric art in the world. They were executed in the Palaeolithic period and date from around 13,800 BC. The caves are about 890 ft. long. After a small ante-cave comes a large natural hall, known as the 'Sistine Chapel of the Stone Age'. On the roof and walls there are representations of lying and running bison, horses and other animals of the chase, which reach lengths of up to 7 ft. The drawings are coloured and occasionally scratched into the rock. In 1879, at the time of their discovery, the authenticity of the paintings was strongly disputed, until caves with similar pictures were discovered in the south of France.

Environs: Quijas (2 km. S.) has an old

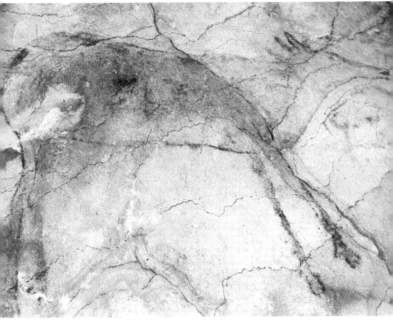

Altamira, cave painting, hind

tower and the *Palacio de Bustamanté*, with a portico of six round arches. **Ibio** (*c.* 4 km. S.) with the *Palacio de Guerra*. **Mazcuerras** (*c.* 6 km. S.) has several *mansions*, for example, Riabeyo. At **Yermo** (*c.* 8 km. SE) there is the Romanesque church of *Santa María*, which was founded in the 9C and rebuilt in 1203; it is single-aisled, with a wooden ceiling and a semicircular apse.

Altea

Alicante/Valencia   p.396☐L 8

Altea, at the head of a bay, is deservedly held to be the most beautiful coastal town in the province. The charming hillside town was a fortress under the Habsburgs. *Fortification systems* from the time of Philip II (16C).

Environs: Following the coastal road NE from Altea, and after crossing the wild gorge of *Barranco de Mascarat*, one finds the small fortified town of **Calpe**, at the head of a bay. This ancient fishing village still has traces of Phoenician, Greek, Roman and Arab settlement. The little Gothic-Mudéjar church, with net vault and pointed horseshoe arches is worth a short visit.

Callosa de Ensarría, on the S. slopes of the Almédia, makes a pleasant excursion from Altea. The stone façade of the church of *San Juan Bautista* is impressive. In a former *monastery* there is a Gothic Madonna, which was left behind by James the Conqueror and is much revered. Desecrated by Moors, it received the name 'Virgen de las Injurias' (The Virgin of Insults).

Altamira, cave painting, bison

Ampudia
Palencia/Old Castile   p.388□F 3

Castle: 15C square Gothic castle with towers at the corners. Inside there are interesting rooms with fine stucco on doors and windows.

Collegiate church: Begun in the 13C, but not completed until the 17C. Gothic pulpit and numerous good altarpieces, including the high altarpiece by Giralte and the Renaissance altarpiece in the Capilla Santa Ana by Francisco Velázquez.

Environs: Valoria de Alcor is *c.* 2 km. S. of Ampudia and has a 12C single-aisled Romanesque church, which has a beautiful portal with interesting capitals. Inside there is a lovely 13C wooden sculpture of the Madonna and a Romanesque sculpture of Christ.

Andorra la Vella
Republic of Andorra   p.390□M 2

References to the 'Andosinos', the Iberian tribe, who obstructed Hannibal's passage over the Pyrenees during his march on Rome in 218BC, go back as far as Polybius. The discovery of Iberian and Roman coins in San Julia De Loria and in Les Escaldes seems to support this tradition. There is some evidence to back up the theory that these valleys were already inhabited in the Iron Age: archaeological remains of the 'Balma Margineda' on the right bank of the river Valira; rock paintings of Ordino; and the burial grounds of Encamp, as well as many other finds. The ceramics of the Sierra d'Enclar and Cedre are relics from the Bronze Age. The first mention of the principality dates from 839, when the cathedral of Seo de Urgel was consecrated, and the six parishes of the principality appeared by name in the 'Acta de consagración'. It has now been proved that the Charter of Charlemagne — in which the founding of the principality was acknowledged—is not genuine; it can be seen in the archives of the Casa de la Vall. At the beginning of the 11C the Count of Urgel handed over the suzerainty of the valleys to the Bishop of Urgel. In 1206 jurisdiction fell to the Counts of Foix, whose protection the Bishops had begged. In 1278, following bloody battles for power, the first agreement between Pedro de Urgo, Bishop of Urgel, and Roger Bernat III, Count of Foix, was signed in the presence of Pedro II of Aragon. In 1288 a second agreement was made, which was signed by Pope Martin IV. These two agreements form the basis of the dual suzerainty of the valleys of Andorra, which holds good to the present day. In 1419 both rulers allowed the inhabitants free election of their own administration ('Consell de la Terra'), the predecessor of the current 'General Council of the Valleys', which is made up of 24 freely elected councillors, who are elected every four years. The rights of the Counts of Foix later fell to the French crown, so that now the government of Andorra is again shared between the Bishop of Urgel (as representative of the Count of Urgel) and the President of the French Republic (as heir to the rights of the House of Foix). The language of the principality is Catalan. The capital, Andorra la Vella, is 3,475 ft. above sea level and, despite the name of la Vella (the Old), is not the principality's oldest foundation.

Casa de la Vall: The seat of the administrative council. A medium-sized building with a simple façade and Romanesque doorway, over which the principality's stone coat of arms (1761) can be seen. Bar-

Altamira, cave painting, bison

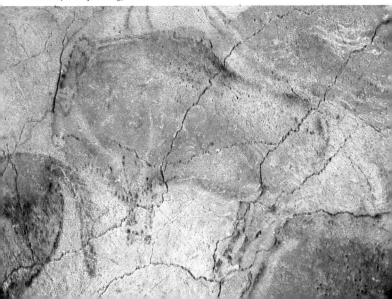

tizans make the building look like a fortress. The square tower on the right side has a pavilion slate roof. To the rear of the building there is another doorway. In front there is a garden, which is separated from the street by an arch, and has two sculptures by Viladomat. Councillors attend Mass before sessions in the *Capilla de Sant Ermengol*, which is part of the Casa de la Vall. The *Sala de Consejos* has interesting murals and the famous cupboard (the 'Cupboard of the Six Keys'), in which the archives are kept. Each of Andorra's six parishes has a key to the cupboard. The great kitchen is also worth seeing. The Court of Justice is completely panelled with wood. On the upper floor is the former councillors' dormitory, which now houses the Museum of Andorra's art and history.

Environs: At **Les Escaldes**, on the edge of town towards Encamp, is the *Chapel of San Miguel de Engolasters*. This little Romanesque church has a three-storey tower with double windows. Judging by the type of ornamentation, the chapel dates from the 11C. **Encamp:** The old 12C *parish church* has a Romanesque bell tower in Lombard style. The *chapel of Sant Romá* is also Romanesque and was consecrated in 1163. In the **pilgrimage church of Nuestra Señora de Meritxell** there is the polychrome Virgin of Meritxell, the patron saint of Andorra (behind the high altar). On the high altar there is a baroque madonna. This pilgrimage church is Andorra's national shrine. **San Joan de Caselles:** This chapel is one of the finest Romanesque buildings in Andorra. It dates from the 13C and has a three-storey tower, which is typically Lombard. The interior has good paintings, including a 14C Gothic painting on wood and a Romanesque Christ on the Cross, the latter consisting of fine 12C multicoloured paintings by Longinos and Estefanon, which were discovered during restoration work. **Santa Coloma**, next to the Romanesque bridge over the Gran Valira, has a 12C Romanesque *church* with a three-storey cylindrical tower and a conical roof. Mozarabic

Andorra, Casa de la Vall

Andorra, Santa Coloma

çade. The free-standing clocktower, the *Torre del Reloj*, is reputed to be the same date as the mosque. Inside there is a painting by El Greco, *Christ on the Mount of Olives*, (second side chapel on the left); the beautiful reja in front of it is the work of Master Bartolomé of Jaén. A further painting, *The Assumption of the Virgin Mary*, is by Pacheco. In the dome there is a 16C fresco.

Casa de Don Gomez (Calle de Maestra): Beautiful baroque palace.

Also worth seeing: A fifteen-arched bridge, originally built by the Romans across the Guadalquivir.

Environs: Porcuna (30 km. SW): The Roman settlement of *Obulco* practised Mithraism. There is also a 15C *castle*. **Montoro** (35 km.W.) has a 16C church, *Santa María*, with Romanesque capitals inside. *San Bartolomé* is late Gothic with a baroque clocktower and panelling within. 14C *bridge* to the old town.

influence can be seen in the polychrome paintings of the triumphal arch. Inside there is an antique font and the 12C *Virgin of Santa Coloma*. The **Castle of San Vincent** was founded by Roger Bernat, the Count of Foix, and has recently been restored.

Also worth seeing: Parish church of *San Julia de Lória, La Cortinada* at Ordino, and the Chapel of *San Cristofor* at Anyos.

Andújar
Jaén/Andalusia   p.394☐F/G 9

Parish church of Santa María la Mayor: A 15C Gothic church, built upon the site of a former mosque; Plateresque fa-

Ansó
Huesca/Aragon   p.388☐K 2

Inhabitants of this little mountain village in the Aragonese Pyrenees have preserved their ancient dialect, customs and costumes to the present day.

Parish church: Post-Gothic, with some baroque altarpieces from the 17&18C.

Antequera
Málaga/Andalusia   p.394☐F 10

Church of El Carmen: Apart from the

Andorra, San Climent de Pal ▷

Churrigueresque altarpiece, there is an exceptionally beautiful Mudéjar artesonado.

Collegiate church of San Sebastián: 16C Renaissance building, with Plateresque portal and elegant baroque tower (1709); inside there are fine choir stalls.

Moorish castle: On the Cerro de San Cristóbal, remains of walls and a tower—*Torre Mocha* or *Papabellotas*—have survived. From here the view extends over the bizarre rock formations of the land around El Torcal.—To the W. the Arab *Puerta de Málaga* with horseshoe arches; now *Ermita de la Virgen de la Espera.*

Arco de Santa María (or *Arco de los Gigantes;* Plaza Alta): A triumphal arch built in 1585 in honour of King Philip II; it stands in front of the church of Santa María.

Town museum (formerly the Renaissance *Palacio Nájera*): In the archaeological sec-tion a beautiful bronze statue of a youth (1C) is displayed alongside a collection of inscriptions and finds from the old 'Anticaria'. On the top floor there is a collection of sculpture, as well as a small picture gallery (Bocanegra, Fray Juan de Correa, Arellano).

Environs: Cueva de Menga (1 km. NW): Vast prehistoric *burial site* dating from *c.* 2000BC. This and the two following examples of earth-covered burial mounds are relics of the late Stone Age (neolithic). The W-E aligned dolmen is a chamber about 82 ft. long and 10 ft. high, the lateral interlocking stone slabs of which are covered by five heavy blocks (the heaviest weighing about 180 tons). Three stone pillars support this enormous weight. In the anteroom on the left symbolic signs and human faces can be made out. Next to this is the 62 ft. **Cueva de Viera** with finely worked stones, which also dates back to the megalithic culture. A stone slab covers the square burial chamber. The **Cueva de Romeral** (a bit off the road by

Andorra, Casa de la Vall, Sala de Consejo

a sugar factory) is a particularly artistically constructed burial mound. It consists of a 75 ft. long gallery, which leads into a domed, round room (the dome effect is created by concentric stone courses); this connects to a further chamber. **Archidona** (14 km. E.): *Castle ruins; medieval town walls; Santuario de la Virgen de Gracia* with traces of a former *mosque*. **Loja** (38 km. E.): Known as 'Lauza' in Moorish times, the town is dominated by the ruins of an *alcázar*, the former residence of Gonzalo de Córdoba, general to Ferdinand and Isabella and known as 'El Gran Capitan'. The 16C church of *San Gabriel* has a fine artesonado. The church of *Santa María* has a 16C baroque façade.

Aoiz
Navarra/Navarra   p.388 □ I 2

A small town on the left bank of the river Iraty.

Parish church of San Miguel: Single-aisled church with groin vault. The original high altar was the work of Juan de Ancheta around 1580; most of the carved reliefs belonging to this old altar were borrowed by the sculptor Juan de Tormes for his baroque altar of 1746. A crucifix is also by Juan de Ancheta.

Aracena
Huelva/Andalusia   p.398 □ D 8

Nuestra Señora de los Dolores: 13C Gothic church of the Knights Templar, on the Cerro del Castillo, with the ruins of an Almohad fort. The beautiful brick tower *Torre Ariosa* (12C) is a remnant of the former mosque; its design with pointed arches and lozenge patterns is reminiscent of the Giralda de Sevilla. The W. façade displays elements of the transition from Romanesque to Gothic. Inside there is a nave, two aisles and a choir and, to the left of the altar, a beautiful grille with praying figures.

Andorra, Casa de la Vall, court of justice

Also worth seeing: Statue by Montañés in the parish *church of the Asunción*. The *Convento de Santa Catalina* has an impressive portal.

Environs: Almonaster la Real (40 km. W.): *Parish church* with interesting portal (16C).

Aranda de Duero
Burgos/Old Castile   p.388☐G 4

Santa María la Real: The façade is a good example of the Isabelline style with the escutcheons of Ferdinand and Isabella and Bishop Fonseca, and sculptures attributed to Francisco de Colonia or Felipe Bigarny. The 15C Gothic church has a nave and two aisles and a beautiful staircase leading to the raised choir. There is a monumental Renaissance pulpit.

Also worth seeing: The remains of the 13C Gothic church, *San Juan Bautista*; a

few 14&15C *mansions*; and the chapel of *Nuestra Señora de las Viñas*.

Environs: Sinovas (*c.* 3 km. N.): The church of *San Nicolás de Bari* has polychrome 13&14C Mudéjar ceiling panelling, which has survived in part. **Gumiel de Hizán** (*c.* 8 km. N.): The *parish church* has an Isabelline portal, a nave and two aisles with groin vaults and a 15C wooden retable. **Pinillos de Esgueva** (*c.* 12 km. NW): 12C Romanesque parish church with a decorated apse and a fine portal.

Aranjuez
Madrid/New Castile   p.392☐G 6

Founded as a small village in the 11C under Arab rule. In the 14C the Grand Master of the Knightly Order of Santiago had a palace built on the bank of the Tagus; this was torn down in 1772. The present palace was commissioned by Philip II and completed under Charles III. The town

Antequera, panorama with Castillo

was laid out in its present form by Ferdinand VI. The court resided here for some length of time.

The Royal Palace: In 1560 Philip II commissioned the architect Juan Bautista de Toledo to build an extension to the hunting lodge built by Charles V. After his death the work was continued by Juan de Herrera. Between 1660–65 the castle was destroyed by fire; Philip V had it rebuilt in 1722. Under Ferdinand VI and Charles III the building was further enlarged by the architect Sabatini. The three-storey main façade has corner pavilions with domes, and the two-storey wings end with arcades. The main building has statues of Philip II, Philip V and Ferdinand VI. Inside, the impressive staircase is by Bonavía. In the *Saleta* one can admire paintings by the Italian Juan Jordani and in the *Antecámara* and *Cámara*, paintings by Lucas Jordán. In the antechapel there are paintings by Mengs and Maella. The *Royal Chapel* is by Sabatini and contains a superb carved marble altar and the well-known

painting *The Immaculate Conception* by Maella. The fresco, *The Virgin and the Evangelists*, is by Baeyeu. The throne room's ceiling is by Camarón and that of the Queen's salon, in Pompeian style, is by Maella. Paintings are by Teniers. The pièce de résistance of the palace is the *Sala de China* (the porcelain room) in the SE tower, which has a large collection of porcelain and, on the walls, priceless Chinese paintings and engravings. The Queen's bedroom and dressing-room are in Italian style with ceiling frescos by Z.G. Velázquez and Camarón. The Arab closet is a copy of the salon of the 'Two Sisters' in the Palace of the Alhambra in Granada.

Casita del Labrador (Farmer's house, at the end of the Calle de la Reina): Commissioned by Charles IV and built by Isidro Gonzales Velázquez (finished in 1803), emulating the Trianon at Versailles. The style is classical with three storeys on a rectangular plan. The façade is flanked by two wings, which form a courtyard, with statues in niches and a beautiful fountain.

Antequera, town museum, boy

Aranjuez, Fountain of Neptune

Aranjuez, Royal Palace

The main staircase has an unusual ramp in gilded bronze. Everywhere there are marble statues and frescos by the best contemporary artists: Duque, Z.G. Velázquez, Maella, Bayeu, Zapelli and others. The rooms are in the style of Louis XVI and Empire style; the Grand Salon is in Etruscan style. The María Luisa Room and the Platinum Room, richly decorated and containing many things of historical interest, are particularly magnificent.

Gardens:

Jardín de la Isla: A park surrounded by a high wall, on an island in the Tagus. It was planned by Isabella the Catholic and Philip II and laid out in the 17C by Sebastián Herrera. It is remarkable for a great abundance of fountains and statues. At the entrance there is the beautiful marble fountain *Hercules and Narcissus*. The *Salón de los Reyes Católicos*, an avenue of plane trees, extends along the left bank of the river; at the end of the avenue are the fountains of Bacchus and Neptune. Within a circular planting of lime trees is the fountain of Apollo, and further on the original clock fountain. The *Fuente de la Espina*, surrounded by Corinthian columns, and further fountains, named after Neptune and Cybele, are partly of marble and partly of bronze.

Parterre: This stretches before the E. front of the Royal Palace and is one of the most beautiful parks in Spain. Begun under Philip V in 1726, fountains, ponds, waterfalls and borders are laid out in French style. Its extension between the old

chapel and the Royal Palace forms the *Jardín de Estatuas* with many busts of Roman emperors.

Jardín del Principe: This garden stretches between the Royal Palace and the Tagus. Dating from the end of the 18C, the park is partly in French style and partly in English, or exotic, style, and made into a most interesting garden by Boutelou. There are splendid fountains (including the fountain of Apollo with a columned hall), various pavilions and the 'Casita del Labrador'.

Churches:

San Antonio: built under Ferdinand VI by the architect Bonavía. Only the atrium, consisting of arches with Ionic columns and a gallery, over which there is a dome, remains. In the middle of the dome there is the royal coat-of-arms.

Parish church de Alpagés: Building began under Carlos III and finished in 1749. It is a simple brick building with a baroque portal and wide-stretched dome.

Monastery of San Pascual: Founded by Charles III and built by the architect Sabatini (finished in 1773). On the wall near the high altar there is a painting of St.Paschal by Mengs. Paintings by Tiepolo and Maella can be seen above the other altars.

Also worth seeing: The *Puente Largo* (Long Bridge) is a beautiful construction with an elegant balustrade, which was finished under Charles III in 1761. The bridge spanning the Tagus is nearly 1,000 ft. long. The *palaces of de Godoy, Medinaceli* and *Osuna* as well as the *Casa de Infantes*, all date from the 18C. Also of great interest is the *Casa de Marinos* with several of the Spanish kings' richly carved ships.

Environs: Ciempozuelos (*c.* 22 km. N. of Aranjuez) was inhabited in prehistoric times, as finds in the region testify. The *parish church of Santa María Magdalena* dates from the 14C and the interior is decorated in the style of 17C Madrid. The ground plan is in the form of a Latin cross and there is a dome over the crossing. The high altar has two oil paintings by Claudio Coello (1682). **Colmenar de Oreja** is *c.* 18 km. E. of Aranjuez. The *parish church of Santa María la Mayor* was built in the late 15 or early 16C. It has an apse and round towers at the corners. Inside there are a nave and two aisles, the nave being most highly finished, with very beautiful groin vaults. The *Museum of Ulpiano Checa* houses a collection of the artist's work. **Pinto** lies 31 km. N. of Aranjuez. The *parish church of Santo Domingo de Silos*, built in the early years of the 16C, contains a beautiful Plateresque pulpit. The altarpieces are baroque, as are the majority of the sculptures and paintings. Of the *castle* there remains a 14C tower, which has furniture and paintings etc. **Valdemoro** (24 km. N. of Aranjuez): The parish church, the *Iglesia de la Asunción*, dates from 1671, and was built on the site of a 14C building. The tower dates from the 18C. The altar is graced with paintings by Goya, and Francisco and Ramón Bayeu. The church also contains other oil paintings and sculptures by various artists.

Aránzazu

Guipúzcoa/Basque Provinces   p.388☐H 2

A popular pilgrimage shrine for 400 years, *Nuestra Señora de Aránzazu* is 2,950 ft. up on Monte Aloña, 8 km. from Oñate. The shrine consists of a basilica of the same

Aranjuez, Casita del Labrador

name and a Franciscan monastery. The monks also run a hotel, as the shrine of the patron saint of the Guipúzcoa province also serves as a holiday resort. The shrine is also referred to as 'Montserrat of Guipúzcoa'.

The **Basilica Nuestra Señora de Aránzazu:** Built to the plans of Laorga and Sainz de Oiza in neo-Romanesque style. The *façade* is decorated with figures of the Apostles and a recently added group of sculptures, by the sculptor Jorge de Oteiza, which represent piety. Inside, there is an *altar* by Lucio Muñoz and paintings by the same artist in conjunction with Carlos Pascual and Nestor de Bastarrechea.

Arbás
León/León   p.386 □ E 2

Collegiate church of Santa María de Arbás: Founded in the 12C under Alfonso VII and built in Romanesque style; later more lavishly developed by Alfonso IX in

1216. In the early 18C various alterations were undertaken. Superb portal with extraordinarily ornate capitals. Next to the church there is a 13C Gothic *chapel* and 12C *hospital*.

Arcos de la Frontera
Cádiz/Andalusia   p.394 □ E 10/11

A picturesque town on a rock on the N. bank of the Rio Guadalete, from which it rises like an amphitheatre. Known as *Medina Arkosh* in Arab times, the name was changed after its seizure by Alfonso X in 1250. The Arab alcázar was succeeded by the castle of the Dukes of Arcos.

Santa María de la Asunción: The church is Visigoth in origin but the present building is in the main 16–18C. Its imposing Plateresque façade dominates the broad Plaza de España. The clock tower with its added bell tower rises above the baroque portal. The W. portal has remained in late Gothic Isabelline style. In-

Aranjuez, Jardín de la Isla, Fuente de Apollo

side, the supporting columns form a so-called palm vault. Diego Roldán made the baroque choir stalls (18C). The *sacristy* contains a silver monstrance (17C), an ivory crucifix (probably by Montañés) and various paintings (Cano, Lagardo).

San Pedro: Late Gothic parish church. In the N. transept two Moorish banners testify to the struggle over Granada. There is a beautiful Gothic retable behind the high altar, as well as paintings by Zurbarán and Pacheco. The baroque side chapels are also interesting.

Also worth seeing: *Hospital de la Encarnación:* Late Gothic portal. *Asilo de la Caridad:* Façade from the time of the viceroys. *Town Hall:* two lovely Mudéjar artesonados and a portrait attributed to Goya. The *Palace of the Dukes of Osuna* has pinnacle towers, which were once part of the former fortifications. *Palace of the Counts of Aguila:* Mudéjar gateway.

Environs: Bornos (12 km. NE): The *church of Santo Domingo* has a painting attributed to Murillo. The baroque choir and 14C choir books are also worth seeing. **Espera:** (12 km. N.) The *parish church:* was begun by Hernán Ruiz (mid-16C) and finished in the early 17C. Baroque high altar has paintings by Pablo Legot. The Chapel of the Sacrament was built in the 18C. *Hermitage del Santo Cristo de la Antigua.* The building served as a parish church up to the 16C and combines various elements of the Romanesque. Arab *fort* with alterations (both Gothic and post-Reconquest); deep cisterns have survived.

Arenas de San Pedro
Avila/Old Castile   p.392□E 6

Arenas de San Pedro is situated in the centre of the vast central massif of the Sierra de Gredos, the peaks of which are almost permanently snow-covered (Pico Almanzor, 8,510 ft.). The beauty and variety of the landscape, as well as the pleasant climate, have made the area one of the most popular summer holiday spots.

Palace of the Infante Don Luis de Borbón: Built in the last years of the 18C by Don Luis de Borbón after his brother, Carlos III, had exiled him from Madrid. The building is not very large and is reminiscent of the Royal Palace in Madrid.

Castillo de la Triste Condesa: The castle of the sad Countess, in which the widow of Don Alvaro de Luna lived and died after her husband was beheaded on the order of Juan II of Castile. Intended to be more a palace than a fortress, it was built in the 15C. It has a square ground plan and a mighty tower; there are also round towers at the corners.

Parish church de la Asunción: Built in Gothic style with a very tall bell tower. Inside there is a fine Renaissance retable and the tomb of San Pedro de Alcántara.

Monastery of San Pedro de Alcántara: Built outside the town by Carlos III in the 18C. The chapel with its octagonal ground plan is the work of Ventura Rodríguez, who also decorated the interior with marble and bronze figures. The chapel contains a remarkable retable by Gutiérrez. Altogether, it is very like the chapel in the Royal Palace in Madrid.

Environs: Cuevas del Valle (c. 16 km. N.): Typically picturesque town of the Sierra de Gredos with unusual architecture; the façades have wooden galleries. **Hoyos del Espino** (c. 20 km. N.): The *parish church*, originally Gothic, has been altered several times. The bridge over the

Aranjuez, Royal Palace, Sala de Papeles Chinos

Tormes is medieval. **Pedro Bernardo** (*c.* 10 km. NE): Founded by Blasco Jimeno 'El Chico' in the 12C. Baroque 17C *parish church*. The *Town Hall* was built in 1589. **Candeleda** (*c.* 12 km.W.): Picturesque village with wooden beams embedded in the walls of the houses, large wooden galleries and enormous awnings. The Gothic *parish church* is 15C. Outside the town is a Romanesque *bridge*. **Navarredonda** (*c.* 18 km. N.): 16C *parish church*; the main chapel was rebuilt in 1805. The massive tower was probably built as a watch tower in the Middle Ages and later converted to a bell tower. Inside there is fine panelling. **Lanzahita** (*c.* 15 km. E.): 16C *parish church* contains an altarpiece dated 1588. The Romanesque *bridge* has been rebuilt.

Arévalo
Avila/Old Castile   p.392☐F 5

A small town situated between endless plains and deep hollows. It is one of the oldest towns in Castile and was the seat of noblemen. Isabella the Catholic and her grandson Ferdinand, the brother of Charles V and Emperor of Austria, spent part of their childhood in the castle. After battles with the Moors (1088) the town regained strength and became of key importance.

San Martín: Built in the 13&14C in Mudéjar style, with a nave, a transept and three apsidal chapels. On the right side, there is a Romanesque portico, which was restored in the 16C. Of particular interest are the two mighty Mudéjar towers. There is a retable by Gregorio Fernández.

Santa María: The church was originally 13C and had a Romanesque apse. However, both church and apse were renovated in the 17C in Mudéjar style, and the apse was given blind arcades.

San Miguel: 13C church completely renovated in the 15C. The square apse

Arenas de San Pedro, Castillo de la Triste Condesa

with barrel vaults is from the original building. Furnishings are Mudéjar. The tower has been truncated. Inside there is a nave framed by two large round arches. The main chapel contains a beautiful 16C retable from the school of Pedro Berruguete.

Gómez Durán or La Lugareja: This 13C church is pure Mudéjar. The Cistercian nuns lived here until they moved into the convent of Santa María in the town. It was probably never completed and all that is left are the three apses and the transept with a vault. The unusual brick decoration is lavish and varied. It is considered one of the best examples of the Mudéjar style.

Other interesting churches: The Emperor Constantine is supposed to have founded the *Iglesia del Salvador*. The present brick building is 16C with a Mudéjar tower. Inside there is a nave and two aisles. The chapel of the alderman Bernal Dávila has a remarkable retable, which was started by Juan de Juni and completed (upon his death in 1573) by his son, Isaac. *San Nicolás* was built on to the Jesuit monastery in 1593 and has a very beautiful stone façade. *San Juan de los Reyes* takes its name from the Catholics, Ferdinand and Isabella, who donated this site (between two of the town wall's towers) for a church. The 16C main gateway has stone vaults. The main chapel has baroque retables. *Santo Domingo* is 16C and has a nave and two aisles. The façade, built in 1572, is very similar to Herrera's work in its austerity. The tower dates from the same time. Inside the decoration is very lavish and there are beautiful baroque retables.

Monastery of Santa María la Real: Built in the 12C on the site of a former royal palace. All that remains of the old palace is a panelled ceiling. The monastery has a fine retable and interesting stucco.

Other monasteries: The monastery *de Montalvas* is 17C and has a beautiful brick façade. The 17C *Hospital de San Miguel* has an interesting baroque façade.

Arenas de San Pedro, medieval bridge

Palaces: The 16C *Palacio de Altamirano* has an unusual corner balcony. The 17C *Palacio del Mayorazgo Verdugo* has a beautiful façade. The *Palacio de los Marqueses de los Altares* is 16C and has reliefs on the walls, unusual grilles on the windows and balconies. The 16C *Palacio de los Cárdenas* has a superb Plateresque façade. In front of the palace is a stone sculpture of a bull. Inside the *Palacio de Villasante* there is an interesting green alabaster sarcophagus.

Castillo de Arévalo: Built in the 14C on the ruins of a previous building. All the rooms in the keep have contemporary 16C furnishings.

Squares: There are three squares altogether: the *Plaza de la Villa*, which has typical buildings with portals; the *Plaza del Arrabal*; and the *Plaza del Real*, which is not as old, but which used pillars from older buildings and ruins in its construction.

Bridges: There are two bridges over the rivers Arevalillo and Adaja, which flow either side of the town. Both are impressive examples of the Mudéjar style of the 14C.

Environs: Adanero (*c.* 20 km. S. on the main road to Madrid): The *Iglesia de la Asunción*, the parish church, is 15C and has a nave and two aisles, which are separated by enormous arches. The Counts of Adanero had the main chapel and transept altered in the 18C. There are some baroque altar-pieces decorated with mirrors, a Plateresque retable, a baroque confessional and a picture of the Madonna and Child with St.Anne by Murillo. The brick gateway dates from the same time as the transept. Outside the town stands the *Palacio de los Condes*, of which only the Renaissance portal remains. **Gutiérre Muñoz** (*c.* 15 km. SE): 16C *Parish church* in the style of Herrera.

Argamasilla de Alba
Ciudad Real/New Castile   p.392□H 7

Castle of Peñarroya (9 km. from the

Arévalo, plaza and towers of San Martín

town, on the road to Ruidera): Moslem in origin, it was handed over to the Order of the Knights of St.John of Jerusalem, after its capture by the Christians in 1251. It is a mix of different styles and consists of two parts, the *Torre del Homenaje* (the keep) and a simple *church* (dated 1229), which has a barrel vault and stands in the middle of the assembly square.

Armentia
Alava/Basque Provinces   p.388□H 2

Armentia was the seat of a bishop from 871–1088. St.Prudent, the patron saint of the province of Álava, was born here.

Basílica San Andrés: A Romanesque church built in the latter half of the 12C and altered in 1276. The church is in the form of a Latin cross and has beautiful capitals. The portico is lavishly carved with biblical figures.

Arnedo
Logroño/Old Castile   p.388□H 3

Santo Tomás: Gothic, built in the first half of the 16C; large rectangular room with stellar vaults.

Monastery of Nuestra Señora de Vico: Baroque interior.

Castle: Very high up. Only the remains of walls and the Puerta del Cristo have survived.

Environs: Munilla (*c*. 15 km. S.): The *parish church* has an altarpiece by Gabriel de Pinedo dated 1622.

Arroyo de la Luz
Cáceres/Extremadura   p.392□D 7

Nuestra Señora de la Asunción: Gothic and Renaissance, built in 15&16C; original façade. Inside there is a large polyptych

Arévalo, Castillo

Arévalo, Iglesia de La Lugareja

columns, some of whose capitals display beautifully carved groups of men and animals. The border of the portal is formed by seven carved consoles, between which beautiful reliefs can be seen. There are also fine capitals supporting the triumphal arch inside the church.

Also worth seeing: A medieval Gothic *castle*, which is in a bad state of repair. The variously decorated waterspouts on the old *houses* are also interesting.

Artajona
Navarra/Navarra   p.388☐I 2

A little medieval town, with imposing, well-preserved defensive walls and twelve prism-shaped watch towers (14C); known as *Cerco de Artajona.*

San Saturnino: A fortified church from the 12&13C. Gothic in structure, but with Romanesque reminders of the Order of Cluny. It has a sculptured façade and a richly carved portal. Inside there is an altar decorated with carvings; paintings dating from 1497–1501 are the work of an unknown master. Paintings originally in the apse are now in the museum of Pamplona.

San Pedro: Built in a style transitional between Romanesque and Gothic. The beautiful portal also dates from this time. Houses a supposed piece of the True Cross.

Hermitage of Nuestra Señora de Jerusalén: Built in the 17C. Houses a beautiful statue of the Virgin Mary, which was probably brought back from a crusade in the Holy Land (together with the above-mentioned fragment of the Cross in the Church of San Pedro), by a knight of Artajona. It is made of gilded and enamelled bronze and may well be a product of the Limoges school, dating from the end of the 12C. It is a most beautifully modelled

by Morales, which has 16 pictures and 4 medallions depicting scenes from the lives of the Virgin Mary and Christ. Morales lived in Arroyo, from 1563–66, during the execution of this fine cycle, which he left to his native Estremadura.

Artaiz
Navarra/Navarra   p.388☐I 2

Parish church of San Martín: Single-aisled Romanesque church built in the latter half of the 12C. Groin vault was added in the 16C. There is a baroque altar and many statues, and in this respect it is similar to the monastery of San Salvador de Leyre. The beautiful portal is particularly striking; at each side there are three

piece with the Madonna on a richly carved throne and the Christ child on her lap. The enamelled throne is also a reliquary.

Astorga
León/León   p.386 □ D/E 3

The seat of a bishop, with a population of *c.*13,000. Beautifully situated on a spur in the Manzanal range of mountains, some 2,850 ft. above sea level. It enjoyed greatest influence in the 9C as a staging point on the pilgrimage route to Santiago de Compostela. As Asturica Augusta it was occupied by the Romans—Pliny the Elder described it as a magnificent city. Astorga was a colony of the Asturians and their seat of justice. It became the seat of a bishop as early as the middle of the 3C. Repossessed by Navarre from the Moors, it was soon under Castilian rule.

Cathedral of Santa María: The original church was consecrated in 1069. Around the middle of the 13C a new church was built on the same site. The present building was begun in 1471 with the choir. In the 16C the rest of the old church was torn down and the construction of the present building started; this was eventually completed in the latter half of the 17C with the building of the two towers and the superb Plateresque W. fa[ce]ade. *Inside:* Gothic nave with fan vaults and clusters of columns. The two large chapels and the sacristy door are attributed to Rodrigo Gil de Hontañón; a 12C statue of the Virgin Mary and a statue of the Immaculate Conception are by Gregorio Fernández. Altarpiece on the high altar is by Bartolomé Hernández and there are fine sculptures by Gaspar Becerra (1558–62). Beautiful 16C choir stalls are the work of several artists (including Juan de Coloniaa and Robert de Mémorancy, who also carved the pulpit). The *Gothic*

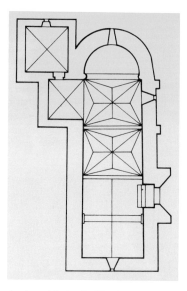

Artaiz, parish church of San Martín The most interesting part of this single-aisled Romanesque church is the fine, highly-decorated portal

transept was restored in 1780. The adjacent *Museo Diocesano-Catedralicio* preserves a considerable treasury, the jewel of which is a wooden reliquary covered with silvergilt, which King Alfonso III, the Great (866–910), donated to the cathedral. The casket was finished in the royal workshops of Gauzon and displays Mozarabic influence. In addition there are: a reliquary (splinter of the True Cross) in gold and silver with jewels (12–13C); a rock crystal chalice; Flemish paintings (16C); ceramics.

Other interesting churches: *San Bartolomé* (founded 11C) with Gothic portal and Romanesque towers. High altar by José de Rozas (16–17C). *El Santuario de Fatima,* formerly San Julián, with beautiful Romanesque capitals on the main portal. Inside there is interesting stucco of the Astorgan school. *San Esteban* and *Santa Marta* together form a complex. The lat-

Astorga, Museo Diocesano, reliquary

ter has fine altarpieces and paintings and an impressive 17C statue of St.Peter of Alcántara (1499–1562). In its present form *San Esteban* dates from the 16C. The *Church of the Holy Spirit* has a splendid Gothic ribbed vault and baroque altars. *San Francisco* dates from the time of St. Francis' stay here. Altered several times, it still has a few ancient capitals, windows and arched vaults. *Santa Clara* was originally early 14C but was destroyed and subsequently rebuilt; portal, arcades in the cloister and windows are 14C.

Palacio Episcopal/Archbishop's Palace (behind the cathedral): Built 1889–1913 in pale granite by Antonio Gaudí (1852–1926) in his unmistakable style, which is based on medieval Gothic and Moorish elements united in his personal form of Art Nouveau. Inside there are four interesting rooms: the *Throne Room* with neo-Gothic windows, the *refectory, office* and the *chapel.* Now it houses the *Museo de los Caminos,* which principally displays souvenirs of the Santiago pilgrims. Paintings (15–16C) and sculptures (12–13C); also Roman finds, including frescos from a villa.

Also worth seeing: *Ayuntamiento/Town Hall,* a beautiful 17C baroque building with clock. The Roman slave prison *(Ergástula Romana),* subterranean vaults (197 ft. long, 32 ft. wide and 28 ft. high). The *town walls* with semicircular towers, of Roman origin, which have survived in part.

Environs: At *Veguellina* (20 km. E. of Astorga, just before the Hospital de Or-

Astorga, Museo Diocesano, 10C casket of King Alfonso III

bigo) is the *Puente de Orbigo*, a 13C bridge of 20 arches. In 1434 the knight Suero de Quiñones and nine companions defended this bridge for 30 days. His deed is celebrated in Spanish heroic epics. *c.* 18 km. N., on the Río Orbigo, lies **Carrizo de la Ribera** with the convent of *Santa María*, built by Cistercians in 1176. The 13C church displays Romanesque and Gothic features. The high altar (1676) is attributed to the school of Gregorio Fernández. Plateresque cloister. Adjacent 18C building.

Astudillo
Palencia/Old Castile   p.388□F 3

Convent of Santa Clara: Founded by Doña María de Padilla in 1365 next to her palace. A Gothic church with Mudéjar roof. In the choir there is a little temple, which is probably the tomb of the foundress; there are also the tombs of her steward, Don Juan González de Pedrosa, and his wife.

Santa Eugenia: Of the original 13C church only the apse has survived. The high altarpiece dates from 1491–1503 and is attributed to Gil de Siloé.

Also worth seeing: The Gothic church of *Santa María* with a 16C high altarpiece by Hernando de Nestosa, several Spanish-Flemish paintings and the tomb of Alonso de Astudillo from the 15C; the Gothic church of *San Pedro* has a 16C high altarpiece with fine reliefs; nearby is the pil-

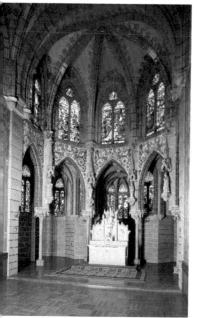

Astorga, Palacio Episcopal, chapel

Astorga, Palacio Episcopal, 16C bust

grimage chapel of *Christus de Torre-Marte*, which has a 15C figure of Christ, a Gothic-Mudéjar pulpit and several 12C Romanesque capitals.

Atienza
Guadalajara/New Castile   p.388☐H 4

Here the child king Alfonso VIII escaped from his uncle, Ferdinand II of León, who wished to contest the young king's throne, an event which is annually celebrated as 'La Caballada'.

Town walls: These date from the 11–13C and encircle the town in double rings. They were defended by numerous towers, parts of which remain. The best known of the town's gates, *San Juan* or *Arrebatacapas*, is still in very good condition.

San Bartolomé: A mixture of dates and styles. It was begun in the 12C, from which time the square apse survives almost unchanged. A century later an aisle was added and this is separated from the original nave by Gothic pointed arches. Both were restored in the 16C. The panelling and altarpiece are 17C, and the *Capilla de Cristo de Atienza* is 18C.

La Trinidad: Of the original church, built around 1200, there remains only the apse, for the rest was rebuilt after a fire in the 15C. Also from this time is the beautiful nave with groin vaulting. The interior is primarily 18C.

San Gil: Originally 13C Romanesque, it was altered in the 16C. Within, nave and two aisles are separated by pointed arches.

San Juan: Late 15C Gothic façade and 16C interior decoration. Nave and aisles

Astorga, Cathedral, detail of choir ▷

are spacious and separated from each other by large cylindrical columns.

Convento de Santa Ana: An interesting Renaissance building with Plateresque portal. Inside there is an 18C work *(Cristo del Perdón)* by the sculptor Luis Carmona.

Santa María del Rey: At the foot of a hill, on which stands a castle. It was begun at the end of the 12C and dating from this time is the Romanesque apse and the two entrance doors, which are decorated with more than a hundred stone figures. The interior was renovated in the 16C; there is a 17C baroque altarpiece.

Plaza del Trigo and Plaza del Mercado y Mayor: Typical squares with arcades and awnings. The buildings for the most part are 16C.

Castle: Built in the 12C on a hill near the town. It is now almost totally ruined. Only the tower is of interest, although one may guess at the original function of some of the ruins.

Environs: Campisábalos is *c.* 28 km. NW. The *parish church* is a building of extraordinary beauty dating from the 12C. The semicircular apse has pillars set against the walls. The tower is very solidly built, but the portico has not survived in particularly good condition. Portal and various arches are Romanesque. Adjoining the S. side is the 13C *Chapel of San Segundo* with a semicircular apse, a door and a frieze. The nave has a simply panelled ceiling and a baroque altarpiece. **Villacadima** (near Campisábalos): The *church* has a Romanesque exterior, apart from the apse and the atrium, which are later, possibly 12C. There are a nave and two aisles, and a groin-vaulted apse, whose altarpiece is composed of 17C paintings.

Aula Dei
Zaragoza/Aragon   p.388☐K 4

12 km. from Saragossa, towards Barcelona, stands a Carthusian monastery of architectural interest.

Astorga, Museo Diocesano, detail of a treasure chest from around 1300

Church: Single-aisled with two choirs and numerous chapels. The high altarpiece is 18C and there is a frieze of eleven paintings by Goya, dated 1774. These form a cycle depicting scenes from the life of the Virgin Mary. The two 16C cloisters at the sides of the building have groin vaults and a painting by Antonio Martínez of scenes from the life of St. Bruno.

Auñón
Guadalajara / New Castile   p.388☐H 5

Worth seeing: The *parish church* is a beautiful early 16C building, in which the late Gothic and Plateresque can be clearly distinguished. Outside the town there is a beautiful medieval *bridge*.

Ávila
Ávila / Old Castile   p.392☐F 5

Capital of the province of the same name,

which covers an area of over 8,000 sq. km. It is the highest town in Spain, standing some 3,700 ft. above sea level. The ancient Roman 'Avela', ringed with walls in the Middle Ages, was built like a cliff-top fortress, on a hill overlooking the river Adaja. The history of the town revolves around wars and acts of heroism; religion and a tendency towards mysticism also played an important role. The town was originally an Iberian-Celtic settlement, which, according to Ptolemy, lay at the eastern periphery of Lusitania and bore the name of 'Obila'. Numerous sculptures depicting bulls and boars can be seen in some of the streets and palaces and these testify to the presence of an ancient Iberian civilization. The 1C AD saw the arrival of Bishop San Segundo, one of the seven apostolic emissaries, who converted the town to Christianity. In the heyday of the Romanesque, during the 'Reconquista' Count Raymond of Burgundy seized the town from the Moors. Thereafter many noblemen from Burgos, León, Asturia and Galicia settled here, giving Ávila the sobriquet 'de los

Astorga, Palacio Episcopal

Caballeros' (Ávila of the Noblemen). It became the residence of several Castilian kings and the seat of the 'Juntas'. St. Theresa, the great mystic and reformer of the Carmelite Order, was born here in 1515. Today the town has some 34,000 inhabitants.

Town walls: Ávila is the very picture of a medieval town, completely surrounded by walls. They are considered the oldest and best-preserved walls in Spain and are impressive for their sheer monumentality. The total length is about 2.5 km., the average height around 40 ft. and the thickness about 10 ft. The walls, built so as to form a trapezium, are defended by 88 towers and crowned with 2,500 merlons (battlements). Nine gates defend access to the city, all are worth seeing and some are of especial beauty, such as San Vicente and Puerto del Alcázar, which are in the E. and oldest section of the wall. The most striking part is the superb 'Cimorro'. This is both the cathedral's apse and also a bastion in the city's ring of fortifications. It is a solid part of the defensive system, which is itself one of the major works of Spanish fortification. The gates Puerta del Mariscal and Puerta del Carmen are in the N. section of the wall, while on the W. side stands the Puerta del Puente or Puerta de San Segundo, which is flanked by two towers. Count Raymond of Burgundy had the town walls built at the suggestion of his father-in-law, King Alfonso VI. They took nine years to construct, from 1090–99. Direction of the work was given to Casandro, a master of geometry, and Florian de Ponthieu, a Frenchman. Materials from earlier buildings, including Roman freestones, and the remains of tombs and former fortifications were used in the construction. Mudéjar features, especially in places in the N. part of the wall suggest that captive Moors may have been involved in the work.

Cathedral: Construction of the cathedral — a Romanesque basilica with a nave and two aisles — began in the first years of the 12C. A few years later, however, the master builder Fruchel took over

Ávila, city walls

direction of the work, altered the plans and built the first Gothic cathedral in Castile, integrating the apse within the defensive walls of the town. The apse forms a large tower in the wall with embrasures and battlements. After Fruchel's death and until the middle of the 14C, further parts were added, including the left aisle, which was built in purest Renaissance style. From the outside the church looks like a granite mountain; inside it is equally unusual, for the walls are made of red and white veined stones, creating strange effects. The cathedral has two *façades:* The W. façade has two towers (one of which is unfinished), built by Juan Guas in the 15C and converted to baroque in 1779. The Apostles' façade dates from the 13C and was altered by Juan Guas. The *nave* is very high and lit by two rows of windows, with beautiful paintings in between. The vaulting, transept and choir gallery are Gothic. The *apse* is a most beautiful example of the Spanish Romanesque. In the nine *chapels* there are interesting Gothic and Renaissance grilles. Renaissance choir stalls are by Cornelis of Holland. The high altar has a painting by Pedro Berruguete, Juan de Borgoña and Santa Cruz, depicting scenes from the life of Christ. The window is 14C. Renaissance altars of Santa Catalina and San Segundo are made from alabaster. There are also two beautiful pulpits of gilded iron, one Gothic, the other Renaissance. Behind the main altar lies the superb alabaster tomb of Bishop Don Alfonso de Madrigal, 'El Tostado'. It is the work of Vasco de la Zarza, who brought the Tuscan Renaissance to Spain. The *Capilla de San Juan Evangelista* has two interesting Gothic tombs. The *Capilla de Nuestra Señora de Gracia* has two tombs from the 12&13C, which are the oldest in the cathedral. The *Capilla de San Antolín* has a splendid 16C altarpiece. The *sacristy], also known as the Capilla de San Bernabé,* has a good alabaster retable, which was made by Isidro Villoldo and Juan Frias (1549–53). Through a Romanesque doorway one enters the 16C *cloister,* originally Gothic but completed with Renaissance decorations. The *cathedral treasury* exhibits in-

teresting carving and painting as well as valuable work in gold. Among the sculptures there is a small 15C figure of the Madonna, which is reputed to be by Vasco de la Zarza. The painting collection is good, particularly a 12C Romanesque panel. Also of interest are two panels from the 15&16C, which are by the Master of Riofrío and depict the Annunciation and the Presentation of Christ in the Temple. A further 15C panel depicts the *Glorification of St.Peter*. An outstanding example of the goldsmith's art is the huge monstrance by Juan de Arfe, which is made up of three parts and is 5ft.8in. high. It was completed in 1571. Of further interest is the chalice by Andrea Petruchi and named after St.Segundo; there are also numerous processional crosses.

San Vicente: Ávila's most important Romanesque building, lying just outside the NE corner of the town wall. It was dedicated to Deacon Vicente of Huesca who, together with his sisters Sabina and Christeta, is supposed to have suffered martyrdom on this site in 304. Essentially Romanesque, there are features of 12&14C Gothic. Coloured sandstone was used as building material. The interior is divided into a nave, two aisles and three large apses. Building started at the beginning of the 12C and by 1109 the three apses as well as the mighty transepts and the lower part of the nave were already practically complete. The *S. portal* is decorated with a particularly beautiful upper ledge, depicting the struggles between Sin and Virtue. The 13C *W. portal*, with its figures of the apostles and Romanesque sculpture, is reminiscent of the famous 'Pórtico de la Gloria' of the cathedral of Santiago de Compostela. Construction began again after the middle of the 12C and Fruchel, who brought Gothic to Ávila, took over. The arcades, arches and triforium galleries above the aisles are Romanesque, but the rest is Gothic. Work finished in the 13C. The interior contains the 13C *tomb* of the saints to whom the church is dedicated. It lies beneath a canopy, protected by grilles and decorated with superb reliefs, which depict

Ávila, city walls

the lives of these saints. The *crypt* has a statue of the *Virgen de la Soterraña*, which Ferdinand III, the Holy (1217–52), particularly admired. The church also contains other beautiful tombs and interesting baroque retables.

San Pedro: Building began in 12C Romanesque and continued in 13C Gothic. The three parallel apses with doors and windows are Romanesque, while the rose-window and the three frontispieces are Gothic. The *W. gate* is a masterpiece of the Spanish Romanesque. In the left aisle there is a painting of *St. Peter in chains* by Morán (1673) and in the right transept a retable (1536) and five pictures from the Berruguete school. The retable in the apse is by Juan de Borgoña. In the *sacristy* there is a beautiful Gothic grille as well as a lavish collection of priestly robes from the 15&16C.

Other interesting churches: *San Andrés* is one of the oldest churches in Ávila and is thought to date from the 11C. It is

Romanesque and has capitals richly decorated in the León tradition. *San Segundo* is also Romanesque. In 1519 the skeleton of San Segundo, the first bishop of Ávila, was found here. The statue of this saint in an attitude of prayer, by Juan de Juni (1572), is one of the artist's best works. In the church of *San Juan* St. Theresa's font is preserved. The main façade has platforms and the coats-of-arms of the town's most important families; from this vantage point they would watch bull fights, which took place in the market-place. *Santiago* is built in Gothic style; the tower dates from the 14C and the façade is pure Renaissance. It houses two retables from the 16&17C. *San Nicolás*, consecrated in 1198, has an apse and three most interesting doorways. Within, there are beautiful 16C retables. The *Chapel of Mosén Rubí de Bracamonte* was built in 1516 and is now part of a Dominican convent; it is a strange mixture of Gothic and Renaissance. The interior contains the 16C tomb of the founder, María de Herrera, and her husband by Váquez Dávila and very beautiful

Ávila, Cathedral (coro), Martyrdom of St. Sebastian

Ávila, Cathedral, St. Paul, 12C

Ávila, Cathedral, font

stained glass windows. The church of *San Esteban* has a Romanesque apse.

Monastery of Santo Tomás: A royal monastery founded by Ferdinand and Isabella. Late Gothic, begun in 1482 and finished in 1494 (after the conquest of Granada in 1492). The church is built in the form of a Latin cross. Sanctuary and the choir are raised, which is unique in Spain, and the vaulting lowered. The altarpiece, dedicated to the life of St. Thomas Aquinas, is the most beautiful of Pedro de Berruguete's works and was painted between 1494–98. The *choir* is probably by Martin Sánchez and with its Gothic decorations is reminiscent of the charterhouse of Miraflores in Burgos. The church has three splendid *tombs*: the alabaster tomb of Prince Don Juan, only son of Ferdinand and Isabella, made by Fancelli of Florence in 1512, and very similar to the tomb he made for Ferdinand and Isabella; the tomb of Núenez de Arnalte, a work by Vasco de la Zarza; and the tomb of Juan Dávila and his wife, which is the work of an unknown artist. The monastery has fine *cloisters*, of which the Kings' Cloister is of particular interest, and an interesting museum of oriental art.

Other interesting monasteries: *Las Gordillas* (1557), with the tomb of its founder María Dávila, a work in the purest Renaissance style by Vasco de la Zarza. *San Antonio*, founded by D.Rodrigo del Aguila (1577): On the left side of this small church is the splendid chapel of the Virgen de la Portería with most beautiful 18C works of art. *Santa Teresa* was built in 1636 upon the site of the house in which the saint was born. Baroque façade by Juan Gómez de Mora, with a three-arched portico and a triangular gable wall. The church has a nave

Ávila, Cathedral, high altar, detail of the ▷
'Epiphany'

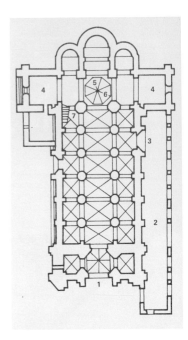

Ávila, Puerta de San Vicente

and two aisles, and inside there are sculptures by Gregorio Fernández. *La Encarnación*, now the St. Theresa museum, is the convent where the saint, who was the new spirit of her order, spent twenty-nine years of her life. In 1630 a chapel was built over her cell and in the convent's cloister some of her manuscripts, as well as a drawing of St. John of the Cross, are preserved. *Nuestra Señora de Gracia* contains a fine 16C altarpiece, probably the work of Juan Rodriguez and Lucas Giraldo. *Santa Ana*, dating from 1350, contains three baroque retables. *San José* or *Las Madres* was St. Theresa's first foundation (1562). The existing church was built in 1608 by Francisco de Mora in the style of Herrera. It has a simple façade with a three-arched portico and a niche containing a statue of St. Joseph, by Giraldo Merlo. Inside, the high

Ávila, San Vicente 1 W. portal 2 *roofed arcade* 3 S. portal 4 transept 5 crossing with dome on pendentives 6 tomb of the church's patron saint (decorated with fine reliefs) 7 staircase to Romanesque crypt.

altarpiece is by Alonso Cano and a praying statue is by Alvaro de Mendoza; the chapel of the Guillamas has two superb tombs and an altarpiece by Pantoja de la Cruz.

Palaces: *De Polentinos* was built in *c* 1535 by a pupil of Vasco de la Zarza. In the façade there is a doorway with a round arch, which is decorated with an escutcheon. Above the windows are two more escutcheons. Embrasures in the façade are similar to those used in fortifications. The inner courtyard is a prime example of Renaissance style peculiar to Ávila. *Los*

Ávila, San Vicente

Águila and Torres Arias has a Renaissance façade with columns, escutcheons and a balcony. *Oñate* or *Torreón de los Guzmanes* has the most beautiful defensive tower in the town. The inner courtyard has a splendid Iberian sculpture of a boar, a cross between a pig and a bull. The *House of the Marqueses de las Navas or the Dávila* has Gothic windows and doorways. *De la Audiencia* was built in 1541; the door and windows are decorated with pillars. *De los Velada* has a mighty defensive tower and sturdy corner columns with escutcheons guarded by lions. Also of interest are the grilles in front of the windows, the Gothic carving on the observation tower and in the inner courtyard. *Del Verdugo*, built towards the end of the 15C, has two mighty defensive towers at the sides. Above the doorway is a frieze with many escutcheons and

a Plateresque window. *La Casa de los Deanes* has a Renaissance façade with two rows of columns with decorated capitals and numerous escutcheons. The inner courtyard has two galleries with beautiful Gothic arches. Nowadays this house is a museum of Celtic-Iberian finds from Ulaca, Las Cogotas and Mesa Miranda. The *Bracamonde House* is 16C Plateresque. Of the two Bishop's palaces, the earlier is Gothic and the later Plateresque. The *Cruz de los Cuatro Postes:* is a stone cross on the road to Salamanca, a site with a superb view of the town.

Also worth seeing: *Ermita de San Martín*, with Mudéjar decorations and Romanesque tower. *Ermita de la Cabeza*, a 16C Mudéjar brick building. The *Inclusa*, formerly a Franciscan convent, has a

Renaissance façade. *Further secular buildings:* Ávila possesses a large number of old houses and palaces. Spread over many streets, they reflect the solemnity and simplicity of the Gothic era of Ferdinand and Isabella.

Environs: *c.* 20 km. E. lies **Aldeavieja** with the Renaissance *Santuario de Nuestra Señora del Cubillo,* built by Juan de Herrera. **La Serrada** (*c.* 9 km. E.) has a 16C Gothic *parish church* with an interesting tower. **Muñopepe** (*c.* 14 km. W.) has a 16C *parish church* which is a mixture of Gothic and Renaissance. The 16C *parish church* of **Villatoro** (*c.* 35 km. W.) bears the Dávila escutcheon on its façade; the apse and the transept are Gothic. Very near to **Solosancho** (*c.* 25 km. SE of Ávila) is the *wilderness of Ulaca,* a fortified area surrounded by a double pentagonal wall 4,020 ft long. It dates from the Iron Age, 4–3 BC, and is attributed to the 'Cogotas' culture. The remains of gateways and sacrificial altars are still visible. All of the carved granite boars of that age come from here and

indeed one stands in the square in front of the church. The 15C *castle of Villaviciosa* is a residential fortress of unique construction. **Cardeñosa** (*c.* 10 km. N.): The *wilderness of Las Cogotas,* outside the town, is Iron Age, dating from some time between the 4–3C BC. It is made up of two fortified areas with walls. One area is surrounded by four rings of walls, the innermost one of which has four gateways flanked by round towers, and served as an acropolis. The other area is a necropolis with more than 1,600 graves. **Sotalvo** (*c.* 28 km. SW): The 15C *castle of Aunqueospese* belonged to the House of the Medinaceli. Its irregular ground plan conforms to the underlying rock, which is its foundation. Inside are three floors of interesting rooms. **Vega de Santa María** (*c.* 30 km. N.) has a 15C *parish church* with a Mudéjar tower. The nave has 16C panelling. **Las Navas del Marqués** (*c.* 50 km. E.): 15C Gothic *parish church*; the 16C *castle* is rather more a palace than a castle. It was rebuilt in order to preserve an exceptionally interesting Renaissance courtyard.

Ávila, San Vicente, vaulting

Avilés

Oviedo/Asturia   p.386☐E 1

Avilés is of Roman origin. In the 12C, under Alfonso VI, the town was granted various privileges, which it successfully defended over a considerable period. Under Alfonso X, the Wise, the citizens were no longer obliged to pay taxes to Oviedo. Nowadays Avilés is a modern industrial town. Nevertheless, in the centre, around the Plaza de España, it has preserved a medieval atmosphere with arcaded streets, narrow alleys and old houses. Pedro Menéndez, Governor of Florida, and the painter Juan Carreño de Miranda were born in Avilés.

San Francisco: A 13–14C Gothic church

near the Plaza de España. Single-aisled, some Romanesque features have survived, e.g. the pillars and stone window arches to the right of the crossing. There are beautifully carved Gothic stone tombs in the church and the remains of remarkable ceiling paintings from the 13–15C to the right of the high altar. The ceiling's supporting beams are decorated with painting and there are stone reliefs forming borders. Above the beautiful old apse are star-shaped wooden beams. To the left of the S. entrance, through a happily designed modern courtyard next to the modern monastery, there is an old wall tomb and a Romanesque figure above two archways. The N. entrance, on a hill with a flight of steps (old fountain on the left), has an old, partly destroyed, tympanum filled with figures.

San Nicolás de Bari (also near the Plaza de España, but on the other side from San Francisco): 12C main portal and the tomb of Pedro Menéndez de Avilés. Attached to the N. façade is the 14C Gothic Capilla de los Alas, which contains 7 Gothic reliefs.

Santo Tomás de Sabugo: An imposing Gothic church, rising abruptly from the middle of office blocks in the Calle de General Zubillaga, the new part of town; it originally dates from the beginning of the 13C.

Ayuntamiento/Town Hall: In the Plaza de España. Two-storey with a late 17C clock tower and a façade by Herrera.

Also worth seeing: The 15C *Palacio de Valdegarzena* (Casa de los Baragañas); the 17C *Palacio de Llano Ponte* and the *Palacio del Marqués de Ferrara,* both 17C; the *Palacio de Camposagrado,* which has a baroque façade between two towers. In 1900 the *Palacio-Valdés* theatre was built.

Environs: Pravia: 24 km. SW of Navés, in a delightful setting, overlooking one of the most beautiful valleys in Asturia. An

Ávila, Cruz de los Cuatro Postes (Cross of the Four Columns)

Ávila, Santo Tomás, marble tomb of the Infante Don Juan

old village with a remarkable collegiate church and the 18C *Palais de los Montas*. At **Santianes de Pravia:** 3 km. behind Pravia lies the former residence of the Kings of Asturia. The 8C *Santes Juanes* (774–83), the oldest church in Asturia, is currently being restored under the care of the King of Spain. It has a nave and two aisles, a wooden-beamed ceiling, arches and square pillars. The altar table, which is the oldest in Spain, is to be found in the El Pito palace museum in *Cudillero*. To the right of the church entrance stands a large *baptismal font* made from a pre-Roman artifact. The window on the left by the choir is also part of the original church. Next to the church you find the Kings' former *summer residence*, a building of 1786 (from the balcony, there is a beautful view). Currently on display in one of the rooms in the house is part of the church's inventory, which is due to be returned to *Santes Juanes*, after the latter's restoration. There is also a remarkable 12C/13C painting of Christ with the Virgin Mary and St.John with 18C baroque figures, dating from the

time of the church's redecoration. **El Pito:** In the crypt of the *parish church* there is an 8C altar, which belonged to King Silo. **Cudillero:** In the 19C *Palacio de El Pito* the Segas collection is on display. This includes a painting by Goya and a superb collection of carpets.

Ayamonte
Huelva/Andalusia   p.394□C 10

Parish church of El Salvador (Calle Real): A 13C building whose high tower is clearly visible. The frescos inside are in good condition.

Capilla del Socorro: A statue of Christ, carved by converted Indians in the 16C, is venerated here.

Convento de San Francisco (Between the old and the new part of town): Convent church with massive Mudéjar tower. Single-aisled, with a superb panelled ceil-

Avilés, San Francisco

ing. Choir and Capilla Mayor are separated by a round arch. 17C altarpiece.

Nuestra Señora de las Angustias (in the 'Ribera', i.e. the new part of town): This church formed part of the fortification system. The Mudéjar interior with 16C ceiling and altarpiece with bas-reliefs.

Also worth seeing: *Convento de Santa Clara:* Façade has twin windows (16C). Remains of the medieval *fortress; the Palace of the Marquis of Ayamonte; Casa Grande* (or Casa del Pintado).

Environs: Cartaya (20 km E.): Phoenician settlement with traces of Roman and Arab past. Interesting Arab fountains.

Ayerbe
Huesca/Aragon   p.388☐K 3

Parish church: In the 16C this church was a Dominican monastery. Inside there is a black marble tomb, decorated with reclining figures, which dates from the 17C. The high altar is dedicated to the Virgin of the Rosary. Its retable, with carving by Juan Miguel de Urliens and painting by Pedro L'Orfelin, dates from 1613.

Hermitage of Santa Lucía: 12C; the chapel contains a beautiful *Madonna and Child*.

San Pedro: Only the Romanesque tower remains of this 12C church; round-arched windows are flanked by columns.

Clock tower: 17C, built on the site of the former church of Santa María de la Cueva.

Palace of the Margraves of Ayerbe (Plaza Mayor): A bank now occupies this building, which dates from the latter half of the 15C. The palace has a beautiful fa-

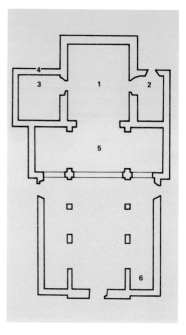

Santianes de Pravia, Santes Juanes 1 E. facing main apse **2** and **3** side apses **4** pre-Romanesque window **5** crossing **6** pre-Romanesque font

çade and was built for Hugo de Urries, a diplomat at the court of Ferdinand and Isabella. Parts of the old inner courtyard and wood-covered ceilings from that time have still survived.

Also worth seeing: The ruins of a *castle* and a Romanesque church, both from the 12C, on the mountain of San Miguel.

Ayllón
Segovia/Old Castile   p.392☐G 4

A picturesque village with interesting remains from different periods.

Ayamonte, view

La Puerta del Arco: This gate still serves as an entrance to the village. It consists of two arches, the inner one of which is decorated with the escutcheon of Don Diego López Pacheco and his wife, Doña Luisa Cabrera y Bobadilla. Of the old town walls the Marina tower still stands.

Palacio de Juan Contreras: The Contreras Palace was erected in 1497 and is the most beautiful building in Ayllón. It is Gothic and has a very beautiful portal with escutcheons and an inscription giving the date of its construction.

San Miguel: A 13C Romanesque church, which was later renovated; several Gothic and Plateresque tombs.

San Francisco: A monastery near the village founded by St. Francis of Assisi.

Museum of Modern Art: Devoted mainly to modern Spanish art, housing paintings and sculptures by Barjola,

Riaza (Ayllón)

Genovés, Venancio Blanco, Alcorlo, Máximo de Pablo and other artists.

Environs: Campo de San Pedro (*c.* 10 km. W.): A 17C neoclassical church, *San Pedro*, has a beautiful portal and an 18C altarpiece. **Cascajares** (*c.* 7 km. SW): Of the church of *San Pedro*, an old Romanesque building, only the portal has survived. 18C altarpiece on high altar, with a 16C wooden figure of St.Peter. Another altarpiece has beautiful 16C sculptures. In **Maderuelo** (*c.* 10 km. NW) there are remains of the old town walls and gates. The Romanesque parish church of *Santa María* has a Renaissance altarpiece upon which scenes from Christ's childhood and the Via Dolorosa (Way of the Cross) appear in colourful reliefs. In a Gothic chapel there is a 15C tomb. Also of interest: the *Capilla de la Vera Cruz*; the church of *San Miguel* as well as several *mansions*. **Fuentemizarra** (*c.* 12 km. NW): The church of *Nuestra Señora del Ejido* has remains from an earlier Romanesque building; also a beautiful altarpiece with various 17C paintings and sculptures. **Riaza** (*c.* 21 km. S.) is a very pretty, typical mountain town with a Gothic *parish church*, which has a 16C Pietá. Also dating from the 16C is the pilgrimage church of *Hontanares*. **Fresno de Cantespino** (*c.* 10 km. S.) has the remains of an old *castle* and a Romanesque *parish church*, which possesses a 16C Spanish oil painting of the *Madonna and Child*.

Azaila
Teruel/Aragon   p.388☐K 4

A little town on the Meseta plateau, occupying a site of historical importance. On a hill *c.* 1 km. away, is an Iberian village from the 1C BC called *Cabezo de Alcalá*. Here one can still see remains of streets and houses, as well as a Celtic burial ground.

Azcoitia
Guipúzcoa/Basque Provinces   p.388☐H 2

Nuestra Señora de la Asunción: Built in the 16C, with a fine altarpiece of 1568.

Also worth seeing: *Casa Consistorial/Town Hall*. From the other side of bridge over the river Urola there is a fine view of the picturesque old houses.

Azpetitia
Guipźocoa/Basque Provinces   p.388☐H 2

The town is known as the town of alpargatas; these are canvas shoes with twisted hemp soles, which have stayed the same for centuries.

Parish church of San Sebastián: Gothic with a classical portico designed by Ventura Rodríguez and erected in 1785 by Francisco Ibero. Of interest within is a marble font, at which St.Ignatius was baptized; also the tomb of Martín Zurbaro, Bishop of Tuy, which is adorned with a praying statue.

Also worth seeing: The little town has fascinating old palaces and mansions e.g. the Mudéjar *Casa de Anchieta* and the 15C *Casa Zuola*, an Aragonese-Mudéjar brick building. Also worth mentioning are the baroque altar by Azpiazu in the monastery, as well as the 16C church, *Nuestra Señora de la Soledad*.

Badajoz
Badajoz/Estremadura   p.392□C 8

Capital of the province of the same name;
it occupies a hill on the left bank of the
Guadiana, overlooking the river and only
6 km. from the Portuguese border.

The original Celtic settlement was known
as *Civitas Pacis* during its resistance against
the Romans. In 1009 the small kingdom
of Batalvoz was established by the Moors
under Abu-Mohammed-Abdallah, and was
the subject of constant Spanish and Por-
tugese aggression. In 1229 it was conquered by Alfonso IX and became the
kingdom of León. Badajoz resisted numerous Portuguese invasions (1385, 1396,
1542), and in 1580 Philip II used it as the

Badajoz, panorama

base for his campaign against the Portuguese, during the course of which, in 1660, Badajoz was beseiged. In 1705 it was besieged by the Allies in the War of the Spanish Succession. In 1810 it was seized by the French, who finally gave way to Wellington's English forces after three months' resistance, leaving the city badly damaged. It was again the scene of bitter fighting in 1936.

There is a fine view of the city from the right bank of the Guadiana, to which Badajoz is linked by a huge granite bridge, the *Puente de las Palmas*. This is 1,909 ft. long and has 32 arches; it was begun in 1440 on Roman foundations and finished in 1596 according to Herrera's designs. Most of the remains of Moorish occupation can be found in the hills of Orinace.

Cathedral of San Juan (in the lower town): The city's main monument, built 1234–84 under Alfonso the Wise. The fortified basilica was often used as a sanctuary by the citizens during troubled times.

There is a nave and two aisles. The choir and the façade, which has a statue of John the Baptist, are 16C Renaissance; the marble portal dates from 1619. Windows in the high square towers (1240-1419) were decorated with Plateresque ornaments by Juan de Ayala in the 16C.

The interior is in a style transitional between Romanesque and Gothic. There are twelve chapels, of which the most interesting is the *Capilla de los Beneficiados*. The Renaissance *choir* is by Jerónimo da Valencia and it has fine choir stalls (1548). The crossing has large bronze chandeliers. The Churrigueresque high altar dates from 1708. In the chapel to its left is a Mary Magdalene by Mateo de Cerezo. The alabaster bas-relief of the Madonna and Child in the *Capilla de la Encarnación*, was designed by the Florentine artist Desiderio da Settignano. The *Capilla de los Duques* contains tombs and the painting 'Christ on the Cross' by Luis de Morales (El Divino); the *Capilla Santa Ana*, third on the right, has two more paintings. The Gothic clois-

Badajoz, Puerta de las Palmas

ter, built 1509–1520, contains the tomb panel (by an Italian artist) of Don Lorenzo Suárez de Figueroa, who died in 1506.

The chapterhouse houses the *Museo Catedralico* (diocesan museum), which has paintings by Luis de Morales, Pedro Orrente and Flemish masters.

Other churches: *Santa Maria:* The city's oldest church containing an altarpiece by the German artist Luchincky. *La Concepción:* Contains two paintings by Morales.

Alcazaba (fortress): By the river. The former seat of the Bishop of Badajoz, it later became the residence of the Moorish kings. All that remains of it is the Mudéjar palace of the Dukes of la Roca. This has huge square corner towers and a vaulted entrance with flat arches. The octagonal *Torre de Espantaperros* is notable for typical Almohaden battlements; it now houses the *Museo Arqueológico Provincial*, which has Roman and Iberian finds, Visigoth stele and some Islamic art.

Badajoz, Cathedral

Palacio de la Disputación: Formerly the Church of Santa Catalina, but now the *Museo de Bellas Artes*, a local museum mostly dedicated to artists from Estremadura, such as Luis de Morales, Zurbarán, Eugenio Hermono Covarsi and Antonio Juez.

Baeza
Jaén/Andalusia   p.394☐G 9

Cathedral of Santa María (Plaza de Santa María): A Gothic cathedral built in the 16C by Jerónimo del Prado. The W. façade has a fine portal, the 13C Mudéjar *Puerta de la Luna*, which has parallel horseshoe arches. The interior, restored in the 16C by Andrés de Vandelvira and his successors, has a superb hexagonal *pulpit*, which is made from elaborately decorated wrought-iron. The *choral gallery* is an ornate 16C work by Bartolomé de Jaén. There are also some fine Mudéjar stucco *pillars* and an interesting *cloister*.

Seminario de San Felipe Neri: The seminary is in the old *Palacio de Benavente* (or *Palacio de Jabalquinto*), which has a splendid ornamental Isabelline façade decorated with coats-of-arms. Over the Gothic door- and window-arches there is a Renaissance *loggia*. The *patio* is also Renaissance and has two-storey arcades, marble pillars and a Baroque memorial staircase. The *archive* contains six Romanesque pillars from the now-destroyed Church of San Juan.

Church of Santa Cruz (opposite the seminary): The Romanesque portal on the W. side used to be part of the Church of San Juan. The interior has been restored many times, but still contains original 15&16C frescos.

Plaza de los Leones: This magnificent

square contains a number of interesting things: the *Fuente de los Leones* (Lion Spring) with four Roman lions lying down and a female figure; the *old slaughterhouse*, a 16C Renaissance building decorated with Charles V coat-of-arms; the Renaissance *Audiencia Civil* (Appeal Court) or *Casa del Populo*, which was begun in the 16C and has windows framed by aedicules; and the *Arco del Populo*, or *Arco de Jaén*, also 16C, which is attached to it. Nearby is the 16C *Arco de Baeza*.

Ayuntamiento/Town Hall: This building dates from 1559 and has also served as prison and abattoir. It has a fine Plateresque façade, whose decorations are concentrated around the doors and windows.

Also worth seeing: *San Andrés* (Calle de Francisco Robles), 16C with a Plateresque S.portal. *Santa Ana* (Calle de Rojo), with a Renaissance portal. The 17C *Los Descalzos* (Calle de Francisco Robles). *El Salvador* (near the Plaza de José León), a Romanesque-Gothic church, which was heavily restored in the 17C. *Convento de San Francisco* (Calle de San Francisco); remains of the 16C Renaissance building, especially the church portal, still display the talent of the major architect Andrés de Vandelvira. The town is enhanced by a number of attractive mansions: the *Palacio de los Condes de Garciéz* (Calle de San Pablo); the *Casa de los Ancuña*, 16C with a Renaissance façade; the *Palacio Montemar*, with a fine courtyard; and the *Casa de los Cabrera*. There is a splendid arched doorway: the *Arco de Barbudo* (Calle del Beato Juan de Ávila), with a Madonna and devotional inscription; the *Puerta de Ubéda* is part of the old fortress, which includes a tower with the coat-of-arms of the Ferdinand and Isabella. The former university building is 16C, and the Mudéjar stucco ceiling is a reminder of the time when Baeza was a university town (1583–1807).

Bagur

Gerona/Catalonia   p.390☐O 3

The beautiful village of Bagur is inland and just a few km. from the finest beaches of the Costa Brava (Sa Riera, Sa Tuna, Aiguablava, Cap-Sa-Sal). The hill-top *fortress*, was an important defensive bastion against the attacks of Norman pirates and the Saracens. Built in 1079, it originally belonged to Ermessenda, the wife of the Count of Foix, Ramon Borell. Totally destroyed by the Duke of Lothringen in the war against Juan II, it was rebuilt immediately. It was finally sacked on 10 September 1810 by the English under Doyle during the War of Independence. In 1934 it was declared a national monument.

Environs: Pals: The *parish church*, originally Romanesque, was rebuilt in 1478 with Gothic features; 18C façade. The *Castle of Monteáspero* dates from 889, but only the tower — known as the 'Tower of the Hours' because it used to have a clock—

Bagur, fortress

survives and the upper part of this has recently been restored. **Peratallada:** The *castle* dates from 1065 and was, as its name suggests (pedra tallada = hewn stone), cut out of the hill. Arabian and Gothic remains have been discovered here. The main rooms have survived in Gothic style. The *parish church of San Esteban* is a two-aisled building with an elegant bell tower. **Palau-Sator:** The *parish church of San Pedro* used to be the castle tower; only one tower and a Gothic portal survive. Also of note are the remains of the Visigoth *church of San Feliu de Boada*, the only such example in the area.

Balaguer
Lérida/Catalonia   p.390☐M 3

This town was founded on the right bank of the river Segre. In 897 it was surrounded by a wall, part of which still survives today. It became the capital town of the region after its conquest by the Lords of

Urgel in 1106. It was the scene of many struggles between the Catalonian nobles and the King of Aragon and in the course of these the knights' castle, 'Castell Formos' (castle beautiful) was destroyed along with the church of Santa María. In 1400 the area came under the crown and Balaguer lost its status as a capital city.

Santa María: Originally consecrated in 1575; in 1856 it was converted into a prison, only to become a church again in 1881. The bell-tower, which is built on a polygonal base, is 14C, as is the stellar vaulting.

Church of San Salvador: Originally Romanesque. The parish church 1351–1557. There is some fine 14C stonework.

Monastery of Santo Domingo: The church was built by Jaime Fabre and used by Dominicans and Franciscans. The Gothic transept dates from 1330–50.

Santo Cristo de Balaguer: This was

Pals (Bagur), town walls

erected in the 17C on the site of the old church of Santa María de Almata. It has a 16C carved wooden crucifix and a fine iron grille near the altar.

Plaza Mercadal: A medieval square with colonnades. The hospital was built in 1480 and restored in the 18C.

Environs: Bellpuig de las Avellanas: The *Abbey of Santa María*, a Premonstratensian monastery founded in 1180 and the result of a merger between two older churches. In the 17C it had a reputation for being an establishment of great religious learning. The church is incomplete —it has no nave—and what we see today dates from the 15-16C. The apse is pentagonal. **Castelló de Farfanya**: Cylindrical towers, which were part of the medieval city wall are still standing. The *church of Santa María* occupies a commanding site above the town. It is a simple 14C building with a tall, elegant tower. **Ager** (25 km. N.): Near the monastery, there are the impressive remains of the walls of the monastery church of *San Pedro*. **Cubells** (15 km. NE) has two interesting Romanesque churches. The monastery of **Santa María de Gualter** (40 km. NE) is also of interest.

Bañolas (Banyoles)
Gerona/Catalonia   p.391 □ O 3

Archaeological Museum (in the house of Pía Almoina): Built 12-17C. It contains two important collections: the Alsíus Collection, including a famous *Neanderthal jaw*, found in 1887 by Pedro Alsíus near Lake Bañolas (the oldest human remains discovered in Catalonia); and the Butinya Collection, which consists of Roman coins found in local excavations.

Monastery of San Esteban: A Benedic-

tine monastery built in 1812 on ruins of a former building, which had probably been burned to the ground by the Normans in 945; the site was reconsecrated in 957. All the Romanesque remains were razed by the French in 1655. The new church is neoclassical, and was built between 1702-40. It has a good *altar painting* by the master of Bañolas, and a Gothic 15C silver *reliquary*.

Also worth seeing: *community church*, a 13C Gothic building; the *marketplace*, with porticos and 15-16C buildings.

Environs: San Miguel de Fluviá: A Romanesque *parish church* with a nave and two aisles, fine apses and a bell-tower. It used to be part of the old monastery of San Miguel. The transept has high vaulting and simple capitals with flower motifs. The *bell-tower* has features of the later fortress wall. **Seriña:** The site of key archaeological finds from the Neolithic and Bronze Ages. The *parish church* is a fine example of 12C architecture; the portal has

San Miguel de Fluviá, parish church 1 main portal **2** bell tower **3** leaf capitals **4** altar

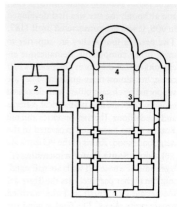

Baños de Cerrato, San Juan Bautista

four archivolts on pillars, which are themselves on bases. **Porqueras:** The Romanesque *parish church of Santa María* is 12C, and although the site was first developed in 906, it was not consecrated until 1182. The *portal*'s four arches are superior to most other comparable Romanesque archivolts in that they form not merely a half circle, but almost three-quarters. They are supported by elegant pillars with decorated capitals; there are also geometrical patterns and medallions. Iberian ceramics and old Roman coins have been excavated in the neighbourhood. Ruins of the 9C *castle* are still visible. **Santa Pau:** An interesting village some of whose old walls are still standing; the higher part includes the Torre del Homenaje (the keep) and the fortified square stone *chapel*. The Gothic windows are very fine, as is the inner courtyard. In

the *Capilla de Oratorio dels Angels* is a wonderfully simple 12C Christ figure.

Baños de Cerrato
Palencia/Old Castile   p.388 □ F 3

San Juan Bautista: A Visigoth basilica, which has been declared a national monument. It was built in 661 on the orders of King Recceswinth and is one of the finest examples of its kind. Nave and two aisles are separated from an older construction by horseshoe arches with Corinthian capitals. Through two of the arches there is a mineral spring; indeed, the sanctity of this spring was the original reason for building the church.

Environs: Some 4 km. N. is **Villamuriel de Cerrato,** with the 13C church of *Santa María.* The portal has two pointed (Gothic) arches. Inside there are a nave and two aisles with some splendid two-pieced dome vaulting. **Hermedes de Cerrato** (*c.* 17 km. SE): A Romanesque-Gothic *parish church* with several quite good altarpieces; the pilgrim chapel *Nuestra Señora de las Eras* is Mozarabic and has an interesting horseshoe arch. **Baltanás** (*c.* 10 km. NE): The 14C church of *San Millán* has a nave, two aisles, a Plateresque choir, several Gothic monuments and a baroque altarpiece with a 15C Gothic figure of Christ. **Magaz** (*c.* 5 km. N.): The parish church has an interesting 14C Gothic chapel.

Barbastro
Huesca/Aragon   p.388 □ L 3

Roman in origin. A former bishops' seat on the Rió Vero and a fortified town. It was originally founded by Decius Brutus, and named *Brutina* after him. The union of Aragon and Catalonia was formally sealed

Baños de Cerrato, San Juan Bautista

in Barbastro in 1137, when Petronilla, the daughter of King Ramiro II of Aragon, and Ramón Berenguer IV, Lord of Barcelona, were betrothed.

Cathedral: Late Gothic, built between 1500-33. Builders found traces of an earlier building in the sacristy and from these signs it was apparent that the spot was once occupied by a mosque. The cathedral has a nave, two aisles and Churrigueresque side chapels under flying buttresses. The church has fine groin vaulting. The construction of the high altar was overseen by Damián Forment; by the time of his death in 1540, the first part of the alabaster relief on the altar was finished. It was then completed by one of Forment's pupils, Juan de Liceyre. The altarpiece is carved wood and dates from 1596-1604. Panel-

ling in the choir and the choir stalls themselves date from 1584 - 94. The 16C altarpiece in the Capilla del Santísimo was originally in the monastery of San Victorián.

Archbishop's Palace: An Aragonese building. Inside: two fine Flemish tapestries and a collection of medieval objects.

Ayuntamiento/Town Hall: A 15C building designed by the Moor Farag de Gali, chief architect to King Ferdinand the Catholic. Restored in the 19C.

Also worth seeing: The *Plaza Mayor* is bordered by beautiful arcades. Barbastro still contains many fine mansions, notably the *Palais of the Argensola family*, a typically Aragonese Renaissance building of the 16–17C; it has a fine roof with carved eaves. The poet Lupercio Leonardo and his brother, Bartolemé de Argensola were born here.

Barcelona

Contents:

I.　Geography and Location

Barcelona has an especially pleasant climate, situated as it is on the plain between the Rivers Besós and Llobregat, and sheltered from the N. by the Collcerola range (including the Tibidabo ridge, some 1,778 ft. above sea level), from the W. by the San-Mateo heights and from the E. by the Garraf massif. The original settlement was on a hill overlooking the Mediterranean. This then extended into the plain —to the N. the only hills are the cluster of Carmelo, Creueta and Puxtet. Barcelona's population is around 1,800,000, (not including suburbs) and now it extends far beyond Tibidabo. Although Spain's official language is Castilian, some natives of Barcelona speak Catalan.

II.　History

Gnaeus Cornelius Scipio conquered the Iberian town of Layi, which was originally founded by the Layetani, and called it Barcino. Its official title as a Roman colony later became Favencia Julia Augusta Paterna Barcino. During the 4C it was sur-

rounded by a wall, which was (and still is) cut across by two roads, the Dardus and the Decumanus. For a time in the 5C the Visigoth King Ataulf used it as his base. In the 8C it was taken by the Arabs and in 801 recaptured by the French King Louis. From this time the Garraf massif became the dividing line between the French and the Mohammedans, and what is now Catalonia became part of the Spanish border. The province became an organized unit, and the Counts of Barcelona held sway over much of the surrounding area. After Wilfred 'el Velloso' (the Hairy, 878 –97) the title became hereditary, and under Borrell II (947–92) Barcelona became the capital of an independent state (988). Ramon Berenguer I and his brother Berenguer Ramón linked the old border territories under their command, and the kingdom of Catalonia was born. The first nobleman to hold the title of king was Alfonso I (1162–96), who reigned over Catalonia, Aragon (united by marriage), Provence, Béarn, Bigorre, Carcassonne, Béziers, Nîmes and Nizza. The Catholic King Pedro I (1196–1213) lost most of its French provinces—as well as his life—by taking part in the Crusades; the Catalans only managed to hold on to Roussillon and Montpelier. His successor, James I, known as the Conqueror, started by moving into the Mediterranean. He took the two largest Balearic Islands (Mallorca in 1235, Ibiza in 1238), and also the province of Valencia. Succeeding kings annexed Corsica, Sardinia, Sicily and Greece. Barcelona remained the capital until the reign of the Catholic King Ferdinand II, after which the royal seat moved first to Burgos and then to Madrid. Barcelona kept a viceroy and remained capital of its province, representing Barcelona in general, until Philip V, on the side of Charles of Austria, stripped it of its rights during the War of

Barcelona, Cathedral

the Spanish Succession (1701-13). In 1860 the city we see today began to develop. In 1888 it was the site of an international exhibition, and during 1914-24 it was again given special rights. From 1931-39 it was the centre of the independent state of Catalonia.

III. 1. Buildings

Barrio Gótico (Gothic Quarter)
The Roman Walls: In the 4C, the N. slope of the *Mons Taber*—the site of the original Iberian settlement, which was later taken over by the Romans—was protected by a surrounding wall. By the 5C the area within this wall included a palace and a cathedral. The wall was 30 ft. high, 12 ft. thick, altogether 4,166 ft. in length and protected by square and polygonal towers. In the 13C, King James I had a new defensive wall built, and gave permission for the building of residential houses backing on to the old wall. The *Roman walls* run alongside the Calle Correo Viejo, the

Barcelona, cathedral, relief by Bartolomé Ordóñez

Bajada Cassador, the Calle Subteniente Navarro, the Plaza del Angel, the Bajada Llibrería, the Calle Tapinería, the Plaza Berenguer III and the Calle de los Condes de Barcelona. There has been a certain amount of 20C restoration. The Plaza de la Catedral has a piece of the Roman wall and the beginning of a Roman aqueduct; there are also fragments of pillars originally found in a villa in the Sant quarter of the town.

Cathedral of Santa Eulalia: In 559, at the time of a council, there was already a cathedral (consecrated to the Holy Cross and Santa Eulalia), on this site. It was damaged by Almanzor in 985 and rebuilt as a Romanesque cathedral by Ramón Berenguer between 1045-58. Eventually, in 1298, it was completed in Gothic style. The San Ivo Gate and part of the transept have survived as Romanesque. The apse was added between 1317-70, the vaulting in the transept was finished in 1381 and further work done between 1417-22. The façade, however, is 19C, built by J.Oriol Mestres and August Font, to the designs of Master Carlí (1405).
The most impressive parts of the cathedral are the two octagonal towers over the transepts. The dome is not in the usual position over the crossing, but at the beginning of the nave—as it is in the cathedrals of Freiburg and Ulm. Inside there are a nave and two aisles with ribbed vaulting constructed in such a way as to give the impression of seven vaults. The *Crypt* of St. Eulalia, under the high altar, has flat, 12 part vaulting. It contains the saint's *marble sarcophagus*, with reliefs by a student of Giovanni Pisano; 14C bishop's stool behind the altar.

The *San Ivo Gate* (3) is the oldest part of the cathedral and its façade has Romanesque arches and windows, as well as ancient reliefs of men and animals in battle posture. Some small chapels (4 to 9) arranged round the apse have good paintings, the most notable of which is the *Transfiguration* by Bernat Martorell. Near the sanctuary, against a wall, is the *tomb of the founder* of the Romanesque cathedral, Ramón Berenguer, and his wife Almodís. The octagonal wooden pulpit near the coro (11) was completed in 1390 and is a fine piece of ironwork. The upper choir stalls, by Pere Ca Anglada (1399) are older than the lower ones, which are by Marcia Bonafe. Baroque features were introduced in the 16C. In 1519 a meeting of the Order of the Golden Fleece was held in the cathedral, and this gave Juan de Borgoña the opportunity of putting the coats-of-arms of the invited monarchs (Henry VIII, Fritz I, etc.) on the stalls reserved for them. The choirscreen (12) is the work of the artists Bartolemé Ordóñez and Pere Vilar, and dates from 1517.

The *San Raimundo Chapel* contains the Gothic *tomb of St. Raymond of Peñafort*, which was retrieved from the ruined church of Santa Catalina. The Porta San Severo (15) leads to the *cloisters*, which has four groin-vaulted galleries and a garden with very old trees (16,17). In the middle of the vaulting there is a terracotta relief of St. George by Antoni Claperós (15C). The *Chapel of Santa Lucía*, at the end of the cloisters, was consecrated to the Virgin Mary in 1268. The chapel's façade (21) has a typically Romanesque portal, including columns with decorated capitals. The font is 14C. Near the chapel is the *chapterhouse* (22). The *Museo Capitular* houses a valuable altarpiece by Bermejo, St. Eulalia's missal by Ramón Destorrent, a predella by Bernat Martorell and a 14C altar from Italy by S.di Pietro. In the *Capilla del Santísimo* (24), the Secretaria del Capitulo, contains the holy shrine of

Barcelona, Cathedral of Santa Eulalia 1 main doorway **2** Baptistery **3** San Ivo Gate **4** Chapel of the Santos Innocentes **5** Chapel of the Aparición **6** Chapel of Our Lord **7** Patrocinio Chapel **8** San Miguel Chapel **9** San Antonio Chapel **10** Sacristy **11** Coro **12** Trascoro **13** San Clemente Chapel **14** Chapel of San Raimundo de Peñafort **15** San Severo Gate **16** Piedad Gate **17** Cloister **18** San Jorge Pavilion **19** Santa Eulalia Gate **20** Santa Lucía Chapel **21** façade of the Chapel of Santa Lucía **22** Chapterhouse **23** Secretaria **24** Chapel of the Santísimo or 'Christ of Lepanto'

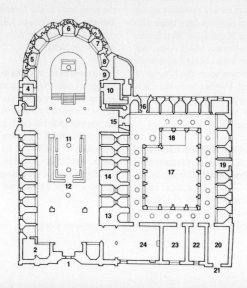

San Olegario, and above it 'Christ from Lepanto' on the cross. The *church treasure* includes a Gothic monstrance, a selection of 15C jewels and a throne of silver gilt.

Casa del Arcediano (the former archdeacon's house): Opposite the chapel of Santa Lucía and near the 14C Casa del Deán with Renaissance façade. The former is a 12C building, a mixture of Gothic and Renaissance, which was restored in 1610. The courtyard has a beautiful Gothic fountain. The fine marble letter-box was made by the architect Domenech i Montaner in the 19C. Upper rooms have exhibitions and collections from Barcelona and Catalonia.

Bishop's Palace: Built in the 12&13C, but much restored. The *baroque façade* facing the Plaza Nueva dates from 1784; the other façade, looking on to the Calle del Obispo Irurita, is much plainer. The inner courtyard has a Romanesque gallery with arcades and columns; the right side is probably the oldest. Some of the windows are 13C, but the Gothic ones are 15C.

Near the Bishop's Palace and opposite the Puerta de Santa Eulalia, on the small Plaza Garriga Bachs there is a *memorial* set up by J. Llimona to commemorate those who died during the Napoleonic War. To the right is a small alleyway which opens into a hidden square with a beautiful *fountain* and then continues on to the Church of San Felipe Neri. Further down the Calle del Obispo Irurita, towards the Plaza San Jaime, is the seat of the Catalonian Regional Council.

Palacio de la Generalidad, (the seat of the ancient Catalonin parliament)/ **Diputación Provincial:** The façade was built from 1610–30 to the designs of the architect Pere Pau Ferrer. The Gothic gate into the courtyard (1416) is by Marc Safont, Pere Joan and Aliot de la Font. The sec-

ond courtyard has a free-standing Gothic staircase leading up to the first floor gallery; there are also late Gothic arcades and elegant columns. The gallery leads to the *Capilla de San Jorge* (1432), whose *façade* rates among the finest examples of Catalonian late Gothic. The chapel has splendid 17C vaulting with a dome and hanging capitals. Among the lovely things in the chapel there is a 15C statue of St.George. From the N. side of the gallery there is access to the splendid marble-floored *Patio de los Naranjos,* built by Pau Mateu and Tomás Barsa around 1532. On the left is a bell-tower, with a bell by Pere Ferrer from 1568. Further on is the *Salón del Consistorio Major* (session room), also known as the 'golden room' because of its gold panelling. It is the work of Ramón Puig (1578). The azulejos are from Talavera. A Renaissance door leads from the S. end of the Gothic gallery into the *Salón de San Jorge,* a three-aisled room with vaults, transept and dome by Pere Blai, (1596). This is where all the most important state decisions were taken. A door on the right of the main entrance opens to reveal a staircase, which in turn leads through an ante-room and out into the Plaza de San Jaime. The Italian-style façade of 1597 has statues of the presidents of the Generalidad: L. de Tamarit, F.Boteller and J.Riu, and also a statue of St.George by Aleu. The balcony dates from 1860.

Ayuntamiento, or **Casa de la Ciudad:** Barcelona City Hall has a neoclassical *façade* and stands opposite the Generalidad. It was designed by Mas i Vila; the upper section was added in 1853. Statues on each side, depicting King James I along with noblemen of Barcelona, are the work of Bover. The building's left façade is Gothic, and forms part of the palace. Entry from this side leads into a room with a poly-

Barcelona, Town Hall, Salón de Ciento

chrome wooden-beamed ceiling, dating from 1401. From here a black marble staircase, with murals depicting a Catalan fable, takes you up to the top floor. From the landing, which has a sculpture by Viladomat, you can see an old 14C façade with a 17C doorway. On the right is the top balcony looking on to the Gothic courtyard. From here a doorway flanked by columns opens to the 14C *Salón de Ciento* ('of the hundred'), and then on to the Salón de Sesiones (session room), which is also known as the Salón de la Reina Regente and has a picture of Queen María Christina and Alfonso XIII of Masriera. The Salón de las Crónicas, next to the staircase, contains paintings by J.M.Sert from 1928.

Palacio Real Mayor: The narrow Calle de Librería leads from the Plaza de San Jaime to the attractive Plaza del Rey, where this palace is to be found; the plaza is also the venue for the 'Gothic Quarter Concerts' in summer. On the left is the *Capilla Palatina*, and on the right the *Palacio del Lugarteniente*, which contains the Archives of the Crown of Aragón, and *Barcelona's Historical Museum*. The palace's façade is a mixture of styles and periods: the upper section has a 13C triangular Romanesque window and a 14C Gothic rose window, above which is a Renaissance gallery of 1555. A staircase leads up to the Romanesque palace door and to the Gothic chapel. In order to visit the palace and chapel, you must go through the Museum de Historia de la Ciudad. The *museum terrace*, leading to Room XVII, gives a splendid view over the entire quarter, including the partially excavated underground Roman town, the columns of the old Romanesque palace, the Visigoth buildings and the early Christian basilica.

Capilla Palatina, or **Capilla de Santa Agueda:** Built on the site of St. María's Oratory. It is single-aisled and has polychrome wooden beams. In the apse you can see the coat-of-arms of James II and his wife, Blanca de Anjou. The *altar*, which is known as 'El Condestable', is a greatly treasured masterpiece by the Gothic sculp-

Barcelona, Palacio de la Generalidad

Barcelona, Palacio de la Generalidad

tor Jaime Huguet and it is reckoned to be one of the finest examples of Catalan art.

Salón Mayor, or **Salón del Tinell:** 56 ft. wide, 110 ft. long and built 1359–62. An assembly room for parliament and the room in which the Catalonian Kings received their most esteemed visitors. The N. wall used to be covered with a 12C fresco and this is now on display in the ante-room.

Also worth seeing: Behind the cathedral, in the Calle del Paradís, there is a stone which indicates the highest point of what used to be Mt.Tabor. Four perfectly preserved Corinthian columns—once part of a Roman temple of Augustus — were found in the house next door.

III. 2. Other religious buildings

Church of Santa María del Mar: King James I vowed that he would erect a cathedral to Santa María after he had annexed the island of Mallorca. After taking Sardinia in 1329, Alfonso I, the Good, laid the foundation stone on the site of an old parish church, which had been consecrated in 998. Santa María del Mar, built by the architect Berenguer de Montagut, was the centre of Mediterranean Catalonia. It is the finest example of Catalonian Gothic with huge, plain surfaces and massive buttresses. Octagonal towers are topped by three storeys having 8 narrow windows per storey. In 1428 the old *rose windows* were destroyed; they were replaced in the 15C by late Gothic ones. The N. wall has a tower with 15C sculptures; the apse was built in 1542 by B.Salvador. *Inside:* the nave and two aisles are of the same height and the nave is twice the width of the aisles. The plain octagonal pillars are so far apart that the overall effect of space and breadth is quite unlike that of any other Gothic cathedral. The sanctuary contains the *tomb of Constable Pedro of Portugal,* King of Catalonia. Some of the *stained glass windows* are particularly fine, especially the 'Last Judgement' (1454) by S.Desmanes in the left aisle, the 'Ascension' in the Mary

Barcelona, Santa María del Mar

Barcelona, Santa María del Mar

Chapel and the 'Last Supper' (1667) by Isidro Julia. The baroque high altar of 1771 was destroyed in 1936. The church treasury contains a 16C silver cross, various other silver pieces and an 18C chalice.

Sant Pere de les Puelles (San Pedro de las Doncellas): The Church of San Saturnino occupied the site in 801; the same spot was consecrated in 945 as San Pedro de las Doncellas, which was attached to a Benedictine convent, whose abbess had a great deal of influence over local matters. The church was destroyed in 986 and later rebuilt. In the 19C it was extensively rebuilt: the Romanesque cloister was dismantled and parts were moved to other monasteries and to museums. It was badly restored in 1911 and now only the 15C Gothic façade is of interest. The vaulting and dome survive from the original 10C church.

San Pau del Camp (San Pablo del Campo—St.Paul in the Fields) : On the Calle de San Pablo, just off the Ronda de San Pablo. A church, cloisters and a 14C Gothic abbey; dating back to 912, although it is not possible to establish the exact foundation date. The façade has Lombard-Romanesque features. The portal's archivolts are supported by columns with Visigoth capitals. The three apses have interesting decoration, and the *cloisters*, which have triple arcades and a garden are among the finest in Barcelona.

Church of Santos Justo y Pastor (Plaza de San Justo):A very old church, which had already been restored in 801. The façade is rather simple. Inside there is a nave and side chapels, with reliefs on the vaulting. The *Retable of San Felix* in the chapel of the same name (the first on the left next to the apse) is by J.de Bruselas and Pere Nunyes (1525), as are the holy water stoups (both originally Gothic capitals). Since the 10C the church has been able to bestow the remarkable *Right of the Holy Testament* (Testamentos Sacramentales). This concerns the deathbed utterance of a critically ill person's will, in the presence of wit-

Barcelona, San Pablo del Campo

Barcelona, La Sagrada Familia

nesses. If the witnesses have been to the altar of the San Felix chapel within the last six months and have sworn the same statement, it takes on the status of a testament, even if there is no written confirmation. This privilege dates from the town by-laws of 1282 and is still in use today.

Church of Santa María del Pino (Plaza del Pino): There was first a church on this site in the 10C; the church visible today was begun in 1322 and consecrated in 1453. Crypt and rib vaulting from the 16C. The *rose-window* is disproportionately large. The octagonal bell tower has Gothic windows and blind arcades. The interior is sober and made up of a nave and side chapels. A Gothic tomb dating from 1394 can be found near to the sacristy.

Monastery of Santa Ana (Plaza de Santa Ana): A Romanesque church from the 12C, which has been a protected monument since 1881. The Gothic portal dates from 1300. The inside is rather plain; rib vaulting dates from the 14C and there is

a *Pietà* by the contemporary artist Pere Bruna in the *Chapel of All Saints*. The cloister on the opposite side is 15C.

La Sagrada Familia/Church of Atonement of the Holy Family (in the Plaza de la Sagrada Familia): In 1891, the architect *Antonio Gaudí* was commissioned to complete the building, work on which had already been started. It was originally designed as neo-Gothic but he changed the designs considerably. The first bell-tower was finished in 1921; Gaudi died in 1926. Three façades symbolize the birth of Christ (W.), his life and death (E.) and his Ascension (S.). Eight towers represent the apostles and the main dome, the Virgin Mary. Three doorways in the only completed façade (that of the birth of Christ), symbolize faith, hope and love. The architect is buried in the crypt. In 1952 work began again, based on his designs.

Convent of Pedralbes: A Poor Clares Convent in the district of the same name. It was founded by James II and his fourth

Barcelona, Convent of Pedralbes, cloister

Barcelona, Casa Milá by Antoni Gaudí

wife Elisenda de Montcada in 1326. From the front garden look at the fine façade and the plain tower. Queen Elisenda's coat-of-arms can be seen over the front portal, as can those of the Montcada family and of Barcelona. The public is only allowed into part of the single-aisled *church*—the sanctuary is for the Poor Clares alone. On the right by the sanctuary is Queen Elisenda's tomb. The large three-storeyed *cloister* is impressive, with late Gothic arches on elegant pillars. It leads to the *Chapel of San Miguel*, where there are frescos by Ferrer Bassa, dated 1343, which have survived in good condition.

III. 3. Secular buildings

Hospital de la Santa Creu (Santa Cruz): Its foundation stone was laid in 1401 by the royal family and representatives of the city guild. The building was extended in 1509. There are four floors. In the 17C a baroque rest house (Casa de Convalecencia) was attached. The third hospital building, the old medical school, now serves as the meeting-place for the *Real Academia de Medicina*. Other buildings include: the *Biblioteca de Catalunya*; the *Escuela Massana* for sculpture; as well as various archives and museums. The most interesting building is the Gothic *main hall of the hospital*, which is now the reading-room of the library, and the Gothic *cloisters* dating from 1417. The *courtyard* of the Casa de Convalecencia, built 1774–1802, is one of the finest designs of its time.

La Lonja (Plaza Palacio, corner of Paseo de Isabel II): Built in the 14C (1358–90)

Barcelona, Museo Picasso

as a market—in the Middle Ages nearly all towns in Catalonia and Aragon would have had such a building—now operating as the centre of the Barcelona *stock exchange*. In the 15C it was a kind of customs office, and the first floor became the office of the 'Naval Consulate'. Between 1774–1802 the façade was restored in classicistic style. The main room is Gothic and very wide, composed of three aisles with round arches, which support a flat wooden roof.

Las Atarazanas and Monumento a Colón: The Atarazanas are the largest and best-preserved *medieval docks* in the world. They are at the end of the Ramblas, opposite the Columbus Monument. Built in 1378 they were continually extended well into the next century to give extra capacity (30 galleys could be built side by side).

Today they house a maritime museum. The *Columbus Monument*, an iron column on a stone base with a statue of the famous discoverer on the top, was built by C.Buigas Monrava in 1886. It commemorates Columbus's presenting himself to the King in Barcelona on his return from his first voyage.

Palacio de la Virreina (Rambla de las Flores): Commissioned in 1772, by the Viceroy of Peru, (the Marquis of Castabell), from the architect and sculptor Charles Grau. The Marquis, however, died and it was his wife, the Vicereine, who moved into the house—hence its name 'de la Virreina'. The reception room is the most impressive, with twin staircases and typically Catalan hanging capitals. The rococo dining-room is also interesting. Today the palace houses the *Museo de Artes Decorativas* and the *Cambó Collection*.

La Casa Milá: Antonio Gaudí, the inspired architect from Barcelona and the mastermind of the Sagrada Familia, built some unconventional residences, whose design caused much controversy. One example is the **Pedrera** (Quarry), a five-storeyed house (in the Paseo de Gracia, on the corner of Calle Mallorca). Dedicated to the Madonna of the Rosary, each floor symbolizes a secret of the Rosary. Gaudí was also responsible for the remarkable wrought-iron balcony. The **Casa Batlló** (Paeso de Gracia, Calle Aragón) has a ceramic roof and is a further example of Gaudí's imaginative work, as is the **Palacio Güell** on the Ramblas.

Gran Teatro del Liceo (Rambla de Capuchinos): One of Europe's biggest opera houses lies hidden behind an unremarkable façade. It was designed in 1848 by Garriga i Roca and, after several fires, was eventually completed by J.Oriol Mestres. The city's greatest realist painter was involved in its construction.
Opera is performed there in the winter and ballet in the spring.

Palacio de la Música (in Calle Alta de San Pedro, on the corner of Calle Amadeo Vives): Barcelona's biggest *concert hall*, built in 1908 by Domenech i Montaner for the 'Orfeo Catalá' choir. It is decorated in Catalan *Art Nouveau* style and, typically, uses polychrome materials (like ceramics and stained glass) and flower motifs. There are sculptures on the themes of Catalan and international music.

Palacio de Pedrables: (on the Avda. Generalísimo Franco): in the Cuidad Universitaria. Formerly a royal residence. It is open to visitors, and has some interesting 18C murals (on the first floor).

IV   Parks and other buildings of interest

Parque de la Ciudadela: Approaching the park from the NW, along the Paseo San

Barcelona, Museo Picasso, bullfight

Juan, you come to a *triumphal arch*, built as the entrance to the 1888 International Exhibition. The route continues down the Allee Salón Victor Pradera, (the Courts of Justice on the left), at the end of which is the memorial to the mayor Rius i Taulet (1901), who was the main promoter of the Exhibition. Opposite is the entrance to the park. The *park* takes its name from the citadel built by Philip V to protect Catalonia. It was captured by the French in 1808 and in 1869 General Prim handed it over to the city. Only the chapel, the arsenal and the governor's palace survive. In 1888 the park became the site of the International Exhibition. The building on the right of the main entrance—designed by Domenech i Montaner as the Exhibition restaurant—houses a *zoological museum*; the *cascada* (waterfall) is on the left. The old *arsenal*, which houses the *Museum of Modern Art*, is in the W. of the park. What was the citadel chapel is today an army chapel.

Parque de Montjuich and Exhibition Grounds: The mountain was inhabited by

an Iberian tribe in pre-Roman times. Later the Romans linked Mons Taber and Mons Jovis (Montjuich) by road. In the 15C there was already a lighthouse on the site of the one visible today. The castle (first built here in 1640), was converted into a citadel in 1694. Today the **Castillo de Montjuich** houses the *Military Museum*. The park was laid out in the 19C. In 1929 the *Palacio Nacional* opened, together with some other small buildings and the *Spanish village*, (composed of copies of the best-known buildings from Spain's major cities, which were on display at the Exhibition). The architect was Puig i Cadafalch; Rubió i Tuduri was responsible for laying out the park, and Carles Buigas, an engineer, designed the *Palacio Nacional*'s fountains. Today the Palacio Nacional houses the *Museum of Catalan Art*. This can be reached from the Traversera de Dalt and the E. side of the parallel street, the Calle de Llarard, or from the Calle de República Argentina, the viaduct and the Calle San Camilo (W. entrance). Eusebio Güell, a patron of the arts, commissioned

Barcelona, Museo Picasso, lithograph

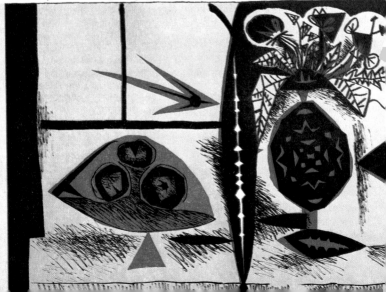

the architect Gaudí to design the park, which was originally going to be a garden city. The work took from 1900–14. The W. entrance is flanked by two pavilions with polychrome roofs. A staircase leads to the Room of a Hundred Columns (which in fact has 86) with the original ceiling, and then through to a square, whose seats are decorated with tile fragments collected by Gaudí himself.

V. Major Museums and Collections

Museo de Arqueología (Archaeological Museum, Montjuich Park, Paseo Santa Madrona): Collections of prehistoric, Iberian, Greek and Roman art, including the valuable finds from the *Excavation of Ampurias*.

Museo de Arte de Cataluña (Palacio Nacional de Montjuich, Avda. Marqués de Comillas): Contains a most important collection of Catalan art, including Romanesque (wall paintings from *Tahull* and from the Pyrenees) and Gothic art (work of Jaime Huguet).

Museo de Arte Moderno (in the arsenal in the Parque de la Ciudadela): An interesting collection of modern Spanish, especially Catalan, painters.

Cambó Collection (Palacio de la Virreina, Rambla de Capuc.): Set up by the politician and patron of the arts F.Cambó; it houses work by Italian, Flemish and Dutch painters.

Since 1963, the **Picasso Museum** has been housed in the Palacio Aguilar (Calle Montcada, 15—a former nobleman's house with fine colonnades), and the nearby Palacio Castellet.

Since 1973, the very modern building in the upper part of the Montjuich Park has housed the **Fundación Miró**. One room

is devoted to art while the other rooms have a variety of exhibitions. In the garden and on the terraces there are fine sculptures by Joan Miró.

The **Museo de Historia de Barcelona** is in the Plaza del Rey and the **Museo Marítimo** is in the Atarazanas on the Plaza de Colón.

Environs: Mataró (30 km. NE): The most interesting sight here is the *Basilika Parroquial Santa María*, which was built in the 16C and restored in 1675. It has a baroque altar of 1693 by Antonio Riera and H.Bonifaci. The Capilla de los Dolores contains paintings by Antonio Viladomat (1737). The city museum is also of interest. **Sabadell** (18 km. N.): The *parish church of San Feliu* is a neo-Gothic building designed by Enrique Sagnier Villavecchia. It was built on the site of a Gothic church of 1420, and was consecrated in 1921. The city museum has an interesting antique collection. 1 km. from **La Garriga** (40 km. N.) is the Romanesque *Church of La Doma*, which has a fine Gothic altarpiece. The Visigoth church of San Esteban also has a 15C Gothic altarpiece. **Canet de Mar** (40 km. NE): The *castle of Santa Florentina*, a 14C building has an interesting art collection, and some *remains of a medieval castle*. The *parish church of San Pons* in **Corbera de Llobregat** is 11C in origin. It used to be attached to a Cluniac priory, which was consecrated before 1068. It is one of the finest rural churches in the province.

Batres
Madrid/New Castile   p.388☐G 6

The Castle: Begun in the 13C. It be-

Barcelona, Museo Picasso, lithograph ▷

longed to the family of Garcilaso de la Vega, who did some writing here. The building, which is square and built entirely of brick, has corner towers with rounded battlements. The Torre del Homenaje (keep) rises up out of the middle of the E. wall.

Bayona

Pontevedra / Galicia   p.386☐B 3

Known as Erizana in the Middle Ages. Its inhabitants were the first people to receive the news of the discovery of America for the caravel La Pinta docked here on her return. This picturesque town has kept many medieval features. There are some fine old mansions, including a baroque building by Don Lope de Mendoza and the Palacio de los Correa.

The Romanesque-Gothic *collegiate church* has a nave and two aisles, rib vaulting, fine capitals and a Romanesque portal. The atrium is framed by crosses from the 16–18C.

The *Castillo de Monterreal*, on a hill overlooking the sea near Bayona, has a fine view. Here, among other things, there is a fine medieval tapestry of the Creation of the World (see also Gerona Cathedral). There is also a large park within the strong defensive walls. Three of the castle's original towers have survived: the Torre de Reloj, the Torre del Tenaza and the Torre del Principe, the last of which is square and has three coats-of-arms over the gate.

Environs: Gondomar is the site of the beautiful *Gondomar Palace*. In **Parada** the church of *Santiago* has a 13C apse decorated with old frescos. **Panjón** has a modern *votive chapel* for fishermen and sailors, built in 1936 by Antonio Palacios. The Romanesque church of *San Juan* was restored in the 18C, but traces of the original wall paintings survive. Corujo: The *parish church* is 12C, but part of the original Monastery of San Salvador (already extant in 1092), still stands. **Oya:** The Romanesque monastery, *Santa María de Oya*, on the sea front was founded by Al-

Batres, castle

fonso VII and attached to the Cistercian order in 1185. Philip IV gave it the name Santa María la Real as a tribute to the monks' successful resistance of a Turkish pirate invasion in 1624. The church has a nave and two aisles, vaulting with pointed arches and five apses. The triumphal arch is decorated with old frescos. The baroque façade was added in 1740; 16C cloister.

Béjar
Salamanca/León   p.392☐E 5

This town lies 3,143 ft. above sea level, on a ridge in the Sierra de Béjar, the range which forms the Castilian border. It has a population of around 20,000 and, as well as a great deal of industry, some fine sights.

Santa María: A brick building erected at the beginning of the 13C and renovated in the 16C. The main altar is mid-17C, and there is a painting, the Madonna de las Angustias, by Luis Salvador Carmona. There

are also various gold articles from the 15–16C.

Parish church of San Juan: Originally 13C; the choir and gallery are 17C, the side chapel 16C, the statue of Bartolemé Lopez de Ávila dates from 1630, and the Italianate altar is 16C.

San Salvador: Built in 1554, with a nave and two aisles; fine retable. On the left in the sanctuary there is the late 16C tomb of Captain Juan de Bolaños praying.

Palacio Ducal/Duke's Castle: The ancestral home of the Dukes of Béjar. There are two round towers and one polygonal polygonal; some of the original fortifications are still visible on the W. side. The interior contains a fine Renaissance courtyard with staircase and gallery. One of the wings houses the *Museo Municipal*, which has interesting Flemish, Dutch and Spanish paintings and sculptures by Mateo Hernández, Pérez Comendador and others.

Bayona, Castillo de Monterreal

Bayona, Castillo de Monterreal, gate

Bayona, Castillo de Monterreal, tapestry from the Salón Principal

Also worth seeing: The *hospital*, a converted Franciscan priory, with various 16&17C sculptures in the chapel, including an Ecce Homo and Dolorosa, Gothic paintings and a retable by a student of Fernando Gallego. There are also remains of a *Roman bridge*, and the *city walls* (11&13C).

Environs: Candelario (4 km. S.) has an interesting *parish church* dating from the beginning of the 16C. The *Capilla Mayor* contains some 16C gold items.

Bellpuig
Lérida/Catalonia   p.390☐M 4

This town has been the centre of the barony of Bellpuig since the 11C. There are remains of a castle and wall, which were built by Berenguer I.

Parish Church of St. Nicolás: Since 1942 this has been the most important *Renaissance mausoleum* in Catalonia. It contains the tomb of Ramón de Cardona y Anglesola y de Requesens (also incorrectly known as Ramón Folch), who was born in Bellpuig in 1467 and died in Naples in 1522. In his time he was famous and influential, becoming Viceroy of Sicily and Naples in 1505. His influence helped to keep the Inquisition out of Naples. He founded the Monastery of San Bartolomé in his native town of Bellpuig and this served as his mausoleum until 1942. His tomb was carved by Merliano de Nola in 1525, and is a superb example of 16C tomb

Belmonte, castle

Belmonte, parish church, W. portal

carving. On top there is a figure in the uniform of a viceroy, reposing as if in sleep; there are also scenes from his life. The mausoleum was restored after the Civil War.

Belmonte
Cuenca/New Castile   p.392□H 7

In the 14C Pedro I, the Cruel, conferred the status of 'villa' upon Belmonte, an act which ushered in a period of growth and prosperity for the town. Its first feudal lord was the young Don Juan Manuel, a famous writer and keen warrior who was responsible for building the castle and the city's defences.

Castle (mid-15C): Comprising three square buildings, meeting so as to form a courtyard in the shape of an equilateral triangle, in the middle of which there is a fine Gothic fountain. The walls have towers, embrasures and parapets. The rooms, windows, chimneys, parapets and courtyards are all very interesting. The castle itself has been declared a national monument and it is one of the best-preserved buildings of its sort in Spain. Today it belongs to the Duke of Peñaranda.

Parish Church: A collegiate church from 1459. It has interesting Gothic altarpieces and choir stalls, which were originally in the cathedral at Cuenca and which are decorated with numerous biblical scenes.

Also worth seeing: Skilfully built archways and impressive mansions embellished with *coats-of-arms*; the main square has typically Castilian *colonnades*.

Environs: Mota del Cuervo has white windmills. **Villaescusa de Haro** has an unusual Gothic chapel, *Nuestra Señora de la Asunción*, which has fine filigree-work, a bell-tower and a Renaissance retable.

Benasque
Huesca/Aragon   p.388☐L 2

Benasque is a fortified mountain village at the foot of the Montes Malditos Massif in the Pyrenees; there are some interesting farmsteads.

Palacio de los Condes de Ribagorza: The palace of the Counts of Ribagorza has a fine Renaissance façade and a huge staircase.

Parish Church: 13C Romanesque, with 17C cloisters and sanctuary.

Also worth seeing: The narrow streets abound with picturesque *mansions*, which belonged to noble families such as Juste and Conques.

Benavente
Zamora/León   p.386☐E 3

A town of some 12,000 inhabitants on the right bank of the Río Esla, about 2,428 ft. above sea level. There is much of interest.

Santa María del Azoque: Built 1180–1220 on the orders of King Ferdinand II; restored several times up to the 16C. It has a fine 12C Romanesque portal, but the main portal is classical and dates from 1735. There are a nave and two aisles, and

amongst the unusual features, five apses, each with a chapel. The church has a 16C baroque retable and a 13C Annunciation.

San Juan del Mercado (Plaza de España): A Romanesque church built in 1182. It has three apses, a S. portal decorated with intricate figures in the style of Master Mateo — including a tympanum with the Adoration of the Magi—and a simpler N. portal with floral carvings in the three archivolts. There are 16C wall paintings.

Also worth seeing: The *Hospital de la Piedad* built by Alonso de Pimentel. It has a fine façade and a Renaissance portal with the coat-of-arms of the founder. — San Andrés has a Mudéjar tower which is late 12C. The *Convento de Santi Spiritus* and the *Convento Santa Clara* are both 13C in origin. There are also ruins of the *Castillo de los Pimentel*, of which a huge square 16C tower, the *Torre del Caracol*, has survived and which has flat window-arches under the decorated battlements.

Environs: Castrogonzalo, to the S., on the way to Madrid, is the site of the church of Santo Tomás, which has a 16C high altar; nearby is the Roman *bridge* over the Río Cea. **Villalpando** (about 20 km. away) has the massive fortified *Puerta de San Andrés*, built by King Ferdinand II in 1170, and restored at the end of the 15C by Ferdinand and Isabella. Also of interest are the churches of *San Lorenzo* (13C), *San Miguel* (mid-12C Mudéjar with a mid-15C retable), *San Nicolás* (13C, with a 16C Capilla Mayor), *San Pedro* (originally Mudéjar, but renovated, and with 17C tombs), *Santa María la Antigua* (12C Mudéjar with three apses) and the *Capilla de Alonso Gómes (16C)*. **Villamayor de Campos** (a little way NE of Villalpando) has a 16C church, *San Esteban*, which has a remarkable high altar, and the church of *Santa María*. **Castroverde de Campos**

(NE from Villalpando) has the church of *Santa María del Río* (13C, restored in the 16C, with a 13C Madonna and Child), *San Nicolás* (13C) and *Santa María la Mayor*, which has a baroque retable. Route 620 W. out of Benavente towards Sanabria leads, after 30 km, to **Santa Marta de Tera** with its 13C Romanesque *parish church*, which contains elements of a previous 10C building. NW of Benavente is **Bercianos de Vidriales**, which has a 12C Romanesque *parish church* with part of a 13C nave and 16C main portal. Also NW of Benavente, still in the province of Léon, is **Alija del Infantado**, with the ruins of the 13–15C *Castillo-Palacio*, and the churches of *San Verisimo* (13C, with a 16C Renaissance portal) and the Mudéjar *San Esteban*.

Berga

Barcelona/Catalonia   p.390□N 3

Livy mentions a pre-Roman tribe, the Bergistani, who came from the old settlement of Castrum Bergium and were conquered by Hannibal in 218. The region was a Roman province and in 998 it became the capital of the independent state of Berga. In 1655 the French destroyed the old parish church, which belonged to the castle. The remains of the monastery and cloisters of the *Cistercian Abbey of Montbenet* (founded in 1338) can be seen near the church of *San Juan*.

Environs: San Jaime de Frontanyá: A parish church some 12 km. NE of Berga. 11C in origin, it has survived as the finest Catalonian church of that date. It is single-aisled with a transept and three apses. The dome is octagonal and has a false gallery; the apses have small round windows. **Pedret** (3 km. NE): The little *church of San Quirce* is 10C and was originally full of wall paintings; these are now on display in museums in Solsona and Barcelona.

Caserras (15 km. S.): As well as a *castle* and the parish church (16–17C), there are some fine medieval mansions.

Berlanga de Duero

Soria/Old Castile   p.388□H 4

La Colegiata: Collegiate church (1526), built by Juan Rasines de Burgos, in a style transitional between Gothic and Renaissance. Hall church with a nave and two aisles, and some fine ribbed vaulting; there are also numerous altarpieces and tombs. The *main chapel* has a retable (with 16C paintings and sculptures) and the Plateresque tomb of the founder. The *Capilla de Santa Ana* has a Gothic retable and the tomb of Gonzáles Aquilera; the *Capilla de Los Christos* has the tomb of Brother Thomas of Berlanga. Fine choir stalls dating from 1580 are the work of Martín de Valdoma, as are the screen and the two 16C pulpits.

Castle: Magnificent 15C castle on a nearby hill. It is encircled by two walls and has a large keep.

Other things of interest: The Plateresque *Palace of the Marqués de Berlanga*; the Renaissance *Palace of the Dukes of Frías*; the Gothic *pillar of justice* with Berlanga's coat-of-arms; and the 16C *hospital*.

Environs: The Romanesque *church* at **Bordecórex** (*c.* 15 km. SE) has a unique apse with small Lombard arches. **Caltojar** (*c.* 10 km. SE): The church of *San Miguel* is 13C in origin and has a beautiful portal, which is decorated with reliefs. The interior contains a fine retable (1576) by the sculptor Martín de Valdopa and the artist Diego Martínez. **Gormaz** (*c.* 15 km. NW): The Moorish *castle* was built in 965 and extended in the 13 – 14C. It has a mighty defensive wall and numerous towers. The gate has horseshoe arches.

Bermeo

Vizcaya/Basque Provinces   p.388☐H 1

Bermeo is a picturesque town laid out like an amphitheatre. It has an attractive harbour and a beautiful beach and is the main fishing town in the province of Vizcaya. Probably of Roman origin.

Church of Santa Eufemia: 13C Gothic, single-aisled with interesting vaulting. In one of the side chapels, there is a fine late Gothic *sarcophagus*, belonging to an important member of the Mendoza family from Arleaga.

Church of Santa María: Neoclassical, built in 1821 by Silvestre Pérez.

Convento de los Franciscanos: A Franciscan monastery with a 16C Gothic church and Gothic cloisters. Originally founded in 1357 by the Lords of Vizcaya.

Other things of interest: *Torre Ercilla:* This tower used to be a refuge for the poet Alonso de Ercilla; today it is a protected monument and houses a fishing museum. At the turn of the century Bermeo possessed other towers but of these there are only the skeletal remains of *Rentería* and *Ugarte*. The Gothic 'Puerta de San Juan', with a statue of San Juan, is all that remains of the town's old fortifications. There are also numerous houses embellished with coats-of-arms.

Besalú

Gerona/Catalonia   p.390☐N 3

Originally the centre of a Roman Province,

it was built at the intersection of two Roman roads. Until the 14C, it was very influential as the capital of the province of Besalú, and the town's finest Romanesque and Gothic buildings, such as the *synagogue baths* and a magnificent restored *bridge*, date from this time. In 1077 Besalú played host to a synod. In 1966 it was eventually placed under national protection.

Iglesia Santa María (once part of the castle of Besalú): Ruins of what was once a bishop's church, only part of the vaulting, arches and nave survive. An early Romanesque *tympanum*, with figures of Christ and tetramorphs, is now in a private collection in Barcelona.

Church of San Vicente: An old parish church with a nave and two aisles in a style transitional between Romanesque and Gothic, with a large Gothic rose window in the façade. The near portal displays motifs which appear in the Ripoll monastery.

Parish Church of San Pedro: Founded in 970 as part of the Besalú monastery (which along with the cloisters was destroyed in 1835). The church was rebuilt in 1160. It has a nave and two aisles, and a huge window flanked by lions. The nave is higher than the aisles. The stonework of the windows is attributed to the school of Roussillon. The unusual construction of the beginning of the nave points to Italian influence.

Also worth seeing: The fine *bridge* over the Fluviá.

Environs: Beuda: The old *castle ruins* and the Romanesque *parish church of San Feliu* (12C with an old font), are both interesting. Some 10 km NW lies **Palera**, a former monastery dating back to the 11C,

Gormaz (Berlanga de Duero), castle

with the *Iglesia del Santo Sepulchro* (Church of the Holy Sepulchre).

Betanzos
La Coruña/Galicia   p.386☐ B 1

Betanzos is on a hill overlooking the estuary. During Roman times it was a harbour, Brigantum Flavium, which is now silted up. There are some fine medieval mansions in the town, as well as very lovely churches.

Santa María del Azogue: A Romanesque-Gothic building from the 14/15C, it has a nave and two aisles, a fine main portal, ornate archivolts and, in the tympanum, the Adoration of the Magi.

San Francisco: One of Galicia's most interesting Gothic churches (14C). Fine portals: the tympanum of the smaller (W.) portal has the Adoration of the Magi; the huge S. portal has most impressive Gothic

stone figures (angels, a Madonna and an Annunciation, which show the influence of French cathedrals) on both sides of the capitals of the columns. The interior is single-aisled with three apses and a huge Gothic window. Here too the capitals have splendid medieval carving. The main chapel has a fine carved sarcophagus, in which the body of Fernán Pérez de Andrade lies (d.1384). The sarcophagus is supported on the backs of a bear and a boar; on top lies the knight's effigy with his sword and his favourite hounds and around the sides there are reliefs of hunting scenes.

Santiago: An interesting church dating from the 11C; the structure we see today, with a nave and two aisles, is largely 15/16C. Fine main portal, with figures of Jesus and the apostles in the archivolts and

Betanzos, San Francisco 1 W. portal **2** S. portal with Gothic stone figures **3** tomb of Fernán Pérez de Andrade **4** to **8** interesting stained-glass windows

Betanzos, Santa María del Azogue

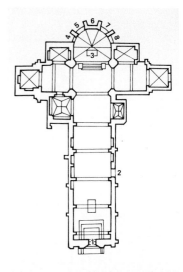

St.James on horseback in the tympanum. The huge pointed arches and rose window are worth seeing, as is the early 16C *Chapel of San Pedro y San Pablo* on the right of the entrance, which has a Plateresque altar by Cornelis de Holanda.

Nuestra Señora del Camine: A single-aisled pilgrimage church. Built in 1568, it has stellar vaulting and a typically Renaissance façade with a gabled roof and medallions.

City Walls: The medieval gates—part of the old city walls built by the Ferdinand and Isabella—have survived, namely, La Puerta del Puente Viejo, La Puerta del Puente Nuevo and La Puerta del Cristo de la Ribera.

Also worth seeing: The *Ayuntamiento* (Town Hall), built according to the designs of Ventura Rodríguez; the *city archives* and the *Colegio de Huérfanas*, which date from the 18C, along with the palaces of Lanzos and Taboada (Orphanage School for Girls).

Environs: Cambre: The church of *Santa María* used to be part of a 10C Benedictine monastery. The building we see today dates from the 12C, and was designed by Michael Petri with a nave, two aisles and five chapels. The church is small, well-proportioned and has a fine portal, bellcote and rose window; other Gothic elements include pointed arches. The *Lema Cross* (1774) is near Cambre. There is a medieval bridge over the Mero. **El Burgo** was part of the territory of the Knights Templar and rivalled La Coruña in the 12C. The Romanesque church of *Santiago* has three semicircular apses, fine capitals and an Agnus Dei in the tympanum over the main portal. El Burgo's Romanesque *bridge* is also worth seeing. **Culleredo** has a 12C *Romanesque church*, with a splendid tower, the Torre de Celas de Peiró, which is decorated with coats-of-arms. **Collantres:** The area around Betanzos between La Coruña and El Ferrol has the largest number of Romanesque buildings in all Galicia, including the 12C Romanesque church at Collantres. **Coiros** is about 5 km. further

Betanzos, San Francisco

out towards Lugo, and also has a 12C church. **Oza de los Riós:** The parish church dates from 1121 and is Romanesque; it is single-aisled and has a square apse.

Bilbao
Vizcaya/Basque Provinces   p.388☐H 1/2

Bilbao, the capital of the province of Vizcaya, has more than 400,000 inhabitants. It is on the bank of the river Nervión ('Ibaizábal' is Basque for 'wider river'), is an episcopal seat and one of Spain's biggest harbours and industrial centres. The city was founded in 1300 by Don Diego López de Haro, Lord of Vizcaya, and by the 15C it had become a major harbour, which was later to be much fought over. Local ore made Bilbao one of the first centres of the iron industry — Shakespeare mentions swords from Bilbao. In 1475 Ferdinand the Catholic conferred the status of 'Villa Noble' on the city. In the 15C it began commercial trading with France, England and Guinea, and later with the West Indies; it also provided part of Philip II's Armada fleet. In the first half of the 17C the city fought off attacks from the Dutch, English and French and between 1808–13 it was taken by the French. During the Carlist Wars it was besieged several times.

Santiago (Plaza de Santiago): Gothic cathedral, built around 1379 and substantially restored after a fire in 1571. The church has a nave and two aisles, a projecting *Renaissance door*, a columned hall from the same period and a Gothic cloister with rib vaulting. The most impressive item left in the church treasury is the *custodia*, a processional monstrance.

Church of San Antón (Plaza del Mercado): Late Gothic, built in the first half of the 15C by Anton Guillot de Beaugrant. Plateresque portal, Renaissance porch and an 18C baroque bell-tower. The *Capilla de los Dolores* has a Plateresque altar by Beaugrant.

Betanzos, San Francisco, tomb

Cambre (Betanzos), Santa María

Church of San Nicolás de Bari (Paseo del Arenal): An octagonal 14C building, completely renovated in the 18C; the old pillars from the shrine serve as the foundations. Inside there is a fine wooden altar and sculptures by Juan de Mena.

Church of Nuestra Señora de Anunciación: A Dominican church with a nave and two aisles, and 15C late Gothic vaulting. The façade and the altar with sculptures are 17C, the late Gothic blind doors on either side of the altar are 15C.

Church of Santos Juanes (Calle de la Cruz): Interesting altarpieces.

Iglesia de la Encarnación: Gothic-Renaissance church belonging to a Dominican convent; built at the beginning of the 16C.

Church of San Vicente Mártir (Plaza de Albia): A late Renaissance building from the 16C.

Museo de Bellas Artes (Museum of Fine Art) with the **Museo de Arte Moderno** (Museum of Modern Art): Two of Spain's most imteresting museums. Both buildings are in the Parque de Doña Casilda de Iturriza, an attractive *park* with waterfalls, pergolas and rose gardens set out in the English style. Exhibited in the museum are painters from the Spanish, Dutch and Italian schools: Cornelius Engelbrechtsen, Jan Gossaert, Tiepolo, El Greco, Goya, Velázquez, Valdés Leal, Ribera, Bassano, Menis, Schongauer, Breughel, Cézanne, Gauguin and many others.

Museo Arqueológico (Archaeological Museum; Calle de la Cruz): Houses some of the more important finds from old Iberian and Roman settlements, such as from the caves at *Basondo*.

Ayuntamiento/Town Hall (Plaza del General Primo de Rivera): An impressive 19C building on the site of an old Augustinian monastery. It has white marble steps and inside there is a splendid Moor-

Bilbao, San Antón

ish reception room (open during office hours).

Environs: Basilica de Begoña: The *shrine of the Virgin Mary*, the city's patron saint, is on a hill close to Bilbao. This attractive and much-visited pilgrimage church was 16C Renaissance originally, but it has been much restored and now possesses a Plateresque *portal*. The modern *bell tower* is a masterpiece by Basterra. Inside there are some large *paintings*, which may be by Luca Giordano; the most interesting is the 'Pilgrimage of Begoña'. Near the church are some fine cloisters. **Galdacano:** *Santa María:* A parish church built between the 12–14C, and the most interesting church to have survived from that time in Vizcaya. The portal is transititonal between Romanesque and Gothic and is richly decorated with figures. The church was rebuilt in the 16C, and the pictures around the high altar, such as the Annunciation, are Renaissance. *Palacio de Urgoiti:* A fine 18C baroque palace, whose façade has a statue of St.Lawrence and various coats-of-arms. **Valmaseda** (*c.* 25 km. W.): A small industrial town on the banks of the Cadagua, which is straddled by three old bridges. *San Severino* is 14C Gothic. Remains of *old fortifications*.

The town flourished in the 15C, after much 14C building, which included a new church, castle, defensive walls, etc. The Countess of Cabrera established a residence here. The Gothic *fountains* of the 'Carre Ample' date from this time. There is an interesting medieval *marketplace*, which is now a fish-market.

Marimurtra Botanical Garden: This was started by the German botanist Karl Faust (b. in Hadamar 1874; d.Blanes 1952) in collaboration with a Swiss called Xenon Schreiber. It has more than 3,500 species of mostly Mediterranean and North African plants. Since 1961 the Aquarium of the Institute for Marine Research has been here.

Also worth seeing: The *parish church of Santa María l'Antigua*, which was first consecrated in 974, and became an independent parish church in 1319. It was restored in the 18C. A splendid baroque altar was unfortunately destroyed in 1936. *Blanes Castle* was already known in the 11C under the name of Forcadell. The *castle of the Viscounts of Cabrera* near the church was built in 1390 and destroyed by French troops in 1694. Only a part of the façade remains.

Blanes

Gerona/Catalonia   p.390☐O 3

The Roman town of Blandae formerly had a reputation similar to that of Tarraco or Emporion. Blanes is the southernmost point of the Costa Brava and on that part of the coast which runs from the French border down past La Selva, Bajo Ampurdán and Alto Ampurdán. The name is well known for literary rather than geographical reasons — in the 1920s the journalist Fernando Agulló was lyrical in his praise of the beauty of this stretch of the coast.

Bosost

Lérida/Catalonia   p.390☐L 2

Capital of the lower Arántales. The original Roman settlement was located in what is now the San Roc quarter. The town lies along the left bank of the Garona.

Parish Church of the Assumption of the Virgin Mary: In the centre of town. One of the finest Romanesque churches in the valley. It has a nave and two aisles, and is structured somewhat like a basilica. Externally the three apses are decorated with

Lombard blind arches. The three-storeyed bell tower has a spire. The N. portal is 12C with three archivolts on four highly decorated pillars with capitals; the S. portal is later. The impressive tympanum depicts Christ in Judgement.

Brihuega
Guadalajara/New Castile   p.388□H 5

Castle of Peña Bermeja: Originally a resort for the Moorish kings of Toledo. In the 18C, on the orders of Archbishop Jiménez de Rada, it was surrounded by defensive walls. Unfinished, it has a rectangular ground plan. Two *chapels* survive: the *Capilla de la Vera Cruz* and the *Capilla Santa María del Castillo*. The latter is in the Torre del Homenaje (keep) and built in a style transitional between Romanesque and Gothic.

Las Murallas (City Walls): These are connected to the castle and are 13C in origin. They have almost entirely collapsed, but two *city gates* remain.

Church of Santa María de la Peña: 13C, built inside the castle; transitional between Romanesque and Gothic. It is simply constructed, with a nave and two aisles, a polygonal apse in the main chapel and groin vaulting. Now much restored.

Church of San Felipe: Gothic, though planned as a Romanesque building.

Church of San Miguel: Also 13C in transitional Romanesque-Gothic style; the portal shows strong Romanesque influence like that of San Felipe.

La Real Fábrica de Paños (the Royal Cloth Factory): Commissioned by Charles III in the 18C in gratitude for the support of the Bourbons.

Briones
Logroño/Old Castile   p.388□H 3

Parish Church: The church dates from 1515, has a nave and two aisles and stellar vaults. The elegant baroque tower was added in the 18C by Agustín de Azcárraga. There is a fine altarpiece on the high altar by Juan Bascardo. The Capilla de la Purísma has a grille, a tomb with a praying statue and a 16C retable. In the Chapel of the Visitation there is a painting by Juan Fernández Navarrete from 1565, and a retable with an oil-painting by Juan de Borgoña. The choir stalls by Juan Ortega are 18C.

Also worth seeing: The *Capilla des Cristo de los Remedios* has an 18C baroque portal. There are numerous *mansions*, such as that of the Quincoces family (16C), that of the Marquis of Terán and that of the Marquis de San Nicolás, which has a splendid façade. The Tor de la Luna and the N. gate are all that remain of the city's defences.

Environs: San Asensio (c. 5 km. SE): A 16C single-aisled *church* with an 18C tower; the *fortress of Davalillo*; the 15C Hieronymite monastery, *La Estrella*, which has Gothic cloisters. **San Vicente de la Sonsierra** (c. 3 km. N.): The church of *Santa María* dates from the 16C and is built on the site of the old castle. It has a portico by Sebastián de Portú (1744) and a 16C retable. The basilica of *Nuestra Señora de los Remedios* has a 13C altarpiece.

Briviesca
Burgos/Old Castile   p.388□G 2/3

Santa María la Mayor: A collegiate church with a huge façade, on which there is an image of Nuestra Señora de Allende. Inside there is a large dome with lavish plaster decorations. The Gothic chapel of *Santa Casilda* has a walnut retable by Pedro López de Gámiz. The baroque *Capilla del Sagrario* has a baroque altarpiece and frescos in the dome and on the walls.

Monastery of Santa Clara: A single-aisled church with a huge Renaissance altarpiece by Diego Guillén and Pedro López de Gámiz (1523).

San Martín: A Gothic parish church built on the remains of an old Romanesque chapel. In the apse there is a highly ornate baroque altarpiece of 1705.

Also worth seeing: The Gothic chapel of the *hospital*, which has a small retable of 1612; *mansions* such as the *Palacio de los Torres*, the baroque *Palacio Abad de Rosales* and the *Town Hall* in the *Palacio de Soto Guzmán*; nearby is the pilgrimage chapel, *Santa Casilda*.

Environs: Aguilar de Bureba (*c.* 5 km. NW): 12C Romanesque parish church, with curious capitals with animal figures. **Vileña** (*c.* 6 km. NW): The 13C monastery church, *Santa María de Real*, has a Renaissance altarpiece on the high altar and the tomb of the founder, Doña Urraca. The *museum* contains more Gothic wooden tombs, and pieces of 14C Gothic panelling. The 16C *parish church* has a tower and groin vaulting.

Buitrago de Lozoya

Madrid / New Castile   p.392 □ G 5

City Walls: Completely surround the city; begun in 11C, frequently repaired; expanded in 15C. That part of the wall built along the banks of the river Lozoya is fairly low and insubstantial, but the rest is high and solid.

The Castle: A 14C Mudéjar building with a rectangular ground plan and towers at the corners. The inside has fallen in.

Santa María: In 1936, the parish church was practically burned down; only the Flamboyant Gothic portal and the severely damaged Mudéjar tower remain.

Environs: Lozoya (*c.* 20 km. E. of Buitrago): The *parish church of San Nicolás*, built in the early 16C, has a nave and two aisles; ceramic altarpiece by Zuloaga. The *Town Hall* is a 17C baroque building. The *Canto Bridge* in the neighbourhood was built by the Romans and is still in splendid condition. **Patonés** (some 15 km. S. of Buitrago): The *caves of Reguerillo* nearby are known as the 'Altamira of Madrid'. They were discovered in 1864, and their passageways and halls extend *c.* 1,000 ft. in all. The walls are covered in pictures of fish, monkeys, a stag, a mammoth and two human figures, which were scratched into the rock. Earthenware vessels and flint implements have been found here. **Rascafría** (some 30 km. SE of Buitrago): The *parish church of San Andrés* is 14C in origin but was extended in the 16C. The nave has Gothic vaulting and 16C panelling. **El Paular** (near Rascafría): The *monastery* was founded by Juan I in 1390 as a tribute to his father Henry, who was killed in France. It was completed in 1440. Since then it has been much altered. The *Kings' Chapel* in the courtyard is part of the original 14C church. It is 15C, has a square ground plan and is groin-vaulted. To enter the church itself you go through a narthex, which is square with groin vaults and has a fine door by Juan Guas (both 15C). In 1755, the original church was destroyed by an earthquake; it was rebuilt in the style of the time. It is single-

Monasterio del Paular (Buitrago de ▷ *Lozoya)*

aisled with side chapels, a polygonal apse and a dome over the crossing. The alabaster altarpiece on the high altar is a highly unusual late Gothic work (15C). The late 15C grille has arches, crosses and coats-of-arms. The cloister, of the same date, has various types of groin vaulting. **Talmanca de Jarama** (some 35 km. S. of Buitrago): The *parish church of St. John the Baptist* has the only remaining Romanesque apse in the province of Madrid. It was built at the beginning of the 13C. The tower (16C) and the portal, with has an interesting late Gothic inscription, were added later. The interior is in two parts, one Gothic with tie-ribbed vaulting and the other Renaissance. The *city walls* are brick. They were begun by the Romans, and rebuilt by the Visigoths, Arabs and Christians. The *Mudéjar brick apse* (on the marketplace) was part of an 11C chapel and has partially collapsed. The 18C baroque *Casa de Labor de los Cartujos* belonged to the monks of El Paular. A barn and a chapel with frescos still survive. **Torrelaguna** (*c.* 25 km. S. of Buitrago): Called 'Barnacis' by the Romans, it was the birthplace of Cardinal Cisneros. The *parish church of La Magdalena* was begun in the 13C but not fully completed until the 15C on Cisneros' orders. The main façade has a Gothic portal; the tower on the right has the coat-of-arms of Cisneros and also that of the town. Inside, the nave and two aisles are separated by pointed arches. The choir is Renaissance, as are the two pulpits. Side chapels house Renaissance tombs and Plateresque-baroque paintings by Eugenio Cagés. On the *marketplace*, in front of the house in which Cardinal Cisneros was born, there is a small monument to his memory.

Burgos

Burgos/Old Castile   p.388□G 3

In 882 Alfonso III of León reconquered the city from the Arabs. Subsequently Count Diego Rodríguez Porcelos built a castle and established a settlement, mostly composed of brave troops. During the course of the following century Count Fernán González, founder of the province of Castile, made Burgos the capital of the province. The area up to the boundaries had to be constantly defended during the struggle with the Arabs, until it became an independent kingdom under King Ferdinand I. In 1075 King Alfonso VI moved the episcopal seat from Oca to Burgos and subsequently had the first Romanesque cathedral built here.

The Cathedral (Plaza de la Catedral): The cathedral we see today stands on the site of the original building and was built in 1221 on the orders of King Ferdinand III (the Holy) and Bishop Mauricio. The building, which dominates the whole of the town, was designed by Master Enrique, who also built the Gothic cathedral at León.

The *Puerta Real* or *Santa María* portal in the main façade is 18C; most of its figures are missing. Above it is a splendid rose-window. The main façade also has two further doors and these have bas-reliefs by Juan Poves (1653). On each side there is a tall elegant tower (276 ft. high); these were built in 1442 by Juan de Colonia and make a wonderful sight with their carvings, arabesques, columns, statues and spires. The *Puerta de Sarmental* on the S. side is the most beautiful of all. It stands at the top of a long grand flight of steps between the sacristy and the cloisters, and this has the effect of reducing the conspicuous height differential between the floor of the church and the street. Built in French Gothic style it has a fine tympanum with Christ teaching together with the Evan-

Burgos, Cathedral ▷

gelists and Apostles. The *Puerta de la Coronería* on the N. side has a 13C bas-relief of Christ in Judgement between Mary and St.John. The left transept has a fine double *staircase by Diego de Siloé* with curious reliefs and gilded bannisters with rich Renaissance decoration. The fourth door, the *Puerta de la Pellejería*, also on the N. side, is Plateresque and the work of Francisco de Colonia. Inside he cathedral there is an unusually large octagonal chapel, the *Condestable Chapel*. This has eight pinnacles and inside, richly decorated walls with coats-of-arms by Simon de Colonia and Diego de Siloé. It dates from the end of the 15C—like the huge dome over

the crossing, also with eight pinnacles, which was finished by Juan de Vallejo. The cathedral has a nave and two aisles, a transept and ambulatory. The nave is 348 ft. long, the transept 194 ft. The *windows* have pointed arches and stained glass. The Plateresque *dome vaulting* was begun by Felipe de Borgoña and completed by Juan de Vallejo. Under the vaulted dome is the *tomb* of El Cid Campeador and his wife Doña Jimena. The *main altar* and altarpiece date from 1562 and are by the brothers Rodrigo and Martín de la Haya. Between carvings of the life of Mary a charming Gothic Madonna sits enthroned. At the foot of the high altar are the *tombs* of the Infante Don Juan, one of Alfonso X's sons, and other members of the royal family. The *grilles* separating the transept from the choir are ornate wrought metal in Castilian-Aragonese style. The *choir stalls*, which comprise 103 separate walnut stalls, are all inlaid with boxwood, a masterpiece by Felipe Bigarny, who also carved the white stone *reliefs* in the ambulatory behind the altar. In the middle of the

Burgos, Cathedral of Santa María 1 Puerta Real **2** Puerta de Sarmental **3** Puerta de la Coronería **4** Puerta de la Pellejería **5** Condestable Chapel **6** dome **7** Capilla del Santísimo Cristo **8** Capilla de la Presentación **9** Capilla de la Visitación **10** tomb of El Cid Campeador **11** high altar **12** Siloé staircase **13** grilles of the choir **14** choir **15** Capilla San Gregorio **16** Capilla San Nicolás **17** Capilla Santa Ana chapel **18** Capilla Santa Tecla **19** cloister door **20** cloister **21** Capilla Santa Catalina chapel **22** sacristy **23** chapterhouse

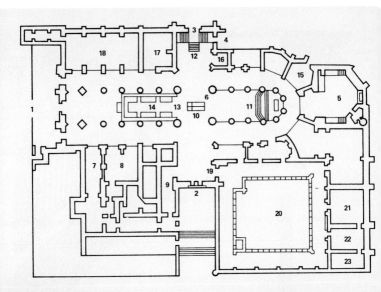

coro is the copper-covered *tomb* of the founder, Bishop Mauricio. The outward-facing side of the coro is decorated with paintings by Juan Rizi. In a corner of the nave is the famous 16C 'Papamoscas' clock, with a figure whose mouth opens and shuts on the striking of the hour.

The Chapels: The *Capilla del Santísimo Cristo* has a 13C *figure of Christ*, also known as the Cristo de Burgos, which legend has it was made by St. Nicodemus. The *Capilla de la Presentación* was built by Felipe Bigarny from 1519–22 and contains *tombs* by Bigarny for González Díez de Lerma and Diego de Bilbao; there is also a neoclassical retable with a *Madonna* by Sebastiano del Piombo. The *Capilla de la Visitación* (1442), attributed to Juan de Colonia, houses the marble *tomb* of Bishop Alonzo de Cartagena by Gil de Siloé. The huge *Condestable Chapel*, built by Simón de Colonia in 1482, is a striking example of German Gothic, with its octagonal openwork dome on a square ground plan. The *grille* is a masterpiece by Cristóbal de

Andino. The tombs of the Condestable and his wife are in front of the *retable*, which is by Felipe Bigarny. Side altars and the small sacristy near the chapel are generously adorned with church treasures, including a *painting of Mary Magdalene* by a pupil of Leonardo da Vinci. The *Capilla Santa Ana*, built by Simon de Colonia in 1488, contains the mausoleum of the founder, Bishop Acuña, and also a Gothic filigree retable of the *Tree of Jesse* by Gil de Siloé and Diego de la Cruz. The *Capilla San Gregorio* contains two 14C tombs. The *Capilla San Nicolás* (13C) is the oldest in the cathedral. The baroque *Capilla Santa Tecla*, decorated by José Churriguera, has a 12C font.

Cloisters: On the entrance door there is a magnificent Baptism of Christ and Annunciation. The cloisters themselves are 13C Gothic and have some interesting *sculptures*, of which the group with Ferdinand III and his wife Beatrix of Swabia are the most impressive. The chapel in the upper part of the cloisters contains important

Burgos, Cathedral, window

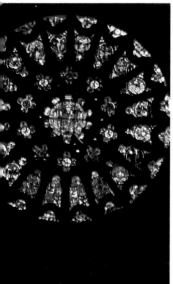

Burgos, Cathedral, dome

tombs. The chapterhouse and the archive house the *Diocesan Museum*, which has exhibits of documents, carpets, wall-hangings, vessels, paintings, miniatures and works in gold, which are of great value.

San Nicolás (C. Fernán González): A Gothic church with a nave and two aisles, built by the Colonia family. It has 16C Flemish paintings and splendid Gothic tombs. In the tympanum above the portal there is a statue of St. Nicholas (seated), which is the work of Juan de Colonia. The door is decorated with scenes from the lives of saints and the huge stone retable behind the high altar is by Francisco de Colonia.

San Gil (C. Trinidad): Rather a plain Gothic church from the outside with numerous things of interest within. The *Capilla de la Natividad* has octagonal vaulting and an altarpiece by Felipe Bigarny. In the *Capilla de Santo Cristo* there is a painting of Christ. The *main chapel* has a baroque retable, a 15C gilded pulpit, a wooden altarpiece by Diego de Siloé, a Madonna by Gregorio Fernández and many tombs.

San Lesmes (C. de San Juan): This richly decorated Gothic church contains a beautiful retable and many tombs—that of San Lesmes, which has a carved figure lying on the top, is worth mentioning.

Santa Gaeda (Plaza de la Catedral): An early Gothic church of great historical importance, for it was here that King Alfonso VI revoked his oath to El Cid. There is a most unusual font.

Other churches of interest: The Gothic *San Esteban* has a rose window in the portal, Renaissance retables and tombs, a cloister and a carpet collection (in the sacristy). *San Cosme* has a Plateresque portal by Juan de Vallejo (16C) and baroque retables. The church of *Santa Clara* is 13C. *Santa Dorotea*, which has the coat-of-arms of Ferdinand and Isabella on its Gothic façade, is 15C. *La Merced* was built by Juan de Colonia in the 15C.

Burgos, Cathedral, Condestable Chapel

Las Huelgas Monastery

Real Monasteria de Las Huelgas (C. La Castellana): Founded in 1187 by Alfonso VIII, and planned as a pantheon for the Kings of Castile. It belonged to the Cistercian order and was under the protection of the royal house. The complex consists of a convent and a church with associated buildings, all of which are surrounded by walls with battlements. The church has a rather simple Cistercian façade, a square tower, an atrium with an arcade, which is built in a style style transitional between Romanesque and Gothic and, on the N. side, a portico. The Gothic church has a nave and two aisles, which were intended as burial places; the nave for kings, the right aisle for Infantes and the left aisle for nuns. The many *tombs* include that of the Infante Don Fernando de la Cerda, Alfonso X's eldest son, and also that of the founder, Alfonso VIII, and his wife. The 13C Romanesque *Cloister of San Fernando* leads to the chapterhouse, where the banner of the Miramamolin, from the Battle of Las Navas de Tolosa, is on display. This in turn leads to the Romanesque 'Claus-

trillas', a small cloister, and on to the *Moorish Chapel of Santiago de la Asunción*, which has horseshoe arches. One room contains a collection of valuable medieval textiles, which is unique in the world.

Cartuja de Miraflores: (4 km. from the town centre): King Henry III's old palace occupied this site, which Juan II later gave to the Carthusian monks. In 1441 they built a charterhouse on the land. This was rebuilt after a fire in 1452. The portal has plain arches, and there is a 15C Pietà in the tympanum. The single-aisled church is 15C, built in the Isabelline style and divided into three parts. The middle part has fine *Renaissance choir stalls*. The *tombs* of King Juan II and his wife Isabella of Portugal are there, along with that of the Infante Don Alfonso, brother of Isabella the Catholic. These tombs and the wooden *retable* (reputedly covered with the first gold brought back from America) are masterpieces by Diego de Siloé. The chapel contains an *Annunciation* by Berruguete and *Magdalena* by Ribera. The

Burgos, Las Huelgas Monastery

Cartuja de Miraflores (Burgos), Last Supper

Chapel of St. Bruno has a *statue* of St. Bruno by Pereira (17C).

San Pedro de Cardeña: From the charterhouse the roads leads to a convent (some 9 km. from the town centre), which is one of the oldest Benedictine monasteries in Spain. It was completely restored in the 17C, but has traces of the original Romanesque—cloisters and chapterhouse are both 12C and parts are even early Romanesque from the 11C. The church is 15C, has a nave and two aisles and contains the impressive *martyr's cloister* and *Chapel of El Cid.*

Casa del Cordón: One of the finest examples of secular architecture in Burgos. Flanked by two towers it was built 1482–92 and named after the stone cordon representing the girdle of St. Francis, which frames the portal. The classical courtyard has triple galleries.

Hospital del Rey: Founded by Alfonso VIII in the same year in which the Monasterio de Las Huelgas was built. It was intended for the poor and pilgrims. The Plateresque portal, *Puerta de Romeros*, and that of the church are both especially striking.

Other things of interest: The town has squares, streets and mansions of unparalleled beauty, of which the following merit special attention: the *Arco de Fernán González*, built as a monument to war heroes in 1592; the 10C Moorish *Arco de San Martín*, which is flanked by towers; the *Hospital Barrantes*, built in 1627,

Cartuja de Miraflores, retable

Burgos, Arco de Santa María

whose portal has round arches; the *Hospital de la Concepción*, built by Diego de Bernuy in 1561 with one Plateresque façade and one in the style of Herrera; the *Plaza Mayor*, with a statue of Charles III and the Town Hall of 1788. On the hill of San Miguel you can see the *remains of one of Spain's most powerful castles* and former royal residence, blown up by the French.

Museums: *The Provincial Archaeological Museum* occupies the Casa de Miranda (1545), which has a fine courtyard and Renaissance staircase. Three large rooms display numerous finds, from prehistoric times through to the present day. Among the Spanish-Roman stele and Visigoth and Arab sarcophagi, there is a decorated enamel *altar frontal*, which is a masterpiece of 12C Romanesque metalwork. The *tomb* of Juan de Padilla is also of interest with a figure of a soldier in an attitude of prayer by Diego de Siloé. Among many other impressive exhibits is a collection of paintings by Berruguete, Rizi, Lucas Jordán and other 15–16C painters. The *Museo Marceliano Santa María* is in the former monastery of San Juan and has about 150 works of these Castilian painters.

Environs: Fresdelval (*c.* 7 km. N.): The Gothic *cloister* is all that remains of the 15C monastery. **Gamonal de Riopico** (*c.* 3 km. E.): The church of *Nuestra Señora de la Antigua* is 14C. **Monasterio de Rodilla** (*c.* 15 km. NE): The 12C church of *Nuestra Señora del Valle* has a single aisle and a semicircular domed apse. **Palacios de Benaver** (*c.* 10 km W.): The *church* has an atrium and a flat tower, and consists of a nave and two aisles and an apse with barrel vaulting; the 14C *church of the Benedictine monastery* has a 13C cross and three wooden statues in a recumbent position.**Sarracín** (*c.* 10 km. S.): The *Palacio de Saldañuela* is Italianate and has a façade with arches and a courtyard. **Bugedo de Juarros** (*c.* 20 km. SE): The *Cistercian monastery* from 1172 comprises a single-aisled church, a semicircular apse, a chapterhouse and cloisters, which were renovated in the 17C. **San Juan de Ortega** (*c.* 15 km. NE): All that remains of the 12C monastery is the *church*, which has a nave and two aisles and the splendid 15C Gothic tomb of Juan de Ortega, which is surrounded by a 16C Plateresque grille.

Cáceres

The Celtic settlement was occupied by the Romans in 54BC and, under the name of Castra Caecilii (after Quintus Caecilius Metellus, Pompey's fellow commander in Spain), was converted to a Roman colony subordinate to the Colonia Norba Caesarea, now Alcantara. Under the Visigoths the town lost importance and in the 9C it was taken over by the Arabs, who called it Al-Cazires or Quazris (Alcazares), on which the current name is based. The town was repossessed four times by the Christians, the first time by Alfonso VII in 1141. In 1170 Cáceres was temporarily occupied by the 'Fratres de Cáceres', who later founded the Knightly Order of St. James. The wars continued until the town was finally incorporated into the Kingdom of Léon in about 1220 under Alfonso IX. In the civil wars between Castile, Léon and Estremadura, Cáceres was hotly disputed and consequently was ever more strongly fortified.

The most interesting part of the town from an architectural point of view, is the **Bario monumental,** or old town, on the SE edge of present-day Cáceres. This is surrounded by a ring of walls with twelve towers (originally there were thirty) and has survived almost intact. The walls' foundations date from Roman times, but the walls themselves were mainly built by the Almohades. Many buildings in the old part of the town are from the Middle Ages and were built on Roman or even Celtic foundations.

Fortifications:*The Torre de Bujaco,* a large clock tower, in good condition, was named after the conqueror Abu-Jacob. It was once part of the Roman walls and is still crowned by a Roman statue of the Godess Ceres. Next to this is one of the town's gates, the *Arco de la Estrella,* built in the 18C by Chirriguera and flanked by the ruins of the old *Torre de los Púlpitos* (15C). To the right stand the towers *El Horno* and *La Hierva,* which both date from Almohaden times. The gate, *Arco de Santa María,* dates from the time of the Reconquista; the *Torre El Postigo* and the octagonal *Torre Redonda* at the NW corner of the walls were built by the Almohades on Celtic-Roman foundations.

In the S. stands the battlemented *Torre de las Cigüeñas,* of 1726, which contains a small baroque chapel with the Virgen de la Estrella. Entering the town from the S. via the *Puerta de la Mérida,* just S. there is another octagonal tower, the *Torre Desmochada*, which stands in front of the gateway in the wall. The only Roman gateway in the town walls to have survived is the *Arco de Cristo*, on the E. side. Entry into the W. side of the town is through the *El Socorro* gate, behind which stands the great tower *Los Espadero* (with a machicolation above the corner).

Basilica Santa María de Mayor (on the square of the same name): Gothic church with a nave and two aisles terminating in a Renaissance choir (16C), with groin vaulting. *Interior:* marble stoup (15C), numerous memorial slabs, tombs and sarcophagi from the 15&16C. Renaissance *Sacristy door* by Alonso de Torralba (1527). The *Retable* behind the high altar is dedicated to the Assumption of the Virgin (as is the church itself) and is by Guillén Ferrant and Roque Balduque (1551). At the foot of the tower there is a *bronze statue* of St. Peter of Alcántara by Pérez Comendador.

Santiago: Outside the town walls. The original single-aisled church was altered by Rodrigo Gil de Hontañón from 1554–6. Two mighty buttresses frame the *pointed-arched portal*, which rests upon fluted stumps of pillars. The tower is of a later date (1738). *Interior:* Gothic arches, baroque columns, Romanesque capitals and pointed arch vaulting from the 16C. The *winged altar* in the Capilla Mayor, was begun by Berruguete in 1559 and completed in his workshop after his death. Plateresque *tomb* of Sancho de Figueroa and 'Cristo de los Milagros' (a painted sculpture from the end of the 15C), *grilles* by Francesco Nuñez (1563).

Monastery church of San Domingo (in the street of the same name): 1526; to the N. outside the town walls; with Graeco-Roman capitals.

San Francisco Javier: In the centre of the old town. An extensive baroque building in Jesuit style, dated 1755.

Monastery of San Francisco (SW of the Old Town): Beautiful monastery church with a nave and two aisles in pure Gothic style from the 15C; dazzling baroque façade, 15C cloister and numerous tombs.

Casa de los Golfines de Abajo (on the square of the same name): The most important of the houses in the style of the late 15C, having defensive towers, balustrades and Romanesque windows. Ferdinand and Isabella resided here.

El Palacio de los Golfines de Arriba (NW of the town walls): in which Franco was made head of state.

Casa de las Veletas (House of the weather vanes): Built on the foundations of the former Alcázar, of which only a cistern (known as 'algibe') remains. Five round-arched vaulting bays rest upon granite columns with horseshoe arches. Interesting baroque façade. Inner courtyard with 17C panelling. The *Museo Arqueológico Provincial* is located here, a regional museum with paintings, archaeological collections, crafts and traditional costumes. Of particular interest are a series of carved stele (from the Bronze Age to Roman times), as well as a collection of coins.

Casa de las Cigüeñas (late 15C): Possesses a slender tower in the style of the Florentine Renaissance, which—thanks to a privilege granted by Ferdinand and Isabella—was alone protected, when all the other towers in the town were torn down as a punishment for the continually warring families. This exception was made because of the service of Don Diegos de

Cáceres, Calle de San Pablo

Cáceres in the battle of Toro (some towers were later given new battlements).

Also worth seeing: The 16C *Casa de Ulloa* (Calle Ancha); *Casa de Paredes* (Calle Ancha), which has large Gothic windows; *Casa del Sol* (late 15C, on the medieval Plaza de San Mateo), which has a little balcony with embrasures; the Gothic *Casa de los Sande.*
The 15C *Casa de los Sachez-Paredes*; the *Casa de los Pereros:*, with beautiful 15C Renaissance patio. *Episcopal Palace* (on the Plaza Santa María), with 16C Plateresque portal. *Casa Ovando* (on the Plaza Santa María), with 16C Plateresque portal. *Palacio de Mayoralgo* (also on the Plaza Santa María), 16C with Gothic elements. *Palacio de Godoy:* Superb palace outside the town walls. 16C Renaissance with a beautiful portal, as well as a picturesque corner balcony. 16C *Palacio de la Isola*, with an interesting façade. It now houses the provincial archives and library. 16C *Palacio de Roco:* has a beautiful corner window with a balcony. 16C *Palacio del Duque de Abrantes* (on the Plaza del Duque), with Gothic and Renaissance galleries. Late 16C *Palacio de los Toledo-Montezuma*, built by a son of the Aztec princess, whose father was received by Hernan Cortés.

Environs: Hermitage of the Virgen de la Montaña (1 km. SE): Early 17C *chapel* with a highly venerated statue of the Madonna, a copy of the Virgen de Montserrat. **Cáceres el Viejo** (4 km. N.): Former *camp of Quintus Caecilius Metellus* during the war against Sertorius (79BC). Laid out in the form of a rectangle and surrounded by a 13 ft. 6 in. wall. So far the praetorium, the praetorian gate and a temple have been excavated. **Monroy** (*c.* 20 km. NE): The parish church of *Santa Catalina* was built in the 15&16C in Gothic and Renaissance style. The interior contains a lovely altar with paintings by Pedro Iñigo and Alonso Paredes. The very well preserved *Castillo* is an impressive building with double ramparts, tombs, five towers of varying sizes, battlements and embrasures. It was hotly contested during the time of Henry IV.

Cáceres, Palacio de los Golfines

Cadaqués
Gerona/Catalonia   p.390☐O 3

A beautiful little town in the Alto Ampurdán, at the N. end of the Costa Brava, on the Cabo Creus peninsula. By the beginning of this century it was already a favourite tourist resort. Salvador Dalí, the Ampurdán-born Catalan painter, chose the neighbouring port of Lligat as his residence and built his singular split-level house there. It became a centre for avantgarde artists such as Max Ernst, Paul Eluard and Garcia Lorca. In 1820 a fishing community already existed here; this then developed into a town next to the old castle of the Counts of Ampuria, which is right on the harbour.

Santa María (16-17C): The old parish church was destroyed in 1543 by Barbarossa and his Algerian corsairs. The present church houses a valuable *baroque high altar*, a work by the woodcarver Pau Costa (1727).

Also worth seeing: Fortress ruins of *Castell de San Jaime*.

Cádiz

Cádiz/Andalusia   p.394☐D 11

A provincial capital and diocesan town, whose praises have been sung by many. This is due not only to its delightful setting—on a small promontory extending 9km. long and 1 km. wide into the bay—and to its neat houses with their balconies and miradors, which huddle within the high walls (up to 50 ft. in places) but also to the lush surrounding vegetation. The 'Señorita del Mar' or the 'Tacita de plata' (little silver cup) was known as Gadir and was an old Phoenician foundation (9 or 8C BC). Here valuable tin, among other things, changed hands. Seized by the Romans (in the second Punic War, 218-01BC, the town, built upon rocks only about 17 ft. above the sea, was renamed Julia Augusta Gaditana or Gades. The town was famous in Roman times, when it had a monopoly in the salt fish trade and was an entrepôt for silver and copper; the art of the dancing girls, 'puellae Gaditanae', was also highly esteemed. Cádiz declined under the Visigoths (6C), the Arabs (711) and again, following the ravages of the Norman attacks (813). In 1262, Alfonso X captured the town and resettled it. It was only with the discovery of America that Cádiz reached its heyday. However, by 1596, after English attacks, its importance had again diminished. Two hundred years later historical events threw Cádiz back into the limelight, for the fleet defeated by Admiral Nelson at Trafalgar in 1805, had sailed from Cádiz. During the Peninsular War (1808-13) the town strongly resisted the French attack; the Junta assembled here,

Cadaqués, view

Cádiz, Cortes Memorial

Cádiz, Puerta de Tierra

and the Cortes issued a constitution—which they were, nevertheless, unable to carry through. Within the 17C city walls, only a few old buildings managed to emerge unscathed from the destruction of numerous battles, sackings, etc.

Cathedral (Catedral Nueva): A monumental classical building of the 18C (completed in 1838). It has a nave and two aisles, separated by bundles of columns, a dome over the crossing and baroque furnishings, including beautiful *Sillería* (choir stalls) by Pedro Duque Cornejo (17–18C), from the Charterhouse of Seville. The crypt has the *tomb* of the great Spanish composer Manuel de Falla, who was born in Cádiz. The figure of *St.Bruno* (Capilla San Sebastián) is by Montañés. The valuable *treasury* contains: a tall silver mon-

strance with a golden tabernacle in Flamboyant style (probably by Enrique de Arfe); a chalice by Benvenuto Cellini; a processional cross; the *'Custodia del Millión'* (a tall 17C silver monstrance, *c.* 13 ft. high) by Antonio Suárez; an ivory crucifix and a painting of the 'Crucifixion', both by Alonso Cano; 'Ecce Homo', a painting by Zurbarán and a beautiful painting by Murillo.

Capilla Santa Catalina (Avenida de Primo de Rivera): The former Capucin chapel has *paintings by Murillo*: on the left, an early work, the 'Immaculate Conception'; on the right, in the Sacristy, a particularly beautiful painting, the 'Stigmata of St.Francis'; and on the high altar, 'The Mystic Marriage of St.Catherine', the artist's last work. When Murillo was paint-

Cádiz, panorama with Cathedral

ing this he fell very heavily from the scaffolding and died shortly afterwards in Seville, in 1682. The picture was completed by his pupil, Meneses y Osorio. The beautiful wood carving 'Five Secrets of the Rosary' is by Francisco Salzillo (first chapel on the right).

Santa Cruz (or **Catedral Vieja;** next to the New Cathedral): The beautiful 13C parish church was destroyed in 1596. In the early 17C it was rebuilt in Renaissance style and converted.

La Santa Cueva (near the Calle Rosario): A round 18C oratory with three beautiful *paintings* by Goya, including the 'Last Supper' and the 'Feeding of the Five Thousand'.

Oratorio de San Felipe Neri (Calle Santa Inés): A plaque on the W. wall commemorates the reading of the constitution drawn up by the Cortes in 1812. It is a small oval building (1671) and contains among other things a *painting* of the 'Immaculate Conception', by Murillo (on the high altar), as well as a *terracotta figure of St. John the Baptist* by Pedro Roldán.

Hospital de Nuestra Señora del Carmen (or de Mujeres; Calle del Obispo Calvo y Valero): A beautiful façade of 1740 and an interesting patio (with an 18C ceramic 'Stations of the Cross'). The *rococo chapel* has a painting by El Greco, 'The ecstasy of St. Francis'.

Museo Provincial de Bellas Artes (Plaza del Generalísimo Franco): An altogether interesting collection, especially the 21 *paintings by Zurbarán* —: several paintings of 'St.Bruno', paintings of Carthusian monks and Evangelists, 'Pentecost', 'St.Anthelm', 'Vision of St.Francis of Assisi' etc. Some came from the Charterhouse of Jerez, which was abolished. Among the works by *other painters* the following are outstanding: 'The Virgin suckling the Infant Christ' by Bernhard van Orley, 'Holy Family' by Rubens, 'Ecce Homo' by Murillo, 'Ecce Homo' by Ribera, the 'Immaculate Conception' by Francisco Rizi, 'Deposition' by Juan Bautista Campaña, a self portrait by Alonso Cano, pictures by van Eyck, a triptych by Rogier van der Weyden and others. In Room IV there is a delightful collection of Phoenician, Greek and Roman glass. The *Archaeological Museum* contains finds from tombs, including: an interesting Phoenician *marble sarcophagus* in human form (from the 5C BC) which is unique in Spain; Phoenician jewellery; Graeco-Roman vases; Roman sculptures; and also Visigoth and Arab exhibits. The museum's oldest exhibit is a capital decorated with volutes, which must have come from the temple of Astarte at Gadir, the ancient Cádiz.

Also worth seeing: *Monastery church of San Augustín* (Calle del Rosario): in the right transept, there is a 17C *sculpture, 'Cristo de la Buena Muerte',* which is attributed to Montañés. The *Church of Nuestra Señora del Carmen,* is 18C with a baroque façade with Indian elements. The *garrison church of La Castrense* (Plaza de Falla) has 18C sculptures. The *Church of la Merced* is 17C; in the sacristy there are frescos by Cl. de Torres. The *Ayuntamiento/Town Hall* (Plaza de San Juan de Dios) is a 19C neoclassical building. The *Archbishop's Palace* (Plaza de la Catedral) is 18C. The *Casa de Viudad* (Plaza de Falla) is also 18C; in the chapel there is a painting of St.John, by the Cretan painter

Johannes Damaskinos. Further classical buildings include the *Gobierno Civil,* (the harbour) 1773, the former *customs station* and the *inner courtyard* (1740) of the *Hogar Provincial.* The *Puerta de Tierra* (Plaza de la Victoria), 1755 is the only old city gate. The *Castillo de San Sebastián, c.* 1620. The *Municipal Historical Museum* (Calle de Santa Inés) there is an interesting model of 18C Cádiz, and also documents concerning the Cortes and the Peninsular War.

Environs: San Fernando (18 km. S.): *Puente Zuazo:* This bridge over the Caño de la Carraca is probably Roman in origin. The *Panteón de Marinos Ilustres* contains 52 memorials to famous mariners. The *Casas Consistoriales* is a beautiful classical 18C building. The *Castillo,* originally Moorish, was later converted.

Calahorra
Logroño/Old Castile   p.388☐I 3

As early as 200BC Calahorra, which bore the Iberian name of *Calagoricos,* was known to be an important place, as archaeological finds (now in various museums), testify. The Romans captured the town in 189 BC, rebuilt it, renamed it *Calagurris* and made it a 'Civis Romanus'. The Roman writers Quintilian and Prudentius came from Calahorra. In the Middle Ages Henry II of Trastamara was proclaimed King of Castile here.

Cathedral: Built 13–15C, with a nave, two aisles and an ambulatory. It is for the most part Gothic; the rest is Renaissance. The interior is lavishly furnished with grilles, altars and retables. The *Chapel of San Pedro* is particularly worthy of attention, due above all to its Plateresque alabaster altar, which is probably the work of

Master Guillén; the chapel also has splendid wrought-iron grilles. The *sacristy*, resplendent with forty-one large mirrors, has copper engravings from the Dutch school, as well as fine paintings such as Ribera's *St.Peter*, the *Immaculate Conception* by Vexés and the *Martyrdom of San Emeterio and San Celedonio* by a pupil of Guido Reni. The chapterhouse also contains good paintings such as *Christ seated upon a pillar* by Zurbarán and *Sta. Margarita de Alejandría* by Titian, as well as alabaster statues from the 17C. Of particular interest in the treasury is the Gothic monstrance *El Ciprés*, of 1467, which was a gift from King Henry IV.

Santiago: The church's façade and tower have strong clasical elements and Byzantine features. Inside there is a groin vault with four domes. The Churrigueresque altarpiece is by Diego Camporedondo of Calahorra; the Gothic painting of Christ, *Cristo de las Maravillas* dates from the 13C.

San Andrés: The church portal is late Gothic. The tower has a base of ashlars above which rises the Mudéjar brick upper section. Inside, there is a 17C baroque altarpiece and a Gothic sculpture of the Apostle St.Andrew.

Also worth seeing: The *Carmelite church* has a sculpture of Christ by Gregorio Fernández; the very simple *Capilla de Casa Santa*, built on the site of a Roman prison; the 18C *Bishop's Palace* and the *Casa de Pedro Antonio Ruiz*, which has a Plateresque portal.

Environs: Alcanadre (*c.* 20 km. NE): Gothic *church* with Renaissance furnishings; Roman aqueduct. **Aldeanueva de Ebro** (*c.* 10 km. SE): Single-aisled *parish church* with groin vaulting; the interior, by Pedro de Troas has a 16C altarpiece.

Calatañazor
Soria/Old Castile p.388☐H 4

Santa María del Castillo: A parish church with W. wall and portal in the original Romanesque. The interior is 16C and has fine works of art, including, Romanesque painting of the Virgin Mary, a wonderful Gothic cross, which forms part of a baroque altarpiece (1699), four 16C Castilian oil paintings, a 13C Madonna and a Romanesque font.

Also worth seeing: Ruins of the *town walls* and *castle*; remains of a 12C Romanesque church, *San Juan Bautista* and the *Iglesia de la Soledad*.

Environs: Nafría la Llana (*c.* 8 km. S.): with a 12C Romanesque church, whose windows, columns and decoration have survived from that time in excellent condition. It is single-aisled, has an apse and, between the nave and the high altar, a triumphal arch, which resembles a portal. **Torreandaluz** (*c.* 12 km. S.): Despite al-

Calatañazor, view

terations the parish church has retained the lovely portal and square tower of the original building.

Calatayud
Zaragoza/Aragon   p.388☐I 4

An old border town in the valley of the Río Jalón. The Moors founded it close to the Roman city of Bilbilis. Ruins of the 8C Moorish castle (Kalat Ayub or castle of Job) dominate the town. The town's Moorish quarter is clearly discernible with its massive gates and crooked alleys; in another part of the town there are cave dwellings. Calatayud was often a bone of contention between Aragon and Castile. In 1461 the investiture of the Infante Don Fernando as Crown Prince (later King Ferdinand the Catholic) took place here.

Collegiate church of Santa María la Mayor: The striking octagonal Mudéjar tower, three storeys high, at one time be-

Calatayud, Santa María la Mayor

longed to a mosque. The mosque was converted to a Mudéjar church, with a nave and two aisles, under King Alfonso I in 1120. It was restored in 1907, burned down in 1933, and subsequently rebuilt. In the 16C side chapels were added under the row of arches. The Plateresque portal, built in alabaster in 1526, is the work of Juan de Talavera and Esteban de Obray. It is decorated with beautiful figures of the apostles and saints. In the tympanum there are the Virgin and Child flanked by angels. The high altar is early 17C. Altarpieces in the chapels of San Juan Bautista and the Virgen Blanca are also baroque. In the first-mentioned chapel there is a painting by Pedro Aibar Jiménez, *The beheading of John the Baptist.* The Gothic cloister has a Mudéjar portal and interesting 15C panels. The chapterhouse is also full of interest, and contains a 15C altarpiece of the Adoration of the Magi, as well as a collection of paintings.

Santo Sepulcro (Calle de Sancho Gil): This church of the Holy Sepulchre was built in the 17C on the ruins of an older church built by the Knights Templar in the 12C. The Gothic cloister belonged to the earlier church. The 18C high altar is graced with a remarkable reclining figure of Christ.

San Pedro de los Francos: There was a church on this site as far back as the 12C, and San Pedro emerged from its rebuilding. Built in brick in Mudéjar style it has a Gothic portal of sober design. In the 19C, the tower, also Mudéjar, had to be reduced in height as it threatened imminent collapse.

Castillo de Ayub: As mentioned above, this is the Moorish castle built in the 8C by the town's founder Ayub.

Also worth seeing: *The church of San Andrés* is 12C with a beautiful Mudéjar tower. The *Church of San Benito* has an interesting gilded dome and beautiful stucco work inside. The *Santuario de la Virgen de la Pena*.

Environs: The ruins of **Bilbilis** are *c.* 5 km. E. of Calatayud. It was a Celtic-Iberian settlement in which the Romans later established themselves. Of the Roman settlement parts of an acropolis can be seen, as can the remains of a theatre, which was discovered during excavations. Bilbilis was also witness to a battle between the Romans Marius and Pompey. Numerous finds from the excavation of Bilbilis are exhibited in the Ram de Viu collection in Calatayud. **Cervera de la Cañada** (*c.* 10 km. NW): The Gothic-Mudéjar church of *Santa Tecla* contains several Gothic altarpieces.

bui. There are the remains of a *Roman thermal spring*, an *archaeological and Romanesque museum*, as well as an old *synagogue* and the gates of the old town walls.

Parish church of Santa María: Built around 1700 on the ruins of the royal castle. The statue of the Virgin on the splendid baroque portal has only recently been added, and rather conflicts with the authenticity of the style. The 12C *Romanesque Majestad de Caldas* (Christ on the Cross), all but the head of which was destroyed in 1936, has since been restored. It is a highly original work; especially fine is the carving of the beard and the hair, which looks almost real and is not to be seen on any other polychrome figure of this date.

Caldas de Montbuy
Barcelona/Catalonia   p.390☐N 4

In ancient times known as Caules de Mont-

Cambados
Pontevedra/Galicia   p.386☐B 2

The church of *Santa Mariña de Gozo* was

Cambados, Palacio de Fefiñanes

founded by Fonseca, Archbishop of Santiago, with the blessing of Doña Maria de Ulloa, the mother of Alfonso III. It was built *c.* 1530 with a nave, no aisles and a side chapel. There now remain nothing more than romantic ruins, which nevertheless retain much of the church's former elegance. The church of *San Benito* was built upon the ruins of a much older church. The two baroque towers to the left and right of the façade date from 1784.

Gardens and palaces: Cambados is renowned above all for its beautiful gardens and palaces. The *Palacio de Fefiñanes* was built in the 17C by Pardo de Figueroa. It has an unusual large corner balcony, coats of arms on the façade, a battlemented tower and a beautiful bridge.

Also worth seeing: The *Palacio de Montesacro* (neoclassical; with a large chapel); the *Palacio de Bazán* and the *Palacio de Figueroa. Santo Tomé de Mar* is on the coast, very near to the town, along with the ruins of the Romanesque lighthouse, *San Santarino,* which played an important part in the defence against the Normans.

Environs: At **La Lanzada**, on the coast, S. of Cambados, there are the ruins of an old fortress, which was destroyed in the 12C, and a small pigrimage church, *Nuestra Señora de La Lanzada.* **Villagarcia de Arosa:** is a little harbour town, which existed in Roman times, and which has especially beautiful palaces. On the *Mirador del Monte,* (with a beautiful view of the town and the estuary), there are the ruins of a medieval castle. The *Palacio de Vista Alegre* was built in 1718. Also of interest are the *Palacio del Rial* which has two small towers and a chapel, and the *Palacio de Rubianes* (on the road to Pontevedra), which has a 16C portal. **Caldas de Reyes,** the Roman *Aquae Celenae,* was famous for its thermal baths in Roman times. Roman finds have been unearthed here, including

jewellery, which can be seen in the museum in Pontevedra. The church of *Santa María* has a Romanesque colonnade and stone reliefs in the atrium. In the tympanum above the Romanesque portal there is the Lamb of God. Inside there are the tombs of the Caamaños, (ancestors of the Portuguese national poet Luís de Camões), and a beautiful statue of the Assumption of the Virgin, by the sculptor Felipe de Castro. **César:** Very near to Caldas de Reyes. The Romanesque church of *San Andrés* has a beautiful 12C apse. **Cuntis:** The old thermal baths are a few kms. further along the road to La Estrada. The 18C church of *Santa María* was built on the site of an older church dating from the 16C.

Cambrils
Tarragona/Catalonia   p.390☐M 4

A fishing village and harbour near Tarragona; it was granted municipal rights in 1155. The parish church of *Santa María* is a 17C building, parts of which are 15C.

Environs: Monastery of Escornalbou and **Hermitage of Santa Bárbara:** On Mount Escornalbou, in the Siuarana mountains and occupying a commanding position over the Ebro plain. The site of a small fortress built by the Romans in order to protect the mines they were working nearby. In 1166 Augustinian monks founded a monastery on the foundations of a ruined Arab castle. In 1580 the Franciscans took over the monastery. The medieval monument is worth a visit. The church, in Romanesque transitional style, was consecrated in 1240; the cloister was rebuilt on another site. Also of interest in the area are **Pradell, Torre de Fontovella, Colldejou and Montroig** in the

Cambados, Santa Mariña de Gozo ▷

Siuarana mountains, the last Arab bastion in the Tarragona region. Also **Pratdip** which has *castle ruins* and the **Hospitalet del Infante.**

Camprodón
Gerona/Catalonia   p.390☐N 3

Benedictine monastery of San Pedro: Founded in 948. The church was consecrated in 1169, has a Latin cross ground plan, five square apses, a cloister and a bell tower.

Also worth seeing: *Parish church of Santa María:* A 14C Gothic building. The so-called *New Bridge* (Pont Nou) over the Fluviá connects the upper and lower parts of the town and was built in the 16C next to a defensive tower.

Environs: Molló: The town is mentioned as far back as 936. *Parish church of Santa Cecilia:* 12C Romanesque church with one of the most beautiful bell towers in the region—square with double round-arched windows in the five storeys. **Baget:** The *parish church* is an equally lovely example of Catalan-Lombard style so often found in the Pyrenees. An unusual feature of this church is the window in the apse, which has fine double columns. The bell tower is four-storeyed with double-arched windows. Inside the church there is a wonderful 12C *Christ on the Cross.* **Llanas:** *The parish church of San Esteban*; consecrated in 1168. Interesting wooden *antependium.*

Canales de la Sierra
Logroño/Old Castile   p.388☐H 3

San Esteban: Dates from 1170 and despite some alterations has retained original characteristics. It has an unusual square

apse and a portico. Inside there is a 12C font.

Environs: Villavelayo (*c.* 3 km. E.): The 12C Romanesque church is single-aisled with a 14&15C vault and a 12C baptismal font.

Cangas de Onis
Oviedo/Asturia   p.386☐E 1

Cangas de Onis is a prettily situated small old town with fine mansions. After the battle of Covadonga (q.v.), it became the residence of the Kings of Asturia.

Parish church: 18C with 15C high altar.

Hermitage church of Santa Cruz: The chapel, originally dating from 437, was rebuilt by King Favila (the son of Pelayo) in 775 and restored in 1635. Inside the chapel there are megaliths with etched pictures of deities.

Also worth seeing: The 16C *Palacio de Cortes.* Nearby, is the 17C tower of the *Capilla de la Concepción,* which has a very beautiful portal. The beautiful and famous *bridge* over the Rio Sella is of Roman origin and was rebuilt in the 13C.

Environs: Cueva del Buxu: 2.5 km. from Cangas de Onis is the Cave of Buxu, in which drawings of animals and geometric patterns from the Palaeolithic Age have been discovered.

Cantalapiedra
Salamanca/León   p.392☐E 4

Santa María del Castillo: A Mudéjar parish church, converted from a former mosque. The apse was rebuilt in the 18C;

mid-17C high altar by the school of Gregorio Fernández. 13C cloister.

Caparra
Cáceres/Estremadura   p.392☐D 6

An area of Roman ruins *c.* 23 km. N. of Oliva de Plasencia. Remains of an amphitheatre are recognizable. On the peninsula there is a former *triumphal arch*, in the form of a small temple about 27 ft. long, which has survived in good condition.

Caravaca
Murcia/Murcia   p.396☐I 9

The Holy Cross is supposed to have appeared here in 1232, an event annually celebrated with religious festivities at the beginning of May.

Chapel of Santa Cruz de Caravaca:

Replica of the Escorial with a relic of the True Cross. Begun under Philip IV and completed at the beginning of the 18C. Inside there is a picture of St. Francis of Ribera.

El Salvador: Renaissance church (1534 –1600).

Environs: Calasparra (10 km. N.): Medieval castle ruins. **Cehegín** (*c.* 15 km. E.): The town has preserved its historical appearance. In the main, local red marble was used for building, see the fine 16–18C mansions. The parish church of *La Magdalena* is a modest Renaissance building, which is remarkable for its reversed order of columns, i.e. the Ionian is beneath the Tuscan, a peculiarity, which can also be seen in Spanish-American churches. Inside there are various works attributed to Roque López and a painting, the *Immaculate Conception*, by Alonso Cano or Bocanegra. The baroque façade is graced with a wooden sculpture of Mary Magdalene (late 15C). Nearby is the *Ermita de la Concep-*

Cangas de Onis, Roman bridge over the Río Sella

ción, built in Renaissance-Mudéjar style and furnished with beautiful coloured Mozarabic artesonado ceilings.

Carcastillo
Navarra/Navarra   p.388 □ I 3

Monasterio de la Oliva: This famous monastery is to be found in the little town of Carcastillo, on the banks of the river Aragón. Founded in 1134 by King García Ramírez, it was put at the disposal of the Cistercians of the Scala Dei Abbey in Gascony, who occupied it in 1150. Until the 15C it was the mother monastery of the Spanish Cistercians and it developed into one of the richest monasteries in Spain, becoming a cultural centre.

Church: Built 1164–98 in the form of a Latin cross, it is the earliest *Gothic building* in Spain, which is still standing. It is also one of the finest examples of Cistercian architecture in Spain. 250 ft. long and 134 ft. wide at the transepts, it has a nave and two aisles. The main portal is Gothic. Inside there is groin vaulting, round-arched windows and five chapels. The central semicircular apse is Romanesque. The Gothic *cloister* is 14–15C.

Monastery: Recently restored, this superb building is most remarkable for its chapterhouse, which has ribbed vaulting supported by columns with pure Romanesque capitals. There is also a refectory and a library.

Environs: Marcilla with the *Monastery of Santa María*. This monastery was founded in 1160 by Cistercians, but was much altered in 1713. Also of interest is the *castle of the Marqués de Falces*.

Cardona
Barcelona/Catalonia   p.390 □ M 3

Church of San Vicente: Built 1019–40.

Carcastillo, Monasterio de la Oliva, chapterhouse

Founded by Bremund de Cardona and his brother, the Bishop of Urgel, who was also his successor. It was consecrated on 23 October 1040 by the Bishop of Urgel. In the 18C the church was converted into a barracks. Repeatedly destroyed and restored. The church has a narthex, nave, two very narrow aisles, transept, dome over the crossing and a crypt. The nave is higher than the aisles, as in a basilica, and the sanctuary is in front of the main apse, which differs from the side apses. The *dome* over the crossing, is the oldest of its kind in the whole of Spain. It has a drum and shell-like stone pendentives; the arches are supported by compound pillars. The *crypt*, which is entered from the crossing, has columns instead of pillars, and simple cushion capitals. Running beneath the transept and the main apse, it has a nave and two aisles. The exterior of the church has blind arches, so typical of Lombard style, of which this church is the most perfect example. In the main apse, in the sanctuary and on the upper part of the transept there is a row of blind windows as in the monastery at Ripoll.

Cariñena
Zaragoza/Aragon   p.388 □ I/K 4

La Asunción: Parish church built in brick at the end of the 18C on the foundations of a previous Gothic church. The proportions of this baroque church are cathedral-like. It has a nave and two aisles and a beautiful *baldacchino* over the high altar. On a side altar in the choir, there is an interesting 16C Renaissance *altarpiece* with reliefs of the Secrets of the Rosary; on an altar in the left half of the transept there is another 16C altarpiece. The *Capilla de Santiago* was part of a former mosque and is Gothic-Mudéjar. The parish church also has an octagonal *bell tower*, a relic from a castle of the Knights of St.John and a replica of the 'Miquelet' tower in Valencia.

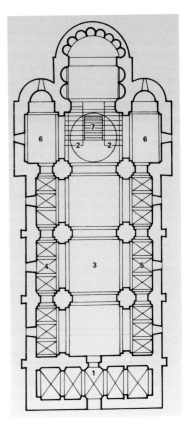

Cardona, San Vicente **1** narthex **2** crypt entrance **3** nave **4** and **5** aisles **6** transept **7** crossing with dome

Also worth seeing: The 13C *Iglesia del Cristo de Santiago. Ayuntamiento/Town Hall:* 16C and very typical of Aragonese-Renaissance town palaces of the time. The façade has an arch supported by columns and is crowned by a roof with deep eaves.

Environs: Fuendetodos (*c.* 22 km. E. of Cariñena): The birthplace of the famous Spanish painter, Francisco de Goya y Lucientes, who was born here on 30 March

1746. The house in which the artist was born has been restored and is now occupied by a small museum. Today it belongs to the family of the painter Zuloaga. The kitchen has been faithfully restored to look as it would have done during Goya's lifetime, with an open fireplace. Beautiful pieces of pottery show the skill with which Muel's potters made their Moorish influenced ceramics. In the 15&16C the Muel workshops enjoyed an international reputation. In front of Goya's house there is a bronze *statue of Goya* by Julio Antonio. The Mudéjar *Iglesia de la Asunción* is in a delapidated condition. The reliquary chapel has frescos which have survived in part. Further frescos in the dome are attributed to Goya. Also to be found here is a *painting of the Virgen del Pilar,* which Goya produced in 1763 at the start of his work under Luzán. Nearby there was a Moorish *castle,* the ruins of which still exist.

Carmona
Sevilla/Andalusia   p.394 □ E 9/10

This town, one of the oldest in Spain, was known as Carmo in Roman times and Karmonaah under the Arabs. The town walls are *c.* 4 km. long and considerable parts are of Roman origin. Even today many buildings in the town still have an Arab air.

Santa María la Mayor: Remains of a mosque, which formerly occupied the site, are visible in this 15C Gothic church, e.g. the *Patio de los Naranjos,* at the N. end of the church. The patio has horseshoe arches and on one of the columns there is a fascinating *calendar inscription* (mid 6C), reputed to be the oldest calendar in Spain. The name day of the town's patron saint also appears on the column. The church has been restored in both Renaissance and baroque styles.

Inside there is a large *Plateresque retable* (1559), which depicts the Passion in four overlapping rows. The choir stalls were carved in the 18C. A beautiful Gothic *winged altar* (15C) stands in the baptistery (1st chapel on the left). In the *Capilla de los Martirios* a Flemish crucifixion altar with carved decorations (1500) and a Plateresque reja are of interest. Also in the *right aisle,* in the Capilla de San José y San Bartolomé, there is a grille in the same style (*c.* 1550). This chapel contains paintings from the mid 16C, which could be the work of Pedro de Campaña. Among other things in the *sacristy,* there is a beautiful processional monstrance (*c.* 1580) by Francisco Alfaro.

San Bartolomé (Calle de los Officiales): Originally Gothic (see S. portal), and with a very big tower; extensive baroque alterations, including four beautiful altars.

San Pedro: 15C, restored in the 17C. The mighty *bell tower,* which is an imitation of Seville's La Giralda, is 17C. Ambrosio de Figueroa decorated the *Capilla del Sagrario* (1760; to the right of the entrance) in the very agitated style of Seville baroque. The *ceramic font* (to the right of the high altar) bears the name of the artist.

Ayuntamiento/Town Hall (Plaza de San Fernando): 18C building; courtyard with a large Roman *floor mosaic* of the head of Medusa and geometrical patterns. The *Plaza de San Fernando* is surrounded by beautiful Mudéjar houses, including the *Cabildo Antiguo* (15C), the former Town Hall, which has a Renaissance façade.

Puerta de Sevilla: Originally a Roman double gateway, which was converted under the Moors and later altered to form part of the *Alcázar de Abajo.* The Roman road, linking Seville and Cordoba, ran through this gate and the Puerta de Córdoba.

Puerta de Córdoba: Restored; flanked by

two massive octagonal towers. Roman in origin. About 5 km. away, a five-arched *Roman bridge* is further evidence of the ancient traffic network.

Roman burial ground: This Roman cemetery (on the W. side of the town) is one of the most important in Spain. Of the 1,000 or so graves from 2CBC–4C AD, some 200 to 300 burial chambers have been excavated; these held interred bodies or funerary urns. Inside some of the chambers there are paintings of flora and fauna. We can get an idea of the burial ceremonies themselves by looking at a large family tomb, the *Triclinio del Elefante* (so named after the painting of an elephant). This consists of a forecourt with benches, where the funeral feast was eaten and a kitchen, where it was prepared. *The Servilia family vault* is particularly magnificent, with separate columbaria (niches for funerary urns) for the servants. The once two-storeyed arcaded courtyard emphasized the high social rank of the family. The *museum* has burial objects, inscriptions, documents, etc. Apart from the Roman cemeteries, *Iberian burial mounds* were also discovered.

Also worth seeing :*Alcázar de Ariba* (or Alcázar del Rey Don Pedro): The Almohaden castle, built high on the hill, and the same size as the palace, can just about be recognized from the ruins. The castle was converted by Ferdinand and Isabella. *Church of San Felipe*, Mudéjar with particularly lovely artesonado. *Church of El Salvador*, 17C, baroque; 18C Churrigueresque altar. *Church of Santiago* (Calle de Calatrava), 14C, greatly altered in the 18C. *Convento de las Descalzas* (barefoot Carmelite nuns): Founded 1629; baroque church, built in the early 18C. *Monastery of la Concepción:* Founded early 16C. The 18C Mudéjar church has late 17C sculptures. *Ermita de San Mateo* (E. side of the town): Showing Moorish influence. *City palaces: Palacio Aguilar* (Calle de Martin

López): very beautiful baroque building (late 17C); the *Palacio los Rueda* (baroque with charming patio) stands opposite. The *Palacio de los Quintanillas* (1755), also called Palacio del Marqués de las Torres (near the church of Santa María la Mayor) and the *Casa del General Freire* are both 18C.

Environs: Alcolea del Río (20 km. N.): The historic *bridge* over the Guadalquivir is 18C and has 17 marble arches. **Villanueva del Río** (21 km. N.): Roman excavations *c.* 6 km. from the town, near the castle of Mulva. **Cantillana** (35 km. NW): Roman *settlement of San Bartolomé;* remains of Roman walls; *Monastery of Nuestra Señora de la Soledad.* **Lora del Río** (23 km. NE): Ruins of a Moorish *fortress castle; Town Hall* with baroque-Churrigueresque façade. **La Campana** (37 km. E.): *Parish church of Santa María:* Late 16C–early 18C. Much work by Antonio de Figueroa, most importantly the main façade. Alonso Cano worked on the high altar, and he is also reputed to have painted the Flagellation of Christ. In the sacristy, there is a fine painting of Christ by the baroque painter Juan Gómez. There are other excellent altars with superb sculpture. The choir stalls are 18C. Interesting liturgical instruments are preserved in the Sacristy. The **church of San Lorenzo:** is an 18C baroque building. **Monastery church of San Sebastián:** The domed *Capilla del Niño Jesús* is of especial interest.

Carrión de Calatrava
Ciudad Real/New Castile   p.392□ G 7

Castle of Calatrava la Vieja: Originally an Arab building, it became the first stronghold of the Knights of Calatrava. Only a few walls remain to suggest the size of the former fortress. The castle was entrusted to the Knights Templar by Alfonso

VII of Castile. They handed the castle back to the King when they found themselves unable to defend it. It was finally taken over by two Cistercian monks, who then founded the Order of Calatrava here. The *Chapel of Santa María de los Maártires* withstood the dilapidation of the castle. It was later called the *Santuario de Nuestra Señora de la Encarnación*. After French occupation and the Carlist War the old wooden ceiling was replaced by a vault. 13C marble statue of the patron saint.

Carrión de los Condes
Palencia/Old Castile   p.388☐F 3

A former royal court and the seat of a count, Carrión de los Condes is one of the most historically interesting towns in Castile. Traces of its former importance can be seen in the churches.

Santa María de la Victoria or **del Camino:** The church's name recalls the victory of Bermudo I over the Arabs. 12C Romanesque; the façade is decorated with carvings. The portico's capitals and archivolts have carvings of bulls and virgins, which, according to legend, recalls the tribute Christians had to pay to the Arabs. Inside there are a number of 17C tombs, a Gothic Christus, and Plateresque high altarpiece; Romanesque cloister.

Santiago: All that remains of the original 12C church is the very beautiful carved Romanesque *portal*: the two capitals show the triumph and damnation of the soul; the archivolts have 22 figures of the brotherhood; and the frieze has Christ the Pantocrator with the twelve Apostles.

Convento de San Zoilo: The 10C Benedictine monastery has a superb 16C Plateresque cloister with lavish carving in medallions and on various tombs.

Also worth seeing: The 13C Convent of *Santa Clara* houses a valuable Pietà by Gregorio Fernández; the Gothic church of *Nuestra Señora de Belén* and the church of *San Andrés* both have baroque altarpieces; nearby, the 11C *ruins of the Benevivere Abbey*.

Environs: Nogal de las Huertas (*c.* 5 km. NW): Monastery of *San Salvador* from 11&12C with a beautiful portal and most interesting capitals. **Santa María de la Vega** (*c.* 7 km. NW): *Cistercian convent* with a Mudéjar church which has a nave and two aisles.

Cartagena
Murcia/Murcia   p.396☐K 9

A city with pop. of 148,000. It is one of the best-protected natural harbours in the W. Mediterranean, with good defences high up on hills. The home port of the Spanish navy, it has large shipyards, a naval arsenal (built by Charles III) and docks. Cartagena, 'Carthago nova', is, as the name implies, a Punic foundation; the Carthaginian general Hasdrubal founded it in the 3C BC. It was seized by the Romans under Scipio in the Second Punic War and named Urbs Julia Nova Carthago. The city became very important thanks to its mineral-rich hinterland (iron, zinc, lead). Later the city took the name 'd'Espartaria'. In 427 it was destroyed by the Vandals. Under the Arabs, who called it 'Cartadjanah', it became an independent principality until 1242, when it was retaken by Ferdinand III, the Holy. The town continued to be hotly fought over, was captured by the Moors again and held for 22 years, before being liberated by King James of Aragon, who transferred the diocese from Cartagena to Murcia. Sacked by English buccaneers who were pursuing the remnants of the Armada on their return to Spain in

Cartagena, Archaeological Museum

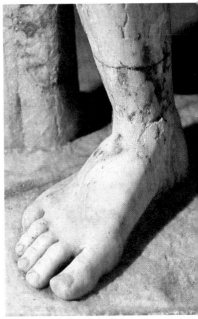

Cartagena, Archaeological Museum

1588, the city sank into insignificance. It played an important part in the Peninsular War. In 1936 Cartagena's fleet declared loyalty to the government, but was nevertheless unable to hinder the landing of General Franco's troops from Africa. There are superb roads into the town. The entrance to the harbour is protected by forts on either side, the *Castillo de Galeras* and *Castillo de San Julian*. The *Castillo de la Concepción*, built in the late 11C by Henry III and rebuilt by Alfonso X, stands on a hill 235 ft. high, and is linked by an old stair to the old cathedral.

Santa María de la Vieja: Former cathedral. 13C Gothic (Romanesque choir screen) and much restored. The crypt houses a small *archaeological collection*, which includes a Roman column, the

Columna pretoriana, further columns (from a former circus) and a Roman mosaic.

Santa María de Gracia: Baroque, begun in the 17C and completed in the 18C. Nave, two aisles, domed chapels and an altar decorated with sculptures by Salzillo and Roque López. There are paintings by Cardona, Cruz and Miguel Muñoz, as well as 'Pasos' by Mariano Benlliure. Salzillo's work can also be seen in the churches of *San Diego* and the *Iglesia de la Caridad*.

Archaeological Museum: This houses Roman finds (statues and stone inscriptions), Moorish art (ceramics from Cartagena), as well as collections of Byzantine and Visigoth finds.

Cartuja Baja
Zaragoza/Aragon　　　　　　　p.388□K 4

A village not far from Saragossa, which developed from a charterhouse. Founded in 1651 by Carthusians, the convent was also known as the 'Cartuja de la Concepción'. It was rebuilt in 1781 and dissolved in 1835. The *baroque church* is splendidly furnished and has an 18C altar. Cloister and church are decorated with beautiful paintings by Francisco Bayeu.

Casalarreina
Logroño/Old Castile　　　　　　p.388□H 3

Convento de la Piedad: Founded by Dominican nuns in 1508. It is a large building with a most beautiful portal and tympanum. The altarpiece on the high altar is 17C.

Also worth seeing: *parish church* with a 17C portal; several 17&18C *mansions*, and a Renaissance palace.

Environs: In the *parish church* of **Castañares** there is a fine retable dated 1544, which is probably the work of the sculptor Damián de Formaent. **Castilseco** (*c.* 15 km. N.): Simple 12C Romanesque church with interesting capitals. **Sajazarra** (*c.* 10 km. NW): 13C *castle* with square ground plan and keep; the Romanesque *Cistercian church* has a 16C retable and 13C painting of the Madonna *de la Antigua.* **Tirgo** (*c.* 10 km. W.): Several *mansions* and an interesting Romanesque *church* with barrel vaulting and two decorated portals.

Castejón de Monegros
Zaragoza/Aragon　　　　　　　p.388□K 4

A little town on a mountainside in the Sierra Alcubierre. It is dominated by a castle, whose chapel has an interesting 15C altar.

Cartagena, Ayuntamiento

Church: 14C; extended in 1591. Inside there is a beautiful 14C high altarpiece, several paintings and a 14C sculpture of the Virgin.

Castellar de la Frontera
Cádiz/Andalusia   p.394☐E 11

A fortress town high on a cliff, within the battlemented walls of a Moorish *fort*. It withstood the onslaught of the Reconquista for a remarkable time. The castle has occupied the site since the 12C.

Environs: La Almoraima: 18C *convent*, in whose chapel there is a figure of Christ (the 'Cristo de la Sangre' or 'Cristo de la Almoraima'), which is much venerated. **Jimena de la Frontera** (14 km. N.): *Santa María Coronada*, 18C; Gothic *church of La Misericordia,* with baroque high altarpiece and Mudéjar ceiling; the *Monastery of Nuestra Señora de los Angeles* is 15C, rebuilt in the 17C, and has a beautiful 15C polychrome statue of the Virgin; large *Moorish defensive complex*: tower portal with horseshoe arch, subterranean storage system with barrel vaulting, and cisterns.

Castelldefels
Barcelona/Catalonia   p.390☐N 4

The town, a few miles from Barcelona, has a sandy beach several miles long. The name, 'Castle of the Believers', comes from the little *castle* (mentioned as early as 967) in which a small Benedictine community settled.

The church of *Santa María,* which is part of the castle, was consecrated in 1011. There are various 16C *defensive towers* some of which have been restored, e.g. the one in the garden of the Hotel Rey Don Jaime.

Castelló de Ampurias
Gerona/Catalonia   p.390☐O 3

Castelló, a walled town with 7 gates, was the capital of Ampurias until the 14C.

Santa María: (Actually a cathedral since the diocese of Ampurias was supposed to have been transferred here.) Building began on the parish church in the 11C; the square bell tower also dates from this time. The main building, nave and two aisles, together with the portal, are 15C. The *high altar* is by Vicente Borrás (1485). The *portal*, is indeed worthy of a cathedral, having six consecutive foliated arches of decreasing size, and figures of the 12 Apostles, each with a baldachino, arranged on either side on a running console. The interior is impressive, dating from the 13–14C, with ribbed vaulting on excessively wide columns. The Gothic alabaster *altarpiece* by Beuda looks like the highly imaginative product of a silversmith. Equally impressive is the Virgin with Child, as much for her natural manner as for the perfect depiction of the clothes. Unfortunately this fine piece has been damaged in recent years.

Castellón de la Plana
Castellón de la Plana/Valencia   p.390☐L 6

Castellón de la Plana (pop. 100,000), capital of the province of the same name, is about 70 km. N. of Valencia on the Costa del Azahar. James I of Aragon founded the town in the 13C. In 1837 the city fought against the Carlists. During the Spanish Civil War (1936–39) Castellón, one of the last strongholds of the Republicans, was extensively destroyed. The rebuilt city, with its clear, tree-lined streets and squares lavishly adorned with plants, looks very modern. The harbour (El Grao) is 4 km. away. It divides two beaches, where mansions stand alongside high-rise apartment blocks.

Castellón lies in the middle of the so-called Huerta de la Plana, a very fertile region, stretching 38 km. from Cabo Oropesa in the N. to Almenara in the S. and up to 12 km. wide. Because many monuments, and especially churches, fell victim in the Civil War, the city has little to offer the tourist.

Church of Santa María: Gothic church from the 14/15C. Altered several times. After 1945 it was rebuilt according to the old designs. The portals are Gothic.The interior contains a few *paintings* by Francisco Ribalta (1555-1628), who was born in Castellón and to whose memory a statue on the Paseo de Ribalta is dedicated. Opposite the church of Santa María stands the 134 ft. *unattached bell tower*, the Torre de las Campanas. This late 16C octagonal tower is known to the locals as 'El Fadri' and, like the Miguelete tower in Valencia, is also the town's emblem.

Museum (in the Diputación): Houses an impressive collection of paintings from the 15 – 20C, including works by Bermejo (15C), Ribalta (16–17C), and Ribalta's pupil, *Jusepe de Ribera* (17C), who was at the court of the Spanish Viceroy of Naples for a long time and was called Spagnoletto by the Italians. He adopted the chiaroscuro style of painting pioneered by Caravaggio. The little museum also contains works by Flemish painters such as Teniers (17C) and various Italians, as well as a collection of prehistoric finds: tools, arms, jewellery, etc.

Capucin convent (Ronda de la Magdalena): A series of paintings of the founders of the order are attributed to Zur-

barán or at least are thought to come from his workshop.

Environs: Benicasim: A few km. N. of Castellón. Some 7 km. above the town, there is a wonderful *view* from the Carmelite convent in the Desiertos de las Palmas, which is some 2,350 ft. above sea level. Towards the town there is the tourist centre *Las Villas de Benicasim*, which has summer houses, numerous hotels and a long sandy beach. **Cabanes:** A former *Roman settlement*, some 25 km. N. of Castellón, which has ruins and a Roman arch, through which the Via Augusta ran. **Oropesa del Mar:** (22 km. N. of Castellón de la Plana). Above the small town there are extensive *castle ruins*; the *Old Town*, which stretches along a ridge, is worth seeing. During the 8&9C Oropesa del Mar developed into an important bastion of the Moorish rulers. It was seized by the Spanish national hero El Cid in 1090, although it was retaken by the Moors shortly afterwards. Not until 1233 did James I of Aragon manage to liberate Oropesa once and for all. Nowadays the town is an agricultural centre, although the last two decades have also seen it build up a thriving tourist trade. *Of interest* are the high-lying Old Town and the ruins of the *Castillo.* **Villarreal de los Infantes:** James I (also called the Conqueror) had this town built on the plain amid orange groves, just a few km. SW of Castellón; the town has a very regular layout. The arcaded *Plaza Mayor* (the main square) is in the middle of the town. *The churches of San Jaime* (16C) and *San Pascual* (18C), which has the tomb of St.Paschal, are interesting. Moreover, the latter is the largest sacred building in the province of Castellón de la Plana and has a fine tall octagonal *brick tower*. The interior decoration is baroque. A beautiful *retable* with 16 separate plaques adorns the high altar. In the sacristy there are 6 15–16C *paintings* by the Italian artist Paolo de San Leocadio. **Burriana,** to

Castellón de la Plana, Cathedral

the S. of Castellón, is also a country town. In the Middle Ages it was of some importance. The Gothic church dates from the 16C. **Vall de Uxó** (*c.* 30 km. SW): The *Iglesia de la Asunción* has an impressive baroque façade.

Castrojeriz
Burgos/Old Castile   p.388☐F 3

San Juan: In the centre of the church's main (baroque) retable there is a painting of St.John. Gothic retable in a side chapel and several tombs. Gothic cloister.

Santa María del Manzano: A collegiate church founded by Doña Berenguela in 1214. On the high altar there is a 13C seated Madonna.

Santo Domingo: 16C church with a valuable collection of Flemish carpets.

Castle: Dominates the entire town and is surrounded by walls and towers.

Environs: About 10 km. N. lies **Villasandino:** The *parish church* has a Spanish-Flemish Gothic altarpiece by Jorge Inglés dated 1465. **Celada del Camino** (*c.* 15 km. W.) has a Romanesque-Gothic church with a 15C painting of the *Madonna de la Parra* and a tomb decorated with reclining figures.

Castro Urdiales
Santander/Old Castile   p.388☐G 1

Santa María: A 14C Gothic church with

nave, two aisles and ambulatory around the choir. The Puerta del Perdón has Romanesque features.

Castle: Originally belonged to the Knights Templar; later converted to a lighthouse.

Celanova

Orense/Galicia   p.386☐C 3

Monastery of San Salvador: The monastery and its church, which has a superb baroque façade, stand on the beautiful Plaza Mayor. The monastery was founded in the 10C by San Rosendo and the monks of the monastery of Ribas de Sil. A vast building complex, which was altered and rebuilt in the 16&18C, it is one of the most important monasteries in Galicia. Until 1681 Melchor de Velasco was in charge of building the church, which then had a nave, two aisles and a dome. The three beautiful altars with partly gilded Churrigueresque altarpieces are particularly

fine. Relics of San Rosendo and San Torcuato are preserved in silver urns. The sacristy is Renaissance and contains valuable liturgical vessels from the 11&12C. The larger of the two cloisters has a ribbed vault and was originally built in 1550, while the smaller one was built in 1611, or possibly 1722.

Capilla de San Miguel: An inconspicuous but very interesting little Mozarabic church in the middle of a garden. It is a 'Monumento Nacional' and has survived in superb condition from the 10C. The interior is rather surprising, reminiscent of the mosque in Córdoba; it is single-aisled with a transept and rectangular apse.

Environs: Vilanova dos Infantes: (3 km. N. of Celanova), has a beautiful baroque church, the *Virgen del Cristal.* At **Allariz:** (*c.* 10 km. E of Celanova) there is the *Convento de la Clarisas,* which houses the curious Gothic Virgen Abridera, a richly decorated, hinged wooden statue of the Madonna and Child. The 10C Mozarabic

Castellón de la Plana, museum

Vall de Uxó, Iglesia de la Asunción

church of *San Martiño* is in the vicinity of Allariz. Side walls and parts of the façade have survived the alterations of the 12&13C. **Junquera de Ambia:** The monastery of *Santa María* was founded in 1164. There is an old church with a massive Romanesque tower built on to the side. The church has a nave, two aisles, rose windows and Gothic pointed arches above the Romanesque columns. The façade is a visual delight and has a beautiful portal. Altars date from the 16C,17C&18C. The cloister is transitional between Gothic and Renaissance. **San Esteban de Ambia:** The church of *Santa Eufemia* was originally 10C and a few features from this time have survived, e.g. parts of walls and arches and interesting windows. **Baños de Molgas:** has a beautiful church, the *Santuario de los Milagros,* built 1713-68. It stands on the Monte Medo and is surrounded by chapels representing the Stations of the Cross. **Maceda:** On a hill, near the town, there is an old fortified complex. **Bande:** (15 km. S. of Celanova) has a 7C church, *Santa Comba,* which is one of the most interesting Visigoth monuments in Spain. Built on a Greek cross groundplan, it has a square Capilla Mayor and a horseshoe-shaped triumphal arch on columns of Corinthian marble. The face of the vault is carved with patterns. Next to the triumphal arch there is a fresco of St.Antony of Padua. **Entrimo:** Near the Portuguese border with an interesting baroque church, *Santa María la Real,* which has particularly beautiful portals.

Cella
Teruel/Aragon   p.388□I 5

Situated in the broad, fertile valley of the river Jiloca, the town flourished during the time of El Cid.

Church: 15C, extensively altered in the 17&19C. 17C tower. In the chapel opposite the entrance there is a 14C *painting of an apparition of the Virgin*, which is greatly treasured. Parts of the former Renaissance

Castro Urdiales, panorama

Celanova, Capilla de San Miguel

high altar (the work of the Aragonese Bernardo Pérez in 1560) are now to be found in the chapel of Christ; further fragments are in the parish museum.

Town Hall: Occupies a 17C building; interior colonnade.

Fountain: Known locally simply as 'Fuente', this is in fact one of the loveliest fountains in Europe. It was built in 1729 by the Italian engineer Ferrari.

Environs: You can see a Roman *aqueduct* on the route from Teruel to Albarracín.

Cervera
Lérida/Catalonia   p.390☐M 4

The town owes its origins to the 13C castle of Cervera. In the period 1718–1842 the University of Barcelona was set up here.

Santa María: Large 14C parish church with a Romanesque portal from an older church (San Martín). It has fine tombs and a 13C Romanesque statue. In one of the chapels a relic of the 'True Cross', which was used for exorcisms (traditional casting out of devils), is venerated. The church also contains the processional cross from the church of San Nicolás by Bernat Lleopard (1435).

Cervera de Pisuerga
Palencia/Old Castile   p.388☐F 2

Santa María del Castillo: The most interesting part of this 16C Gothic church is the *Chapel of Santa Ana*, which was built as the burial place for Gutiérrez de Mier and his wife. The chapel has a Gothic altarpiece with a painting of the Madonna and Child with St.Anne, attributed to Felipe Bigarny. The high altarpiece is a picture of the Madonna from the 13C.

Environs: Villanueva de Pisuerga (*c.* 12 km. W.): The little Romanesque *parish church* is one of the best examples of this style in the province. It has a remarkable portal with carved archivolts and capitals. **Perazancas** (*c.* 8 km. S.): The Romanesque *parish church* has a beautiful Romanesque chapel behind the high altar and an interesting portal with archivolts; the *pilgrimage chapel of San Pelayo* is Romanesque with Mozarabic capitals and 11C wall paintings. **San Cebrián de Mudá** (*c.* 4 km. N.): 13C Romanesque church with a barrel-vaulted nave and a square apse with ribbed vaulting and Gothic wall paintings. **Celada de Roblecedo** (*c.* 8 km. N.) with a Romanesque church from 1174. **San Salvador de Cantamuda** (9 km. N.): A Romanesque church with three apses, and interesting altars with columns and capitals. Nearby is the 10C *Abbey of Lebanza*, which was so completely rebuilt in the 18C that nothing from the old building has survived.

Cervera del Río Alhama
Logroño/Old Castile   p.388☐I 3

Santa Ana: A 16C Gothic church with Renaissance carving.

Also worth seeing: The Gothic church of *San Gil* with Romanesque remains; the church of *Nuestra Señora del Monte* with a 12C Romanesque Madonna; the ruins of a Moorish-Christian *castle*; numerous 16&17C Mudéjar brick buildings; near the town are the ruins of *Contrebia Leucade*, a Celtic-Iberian town.

Chantada
Lugo/Galicia   p.386☐C 2

A charming little town. 2 km. away is the

Monasterio San Salvador de Asma (or de Chantada), an 11C Benedictine monastery. According to tradition, it was commissioned by Count Don Ero and Countess Adosinda, on the ruins of the Castillo de Chantada, after the latter had been destroyed by the Normans. The cloister and the church have survived. In spite of several restorations the portals, capitals and vaults with Romanesque decorations have survived. The old frescos are most beautiful.

Chelva
Valencia/Valencia   p.396☐K 6

A town about 75 km. NW of Valencia on the Río Tuéjar, in a delightful and secluded setting, (the Pico de Chela, 3,530 ft. rises to the N., behind the town); it is a veritable oasis. The huge Roman *aqueduct*, called 'Peña Cortada', is most impressive. Chelva has a splendid *baroque church* with an imposing façade and beautiful interior decoration. In the neighbourhood there are several *hermitages, waterfalls* and an *artificial lake*, all in picturesque settings.

Chinchilla de Monte Aragón
Albacete/Murcia   p.396☐I 8

A hilltop town, about 15 km. from Albacete on the road to Valencia, with about 9,000 inhabitants. Known as Saltigi in antiquity, it was the capital of the county of Villena before Albacete. The town spreads out in a semicircle around the Plaza Mayor, at the foot of a hill (*c.* 670 ft. high). On top of the hill there are the ruins of the historic *Castillo*, which dominate the town. The 15C fortress is much restored and was formerly the seat of the earlier Marquesadas (border counts). The castle occupies the site of a Roman fort but no

traces remain of the latter. Today it is a prison. Numerous cave dwellings have been carved out of the hill.

Santa María del Salvador: One of the most beautiful buildings in the whole province. 15&16C Gothic, the façade dates from 1440 and the tower is 15C. The apse has superb Plateresque decorations. Between the buttresses, which are decorated with carvings down to the ground, there are pilasters and grotesques. Across the top there is a balustrade, with figures of the Apostles and candelabras (1540). Inside: a Plateresque altar; the Renaissance *Capilla Mayor* with an oval dome and shell vaulting, statues, grilles dated 1503 and a choir desk of 1560.

Monastery of Santo Domingo (14C): The church has a Renaissance portal, 14 – 15C cloister and beautiful Mozarabic panelling.

Also worth seeing: The *Town Hall* (18C)

Chinchilla de Monte Aragón, Convento de Santo Domingo

with fine Renaissance façade (1590). Gothic houses line the alleys leading up the hill from the Plaza Mayor. The *Casa del Colegio* has a courtyard dating from the late 15C.

Chinchón
Madrid/New Castile   p.392☐G 6

Parish church, **Iglesia de la Asunción:** Begun in 1537 as a count's chapel, it was finished in 1626. It is a massive building with a very restrained baroque portal. The interior is single-aisled, initially Gothic, but completed in Renaissance style. Above the main altar, there is a painting, the Assumption of the Virgin by Goya.

Plaza Mayor: The best example of an arcaded market square in Castile. An irregular ground plan and the covered ways and loggias give the square a unique appearance and an unmistakable atmosphere.

Cifuentes
Guadalajara/New Castile   p.388☐H 5

Parish church of San Salvador: Building began in the mid 13C and this accounts for the style, which is transitional between Romanesque and Gothic. The roof is late 13C Gothic and there is a rosette in the gate of St.James. In the 16C the main door was replaced by the existing Renaissance door. Inside there is a beautiful alabaster pulpit and the remains of a 16C altarpiece.

The castle: extensive on a nearby hill. Its building was ordered by the Infante Don Juan Manuel. Roughly rectangular it has square defensive towers at the corners and an impressive keep, the 'Torre del Homenaje'. Between two towers, there is a knee-shaped Moorish entrance gate. On

one wall you can see the Infante's coat-of-arms. The *town walls*, which start here and once surrounded the whole town, have survived in part.

Plaza Mayor: An arcaded square with an unusual, triangular ground-plan.

Environs: Arbeteta SW of Cifuentes. Simple *parish church* with an 18C tower surmounted by a weather-vane in the shape of a warrior, called 'Mambru'. The *castle* on a nearby hill probably dates from the 15C and was a mountain fortress. **Yela:** *c.* 15 km. NW of Cifuentes. The *parish church* is Romanesque from the early 13C. Outside there are colonnades running along both sides, and a semicircular apse. At the entrance, arches are supported by pillars, the capitals of which are decorated with acanthus leaves. The nave has a panelled ceiling.

Ciudad Real
Ciudad Real/New Castile   p.392☐G 7

The town was founded in 1255 and has preserved monuments from its historic past. Its early history is much concerned with the Knightly Orders. The 'Gran Priorato de San Juan', the Knights of Calatrava and the Knights Templar acquired great influence in the area and threatened the authority of the King. Alfonso X, King of Castile, therefore, had 'Villa Real' fitted with defensive walls and 21 watch towers in order to stop the growing feudalism of the Orders. As a reward for the good administration of the town, the king later granted privileges and gave it the title 'Ciudad Real' or Royal Town.

Town gate of Toledo (Puerta de Toledo): Important example of Castile's Mudéjar architecture.

Cathedral of Santa María del Prado:
Built in 1531, it is one of three Spanish
Gothic cathedrals to be single-aisled. As
a result of later conversions it is a mixture
of architectural styles. The last addition,
which was in the 19C, was the slender
tower 'Torre Nueva'. The single, outsized
nave receives light from a large *rose window*.
The *high altarpiece*, a picture of the 'Virgen del Prado' is by Giraldo de Merlo.

Church of Santiago: In the main 13C.
The town's oldest building, dating back to
the time Ciudad Real was still a royal town.
Nave and two aisles, pointed arches,
Romanesque window and a 13C statue of
the Virgin and Child.

Church of San Pedro: 14&15C. From
some angles it has the look of a fortress.
The church has many fine features. In the
main façade there is a Gothic entrance door
and five archivolts with Byzantine decoration. The *tomb of the Choirmaster Coca*, the
founder of the church, can be found in the
Chapel of the Sacrament. It is one of the

most beautiful examples of Spanish sculpture; the reclining figure in Spanish-
Flemish style is finely executed and
reminiscent of the 'Doncel' sculpture by
Sigüenza.

Deputación: A classical building, built
at the end of the last century, housing a sort
of provincial museum. It contains paintings and sculptures by La Mancha's most
important artists, including Carlos Vázquez, Lizcano, Gregorio Prieto, López
Torres, Palmero, Iniesta, López Villaseñor,
Obon, García Coronado, as well as other
famous Spanish painters.

Also of interest: A visit to the *insect collection* donated by the Mancha-born natu-
ralist José María de la Fuente.

Environs: Daimiel about 31 km. NE.
The Gothic church of *Santa María* is 14C
and has a Renaissance façade. The colonnade has semicircular arches resting upon
square plinths, the so-called spurs. Inside
there is a nave and two aisles with groin

Ciudad Real, San Pedro

Ciudad Real, Puerta de Toledo

Ciudad Rodrigo, Cathedral

vaults. The *church of San Pedro* is late 16C, and has an interesting octagonal tower with semicircular windows and battlements. Inside: baroque retable and beautiful groin vaulting.

Ciudad Rodrigo
Salamanca/León　　　　　　　p.392□D 5

Occupies a picturesque location on a hill 2,180 above sea level and overlooking the right bank of the Agueda. It was founded in the 12C by Count Don Rodrigo González on the site of the ancient Celtic settlement of Mirobriga.

Catedrale de Santa María: The cathedral was founded on the 17 July 1165 by King Ferdinand II of León. It was completed in 1230 under Ferdinand III, the Holy, in the year of the unification of the kingdoms of León and Castile. The basilica, with nave, two aisles, groined arches and three vaults, was built along the lines of the basilica in Zamora. The cathedral's S. portal is 12C, dating from the earlier period of construction. In the tympanum, above the pure Romanesque portal is Christ in an act of blessing; he is flanked by St.John and St.Peter on his right and by St.Paul and St.James on his left. Above the tympanum, in an arcade of pointed arches, there are twelve figures from the Old and New Testament; these, like the W. portal, were carved in the early 13C. The W. portal, which probably dates from 1220–25, makes an splendid impression, the originality and brilliance displayed making it a decorative pièce de résistance. The 14C saw further construction, including the Gothic cloister, which was completed in 1525. The NW wing, by Benito Sánchez, was completed in 1526. The Capilla Mayor dates from 1550 and is the work of Rodrigo Gil de Hontañón. The painting on the high altar is by Fernando Gallego (1480-88). Splendid choir stalls with wood carvings are the work of Rodrigo Alemán (1498).

Capilla del Cerralbo: Founded in 1561 by Cardinal Francisco Pacheco, Archbishop of Burgos. It is a classical building, radiating majesty. Excellent paintings by Ribera.

Other interesting churches: *San Pedro,* originally 12C, was much restored in the 16C. The most interesting features are the Romanesque portal and the Mudéjar apse. *San Andrés* has two interesting Romanesque portals. The *ruins of San Francisco,* the former Franciscan monastery was supposedly founded by St. Francis himself. The ruins suggest a construction date some time in the 16C. *San Augustin,* the Au-

Ciudad Rodrigo, Cathedral, capitals

gustine monastery, was established by Francisco de Chaves in 1483; the existing building dates from the 16C (Hontañón). The monastery of *Santa María de la Caridad,* 4 km. outside the town, has a 16C façade.

The three columns: Dating from Roman times, they have become a symbol of the town. Their significance, however, has yet to be established.

Town walls: The defensive walls were built on the orders of Ferdinand II, by Juan de Cabrera, a Galician, probably in the middle of the 12C. They are about 6,000 ft. long, 44 ft. high and 7 ft. thick. Defensive towers and gates are later (18C) additions.

Castillo de Enrique II de Trastamara/Alcázar: Built for Henry II of Trastamara in 1372 on the site of a Roman fort, by the architect Lope Arias from Zamora. It is a superb fortress with battlemented walls, embrasures and a keep. It has been restored and part of it has been converted into a Parador Nacional.

Ayuntamiento/Town Hall: Built in the mid 16C, it has a two-storey colonnade with wide arches. Round towers at the corners bear the town's arms.

Also worth seeing: Ciudad Rodrigo abounds in fine buildings; there are houses along medieval streets and mansions with coats-of-arms in squares, etc. The most important are: the *Casa de los Castros* (16C fa-

Ciudad Rodrigo, Cathedral, façade

çade and two simple towers); the *Casa de los Aguilas* (a 16C estate) and the *Casa de la Colada*, both the latter being the work of Pedro de Güemes. In the chapel of the *Casa del Principe,* the palace of Prince Mélito de Mendoza, there is a Calvary by Juan de Juni (1557). The *Hospital de la Passion* has an interesting Italianate painting, 'The bitter path to the Cross' (1563) in the chapel.

Environs: El Bodón (14 km. in the direction of Cáceres) has a parish church with an interesting 16C portal. In the *Eremita del Santo Cristo* there is a 16C crucifix, probably by Lucas Mitata. About 10 km. further SE is **Fuenteguinaldo** with a Gothic parish church, containing a Renaissance retable. Nearby are the remains of a ruined Celtic-Iberian town,

Urueña, or Yrueña, which has walls over a mile long.

Clavijo
Logroño/Old Castile   p.388☐H 3

Castle: The castle was the setting for the legendary battle against the Arabs in 844; during this battle James the Apostle was said to have appeared upon a white horse. There are remains of the walls and the keep.

Parish church: 16C, with stellar vault and baroque altarpiece.

Basilica des Laturce: Built on the site of

an older church. Inside there is a baroque altarpiece, with a huge oil painting of the battle of Clavijo.

Coca
Segovia/Old Castile   p/392☐F 4

The Roman town of *Cauca*, birthplace of the Emperor Theodosius, was important in pre-Roman times, when it was a Celtic-Iberian enclave.

Castle: In splendid condition and one of the most beautiful castles in the whole of Spain. Gothic with strong Arab influences, it was built in the 15C by Moors on the orders of Bishop Don Alonso de Fonseca.

Built in brick, the castle is finely pattened to produce lovely tonal effects. The fortress has a square ground plan and is surrounded by a moat. The keep has four octagonal towers. A bridge crosses the moat to the main gate, which has a pointed arch to the outside and a horseshoe arch within.

Santa María: A Gothic church built in the early 16C with groin vaults. Inside are the splendid tombs of the Fonseca family; the tombs of Alonso de Fonseca and Doña María de Avellaneda (transept and main chapel), the work of Francelli and Bartolomé Ordóñez, are especially fine.

Arco de la Villa: The old entrance gate to the town is in good condition and has pretty arches and two beautiful towers.

Ciudad Rodrigo, Cathedral, window

Ciudad Rodrigo, Celtic 'boar'

Cogull

Lérida/Catalonia   p.390☐L 4

The village originally grew up around the castle of Cogull, whose ruins still dominate the town. The *parish church* has a baroque façade of little distinction. Interesting 16&17C houses. Cogull owes its fame to *prehistoric wall paintings*, which were discovered in the *Cueva de los Moros*, 500 m. from the village, on the left bank of the river Set. They were one of the first finds of this kind in the whole peninsula, but they only became known in 1908, through the efforts of Ceferino Rocafort. The cave is one of the northernmost in Catalonia to contain wall paintings. The paintings display 45 dancing figures (women, hunters, deer), scratched into the stone and coloured in red and black; 10 of these are simply engraved without paint. Some seem to belong to a later date, and this fact adds weight to the theory that this was a holy place, which was in use for centuries. There are also Iberian and even Roman inscriptions.

Colera

Gerona/Catalonia   p.390☐O 2

On the Alto Ampurdán and one of the last towns on the Costa Brava before the French border. Until 1934 it formed a single community with Port Bou. There are some megalithic tombs in the vicinity.

Environs: Near **Rabós de Ampurdán** is the restored monastery of *San Quirce de*

Ciudad Rodrigo, Castillo with bridge over the Río Agueda

Colera, which was mentioned as early as 844. In 927 construction was started on a new church, which was consecrated in 935 and restored in 1123. It has a nave and two aisles with barrel-vaulting above the nave and quadrant-vaulting above the aisles. Externally the three apses have Lombard decoration, as in Cardona and on many Catalan churches of this date. One can also see the ruins of a former cloister.

Comillas
Santander/Old Castile   p.388□F 1

A little castle-like town, dominated by an impressive complex of buildings, which was erected by the first Count of Comillas in the 19C. The complex consists of an *Ec-*

clesiastical University, built by Domenech Montaner and Cascante, as well as the *palace* and the little castle, *El Capricho*, by Gaudí. Also of interest are the old 17&18C *Seminario Cantábrico* and some mansions, such as the house of *Fernández de Castro y Cueto*.

Constantina
Seville/Andalusia   p.394□E 9

This town, founded by the Emperor Constantine, is a departure point for visits to two places of artistic and historical interest.

Las Navas de la Concepción (16 km. NE): 18C *parish church* , with baroque altar. Inside some figures are reputed to be the work of Luise Roldán. 2 km. from the village there are ruins of a monastery.

Cazalla de la Sierra (19 km. NW): This town also goes back to a Constantine foundation. The church of *Santa María de la Consolación* is a mixture of Gothic and Mudéjar. It has a 16C *statue of St. Bruno* by Juan Hernández.

Córcoles
Guadalajara/New Castile   p.388☐H 5

Things of interest: The *parish church* has a simple 13C Gothic portal. Inside there is a beautiful 15C statue of 'Señora de Monsalud'. Outside the town there is the dilapidated *Monastery of Monsalud*. The 12C church is in Romanesque-Gothic transitional style. The 13C chapterhouse has beautiful columns with Gothic capitals. 16C cloister and 17C sacristy.

Córdoba
Córdoba/Andalusia   p.394☐F 9

Situated at the foot of the Sierra de Córdoba on the N. bank of a sharp bend in the Guadalquivir. A provincial capital with a very strong Moorish character, it is one of the most interesting cities not only in Andalusia but also in the whole of Spain. Indeed, Córdoba developed into one of the most magnificent cities in the western world. The town had already been settled in Iberian times. It became capital of the province of Hispania Ulterior in AD 152 and was later again a capital, this time of the province of Baetica (Baetis was the name of the Guadalquivir), which covered approximately the same of area as present-day Andalusia. At around the time of Christ the town produced great figures of Roman culture such as the orator L.A. Seneca the Elder (born about 55 BC), and above all his son L.A. Seneca the Younger (born about 4 BC), the important philosopher and tutor of Nero, as well as his

Coca, castle

nephew, the poet M.A. Lucanus (born about AD 39). Visigoth rule began in the middle of the 6C and bequeathed a legacy of buildings. Buildings continued under the Islamic conquerors (711). The Arabs made Córdoba the centre of a great empire stretching as far as the Pyrenees. Under the Omayyad ruler Abd ar Rahman I, Córdoba became an emirate (756), and under Abd ar Rahman III (912–61) a caliphate. This period was the city's historical and influential heyday, and it continued until 1010. There was a superb irrigation system, a population of about half a million and a blossoming economy, of which the leather industry (cordwain) was particularly famous. The lovely Great Mosque became a centre of Arab pilgrimage. The town had a further 300 mosques, numerous palaces and equally numerous free schools, universities and public libraries, hospitals and baths. Córdoba's cultural life was so great that it became of European importance. The mighty caliphate ended in 1031, after which the harsh religious attitude of the Almoravide rulers destroyed many of the magnificent buildings from the Omayyad era. Decadence set in and this resulted in a gradual shift of power to Seville. The cultural life of Córdoba shone once more in the 12C with the great Islamic philosopher Averroës, who was a son of the city and who made the works of Aristotle famous in the west. His contemporary was the notable Jewish scholar Maimonides. Arab supremacy came to an end in 1236 with the victory of the allied Christian kings in the course of the Reconquista. Ferdinand III, the Holy, conquered the town. Above all, the breakdown of the irrigation system in the fertile campiña meant economic collapse. With the end of Córdoba's great era came the rise of Granada under the Arab Nasrite dynasty.

Under Ferdinand and Isabella, General Gonzalo Fernández de Córdoba became particularly famous. He was born near the city in 1453, and successfully fought against Moorish Granada. Later he was known as 'El Gran Capitán'.

Mosque/Cathedral: This world-famous

Comillas, aerial view of the university

building, also known as the Mezquita, was the principal mosque of western Islam and is the largest and most beautiful mosque of all. It was begun in 785 (under the rule of the first Emir of Córdoba Abd ar Rahman (756–88), on the foundations of a Roman temple of Janus and a Visigoth church. The mosque originally had 11 aisles but, by the end of the 10C, after various extensions, there were 19 aisles and it was 600 ft. long and 430 ft. wide—including the Patio de los Naranjos, the Courtyard of Orange Trees. The mosque became a Christian church in 1236 after the conquest of Córdoba. The first church insertion was made at the end of the 15C. Emperor Charles V then set about the insertion of a larger church, which is, nevertheless, dwarfed by the Arab mosque. This intrusion, later—but too late—regretted by the Emperor was halted in 1599. The whole complex is surrounded by a battlemented and buttressed fortress-like wall, broken by several gates. The sole surviving Arab gate, the *Puerta de San Esteban* (8C) is on the W. side. On the E. side

there is the *Puerta de Santa Catalina* (Renaissance), which has reliefs of the old minarets on the *Puerta del Perdón*, which latter gate forms the main entrance to the mosque, on the N. side. Next to the 'Gate of Mercy' (14C Mudéjar, with horseshoe arches in customary rectangular 'alfiz' frames and lavishly carved with reliefs), there is a balustraded Renaissance *bell tower* of six storeys. This has a fine view and was built on the site of the minaret or alminar of 951. A statue of the Archangel Raphael, patron saint of the town, stands on the very top of the tower. In the N. wall there is the *Capilla de la Virgen de los Farandoles*, which is no more than a recess with lanterns. The *Patio de los Naranjos* with its palms and orange trees forms the extension on the N. side of the mosque; formerly this had been open, but it was walled after the conquest of the town. On the courtyard walls there are remnants of beams, and these give some impression of the mosque's old, carved ceiling.

The Mudéjar *Puerta de las Palmas* (Roman boundary stones on each side) leads inside

Córdoba, Mosque, nave

he mosque. The prayer hall is relatively
ow (only 38.5 ft. high) and there is an overwhelming impression of a 'forest of
columns' (c. 850). These form 19 transepts
and 36 aisles, without giving the impression of any particular alignment usually so
apparent in Christian churches. The
columns of marble, jasper or granite have
lavish and varied capital decorations (in the
main they came from Roman and Visigoth
buildings). Resting upon the columns and
crossing over each other, are round and
horseshoe arches; these are rendered par-
icularly attractive by the alternate use of
red and white marble—an effect not originally intended in the mosque. Arches from
a later date in the S. and E. of the mosque
have preserved their particularly rich,
somewhat fan-like arrangement. There are
elegant columns between the upper rows
of arcades and extraordinarily lavish ornamentation on the intrados and on other
surfaces of the arches. The wider aisle leads
from the Puerta de las Palmas (originally
he central aisle of the 11-aisled building)
to the *Capilla Villaviciosa*. This was formerly the second *Mihrâb* (the extension
under Abd er Rahman II, mid 9C), and it
has architecturally interesting ribbed vaulting, which was only found in Christian
churches 200 years later. Next to this is the
Capilla Real (14C), which was the burial
chapel of the Castilian Kings Ferdinand
IV and Alfonso XI. The beautiful Mudéjar stucco, as well as the faïence exemplify
the art of Granada. On the S. wall of the
10C addition (under Al Hakam II) is the
splendid *Mihrâb* (Nuevo), which dates
from the time of the most dazzling development in Arab art. Originally the
Mihrâb was just a small niche marking the
direction of Mecca for worshippers; now
this room's splendour encapsulates Córdoba's fame. The gloriously colourful mosaic decoration of the octagonally-domed
Kebla, which precedes the Mihrâb, also ex-
emplifies the superb original artistic skill.
Even walls and ceiling are covered with the
finest arabesques, blind arches and filigree
work. On the friezes of the alfiz there are
Arabic texts in Kufic script. A horseshoe
arch opens into the Mihrâb, the shell-

Córdoba, Mosque, Abd-ar-Rahman-I aisle

Córdoba, Mosque

shaped dome made from a single block of marble. The walls are faced in marble and there are fan-shaped blind arches on the sides. To the left and right are rooms for the Caliphs, the *Makshura*, which is closed off by grilles. To the left stands the round baroque *Capilla de Santa Teresa*, or the *sacristy*, with the church treasury. This includes: a Gothic silver monstrance by Enrique de Arfe (1517), rare *Arabic manuscripts* of the 9&10C, statues by Alonso Cano and a beautiful Mudéjar reliquary, the 'Sta. Teresa' by José de Mora. In the *Capilla del Santo Cristo del Punto* (left of the sacristy) there is a painting of the Annunciation by Pedro de Córdoba, dated 1475. In the *Capilla de San Pablo* there is a retable and a statue of St. Paul, both by Pablo de Céspedes; there are also beautiful grilles. Of particular interest

among the over thirty chapels is the *Capilla Nuestra Señora del Rosario*, which has three paintings by Alonso Cano.

The inserted *Cathedral* (16C, primarily Plateresque), also called 'Crucero', for which 63 columns were sacrificed, has a Latin cross ground plan. This violent insertion was carried out against the wishes of the city council and the citizens. The cathedral consists of the *Capilla Mayor, transept and choir*. Construction started under Hernán Ruiz the Elder (1523–39), was continued by Hernán Ruiz the Younger and El Moro, and was only completed in 1599. The Christian insertion unites the Gothic emphasis on height with the Renaissance arrangement of the walls. Further details include: a red marble altar; two interesting baroque pulpits (1760); and the excellent Churrigueresque-baroque *choir*

stalls in mahogany, with scenes from the Old and New Testament, by Pedro Duque Cornejo (a pupil of Roldán).

Church of La Compañía (Plaza de la Compañía): The church of the Jesuit college was built in the 16C. There is a Churrigueresque high altar with statues by Pedro Duque Cornejo. In the Renaissance patio there is an impressive baroque staircase.

San Agustín (Calle San Agustín): Originally a Gothic church with a polygonal central apse; restored in the 16C. Inside there are frescos, paintings by Nino de Guevara and Antonio del Castillo, and a figure of the Virgin Mary by Juan de Mesa.

San Hipólito (Paseo del Gran Capitan): 14C Gothic collegiate church, with 18C baroque restoration; marble sarcophagi of Alfonso XI of Castile (who had the church built), and of his father Ferdinand IV.

San Lorenzo (Plaza San Lorenzo): Romanesque-Gothic church (altered in 1687), whose best feature is the beautiful rose-window in the façade. Inside there are 15C frescos with scenes from the Passion.

San Miguel (Plaza de José Antonio): Built under Ferdinand III, the Holy. On the S. side there is a beautiful early Gothic portal and also a fine horseshoe arch.

San Nicolás de la Villa (Paseo del Gran Capitán): 13C, restored in the 15C, with a beautiful octagonal *bell tower*. Sumptuous church treasure.

Córdoba, Mosque, patio

Córdoba, Mosque, Capilla Real

San Pablo (Calle de San Pablo): A beautiful Romanesque-Gothic church founded in 1241 under Ferdinand III, the Holy, as the church of a Dominican monastery. The main portal is on the Calle Salvo Sotelo. The building is distinguished by numerous additions and conversions in various styles (baroque side portals) as well as by the use of Arab capitals (main portal and apses) and parts of walls. The interior is roofed by a most beautiful stucco *artesonado* with Mudéjar decoration. The Arab *dome* is reminiscent of the vaulting in the Mihrâb in the Great Mosque. The walls are adorned with azulejos and stucco scrolls. Juan de Mesa carved the *statue* of the 'Virgen de las Angustias'. The *Capilla del Rosario* contains sculptures by Pedro Duque Cornejo and there is a baroque Camarín (shrine).

San Pedro (Plaza de San Pedro): This was the *cathedral of the Mozarab Christians* under Muslim rule. Apse and two side portals are 13C. Inside there is a beautiful 16C artesonado. The Capilla Mayor has an 18C Churrigueresque altar.

Santa Marina (Calle Mayor de Santa Marina): The town's oldest Gothic building (*c.* 1236) with a harshly buttressed façade and a Renaissance tower. Inside: nave and two aisles; converted in the 18C. In the *Capilla de la Virgen del Rosario* there are paintings by Castillo the Younger (St. Francis, John the Baptist), Fray Juan del Santísimo Sacramento and A. Gómez de Sandoval. The *sacristy* has beautiful Mudéjar decorations at the entrance. The church's W. entrance on to the square, is decorated with a *bronze statue* in honour

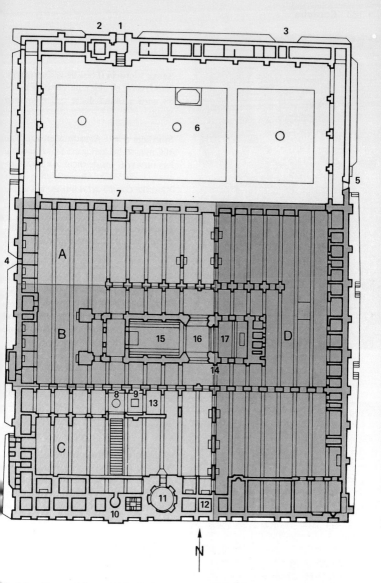

Cordoba, Mosque 1 Puerta del Perdón **2** bell tower **3** Capilla de la Virgen de los Farandoles **4** Puerta de San Esteban **5** Puerta de Santa Catalina **6** Patio de los Naranjos **7** Puerta de las Palmas **8** Capilla Villaviciosa **9** Capilla Real **10** Mihrâb **11** Sacristy or Capilla de Santa Teresa **12** Capilla del Santo Cristo del Punto **13** Capilla de San Pablo **14** Cathedral **15** Coro **16** Transept **17** Capilla Mayor

A built under Abd ar Rahman I **B** first extension by Abd ar Rahman II **C** second extension by Al Hakam II **D** third extension by Almansor

Córdoba, Mosque, window

Córdoba, Mosque, Puerta de Al Hakam II

of the famous matador *Manolete* of Córdoba, who died in 1947.

Santa Victoria (Plaza de la Compañía): Neoclassical church built between 1761–88 with a round dome and columned façade.

Santiago (Calle Agustín Moreno): The 10C minaret belonging to a former mosque has survived. Inside there is a stucco *artesonado* (1635) by Alonso Muñoz de los Ríos; the *Capilla del Bautismo* has a 16C altar.

Convento de San Francisco (Plaza del Potro): This 13C monastery was founded under Ferdinand III, the Holy (a statue of whom is in the inner courtyard). Neoclassical church portal and Churrigueresque interior decoration. Of the paintings, 'St. Andrew' by Valdés Leal is most noteworthy. There are figures by Alonso Cano and a beautiful work by his pupil, Pedro de Mena of 'St. Peter of Alcantara'.

Convento de Santa Clara (Calle del Rey Heredia): Founded by Alfonso X (1262). Of the former mosque, only the mighty minaret (*c*. 1000), which has a muezzin's staircase, battlements and corner towers, remains.

Convento de Santa Isabel (Cuesta del Rincón): Founded by the Count of Priego in 1491. Renaissance church portal. Domed interior with lavish baroque furnishing, which was subsidized by the de Figueroa family.

Synagogue (Calle de Maimónides, No. 18): An undamaged Mudéjar building built by Isaac Mejeb in 1315 and decorated within with stucco. In the patio there is a *memorial slab*, commemorating the Jewish

Córdoba, Mosque, detail

Córdoba, Mosque, Puerta de la Paloma

Córdoba, Mosque, Puerta de San Esteban

scholar and doctor *Maimónides*, who was born in Córdoba in 1135. The house where he lived is supposed to have occupied the site of the Casa de las Bulas (Plaza de las Bulas), now the Museo Municipal Taurino.

Roman bridge (Puente Romano): Approaching the bridge you pass under the *Puerta del Puente*, a Renaissance triumphal arch, built by Hernán Ruiz in 1571. The bridge, which crosses the Guadalquivir, is of Roman origin and some 800 ft. long with 16 arches; rebuilt in Arab times. At the S. end of the bridge there is the *Torre de la Calahorra*. Downstream are the remains of old *Arab mills*, such as the Albolafia, the paper mill and the Enmedio mill.

Torre de la Calahorra: A battlemented tower and part of a massive defensive system. The latter, based on a Moorish complex, was fully extended in 1369 (along with the tower) by the Castilian King Henry II. Nowadays the *city museum* is to be found here. This houses the city's archives and also mementoes of 'El Gran Capitán', Gonzalo de Córdoba, and of the Spanish poet Luis de Góngora (1561–1627), among others.

Alcázar de los Reyes Cristianos (Alcázar Nuevo; Calle de Amador de los Ríos): A fortified palace, bordering on the Campo de los Mártires (also Arab baths). It was built in the 14C under Alfonso XI on the site of an older Arab castle. The magnificent park has survived in Arab style. In the 19C the Alcázar was used as a prison; today it contains a *museum*, with Roman mosaics, and an unusual large Roman sarcophagus (3C AD) with reliefs of figures, etc.

Alminar de San Juan (Calle Barroso): The badly damaged *minaret* is all that is

Córdoba, Alcázar, Roman mosaics

left of a mosque, which was handed over to the Knights of St. John after the conquest of the town. The minaret has most beautiful twin windows, with marble columns and 9C capitals. Muezzin's staircase inside.

Palacio del Marqués de Viana (Calle San Agustín): A lovely palace with 14 absolutely beautiful courtyards and gardens. It is one of the most beautiful residential buildings in Córdoba. Standing on the site of a former building belonging to the Caliphate, its rooms house various *collections*, including: Roman finds from the area, cordwain leather goods, silver work, weapons, porcelain, paintings and also an interesting library on the subject of hunting.

Casa del Carpio (Calle de Romero de Torres): 15C palace. Arab capitals in the patio. Roman mosaics.

Casa de los Ceas (or Casa del Indiano; Plaza Angel de Torres): The beautiful 15C

Mudéjar façade deserves particular attention; Plateresque entrance and twin windows.

Casa de los Villalones (Plaza Orive): Superb Renaissance palace (1560) with finely ornamented portal. The Italianate *loggia* on the façade is especially interesting.

Casa del Marqués de la Fuensanta del Valle (Calle Angel de Saavedra): Nowadays this palace houses the *Conservatory* and the *School of Dramatic Art*. The door has waffle-patterned stucco.

Palacio Episcopal (Calle de Torrijos): This spacious palace stands on the site of an Arab alcázar. It was restored in the 15C and in 1745 and has 16C tapestries. Beautiful Gothic portal on the Plaza de la Pacienca. Nearby stands the splendid Gothic-Plateresque *San Jacinto Gate*.

Ayuntamiento/Town Hall (Calle Claudio Marcelo): A Renaissance building dating from the beginning of the 17C. A black

Córdoba, Alcázar, garden

marble baroque staircase leads up to its beautiful rooms. There is a large painting of the city's patron saint, the Archangel Raphael, by Antonio del Castillo.

Roman temple (1C AD; near the Town Hall): A large and interesting building, which has been restored. The façade is decorated with Corinthian columns.

Torre de la Malmuerta (Plaza de Colon): This massive, octagonal, battlemented tower (1406–8) was once part of the city walls. Under Ferdinand and Isabella it was a prison and later, in the 18C, an observatory.

Puerta de Almodóvar: A Moorish gate in the battlemented city walls; flanked by square towers. It leads into the former Jewish quarter, the *Judería*, whose Jewish inhabitants were driven out in 1492.

Barrio de la Judería (the Jewish quarter): Here the oriental character of the city has survived up to the present day. There are picturesque narrow alleys, mansions and beautiful squares. Especially interesting are the Calle de Cabezas with its many mansions, the Calle de Feria with the so-called 'Portillo', and the Calleja de las Flores.

Plazuela de los Dolores: An exceptionally charming little cobblestoned square, surrounded by white walls and the whitewashed front of the Capucin monastery, with a typically Andalusian atmosphere. In its centre stands a cross, surrounded by eight wrought iron lanterns, and the marble figure of *'Cristo de los Farandoles'* (or 'Cristo de Agonía').

Plaza del Potro: This square gets its name from the foal above the basin of the charming 16C *fountain*. The square once served as a livestock market, but was made famous by *Cervantes,* who mentions the square in 'Don Quixote'. The writer is supposed to have lodged at the old *inn,* the 'Mesón del Potro', which is rather like an Arab 'fonduk' with its cattle yard. Also in

Córdoba, Alcázar

Córdoba, Alcázar, Provincial Archaeological Museum

the square is the old hospital foundation 'La Caridad', which is now the *History of Art Museum*. An 18C *statue* of the Archangel Raphael is the work of M. Verdiguier.

Plaza de la Corredera (or Plaza Mayor, Plaza del Mercado): A large square with red flower-decorated brick buildings with arches. It was used as an arena for bullfighting for many years.

Provincial Archaeological Museum (Plaza de Jerónimo Paez): This important Andalusian collection is housed in the rooms of the *Casa Paez,* a 16C Renaissance building designed by Hernán Ruiz. It contains prehistoric and Iberian *finds* (including a relief from Almodóvar del Río) and finds from Roman and early Christian ex-

cavations (in the second courtyard: carvings of Mithras, sarcophagus with scenes from the Old Testament) etc. Also there is the delightful, beautifully modelled and enamelled 10C *bronze stag*, which came from a fountain in Medina Azahara. It was a gift from the Byzantine Emperor Constantine VII to Abd ar Rahman III. Also of interest is a collection of so-called 'braseros', or iron braziers with Arab inscriptions.

Museum of Art (Plaza del Potro): The *chapel* of this former hospital 'de la Caridad' (15C) contains *paintings* from the *Córdoba School of the 17C* and includes works by Agustín and Antonio del Castillo, Valdés Leal and Bocanegra. A whole room is reserved for the work of Mateo Inurria, a sculptor from Córdoba (the equestrian

statue in the Plaza de José Antonio is his work). The top floor of the hospital has work from the *School of Córdoba of the 15&16C*: a triptych of 1494; 'Flagellation of Christ' by Alejo Fernández; 'St.Nicólas of Bari' by Pedro de Córdoba; paintings by Pedro Romano; 'The Immaculate Conception', a painting by Murillo, and paintings by Francisco Pacheco, among others. Flemish and Italian painters are also represented, as is Goya, with two portraits. There is further a collection of graphics and modern paintings. The baroque façade of the *Museo de Julio Romero de Torres* (1880-1930) looks on to the patio; it houses his works, which include portraits and Andalusian landscapes.

Museo Municipal Taurino (bullfighting museum; Plaza de las Bulas, Casa de las Bulas:) 16C; with bullfighting exhibits and mementoes of the city's famous toreros, such as Manolete, Lagartijo, El Córdobés and others.There are also leather and silver articles.

Also worth seeing: *Church of San Andrés* (Calle San Andrés): 13C, converted 18C, with an early 16C altar in the left transept chapel. *Church of San Pedro de Alcántara* (Calle Salazar): 16C portal; converted to baroque in the 17C. A 'Mater Dolorosa' painted by Pedro de Mena. 18C *Church of San Raphael. Church of la Trinidad* (Calle Sanchez de la Feria) with 17C Churrigueresque altars and sculptures by José de Mora. *Church of El Sagrado Corazón* (not far from the Plaza de Sevilla) with a 10C minaret. *Ermita de la Magdalena* (Plaza de la Magdalena): One of the oldest

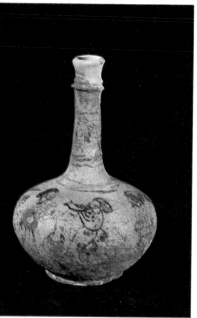

Córdoba, Alcázar, Arabic vase

Córdoba, Alcázar, Iberian lion

churches in Córdoba. It has remarkable early 13C Romanesque-Gothic portals; 18C baroque alterations. *Capilla de San Bartolomé* (13–14C): Stucco-decorated interior with especially beautiful azulejos and interesting Visigoth columns. *Capilla San Jacinto* (Calle de Torrijos): Beautiful late-Gothic portal. *Oratorio of San Felipe de Neri* (Calle de San Felipe): 16C, nowadays Gobierno Militar. The façade was probably by A. Berruguete. The *Convento de Carmelitas Calzadas* (Puerta Nueva): A Mudéjar church (1580) with a retable of 12 good paintings by Valdés Leal. The baroque *Monastery of La Encarnación.* The *Convento Jesús Crucificado* (Calle del Buen Pastor): Monastery founded in 1588; lovely artesonado and fine capitals. Former *Carmelite monastery* (Calle del Buen Pastor), where St.John of the Cross lived. *Monastery of Jesús Nazareno:* Sculptures by Antonio del Castillo. *Monastery of San Cayetano* (Calle de A. El Sabio): Founded (1580) by St. John of the Cross. 17C church. *Convento de Santa Ana* (Alta de Santa Ana): 16C; 18C figures on the portal. *Colegio de la Merced* (Plaza de Colón): The former monastery church has a very beautiful baroque façade (1745) and also an extraordinarily beautiful Renaissance patio. The baroque church was gutted by fire in 1978. *Hermitage of los Mártires* (R. de los Mártires, on the Guadalquivir): The church's altar is a 3C Roman sarcophagus. The *Santuario de Nuestra Señora de la Fuensanta is a pilgrimage church* dated 1641; paintings by Pablo des Céspedes and A. del Castillo. The *Hospital de Agudos* (near the Plaza de las Bulas) is 18C: The beautiful Gothic-Mudéjar *Capilla de San Bartolomé* (13–14C) has stucco decorations, especially lovely azulejos and remarkable Visigoth columns. The *Casa de Hernan de Oliva* (Calle de San Pablo): Plateresque fa-

Córdoba, Museo de Julio Romero de ▷
Torres

çade. *Mansion of the Fernández family of Córdoba:* A magnificent Renaissance building near the Plazuela de los Dolores.

Environs: Medina Azahara (8 km. SW): Here stood the famous palace town of the Omayyad Caliph Abd ar Rahman III, which was one of the most beautiful complexes of Arab secular architecture. The numerous buildings were spread over a large area (some 1,675 yds. by 840 yds.), on three terraces on the slopes of the Sierra Morena. They were surrounded by a double wall defended with towers. Building began in 936 at the suggestion of Abd ar Rahman's favourite wife Azahara ('the flower') and was completed in 960. The entire court and council was transferred here—a complex for about 1200 people. The lower terrace had the *mosque,* municipal buildings, stables and accommodation for soldiers; the middle terrace had *gardens* and *pavilions,* and the upper terrace, which had the most beautiful *palaces,* was the site of the alcázar itself.

A workforce of *c.* 10,000 men was employed on the project. Some 4,000 columns with lovely capitals were used. The irrigation system, for the gardens, baths and also for Córdoba itself, was supplied by an 11 mile long aqueduct. By 1010, however, the dazzling court had already been plundered and destroyed by the Almoravide invaders from Morocco, whose strict religious attitudes were opposed to luxury. The area then served as a quarry and undamaged parts were employed in new buildings (in Seville and Granada). Following finds like marble slabs, fragments of stucco and jewellery, restoration work is now underway on the mosque, the 'Salón Real' or the 'Salon de los Visires', and on a three-aisled and a five-aisled pavilion. A small *museum* gives some idea of the excavated treasures, which are of great importance, above all for the reconstruction. **San Jerónimo el Real de Valparaíso** (1.5 km from Medina Azahara): A monastery of the order of St.Jerome built in the early 15C almost entirely from the ruins of an Omayyad castle. It has a beautiful Gothic *cloister.* The church is early 18C.

Córdoba, Alcázar de los Reyes Cristianos, 3C Roman sarcophagus

The monastery's inner rooms are decorated in an interesting fashion, particularly the room of Isabella the Catholic. The monastery's history has clear parallels with the political development in Córdoba. **Las Ermitas** (14 km. NW): Judging by finds from the 4C AD, these hermitages, which are in the lovely countryside of the Sierra de Córdoba, were already known settlements in early times. Then they provided refuge for those fleeing from the Moors. They are still partly inhabited today by Carmelites. The church is 18C. **Santa María de Trasierra** (16 km. NE): Probably a former Almohaden mosque (12C), on the ruins of the castle. **Almódovar del Río** (24 km. W.): The imposing (restored) castle rises high above the town, with massive walls, battlements and tower. **Posadas** (32 km. W.): *Capilla Santiago* with 13C tombs. **Bujalance** (45 km. E.): An ancient foundation (the Romans called it Vogia) with a Moorish name; remains of a *castle complex* with seven *towers*, built by Abd ar Rahman III in 935, have survived. **Bélmez** (71 km. NW) has an imposing castle.

Hinojosa del Duque (100 km. N.): Church of *San Juan Bautista*, or the 'Cathedral of the Sierra', with a Plateresque façade and beautiful Gothic interior. **Belalcázar** (9 km. N. of Hinojosa del Duque): Interesting, massive castle.

Coria
Cáceres/Estremadura   p.392☐D 6

Picturesque little town on a hill overlooking the right bank of the Alagón, 68 km. N. of Cáceres. An episcopal seat. The ancient Celts called it Caura; the Roman name was Cauria Vetona. Under Viriatus it was the centre of opposition of the Lusitanian rebellion against Rome. The town prospered under the Visigoths and became the capital of a small independent kingdom under the Arabs in the 9C. After several attempts, the Christians (under Alfonso VII), finally managed to retake the town.

Town walls: One of the best preserved Ro-

Medina Azahara (Córdoba)

man defensive systems in the whole of Spain. The granite walls are 27 ft. thick and 1,608 ft. in length. Four gates, flanked by small, semicircular towers have survived, as also have further corner and defensive towers. There is a 15C tower-like, pentagonal fort with battlements.

Cathedral: A very tall, single-aisled building. It was founded in 1108 and completed in the 16C; the double Plateresque *main portal* with its bizarre decoration is also 16C. The ground plan is a simple rectangle, and the long, tall nave has neither a transept nor an apse. The *side portal*, which is at the foot of the bell-tower (rebuilt 18C) displays a mixture of late Gothic and Plateresque elements (15–16C). *Inside: Baroque winged altar* by Juan and Diego de Villanueva (1749). Churrigueresque *high altar*. Beautifully carved late Gothic choir stalls with 45 high and 28 low seats, some of which were reserved for the Dukes of Alba alone, who once ruled the town. The choir, ending in a Gothic *grille* made by Hugo de Santa Ur-

sula (1503), has beautiful panelling. There is a baroque choir desk, and in the retrochoir sculptures by Miguel Villarreal (1512). The *Capilla Mayor* has tombs of the bishops Pedro Jiménez de Préxamo (d. 1495), by Juan Francés and Garcia de Galarza by Lucas Mitata and Juan Bravo (1596). The *Capilla del Relicario* (1783) has goldsmith's work from the 13–18C.

Also worth seeing: The *Palacio del Duque de Alba,* formerly an alcázar, which was converted to a Gothic-Renaissance palace. There are also a few notable mansions, the *Hospital de Bardales* and the *Episcopal Palace.*

Environs: Hoyos: 15C Gothic church with Romanesque portal.

Corullón
León/León   p.386☐D 2

San Esteban: This church was consecrated in 1086; building began in 1093

Medina Azahara (Córdoba)

and lasted until 1100. The portal is strongly reminiscent of the Pórtico de las Platerías of the cathedral of Santiago de Compostela. There are a nave and two aisles, an 18C apse and a simple tower.

San Miguel: 12C Romanesque church with good sculpture on consoles. One of the portal's capitals is possibly Visigoth.

Castillo: 14C castle complex, which belonged to the Counts of Villafranca.

Covadonga
Oviedo/Asturia   p.386 □ F 1

Covadonga is something of a national shrine for Spaniards. In 711, after his defeat by the Moors in the battle of Guadalete, the Visigoth Prince Pelayo fled here, along with 300 warriors, and they all hid in the cave of Auseva. Later, in 718 at the Deva gorge, he defeated the Moorish troops, who had victoriously marched through the whole of Castile under the

Córdoba, city walls

command of the Omayyad Caliph. Subsequently a commemorative altar to the Virgin was set up in the cave in gratitude for this victory. The cave, which was named Covadominica (later Covadonga), is high in a rocky cliff and contains the tombs of King Pelayo, his wife and his sister. A figure of the Virgin Mary (La Santina or La Virgen de las Batallas, the patron saint of Asturia) stands upon the altar. Originally 12C, it was clothed and fussily decorated in the 18C.

Basilica of the Virgen de las Batallas: In a very picturesque setting on a spur halfway up the cliff which has the cave shrine. It was built between 1877–1901 in neo-Romanesque/neo-Gothic style. Treasure chamber with historical mementoes.
On the left, before you reach the basilica, there are several buildings, including hotels and a 16C *abbey* with a collegiate church. Part of the walls of the *cloister* come from the original 10C building; the cloister has two 10C tombs with sculptures.

Environs: Corao: 9 km. from Covadonga towards Carrena de Cabrales you come to the village of Corao. 2 km. along the road to Abamia is the small 12C single-aisled church, *Santa Eulalia*, which is just off the road and very isolated. The tympanum of the W. portal has figures and on the N. side there is a tiny Gothic window. Inside the church there are remnants of frescos and an eight-pointed star vault above the choir. Today, it is quite inaccessible and totally empty. According to tradition the tomb of the Asturian Gothic Prince Pelayo was placed here (cf. Covadonga).

Covarrubias
Burgos/Old Castile   p.388 □ G 3

Collegiate church: This 14–16C Gothic building has a nave, two aisles, four side

Covadonga, Auseva caves

Covadonga, basilica

chapels, three apsidal chapels and a beautiful cloister. The original Gothic altars were replaced by the present baroque altars in the 18C. The 17C organ is also worthy of mention. The *Capilla de los Reyes* has a wooden Flemish *triptych* whose central painting of the Adoration of the Magi is attributed to Gil de Siloé. The church also contains over 30 *tombs,* of which those of Count Fernán González, his wife Doña Sancha, and Princess Christina of Norway, are particularly notable. The *parish museum* is housed in the sacristy and contains a 15C retable, oil paintings by Berruguete, van Eyck, Ribera, El Greco and Zurbarán, as well as documents, examples of the blacksmith's craft and cult items.

Also worth seeing: The splendid 10C tower, known as *Doña Urraca;* the archives,

the *Adelantamiento de Castilla*, in Herrera style with Plateresque decorations; the 15C Gothic church of *Santo Tomé*, which has a nave and two aisles, an interesting altarpiece and several tombs; the *Palace of Count Fernán González* and the *house of Doña Sancha.*

Covet
Lérida/Catalonia   p.390□M 3

A little town, near Tremp in the Alta Cerdaña. Perhaps surprisingly, it is the site of an exceptionally beautiful Romanesque church. However, this is typical of this part of the Pyrenees. The church has three apses and a ground plan of a Latin cross. The carved portal is unusual, especially

Covadonga, altar, detail

with such an abundance of figures. In the tympanum there is a figure of Christ and angels playing musical instruments, while the archivolts have monstrous figures and robbers; also carvings of the Holy Family and the Fall of Man.

Environs: Isona (4 km. N.): You can see the remains of the town walls and towers. The parish church of *Santa María* is Gothic. The *Monastery of San Vicente*, first mentioned in 971, is a Visigoth foundation.

Cuéllar
Segovia/Old Castile   p.392□F 4

Cuéllar was an important town in the Middle Ages. The skyline is dominated by church towers.

Parish church of San Martín: Mudéjar with a nave, two aisles, three polygonal apses and doors with round archivolts.

Parish church of San Esteban: Also Mudéjar, with a very beautiful brick apse. The tombs on either side of the sanctuary have lavish plaster decorations. The church also contains two 16C altarpieces.

Parish church of San Andrés: Church with a nave and two aisles, three polygonal apses and two Romanesque portals with round arches.

Iglesia del Salvador: 13C Mudéjar church.

Santuario de Nuestra Señora del Henar: On this spot the Virgin Mary is supposed to have appeared to a herdsman. Originally a small pilgrimage chapel marked the site. The present building dates from 1642. Inside there are baroque altarpieces, and both dome and vaults are covered with paintings.

Monastery: 13C; Don Beltrán de la Cueva converted *San Francisco* into a mausoleum for his family. Remains of the tombs can be seen in the museum in Valladolid. *Santa Clara* is a single-aisled church dated 1244.

Hospital Santa Magdalena: Founded by Gómez Gonzáles towards the end of the 15C. The portal is decorated with escutcheons and a stone slab with Gothic lettering. There used to be a fine diptych by Juan Fernández, but this is now in the town hall; the Via Dolorosa and the Annunciation are depicted on one panel and the Assumption of the Virgin and St.Mark and St.Catherine are on the other.

Castillo: The castle, in the upper part of the town, was built in the late 15C by Don Beltrán de la Cueva, Duke of Alburquerque; it was converted in the 16–18C. It has a square ground plan; at the corners there are three round defensive towers and one square. Inside, there is a large courtyard with a double, nine-arched gallery and several rooms with very beautiful panelling.

Cuenca
Cuenca/New Castile   p.396☐I 6

Cuenca is officially considered a 'picturesque town'. The houses of Old Cuenca are huddled together on a rocky massif, which frames the Júcar and Huécar rivers. The most interesting feature of this unusual town is its steep location and asymmetrical terraced lay-out, with delightful spurs jutting across each other.

Cathedral: A national monument. Begun in Gothic-Norman style (main chapel and

Covarrubias, collegiate church

transept) and continued in Anglo-Norman style (particularly the central nave). The 18C high altar is by Ventura Rodríguez. The grille, made by Sancho Muñoz in 1557, is particularly splendid. The 16C choir grille is the work of Hernando de Arenas. The *Arco de Jamete*, an arch in the transept is an ambitious Renaissance creation. There are fine tapestries, some of which are Flemish. There are two paintings by El Greco, paintings by Yañez de la Almedina and Juan de Borgoña, a Mater Dolorosa by Pedro de Mena, the 12C statue of the *Virgen del Sagrario*, a Byzantine Calvary (12C), fine panelling in the *Capilla Honda* and a 14C Byzantine diptych, which is unique in Spain.

San Miguel: This church is picturesquely situated in the Júcar ravine. It is used as an auditorium for church music festivals, in which Spanish and foreign orchestras and top class choirs take part. Mudéjar ceiling.

Chapel of the Virgen de las Angustias:

Interesting chapel on a most beautiful pathway along the cliffs.

Museum of abstract Spanish art: Housed in one of the 'hanging houses', this contains pictures and sculptures by such important Spanish artists as, Chillida, Tapies, Saura, Cuixart, Serrano, Feito, Sempere, J. de Ribera, Torner, Conogar and Zóbel. Inside the building you can admire beautiful wall paintings, Gothic window grilles and a piece of remarkable Mudéjar panelling.

Archaeological Museum/Casa Curato (at the foot of the Old Town): Finds from excavations in the province, particularly from Valeria, Segóbriga and Ercávica. There is an important collection of coins, large statues, Roman mosaics and ceramics.

Casas Colgadas/'Hanging houses': Dating from the 14C, these are built on the cliff directly above the chasm. Their charming wooden balconies afford a lovely

Covarrubias, collegiate church

Covarrubias, collegiate church

Cuéllar, El Salvador

Cuéllar, Castillo

view. They have been variously fitted out, one as a museum, another as a typical inn, which is known as *Mesón*.

Environs: The *Ciudad Encantada* (Enchanted Village): This is a nature reserve covering an area of over 20 sq. km. Geological phenomenon include a rock labyrinth, resembling a ruined town.

Cuerva
Toledo/New Castile   p.392□F 6/7

Parish church: This church is built of ashlars and masonry older than the church itself. It is single-aisled, has several chapels, a tower and various other additions. The tower is not of uniform style;

it was almost entirely built in the first half of the 16C, but was greatly altered between 1565-70. The apse and the nave are late Gothic. The S. portal, with a statue of St.James the Great (St.James is the patron saint of the church), has survived in Plateresque style. In the sanctuary there are tombs of the Counts of Arcos (17C) and Doña Aldonza Niño de Guevara.

Castle: 13C, in a dilapidated state. Only the incomplete outer walls and the round outer towers are still visible.

Cullera
Valencia/Valencia   p.396□L 7

This town (36 km. S. of Valencia) lies at

Cuenca, Cathedral

Cuenca, Casas Colgadas

the mouth of the Júcar. Its terraces are cut into the slopes of the *Monte del Oro* (780 ft.). Iberians settled here around 400 BC, as some ruins still testify. Phoenicians, Greeks, Carthaginians and Romans followed, turning Cullera into an important trading town. **Fortress:** In the 8C the area was taken over by Moors, who built their fortress on the mountain, the imposing ruins of which cover an area of *c.* 32,000 sq. ft. It is particularly worthy of an excursion, on account of the beautiful view you get of the Júcar valley, as well as of Albufera and the sea. **Torre de la Reina Mora:** The tower of the Moorish queen, which rises above the former Arab quarter.

Also worth seeing: 17C *parish church* with Gothic remains of the original church and two old *fortress towers*.

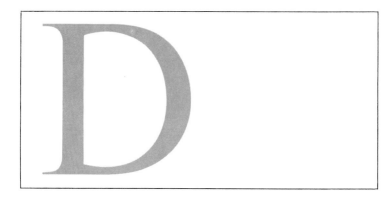

Daroca
Zaragoza/Aragon   □ p.388J 4

The town, which has Oriental characteristics, is set in hilly countryside on the bank of the Jiloca. Originally an Iberian settlement, the Romans used it as a military station known as *Agiria* in the province of Caesaraugusta, now Saragossa. Under Moorish occupation it was called *Kalat-Daruca* and was the scene of heavy fighting for control of the province between rival Moorish families, a struggle which was finally ended by the Emir of Córdoba. Daroca was finally liberated from the Saracens in 1122 by King Alfonso I, and received city status from Pedro IV in 1366.

Collegiate Church of Santa María: Of the original Romanesque structure, only the main apse remains and this has been incorporated into the *Capilla de los Corporales*. It became a very popular place of pilgrimage, and was consequently extended in the 15C. An additional building was constructed in the 16C. The church itself has a nave, two aisles and stellar vaults, with an unusual dome over the crossing. The *Puerta del Perdón* dates from the time of the 15C alterations, and has an upper arch, which ends conically. Al-

together there are four arches, each of which is supported by four pillars with decorated capitals. In the *tympanum* above the door there are fine sculptures. The *main altar* is alabaster, is flanked by figures of angels and has a baldacchino above. The walls of the *Capilla de los Sagrados Corporales* are decorated with reliefs. There is also a silver Gothic shrine engraved with flowers. Side chapels, dedicated to St. Thomas and St. Michael, have 15C Plateresque altarpieces.

Museo del Santísmo Misterio: The parish museum, which is near the Church of Santa María. It houses numerous wood carvings of various dates, including representations of Ferdinand and Isabella, many of which are attributed to Bartolomé Bermejo. There is an interesting alabaster altarpiece showing Flemish influence. Among the fine liturgical paintings and splendid gold items, a silver monstrance (1384) is outstanding. It was commissioned for the church by King Pedro IV, and made by Pedro Moragues.

San Miguel: A 12C Romanesque church, with a fine Mudéjar tower. Inside there are

Daroca, collegiate church of Santa María

interesting 13–15C wall paintings. The portal is plain with a tympanum and round arches, each of which is supported by four columns with undecorated capitals.

San Juan Bautista: Of the original Romanesque church, only the apse (with 13C murals) remains; the rest has been restored in baroque style.

Santa Domingo de Silos: A 12–13C church.

La Mina: A 16C tunnel cut from the side of the mountain to channel off excess water; barrel-vaulted it is altogether a remarkable architectural achievement.

Casa de Don Juan de Austria: The house originally belonged to the Luna family. The courtyard with Mudéjar stucco is still in good condition, as is one of the rooms, which has a fine carved wood ceiling.

La Muralla: Daroca is surrounded by a wall, *c.* 1.5 m. long, and is complete with battlements and 114 separate watch-towers. It was much restored in the 13&16C. Two of the gates are still standing—the *Fondonera (or Alta)* and the 15C *Baja* Gate.

Denia
Alicante/Valencia   p.396☐L 8

This small town lies at the northernmost point of the province of Alicante, 2,460 ft. above sea level on the slopes of the Montgó. It is famous for its fiesta, which takes place from mid-July to mid-August. It was originally founded by the Phoenicians, the Greeks knew it as *Hemeroskopeion* and the Romans, for whom it had much significance, as *Dianium*, after the temple of Diana there. The Visigoths made it an episcopal seat and the Moors, the capital of a kingdom. It later became the capital of a duchy, under the Dukes of Lerma, one of whom was chief minister to King Philip

Daroca, Santa María

Daroca, Santo Domingo, apse

III. There are, however, few reminders left of the city's distinguished past.

Citadel: Perched above the town with a a splendid view over the Bay of Valencia. Among the ruins are both Roman and Arab remains. The French used it as a base during the Napoleonic wars.

Also worth seeing: *Les Roques*, in the most picturesque quarter of the city, close to the remains of the castle. It has become an arts and crafts centre, along with the *Baix la Mar*, an area near the harbour. There are some interesting 18C buildings in the Plaza de los Caídos (Square of the Fallen), e.g. the church of *Santa María* and the *Town Hall*. On the steps leading up to the castle you can see two Roman altars.

Environs: On the bluff near **Las Rotas** there are caves which are accessible only from the sea. Two hours' walk will get you to the **Poblado Ibérico**, in the Sierra de Montgó, the site of the remains of an Iberian settlement dating back to the 7–8C BC.

Deva
Guipúzcoa/Basque Provinces   p.388☐H 1

Deva is on the Cantabrian coast by the mouth of the river of the same name. It is a small fishing village and, in summer, a popular resort.

Santa María la Real: 13C, with a splendid portal of the same date, which is decorated with fine polychrome sculptures of the twelve Apostles. The high nave is supported by columns decorated with 13C Romanesque bas-reliefs. In a side chapel there is a tomb from the same period as the church and this is decorated with reliefs. There is also a winged altar and various gilded altars.

Dueñas
Palencia/Old Castile   p.388☐F 3

This was the site of the first meeting be-

Deva, Santa María la Real, portal

tween Isabella the Catholic and Ferdinand of Aragon. In the town there are the ruins of the old castle, as well as some old mansions.

Santa María: 13C parish church with fine altarpiece (in the main chapel), which is attributed to the craftsman Master Antonio. There are also the Gothic tombs of the Lords of Buendía, and the tomb of Lord Don Pedro with a Plateresque praying figure.

Convento de Teresianas: The old abbey has a church with two naves, baroque altarpieces and Gothic tombs.

Abbey of San Isidro de Dueñas: The abbey was founded by the Benedictines in the 12C, but stands on the site of an older building from the 7C. Of the original Romanesque structure, only the portal remains.

Environs: Calabazanos (*c.* 5 km. N.): The nunnery is famous as the setting for the opening of the Castilian play 'Auto del Nacimiento' by Gómez Manrique. The abbey has Gothic and Plateresque panelling.

Durango

Vizcaya/Basque Provinces   p.388□H 2

A small industrial town in the fertile plain between the mountains and the River Durango. Four gates still stand from the original city defences.

Santa María de Uribarri: A sprawling Gothic church begun in the 15C, but not fully completed until the 17C, consequently parts are baroque. The present bell tower is built on the foundations of the original tower, the *Torre de Arandoño*. The *main altar*, a fine Renaissance piece by Martín Ruiz de Zubiate, has a 14C Gothic madonna.

San Pedro de Tavira: A 13C Romanesque building and one of the oldest church buildings in the Basque area. Arab influence is apparent in the choir.

Santa Ana: This Herrera-style church was completed in 1626. It has a splendid high altar and Tuscan columns which look like pilasters. The high *bell tower* with its baroque conclusion is by Pedro de Dueña.

Gate of Santa Ana: A baroque gate and part of the original defences; it has two small side-towers and a statue of St.Anne. It was rebuilt in 1744.

Also worth seeing: In the town there is a Gothic stone *crucifix* with an inscription. The most impressive mansions are those belonging to the following families: Aguirrebengoa, Ampuero, Láriz and Olalde. The house in which the *founder of Montevideo*, Don Bruno Mauricio de Zabala, was born is still standing.

Ecija
Seville/Andalusia — p.394 □ E 9

Originally a Greek settlement, the Romans called the town *Astigi*. A fortress with towers and gates testifies to Moorish occupation. Ecija has been a diocesan town since 3C. The town's skyline owes its distinctive silhouette to numerous towers (covered with colourful azulejos), which have earned Ecija the title, 'Ciudad de las Torres'. As the town was severely damaged by the great earthquake of 1755, most of the towers date from the second half of the 18C and some are modelled on the Giralda of Seville.

Parish church of Santiago el Mayor: Early 16C Gothic-Mudéjar church; Renaissance and baroque alterations and extensions. The tower was rebuilt in Mudéjar style after the earthquake. Inside: a very beautiful late Gothic *retable* with panel paintings and sculptures (16C); in the N. aisle, there is a *Crucifixion* by Pedro Roldán.

Parish church of Santa Cruz (Calle de Más y Prat): The present 18C building is classical but a succession of buildings have occupied the site since Visigoth times. First there was a cathedral, then a mosque, followed by another Christian church, and finally the present one. The *patio* has a decorated Mudéjar horseshoe arch, with coats-of-arms. The bell tower has two panels of Arabic inscriptions. Inside, there is a 14C statue of the Virgin Mary, *Nuestra Señora del Valle*. Nearby, to the right of the high altar, there is another altar, which is actually a Christian Visigoth *stone sarcophagus* (5–6C). It has Byzantine reliefs of the following subjects: the Good Shepherd; the Sacrifice of Isaac; and Daniel in the Lion's Den. A 16C figure of the Virgin Mary near the *high altar* (which has an 18C altarpiece) is the work of Francisco Hernández.

Plaza Mayor (or Plaza de España): A beautiful square surrounded by arcades and houses with oriels. The *town hall* has a colourful Roman mosaic.

Palacio de los Marqueses de Peñaflor (Calle Castellar): The painted *façade* with its monumental portal and Seville-baroque columns creates an extraordinary impression, especially as the façade follows the bends in the narrow streets. The upper storey has a particularly long balcony, 'los Balcones largos'. A large patio leads to the splendid domed *stairwell*. A small courtyard opens into the *stables*.

Also worth seeing: *Parish church of Santa María,* (behind the town hall): 18C with tower in the style of the Giralda of Seville. Inside: in the Capilla Mayor there is a painted panel of Byzantine influence, the *Virgen de la Antigua,* (1610); to the right of the entrance there are two tombs dated *c.* 1400; the cloister has a collection of stone monuments. *Santa Barbara* is 17C and has a portal with Roman columns. The 14C monastery church of *San Pablo y Santo Domingo* (Plaza de José María López) was originally Dominican. It was considerably altered in the 17C. Inside there is the superbly furnished *Capilla del Rosario* (early 18C). The Camarín has a statue of the Madonna (early 16C) by Pedro Millán. The *Church of the Discalced Carmelite Nuns* is a beautiful baroque building of *c.* 1700. *Palacio de Vilaseca* (Calle Castellar); The *Palace of the Marquis of Cortes* has a Plateresque portal; the *Palacio Benameji* has a baroque portal and stairwell; the *Palace of El Conde de Aguilar* has a baroque portal and a massive tower.

Environs: Palma del Río (31 km. NW): Castle ruins and interesting churches. **Peñaflor** (35 km. NW) was established by the Romans; fine tower.

Eibar
Guipúzcoa/Basque Provinces   p.388☐H 2

Eibar is a medium-sized town, principally famous for its bicycle and weapon factories. The latter produces the famous damascened iron blades, a tradition going back to the 15C. The Republic was proclaimed here on 14 April 1931. Extensively damaged during the Civil War, it was quickly rebuilt.

San Andrés: An old parish church built on the orders of Juan de Aguirre in the 17C. It has a Plateresque side portal. Inside there is an extremely beautiful altarpiece (1587) by Andrés de Araoz. The church contains two 15C Flemish bronze lecterns.

Also worth seeing: The *town hall* in French rococo style. The *Palacio de Isasi* (a holiday residence of the princes Baltasar Carlos and Francisco Fernando, sons of King Philip IV), and the *Casa de Orbea are the finest houses.*

Environs: El Santuario de la Virgen de Arrate: A settlement *c.* 8 km. away on Mount Arrate, which was a stopping place for pilgrims on the way to Santiago de Compostela. Inside there are four oil paintings by the local painter Ignacio Zuloaga. A week-long festival with Basque dancing takes place here from 8 September.

Ejea (Egea) de los Caballeros
Saragossa/Aragon   p.388☐K 3

Ejea, the ancient Iberian *Segia*, is situated at the confluence of the Arba de Biel and the Arba de Luesia, on the border of the Pyrenees and the rest of the province.

El Salvador: A fortified Romanesque church, which was built in 1222 and is now a protected national monument. Its fortress-like impression is underscored by a battlemented tower and four small watch towers. There are two interesting, lavishly carved Romanesque portals. In the tympanum of one of the portals there is a Last Supper, while in that of the other portal there is a circled monogram of Christ decorated with figures of angels. Originally the church had a beautiful 15C altarpiece by Miguel Ximénez, but this was dismantled and the individual parts are now in various museums (including the Museo del Prado in Madrid), leaving just one panel of the Stations of the Cross in the church.

El Barco de Avila, Castillo

Nuestra Señora de la Oliva: 18C church, dedicated to the town's patron saint. Inside there is a 13C sculpture.

Santa María (town centre): A fortified church built in 1174 and part of King Alfonso I's fortress. 16C façade. Romanesque N. portal. Inside there are 15&16C altar pictures, as well as a beautiful 15C Mudéjar alabaster pulpit.

Also worth seeing: Several typically Aragonese *houses* in the town.

El Barco de Avila
Avila/Old Castile   p.392☐E 5/6

Parish church: 14C Gothic. The façade is dominated by a mighty tower and three Gothic gates. Inside there is a splendid nave and two aisles which have Gothic vaulting; 15C choir; apses are decorated with crosses. There are also fine altarpieces, paintings and grilles.

Castillo de Valdecorneja: Late 14C castle with square groundplan.

Environs: Becedas (*c.* 10 km. W.): 16C Renaissance *parish church*; main façade has escutcheons and busts of the Counts of Béjar. The tower is very tall and the church interior has a barrel vault.

El Bollo
Orense/Galicia   p.386☐C 3

Of the former castle only the keep remains.

Environs: Las Ermitas: The 17C *Santuario de Santa María* is *c.* 3 km. S. of El Bollo, in barren countryside. It has a splendid façade decorated with columns and figures. NE of El Bollo is **El Barco de Valdeorras** (via Freijido and La Rua), with a keep, which belonged to an old *fortress*.

El Burgo de Osma
Soria/Old Castile   p.388☐H 4

This little town in the Duero valley was founded by Visigoths and is one of the oldest diocesan towns in Spain.

Cathedral: Few remains of the original 12C Romanesque church have survived, as materials from it were used in the construction of the 13C Gothic cathedral. The latter consists of a nave and two aisles and has a Latin cross groundplan. The 13C carved portal in the transept is very beautiful. The 240 ft. high baroque *tower* of 1739 dominates the town. Inside there are beautiful 16C filigree grilles (in the sanctuary and the choir) by Juan Francés. The high altar's retable (*Capilla Mayor*) is an excellent work by Juan de Juni and Juan Picardo (1550). In the *transept* there is a carved white marble pulpit, which has reliefs and the escutcheon of Cardinal Pedro Diego de Mendoza.

The 16C *choir stalls* are the work of Pedro de Palacio. Frescos in the vaults are by Salvador de Maella. Some of the *chapels* are particularly interesting: *San Ildefonso*, containing several 16C paintings of the Castilian school; *San Agustin* with the Gothic tomb of the Montoya family; the *Capilla del Cristo* with a beautiful sculpture by Juan de Juni; and *San Pedro de Osma* with a 13C tomb decorated with carvings. The cathedral has a most beautiful Gothic *cloister* dated 1512. The 18C *sacristy* by Juan de Villanueva is lavishly

decorated and contains a sacristy cupboard with fine horseshoes and English bronzes. The cathedral *museum* houses a valuable collection of Romanesque and Gothic miniatures, including the famous 'Beato' by Martino (1086) as well as valuable sculptures, paintings and cult artefacts.

Also worth seeing: The *University of Santa Catalina*, founded by Bishop Acosta in 1541, with a Plateresque façade; the *Hospital of San Agustin* with a beautiful baroque façade dated 1699; the *town wall* with the 15C San Miguel gate, the *Plaza Mayor* (1768) with several interesting buildings, such as the *Town Hall* and the *Episcopal Palace*.

Environs: Osma (*c.* 12 km. S.): Known to the Romans as *Uxama Argalae*. Mosaics and fascinating remains of fine buildings have survived from Roman times. **Ucero** (*c.* 15 km. N.): A simple *church* with a Romanesque Madonna, a 14C crucifix and a 15C painting of the *Virgin and Child*; the early 13C Romanesque *chapel of San Bartolomé* was originally part of an old monastery, which belonged to the Knights Templar; the ruins of the old *castle* can also be seen.

Elche
Alicante/Valencia   p.396☐K 8

The town is of Iberian origin and was known as *Helice* under the Greeks and *Colonia Julia Ilici Augusta* under the Romans. However, long Moorish rule gave the town its character. Today, with its narrow streets and alleys, white houses and flat roofs, Elche still seems African. In the mid 13C Ferdinand III of Castile seized the town for Christian Spain. From 1296 on

El Burgo de Osma, Cathedral

wards it belonged to the Kingdom of Valencia. Elche is famous for three things: its palm forest, its medieval mystery play and the 'Dama de Elche'.

Palm Forest: The largest palm forest in Europe, surrounding the town on three sides, with around 170,000 date palms. Some of the palms are over 200 years old and have been known to reach a height of 134 ft. Every year Elche supplies the whole of Spain with palm fronds for Palm Sunday. The palm plantations can be traced back to the Carthaginians, but they were particularly well cared for by the Moors, who must have seen them as the trees of their homeland. In one part of the palm forest, the *Huerto del Cura*, there is a particularly splendid specimen, the 'Palma Imperial', from whose trunk branch seven smaller stems.

Mysterio de Elche: The medieval mystery play is staged annually on the 14&15 August in the church of Santa María. It is a lyrical drama performed solely by men in the old Catalan tongue and it describes the death and assumption of the Virgin Mary. Apart from Mary, apostles, angels, saints, Jews and the Holy Trinity also appear. It is often said that the mystery play of Elche was the model for Italian operas.

Dama de Elche: A limestone bust of a woman, which seems once to have been polychrome. It was discovered in 1897 in La Alcudia, 2 km. S. of Elche, and has made the town famous throughout the world. Dating from the 4–3C BC it is a product of the Graeco-Iberian culture. Now it can be seen in the Archaeological Museum in Madrid. There is a copy of the bust in Elche's archaeological museum.

Santa María: This basilica is the location for the above-mentioned Misterio de Elche. The 17C church was extensively damaged in 1936, but was later rebuilt. The splendid two-storey main portal with its lavish ornaments and alternately smooth, fluted and winding columns remained intact. Inside there is a sumptu-

Elche, palm grove

ously decorated high altar. The bell tower offers a beautiful view of the palm forest.

Also worth seeing: The *Calahorra Gate*, near the church of Santa María, is part of the Moorish quarter. Its present form dates from the 15C. The *Casa del Ayuntamiento/Town Hall*, on the Plaza Mayor dates from the 17&18C; its façade has splendid balconies. The *Torre del Consell*, dates from the 15C. Also of interest is the *Fortaleza de la Señoría* (or Palacio de Altamira). A 15C fortress and the seat of the Counts of Altamira. Formerly the site of a Moorish castle, which was the occasional residence of the Kings of Aragon and Ferdinand and Isabella.

Environs: The Iberians, in fact, settled in nearby La Alcudia, rather than in present-day Elche. Since the 15C there have been repeated excavations of the site, which the present owner of the area intends to continue. Several settlement strata, primarily Roman, have already been uncovered. A small private museum contains interesting finds from Iberian, Carthaginian and Roman times. **Crevillente** (10 km. W. of Elche): A little town dating back to a Roman foundation. Its white houses, *domed church* and palms give the place an oriental appearance. Alongside modern *irrigation systems* there are some from Moorish times. There are also *cave dwellings*. During Holy Week the 'pasos' (or depictions of the Passion), by the sculptor Mariano Benlliure are carried through the streets. **Novelda:** The medieval *Castillo de la Mola* with its curious triangular tower (14C) and its even older massive bastions, is supposed to have been the prison of the disgraced Alvaro de Luna (Lord Constable of Castile and favourite of King John II of Castile), before he was beheaded in Valladolid in 1453. Not far from the castle stands the *pilgrimage chapel of St. Mary Magdalene*. This was built recently and it is easy to see the influence of the Sagrada

Familia church in Barcelona. At **Monforte del Cid** (4 km. E. of Novelda) there are the *ruins* of an Iberian settlement. An excursion to *Sierra del Cid*, N. of Novelda, is worthwhile for the view from *Silla del Cid*, which is 3,685 ft. high. A few km. NW of Novelda is **Monóvar.** The town nestles between two hills, on one of which the remains of a Moorish *fort* can be seen. Monóvar was the home of the Spanish writer Azorín, a master of the pure Castilian tongue, who died a few years ago.

El Ferrol del Caudillo
La Coruña/Galicia   p.386☐B 1

The Old Town with its narrow, twisting alleys, was founded in the 13C. In the 18C, when El Ferrol became Spain's most important naval port, the famous Arsenal de la Graña was erected (1726) and a new town was built (with a geometrical lay-out and symmetrical alignment of streets).
The cathedral, *San Julian*, is 18C, as are

Elche, Santa María

the churches *De los Dolores, Las Angustias, San Francisco* and *El Socorro* (which houses the famous statue of Christ walking on the water). The church of *Espiritu Santo* has paintings by Zacaríus Vásquez. Also worth seeing are the fortresses near El Ferrol, which protected the town in the 16&18C: *Castillo de San Felipe, Castillo de San Martin, San Carlos* and *La Palma.*

Environs: El Couto, 5 km. from El Ferrol, with a Romanesque *church.* In **Jubia,** 10 km. from El Ferrol, there is the *monastery of San Martin,* established in the 10C and the only Cluniac monastery in Galicia. In the 16C it became part of the monastery of San Salvador de Lorenzano and lost its importance. The 12C *church* with nave and two aisles has survived in good condition. There are fine capitals, symbolically decorated with figures of men and animals. It also houses the tomb of Count Froila and his son, the patron of the monastery. The monastery was rebuilt in the 18C. **Neda** to the S., near Jubia, has beautiful old mansions. The parish church

of *San Nicolás* is 14C. **Narahío:** Further towards Lugo, on a cliff above the Neda valley, there is a 14C *fortress.* At **Moeche:** SE of Narahío there is a 14C *fort,* surrounded by a wide defensive wall.

El Pardo

Madrid/New Castle   p.392□G 5

Palacio Real (Royal Castle): Built in 1568 by Charles V on the foundations of a hunting lodge, which had been built for Henry III. It was almost totally destroyed by fire in 1604 and subsequently rebuilt by the architect Francisco de Mora. It remained unaltered into the 18C. The royal chapel, designed by the architect Francisco Carlier, was added by Philip V. Charles III extended the castle to the designs of Francisco Sabatini in 1772. It has a square ground plan and corner towers with conical slate roofs. Inside there are numerous works of art, including above all a *collection of wall tapestries*, which is one of the

Elche, excavations in La Alcudia

Elche, Dama de Elche

best in Spain. *Frescos* by Gaspar Becerra, show the palace furnishings of the 16C; there are other frescos from the 17&19C, as well as a collection of neoclassical furniture.

Casita del Príncipe (the Prince's Cottage): A small building built by Juan de Villanueva for the future King Charles IV. Inside there are a number of rooms open to the public, which have been maintained in a style typical of the Spanish Bourbons. They are similar to the rooms of the Escorial and those of Aranjuez.

Palacio de la Zarzuela: Originally a hunting lodge. Designed by Juan Gómez de Mora and Alfonso Carbonell in the 17C. Rebuilt by Charles IV in neoclassical style in 18C. It was almost totally destroyed during the Civil War. Rebuilding began in 1960.

Environs: El Convento de Capuchinos (Capucin convent): On a nearby hill. Although it was founded by Philip III, the foundation stone of the existing building (much altered), dates from 1638. There is an unusual *statue of a reclining Christ* by Gregorio Fernández. *Paintings* by Ribera, Francisco Rizi and other artists.

El Tiemblo
Avila/Old Castile   p.392☐F 5

Parish church: A massive 16C building, resembling a fortress.

Toros de Guisando: These are most unusual granite sculptures of bulls in a meadow just outside the town. They are probably of Celtic-Iberian origin, though some Latin inscriptions suggest they could be Roman.

Monasterio de Guisando: Here Henry IV and his sister Isabella, signed their famous pact, which was the foundation of Spanish unity. The monastery was founded by King Henry IV in 1464. It was

El Tiemblo, Toros de Guisando

later gutted by fire; only the Gothic chapel of San Miguel remains. The existing building dates from the 16C. In the cloister there are the escutcheons of the Count of Villena.

Environs: The 16C *parish church* in **Cebreros** (*c.* 10 km. NE) has remained in pure Renaissance style. Inside, nave and two aisles are separated by round arches. The town also has the *ruins of a monastery* and several *mansions.* **La Adrada** (*c.* 20 km. SW) is a charming village dominated by the ruins of an old *castle*, which has a Gothic chapel. The *parish church* dates from the 16C and is built in the style of the Escorial.

El Toboso
Toledo/New Castile   p.392 □ H 7

15C **parish church:** Late Gothic with a nave and two aisles divided into three strings and crowned by groin vaults. The latter are supported by wide cylindrical columns where they meet the nave and by half columns at the walls. Externally, the S. and W. fronts are Renaissance (late 16C), the latter is interrupted by a large gate with a barrel vault.

House of Dulcinea: Immortalized in *Cervantes' 'Don Quixote'.* In the middle of La Mancha, the house is typical of the period, having a large inner courtyard, kitchen, storeroom and mill.

Erill la Vall
Lérida/Catalonia   p.390 □ L 2

In the 8C the Counts of Toulouse took the Pallar and Ribagorza regions under their protection. A feudal lord settled in the valley of Bohí, founded the barony of Erill and built a castle at Erill-Castell (in neighbouring Viu-Tal), of which there are, however, no remains. The valley enjoyed its heyday in the 12&13C, as the numerous fine Romanesque churches testify.

Parish church of Santa Eulalia: Early 13C, it is famous for its slender five-storey bell tower, which has Lombard decoration, elegant round-arched windows and narrow window bars. Originally single-aisled, later small apses were added on both sides. The porch, also added later, has arcades along the N. wall. It has been restored.

In order to view the church, you must find out which family in the village has the key, as it is handed on to a different village family each month. During early restoration work in 1905, a *tomb* (from the Ribagorza school) was discovered and this is now in the museum in Vic.

Environs: Barruera (3,670 ft.): Centre of local administration for the Bohí valley. The Romanesque *parish church, San Felix,* in ancient Vallis-Orcera has a nave and two aisles; porch and portal were added later. The main apse has Lombard blind arcades. Inside is a 13C *Christ* and an interesting font. **Durro** (4,640 ft.): *Parish church* of the same date as those of Erill, Tahull and Bohí. Unfortunately it awaits restoration. Single-aisled, with Lombard decoration, it has a four-storey tower. **Coll** (3,950 ft.): The *parish church,* one of the smallest, but loveliest in the valley, is a 12C single-aisled Romanesque building, with small transept-like side chapels. Barrel vaulting is supported on columns. There is a blind arcade around the apse and the nave up to the front of the building. The tower is lower than those of the other churches in the valley. The *portal* is simple with good archivolts and an interesting cast-iron lock. Carvings and fragments of a Gothic *altarpiece* are currently being restored in Lérida.

Escalona
Toledo/New Castile   p.392☐F 6

Fortress: Occupied by Alfonso VI. From 1085, after the capture of Toledo, it probably became the fief of the King's vassals. In 1424 Juan II of Castile handed it over to his commander, Don Alvaro de Luna, (together with the village and other castles). The latter then had a palace built within the fortress. In the course of turbulent, internecine battles the fortress was to play an important role in 15C Castile. The entire complex is surrounded by a high wall with battlements and towers a short distance apart. Inside, the fortress consists of a large parade ground and the castle, or palace, which was built 1435–7 by Alvaro de Luna on a rectangular ground plan. The *façade* is framed by two rectangular towers, the left-hand being the *Torre del Homenaje* (keep). Inside the palace there is a cloister-like *courtyard*, of which there remains but a few columns. These are octagonal and their capitals are decorated with thistle leaves and coats-of-arms. The staircase has Gothic ornaments. On the façade there is round tower, which originally was probably an oratory or archive room. It has pointed arches and is roofed by a groin vault, which is decorated with red and white stucco and curious ornaments.

Town walls: These still enclose the whole town and form an uneven polygon. Battlements have only partly survived. Of the three *gates* only that of St.Michael (the castle gate) is of interest, having large pointed arches made of ashlars, and vaulting.

Parish church of San Miguel Arcángel (the Archangel Michael): Painting of the Madonna and Child (choir stalls).

Convento de Immaculada Concepción: Franciscan. Begun in 1521, it was finished by 1525. A brick building, its style

is transitional between Gothic and Renaissance. Latin cross ground plan. There is a beautiful Plateresque portal on the S. side. At each side of the façade there is a small *medallion* with the symbol of the church of Toledo—white lilies in a vase. The single-aisled interior is divided into three parts with groin vaulting and articulated by pointed arches. Beneath the choir there are two white marble *tombstones*—fine Renaissance pieces from the 16C. In the *refectory* there is a 15C Mudéjar-Gothic pulpit.

Capilla des Hospitals de San Andrés Apóstol: *Mid-16C altarpiece* in Plateresque-Renaissance style.

Environs: Fuensalida (*c.* 35 km. SE of Escalona): The *parish church* dated 1455 is Gothic with Mudéjar influence and is built of brick and stone. The bottom of the tower is in two styles: the first and older part has a Mudéjar arch and the second resulted from renovation in 1820. The church is single-aisled with groin vaulting. Three chapels were later added to each side of the old building, which was itself greatly altered in the 16C and again in the 19C. *The castle of the Counts de Fuensalida:* Begun at the end of the 15C in a style transitional between Gothic and Renaissance. A few shapeless remains still survive, such as the main courtyard and the N. and W. buildings. The castle was restored at the end of the 16C and the main portal and the two towers may date from this time. In one of the rooms there is 16C Mudéjar panelling and a Mudéjar door. Other rooms have tiled floors, which came from Talavera (*c.* 1600). **Hormigos** (*c.* 10 km. S. from Escalona): The *parish church* with an early 16C main chapel with pointed arches, is built in half-timbering and brick, probably from the same century. The nave and two aisles are formed by half arches, supported by early Renaissance columns; wooden ceiling. **La Torre de Esteban**

Hambrán (*c.* 40 km. E. of Escalona): *Parish church:* Of the original building, only the Gothic main chapel from the second half of the 15C remains. Inside the groin vault and apex ribbing heralds the Renaissance. The existing nave was built at the end of the 15C; the tower was rebuilt in 1666. The portal and double flight of stairs date from 1675 and in the same year two small chapels were added on the N. and S. sides. **Maqueda** (12 km. S. of Escalona): The *castle* (late 15C), built by Don Gutierre de Cárdenas, has a rectangular ground plan, with cylindrical towers at the corners. Above the portal there are the coat-of-arms of Cárdenas and Enríquez. The *Church of Santa María,* whose towers were part of the town's defences, stands in front of the castle. *The castle of San Silvestre,* six km. away, was also built by Don Gutierre de Cárdenas (late 15C). The ground plan is very similar to that of the castle of Maqueda. The interior is almost totally dilapidated.

Espinosa de los Monteros
Burgos/Old Castile   p.388 □ G 2

Churches: 16C Gothic *parish church* with beautiful vaulting and a modern tower; the church of *San Nicolás* has a superb 15C retable with Castilian paintings; the 18C church, *Nuestra Señora de Berruera.*

Palaces and mansions: The 13C *castle* or the *Velasco tower* with very high battlemented walls; the *Palace of the Marqués de Chiloeches* has a huge façade flanked by two towers.

Environs: About 3 km. S. you come to **Butrera** and its 12C Romanesque church. At **Bercedo** (3 km. E.) the 12C Romanesque church has a most interesting portal. **Siones** (*c.* 10 km. E.) has a 12C Romanesque church, *Santa María* (rectan-

gular groundplan). **Vallejo de Mena** (*c.* 12 km. E.): The 12C church of *San Lorenzo* was renovated in the 13C and has an interesting portal.

Estany
Barcelona/Catalonia   p.390 □ N 3

Parish church of Santa María: There is mention of an church on this site in 990. The Augustinian monastery was founded by the Bishop of Vich in 1080 and the new church was consecrated on 3 November 1133. In 1448 a powerful earthquake destroyed most of the arches, and during reconstruction (1451), these were replaced by pointed arches. In 1966 work began on restoring the church to its original form. The church has a Latin cross ground plan and is single-aisled with a transept. The bell tower rises over the crossing. The middle of three apses is the largest; outside it has a decorative band and a double-arched window supported by columns with capitals.
The most interesting feature of the whole complex is the 16C *cloister,* which you enter from the right side of the nave. There seem to have been various different schools of sculpture at work. The N. side was begun in the 12C, and the cloister was completed with the S. side in the 13C. Each side has 10 round arches supported by pairs of columns with superbly carved capitals. Four columns replace the more usual pillars in the corners. The capitals of the N. side, which abuts on to the church, have scenes from the Old and New Testaments, from the Creation to the Crucifixion (e.g. St.Michael weighing the soul in the presence of the Devil). The capitals on the W. side have scenes of war and hunting; on the E. side there are scenes of court life, with dancing or kissing couples, but even these are not without religious symbolism. The capitals on the S. side are much more ab-

stract, having animal figures or geometrical motifs.

Within there is a three-foot high alabaster Virgin, the 14C *Virgo Lactans*, which is much venerated. An embroidered *silk cloth* in carmine, blue and dark green from the attached monastery is now kept in the *Museo de Arte de Catalunya* in Barcelona.

Estella

Navarra / Navarra   p.388 ☐ I 2

The town is of Roman origin and was established as a free market town on the bank of the Ega by Sancho Ramírez in 1090. Its importance grew when it became a stopping point for pilgrims on the way to Santiago de Compostela, but above all when it became an important trading centre. By 1236 Estella already had a market organization and in 1251 an annual fair. The Jews and the Franks, who had their own quarter, also contributed to the wealth of the town. The Kings of Navarre resided here and during the Second Carlist War Estella was the headquarters of Don Carlos, Conde de Montemolín. The town has so many churches and palaces that it was given the name 'Toledo of the North'.

San Pedro de la Rúa: On the pilgrim route to Santiago de Compostela, the church dominates the whole town. It dates from the time of King Sancho el Fuerte (12C) and is Estella's oldest church. Several architectural styles are combined here and in form it is very like a fortress. The *portal* is most interesting with many overlapping archivolts, which show obvious Moorish influence. The church is dominated by an imposing *tower*. Inside, the main *apse* is particularly interesting, having a double row of arches, with columns and capitals, —perhaps the oldest part of the church. There are a nave and two aisles with three semicircular apses. Other in-

teresting details include a column made up of three intertwined snakes, the Romanesque choir stalls and a font. The most interesting of the sculptures are those by Dominique de Guzmán (16C), of St. Andrew and St.Peter (17C), a *Romanesque Madonna* in the side apse of Mary of Bethlehem and the the Gothic statue 'Nuestra Señora de la O'. The church has a *reliquary of St.Andrew*, brought over by the Bishop of Patras (Greece) in the 13C, as well as that Bishop's enamelled crozier (13C, School of Limoges). The *capitals* of the partly destroyed *cloister* are superb; only two colonnades are intact, the cloister having been almost totally destroyed in the 16C by an explosion in the fortress above the church. The life and sufferings of Christ are finely carved on the capitals of the N. side and the capitals on the S. side have carvings of the deaths of St.Andrew and St.Lawrence and the imprisonment of St.Peter. Capitals from the W. side have symmetrical designs of plants and pairs of birds.

San Miguel: A simple but most beautiful church from the transitional period between Romanesque and Gothic. The church is first mentioned in documents of 1175 and 1187. The Romanesque *N. portal* is extremely interesting and its lovely carving makes it one of the three most beautiful examples in Navarre. On each side there are five columns, the capitals of which show the childhood of Christ and two hunting scenes and are of the greatest stylistic refinement. Each column supports an archivolt, whose individual voussoirs each tell a different story. In the middle the tympanum depicts Christ and the Evangelists. However, best of all are the two *reliefs* on either side of the portal: on the right, the Resurrection of Christ, with two angels and the three Holy Women bearing ointment vessels; on the left, the Archangel Michael's battle with the dragon, and also his battle with the devil over souls. Inside, a 14C altar of painted stucco, has scenes of the burial of the Counts of Muruzábal and Eguía. Other interesting things in the *side chapels,* include a statue of St.Crispin from the early 17C, which is attributed to Juan de Imberto.

Iglesia del Santo Sepulcro: Also built in a style transitional between Romanesque and Gothic. The church is single-aisled with a semicircular apse. Of particular interest is the Gothic *portal,* with an arch and tympanum, which is divided into three parts and shows the sufferings of Christ. On both sides of the portal there is a *frieze* with figures of the Apostles.

San Juan Bautista (Plaza de los Fueros): Originally Romanesque—see parts of the triforium, the N. portal and the vault. The other parts of the building are of various dates, but are essentially Gothic. The columns of the *N. portal* have beautiful capitals with geometrical figures and plant motifs. The *Renaissance high altar* is by Pierre Picart, who begun it in 1562 and

Estella, San Pedro de la Rúa 1 highly decorated portal **2** left apse with various statues **3** choir with three small chapels **4** right apse with Romanesque Madonna **5** entrance to cloister

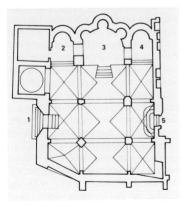

Juan de Imberto, who finished it in 1573. It is divided into four sections, which show scenes from the life of Christ and John the Baptist. To the right of this altar is a 13C Madonna, known as the 'Virgen de las Antorchas'.

Santa María Jus del Castillo: A pure Romanesque church from the 12C, which was also the Court chapel. From 1265 to the beginning of the 15C it was the church of a monastic order.

Basilica of El Santuario de la Virgen del Puy: As its name suggests, this church houses the *statue* of the Holy Virgin of Puy, which was found *c.* 1085 on the site of the church. The statue is silver-plated and decorated with valuable jewels. The church *treasure chamber* has a valuable copy of a finely carved Gothic chapel, as well as a 13C painted shrine, the sword of Charles III and other interesting items. The basilica was converted in 1951.

Nuestra Señora de Rocamador: This little church belongs to a Capucin monastery founded in 1201. In the 12C it was part of a hospice for pilgrims on their way to Santiago de Compostela, during which time the Romanesque apse was built. The high altar has a beautiful medieval painting.

Monastery of Santo Domingo: Once the site of a synagogue. This early Gothic monastery was built in 1259 by Teobaldo II and received numerous privileges from the Kings. The 'Cortes' was also convened here.

Convent of Santa Clara: The founding of this convent in 1253 owed much to the wife of Teobaldo II, who was also the daughter of St.Louis of France. It was converted in 1285. In the 14C the Princesses of Navarre were brought up here. The buildings were restored in the 17C.

Monastery of San Benito: 13C, rebuilt in the 17C. The church originally bore the name, 'Nuestra Señora de la Orta y de las Donas'. Houses a fine Romanesque sculpture.

Monastery of Recoletas: Early 18C. The monastery has the reputation of following the rules of the Augustinian Order to the very letter.

San Pedro de Lizarra: Originally 14C, but over the years, it has been so altered that few interesting features remain, apart from the *Renaissance altar* (1585) by the native artist Juan Imberto and a 15C Christ.

Palacio de los Duques de Granada de Ega: This palace is a superb and rare example of Romanesque secular architecture. It is on the pilgrim route and stands opposite the church of San Pedro. The façade on the Plaza San Martín is more or less undecorated. In its original 12C form the palace consisted of the ground floor with an entrance hall beyond four large round arches. Later the first floor was added. This has four large windows, each of which is divided in two by a column. The *capitals* of these window columns are richly decorated with plants, pairs of birds and wild animals. The capitals of the columns on the façade overlooking the pilgrim route have scenes of Roland's battle with Ferragut, by Martinus de Logroño. These heroic scenes are taken from the story by Turpín and the songs of the Carolingian cycle. The upper right capital has a grotesque caricature depicting the punishment of misers with gesticulating devils and a band of animal musicians. The palace houses the *Museum of the painter Gustavo de Maetzu,*.

Ayuntamiento/Town Hall: In the 11C this was the place where the first foreign settlers, the Franks of San Martín, used to meet. The present building is late Renaissance (16C). The façade has fine rain spouts and coats-of-arms.

Palacio de los Condes de San

Estella, San Pedro de la Rúa, cloister

Estella, San Pedro de la Rúa

Cristóbal: A Renaissance palace with a lavishly decorated Plateresque façade. The Franciscan monk and famous writer, Brother Diego de Estella, was born here in 1524.

The Governor's palace: An interesting secular building of 1613, belonging to the church of San Pedro de la Rúa.

Casa de los Santos: Belonged to the Eguía family. St.Francis Xavier lived here as a child—only part of the Renaissance staircase remains from that time. A spiral staircase led from here to the Jaso family pantheon in the Chapel of San Jorge.

House of Carlos VII (No. 13 on the Plaza de los Fueros): Carlos VII lived here from 1872–76 during the Third Carlist War.

Also worth seeing: Near the church of Santa María Jus del Castillo stood the *castles of Belmecher, Atalaya and Zalatambor,* of which there are but few remains; a simple iron cross stands in their memory. The castle of Belmecher was an imposing defence system of enormous proportions. In 1451 it was the scene of the clashes between the rightful heir to the kingdom, the Prince of Viana, and his step-mother.

Estepa
Sevilla/Andalusia   p.394☐F 10

Virgen de los Remedios: Decorated in the characteristic baroque style of Andalusia it contains a multi-coloured Italianate marble pulpit and a very fine 18C *shrine* behind the high altar, the *Camarín de la Vera Cruz,* by Nicolás Bautista Morales.

Castle: Estepa was the 'Astapa' of the Iberians and the castle ruins are evidence of their desire to defend themselves. However, later on, in BC 207, the Punic inhabitants' embittered resistance against the Roman troops was broken here. The Roman presence is still visible, as is the Arab extension of the fort. The massive keep is late 13C.

Also worth seeing: The baroque *church of El Carmen* (town hall square) from the 18C baroque, with an interesting portal. *Santa María la Mayor* is a 16C Gothic church within the confines of the castle; polychrome marble pulpit with alabaster figures of the Evangelists; 18C high altar and font. *Santa Victoria* has a beautiful baroque tower. The *Monastery of San Francisco:* has a 17C statue of St.Francis. The baroque *Convent of Santa Clara* has a Renaissance portal. Both convent and the monastery stand on the Cerro de San Cristobal. The *Palacio de los Marqueses de Cerverales* has an interesting baroque façade with twisting columns at the portal; patio.

Estíbaliz
Álava/Basque Provinces   p.388☐H 2

Santa María: An old 11C Romanesque convent church standing on a hill on the road to San Sebastián, 3 km. from Vitoria. Latin cross groundplan. The nave is barrel-vaulted and has beautiful capitals and three semicircular apses. There is a lovely early 13C *portal.* At the high altar there is a *statue of the Virgin Mary,* the patron saint of Álava. Carved from wood it probably dates from the 12C, as does the font.

Eunate
Navarra/Navarra   p.388☐I 2

Church of Santa María: The church of Santa María de Eunate stands on open ground near Puente la Reina. Built by the Templars, its unusual octagonal form suggests that it is probably a copy of the Church of the Holy Sepulchre in Jerusalem. Some believe it to be a cemetery church on the edge of the pilgrim route to Santiago de Compostela, a theory strengthened by the discovery of graves near the ring of arches. However, what is certain is that this is an interesting and beautiful Romanesque church, probably dating from the second half of the 12C. The church is surrounded by a ring of arches in the same octagonal form as the church. At one time, this was probably joined to the church by a roof. Some of the pillars are rectangular and some are composed of double columns with capitals, which may be decorated with figures and plant ornaments. The corners of the church are formed by strong columns flanked by two more slender columns. The single windows have round

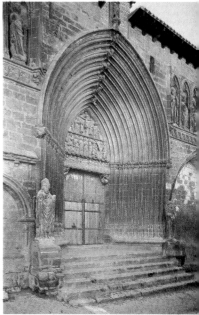

Estella, Santo Sepulcro

arches, which are supported by two smaller columns with capitals. The short tower, to one side of the building, has a stair leading to the roof. The main portal has four archivolts and these are supported on each side by two columns with interesting capitals. Inside there is a domed vault with eight ribs and a concluding keystone. The apse has an upper row of arches and a lower row of blind arches, which have the oldest of the church's capitals.

Ezcaray
Logroño/Old Castile   p.388

Parish church: 16C. The façade is decorated with escutcheons, which have come from the remains of old mansions. The tympanum has an Annunciation. Round towers at the corners make it look very like a fortress. Inside there is a nave and choir, the stalls of which are baroque. There are three Gothic altarpieces and another from the 16C.

Also worth seeing: The *Chapel of Nuestra Señora de Allende* with 10 paintings from the 17–18C, dedicated to the Archangel Michael. 17&18C *mansions,* the most outstanding of which is the *Palace of the Count of Torremúzquiz.*

Environs: About 3 km. N. is **Ojacastro:** Single-aisled 15C Gothic *parish church* with remains from an older Romanesque church. Of particular interest are the baroque high altarpiece, the grille of the chapel of San Pedro and a Flemish triptych from the Gossaert school. **San Asensio de los Cantos** (*c.* 8 km. N.): The *Eremita de la Ascensión* contains many Gothic murals. **Zorraquín** (*c.* 3 km. W.): The Romanesque *church* contains a retable with 15C oil paintings. **Valganón** (*c.* 8 km. W.): Fine

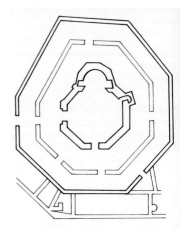

Eunate, Santa María The church has an unusual octagonal ground plan and is surrounded by an arcaded courtyard, which is also octagonal

grilles and drawings can be seen in the Romanesque *Capilla de Nuestra Señora de tres Fuentes.*

Eunate, Santa María

Figueras

The main town of the Alto Ampurdán region. Originally it was the ancient *Juncaria*, which had itself developed from a small walled settlement. The name *Ficaris* is Visigoth. Until 1267 it was governed by the Lords of Besalú, but then it was given the status of an independent 'Royal City' by King James I. Figueras served the royal purpose by holding back the ambitious Lords of Besalú and Ampurias, until, in 1274, Hugo IV, Lord of Ampurias, attacked and set fire to it. Only a single tower remains of what must once have been one of the most remarkable old city walls.

San Pedro: 14C parish church in the old city centre. Several kings were married here. It has a Gothic nave and, at the NE corner of the façade, a Romanesque chapel. Restored 1936.

Teatro Principal: Built in 1826, and converted into the *Museum Dalí* in 1974. Dalí was born in Figueras in 1904. There are regular exhibitions of Dalí's work along with other artists.

The fortress of San Fernando: Named after Ferdinand VI, who ordered it to be built. It was conceived on a huge scale, with seven ramparts a surrounding moat and 5 km. of wall set out in a star shape. It has survived in fine condition.

Other things of interest: *Memorial* to the inventor of the U-boat, Narcisco Monturiol, who was born in Figueras; the *Museo del Ampurdán*, with collections of Iberian, Greek and Roman art.

Environs: Cistella: The *parish church of Santa María*, consecrated in 947, and originally Romanesque; restored in the 18C. There are some fine carvings on the portal and on one of the windows. **Lladó:** the *parish church of Santa María* is an important example of Romanesque architecture. The portal has six archivolts supported by columns. Inside, the nave and two aisles show elements of the transition to Gothic. The area around **Bassagoda** has numerous 10&11C churches.

Fitero

Monastery of Santa María la Real: Founded in 1147 by Cistercians from the

Abbey of Scala Dei, under the supervision of St.Raymond (1090–1163). Here, in 1158 St. Raymond also founded the military-religious Order of Calatrava. Most of the buildings date from 1152–1287. The *church* was built in 1247, with a nave, two aisles and a Romanesque-Gothic transept. It is one of the largest to have been built by the Cistercians in Spain, and has survived largely due to the efforts of Archbishop Rodrigo Ximénez de Rada. The basic structure, like both interior and exterior decoration, is plain and simple. The *portal* consists of a single arch, supported by four columns on each side, and capped by three more arches with a fourth on top. The arches are undecorated, but the capitals are covered with carvings of flowers. The *apse* is Romanesque. The *high altar* has a work of 1550 by Roland de Mois. To its right is the tomb of Archbishop Rodrigo Ximénez de Rada (his remains are in the Abbey of Santa María de Huerta). The *cloister* was built in the 16C, in a style transitional between Gothic and Romanesque; it leads to a 13C chapterhouse. The cloister has an impressive *treasury*, with a 13C enamelled *reliquary* of St.Blasius. Also interesting is a 10C Hispano-Arabic *ivory casket*.

Other things of interest: Nearby there are the remains of old Roman baths.

Environs: Cintruénigo: The *church of San Juan Bautista* (16C) is of interest. The altar in the main chapel is by Esteban de Obray and was completed in 1530. There are sculptures by Gabriel Yoli and Guillaume Lévèque and paintings by Pedro de Aponte.

Fraga, view

Formentera
Balearics/Balearics   p.396 □ M/N 8

Formentera is a hammer-shaped island, and the smallest in the Balearic group (about 100 sq.km. of land with some 4,000 inhabitants). The islanders, who enjoy an unusually high life expectancy, claim that the climate is healthier than anywhere else in Spain. The countryside is beautiful and varied. The S. and E. are covered in rolling hills, which fall away to sheer cliffs where they meet the sea and there is also a fine selection of beautiful beaches and bays. However, tourism has been greatly restricted by the undeveloped road system and this makes the island particularly attractive to travellers who enjoy isolated locations. Its history is very similar to that of Ibiza. The name, Formentera, derives from the fact that wheat ('forment') used to grow abundantly on the island.

San Francisco Xavier: The island's capi

tal and administrative centre. The 16C *parish church* was consecrated by St. Francis Xavier. There are huge walls, a plain façade and a small bell tower. The high altar has a carved statue of the patron saint, and a Madonna and Child.

Nuestra Señora del Pilar: The most remote corner of the island has a fine *parish church*, built in the Moorish style typical of the island. In a niche in the marble-topped high altar there is a painting of the Madonna; there are other Madonnas and saints in side niches. Looking across the beautiful bay of Cala Codolá, you can see the *Faro de Formentera*, a lighthouse, on the top of La Mola, which is 630 ft. above sea level. *Es Caló* is an interesting little fishing village.

Fraga
Huesca/Aragon   p.388 □ L 4

A picturesque little town, which was originally an Iberian fortification. Ptolemy mentions the town, calling it Gallica Flavia. It is situated on the river Cinco, a tributary of the Ebro and is in the middle of a fertile valley. The town itself has a medieval ambience and typical Aragonese brick buildings.

San Pedro: A parish church, which was once a mosque; it was rebuilt in Romanesque style in the 12C. The portal has capitals depicting the life of St. Michael. Restoration occurred at the end of the 15C, and again at the end of the 18C, when the façade was given a fine roofed gallery. The interior is mostly 16C, although the rib vaulting is 15C. The three-storey bell tower displays elements of three styles: Romanesque and both early and late Gothic.

Other things of interest: The *Ayuntamiento/Town Hall*, with the portraits of several kings (painted by a student of Velázquez); *La Casa de Junqueras* with a fine Renaissance portal; the *houses of Monfort and Forada*; and the *Palacio del Gobernador* (the Governor's palace).

Environs: Local excavations have turned up the remains of a Roman settlement, known as **Villa Fortunati**, which dates from the 2 – 4C. There are Roman bedrooms, with mosaic floors, whose designs are picked out in marble and glass. The villa is surrounded by colonnades. Further excavations have revealed an *early Christian monastery* on the same spot (probably 7C in origin), and a small *basilica*, which is probably of the same date. A large **Iberian burial ground** was discovered in Santa Quiteria.

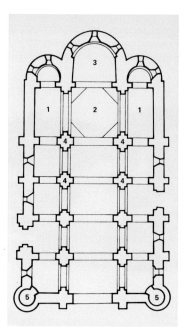

Frómista, San Martín **1** transept **2** crossing with semicircular dome and tower **3** main chapel **4** pillars with semi-columns, with richly ornamented capitals **5** two round towers on the W. side

---

Frómista
Palencia/Old Castile   p.388☐F 3

San Martín: A fine example of Romanesque from the 11C. It has a nave and two aisles, barrel vaulting and a transept. The highly decorated chapels are especially interesting; pagan and Roman themes suggest the origin of the building to be pre-Christian. There is a tower over the crossing and two more towers, which are round.

Santa María del Castillo: 15C Renaissance church with fine Plateresque portal. Inside there is a fine retable with 29 Spanish-Flemish pictures.

Environs: Villalcázar de Sirga (*c.* 5 km.

NW): *Santa María la Blanca* is transitional between Romanesque and Gothic. It has a fine portico and splendid tombstones. **Boadilla del Camino** (*c.* 2 km. E.): The 15–16C church of *Santa María* has a number of interesting altarpieces, a Plateresque high altar and a highly ornamented Romanesque font. There is a wonderful 15C obelisk in one of the streets. **Santoyo** (about 3km SE): The parish church displays features which are Romanesque, Gothic and Renaissance. The altarpieces have some excellent reliefs and sculptures. **Támara** (*c.* 4 km. SE): The parish church of *San Hipólito*, is transitional in style be-

Frómista, San Martín

tween Gothic and Renaissance. It has a nave, two aisles and a transept; interesting choir, pulpit and gallery in the main chapel. There are remains of the 11–13C *city walls*, and there is a Romanesque church attached to the castle. **San Cebrián de Campos** (*c.* 10 km. S.): The *parish church* has numerous baroque and Gothic altarpieces, and a fine Plateresque high altar.

Fuensaldaña
Valladolid/Old Castile   p.388☐F 4

Castle: Built in the 15C on the site of a previous 13C building, on the orders of Juan II's secretary. It has a square keep and four round towers.

Parish church of San Cipriano: A 13C Gothic church with an interesting rococo altarpiece by Manuel de Sierra, and a sculpture of St.Cristobal in a retable by a pupil of Juan de Juni.

Environs: Villalba de los Alcores (*c.* 10 km. NW): 12C Gothic *castle*, restored in the 15C; the Cistercian church of *Santa María* is Romanesque; 15C church of *Santiago*. **Mucientes** (2 km. N.): Gothic *parish church* with stone vaulting, a huge 16C tower by Alonso de Tolosa and a number of interesting retables, including one by Pedro de Correas. **Cigales** (*c.* 4 km. N.): The *parish church*, one of the finest in the province, is a Renaissance hall church and has several 17C retables. **Cabezón** (*c.* 8 km. NE): A spacious *parish church* with a huge tower, a Gothic tomb and numerous

16 – 17C sculptures and paintings. **Palazuelos** (*c.* 9 km. NE): The Gothic church of the *Benedictine monastery of Santa María* has a nave and two aisles; within there are impressive Gothic monuments to the Meneses family. **Valoria la Buena** (*c.* 15 km. NE): a large classical 18C parish church. **Trigueros del Valle** (*c.* 17 km. NE): The Romanesque church of *San Miguel* has barrel vaulting and a 12C portal; the church of *Santa María del Castillo* is 10C and gives the impression of a fortress; its portal has Mozarabic horseshoe arches. The *castle* is large with square towers at the corners; above the main door there is a coat-of-arms, together with the date 1453.

Fuente del Maestre
Badajoz / Estremadura   p.392☐D 8

Fuente del Maestre is *c.* 9 km. from Badajoz. The name comes from the *Casa del Maestre* (manor house), a fine building which belonged to a Knight of St. James of the Figueroa family.

Nuestra Señora de la Candeleria: A 15C Gothic church with 16C Plateresque additions, a Mudéjar *brick tower* and an impressive granite portal set against white walls. Inside there is a highly-ornamented main retable with mouldings, pedestals and columns.

Monastery of San Pedro: 13–14C monastery with Mudéjar gallery and 17C baroque chapel.

Fuentelapeña
Zamora / León   p.386☐E 4

Parish church: The apse is mid-16C; the building was not completed until 1618.

The portal is by a pupil of Gregorio Fernández. Inside there are a nave and two aisles, with transept and crossing, and a 16C main altar. In the sacristy there is an interesting Madonna and Child.

Environs: W. of Fuentelapeña is **Fuentesaúco**, with the church of *Santa María del Castillo*, which has a 16C chancel and further 17C additions. The portal is very fine, with carved figures of St. Peter and St. Paul at the sides. The main altar is mid 16C, with a baroque figure of John the Baptist.

Fuenterrabía
Guipúzcoa / Basque Provinces   p.388☐E 4

Situated at the point where the River Bidasoa forms a natural boundary between France and Spain. Fuenterrabía's strategic position made it an important fortress-town and the scene of a many battles. Picturesque medieval streets and old houses combine with fine beaches to make it a very popular resort. The old town, within the city walls, is under national protection. The *Puerta de Santa María* is a 15C gate decorated with the city's coat-of-arms and an image of the patron saint, Nuestra Señora de Guadalupe.

Nuestra Señora de la Asunción: A Gothic church with nave and two aisles. Originally 11C, it was rebuilt in the 16C in Renaissance style. The *Pyreneean Alliance*, concluded in 1659, was sealed by the marriage of Louis XIV of France to Princess María Teresa in this church. The *bell tower* platform and the balcony 'de los Apóstoles' (in the sacristy) both give a splendid view over the city and neighbouring areas.

Castillo de Carlos V. (Royal Palace): Today this building is the *Parador Na-*

cional El Emperador on the Plaza de Armas. It was begun in the 12C, continued under the influence of Ferdinand and Isabella and completed by King Charles V. The palace façade is 15–16C.

Burg San Telmo: A 16C fortress right on the sea front, which was built during Philip II's reign. It was intended to protect the town from pirate attacks common at the time. The entrance bears Philip II's coat-of-arms.

Other things of interest: The *old town* has a medieval atmosphere, largely because of the narrow streets—the area within the defensive wall was too small to allow for anything wide. The Calle Mayor, or main street, still has old mansions. They are most attractive, with coats-of-arms, wrought-iron work and charming bay windows. The Town Hall and some of the other houses, such as the *Torrealta* and the *Casadevante*, are also delightful. In a street called Pampinot there are old factories. On 7 September each year there is a feast in honour of the Madonna of Guadalupe. A Renaissance story describes the historical event. In 1683 the city was heavily besieged for two months by the army of Prince Condé de Saint-Simon. Exhausted and nearly at the end of its strength, the city was relieved by the arrival of the Spanish army on the eve of the holy day of the Madonna of Guadalupe. Thus the people of Fuenterrabía felt their faith in the Madonna had been rewarded.

Environs: Nuestra Señora de Guadalupe: Outside the city, about 5 km. W., in the shadow of the Jaizquíbel. The *miraculous image of the Madonna of Guadalupe*, the city's patron saint is surrounded by a golden altarpiece. The painting shows a number of model ships and sailors surrounded by sacred objects.

Fuentidueña
Segovia/Old Castile   p.392☐G 4

Parish church of San Miguel: Single-

Fuerteventura, Betancuria

aisled Romanesque church with barrel vaulting and a baroque altarpiece. The chapel contains a 17C wood carving of the crucified Christ.

La Concepción: A Romanesque church with two portals, which have finely decorated capitals, and a 15C altarpiece.

Castle: There are only scattered remains of the castle and its walls, but you can still see that the four corners of the original building had round towers.

Environs: The Romanesque *parish church* in **Sacramenia** (*c.* 8 km. N.): has a 13C font and baroque pulpit. The church of *San Miguel* is also Romanesque, and that of *Santa María* has a Romanesque font. Near the village is the Cistercian monastery of *San Bernardo,* which was founded by Alfonso VII in the 12C.

Fuerteventura
Las Palmas de Gran Canaria/
Canary Islands   p.396☐N/O 10

Shaped like a half moon, this is the second largest of the Canary Islands (*c.* 1,735 sq. km.), and the one closest to Africa. How-

ever, because of its parched climate, it has only around 20,000 inhabitants—the permanent water shortage forces many of them to emigrate. The *Isla de los Lobos* (Seal Island, 5 sq. km.) lies to the NE.

Puerto del Rosario: The main town is also the port, but has no sights of particular interest.

Betancuria: Former residence of the Norman conqueror Béthencourt (who came to the island in 1402) and later the episcopal seat. However, this village is of little importance today. The 15C cathedral, *Santa María,* has a fine wooden ceiling, a small *museum,* and nearby, the remains of a *Franciscan monastery.*

Pájara: A charming African village with a *village church,* whose façade is reminiscent of an Aztec motif. The portal has interesting 17C animal motifs, and the interior has a fine wooden ceiling.

Rio de las Palmas: The *village church* has a fine Gothic alabaster statue.

La Olivia: The *Casa de los Coroneles* is an 18C building and was formerly the Governor's residence.

G

Parish church: Tall, early 16C Mudéjar brick tower, with rectangular ground plan.

Palacio de Gálvez: Called a palace, but actually a castle or fortress (12–13C). The date and circumstances of its founding are unknown. It has a rectangular ground plan and a round tower at each corner. You can still see the towers' simple masonry, held together by ordinary lime mortar.

Environs: Los Castillos: 4 km. NW of Gálvez, with a castle very similar to that in Gálvez. Its ground plan is also rectangular. Originally there were four corner towers, but only three have survived; these are round, but they have unfortunately lost their battlements.

A medium-sized town surrounded by orange groves on the river Serpis, on the Costa Blanca. The *harbour* (Grao de Gandía) is 4 km. from the town, which has a tourist centre and a beautiful beach.

Festivals: The 'Fallas' takes place in March; there are famous processions in Holy Week; the Summer Festival in August; and 9–20 October the Festival of St.Francis Borgia, who is the patron saint of Gandía.

History: The Moors founded the town. In 1252 King James I of Aragon captured it. In 1485 Ferdinand the Catholic gave the

Gerona, Río Ter, cathedral and San Félix

Dukedom of Gandía to the Borgia (Borja in Spanish) family, which produced Pope Alexander VI.

The fourth Duke of Gandía was St.Francis Borgia, Viceroy of Catalonia.

The expulsion in 1609 of the Moriscos (partly christianized Moors), left such gaps in the population that new settlers had to be brought in from all over Spain.

The Ducal Palace: Paseo de las Germanías. The ancestral castle of the Borgia family. Built *c.* 1600 with Gothic and Renaissance features. It now belongs to the Jesuits. There are some splendid rooms and a small museum with famous paintings, works of art and relics of St.Francis Borgia. The latter gave up his positions as duke and viceroy and joined the Jesuit order.

Colegiata (14–16C): This church is a good example of Catalan Gothic. It has two beautiful Gothic portals. The single-aisled interior is simple and of impressive proportions. The large retable is the work of Damián Forment and was painted by the Italian Paolo de San Leocadio. Also worth seeing is the coat-of-arms of Doña María Enríquez, the grandmother of St.Francis Borgia.

Environs: Castillo de Bayrén (on the road to Valencia): A 12C Moorish castle. **Cova de Parpalló** (8 km. W. of Gandía) has prehistoric caves. The **Monastery of Jerónimo de Cotalba** (towards Játiva) is an impressive 14C Gothic building.

Gerona

Gerona/Catalonia　　　　　　　p.390☐O 3

The province of Gerona, on the NE coast of Spain is the easternmost of the Spanish provinces. Bordered by the Pyrenees on one side and the Mediterranean on the

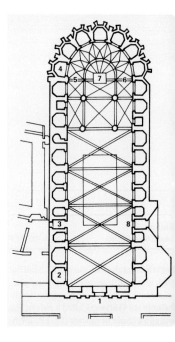

Gerona, cathedral 1 baroque façade by Pedro Costa (1604–16), altered in 1725 **2** tomb of Bernardo de Pau by Lorenzo Mercadante (15C) **3** entrance to cloister and chapterhouse **4** baroque altar by Pablo Costa (16C) **5,6** tombs of Ramón Berenguer, Count of Barcelona, and his wife Mahalda, by Morey (1385) **7** high altar with retable and baldacchino **8** side portal by Morey (1394)

other, it is quite different from the rest of Spain, both as regards climate and scenery. Its capital, Gerona, is divided by the river Oñar; the beautiful old town on the right bank has kept its medieval character. Today, historians have abandoned the notion that this was the ancient city of 'Gerunda' referred to by Pliny and Caesar. It is more likely that Gerunda is a latinized form of Gironda in southern Gaul. Thus the origins of Gerona have still not been exactly established. It was known from early times

Gerona, cathedral

as a diocesan town and due to its strategic setting, often became a theatre of war, earning it the name 'Ciudad de los Sitios' or town of sieges. Between the 17–19C it was besieged no less than 34 times, first by Muslims and later mainly by French troops.

Cathedral: On the right bank of the Oñar, in the Plaza de la Catedral, from which 96 steps lead up to the church. To the right is the *Casa de la Pia Almoyna,* an austere 15C Gothic building. To the left is one of the gates in the medieval walls; known as *Sobreportas,* it is flanked by two cylindrical towers. Opposite stands the *Palace of Justice,* a 16C Renaissance building. All these buildings are in local materials from quarries nearby. The steps date from 1690 and the *cathedral façade* from 1604–16, ac-

cording to the plans of Pedro Costa. The façade was altered in 1725 and the tower was added at the end of the 17C. The *church* itself was built in 1312 on the site of an older Romanesque building, which was consecrated in 1038 by Bishop Pedro Roger, brother of Countess Ermessinda of Barcelona. Of this building all that is left is a part of the tower, which was named after Charlemagne, as well as a splendid *cloister,* which is considered to be the finest in Catalonia. The *inside of the church* originally had a nave and two aisles, as can be seen from the apse (1347). In 1417 Guillom Bofill took charge of the project and decided to make it single-aisled, to retain the feeling of space typical of Catalan-Gothic architecture. The problem of unifying the single nave with the previous three aisles and apse was solved by the addition

Gerona, cathedral, marble throne of Charlemagne, detail

Gerona, throne of Charlemagne

of a beautiful gallery of Gothic windows. The 12C cloister is similar to the cloisters of San Cugat and San Pedro de Galligans, having round arches supported by slender pillars with decorated capitals. Some of the capitals—with animal and plant motifs or battle scenes between man and beast— seem oriental or Islamic in origin; others have biblical scenes. We now know that the sculptors took their inspiration from two 11C Catalan bibles (in San Pedro de Roda, Ripoll). The most beautiful carvings are found in the S. wing, which is probably the oldest. Because of its carvings the cloister is considered the finest example of Catalan-Romanesque architecture. The *side portal* was begun in 1394 by G. Morey; only two of the clay figures have survived. There is an *alabaster high altar* and a 13C silver retable of 1320–57 by Bartomeu, Ramón Andreu and Pedro Bernec. The baldacchino dates from the end of the 14C. Among the splendid pieces in the *church treasury* there is an illuminated manuscript dated 974, a 12C Madonna, a painting of Christ, a 15C Custodia by Pere Artau and a superb *wall hanging*, — the Tapiz de la Creación—from the 11–12C. The tapestry shows Christ Pantocrator and the story of the Creation along with depictions of the seasons and the months of the year (cf. the slightly different tapestry in Bayona).

San Félix (or San Felíu, on the right bank of the Oñar, in the Calle de la Colegiata): The church was built on the site of its predecessor, to which reference was made as early as the 6C. The beautiful Gothic *bell tower* was struck by lightning in 1581 and this destroyed its upper part. *Inside*, the pillars and arches are Romanesque and the rib vaults are Gothic. Apses in the right transept are also Romanesque. In the left transept the baroque *Capilla de San Narciso* is dedicated to the town's patron saint.

Gerona, museum, manuscript (975)

ECLOCVSTE VBIAGELVS PDICTTIONI IПPERAT EAS.

VBILOCVSTE ...

Gerona, cathedral, Retablo Mayor

Next to the *high altar,* which has a Gothic retable, there is a Gothic door and eight sarcophagi; these date from the 2–6C and have beautiful carvings.

Monastery of San Pedro Galligans: Mentioned as early as 992. The church of 1130, with a nave, two aisles and a basilican ground plan, is a beautiful example of the Catalan-Lombard style of architecture. The *bell tower,* square in its lower sections and octagonal higher up, rises above the transept. The *cloister* is rectangular and has fine columns and capitals, with carvings of plants of the region. The *portal,* which has archivolts, columns and capitals shows Visigoth influence. There is a remarkable rose-window in the *façade.* The 12C *Virgen de la Esperanza* (The Virgin of Hope —a pregnant Virgin Mary) can be seen in

the apse. The *Archaeological Museum* is housed in the monastery.

San Nicolás (opposite San Pedro): A well-restored Romanesque church with apses and an octagonal dome.

Episcopal palace (on the Plaza de los Apóstoles): The palace combines Romanesque, Gothic and Renaissance features.

Monastery of St. Daniel: The little church was renovated in the 17C. However, the remarkable Romanesque cloister with Corinthian capitals has survived. The Gothic upper storey was added in the 15C.

The upper part of the town is the so-called *Ciudad Antigua* (Old Town). On the Plaza de Santo Domingo there is a modest building, which was the old **University** (15C). Next to it is the **Monastery of Santo Domingo,** which has a church and 14C Gothic cloister, the carved capitals of which depict biblical scenes.

San Martín Sacasta (next to the Viscount's palace): This church was founded in the 3C. 7C remains from the Visigoth period can be seen. The 11C bell tower is Romanesque and there is a 17C Renaissance façade.

Baños Árabes (Moorish baths): These baths, which are 12C Mudéjar with 13C renovations, can be found in the Capucin monastery between the churches of San Félix and San Pedro. The complex consists of several rooms. The small basin with eight fine columns and capitals supporting an octagonal dome is especially delightful.

Diocesan Museum (Plaza de España): This houses Iberian, Greek and Roman archaeological *collections,* as well as Romanesque *frescos* and various altar paintings from churches in the region.

Gerona, cathedral and San Félix

Provincial Archaeological Museum in the Monastery of San Pedro de Galligans): Mainly finds from Palaeolithic caves in the province and from the excavations in Ampurias.

Environs: Palau Sacosta: A small town, now part of Gerona, with a fortress, the *Torres de Palau*, which was built in 1495 on top of an older one, to which there is a 14C reference. It is the private property of the Sarriera family.

Gibraltar
Cádiz/Andalusia   p.394☐E 11

In antiquity, this massive rocky peninsula was thought to be one of the pillars of Hercules. (Mount El Acho, on the Moroccan coast opposite and part of the Spanish exclave Ceuta, was the second.) Before the Arab invasion in 711, the old name was Calpe. It was the base from which the conquest of Spain began, and was renamed Djebel al Tarik (Mount of Tarik), after the Arab leader, the Berber Tarik; it was later shortened to Gibralta. Until 1309 the town remained securely in Moorish hands. It was taken over by the Spaniards after many bellicose clashes in the mid 15C. Emperor Charles V revamped the defences. During the Spanish War of Succession it was taken by the British and from 1783 onwards it became a British crown colony. Spain's claim to the rock still persists. In 1969 access to the mainland was blockaded at the border town of La Línea de la Concepción. The historical buildings are in the *North Town:*

Catholic cathedral (Calle Real or Main Street): 16C Gothic building, a conversion of the former mosque.

Anglican cathedral (Cathedral Square): Built in 1821 in Moorish style.

Franciscan monastery (Main Street): Founded 1531. Now the *Governor's Palace*. The 14C **Moorish castle** has evidence to suggest that it was already laid out in the 8C.

Environs: Ceuta (North African coast, opposite Gibraltar): A Spanish exclave of the province of Cadiz. The town came under Spanish rule in 1580. 18C church of *Nuestra Señora de Africa* and the *Hermitage of San Antonio* (1540). **Melilla** (NE African coast): This town has been in Spanish hands since 1497 and is part of the province of Granada. It was a trade settlement as early as Phoenician times, but was unable to develop any architectural continuity due to intermittent warfare. A 16C *ring of walls* round the upper town, the

'Pueblo', survives from the time of the occupation of the Duke of Medina-Sidonia. The 17C church, the *Iglesia de la Purísima,* has baroque altars, an 18C figure of the Madonna, the 'Señora de la Victoria', and a 15C statue of Christ the Saviour.

Gijón
Oviedo/Asturia   p.386☐E 1

Gaspar Melchor de Jovellanos y Ramírez, one of the country's greatest clerics and diplomats, who established himself as poet, reformer, encyclopaedist and mathematician, was born in Gijón in 1744. Severely damaged in the Spanish Civil War, the town has since been rebuilt along modern lines. It is also famous as a seaside resort.

The Plaza del Marqués, at the foot of the cliff of Santa Catalina, and at the head of the beach of San Lorenzo, is in the fishing quarter of the town. On the square there are two buildings, the interiors of which

Gerona, cathedral, 16C font

are semi-dilapidated: a *collegiate church* with 16C façade and the *Palace of the Count of Revillagigedo*, which has a 16C façade between two imposing towers.
At the other end of the town, in the beautiful park of Isabel la Católica, stands the *Parador del Molino Viejo*, which is built above an old restored mill—the only surviving one of its kind in the Gijón area.

The *Universidad Laboral José Antonio Girón* is at the edge of the town. It is a monumental, inferior and imitative 20C building, designed by the architect Luis Moya. A rotunda with side wings, it is almost baroque in style with pink marble, granite columns and huge stone figures. The clock tower (including lantern) is about 340 ft. tall. The courtyard is over 100 ft. long. In the main hall there are murals of 377 life-size figures by Enrique Seguva.

The *Instituto Jovellanos:* Founded by Jovellanos in 1794 it is now housed in the 16C palace where he was born. The building serves as study centre and museum, containing, among other things, documents relating to the history of Gijón and a specialist library of periodicals, newspapers, etc.

Even though some of Gijón's beautiful old churches have been destroyed (9C San Pedro and the Gothic church of San Lorenzo) and the vast and valuable collections of Jovellanos have been substantially burnt in fires during the Civil War, Gijón is still a very beautiful town, which, with its bullfights and numerous festivals, exudes charm.

Gomera
Santa Cruz de Tenerife/
Canary Islands   p.396☐L 10

The second smallest of the Canary Islands (378 sq. km.) is dry and bare in the S. and lush and fertile in the N.—as are almost all the islands of this archipelago.

Gijón, San Lorenzo

Gijón, Universidad Laboral

San Sebastián: Harbour and capital of the island. Christopher Columbus berthed here on several occasions and is reputed to have stayed in a yellow stone house, No. 60, in the main street. The *Iglesia de la Asunción* has a pretty Gothic portal of red lava stone. A small painting of the Virgin and Child is attributed to Velázquez. The oldest building in the town is the 15C square tower, the *Torre del Conde*.

Gradefes
León/León   p.386□E 2

Monasterio de Santa María: A Cistercian nunnery founded in 1168, although the foundation stone was not laid until 1 March 1177. The E. end, with an ambulatory around the apse is a fine example of Romanesque. Other parts are 13&14C Gothic with Mudéjar features and there is a 17C gallery on the W. side. Good tombs with reclining figures and statues. Interesting altar.

Environs: San Miguel de Escalada: A monastery church on the Río Esla and one of the most beautiful Mozarabic buildings in Spain. The monastery, dedicated to St. Michael under the Visigoths, fell into disrepair after the Arab invasion in 711. Alfonso III handed it over to refugee monks from Córdoba for rebuilding. On 20 November 913 the new church was consecrated. The basilica has a nave, two aisles, horseshoe arches, open roof trusses, vaulted apses and an arcade of 12 arches on the S. side. Arches of both portico and nave are horseshoe-shaped in Moorish style. Columns and Corinthian capitals with acanthus motifs are very lovely. In the 11C the monastery was converted to a priory. The sturdy tower on the S. side (near the arcade) was added in the 13C. **Eslonza:** The monastery of *San Pedro*—formerly one of the richest in León—dates from the 10C. The present church is mainly 16C and was completed in 1711 **Villarmún:** The *parish church* is one of the few examples showing the transition from Mozarabic to Romanesque style. The

San Miguel de Escalada (Gradefes)

Capilla Mayor is horseshoe-shaped inside, but square on the outside (as in Peñalba). Carving on capitals is partly early Romanesque, partly Mozarabic.

Grado
Oviedo/Asturia   p.386☐E 1

Grado, a town of particular importance in the Middle Ages, dates back to a Roman settlement. There are numerous features testifying to the town's past, including the remains of castles, palaces and houses, e.g. the palace of the Count of Valdecarzana and the adjacent 18C Capilla de los Dolores. The area around Grado is also interesting.

Environs: Cueva de San Roman de Candamo: These caves, beautifully situated above the Pravia valley, 12 km. from Grado, have prehistoric drawings of horses, bison and deer. (Closed on Mondays) **Dóriga:** The Romanesque church of *San Esteban* was converted in the 18C, but some medieval features have survived. *Santa Eulalia* is a Romanesque church with a 12C portal. The *Palacio de Dóriga* is an imposing 16–17C building with a square fortress tower. **Cornellana:** The church of *San Salvador*, part of an earlier Benedictine monastery, was built in 1024. The 12C building has been restored several times; the façade is 18C and the cloister, (with Gothic tombs), is 19C. **Salas:** In 1120 the town of Salas was given to the Counts Sueró and Anderquina by Queen Doña Urraca. The collegiate church of *Santa María la Mayor,* is a 16C single-aisled church with side chapels, which was built on top of an older building. It contains the famous tomb of Fernando de Valdés, Grand Inquisitor and founder of the University of Oviedo. Made of marble, it has realistic figures of 1576–83 by Pompeyo Leoni. There is also a beautiful

Renaissance altar. *San Martín:* This church dates from 896 and still has pre-Romanesque windows, reliefs and inscriptions; the portal is 15C. **Also worth seeing** are the late-17C *Palacio de los Condes de Casares* and above all the imposing watch tower, the *Torre de los Valdés,* part of the 14C castle of Miranda. According to tradition this castle is very old and possibly of pre-Romanesque origins.

Grajal de Campos
León/León   p.386☐F 3

San Miguel: The parish church has a nave, two aisles and arch vaulting supported by Tuscan columns. The Capilla Mayor is 16C, (as is the palace). 17C high altar with sculptures in the style of Gregorio Fernández. 16C paintings.

Castillo: Interesting early 16C defensive system. The fortress consists of a large

Grajal de Campos, Castillo

building with round towers at the corners and numerous embrasures.

Palacio de los Marqueses de Grajal: Built in 1540 by the Count of Grajal in imitation of the Alcalá of Henares. Its ground plan is a large rectangle with corner towers. The façade is made less severe by a gallery in the S. The palace courtyard is framed by semicircular rows of arches, two storeys high.

Granada
Granada/Andalusia   p.394□G 10

Almost unrivalled for beauty and architectural splendour, the entire city has been declared a national monument. It lies at the foot of Spain's mightiest massif, the Sierra Nevada, and on the edge of an extraordinarily fertile plain. A provincial capital with a university and an archaepiscopal see, the city is divided by the Darro which runs underground in the city centre. On the right lies Albaicín, the city's oldest quarter; on the left rises the imposing Alhambra. To the S. the city is bordered by the Río Genil into which the Darro flows. This fertile area was already settled in the 5C BC and was known as Iliberis in Roman times. The city was founded under the Visigoths, whose domination ended with the Arab victory in 711. 'Elvira' (Granada was just a nearby settlement) was ruled by a viceroy dependent upon Córdoba until the fall of the Caliphate in Córdoba in 1031. During the next two centuries Granada was ruled first by the Berber dynasty of the Almoravides and then Berber Almohades, until the first Nasrite king, Mohammed I, established a kingdom in 1241. After the capture of Córdoba by the Christian armies in 1236 the town increased in importance, reaching its brilliant zenith under the rule of the Moorish Nasrites, who were tolerated by the Castilian kings. It was the only surviving bastion of Islam in Spain until the last king of Granada had to relinquish the city to Ferdinand and Isabella at the treaty of Santa Fé in 1491.

The famous humanist Diego Hurtado de Mendoza (1503 – 75), who was born in Granada, described the capture of the town. In the same way that the Alhambra palace was built during the Nasrite dynasty and a lively cultural environment was able to develop in the densely populated and wealthy city, so too were the new Spanish powers able to enrich Granada with splendid Renaissance and baroque buildings. However, from 1570, following the expulsion of the Moors who had rebelled against the repressive measures of Philip II, the economical and historical importance of Granada declined. Vital irrigation systems which were destroyed at that time were not rebuilt until the 20C.
In the 17C the versatile Granada-born artist, Alonso Cano, who was painter, sculptor and architect, made an important contribution to the appearance of the town. His buildings were of a stylistic importance which reached beyond the confines of Granada itself. The sculptor Pedro de Mena, who was also born in Granada was Cano's pupil.

Alhambra: A complex on the high plateau, the Cerro del Sol, which overlooks the town to the SE. It includes the superb palace of Granada's Moorish kings, which was built principally under the Nasrite rulers Yusuf I (1333-54) and Mohammed V (1354-91). Massive towers and gates surround the palace complex emphasizing its fortress-like character; there are also ring walls and the remains of the *Alcazaba*. The latter was built by Mohammed V in 1238 in a shimmering red stone, which led to the

Granada, Alhambra, Court of the Lions

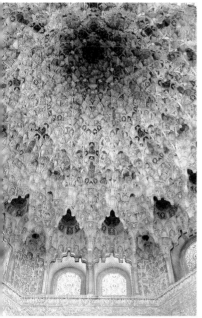

Granada, Alhambra, Mozarabic dome

Granada, Alhambra, dome of the Sala de los Abencerrages

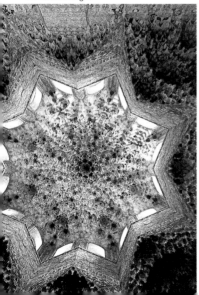

description 'Calat Alhambra' (red castle). From the top of the *Torre de la Vela*, which is 87 ft. high, you get a panoramic view over the Sierra Nevada. The road up into the Alhambra park passes through the *Puerta da las Granadas*, a triumphal arch decorated with three pomegranates, and designed by Pedro Machuca. To the right, on Monte Mauror, the 12C *Torres Bermejas* can be seen; this is part of the fortification linking with the Alacazaba. Walking through the wood you come to the *Puerta de la Justicia*, built by Yusuf I in 1348. Above the gate's first horseshoe arch there is a carved hand to symbolize defence against evil. The second horseshoe arch is decorated with many Arab inscriptions. There are beautiful blue and green azulejos. After four right-angled bends (for reasons of defence), you come to the entrnce to the Alhambra Palace itself. Nearby the Renaissance fountain (1545) dates from the time of Charles V and is the work of Pedro Machuca. The 14C *Puerta del Vino* leads to the *Plaza de los Aljibes* (square of wells). The 'Gate of Wine' displays the Nasrites' artistic style to great advantage. To the W. of the square there are the former buildings of the Alcazaba; to the E. there is the *Palace of Charles V* and to the N. the *Palacio árabe (the Alhambra Palace)*.

Palacio árabe de la Alhambra: The complex is divided into three areas (characteristic of Arab palaces), the rooms of each of which are grouped around a central courtyard (patio): *Mexuar* (department for the administration of justice and all public interests); *Diwân* (official palace with throne room); and *Harim* (private rooms). The Alhambra palace is famous above all for its superb interior decoration, which has given its name to an entire style, the 'Alhambra style'. Essentially this style in-

Granada, Alhambra, Sala de los Reyes

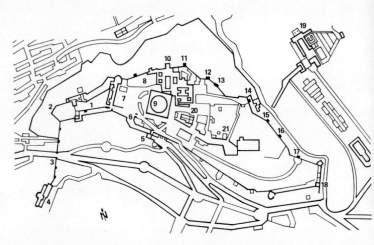

Granada, Alhambra, surroundings 1 Alcazaba 2 Torre de la Vela 3 Puerta de las Granadas 4 Torres Bermejas 5 Puerta de la Justicia 6 Puerta del Vino 7 Plaza de los Algibes 8 Palacio Arabe de la Alhambra 9 Palacio de Carlos Quinto 10 Torre de Comares 11 Torre del Peinador 12 Torre de las Damas 13 Torre del Mihrab o de la Mezquita 14 Torre de los Picos 15 Torre del Candil 16 Torre de la Cautiva 17 Torre de las Infantas 18 Torre de Agua 19 Generalife 20 Santa María 21 San Francisco

Granada, Alhambra 1 entrance 2 Mexuar 3 Patio del Mexuar 4 oratory 5 Cuarto Dorada 6 Patio de los Arrayanes 7 Torre de Comares 8 Sala de Embajadores 9 Sala de la Barca 10 Patio de la Reja 11 Departamentos de Carlos V 12 Peinador de la Reina 13 baths 14 Patio de los Leones 15 Sala de los Reyes 16 Sala de los Abencerrages 17 Sala de las Dos Hermanas 18 Sala de los Mozárabes 19 Sala de los Ajimeces 20 Mirador de Daraxa 21 Jardín de Daraxa 22 Jardínes del Partal 23 Palace of Charles V

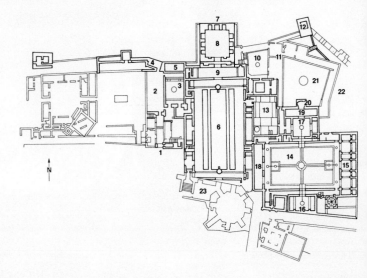

volves two-dimensional surface ornamentation covering whole areas of walls, the space between arches, etc., throughout the alcázar. (Realistic three-dimensional representation, especially of people, is absent.) There are stucco arabesques and filigree lines. Texts from the Koran and eulogies to Mohammed V, as well as the Nasrite slogan 'Allah alone will conquer', in tall Kufic characters and in the rounded, flowing Naskhi script, are worked into a whole network of decorative ornamentation. There are a seemingly endless interaction of forms reminiscent of oriental carpets and including tendrils, rosettes, palmettes, leaf and star patterns, and lozenge patterns. The latter were also called sebka decoration and were very popular during the Almohaden era; see the Giralda in Seville. Protecting the greatly valued and delicate decoration there are fine, tiled wooden roofs with awnings. There are recesses with arches and delicate, slender columns, totally in keeping with the ornamental forms on the walls; the capitals are decorated with similar designs. Columns themselves serve only rarely as supports. Pedestals, plinths and dados are covered in tiles. Other of the palace's exceptional features are the massive so-called stalactite domes with honeycomb cupolas. The oldest part is the *Palacio Mexuar* which housed the former council-chamber (a chapel since 1629 and now restored) and a small prayer-room, the *Oratorium.* The mihrab faces E. The *Patio del Mexuar* with marble slabs opens on to the *Cuarto Dorado* (golden living-room) through three arches. From this patio you enter the heart of the whole palace, the rooms of which are grouped around the *Patio de los Arrayanes* or *Patio de los Mirtos.* Two rows of arcades line the long pool in the middle of the Court of Myrtles. At the N. end stands the battlemented *Torre de Comares* (150 ft. high), which contains the throne room, the *Sala de Embajadores,* the most sumptuous room in the palace. Before this there is a smaller reception room,

Granada, Alhambra, rest room

Granada, Alhambra, Court of the Lions

Granada, Alhambra, lion fountain

the *Sala de Barca* (the Hall of Mercy or of Blessing), *c.* 130 sq. ft., *c.* 60 ft. high and decorated extremely lavishly. Crowned by a cedar dome, a masterpiece of Arab carving, and with a fine artesonado in cedar, the room looks like the nave of a church. Stucco-decorated windows are particularly beautiful.

Passing through the *Patio de la Reja* you come to the *Departamentos* (chambers) *de Carlos V,* the *Peinador de la Reina* (boudoir, in the Torre del Peinador), and to the *baths*, which are actually a series of rooms beneath the palace, built under Yusuf I. The most splendid part of the palace is the *Patio de los Leones* (the Court of Lions) with the harem. Building began here in 1378 under Mohammed V. 124 delicate marble columns support the surrounding arcades. At the E. and W. ends there are two enchanting pavilions ornamented with exceedingly fine stalactite decorations. Between the pavilions is the *Lion Fountain*, whose 12 marble lions support the fountain basin. An Arab poem by Ibn Zamrak, engraved around the edge of the basin extols the beauty of the court, which was formerly enhanced by shady palms.

The *Sala de los Reyes* (or Sala del Tribunal) has a row of seven alcoves roofed by semicircular domes. Stalactite arches connect successive rooms, three of which contain pictures painted on leather.

The *Sala de los Abencerrages* to the S. has a beautiful stalactite dome with interesting carvings on the doors, particularly finely carved capitals and a twelve-sided marble fountain. The room was named after a powerful noble family. To the N. is the *Sala de las dos Hermanas*, another very

Granada, Alhambra, Palace of Charles V

beautiful room, which takes its name from two large, twin marble slabs in the floor. The water in the central fountain flows to the Lion Fountain. It has the largest honeycomb dome of its kind, with some 5,000 cells. Above the azulejo wall decoration there is an Arab poem in homage to the sultan, again by Ibn Zamrak, Mohammed V's vizier.

Behind the Sala de las dos Hermanas, there is the *Sala de los Ajimeces* , so named after its twin windows. This room also leads to the charming little oriel *Mirador de Daraxa* (from 'dar Aischa'—Aischa was the young, favourite wife of the Prophet), also known as 'Mirador de Lindaraja'. The black, yellow and white paving is particularly fine. Large arched windows give a clear view into the *Jardín de Daraxa*, with its cypresses, lemon and orange trees, hedges

and the large 17C fountain in the middle. The *Jardínes del Partal* (partal is the Arabic for 'portal'), on the E. side, are surrounded by a wall. In the garden the *Torre de las Damas*, a tower with a loggia, opens on to a rectangular pond. The complex has many **fortress towers**, including: the *Torre del Mihrab*, near which there is a small early 14C mosque and a subterranean passage; the battlemented *Torre de los Picos*; the *Torre del Candil*; the *Torre de la Cautiva*, the Captive's Tower, decorated under Yusuf I, with stucco and stalactite work, fine flagstones and a superb ceiling; the *Torre de las Infantas*, which is late 14C with splendid chambers; and to the E., the *Torre del Agua* with the aqueduct.

Palacio del Generalife (actually Djennat al Arif, or Architect's Garden): Further

Granada, Alhambra, Jardines del Partal with the Torre de las Damas

E. and higher than the Alhambra. Essentially it is a simple 14C building, which was designed as a summer residence for the Kings of Granada. You approach it through a beautiful cypress avenue. The lovely gardens with the canal and the numerous fountains, grottoes and terraces afford most beautiful views, in particular from the 'Silla del Moro' (Seat of the Moor).

Palace of Charles V: On the S. side of the alcázar. It is the most beautiful Renaissance building in Spain, even if its massive square proportions (210 ft. by 210 ft. and 57 ft. high) are incongruous beside the neighbouring Moorish buildings. The Italian-educated Pedro Machuca of Toledo designed the palace in 1526. It was never completed. The lower parts of the build-

ing are heavily rusticated in a style reminiscent of Florentine palaces; the upper part has windows and pilasters. W. and S. fronts each have beautiful grey marble portals. The round two-storeyed colonnaded courtyard is most impressive. With a diameter of 100 ft., it was used as a bull ring. A dome was planned for the chapel but never executed.

Museo Provincial de Bellas Artes (in the Palace of Charles V): The collection is composed of sculptures and a particularly fine group of paintings, including some by Fray Juan Sánchez Cotán, who lived and worked in the Carthusian monastery in Granada from 1612 onwards. In the Entrance Hall, an 'Adoration of the Shepherds'; in Room II 'Regina Coeli'; in Room III, paintings from the Carthusian

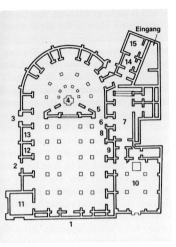

Granada, cathedral **1** main façade **2** Puerta de San Jerónimo **3** Puerta del Perdón **4** Capilla Mayor **5** altar of Santiago **6** portal of Capilla Real **7** Capilla Real **8** altar of Jesús Nazareno **9** Capilla de la Trinidad **10** Sagrario **11** treasury **12** Capilla de Nuestra Señora del Carmen **13** Capilla de Nuestra Señora de las Angustias **14** ante-sacristy **15** sacristy

Granada, Capilla Real, high altar

Monastery, particularly 'Bodegón del Cardo'. The School of Granada is especially well represented in Room I. Also in Room I there is a lovely enamel triptych by Léonard Pénicaud of Limoges, a 15C 'Madonna and Child' by Roberto Alemán, a very beautiful sculpture ('Entombment') by Jacobo Florentino el Indaco, and 'Madonna and Child', a superb bas-relief by Diego de Siloé. In Room V there are paintings by the influential Granada-born Alonso Cano: 'St. Bernardino of Siena', 'St. John of Capistrano' and a 'Madonna and Child'. Additionally there are some of his sculptures such as the 'Head of St. John of the Cross'; as well as sculptures which he executed together with Pedro de Mena. In the same room there are paintings by Pedro Anastasio Bocanegra, who was himself much influenced by Cano; the former

also has work in the Entrance Hall and in Room VII. In one room there is an Italian polychrome marble fireplace (16C Genoese) as well as paintings from 17-20C.

Museo Nacional de Arte Hispano-Musulman (Museum of Spanish-Arab Art); also in the Palace of Charles V: Many interesting exhibits (tombs, ceramics, glass, capitals, etc.) as well as the beautiful and famous *Alhambra Vase*. This clay vase is a superb example of 14C Moorish ceramics. 4 ft. 4 in. tall, it is decorated in gold and blue, with leaping gazelles.

Santa María: A 16C church by Juan de Herrera. Part of the Alhambra complex, it occupies the site of a mosque. *Columns* (on the right of the main portal) stand in memory of two Franciscan martyrs. There are three *statues* by Alonso de Mena inside: 'St.Ursula', 'St.Susan' and 'Christ on the Cross'. Marble font.

Monastery of San Francisco (also in the Alhambra complex): Founded in 1495 on the site of a Moorish palace; it has undergone several conversions and is now a 'Parador Nacional'.

Cathedral of Santa María de la Encarnación: Enrique de Egas started building this massive and most beautiful of all Spanish Renaissance churches in 1523 to Gothic designs. Five years later and until 1563, Diego de Siloé continued the building in Renaissance style. He built the two *N. portals: the Puerta de San Jerónimo* and the *Puerta del Perdón*. The massive *main façade*, on the W. side and its portal, (very like a Roman triumphal arch), were the work of Alonso Cano (1664). Reliefs depict the Birth of Christ, the Visitation of Mary and the Assumption of the Virgin. Cano's brilliant work resulted in the façade becoming the model for other contemporary churches. The *interior* is 390 ft. long and 225 ft. wide, with a nave and four aisles and mighty compound pillars. The *Capilla Mayor* is 158 ft. high with a dome, and contains much fine art. In 1929 the coro in the middle was removed and now there is an unusual through view. In the *Capilla Mayor* 12 pillars form a rotunda with a diameter of 74 ft., which opens into the ambulatory. There are 14 very beautiful 16C Flemish glass windows with scenes from the Passion. Other windows were made to the designs of Diego de Siloé. Two praying figures of the Catholic Monarchs Ferdinand and Isabella are by Pedro de Mena 1675-77. The 12 gilded statues of the Apostles are by Alonso de Mena and Martín de Aranda (1614). Alonso Cano is responsible for the monumental busts of Adam and Eve in niches (painted by Juan Vélez de Ulloa),

as well as the large paintings from the life of the Virgin Mary in the upper storey. Above the arcades there are paintings by Juan de Sevilla and Bocanegra. The transept altar paintings are the 'Milagro de San Benito', by Juan de Sevilla, 'St.Bernard's Vision of Christ', and the 'Martyrdom of St.Cecilia', by Bocanegra. In the *choir* there is an 18C baroque organ. The *Altar de Santiago* has a statue of St.James (1640) by Alonso de Mena and the painting of the Virgen de los Perdones, which was given to Isabella the Catholic by Pope Innocent VIII in 1491. *Left side: The Capilla de Nuestra Señora de las Angustias* has a 15C Statue of the Virgin and a Churrigueresque altar. The *treasury* (the former chapterhouse) has Flemish tapestries, items in gold, a silver monstrance given by Queen Isabella and two sculptures by Alonso Cano, the 'Virgen de Belén' and 'St.Paul'. The *Capilla de Nuestra Señora del Carmen* contains 'St.Mary the Carmelite' by José de Mora. On the *right side*: there is the entrance to the *Sagrario* which was added in the 18C. Now a parish church, it was built on the site of an old mosque; Italian *marble font* (1522). The *Capilla de la Trinidad:* has an altar triptych by Alonso Cano. The *Altar de Jesús Nazareno* has paintings by Alonso Cano ('St. Augustine', 'Virgin Mary', 'Christ' and the 'Stations of the Cross') and by Ribera ('Martyrdom of St. Lawrence', 'St.Mary Magdalene', 'St. Anthony's Vision of the Infant Christ' and 'St.Anthony the Hermit' [copy]). The *portal of the Capilla Real* is a fine late Gothic work by Enrique de Egas, *c.* 1500. A beautiful door made by Diego de Siloé in 1534 leads into the *antesacristy*. In the *sacristy* there is 'The Assumption of Mary' by Alonso Cano and a fine sculpture, the 'Immaculate Conception' of 1656; also a wooden crucifix by J.M. Montañés.

Granada, Capilla Real, Botticelli, 'Christ on the Mount of Olives'

Capilla Real: The royal funerary chapel. Built 1504–21 in late Gothic Flamboyant style by Enrique de Egas, 12 years after the capture of Granada. The former entrance is from the cathedral; however, the main entrance is the Plateresque portal in the later completed *façade* on the Plazuela de la Lonja. The initials Y and F (for Isabella and Ferdinand) can be seen everywhere. The interior is single-aisled with a splendid *reja* (1518) by Master Bartolomé de Jaen, which is probably the most beautiful in Spain. The gilded and painted wrought-iron grille is divided into three parts; the upper part is the most beautiful with scenes from the life of Christ and the Crucifixion. The Carrara marble *tomb of the Catholic Monarchs* (Isabella of Castile died in 1504, Ferdinand of Aragon in 1516) was made by the Italian craftsman Domenico Fancelli, while the *tomb* of Philip the Handsome and Juana 'the Mad' was made by Bartolomé Ordóñez (commissioned in 1519 by the future Charles V). The *high altar* has excellent carvings on historical episodes (*c.* 1520) by Felipe de Borgoñia, including in particular paintings of the compulsory conversion of the Moors (1502) and scenes from the capture of the city. The *praying figures of the Catholic Monarchs* on both sides of the altar are by Diego de Siloé. Two relicarios or side altars of 1632 in the transepts are by Alonso de Mena. Also in the left transept there is a *triptych* by D. Bouts. The *sacristy* has fine paintings: 'Christ on the Mount of Olives' by Botticelli, 'Birth of Christ' and 'Pietà' by Rogier van der Weyden, 'Madonna and Child' by D. Bouts, 'Descent from the Cross', 'Birth of Christ' and 'The Holy Women at the Sepulchre', etc. by Hans Memling as well as other paintings from the Flemish school. There are also the sword of King Ferdinand and the crown and sceptre of Queen Isabella. The *crypt* has the simply maintained sarcophagi of the Royal Family.

San José (Plaza de San José): Of the former 9C mosque parts of walls and the lower part of the minaret (11C) can be picked out; the mosque's cisterns have also

Granada, Capilla Real, crown of the Catholic Queen Isabella

survived. The *interior* (early 16C) has a splendid Mudéjar octagonal dome and a gilded wooden ceiling; fine crucifix by José de Mora.

San Juan de los Reyes (Calle San Juan de los Reyes): The church's tower is the former minaret of a 13C mosque and it has survived in good condition; sebka ornamentation and blind arcades. The church itself is late 15C by Rodrigo Fernández.

San Matías (Calle San Matías): 16C Plateresque church with a splendid baroque altar and a remarkable sculpture of *St.John of God* by José Risueño; also other works by the same artist and paintings by Bocanegra.

Santa Ana (Plaza de Santa Ana): A sober 16C Renaissance church by Diego de Siloé with a beautiful Plateresque W. portal; the *tower* of 1563 is a converted Arab minaret: ajimez, alfices. Inside: the ceiling is beautifully carved; the fine sculpture of the 'Mater Dolorosa' or 'Virgen de la Soledad' is by José de Mora.

Santo Domingo (Plaza de Santo Domingo): An impressive church founded by Ferdinand and Isabella, in a style transitional between Gothic and Renaissance; part of the monastery of Santa Cruz la Real. Beautiful triple-arched *portal* with the royal emblems—yoke and bow. In the *baroque interior* there is a Churrigueresque altar with the Virgen de la Esperanza, a 16C alabaster figure, and paintings from the school of Granada (in particular by Juan de Sevilla, Bocanegra and Pedro de Raxis).

San Jerónimo (Calle del Gran Capitan): Former monastery, founded by Ferdinand and Isabella in 1492. There are two courtyards, one of which by Diego de Siloé is particularly fine, having 36 arches and 7 carved gates. The single-aisled *church* from the early 16C is also by Siloé. The Renaissance façade has a Gothic portal, with St.Jerome above. Inside: 18C frescos

Granada, Cartuja, cloister

Granada, Santa Ana

and a large *Renaissance altar* with scenes from the life of Christ; at the sides there are *statues* of 'El Gran Capitán' and his wife (Duquesa de Sessa) kneeling in prayer. The tomb of Gonzalo Fernández de Córdoba, El Gran Capitán (d. 1515) is in the *Capilla Mayor*. In the vaults there are ancient heroic figures.

Monasterio de la Cartuja (Calle Real de la Cartuja): Remains of the 16C monastery include church, sacristy, cloister and refectory. The *church* with its over-ornate white stucco was completed in the 17C in Churrigueresque style. Late Spanish baroque is seen here in its most elaborate phase. Paintings by Bocanegra; statue of St.Bruno by José de Mora. The domed *sagrario* (with the tabernacle) behind the choir, is of great beauty. The *sacristy*, whose sweeping baroque design is by Luis de Arévalo (18C), became famous as an outstanding example of Churrigueresque style. Indeed the whole interior is under the all-dominating sway of the fine stucco decoration and the effect of changing light as it plays upon the complicated shapes. Inlay on cupboards between pillars is in precious materials. On the marble altar there is a statue of St. Bruno. The *refectory* has paintings by Fray Juan Sanchez Cotán. Other rooms have paintings by Bocanegra and the Italian Vicente Carducho. (Many pictures concern the history of the Carthusians.)

Convent of Santa Isabel la Real (Calle de Santa Isabel la Real): Founded by Isabella of Castile in 1501 and part of the Palacio Daralhorra (see below). The church has a superb portal (with the royal emblems of yoke and pillar) and is probably by Enrique de Egas. Inside there are Mudéjar ceiling, carvings by Caspar Becerra and José de Mora.

Convent of Santa Catalina de Zafra (not far from the 'Arab Baths'): An Arab palace, converted in the 16C; Mudéjar

courtyard. Renaissance church portal. Inside: paintings by Bocanegra among others and sculptures by Risueño.

Hermitage of San Sebastián (Paseo del Violón): A small hermitage, which was formerly an Arab prayer house—'Murabit'. In 1492, before the Christian armies engulfed the town, Ferdinand of Aragon confronted King Boabdil here. Restored in 1615.

Hospital Real (Ancha de Capuchinos): A beautiful building which was begun in 1504 by Enrique de Egas and completed in 1522 by Juan Garcia de Prades. It is actually a complex of *three hospital buildings*. Renaissance façade with statues and a baroque main portal. The upper floor has interesting *Mudéjar ceilings*. There is a beautiful *patio* with arcades; other courtyards were planned but not completed. The hospital cared for the sick, including the mentally disturbed, and also received pilgrims.

Hospital de San Juan de Dios (Calle de San Jerónimo): Established in 1552 as the Hospitallers' first hospital. Very beautiful *marble portal* of (1609) and a splendid tiled *Renaissance courtyard*. The Baroque *church* (1737–59) has double towers. Relics of St.John of God. The statue of the order's founder is by Alonso Cano.

Alcaicería (Plaza de Bibar Rambla): An exact copy of the former Arab bazaar for silk, built in 1845.It has narrow alleys with horseshoe arches in front of the shops and twin windows on the façades.

Alcázar Genil (near the Hermitage of San Sebastián): The 14C castle has a beautiful room with an *artesonado ceiling* and stalac-

Granada, Cartuja Vieja, sacristy, painted ceiling

tite moulding. The alcázar belonged to King Boabdil's mother.

Arab baths (Carrera del Darro, 37): One of the best preserved of such complexes. 11C, restored 20C. Roman, Visigoth and Arab capitals; horseshoe arches on marble columns.

Casa del Carbón (Calle Mariana Pineda): An important historical building, unique in Spain, having been built as an *Arab caravanserai* or hostelry in the 14C. It later became a home for charcoal burners (hence the present name) and was converted into a theatre in the 16C. The entrance has a brick horseshoe arch with an ajimez window above, and an inscription in Kufic characters; gateway with stalactite decoration. The square courtyard has three storeys of arcades.

Casa de Castril (Carrera del Darro): A *corner building with corner balconies* and an impressive Plateresque façade (16C) with much carving. At the present time it houses the regional *archaeological museum* with finds from the province of Granada. There are carved wooden columns in the second courtyard.

Casa del Chapiz (Cuesta del Chapiz, 14): The *Arab country house* of the Moor Lorenzo el Chapiz (early 16C, restored) now houses a school for Arab studies. Beautiful Mudéjar and Renaissance patio.

Casa de los Girones (Ancha de Santo Domingo): Remains of a 13C *Moorish palace*. In one room there are Arab inscriptions. 16C upper storey and patio.

Casa de los Tiros (Plaza de los Tiros): Originally part of the defensive wall. The 16C Mudéjar house has five mythological figures on the *façade:* Hercules, Theseus, Jason, Hector and Mercury. It now houses the *tourist office,* and an interesting *museum*

of local art. On the second floor there is room with a carved ceiling (16C); anothe room is dedicated to Washington Irving who described the Alhambra in such glow ing terms. A further room commemorate the Granada-born future Empress Eugénie.

Audiencia (Plaza Nueva): The forme *chancellery* has a very beautiful Renaissanc façade (completed 1587). Doric and Ionia columns in the large *patio. Stairwell* wit coffered ceiling.

Cuarto Real de Santo Domingo (Call de Santo Domingo): This former *Mooris palace* in a most beautiful laurel garden wa converted to a monastery under Ferdinand and Isabella and is now in private owner ship. The *tower,* belonging to the forme defensive system (13C), has a large *roon* with a most impressive entrance archway arch niches, fine stucco work and super azulejos with fine blue, white and gol decoration. Light falls through 2 horseshoe-shaped windows with or namented wooden grilles. The carve wooden doors leading to the three balco nies are also beautiful. Interesting ceiling valuable furniture.

Palacio Daralhorra (Callejon del Ladró del Agua): Focus of the vast old defensiv system — until the development of th walled Alhambra area. The 15C buildin is part of the Convento de Santa Isabel l Real and once belonged to King Boabdil mother. Beautiful large *patio* with arcade and fine polychrome wooden ceilings.

Casa del Cabildo Antiguo (former Tow Hall, opp. the Capilla Real): Also know as the Palacio de Tovar or *Palacio de l Madraza* (a madrasa is a Koranic school) 14C, various conversions, baroque façade

Granada, Cartuja Viej

Houses the offices of the *Festival Internacional de Música y Danza.*

Lonja (East, near the Sagrario): The former *exchange* (16C) was a Genoese banking establishment. The building was designed by Enrique de Egas. Beautiful façade.

University (Plaza Universidad): In the 16C Emperor Charles V founded the university, which has been housed in this former baroque Jesuit college since 1759.

Puerta de Elvira: 12C. The most important *gate* (named after the neighbouring town of Elvira) in the Arab fortress wall, built upon Roman remains. Only a monumental horseshoe arch has survived.

Albaicín: On a hill, along with the neighbouring quarter, Alcazaba Cadima. The *district of Albaicín* (Rabad al Baecin, so-called after immigrant Moors from Baeza) is N. of the Alhambra and bounded by the Calle Elvira and the northern part of the *Arab fortress wall.* The *old Arab quarter* has a multitude of narrow, twisting alleys streaming up and down the hill, white-washed Moorish-style houses and quiet gardens. There are beautiful views of the Alcazaba of the Alhambra, particularly from the altogether enchanting Carrera del Darro, which has many bridges and is one of the oldest streets in the city. Beyond the Darro (extended to the Plaza de Santa Ana in the 19C), is the *Plaza Nueva*, which the Arabs used for bullfights and also for executions; today it is a good starting point for a round tour.

Also worth seeing: *Church of San Bartolomé* (Plaza de San Bartolomé): 16C, on the site of a mosque; very beautiful portal. *Church of San Cristóbal* (Carrera de San Cristóbal): Gothic building; view on to the Alcazaba Cadima. *Church of San Ildefonso* (near Gobierno Militar): 16C; beautiful

sculptures by Juan de Alcántara (1554). Mudéjar ceiling, 18C baroque altar. *Church of San Nicolás* (Plaza de San Nicolás): Gothic building, 16C; restored in the 20C. *Church of San Pedro y San Pablo* (Carrera del Darro): 16C. *Church of San Salvador* (Plaza de San Salvador): Mudéjar building, late 16C, on the site of a former mosque. Arab cisterns in the patio. *Colegiata Santos Justos y Pastor* (Plaza Universidad): Baroque church in Spanish Jesuit style. *Basilica de Nuestra Señora d' las Angustias* (Acera del Darro): A large twin-towered 17C church in the baroque style of Granada with the 'miraculous image' of the town's patron saint, an altar figure of the Virgin lavishly ornamented marble shrine. *Casa de los Duques de Abrantes* (Plaza de Tovar): 16C Gothic façade with some Moorish elements. *Casa de los Mascarones* (Calle de Pagés): A Moorish building taking its name from two grotesques on the façade. *Casa Morisca* (near the Plaza Albaida): Old Moorish houses. *Casa de los Pisas* (Plaza de Santa Ana): In 1550 *St.John of God*, founder of the order of Hospitallers, died here. The room in which he died has been turned into an oratory. *Palacio Arzobispal* (Archiepiscopal palace; Plaza de Alonso Cano): 16–17C. *Plaza del Triunfo:* Statue of the Virgin by Alonso de Mena, 1631. *Plaza de Alonso Cano:* Bronze statue of the artist, born in Granada in 1601. *Plaza de Bibarrambla:* Arabic Bâb ar raml, i.e. sand gate, so-called because the sandy bank of the Darro once extended this far. It was dismantled and rebuilt near the Alhambra. The *Neptune fountain* is 17C. *Puerta Monaita* (or Puerta de la Era): The first gate in Spain with a right-angled corridor (for defence). *Gobierno Militar* (Plaza de Triunfo): formerly the monastery of La Merced (founded 1515) with a broad courtyard and a monumental flight of steps (early 17C). **Sacromonte:** The famous gypsy suburb with the *Cuevas del Sacromonte*, gypsy dwellings carved out of the cliff; the

Granada, Alcazaba Vieja

gypsies perform their famous dances—flamenco, zambra. *Abbey of Sacro Monte:* A Benedictine abbey on a hill. In caves nearby, skeletons were found; these were thought to belong to the martyrs St.Cecilio and his companions and to date from the 1C AD. There is an adjoining *museum*, containing works by Sánchez Cotán and Vicente López.

Environs: Gabia la Grande (7 km. S.): An early Christian *crypt* (5C), baptistery, a room and a tower with Moorish furnishings (15C). **Ogijares** (6 km. S.): In the *Iglesia del Barrio Alto* there is a painted figure of the *Immaculate Conception* by Pedro de Mena. **Viznar** (8 km. N.): *Tomb of the poet Federico García Lorca.* The *castle* has a series of frescos with scenes from Cervantes' 'Don Quixote'. **Atarfe** (7 km. NW): *The*

ruins of Elvira, which was important before Granada became capital of the emirate. **Santafé** (12 km. W.): Established by Ferdinand and Isabella during the siege of Granada in 1491, on the site of a Roman military camp; it is square with four gates, which Ferdinand ordered to be surmounted by chapels. Granada's surrender was signed here, so too was an agreement between Ferdinand and Isabella and Columbus, in which they supported his voyages of discovery (1492). 18C *church.* **Pinos Puente** (22 km. NW): Fine *Visigoth bridge* over the Río Cubillas with an imposing central horseshoe arch and two smaller arches to either side. **Moclín** (40 km. NW): Arab castle, *La Mota,* and Moorish *town wall* with round defensive towers. **Lanjarón** (50 km. S.): Ruins of an Arab *Alcázar.* **Alhama de Granada** (55

km. SW): A thermal spring, some 2,850 ft. up; used by both Romans and Arabs. Ruins of *thermal baths, bridges and a Moorish bath*. 16C *parish church*: with façade by Enrique de Egas and tower by Diego de Siloé the Younger; beautiful artesonado ceiling within. In the sacristy embroidered robes are preserved. **Orgiva** (63 km. S.):*Castle* of the Counts of Sástago. Parish church on the site of a former mosque.

Gran Canaria

Las Palmas de Gran Canaria/
Canary Islands   p.396□M/N 10/11

The third largest island of the archipelago. It is almost round and is often described as a miniature continent because of the stark contrasts of its landscape; the S. coast is very like Africa, while the N. is heavily wooded and mountainous, rather like the Alps—the *Pozo de las Nievas* 6,540 ft is the highest point.

Las Palmas: The island's capital and the largest town in the archipelago. One of Spain's most important ports, it extends over a 12 km. stretch of coast. The town was founded in 1478 by the Spanish general, Juan de Réjon, who drove the surviving Guanches (the native people) from the island. In 1492 Christopher Columbus—en route for the Indies, on the journey that was to lead to the discovery of America—first put into the island, as he did on his return and also on his second voyage. At around this time work began on the *cathedral* and the *Castillo Nuestra Señora de la Luz* was built to protect the harbour entrance. Assaults by pirates and the attempted landing by the English under Sir Francis Drake were successfully

Granada, Hospital de San Juan de Dios, high altar

repulsed in the 16C. During the following centuries, when most of the churches and palaces were built, there was a big economic upswing. In 1826 Las Palmas became capital of the island and in 1927 capital of the province of Gran Canaria (which included Fuerteventura and Lanzarote).

Cathedral of Santa Ana: Started in Gothic style in 1497 and consecrated in 1570; baroque conversions during 1781–1820. Like many buildings on the island it is built in basalt. The *façade* is primarily classical and the high Gothic nave still has rib vaulting. 18C carved pulpits. Silver chandeliers in the nave are Genoese. The portrait of Bishop Codina is attributed to Goya. In the *treasure chamber* (sacristy) there a gold-plated silver monstance, which is probably by Benvenuto Cellini. The *chapterhouse* has azulejos and the *cloister* has wooden galleries and tropical flora.

Casa de Colón (House of Christopher Columbus, Calle de Colón): Former house of the Governor in which Columbus stayed on several ocasions. Built at the end of the 15C in Spanish colonial style found so often in the Canaries; splendidly decorated portal. Nowadays it houses a *museum* with old furniture, tapestries and *paintings* (by Morales, Reni, Veronese, etc.), coins, weapons and robes, which belonged to Columbus. There are two patios; the first has a pine balcony, the second a wonderful Gothic fountain.

San Antonio Abad: A little chapel very near to the Casa de Colón; built in the 15C and rebuilt 18C. Columbus is supposed to have prayed here before setting off in 1492.

Museo Canario (Canary Islands' Museum): Devoted to finds from the time of the *Guanches*, e.g. mummies, skeletons, skulls, weapons and tools of obsidian, ba-

Arucas, Gran Canaria, parish church

salt and horn, and tattooing tools. Also a natural history collection.

Santo Domingo: 16–17C church of Santo Domingo NE of the Museo Canario.

Pueblo Canario (The Canary Island village): In one of the island's most beautiful parks, the Parque Doramas (named after the last native chieftain), and on the main Parque Doramas road. It was laid out to the designs by Néstor de la Torre, a native artist, and displays important types of Canary architecture.

Museo de Néstor: In the painter's former home, it contains, paintings, watercolours and drawings as well as personal mementoes.

Gáldar: Small town about 40 km. from Las Palmas on the N. coast and at the foot of the volcano of the same name. Formerly an important principality of the Guanches. Near the church there are cave dwellings, one of which, the *Cueva Pintada*, has geometrical decorations.

The *baroque church of Santiago de los Caballeros* has a dome and lavish interior decoration. In the front, on the right, there is an old Spanish font and an 18C statue of the Virgïn, known as *Nuestra Señora la Candelaria*.

A small archaeological collection is housed in the *Ayuntamiento.* The patio has a particularly beautiful dracaena palm.

The Guanches dug caves out of the side of the volcano, the *Montaña de Gáldar*. Their *necropolis* is a collection of round tumuli on the W. slope of the volcano.

Arucas (*c.* 10 km. W. of Las Palmas): *Parish church of San Juan Bautista* (19C).

Artenara: The island's highest village, which has a cave church, the *(Cueva Iglesia)*, dedicated to the patron saint of travellers.

Cenobio de Valerón (on the N. coast 29 km. from Las Palmas): Here, beneath a rocky slope, there are *c.* 350 cave dwellings, arranged on seven levels. They are thought to have been quarters for the *Harimuguadas,* who were a kind of priestess of the Guanches.

Montaña de los Cuatro Puerta (Mountain of the Four Gates): Four caves carved out of the mountain lead to a place sacred to the Guanches and which probably (as in Cenobio) served the priestesses as a 'convent'.

Telde (14 km. S. of Las Palmas), the second largest town on the island, has largely preserved its old Spanish character. Before the conquest it was the main seat of the *Guarteme,* the chiefs of the Guanches.

San Juan Bautista: A late 15C church, built in lava of various colours; modern façade. Inside: nave and two aisles, chapels with artesonado ceilings. The 15C carved, gilded altarpiece on the high altar has scenes from the life of Mary on six panels and is the island's most valuable work of art. Above the high altar there is a 16C life-size figure of Christ in maize stalks and leaves, which was made in Mexico by Tarasco Indians.

Teror (21 km. E. of Las Palmas): An architecturally enchanting town, in which the Virgin Mary is supposed to have appeared in the branches of a pine tree in 1480. All that remains of the original building of the *church of Nuestra Señora del Pino* is a tower of 1740 and the classical façade. The interior is 18C, has a nave and two aisles and a shrine with a 15C painting, which is claimed to have miraculous properties. Valuable church treasure. The *Casa Manrique de Lara* (16–17C) has been a museum of local history and culture since 1970.

La Atalaya: Picturesque cave village. Known above all for its pottery, which is still made without a potter's wheel, as it was by the Guanches.

Graus

Huesca/Aragon   p.388 □ L 3

A picturesque little town of twisting alleys and old houses decorated with coats-of-arms.

Parish church: 13C. Inside there are *panels* by the painter Pedro Espalargues, which show the saints Victorián and Benito surrounded by nuns and angels and also Christ's Passion.

Santuario de Santa María de la Peña:

A shrine just outside Graus. It was built in the middle of the 16C by Juan de Marta and Juan Zeant.

La Casa de Rodrigo de Mur: A 15C house and the most interesting of the town's secular buildings.

Environs: La Puebla de Roda: *Fortified church* of 1067; 12C crypt, Romanesque cloister and 16C retables. The church treasure consists of several reliquaries and a 12C bishop's throne. **La Puebla de Castro** is a village built on the ruins of a Roman settlement. It has an 11C Romanesque church, with a painted winged altar of 1303.

Guadalajara

Guadalajara/New Castile   p.388 □ G/H 5

The town was already settled in Iberian times. Subject to the Moorish rule of Toledo, it was recaptured under Alfonso VI by Alvar Fañez de Minaya, a relation of El Cid. During the Middle Ages Guadalajara was the scene of important historical events. From the 14C the town was owned by the great Mendoza family, which supplied Spain with cardinals and accomplished generals. They made the provincial capital the centre of their power.

Palacio del Infantado (Prince's palace): Gothic-Mudéjar, built at the end of the 15C for Duke Don Iñigo López de Mendoza under the direction of Juan Guas. The size and splendour of the rooms is impressive. In 1480 the palace was extended and in *c.* 1570 clumsy alterations were carried out. Francis I of France was received here with great ceremony, when he came from Pavia, although he was at the time a prisoner. Philip II married Elisabeth of Valois in the palace. In 1936 it was damaged by fire.

Santa María de la Fuente: Formerly a mosque with a minaret, the church now ranks as a semi-cathedral. There are two portals with ogee arches. The nave is divided into three parts. 16C sarcophagi.

San Ginés: 16C church, built under Bartolomé de Carranza, Archbishop of Toledo. Some fine sarcophagi were badly damaged during the Civil War.

San Nicolás: Jesuit church with beautiful altar by Churriguera and a lovely tomb statue of Rodrigo de Campuzano. Fine 18C paintings in the sacristy.

San Francisco: 13C; former church of the Knights Templar, now a historical monument. Beneath the altar is the mausoleum of the Dukes of the Infantado.

San Luis de Lucena: A chapel built entirely of brick. Now a protected monument. Inside there are paintings by Rómulo Cincinato, which have been severely damaged; also other valuable items. Together these are to be the basis of the planned provincial archaeological museum.

Santiago: Former convent church of the Poor Clares. 14C panelling and Mudéjar frieze. The Zúñigas Chapel is Plateresque with Gothic influence and was designed in the 16C by the architect Alonso de Covarrubias.

The **Instituto,** formerly the **Convento de la Piedad:** A particularly interesting early Renaissance building with two good portals, one of which is by Lorenzo Vázquez, Cardinal Mendoza's architect and the other, opening into the chapel, is by Alonso de Covarrubias.

Environs: Lupiana (c. 10 km. E.): The two-storey *monastery, San Bartolomé,* was founded in 1370 and is built on a square ground plan. The upper gallery has late Gothic arches and Gothic influence is clearly visible in capitals and balustrades.

Guadalajara, Palacio del Infantado

The 16C cloister is one of the most beautiful in New Castile.

Guadalupe
Cáceres/Estremadura   p.392□E 7

A small town in a picturesque mountain setting on the SE slopes of the Sierra de Guadalupe. It is famous above all for its Spanish Hieronymite *monastery*, which, next to Montserrat is the most important of Spain's shrines to the Virgin Mary. According to legend its founding goes back to a shepherd's miraculous rediscovery of the image of Our Lady of Guadalupe. Reputedly carved by St.Luke, it had been buried in the Sierra Mariani before the Arab invasion of 711. The town's name comes from the Arab 'guada', meaning wadi or river and 'lubein', meaning hidden. The image was a gift to St.Isidore of Seville from Gregory the Great who carried it through the streets to ward off the plague in the Holy City. First a hermitage was built on the site of the discovery, in place of which Alfonso XI founded a monastery in 1340 to fulfil a vow made before the victorious battle of El Salado against the Moors. In 1386 the monastery was handed over to the Hieronymites, who were also granted many privileges. It soon became the wealthiest Hieronymite monastery in the whole peninsula. A school of medicine was started, which had three hospitals with over 150 beds at its disposal. The monastery's famous doctors were the first to perform a human autopsy in the West. There were also workshops with goldsmiths, embroidresses working on silk, a printing press and a school for book illustration. Particularly fine are the embroidered altar antependia or *frontals,* with religious scenes (14–15C). The kings of Castile, who made pilgrimages here, had the excellent *Hospederia de Real* built for the education of their children. Guadalupe was also much visited by the great explorers, who received their permission to sail here, e.g. *Columbus* who named an island he discovered in the New World af-

Guadalajara, Palacio del Infantado, detail

ter the monastery. *Hernan Cortés*, who conquered Mexico, spent nine days before his departure praying before the 'miraculous' image of the Madonna, and subsequently dedicated the greatest pilgrimage shrine in America north of Mexico City, to Nuestra Señora de Guadalupe. According to Tetzel, the monastery's wealth was astounding, for Conquistadors and Princes used to donate part of their booty to the Madonna ('Buckets and broomsticks of purest silver'). In the 18C 120 lamps of silver and gold hung before the image of the Virgin. However, thousands of pilgrims were looked after daily at no cost to themselves. In 1808 the French stole much of the treasure and in 1835 the monks were driven out and most of the buildings were turned into sheds and stables. In 1908 it was taken over by the Franciscans and restored.**Monastery and church:** The *church*, with a nave and two aisles, is in the form of a Latin cross. Gothic main façade from 1349–69. The entrance portal is on the long S. side, and the bronze door by Juan Francés (1402) depicts the Virgin Mary crowned by angels. To the right of the entrance is the *Capilla de Santa Ana*, which has the tombs of the founder and his wife by Hanequin of Brussels. *Interior:* The nave and aisles are concluded by splendid wrought-iron grilles by Francisco de Salamanca (1510). The *Capilla Mayor*, whose stellar vaulting was painted by Juan de Flandes, 'El Flandesco', Isabella of Castile's court painter, has a beautiful early 17C retable by Juan Gómez de Mora, statues and alto rilievo by Giraldo de Merlo, six large paintings by Carduccio and Caxés, and a bronze tabernacle with silver and gold inlay by Glamin, who was a pupil of Michelangelo (1569). The tombs of Enrique IV and his mother Doña Maria de Aragón by G. de Merlo occupy either side of the high altar. The sumptuous *sacristy*, in gold and white, has ceiling paintings by anonymous artists and eight famous paintings of people associated with the monastery by Zurbarán (1638–47), including 'The Vision of Father Salmerón' and 'Father Gonzalo de Illescas at work'. Above the altar in the little Chapel of St. Jerome in the sacristy is one of Zurbarán's most famous works, 'The Apotheosis of St.Jerome', also called 'Perla de Zurbarán'; other paintings are by one of his pupils. The lamp of the Turkish flagship captured in the battle of Lepanto hangs in this chapel; it was donated to the monastery by Don Juan of Austria. Leading up to the *Camarín de la Virgen* (Chamber of the Virgin) is a *stairway* of 42 red jasper steps. On the walls there are 18C paintings of scenes from the life of the Madonna by Luca Giordano, which were commissioned by Charles VII. The *Rococo Room* is trefoil and has a dome with a lantern 65 ft. high. The statue (her face blackened by the smoke of the lamps) is dressed for the feasts in this room. The Christ Child on the Virgin's arm is of a later date. The Virgin's several cloaks are to be found in the adjacent treasure chamber and they include a coat which Isabel Clara Eugenia, the daughter of Philip II, herself embroidered on gold material. The *reliquary chamber*, a classical design by Nicolás de Vergara (1595), has azulejos from Talavera, a painting of Father Juan de la Serena (1620), a collection of rock crystal mirrors in gilded bronze frames (1687), and a chased silver shrine by Juan de Segovia (mid 15C) with enamelling (late 14C). The *coro* in the apse has Churrigueresque choir stalls by Alejandro Carnicero (1742–44), four paintings attributed to Zurburán, a tenebrario (a carved 14C candelabra) and an 18C choir desk. Magnificent organ. The *Mudéjar cloister*, which has horseshoe arches is in contrast to the austere Gothic style of the monastery; Renaissance gate. In the middle of the cloister the Gothic-Mudéjar *well*

Lupiana (Guadalajara), Monasterio San Bartolomé

house is by Juan de Sevilla (1405) and in the SE corner, there is the alabaster tomb of Illescas de Annequin Egas, who built Toledo Cathedral (1458). Wall paintings illustrate the story of Our Lady of Guadalupe. The greatly restored smaller *Gothic cloister* (or the Patio de la Botica, as the pharmacy was housed here) has two galleries and is 14&15C with Mudéjar doors and windows. The upper gallery has beautiful stucco ceilings.

Museo de Bordados: In the former refectory, has superbly embroidered chasubles and other embroideries from the 14–18C, as well as an abundant collection of paraments.

Museo de Libros Corales: A museum of illuminated books in the Gothic chapterhouse, the ceiling of which is decorated with arabesques. Formerly a dancing room, it now houses 15&16C missals, the priory book of hours (16C), an alabaster Madonna (15C), tapestries and paintings, including 'Taufe Christi' by Juan de Flandes, and a triptych of the 'Magi' attributed to Adrien Isenbrant (d. 1551).

The Joyel (treasure chamber) is a small room of 1651 in the bell tower. It is lined with red satin and houses the *church treasure:* an ivory crucifix attributed to Michelangelo, which was formerly on Philip II's desk, a crown beloning to the image of the Virgin, 15&16C prayer books, richly embroidered liturgical robes and paraments, a cross with lignum crucis, monstrances, jewels, miniatures and a painting of 'Christ on the Cross' by Morales.The **Antesacrestia** in the tower of Santa Ana contains a portrait of Charles II and his wife Maria Luise of Orleans by Juan Carreño de Miranda, as well as a 'Last Supper' and 'Christ washing the disciples' feet', both painted on copper. Below this complex of buildings there is the *new church* of 1730, two old pilgrim hostels, the *Hospedéria de Nobles* with Mudéjar cloister (1512), and a 16C building, which is now a Parador hotel.

The streets of this picturesque town are lined with 15&16C houses, the projecting

Guadalupe, monastery, façade

Guadalupe, monastery, fountain

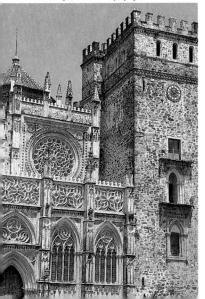

upper storeys of which are propped up with wooden supports.

Environs: Hermitage of El Humilladero (4 km. N.): Square early 15C chapel in brick and ashlar, whose three portals have carvings in the tympana. **Granja de Mirabel** (6 km. W.): Recently restored *palace*, built in the 17C for the Catholic Kings. Interesting patios. **Granja de Valdefuentes** (5 km. SE): *Palace*, built 1552-54 for Philip II with Gothic-Mudéjar W. façade, Gothic chapel with artesonado ceiling and Mudéjar tiles, baroque altars and altar antependium with azulejos from Talavera. **Herrera del Duque** (*c.* 50 km. S.): The parish church of *San Juan* (early 16C) has a Gothic Apostles' gate. The interior has a nave and two aisles with groin-vaulted chapels. The *Convento de San Jerónimo*, a late 16C Renaissance building stands in ruins. On a nearby hill there is the towerless Alcázar with horseshoe-arched windows. **Logrosán** (*c.* 30 km. SW): The parish church of *San Mateo* (late 13C or early 14C) was converted several times in the 15&16C; stellar vaults. The *Ermita de Nuestra Señora del Consuelo* is a 17C building with Gothic-Mudéjar elements from the 15&16C. On the hill of San Cristóbal there are ruins of a medieval *castillo*.

Guadamur
Toledo/New Castile
p.392☐F 6

Guadamur Castle: Splendid example of a 15C fortress; some Italian influence. It was built in the middle of the 15C by Don Pedro López de Ayala. The castle stands upon a hill, has a square ground plan, bulwarks, reinforced corners and revetments. These consist of two rings of walls surrounded by a steep-sided fosse. The tower stands in the W. corner, where two wings meet. The entrance portal on the W. side has a vaulted arch and an embrasure, two round towers, one on either side of the gate, with embrasured turrets. The interior was skilfully restored at the end of the last cen-

Guadalupe, monastery

tury and careful consideration was given to both style and atmosphere. The castle has a considerable collection of old weapons, 15&16C paintings on wood, fabrics, carpets and the objects crafted in gold.

La Ermita de Nuestra Señora de la Natividad: Hermitage chapel with a 15C Mudéjar stone apse. Inside, there is a painting in tempera on canvas, which is probably 14C, and shows St.Anne with the child Mary in her arms.

Environs: Layos, S. of Guadamur. The *Castle of the Counts of Mora*, the Lords of Layos, which has been restored several times. Rectangular ground plan. Building probably began in the late 14C or early 15C, from which time the main façade, with its flat entrance of ashlar, on the W. side survives. In the 16C, the castle changed ownership and the coat-of-arms of the Rojas, with five stars, was added above the entrance. The main building has a Plateresque ceiling of painted wood from the same time.

Guadix
Granada/Andalusia　　　　　　p.394 □ H 10

An old Iberian settlement, which became a military base under Roman rule and was called Julia Gemella Acci. Guadix was one of the oldest of the Visigoth bishoprics. The Arab conquerors called the town Wadi-Asch — which led to the current name—and built a fortress there. After being reconquered by Ferdinand and Isabella, it became a cathedral city once more.

Cathedral: As has commonly happened in Andalusia, it was built on the site of a former mosque, in a style combining both Gothic and Renaissance elements. Diego de Siloé laid out the nave, two aisles and

the ambulatory. The baroque façades have classical characteristics and date from 1713 following the designs of Vicente Acero y Cayón. The interior with stellar vaulting and baroque chapels is interesting above all for *choir stalls* by Ruiz del Peral, which are lavishly decorated in Churrigueresque style. The *cathedral museum* has relics of of the martyr Torcuato.

Convent church of Santiago: The beautiful Plateresque portal with Charles V's coat-of-arms stands out from a sober, buttressed façade. Inside, there is remarkable *stucco*, in semi-geometric patterns, picked out with gold. The *Barrio de Santiago*, has famous cave dwellings.

Also worth seeing: *Alcazaba* (fortress): Originally 9C; the 15C building lies within one of the tower-topped rings of walls, which is 10C. *Plaza Mayor:* (Restored following damage during the Civil War). Dates from the time of Philip II.

Environs: Lacalahorra (15 km. S.): The *castle* is some 4,211 ft. up and has four massive round towers. Originally it was a Renaissance building of the early 16C; Italian artists from Lombardy and Liguria designed the very beautiful *patio* with its marble furnishings. At **Purullena** (7 km. W.) there are remains of Arab baths. **Baza** (48 km. NE): *Collegiate church of Santa María:* Late Gothic, in imitation of Murcia cathedral; Renaissance portals (1561). Also ruins of the Moorish fortress.

Guardamar del Segura
Alicante/Valencia　　　　　　p.396 □ K 9

A picturesque fishing village, at the mouth of the Segura. A *necropolis* provides evi-

Guadalupe, monastery, Zurbarán, 'Pater Gonzalo de Illescas at work'

dence of the Roman presence. The village used to be in the foot hills, where there is a fort, but the earthquake of 1829 destroyed it. Rebuilding took place on the plain and the streets were wide and the houses low to minimize the danger from another earthquake. Shifting dunes, however, next threatened to erode the village bit by bit. This new danger was averted by the planting of pines, eucalyptus and palms, which helped bind the sand. This process, which took place at the beginning of the century has resulted in a thick belt of trees over 10 miles long.

Guernica y Luno

Vizcaya/Basque Provinces   p.388☐H 1

Guernica, the 'holy town of the Basques', lies in the fertile plain of the Río Mundaca, which opens into the Bay of Biscay. The Basque assembly, the so-called Batzarrak, whose form and function was reminiscent of the Germanic 'Thing', used to meet here as early as the 9C. They would congregate beneath an oak, the famous tree of Guernica. The stump of this tree now stands in the courtyard of the Casa de Juntas. For centuries the kings of Castile had to take the oath of the 'Fueros'—the Basques' right to partial self-government—on this spot. On the 16 April 1937, during the Spanish Civil War, Guernica fell victim to the first air raid in the history of war. Within three hours, aircraft of the German Condor Legion reduced the town to rubble, claiming some 2,000 lives. Deeply moved by this terrible event, Pablo Picasso produced his famous picture 'Guernica' in the same year (up to Franco's death it was in New York but since 1981 it can be seen in the Prado in Madrid). During reconstruction of the town attention was paid to old traditions and efforts were made to recreate the town's original character.

Santa María: Building began in the 14C and finished in 1715. A flight of steps leads to the Gothic *portal* of 1449, which is decorated with sculptures and crowned by a

Guadix, Alcazaba

beautiful image of the Virgin Mary. The church has a nave and two aisles, which end in an apse with a triforium. In one of the chapels, there is a Gothic *sarcophagus* with reclining figures, which is the tomb of the Albiz family. The church has sculptures by contemporary artists, e.g. José Capuz, Alberto Brodzky, Moisés Huerta and Mateo Inurria.

Casa de Juntas Forales (Parliament): Built in classical style from 1824–1833 by Antonio Echaverría. The architect simultaneously incorporated the simple convent of Santa María la Antigua within the building complex. Two Tuscan columns form the entrance to the large *Assembly Room*, which is like an amphitheatre. Here also are the *chapels*, the walls of which are decorated with polychrome tiles and the portraits of the Lords of Biscay. To one side of the main entrance there is a small temple, which has eight Corinthian columns and seven stone benches, symbolizing the patriarchs. Inside, there is a part of the Basques' thousand-year-old oak tree. Also housed here in the Assembly building are Biscay's most important historical archives.

Also worth seeing: The mansions of some noble families e.g. the *Palacios de Alegría* and *Ciarreta.*

Environs: Caves of Santimamiñe (4 km. NE): Stalactite caves with rock paintings and finds from the late Palaeolithic age.

Guetaria
Guipúzcoa/Basque Provinces   p.388☐H 1

A small but picturesque fishing village lying on a steeply dropping spit of land, shaped like a mouse, which is thus referred to in the local tongue as 'ratón', i.e. the mouse. Guetaria is the birth-place of Juan Sebastián Elcano, Magellan's companion on the first circumnavigation of the world in 1519–22. Elcano was captain of the 'Vic-

Guadix, cave dwellings in Barrio de Santiago

toria', the only one of Magellan's five ships to return to Spain.

San Salvador: A Gothic church dating from the 13-14C. The irregular ground plan was dictated by its site. It had a nave and two aisles, the side aisles originally being 14C. The central nave is 15C and the main chapel stands higher than the rest. The main portal is surrounded by columns and dates from 1605, as does the tower. The *tower* was designed by Pedro de Alzaga, while the *portico* was built by Domingo de Cardaveraiz. The interior contains interesting altars, which have sculptures by Domingo de Gora of 1625. Subterranean passages lead from the church to the harbour.

Also worth seeing: *The town hall*, which was decorated with frescos by the Basque painter Zuloaga, on the theme of the circumnavigation of the world. The nearby *island, San Antón,* offers superb views and has a lighthouse. There are also remains of defensive systems.

H

Haro
Logroño/Old Castile   p. 388 □ H 2/3

Santo Tomás: 16 – 17C church with Plateresque portal of 1516. The interior has a nave and two aisles with stone vaulting; 17–18C baroque retables.

Also worth seeing: The basilica of the *Virgen de la Vega*, with nave and two aisles; ancient statue of the Virgin. The *Town Hall* of 1769 was built by Juan de Villanueva. There are also a number of interesting mansions, such as the *Casa de Paternina* and the *Palace of the Lords of Haro*.

Environs: Abalos (*c.* 8 km. N.): Gothic *parish church* with 18C baroque tower.

Haro, view

Single-aisled interior with rib vaults, a fine 16C high altar retable and Gothic choir stalls. The *Palace of the Lords of Legarda* has some interesting pictures, including a fascinating portrait of the sailor Martin Fernándes de Navarrete by Vicente López, Entombment by Lucas Jordan and St. Francis by Zurbarán.

Hernani
Guipúzcoa/Basque Provinces   p.388☐l 2

San Juan Bautista (on the Plaza Mayor): The baroque main portal is decorated with intricate figures. The 16C single-aisled interior has an impressive Churrigueresque altar, which is tripartite and decorated with gilded woodwork. A side altar has an altarpiece of 1656 by Bernabé de Cordero. The church also houses the tomb of the Spanish war hero Juan de Urbieta (1553), who captured the French King Francis I at the battle of Pavia.

Also worth seeing: The *Town Hall* (the Casa Consistorial) built in 1874. It stands next to the church on the Plaza Mayor. The Calle Mayor (main street) has a number of fine *palaces* with coats-of-arms on the façades and wrought-iron balconies with carved wooden balustrades. The quarter of the town known as *Los Alfueros* has a typical Basque atmosphere.

Herrera de Pisuerga
Palencia/Old Castile   p.388☐F 2

A town in a position of strategic importance, which fact is reflected in its history. It was at the height of its power during Visigoth times. The remains of the medieval castle and walls are still visible, and there is a 16C gate with the coat-of-arms of Charles I. A number of mansions have survived. The surrounding area has proved rich in archaeological remains.

Environs: Some 2 km. N. lies **Zorita de Páramo**, with the 13C Romanesque church of *San Lorenzo*. It is single-aisled with a transept. The portal has eight archivolts and intricate capitals. On the S. side there is a Plateresque portal with Romanesque figures of the Apostles. **Moarves de Ojeda** (*c.* 7 km. N.): The church of *San Pedro* has one of the best Romanesque façades to be seen in the province, with five archivolts decorated with geometric motifs, and exquisitely carved capitals. The frieze depicts Christ and his Apostles. **San Andrés del Arroyo** (*c.* 8 km. N.): The 12C *convent* has a single-aisled church with three apses. Outstanding carving on the capitals, portals and cloisters. **Olmos de Ojeda** (*c.* 9 km. N.): The 10C monastery, *Santa Eufemia de Cozuelos* has an 11C church with fine carvings on the windows, doors and capitals. **Osorno** (*c.* 10 km. S.): Renaissance parish church with impressive features, including a Romanesque-Gothic Way of the Cross, a 13C picture of Mary and a Romanesque font. **Arenillas de San Pelayo** (*c.* 7 km. W.): *Church* (part of an old abbey), with a fine portal. Inside, there is an interesting Visigoth font with a frieze.

Hierro
Santa Cruz de Tenerife/
Canary Islands   p.396☐K/L 10/11

Hierro, formerly known as Ferro, covers an area of 279 sq. km., which makes it the smallest of the Canary Islands — lack of water also makes it the poorest. It was once known as the 'End of the World'.

Valverde: The island's capital is laid out on a terraced slope. It has a fine *plaza* and an old *fortress church* with a small *bell tower*.

Punta Orchilla: French geographers called this the westernmost point of the known world, the zero meridian, in 1634.

Hita
Guadalajara / New Castile   p.388☐H 5

City Walls: Commissioned by the Marquis of Santillana in the 15C, and much of them, including the Santa María Gate, are still standing. All the *churches* were destroyed in the Civil War, and only a few Gothic gravestones have survived.

Environs: Torija (*c.* 10 km. S.): 16C *parish church* with Gothic interior; there is also a 13C *castle*, (restored).

Huarte-Araquil
Navarra / Navarra   p.388☐I 2

Santuario de San Miguel in Excelsis:

A 12C building about 1 km. N. of the town centre, on the Monte Aralar. Evidence suggests that it was already consecrated in 1031. In the same place is Navarre's oldest and most traditional monastery, Zamarce. San Miguel is a popular pilgrimage destination. The S. portal is part of the monastery; it has three arches and some fine carving. The interior is single-aisled with a particularly fine apse. Forming the altar wall is one of Europe's most famous pieces of enamel-work; a 13C Limoges piece, it is rich in colour, ranging from blue through green to gold, with figures in relief. In the centre there is an oval with the Virgin and Child.

Huelva
Huelva / Andalusia   p.394☐C 10

Cathedral: Begun in 1605. Fine baroque facade.

San Pedro (Calle de Milan Astray): Origi-

Torija (Hita), Castillo

Huelva, cathedral

Huelva, cathedral, Virgen de la Cinta

nally a 16C church; rebuilt after the Lisbon earthquake.

Also worth seeing: The 16C *Iglesia de la Concepcíon*, the 16C *Iglesia de San Francisco* and the *Museo de Bellas Artes* (Provincial Museum, Avenida de Montenegro), which has a collection of local archaeological finds.

Environs: Monasterio de la Rábida (10 km. SE, the other side of the estuary of the Río Tinto): This well-known *Franciscan monastery* was built in the 15C on a hill. The 14C church contains the remains of some 15C frescos, and the cloisters have elements of Mudéjar style. It was in this monastery that Columbus prepared for his voyages and the prior, Juan Pérez de Marchena, mediated on his behalf between

the Genoese and the Catholic Church. There is a museum with Columbus memorabilia: model boats, objects brought back from the voyage, pictures of the crew, a 13C Madonna, known as Nuestra Señora de Rábida, and a 14C crucifixion on a processional cross. **Palos de la Frontera** (6 km. from the Rábida monastery): This harbour, no longer in use, is the place from which Columbus' and his three ships sailed on 3 August 1492 on his voyage of discovery; he returned here on 15 March 1493. The owner of the ship, Martín Alonso Pinzón was born here, and both he and his brother accompanied Columbus on his first voyage. The old town has *remains of Roman defences* a Stone Age burial mound, and the interesting *church of San Jorge*, which is a 15C building on the site of an early Christian church; Mudéjar W.

Huelva, Santuario de Nuestra Señora de la Cinta

portal. The **pilgrimage church of Nuestra Señora de la Cinta** (3 km. from Huelva) is a seaman's church, which Columbus often visited; it possesses a faience image known as the Madonna with Girdle. At **Gibraleón** (15 km. N.), the Phoenician 'Olont' has the remains of a huge Moorish castle and city defences.

Huesca

Huesca/Aragon   p.388□K 3

Huesca is the seat of a bishop and capital of the province of the same name, which together with Zaragoza and Teruel formerly made up the kingdom of Aragon. The city is on a hill by the banks of the Río Isuela. The site was originally occupied by an Iberian settlement called Osca.

Under the Romans Osca became an Urbs Victrix. In the Roman civil war of 1C BC, it was the centre of Praetor Quintus Sertorius' resistance against Sulla. Sertorius founded Spain's first university here. Later, under Moorish rule, it was known as Vechca and became one of the most important fortress-towns. For 25 years King Sancho Ramírez tried to capture it and Pedro I of Aragon eventually freed it from the Moors in 1096. Four Saracen princes died in the struggle, and their heads were incorporated into the city's coat-of-arms. From that time on until its defeat by Saragossa under Alfonso I in 1118, Huesca was the capital of Aragon.

Cathedral: Gothic building built between 1273–1515 on a site formerly occupied by a Roman temple, a Visigoth church and a mosque. It has a nave and two aisles, a transept, five apses and an octagonal tower; the nave is twice as high as the aisles. Under an arched passage there are a number of side chapels.

The church was built under the direction of Juan de Olotzaga and Pedro Jalopa. The *main portal* of 1305 has seven Gothic archivolts and fine life-size statues. Above the Madonna and Child in the tympanum there is a Gothic baldacchino, on top of which is an Adoration of the Magi.

Inside there is a remarkable Romanesque-Gothic alabaster *high altar*, of 1520–33 by Damián Forment; it has reliefs of the life of Christ and a medallion with a self-portrait of the artist. The *main chapel* has fine carved *Renaissance choir stalls*, from the late 16C, by Juan de Berrueta and Nicolás de Berástegui. The *Chapel of Santa Ana* contains a fine screen by Armán Guillén from 1525, and a Renaissance altar from 1522, which is attributed to Alonso Berruguete. Many of the other *side chapels* have fine things e.g. the Chapel of the Madonna of the Rosary has a 14C Madonna. The Lastanosa Chapel and the Chapel of Saints Orienco and Paciencia are consecrated to their founders. The cathedral's *stained glass*, which is early 16C by Francisco de Valdivielso, is also remarkable. The *sacristy* houses some valuable silver pieces, a monstrance in four sections, made by José Velázquez in 1596, and a number of other intricate silver pieces including some fine reliquaries. The *crypt* has 17C tombs, and is the Lastanosa family mausoleum. The *chapterhouse* dates from the same time, and today houses the interesting *diocesan museum*, where a number of valuable enamelled 12–13C Limoges reliquaries are on display. Also on show: a 14C silver relief with an image of the Virgin Mary and an alabaster group of the Adoration of the Magi by Damián Forment. There are also Gothic murals from the church at Bierge, and other interesting

objects, including a 14C figure of St.Peter. The Romanesque *cloisters* were built before the cathedral, except for one section which is Gothic and was built in 1453. In the cloisters there is a fine 13C bas-relief and more tombs. From the cloisters you can get to the former *parish church*, an 18C building and the cathedral's daughter church. Inside is a famous *alabaster altar*, which came from the monastery on Monte Aragón, and was made by Gil Morlanes in 1507–9. Both buildings and furnishings are a mixture of Gothic and Renaissance. The cathedral complex also includes the *episcopal palace*, a medieval building with a fine 15C room.

San Pedro el Viejo (Calle de los Mozárabes): A Romanesque church on the site of an earlier Visigoth building. Built in 1117 and restored in the 17C. It has a nave, two aisles and three apses. The main portal is original, and in the tympanum there is Chi-Rho monogram, a lamb and angels. The choir stalls date from 1506 but have a number of Gothic features. The *high altar* (1602) is by Juan de Verrueta. The Romanesque *cloister* of San Pedro is one of the finest in Spain and dates from 1140. The old church was part of a Benedictine monastery, to which King Ramiro II retired at the end of his life. He died in 1157 as a monk and was buried in the Romanesque *Capilla de San Bartolomé*. His tomb is next to that of his brother, King Alfonso I el Batallador (the fighter), along with many other 13–14C tombs.

San Vicente or La Compañía: An 18C brick church in baroque style, with a fine portal and spacious nave. The site was formerly occupied by Roman baths.

San Miguel or Las Miguelas: Built in transitional Romanesque-Gothic style

Huesca, cathedral, miniature

1150–60; today it is part of a Carmelite monastery. Gothic apse and a square tower with Romanesque windows; 14C restoration.

San Lorenzo/Calle San Lorenzo: Church with nave and two aisles; built in 1339 and subsequently renovated. The site was previously occupied by a Romanesque church. The rebuilding in 1607 added a brick tower and a baroque façade. The interior contains a baroque altarpiece carved in wood, by Sebastián de Ruesta (1650), with a painting by Bartolomé Vicente. The sacristy has a number of 17C paintings by Jusepe Martínez.

Santo Domingo y San Martín: Originally 14C Gothic, this church was rebuilt in baroque style in the 17C under the supervision of Antonio Falcón. The 17C painting on the high altar is by Vicente Verdusán.

Santa María de Foris: Much restored at various times; of the original Romanesque building only the apse and tower remain. The Gothic main portal is 15C, and the 17C high altarpiece is by Bartolomé Vicente.

Seminario de Santa Cruz: The seminary chapel dates from 1571 and is part of an older church of which only the semicircular apse survives.

Convento de Santa Clara: The origins of this monastery go back to 1262, but it has been frequently restored; inside there is a 14C Gothic Madonna.

Convento de Santa Teresa: 17C baroque.

Ermita de San Jorge: A 16C hermitage with an original altarpiece by Juan Miguel de Orliens. The hermitage is said to have been built on the site of the battle of 1096 between King Pedro I and the Saracens.

Ayuntamiento/Town Hall (opposite the cathedral): Renaissance, built in 1578 by

Huesca, cathedral, portal

Huesca, cathedral, high altar

Miguel de Allué. The decoration, which includes sculptures in the entrance hall and staircase, is by Juan Miguel de Orliens.

Colegio Imperial y Mayor de Santiago (near the Town Hall): Renaissance façade; built in 1534.

Universidad Sertoriana (Calle de Quinto Sertorio): Refounded by Pedro IV (Spain's first university had been founded by the Romans under Sertorius). It includes parts of much older buildings, such as the 12C *Palace of the Kings of Aragon* and the Moorish *Zuda*. By the 17C it was practically complete. Visitors can see the 12C vaulted room where the decapitation of 16 nobles is supposed to have taken place on the order of Ramíro II, an incident referred to as the 'Bell of Huesca'. In 1136 Ramíro II invited all the lords of Aragon to see a bell, which he said everyone in Aragon would be able to hear. When the lords were assembled, the decapitation began. Fifteen heads were placed on the floor in the shape of a bell and the sixteenth was hung as the clapper.
  There are fine capitals in the Romanesque room, which belonged to Doña Petronilla (the daughter of Ramíro II).

Museo Provincial: Within the same building, the local museum houses an interesting collection of paintings, architectural exhibits, sculptures and archaeological finds. There is a collection of 16C *Gothic frescos* from the churches at Bierge and Jaso. The collection of painting includes four pictures by the Master of Sigena, an unknown painter, who worked on the high altar of the Sigena monastery in 1519. The influence of the Italian school is unmistakable. There are numerous works by painters such as Maella, Mengs, Francisco Bayeu, Federico de Madrazo, Juan de Pareja, Carreño, Cerezo and Angelo Nardi. The print collection includes lithographs by Goya.

Also worth seeing: Behind the church of San Miguel you can still see remains of the *Muralla*, or old city wall. These include parts of the Roman fortifications, and also the single survivor of the original 99 towers from the 12C. There are also a number of fine old *mansions*, including the *Casa de los Oña* and the *Casa de los Climent*, with 16–17C Plateresque façades. The *Colegio de San Bernardo* and the *Colegio Universitario de San Vicente* have interesting baroque façades. The *provincial hospital* has a fine 15C Gothic portal.

Environs: Santuario de Loreto: This former church lies some 5 km. from Huesca; it was built to the design of Juan de Herrera, but was not completed until 1777.

Ibiza

Balearics/Balearics   p.396 □ M 7

With an area of 221 sq.miles Ibiza is the third largest of the Balearic islands. It has a population of about 40,000. Originally an island hideaway for artists, the combination of picturesque countryside, temperate climate and perfect beaches has made it a universally popular holiday resort.

Ibiza's strategic position has meant that it has been subjected to the influence of a variety of cultures. Very few prehistoric remains have been discovered on Ibiza, but Carthaginians, Romans, Vandals, Byzantines and Moors all settled here. In 1235 James I won it back for Spain. However, the Ibizans have maintained their old traditions, and any visitor should be sure to see one of the many folk festivals.

Cueva de Fontanelles: Caves to the S. of Caba Nonó with interesting Bronze Age paintings.

Ibiza (the town): The capital, it bears the same name as the island and was founded by the Carthaginians in 654BC. Lying on a hill overlooking the sea, it consists of the picturesque fishing/harbour quarter of Sa Penya (lower town) and the original city centre, Dalt Vila, which is encircled by seven towers. The 16C city walls were erected on the orders of Charles V, and have survived in full.

Ayuntamiento/Town Hall: Originally part of the monastery of Santo Domingo, which was dissolved in 1834. The session-room has a series of pictures illustrating the history of Ibiza (including portraits of Antonio Riquers and General Vara de Rey).

Cathedral: This was begun shortly after the island's conquest by James I in 1235. Heavily restored in the 17&18C, now only the bell tower and sacristy survive from the original building. It was probably built on the site of a Moorish mosque. The high altar is of interest, as is a Madonna, the Virgen de la Nieves, by Adrían Ferrán. There are some historical exhibits in the sacristy, including a 13C silver reliquary. The *Archaeological Museum* contains interesting collections of Phoenician and Carthaginian art (earthenware figures, masks, urns, tombstones, coins etc.), which date back as far as the 7CBC. Most of the collection is now housed in a new building in the Via Romana. Some of the exhibits were found in the Puig des Molins (Windmill Mountain) and in the Cuyeram caves near San

Vicente. The church of *El Salvador*, with a square bell tower is also interesting; it stands on the site formerly occupied by the fishermen's church, San Telmo. *Santo Domingo* is a fine baroque church, whose dome was restored in Byzantine style in 1973. An obelisk is dedicated to the memory of Antonio Riquers, the sea captain. There is also a monument in memory of the Ibizan general, Vara de Rey. The *necropolis* is one of the largest Punic burial grounds. The Botafoch lighthouse stands on a projecting cliff.

San José: A town with a population of around 1,400. The parish church of *San José*, was built in 1732. The porch has three round arches and there is a sun-dial over the entrance. The interior decoration is baroque, with an impressive high altar flanked by images of saints and a depiction of the patron. The side chapels are interesting and the wooden pulpit is very fine. The *Ermita Es Cubellas* lies outside the town. It was originally founded by Palau, a Carmelite monk from Catalonia.

San Antonio Abad: A village of some 800 inhabitants on the Bay of Portmany. A natural harbour, it was known to the Romans as Portus Magnus. The parish church, *San Antonio*, was built on the site of a mosque in the 14C and was converted into a fortress to protect the villagers. The main portal has an image of the patron saint and leads to a courtyard with round arches. The nave is supported by huge buttresses. The ruined church of *Santa Inéz* was an old chapel with catacombs.

San Juan Bautista: A town of 5,000 inhabitants on the northern slopes of Furná: The parish church we see today is 18C in origin. In front of the church there is a square, which has arches on columns and terraces. The main building has a bellcote but no other decoration. The dome shows the Crucifixion.

Santa Eulalia del Rio: This village of 7,500 inhabitants has a sheltered location, which gives it an especially favourable climate. There has been a settlement here

Ibiza, view with cathedral

Ibiza, city wall, Portal de las Tablas

since Roman times. The Puig de Missa district lies above the modern settlement. The 14C parish church of *Santa Eulalia* was built on the foundations of a Moorish mosque, and expanded into a fortress in 1548 by Juan Bautista Calvi. The porch has round arches. Inside there are a nave and two aisles; the baroque high altar has an image of the patron saint. From the round tower, there is a splendid view. The *Museo Barrau* has a permanent exhibition of the Catalonian painter Lauereano Barrau.

Igualada
Barcelona/Catalonia   p.390☐M 4

Santa María: This chapel was consecrated in 1059, when the town was founded. It was attached to the monastery of San Cugat. The new parish church of Santa María, consecrated in 1627, was designed by Rafael Planzo and combined Gothic and Renaissance elements. Inside, there is a fine baroque retable by J.Moretó and J.Sunyer from 1718, which has been restored.

Environs: Santa Margarita de Montbuy (3 km. S.): The *Castell de la Tossa de Montbuy* was consecrated around 970 and destroyed in 987 by the Moors under Almanzor. It was later rebuilt as the castle chapel. After a further sacking by the Moors under Abd el Malik in 1003, only the square tower and a few other sections were left standing. The *church* is basilican, which makes it unique in Catalonia. Belltower and plain portal are later additions.

Illescas
Toledo/New Castile   p.392☐G 6

Santa María: A parish church built at different times and in different styles. It has a nave, two aisles, two side chapels and a tower. It was begun in the 13C, the nave is 14–15C, and the choir and sacristy are 16C. Both aisles and the nave end in an apse—the nave's is rectangular, the other two semicircular. There is an unusual range of vaulting styles and effects, including some fine groin vaulting. There are four chapels on the left and three on the right. The *Capilla de la Virgen de la Soledad* in the N. aisle is the most interesting; the *Capilla del Rosario* has two 14C Gothic-Mudéjar style plaques. The 14C bell tower is also Mudéjar.

Hospital Santuario de la Virgen de la Caridad: This has some fine altarpieces and altar paintings, sculptures, painting and work in gold. It was founded by Cardinal Cisneros and re-established in 1592. The *main chapel* has a painting by El Greco from 1603. In the *main shrine* there is the 17C throne of the Virgen de la Caridad, which is made of silver. The simple *altarpieces*, which are supported by the walls of the cross-vaulting, are also attributed to El Greco. They consist of two unsigned pictures dating from 1600 and 1604. The right one depicts love of one's neighbour (Caridad) and that on the left St.Ildefonso, Archbishop of Toledo. The *Capilla de las Reliquias*, which adjoins the sanctuary, contains El Greco's 'Annunciation', 'Birth of Christ' and 'Crowning of the Virgin'.

Puerta de Ugena: 11–12C city gate, Mudéjar in style and the only remaining part of the original city fortifications.

Environs: Casarrubios del Monte (*c.* 20 km. NW): The *Castle of Casarrubios* is 14C and of Mudéjar influence. The groundplan is square with corner towers

Ibiza, Archaeological Museum

and all four walls have survived. The gate is decorated with three striking coats-of-arms. Some doors, both exterior and interior, have survived. The tower, with an impressive slate dome, stands in the middle of the parade ground. The 15C Gothic *castle* itself belonged to the Lords of Casarrubios and has a fine façade incorporating coats-of-arms. It was heavily restored at the end of the last century and has since collapsed. There is a lone round tower on the N. side. **Esquivas** (*c.* 10 km. E.): The *parish church* contains a painted 17C statue of St.Francis of Assisi, which was wrongly attributed to Alonso Cano. There is another figure, the 18C painted 'Virgen de la Leche' and an 18C Pietà. In the *Capilla Santa Bárbara* there is a 16C Castilian-Plateresque altarpiece.

Infiesto
Oviedo/Asturia   p.386□E 1

A small industrial town with a fine pilgrimage church, the *Virgen de la Cueva*, and a Roman bridge over the Piloña.

Environs: Nava: The 12C Romanesque church of *San Bartolomé* used to be part of a Benedictine monastery. There are also two interesting *mansions*, which belong to the family, Alvarez de las Asturias. The older, the *Casa de la Ferrería*, has a 14C tower, which was partially rebuilt in the 16 – 17C, while the 16C *Palacio de la Cogolla*, was restored with an exceptionally lovely façade in the 17C. 2 km. from Nava is the Renaissance church, *Santísima Virgen de los Remedios*.

Iranzu
Navarra/Navarra   p.389□I 2

Nuestra Señora de Iranzu is one of

Spain's oldest monasteries — there is documentary evidence for its existence in 1176, when the Bishop of Pamplona wrote a letter to the Cistercians emphasizing that the monastery was subject to him. It was originally the centre of the Cistercian movement in Navarre; nowadays the monastery houses a community of Theatine monks. The whole complex is quite simple and without ornamentation.

Church: Nave and two aisles, dome vaulting and three square apses, conforming to the strict rules laid down by the Cistercians.

Monastery: Romanesque entrance decorated with pillars; 13–14C Romanesque-Gothic *cloister*; *chapterhouse* with interesting windows. The huge *kitchens*, with massive ovens, are remarkable, and reminiscent of those in the Cistercian monastery of Santa María at Huerta.

Environs: Abárzuza (*c.* 5 km. SE): The parish church, *La Asunción de Nuestra Señora* has a fine Plateresque-Renaissance altar by the sculptor Juan L.Imberto from 1586. There are also three picturesque *hermitages*, dedicated to Santa Bárbara, San Sebastián and San Miguel.

Irún
Guipúzcoa/Basque Provinces   p.388□I 1

A border town lying between Monte Jaizkibel and the ridge of Monte de la Haya, on the banks of the Bidassoa delta. It was devastated in 1936 during the Spanish Civil War, but has since been rebuilt.

Nuestra Señora del Juncal: A fine example of late Gothic church architecture in the Basque region. Its exact date is unknown; it was restored in 1508 and is now under national protection. Nave and two

...ava (Infiesto), San Bartolomé

Irún, Nuestra Señora del Juncal

...sles are separated by high pillars. There a *gallery* with fine segmented vaulting, ...ut the masterpiece is the winged *high ...tar*, begun by Bernabé de Cordero in ...547 and eventually completed by Juan ...ascardo. The altarpiece, which has scenes ...om the life of the Virgin Mary, is basi-...lly baroque, but has traces of the ...enaissance. Work in gold also shows the ...aftsmanship of the 17C master. The ...hurrigueresque *lower altar* is also interest-...g. The church contains the *tomb* of Ad-...iral Pedro Zubiaurre (1508).

...yuntamiento/Town Hall: Built in the ...7C on the Plaza de San Juan. The ba-...que extension of 1763 has an ornate ...rought-iron balcony on the first floor.

...lso worth seeing: Although the

majority of the old mansions were de-stroyed during the Civil War, the *Palace of the Olazábal family* has survived. It has a plain Herrera-style portal. Many important people stayed here, including the Prince of Condé and King Ferdinand VII.

Itálica
Seville/Andalusia   p.394☐D 10

A ruined city near Santiponce (q.v.) of im-mense archaeological importance. A former Roman colony, it was founded by P.C.Scipio Africanus in 206BC for veterans of the Second Punic War. It was the birth-place of the Emperors Trajan (53AD) and Hadrian (76AD). The town enjoyed its peak of civilization and development in the

2C, when it became a municipium. Itálica eventually fell in the barbarian invasion of the 5C, and was further ravaged during the Moorish invasions. Thereafter the ruins were plundered for raw materials, which were used in the development of Seville. However, foundations of houses with courtyards and fountains are still discernible, as well as traces of a paved *street system*, remains of the city wall including a *city gate*, a major street with colonnade, a gymnasium and a *mosaic floor* with themes from classical mythology. The most impressive building is the elliptical *amphitheatre* (with a capacity of 30,000 people), where gladiator fights were held. The archaeological museum in Madrid has a tablet from the Emperor Marcus Aurelius with information as to the frequency of such games. Contests with animals were also staged, as a *fossa bestiaria* (leading to a complex of underground cages) in the middle of the arena shows. Many statues and busts have been found and there is a small *archaeological museum* which has some on display.

Jaca
Huesca/Aragon   p.388☐K

A town on a hill above the left bank of th Río Aragón. It was the seat of a bishop an has kept its medieval characteristics. During the summer the University o Saragossa holds courses for foreign students here. When Jaca was under contro of the Romans, it had municipal defence and was known as Jacca. It was never taken by the Moors, who attempted to seize i while in command of Huesca, but whe were themselves defeated close to Jaca by King Iñigos and Count Aznar Galíndez i the Battle of Río Aragón. In 824 the province of Aragon was founded, only to be subsumed into Navarre in the 10C. In 1035 it became independent again, an Jaca was made the capital, largely due t the strategic significance of its position. I was also an important stage on the pil grimage route to Santiago de Compostela

Cathedral: The first important Roman

Jaca, cathedral, capital

Jaca, cathedral, Museo Diocesano

esque building in Spain. Built under King Ramiro I 1040–76; partial Gothic restoration and later decorated in Plateresque style. What remains of the original Romanesque includes the square bell tower, the exterior walls, the main and S. portals, one of the apses and the pillars of the nave. The cathedral is basilican with a nave and two aisles separated by columns, a transept and three semicircular apses; the main apse is 18C. It was originally barrel vaulted but during the 16C this was removed and replaced by rib vaulting. The Romanesque *main portal* has an interesting *tympanum* in which Chi-Rho monograms are flanked by lions, snakes and a basilisk. *Frescos* on the walls and vaults of the main apse and choir are by Manuel Bayeu. The thin pillars have remarkable *capitals* with scenes from the Old Testament and include the 'Sacrifice of Isaac by Abraham' and the 'Calling upon the false god Baal'. There are numerous *side chapels* containing some fine pieces: the *Chapel of San Miguel* has a Plateresque portal and contains an alabaster figure by Juan de Moreto and Gil de Morlanes. The altarpiece dates from 1523 and is the work of Gabriel Yoli and Juan de Salas. The domed Plateresque *Capilla de la Trinidad* has a late 16C alabaster altar by Juan de Ancheta. The Romanesque *chapterhouse* leads into the *cloisters*, which are 12C. Rooms off the cloisters house the *Diocesan Museum*, where there are exhibits from the diocese's Romanesque churches.

Iglesia del Carmen: Late 17C with a huge Plateresque portal and fine baroque altar.

Monasterio de Monjas Benedictinas (Plazuela de las Monjas): A 12C Benedictine monastery, with 12C *portal* and many 12C sculptures; also a number of Romanesque *capitals*. A fine and somewhat remarkable Spanish-Romanesque *sarcophagus* contains the remains of Doña Sancha, the daughter of King Ramiro I,

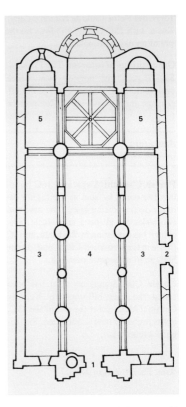

Jaca, cathedral **1** main portal **2** S. side portal **3** left and right aisles **4** nave with sexpartite rib vaulting **5** transept **6** crossing with dome on squinches

the first King of Aragon. Doña Sancha was the founder of the monastery of Santa Cruz de la Serós. She died in 1096.

Ayuntamiento/Town Hall (Calle Mayor): A mid-16C building in Plateresque style with fine wrought-iron screens in front of the windows.

La Ciudadela: Citadel with 17C church, in the N. of the city. Begun by Philip II in 1571, and completed by Philip III.

Torre del Reloj (Calle de Ramón y Cajal): Tower with 15C Gothic windows on the site of an old royal palace.

Other things of interest: The *Puente de San Miguel*, just outside Jaca, which bridges the Río Aragón is part of the pilgrimage route to Santiago de Compostela.

Jadraque
Guadalajara/New Castile   p.388□H 5

Parish Church: A spacious 16C building; the portal is later, as the highly baroque decoration suggests. The nave and two aisles are all on a large scale. The church has a painting by Zurbarán, an 18C figure of the Crucified Christ and, on the high altar, a baroque painting.

Castle Cid: Stands on what has been called 'the finest hill on earth'. Built by Cardinal Mendoza at the end of the 15C, it was probably never completed. Rectangular groundplan.

Environs: Cogolludo (E. of Jadraque) The parish church of *Santa María* is Plateresque and was built in the early 16C. It has a splendid façade. The interior consists of a nave and two aisles with complex groin vaulting. There is a fine painting by José Ribera in the left side altar of the main chapel. The *palace* is an excellent example of secular Spanish Renaissance architecture; it was commissioned by the Lords of Medinaceli in 1492. The façade, which is by Lorenzo Vázquez, displays Italianate elements together with Flamboyant Gothic. N. of Jadraque lies **Pinilla de Jadraque:** 12 – 13C Romanesque *parish church*, whose portal was altered but which is still in Romanesque style. The Romanesque apse was replaced in the 17C. Single-aisled interior. Just outside the village the remains of the *Monasterio de San Salvador de Pinilla* (1218) can be seen. It is Romanesque, as is clearly visible in the semicircular apse and arches leading into the chapterhouse. In the 16C it was extended, when the coat-of-arms of King Charles V was added to the entrance.

Jaca, Puente de San Miguel

aén

aén/Andalusia   p.394☐G 9

A provincial capital and episcopal seat. It
is picturesquely situated at the foot of the
Sierra de Jabalcuz, under the shadow of the
castle on the hill of Santa Catalina. In
Iberian and Roman times, Jaén was known
as 'Auringis', and was famous as a source
of silver and olives; the Moors knew it as
'Geen', which means 'caravan route' and
refers to its strategic location between Andalusia and Castile. It was formerly the
capital of the small province of Jayyan,
which was controlled first by an ambas-
sador from Córdoba and later from the
Moorish kingdom of Granada. In 1246
Ferdinand III, the Holy, conquered the
town, which success was of great importance for the Reconquista and earned Ferdinand the title 'Defender of the Kingdom
of Castile'.

Cathedral: Renaissance building with
two towers and a dome, occupying the site
of an old mosque. It was built in 1500 in
accordance with plans of the architect
Andrés Vandelvira. Although not fully
completed until the 18C, the original
stylistic intentions were adhered to. The
façade has statues and bas-reliefs by Pedro
Roldán, and his baroque figures on the balustrade soften the harsh lines of the structure as a whole. The *interior* has a nave and
two aisles and bundles of Corinthian pillars, which give an impression of majestic
dignity. There are some good pieces in the
side chapels, e.g. the 'Virgen de las Angustias' by José de Mora in the fifth chapel
on the right and 'St.Hieronymus' by An-
tolínez in the third chapel on the right.
The *choir stalls* of 1520 have finely-carved
scenes from the Old Testament and the
Life of Christ. The *chapterhouse* has an
altar retable of 'San Pedro de Osma' by
Pedro Machuca. The *sacristy* houses the
Cathedral Museum, which contains
around 100 pieces: a *'Tenebrario'* or fifteen-
armed candlestick by the famous craftsman, Master Bartolomé de Jaén; a sculpture, 'El Calvario', by Jacobo Florentino;

Jadraque, Castle Cid

'St. Jacob' and 'St. Matthew' by Ribera; 'St.Lawrence' by Montañés; reliquiaries of St.Cecilia, etc. The *main chapel* has the famous relic—'the scarf of Veronica' (Santa Faz).

San Bartolomé (Plaza de San Bartolomé): A 15C church built on the site of a mosque and attached to the city fortifications. It contains wall paintings, a fine Mudéjar ceiling, an interesting Gothic font and a crucifix, 'Cristo de la Expiración', which is atributed to Montañéz.

San Andrés (Calle San Andrés): 16C Mudéjar chapel founded by Gutiérrez González Doncel, Treasurer to Popes Leo X and Clement VII. The courtyard has a bust of the founder. The *Capilla de la Purísima* contains a fine gilded wrought-iron *reja* (early 16C) by Master Bartolomé.

Santa Magdalena (Plaza de la Magdalena): A parish church with a late Gothic portal. It is the city's oldest church and was built on the remains of an even older mosque—in the patio there is a Moorish water-jug, which was used in ritual cleansing. The interior has a nave and two aisles and a splendid altar with a Crucifixion by Jacobo Florentino, el Indaco; 'Mater Dolorosa' by José de Mora; 'Virgen del Pilar' (16C) by Pedro Machuca; and 'St.Mary Magdalene' by Mateo Medína.

Castillo de Santa Catalina: Originally a Moorish fortification, it was converted into a medieval castle (with a Gothic chapel) by Ferdinand III after the Reconquista. It has survived unchanged since that time; today it also contains a Parador (hotel).

Also worth seeing: The *church of San Ildefonso* a huge 14C Gothic church, which is part of the city wall. The N. side has a fine classical portal by Ventura Rodríguez (18C). The *church of San Juan* (Plaza de San Juan) with a Romanesque tower, th Torre del Consejo. The *Church of L Merced* is the home of the famous statue 'J sus de los Descalzos'. The 17C *Monaster of Santo Domingo* is now a school buildin A fine Moorish *palace*, later used by Fe dinand III has a beautiful *portal* from 158 by Vandelvira. Plateresque courtyard wit Corinthian columns arranged in Tusca style. The *Monastery of the Discalce Carmelites* houses the 'Cántico Espiritual the original manuscript of St.John of th Cross'. The 13C *Monastery of Santa Clar* has fine cloisters. The *Ayuntamiento* stand next to the cathedral and has a fine 17C fa çade. The *Arco de San Lorenzo* (Plaza Arc is 15C, with a Mudéjar chapel in the towe The *Palacio del Condestable* (Calle de Ma inez Molina, 22) is also 15C, with interes ing panelling in the Moorish style Granada. The *Provincial Museum* (Aven ida de Generalísimo Franco) has a colle tion of paintings, archaeological exhibi —including an image of a bull from Po cuna—and an early Christian sarcophagu from Martos.

Environs: La Guardia de Jaén (15 km SE): The *Dominican monastery* wa founded in 1530 and designed by André de Vandelvira, but only the arcades aroun the courtyard and one of the fountains su vive. The *church* has a most impressiv crossing and sanctuary, again by Vande vira. The *castle* dates from the 8C, but th ruins we see today are from a later dat There is a Visigoth *necropolis* on Mt.Salid and finds excavated here are on display i Jaén. There are also Moorish burial site nearby, and Roman marble pillars.

Játiva
Valencia/Valencia   p.396 □ K

Játiva is 56 km. S. of Valencia, at the fo of the Sierra des Aguyas, which ensures lentiful water supply, and on the NW slopes of Mt.Bernisa. It is picturesquely situated on the edge of a large vine and orange growing area. Such a location meant that it was originally settled at a quite early stage. Founded by the Iberians, the Romans referred to it as Saetabis, the Visigoths made it an episcopal seat and the Moors knew it as Medina Xateba. In 1249 James I of Aragon recovered it from the Moors and handed it over to the Borja family, who produced two popes, Calixtus III and Alexander VI (born 1431 and the father of Lucretia and Cesare Borgia), and also 7 cardinals and 8 bishops, and finally St.Francis of Borja. Játiva is also the home town of the artist Jusepe de Ribera, who was born in 1591 and died in Naples in 1656. During the War of Spanish Succession, Játiva fought with Charles of Austria, and was consequently put to the flames by the Bourbon King Philip V. It was also severely damaged in the Napoleonic Wars. In spite of these vicissitudes the town has kept its charm; much has been rebuilt on the original foundations, so that the narrow streets and alleys of the old town have been preserved. The *Calle de Monteada* is the finest street and has a number of old mansions. Battlemented walls date back to the fortifications raised during the time of the Borjas. You can take a route through the town which leads past numerous *palaces* and Gothic churches. The *hospital* has a façade with a late Gothic portal and plateresque windows.

Castillo (Castle): An imposing building on the slopes of Mt.Bernisa. Gothic building around Roman and Moorish fortifications; later improved and extended. Splendid view over the city and its environs.

Colegiata: (Collegiate church opposite the hospital): Begun in the early 15C and heavily restored in 1596. The tower, which is 97 ft. high, dates from 1796. The imposing interior has a Tuscan-Renaissance air with three aisles and a high dome over the crossing. The 18C *high altar* is freestanding, with marble columns by Ventura Rodríguez. There is a 14C Gothic figure of Mary. On the left is the *Chapel of Pope Calixtus III*, and the *tomb* (late 15C) of Archbishop Juan Borja. There are also fine altar paintings by Jacomart(15C) and Paolo de San Leocadio (16C).

Ermita de San Feliú: Hermitage built in a style transitional between Romanesque and Gothic on the foundations of a Visigoth basilica. The portal is round-arched. *Inside* there are ancient pillars, fine capitals, Roman and Visigoth lapidaries and an exceptional Gothic retable. A *processional cross*, which is covered with scenes from Christ's Passion is late 13C and extremely valuable.

Museo Municipal: Roman and medieval collections including paintings, coats-of-arms, etc. The most interesting piece is known as the *Pila de Játiva*, and is a fine Moorish water jug made of marble, which was used for ritual cleansing. The fine reliefs, reminiscent of ivory carvings, display a variety of motifs: knights with lances, musicians and dancers, mothers with children, and animals such as goats and peacocks.

Jávea
Alicante/Valencia   p.396 □ L 8

Jávea is situated between the Cape of San Martín and the Cape of San Antonio, on one of the Costa Blanca's finest bays; it was founded by the Iberians. Numerous watchtowers and *fortifications* bear witness to the former rampant piracy, especially of the Berbers. The surviving *city walls*, with the huge towers and Moorish gateways, narrow alleyways and the old castle all give the

Jávea, church, portal

town a medieval ambience. This is also true of the Isabelline (late Gothic) *parish church*, whose crenellations and slit windows make it look like a castle. It has fine portals and Gothic rib vaulting.

Environs: A few km. N. is the **Cape of San Antonio**, which has a *lighthouse* and the finest view on the Costa Blanca. The rocky coast has numerous *caves* with stalactites and stalagmites, some of which can only be reached by sea.

Javier

Navarra/Navarra   p.388☐I 2

This popular pilgrimage destination lies 1,560 ft. above sea level. St.Francis Xavier was born in the nearby cliff-top castle on 7 April 1506. He is the patron saint of Navarre, and worked as a missionary in Goa, India, Japan and China.

El Castillo (Castle): This 11C fortress has high walls and crenellated towers. In the 16C, the *Palacio nuevo* was added to the living apartments and so was a tower, the *Torre del Cristo*. The Great Hall, an oratory and the Chapel of San Miguel are to be found here in addition to the *room where the Saint was born*. There are Moorish fortifications near the castle.

Also worth seeing: The church of *Santa María* houses a 13C Gothic Madonna.

Jerez de la Frontera

Cádiz/Andalusia   p.394☐D 1

The Romans knew the town as Asta Regia. The area has been the scene of fierce fighting, such as the battle in 711 between the Visigoth King Roderick and the Moors around the Río Guadalete. The victorious Moors fortified the city. The struggle between the Christians and Moors during the Reconquista in the 13&14C ended in victory for the Spanish kings. Jerez de la Frontera has gained a worldwide reputation for its bodegas (cellars) where sherry is stored. The town is also famous for the breeding of riding horses.

San Salvador (Plaza de Arroyo): Wide steps lead up to the W. front of this collegiate church, which was built above an old mosque. The free-standing *bell tower* is Mudéjar in style, but the whole church, including the façade, was completely rebuilt during the 17&18C. The interior has a nave and four aisles, with an octagonal dome over the crossing. The *works of art* in the side chapels include an outstanding

Javier, fortified church

Javier, Castillo

painting by Zurbarán, and another in the style of the 16C Spanish school.

San Miguel (Plaza Primo de Rivera): This church is 15&16C late Gothic-Isabelline, and has a most impressive, richly ornamented W. façade. The Mudéjar tower is covered with blue tiles. The interior contains an impressive variety of net vaulting styles and a large 17C *retable* with sculptures by M.Montañés and José de Arce. The reliefs in the middle section and the sculptures of St. Peter and St. Paul are all by Montañés. The sacristy and the baptistery both have Plateresque portals.

Santiago: This late Gothic church from the second half of the 15C has an especially fine Gothic portal. The slender tower is 17C. The interior contains excellent *choir stalls* (1574) which are the work of Jerónimo de Valencia and Cristóbal Voisin and were originally in the nearby Carthusian monastery.

Alcázar: The remains date back to the 11C; the octagonal tower is late 12C in origin. There are *Moorish baths* in the 15C keep, and a 12C former mosque was converted into the *Capilla Santa María la Real*. There is a more recent chapel, *Las Conchas*, which has Mudéjar features.

Casa del Cabildo Viejo (Plaza de la Asunción): This 16C Renaissance building used to be the Town Hall; it was built by Andrés de Ribera. Today it contains a *library* (25,000 volumes) and an *archaeological museum*, amongst whose finest exhibits is a 7C BC Greek helmet.

Jerez de la Frontera, Bodega

Also worth seeing: The church of *San Dionisio* (Plaza de la Asunción) is 15C, with a Gothic-Mudéjar tower ('Torre de la Vela'), a patio and a high rococo retable inside. The late Gothic church of *San Marcos* has three portals in different styles and a 17C baroque altar with older panel paintings. It also has fine Mudéjar side chapels. The church of *San Lucas* (Calle de San Lucas) is 14C and has Mudéjar portals and an early-18C baroque altar; the *Capilla de las Ánimas* has an altar which is attributed to Luise Roldán. The church of *San Juan* (Plaza de San Juan) has interesting Mudéjar chapels. The church of *San Mateo* (Calle del los Córdobeses) is 16C late Gothic with an 18C altar. The *Santo Domingo Monastery* (Alameda de Cristina) is a mixture of Romanesque, Gothic and Mudéjar, with a fine Gothic cloister. The

Hospital de la Merced (Calle de la Merced) has a 13C church with an altar (1564) by Francisco de Ribas. The shrine is of embossed silver (17C), and the Madonna inside it is probably Gothic. The sacristy has a Madonna which has a coloured mount and is known as 'Santa María la Real'. The town has a number of very fine **palaces:** the *Palacio de los Marqués de Montana* (18C), which has a rich baroque façade and a superb patio; the *Casa de Bertemati*, with another impressive baroque façade; the *Casa de Riquelme*, whose Renaissance façade has columns with statues of Hercules; the Renaissance *Casa de Ponce de León*; the 18C *Casa Domecq*; the *Palacio de los Marqués de Campo Real*, an 18C building with a superbly articulated façade and patio.

Environs: La Cartuja de Nuestra Señora de la Defensión (5 km. S.): This Carthusian monastery was founded in 1477 and abolished in 1835. In 1949 it was returned to the Order. The once-famous stud farm of the Carthusians no longer exists. There is a remarkable *entrance doorway*, transitional in style between Gothic and Renaissance, which leads through to the 15C late Gothic *church*, with its finely articulated façade. The figures of saints in the niches are attributed to Alonso Cano. Some of the monastery buildings are not open to the public at present. These are: a 'claustrillo', or small cloister, with arcades; the Gothic 'Claustro Grande'; a refectory; and a chapterhouse. **Torre de Melgarejo** (10 km. E.): The ruins of a former Moorish castle with a crenellated wall, a horseshoe arch and a tower. **Sanlúcar de Barrameda** (23 km. NW): This was the starting point for Columbus' third voyage of discovery to America (1498), and Magellan's first circumnavigation of the world in 1519. The parish church of *Nuestra Señora de la O* has a fine Mudéjar portal with a Gothic arch in a richly decorated alfiz with lions bearing coats-of-arms. The interior contains outstanding 16C *stucco*,

La Cartuja (Jerez de la Frontera)

Jerez de la Frontera, San Miguel

an 18C retable, and Flemish and Italian paintings. The *Monastery of San Francisco* was founded by the King Henry VIII of England as a hospital for sick seamen. It has a fine baroque façade and a Renaissance dome. Also of note are the *Palace of the Dukes of Medina Sidonia*, the *Castle of Santiago*, and the churches of *La Trinidad*, *San Nicolas* and *Desamparados* and the *Monastery of Santo Domingo*.
Chipiona (33 km. NW): The *Capilla de Nuestra Señora de la Regla* has a Gothic cloister with tiles dating from 1640.

Jerez de los Caballeros
Badajoz / Estremadura   p.392 ☐ D 8

The name is derived from the *Caballeros*

Templarios, or Knights Templar, who wrested the town from the Moors in 1229. In order to resist the dissolution of their Order, they defended themselves here against Ferdinand IV's troops, to whom, however, they were soon forced to surrender. The survivors were beheaded in a tower which has since been known as the *Torre Sangrienta* (the Bleeding Tower). The seafarer Vasco Nuñez de Balboa was born here; in 1513 he became the first European to reach the Pacific, but was finally beheaded for various crimes of violence. Hernando de Soto, the hero of Florida, was also born here. Two of the six gates of the town still stand, including the *Puerta de la Villa* which is partly hidden by buildings. The SE section of the town walls incorporates the *castle* of the Knights Templar (13C, largely rebuilt in 1471).

Jerez de los Caballeros, view

Jerez de los Caballeros, San Bartolomé

Santa María: This building stands beside the castle and was consecrated in 556, making it the oldest church in Estremadura. It was rebuilt in the 16C and altered in predominantly baroque style in the 17C. The *interior* is basilican with a nave and two aisles, and contains Romanesque pilasters and some Gothic details. The gorgeous baroque decoration is 17C.

San Miguel (town centre): This church is remarkable for its massive *tower*. The higher the tower rises, the more richly decorated and narrower its storeys become. The church was rebuilt in the 16C, and altered in baroque style in the 17C. The interior contains a large baroque altar, a wrought-iron pulpit, a shrine dating from 1791, and numerous sculptures. The dome has 17C Italianate frescos.

San Bartolomé: This church in the upper part of town also has an ornate 17C *tower* which, like that of San Miguel, is reminiscent of the Giralda. A massive substructure supports a storey with large windows, balconies, and a variety of niches and volutes. This storey is topped by two slender, circular ones. The polychrome decoration, consisting of blue and yellow glass and ceramics, glitters in the sunlight. Blue azulejos also appear in the extravagantly decorated *baroque façade*. There are large pictures made of tiles to the left and right of the main balcony, and there are also further balconies, niches, pilasters and painted stucco arabesques.

Santa Catalina: This church is in the lower town and has groin vaulting, an 18C baroque tower and, in the *interior*, a var-

Jerez de los Caballeros, view

iety of 17C sculptures and an 18C baroque altar.

Environs: Fregenal de la Sierra (*c.* 22 km. away): This town, surrounded by olive groves, is built on the site of the Iberian-Roman settlement of Nertobriga. It clusters around a massive 13C *castle*, which was formerly a fief of the Knights Templar. The *church of Santa María* was founded in the 13C but was frequently rebuilt up to the 17C. One of the castle's towers serves as the church's bell tower.

Jumilla

Murcia/Murcia   p.396□I/K 8

Santiago: Late 15C Gothic-Renaissance

church; not fully completed until 1562. The huge tower is later.

Also worth seeing: Some *16C castle ruins* on the hills above town. The old *prison* is interesting, and today serves as the Town Hall. It has a mid-16C Renaissance twin portal and a high gallery with strange spiral pillars. In the mountains 6 km. away from the town lies the *Franciscan monastery of Santa Ana*, which has a church (1580) with fine painted sculptures. The figure of St. Anne 'La Abuelica' ('The Grandmother') is 15C. Near the entrance is *'Flagellation of Christ'* by Salzillo. 18C azulejos.

Environs: Yecla (28 km. W.): The church of *San Francisco* has a group of sculptures by Salzillo.

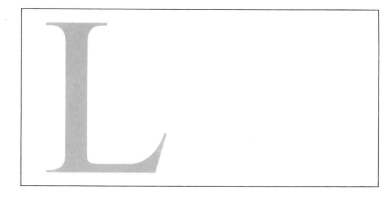

La Alberca
Salamanca/León   p.392□D 5

This village of some 1,500 inhabitants lies at an altitude of 3,444 ft. and is one of Spain's most charming spots. It has kept much of its medieval character and is now under national protection. Outside the idyllic village, with its narrow streets and fine squares there are some fine farmsteads with canopy roofs and bay windows. Most impressive of all, however, is the village's main square with its arcades of wood and granite. Many of the interesting village customs have survived.

Parish Church (on the main square): An 18C church with a nave and two aisles separated by columns; the Capilla Mayor is 18C, the pulpit 16C, the Gothic processional cross 13C and there is a 16C Calvary.

Environs: Las Batuecas: The route from La Alberca to Las Batuecas is very picturesque. The Convent of Discalced Carmelites, founded in 1597, was destroyed by fire in 1872. Nearby are the Cabras Pintas, prehistoric caves. **Miranda del Castañar:** The *parish church* is 13C Gothic, with a nave and two aisles and Mudéjar decoration. It has an 18C tower and Gothic tombs. The *castillo* is 15C, and the *town walls* and single surviving gateway are 16C. The *Plaza de Toros* contains the remains of a *medieval aqueduct*. **San Martín de Castañar** has a 15C *castillo* and a 13–17C *parish church* with a 16C Mudéjar nave, mid-17C high altar and a number of other interesting pieces.

La Bañeza
León/León   p.386□E 3

La Bañeza lies on the route between Astorga and Benavente and contains a few interesting religious buildings.

San Salvador: Most interesting for its fine 11C Romanesque apse. 13C nave and two aisles. The vaulting is 18C, the Renaissance portal late 16C and the high altar mid 17C.

Santa María: This church has an 18C W. tower, 17C nave and aisles, and 16C transept, choir and crossing.

Capilla de la Piedad: Restored in the 18C. It has a fine Romanesque portal, which bears the hallmarks of the school of Maestro Mateo.

Environs: Castrocalbón has the ruins of an old castle. The church of *San Salvador* has three E. apses in typical Romanesque-Mudéjar style. The aisles are somewhat later, dating from the 13C. The *Ermita de la Virgen del Castro*, which adjoins the fortress, has a seated Madonna and Child in the Gothic style.

La Bisbal
Gerona/Catalonia   p.390□O 3

This town, situated 20 km. inland from the heart of the Costa Brava, is known as a centre for ceramics. First mentioned under its present name in 1019, when it was a bishop's seat.

Bishop's Castle: Built in the 12C and rebuilt in the 16&17C, the Romanesque chapel has survived from the original castle.

Parish church: Founded in 901 and rebuilt in its existing Renaissance style in the 17C.

Environs: Cruilles (2 km. SW): Once the seat of the Counts of Cerdaña, all that remains of the old *castle* is a wall and watchtower. The *parish church* was consecrated in 1035 and has a nave, two aisles and three apses. The *parish museum* contains a Romanesque 'Majestad' (crucifix) and panel.

La Coruña
La Coruña/Galicia   p.386□B 1

This, the capital of the province of the same name, is the largest city in Galicia.

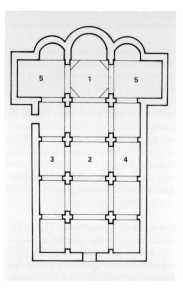

Cruilles, parish church of San Miguel **1** crossing **2** nave **3** and **4** aisles **5** transept

It was founded by the Iberians, and later taken over by the Phoenicians. The Romans knew it as Ardobirum Coronium; Trajan was responsible for its extensive development. It was destroyed under Almanzor in the 10C but was rebuilt and flourished spectacularly in the 13&14C. In 1588 it was the point of departure for the Spanish Armada against England. In 1589 Drake led a counter-attack and attempted to sack the city. During the War of Independence in 1808, the English were defeated and the French took the town.

Iglesia de Santiago: The oldest building in La Coruña dating from the 12C. It is single-aisled and has three apses, and its unusual width is supported by the cross arches. The side columns and the windows are particularly interesting and the capitals are decorated with animal motifs. The first chapel on the right contains a large wooden statue of St. James seated, a 14C work by García Felipe. On the left, over the entrance to the second chapel there is a wooden statue of St. James on his horse by Nicolás Manzano. Much of the furnishing is more recent, such as the baroque high altar, but the two old portals are especially fine. The W. façade is well-proportioned, and the tympanum has a late Gothic St. James with decorated archivolts and figures on either side of the portal. To the left of the portal is a badly damaged Gothic tomb; there are two more under the round arches near the N. portal, which is finely decorated with archivolts and has an Agnus Dei in the tympanum.

Colegiata de Santa María: This 12/13C church has a nave and two aisles and is situated at the highest point of the old city. It has a semicircular apse below a stone rose-window (without glass) and exceptionally fine portals, especially the main one which depicts the Adoration of the Magi in the tympanum. There is a fine crucero to its left. The façade is harmonious and balanced, with a rose-window, a decorated gable and two windows on either side in Romanesque-Gothic transitional style. A number of steps lead up to the main entrance. The N. portal shows the martyrdom of St. Catherine. The most interesting features of the interior are the storiated capitals and the 15C statues of Mary and the archangels on the columns; there are also 14,15&16C sarcophagi.

Santo Domingo: This church has a fine 18C baroque façade. The most interesting aspects of the interior are the *Capilla de la Cofradía de los Remedios* (1663) and the *Capilla de la Virgen de la Rosario* (1661), the patron saint of La Coruña. The altar is by Alfonso Rodríguez and dates from 1688.

San Jorge: Built in 1693, the church has a nave and two aisles. The façade, with fine columns, has a tower on either side and large figures of saints.

San Nicolás: Built in the 18C to plans by

La Coruña, Santiago

Fernández Sarelas, this church contains the *Capilla de los Dolores* with an 18/19C Madonna.

Convento de las Bárbaras: This 15C monastery stands on the attractive little Plaza de Santa Bárbara, along with a cross and some old buildings; one of the portals on the façade has a Gothic relief of figures.

Other religious buildings worth seeing: The *Capuchin monastery* contains a painting by Zurbarán. The *Franciscan monastery*, now in ruins, is a national monument. Originally built in 1214 it was destroyed in the 17C. All that remains of *San Andrés* is a crucero on the Campo San Andrés.

Secular buildings: The most eyecatching buildings in La Coruña are the numerous large-windowed 19C houses by the harbour, the *Galerias de Cristales*, which earned La Coruña the nickname of the 'crystal city'. The most interesting secular work, however, is the 2C *Tower of Her-*

cules, an imposing Roman lighthouse which is still in use. Some of the medieval *town walls* still stand, including some of the gateways such as the *Puerta del Mar* on the Paseo del Parrote (17C) and the *Puerta de San Miguel* (1595). The ruins of the medieval fortress are now covered by the *Jardín de San Carlos Park*, which contains the grave of the English general Sir John Moore. There is a small island at the entry to the harbour on which lies the 16C *Castillo de San Antón*, which is today a *historical and archaeological museum*. The provincial art museum (*Museo Provincial de Bellas Artes*) is housed in the 18C *Consulado del Mar* and includes good paintings by Goya, Velásquez, Ribera, Morales, Murillo, Rubens, Breughel, Veronese, Tintoretto and van Dyck.

Also worth seeing: There are a number of old mansions in La Coruña, such as the 18C *Palacio de Capitanía General*. The *Ayuntamiento/Town Hall*, an early 20C building and the seat of the Real Academia Gallega, stands on the Plaza María Pita.

La Coruña, Santiago, tympanum

Environs: Meirás (Mera): This town lies to the E. of La Coruña and has a well known 16C *castle* with three towers and a chapel renovated in 1893. **Dexo** (NE of Meirás): A coastal town with a Romanesque church. **Bergondo** (SE of Meirás): Has a church which was once part of a 12C Benedictine monastery. It has a nave and two aisles and was rebuilt during the Gothic period. The interior contains some interesting Gothic tombs; the 15C Chapel of Santa Catalina has groin vaulting. There are a number of old mansions in the area, including the fine *La Lancara* palace; also the prehistoric settlements of Reboredo and Bergondo. **Pastoriza:** The road from La Coruña to Carbatio runs past Pastoriza, Oseiro and Monteagudo. *Nuestra Señora de Pastorizia:* On Mt.Suevos, the site of an old Celtic settlement, there is an old hermitage which was destroyed in the 10C. A pilgrimage church was built on the same spot in 1589, and rebuilt during the 18C under Domingo Maceiras; it became one of Galicia's most visited pilgrimage churches. It is well situated, and has a huge

atrium, unique baroque decoration and a façade by Domingo Perez and Blas de Pereiro. **Oseiro:** The 12C single-aisled church of *San Tirso* is interesting: it has a fine square apse and decorated portal. Nearby is the 12C Romanesque *church of San Esteban de Morás*. **Monteagudo:** The 12C church of *Santo Tomé* has a nave and two aisles, three semicircular apses and interesting windows.

La Escala
Gerona/Catalonia   p.390☐0 3

This village was built as the fishermen's quarter of San Martín de Ampurias.

Environs: Near the village is the excavation site of **Ampurias**, known to the Greeks as *Emporion*. It is next to the Roman town, whose original harbour has now silted up. It was first founded on San Martín, then an island, in 575 BC by

La Coruña, Santo Domingo

La Coruña, Colegiata de Santa María

Phocaeans from Asia Minor and later moved to Ampurias. Archaeologists refer to the original settlement as *Palaia Polis* and to the later one as *Neapolis*. Until the 2C AD it played an important role in Mediterranean culture; the Roman settlement was ten times the size of the Greek one. The foundations of many of the houses survive, as do mosaic floors, remains of columns, capitals, a wall with a gateway with pointed arches and the elliptical foundations of an *amphitheatre*. The old *city gate* was commissioned by Titus Livius. Also of interest are the remains of temples, such as those of *Aesculapius* and *Serapis*, where replicas of statues have been found. The *Museo Monográfico*, which is near the Greek settlement, contains ceramics, arms, tools, jewels, statues and mosaics. The most interesting exhibit is a mosaic depicting the sacrifice of Iphigenia from the 1C BC. Also on display are replicas of the *statue of Aesculapius* and the *torso of Aphrodite*, the originals of which are on display in the Archaeological Museum in Barcelona.

La Espina

Valladolid/Old Castile   p.386☐F 4

Monastery of la Santa Espina: Founded by Doña Sancha in the 12C, this monastery takes its name from a thorn of Christ's crown which is preserved here. The church has five apses and was originally built in Cistercian style, although it has since been altered several times. The chapterhouse is one of the finest in Spain. One of the two baroque cloisters is 16C and was built by Juan Nates; the twin-towered façade is 18C. The interior includes an high altarpiece with fine 16C sculptures and a Gothic Madonna.

Environs: Urueña (*c.* 2 km. S.): This town is still completely surrounded by *walls*. It has the remains of a *castle* and a Gothic *parish church* with a 17C altarpiece. Nearby is the 12C Romanesque *Iglesia de la Anunciada*, which has a nave, two aisles and horseshoe arches which appear to be remains of an older building. **San**

La Coruña, Ayuntamiento

Ampurias (La Escala)

Cebrián de Mazote (*c.* 3 km. S.): The 10C Mozarabic church of *San Cebrián* is the most impressive example of this style in the whole of Spain. It has a nave, two aisles and three apses separated by horseshoe arches. There is an interesting Mozarabic relief in the portico.

La Estrada
Pontevedra/Galicia   p.386☐B 2

The most striking building in La Estrada is the *Torre de Guimarey*, which is square and built of ashlars. The baroque palace formerly attached to it, today lies in ruins.

Environs: Moreira (NE of La Estrada, on the road to Oca and Castro): The single-aisled Romanesque church of *San Miguel*

has numerous pillars with intricate capitals and the remains of a 16C fresco in the apse. **Oca:** Has a most interesting palace known as 'Pequeño Versalles' or little Versailles. The gardens are also epecially fine, as is the baroque church which contains sculptures by José Gambiano. **Castro:** The Romanesque church of *San Miguel* contains 16C frescos. **Camanzo** (NE of Castro): The site of a much-renovated 12C *parish church* with a particularly fine old portal. **Carboeiro** (SE of Castro): One of Galicia's finest monasteries, the *Monasterio de San Lorenzo*, which was founded in 936, destroyed in 997 and rebuilt in 1174. Its remains are remarkable; the apse and façade of the church, which originally had a nave and two aisles, are still beautiful; portal and window are also fine. Interesting crypt with three chapels. **Losón**(near Carboeiro): The 12C Romanesque church of Santa Eulalia has an especially fine apse and 15C frescos. **Acibeiro** (SE of La Estrada): The site of the *Monasterio de Santa María*, one of Galicia's oldest Cistercian monasteries. Founded by Alfonso VII in 1135, it was seriously damaged by fire in 1649. All that stands today are the monastery's remains and the church with its more recent bell tower.

Lage (Laxe)
La Coruña/Galicia   p.386☐B 1

Lage is an old seaside town with narrow streets and some fine palaces (the Palacio Moscoso and the Palacio Castro or de Los Caamaño). On 17 August there is a procession when thanks are given to the Virgin for protection against shipwrecks. The church has a single aisle with a fine crucero and dates from around 1600. The most interesting part is the portal, which is decorated with fine reliefs. The interior is groin vaulted and contains some splendid coats-of-arms, reliefs and statues, including a

La Granja de San Ildefonso, Palacio de la Granja

15C statue of St.Ines. In place of the retable in the apse there is a 15C relief depicting the Resurrection of Christ and subsequent events.

Environs: The surrounding area contains a number of 15&16C buildings, especially towards Bayo. Past Cabanas is **Mens**, which has a 12C *parish church* with a nave and two aisles, which was originally part of a monastery, and the celebrated *Torres of Mens*, three square towers surrounded by a thick wall with a walkway, which were destroyed in the 15C and later rebuilt.

La Granja de San Ildefonso
Segovia/Old Castile   p.392☐ G 5

The origin of La Granja de San Ildefonso

dates back to King Henry IV. In 1450, as he was hunting in the woods of Balsain, it occurred to him to build a hunting-lodge and a Chapel to San Ildefonso on a beautiful spot known at the time as *Casar del Pollo*. In 1447 Ferdinand and Isabella gave the site to the monks of the El Parral monastery in Segovia, and they built a *Granja* and rest-house for guests. The Granja was near the village of San Ildefonso. When Philip V was hunting around Balsain castle and came upon the spot with its chapel and houses he was so impressed by its picturesque setting that he decided to buy it from the monks and build his own 'mini-Versailles' to serve as his summer residence and, later, as a place of retirement after his abdication. He entrusted the work to his court architect, Teodoro Ardemáns, giving instructions that the monks' buildings

La Granja de San Ildefonso, Palacia de la Granja

should stand unaltered. The work began in 1721 and was completed in 1723, although the façade took until 1739. Responsibility for the gardens was given to Carlier and Boutelou. Near the castle is the collegiate church, where the king and his bride were married.

Castle: La Granja is a monumental building with four parallel wings, in the middle of which the old monks' guest-house survives. Ardemáns began the work in 1721. The main façade, 509 ft. long and 43 ft. high, was completed by Sachetti in 1736 to the designs of Juvarra. It has a fine portal with the four seasons in the form of caryatids. The side façades are 148 ft. long and the two inner courtyards, the *Patio de los Coches* and the *Patio de la Herradura*, were added later by Andrea Procaccini and Sempronio Subisati; the rear façade encloses the church. The interior, in spite of rearrangement and damage sustained in fires, still has well-furnished rooms with many interesting and valuable pieces. The following rooms are the most interesting: on the ground floor, the *Sculpture Gallery*, whose ceiling is decorated with mythological themes by Bartolomé Ruscha; the *Marble Room*, with splendid marble pillars and columns and a decorated ceiling; the *State Gallery* on the first floor, which consists of a number of rooms with elegant marble floors, Empire furniture and exquisite painted ceilings by Sanni, Saxo and Fideli; the *Throne Room*, with an Ascension; the *Japanese Room*, beautifully furnished and containing four paintings with Biblical themes by Juan Pablo Panini. Other rooms contain 18&19C paintings, including some with folk themes by Houasse, and portraits of Philip V and Isabel de Borbón by van Loo; also Biblical and allegorical works by Lucas Jordán. The collection of Flemish and Spanish tapestries from the 16C onwards, deserves special attention.

Colegiata: Laid out as a Latin cross, it has a high dome over the transept and a façade with two towers. The interior contains a number of fine works of art: *Immaculata* by Maella (1774), *Imposición de la Casulla a San Ildefonso* (Presentation of the Chasuble) by Bayeu and a processional cross by Antonio de Oquendo. The dome and vaulting were covered with frescos, but these have since been destroyed by fire. The finest piece in the church is the tomb of Philip V and his wife, which was completed in 1756. It is made of marble, and has busts of the royal couple in medallions. It was built by Sempronio Subisati and Pedro Sermini, with the sculptors Dumandré and Pitué. Opposite the tomb is an 18C stucco relief by Salvador Carmona of the Victory of Christ.

Park and Grounds: The beautiful grounds are perhaps the most attractive feature of La Granja. They were designed in classical French style along the lines of Le Nôtre's gardens at Versailles and cover a total area of some 360 acres surrounded by a fence nearly 4 miles long. The paths and squares were finished in 1723, at a total length of 22 miles; the elm and wild chestnut trees were planted in the same year. The garden was planned by René Carlier, whose task was helped by Marchand's preparation of the soil and construction of channels. After Carlier's death, Esteban Boutelou took over; he had been the resident garden designer at Aranjuez since 1716. The gardens have 26 enormous fountains, as well as numerous smaller ones, and there are sculptures everywhere, mostly of animals and children. *El Mar*, the lake which supplies the water to the fountains, is artificial, and lies on a 4,000 ft plateau in the centre of the park. The following fountains are of particular interest: the *Gran Cascada* (great cascade), by Thierry and Fremin, in front of the castle's main façade has twelve basins which form an allegorical image of the Earth and the four seasons; the group of three symbolizes the *Tres Gracias* (three Graces); the *Carrera de Caballos* (horse race) is a mixture of fountains and basins, which form a cascade; *Los Caracoles* (the snails); *El Abanico* (the fan); the huge basin of the Fountain of Neptune; the titanic Fountain of Apollo; and the group depicting Andromeda being freed by Perseus, set amidst enormous fountains, by Thierry and Fremin. *Las Ocho Calles* (the eight paths) consists of eight fountains grouped round a paved circular area, with a statue of Pandora and Merkur in the centre and eight more statues around the outside, all by Fremin. Other interesting fountains include *La Fama*, with a jet height of 155 ft., *Los Baños de Diana*, *Latona*, *El Canastillo* and *Las Ranas*.

San Ildefonso: The village contains a number of interesting buildings, such as the *Cuartel de Guardias*, built 1762-5, *La Casa de los Infantes* (1770), *La Casa de los Canónigos* and the royal *Marstall*. The famous *glass factory*, which was built by Juan de Villanueva and Bartolomé Real on the orders of Philip V in 1746, was one of Europe's first crystal manufacturing centres.

Environs: A few km. away from San Ildefonso is **Balsaín**, a picturesque village with the remnants of a royal *palace*—a half-collapsed tower and some remains of walls. **Riofrío** (*c.* 12 km. SW): Isabel Farnese, Philip V's widow, used the famous hunting enclosure to build a huge *palace*; work began on it in 1754 to the plans of Virgilio Ravaglio. It was continued by Carlos Fraschina and José Diaz Gamona and was eventually completed during the reign of Charles III. It is set in a chestnut oak wood of over 1,700 acres and is constructed in Italian baroque style. It has a square ground plan and four equal sides, each 275 ft. long. The most impressive parts are the *inner courtyard*, the huge *staircase* and the *chapel*, which has a fine coloured marble pavement and an elliptical ground plan. The many rooms contain paintings and frescos by Jordán, Canducci, Bayeu, Houasse, Maella, Ribera and the oil-painting *La Caza* (The Hunt) by Velázquez. **La Losa** (*c.* 15 km. S.): The 15C church of *San Juan Evangelista* has a single aisle, a pentagonal apse, an interesting Gothic altarpiece depicting St. Gregory and a Renaissance high altarpiece.

Laguardia
Álava/Basque Provinces   p.388☐H 2/3

This small town was founded in 908 by Sancho Abarca of Navarre to defend the frontier, when it was known as *La Guarda*. It was originally laid out in the shape of a ship, with the bow facing N. and the stern S. In 1164 it achieved town status under Sancho el Sabio. In 1194 its fortifications were extended by King Sancho el Fuerte. From 1367–1461 it was taken many times by the Kings of Castile. In 1461 it finally fell to the Crown of Castile through Ferdinand and Isabella.

Santa María de los Reyes: The site was probably occupied by the monastery of a military order of monks. The church tower of the building visible today looks as if it was once part of a fortification. The church itself was begun in the 12C in Romanesque style and has a nave, two aisles and a cloister. Building continued into the 13&14C, when Gothic elements were introduced. The unusual *portal* is late 14C and a masterpiece of

Spanish Gothic carving. There are larger than life-size statues of the Apostles standing on intricately decorated pedestals and covered by splendid tabernacles. The *tympanum* is in three parts and depicts scenes from the life of the Virgin Mary. The *high altar* of 1618–22 is by the sculptors Lope de Mendieta and Tomás Manrique; Juan de Bascardo also collaborated on it. There are two more altars, which are late-17C baroque, by Diego Jiménez and Martín de Arenalde. The choir stalls (1720) are by Antonio de Herrera. The *church treasure* is kept in the sacristy. The furnishings are 18C.

San Juan Bautista: This church was begun in Romanesque style and work continued through the 13&14C in Gothic. It was extended in the 16C and further altered in the 17&18C. On of a Latin cross groundplan, it has a nave, two aisles, two apses and a large Gothic chapel. The *S. portal* is 12C Romanesque with sculptures of the Annunciation. The Gothic *tower* is fortified and may have been part of the town defences. The baroque *high altar* dates from 1694 and is by Francisco Jiménez. There are many interesting works of art in the church, including a Christ, a Mater Dolorosa and a St.John opposite the baptistery, all 15C. The Renaissance choir stalls are by Esteban Bertin and Nicolás von Harlem and date from 1558. The *sacristy*, which has wall paintings by Pedro Baldini, has some fine Renaissance furniture. The *Capilla Nuestra Señora del Pilar* stands on the site of the original main entrance; it is an octagonal baroque structure of 1732–40 by Juan Bautista de Arbayza. There is a 14C image of the Virgin Mary (painted in 16 – 17C) over the original portal.

Environs: There are some *dolmen* along the Haro-Logroño road, including the largest in the Pyrenees. There are also some interesting remains of Celtic and Ro-

Laguardia, Santa María de los Reyes, portal detail

man settlements, finds from which are on display in the Laguardia archaeological museum.

La Guardia
Toledo/New Castile   p.392☐G 6

Iglesia Parroquial: The parish church contains the 14C *Virgen de Pera*, a polychrome carving. The Virgin is uncrowned and holds a pear (Spanish *pera*) in one hand and the Child in the other.

Capilla de la Concepción: Built 1631–2; attached to the church and decorated with *frescos* by the Italian painter Angelo Nardi. The vaulting, dome and arches are decorated with angels. The sacristy con-tains two oil paintings from the Neapolitan school, probably workshop replicas or copies of works by Caravaggio.

Ermito del Santo Niño: This hermitage is outside the city walls and contains a 16C Castilian altarpiece which narrates in eight panels the story of the martyrdom of *Niño de La Guardia*.

Environs: Corral de Almaguer (*c.* 30 km. E.): The *parish church*, which was originally Gothic, has a nave and two aisles; the S. door is 16C Plateresque. The gilded and painted portal of the *Capilla de los Gascó* is also 16C Plateresque. The *Capilla de los Collado* has a small carved and gilded Plateresque altarpiece from 1535. **Tembleque** (10 km. S.): The single-aisled 16C *parish church* is transitional

Gothic-Renaissance, and has a Latin cross ground plan. The Gothic main portal is to the W.; the N. portal is 17C Renaissance. The interior is divided into four sections and the ceiling has pointed groin vaulting supported on Renaissance columns and Gothic pillars. The *Capilla del Baptisterio* and the *Capilla de San Ramón* have remained unaltered.

La Junquera
Gerona/Catalonia   p.390□O 2

This town is in Alto Ampurdán and stands on the French border. Numerous *dolmens* have been discovered here, as elsewhere in the region, e.g. Can Boleta and Can Nadal.

Environs: Requesens (12 km. NE): *Castle and Sanctuary of Santa María de Requesens*: The old church was built in 844 and remains are still standing; the new one dates from the 17C. The castle, built under the Counts of Roussillon to mark the Ampurian frontier, was restored in the 19C.

La Ñora
Murcia/Murcia   p.396□K 9

San Jerónimo de Ñora: This monastery, known as the 'Escorial de Mercia', was built in Herrera style in 1579. The church, which dates from 1790, has a statue of *The Penance of St. Jerome* (1795) by Francisco Salzillo, which is one of the artist's finest pieces.

Lanzarote
Las Palmas de Gran Canaria/
Canary Islands   p.396□O 9

The fourth largest of the islands with an area of 307 sq. miles. It is actually a small archipelago with six smaller islands off its coast.
Lanzarote was discovered by the Mauritanian King Juba in 25 BC, but took its name from the Genoese Lanzarote Malocello, who landed here in 1312. After its conquest by the Normans under Jean de Béthencourt in 1402, it became the seat of the Bishop of the Canary Islands (1404).

The bare, stony countryside contains some 300 volcanic craters. Despite the shortage of water, the lava-free areas, such as the NE corner, are surprisingly fertile. The cause of this fertility is the black volcanic ash from the craters which has been spread over the soil. This ash absorbs the moisture from the sea air at night and then passes it on to the plants.

Arrecife: The island's capital is set on a broad plain on the E. coast; the *Castillo San Gabriel*, which can be reached from the town by a drawbridge, was built by Torriani in the 16C. The *Castillo San José* dates from 1779. The *Iglesia San Ginés* is dedicated to the patron saint of the island.

Teguise: Situated at the foot of the Guanapay volcano in the centre of the island, Teguise was for centuries the island's capital. The *church of San Miguel* has a statue of the Madonna. The 15C *Castillo de Santa Barbara* on the mountain summit was altered by Torriani in 1596.

La Palma
Santa Cruz de Tenerife/
Canary Islands   p.396□L 9/10

This island, which is barely 30 miles long and shaped like a human heart, was formed from one of the world's largest craters, the *Caldera de Taburiente* (5.5 miles across,

arms and examples of the balconies so typical of the islands, leads into the Plaza de España, with the *Ayuntamiento*, a fine Renaissance building from Philip II's reign (1563). The *Castillo Santa Catalina* was built in the second half of the 16C according to plans of Juan Bautista Antonello, and then rebuilt in 1685 by the engineer Miguel Rosell. The *Museo Provincial de Bellas Artes* contains ancient finds and 19C paintings.

Environs: Santuario de las Nieves (*c.* 4 km.): Consecrated to the island's patron saint, the small 15C church contains the *Virgen de las Nieves* (Virgin of the Snow), which stands on the high altar and is made of heavy Mexican silver. **Cueva del Belmaco:** A cave 12 km. from Mazo, where the last king of the native population sought refuge from the Spanish. There are spiral patterns on the walls which are as yet undeciphered, but which seem to be inscriptions from the Guanche civilization.

Santa Cruz de la Palma, parish church

6,560 ft. deep). It was the last of the Canary Islands to be captured by the Spanish, falling in 1492, after seven months' heavy fighting. Rich vegetation has led to its being known as the 'green island'.

Santa Cruz de la Palma: The parish church of *El Salvador* has a Renaissance portal, and a coffered pine Mudéjar ceiling. In the sacristy there is Gothic vaulting, the only example on the island. The panel of the *Transfiguration of Christ* on the wall behind the altar is by the painter Esquivel. The church of *Santo Domingo* has the original tower. Further religious buildings include, the monastery of *Santo Domingo* with a fine baroque retable on the high altar, *Santa Catalina*, *San Francisco* and *Santa Clara*. The *Calle Real*, which contains some old houses with coats-of-

La Puebla de Montalbán
Toledo/New Castile   p.392☐F 6

Parish Church: Dedicated to the *Virgen de la Paz*, a polychrome Gothic carving. The *Capilla de las Reliquias*, or *Sagrario* contains a polychrome reclining Christ, a 17C Castilian work.

Church of the Convento de Nuestra Señora de la Concepción: This 16C Renaissance church in Plateresque style is built of ashlars and has a Latin cross ground plan. The *interior* contains various forms of pilasters: the shorter ones are Corinthian, the longer ones are decorated with nude male and female torsos, and display Italian influence.

Ermita de Nuestra Señora de la

Laredo, fishermen's memorial

Soledad: The interior contains *frescos* by the brothers Luis and Alejandro González Velázquez (painted in 1741–2). There is a marble and jasper piece on the end wall. One of the altarpieces in the transept contains an oil painting depicting the *Tears of St.Peter*; it is dated 1635 and signed by José de Ribera.

Torre de San Miguel: This early-17C tower is Renaissance in style and has a square ground plan. The lower section, which rests on stone foundations, is made of rubble masonry and bricks. The W. side is interrupted by a semicircular arch.

Castle of the Condes de la Puebla de Montalbán: Built in the mid-15C by the first Lord of la Puebla de Montalbán and continued by his successors. The most remarkable part is the *portal*, a 16C Plateresque Renaissance work. The *interior* contains an unusual 16C pine ceiling, gilded and painted in Gothic, Plateresque and Mudéjar styles.

Environs: Erustes (*c.* 20 km. NW): The *parish church* has a 15C Mudéjar tower; the sanctuary ceiling and the ends of the aisles are in the same style. The sanctuary is richly decorated with star patterns, but the ceiling of the nave is in squares with simple motifs. **Torrijos** (15 km. N.): The *parish church*, an early-16C collegiate church, is in transitional Gothic-Renaissance style, with a Plateresque portal over the main, W. entrance. There is another door in the same style, although more simply decorated, on the S. side. The bell tower is Gothic with Plateresque decorations and has a slate roof. The church has a nave and two aisles, and the altarpiece of the high altar is 16C Plateresque. The *Hospital de la Santísima Trinidad*, also known as 'del Cristo de la Sangre', is in early-16C Gothic-Renaissance transitional style and, although it has been much renovated, part of the church and courtyard are original.

Laredo
Santander/Old Castile   p.388□G 1

Nuestra Señora de la Asunción: This 13C church has a 16C Gothic portal which still shows Romanesque influence. It has a nave and two aisles, groin vaulting and two chapels. The 18C sacristy is behind the two polygonal apses and contains two large gilded bronze lecterns, a gift from Charles I.

Also worth seeing: The 16C *Town Hall*, which has a large portico and a bust of Charles I by Pérez Comendador; remains of the old *town walls*, as well as several *mansions* and *palaces*.

Environs: About 20 km. S. of Laredo is **Ramales de la Victoria:** The *parish church* has a baroque altarpiece; other sights include the 18C *Palace of the Counts of Revillagigedo*, and the *Caves of Covalanas, la Haza, Sotarriza* and *Cullalvera*, which contain prehistoric rock paintings. **Santoña** (*c.* 10 km. N.): The church of *Santa María del Puerto* dates from 1135 and contains a nave, two aisles, groin vaulting and a transept with a stellar vault. It has a neo-Gothic altarpiece with 16C Flemish paintings and another altarpiece, in Plateresque style, with four reliefs and six Flemish paintings; the *Monastery of San Sebastián de Ano* contains the tomb of Barbara Blomberg of Regensburg, the mother of Don Juan of Austria.

Las Ventas con Peña Aguilera
Toledo/New Castile   p.392□F 7

Iglesia Parroquial: This parish church was built in Gothic style in the 15/early 16C; it has a nave and two aisles and a main chapel with a square apse. The *interior* of the main chapel has groin vaulting, with carved and painted key-stones depicting the Keys of Peter, the patron saint of the church. The altarpiece of the high altar is Renaissance (early-17C Plateresque); the Renaissance main portal is late 16C and made of granite. In the 17C the *Capilla de la Concepción* was added on to the right side. This square Renaissance chapel has a dome. The 14/early 15C tower is also of interest: it is Mudéjar with a rectangular ground plan.

Ermita de Nuestra Señora del Aguila: A hermitage just outside the village dedicated to the Virgin of Aguila; the image is made of an alloy of silver and tin and dates from the late 12C/early-13C. There is also a Renaissance reliquary of 1577 by Pedro Angel, which is finely crafted in gilded and chased silver.

Also worth seeing: At the foot of the Cerro del Aguila, in the barren area of Peña Aguilera there is an old Medieval necropolis with 20 graves in the hillside.

Environs: Hontanar (*c.* 30 km. W.): The *Torre de Malamoneda*, a square 14C tower, whose lower section is made of large stones and the upper part of masonry and ashlars. Only the N. wall still stands. The *necropolis* in the NW, near the tower, comprises 100 graves cut in the granite cliffs and shaped in rectangles like sarcophagi. The *castle* is 440 yards from the tower. The four ramparts have neither windows nor projections. The entrance, a semicircular arch, is in the W. wall. The interior is in disarray, without roof or vaulting. **Navaher-**

mosa (*c.* 26 km. W.): The *Castillo de las dos Hermanas* to the E. of the village is Moorish in origin and dates from 11–12C. Its name derives from its location on one of two crags. Much of the wall has been preserved, and there is an entrance with a pointed arch on the E. side. **San Martín de Montalbán** (*c.* 20 km. NW): The *Castillo de Montalbán* is one of the oldest fortifications still standing on the left bank of the Tajo; it was rebuilt in the 12C by the Knights Templar and then later renovated. **Melque** (near San Martín de Montalbán): the *Hermitage of Santa María* is 9–10C Mozarabic and in a state of disrepair.

Lebrija
Sevilla/Andalusia   p.394 □ D 10

Santa María: This 16C parish church is a converted Almohaden mosque: the 18C *tower* was clearly once a minaret. The Mudéjar interior, has a nave, two aisles and horseshoe arches; the aisles are vaulted over by four domes. The fine *retable* (1636) is by Alonso Cano.

Ermita del Castillo: A hermitage founded in 1535. The interior consists of two aisles, with a splendid artesonado ceiling.

Also worth seeing: The *church of La Vera Cruz* with a crucifix by Martínez Montañés.

Ledesma
Salamanca/León   p.386 □ D/E 4/5

Santa María: The church was built during Ferdinand II's reign in the 12C, but the nave is 15C. The *Capilla Mayor* is in the style of Rodrigo Gil de Hontañón, and there are Gothic and Renaissance tombs dating from the 14–16C.

Also worth seeing: The 16C church of *San Pedro*; the Romanesque parish church of *Santa Elena* with a 16C nave; the Romanesque churches of *San Miguel* and *San Pedro*, both in a state of disrepair. The medieval *town walls*, however, are well preserved. There is a medieval *bridge* with pointed arches. 7 km. away is the *Baños de Ledesma*, a warm sulphur spring and a Roman brick vault.

León
León/León   p.386 □ E 2

León is the provincial and regional capital, and has some 120,000 inhabitants. It is situated 2,736 ft. above sea level on a picturesque plain with an attractive view over to the nearby Cantabrian mountains. Its history goes back to Roman times. In 68 AD the Emperor Galba made it the seat of a procurator and stationed the VII legion there to ward off the Asturian advance. From 910 until 1230 León was the capital of the kingdom of the same name. After its sacking by the Moors under Almanzor in 988, when half of it was destroyed, it recovered and flourished under Alfonso V (999–1027) to became the most important city in Christian Spain, partly because of its role as a trading post and stopping-off point on the pilgrim route between Mont-Saint-Michel and Santiago. It retained this status until the kingdoms of León and Castile merged, after which its importance diminished.

Colegiata de San Isidoro: The original building was probably a simple 9C church (it is mentioned in 966) and is dedicated to John the Baptist and St.Pelayo of Córdoba. Destroyed by Almanzor in 988, it was later rebuilt by Alfonso V and subsequently rebuilt in stone by his daughter, Doña Sancha, and her husband Ferdinand I, the first king of León and Castile. Fer-

León, San Isidoro

León, San Isidoro, interior

dinand had the relics of St.Isidore transferred here from Seville and also St. Vincent's from Ávila. The church was consecrated on 21 December 1063; Ferdinand I died in it five days later. The church was rebuilt and enlarged in the late 11C/early 12C, and reconsecrated in 1149. The building we see today is largely from this period. Its ground plan is in the form of a Latin cross with a nave, two aisles and three apses, of which the central one was replaced by a Gothic choir (by Juan de Badajoz, 1513). The chief architect was Petro de Deo, to whom there is a plaque in the SW corner of the church. As befits the importance of this church, its capitals are of exceptionally high quality, and include warriors, beautiful lattice-work, mythical beasts and strange monsters. The two S. portals are 12C; the W. one, the

Puerta del Cordero, is the more richly decorated. On either side of the tympanum are the figures of St.Isidore and St.Pelayo, both of which date from around 1064, along with the friezes with animal figures, which are probably from the original building. The tympanum itself depicts Abraham sacrificing Isaac, over which there is a Lamb of God (El Cordero) flanked by two hovering angels. The gable has an 18C equestrian statue of St.Isidore. The portal of the S. transept, the *Puerta del Perdon* (Door of Forgiveness), is by another artist. Its tympanum depicts the Crucifixion, with the three Marys on the right and Christ's Ascension on the left. Opposite this, in the N. transept, is the *Puerta de la Sala Capitular*, which is similar in construction. The four capitals are decorated with flower and animal motifs. They seem

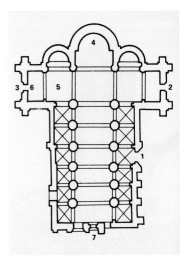

León, Colegiata de San Isidoro 1 Puerta del Cordero (main portal) **2** Puerta del Perdon **3** Puerta de la Sala Capitular, which leads to the chapterhouse **4** Capilla Mayor, with 16C retable **5** Capilla San Martín **6** Capilla de los Quiñones **7** original entrance to the Panteón de los Reyes

León, San Isidoro, Panteón de los Reyes

to be by the same hand as the main portal, although the N. portal is somewhat earlier. Of the 28 windows (10 below, 18 above) illuminating the 56 ft. high interior, 15 are Romanesque, as indeed is much of the interior. The *font* on the left of the entrance has some interesting 11C sculptures; the altar retable in the *Capilla Mayor* is 16C. There is a silver casket on the altar with the relics of St. Isidore; the 16C *Capilla San Martín* contains the bones of St.Martin. It leads into the Romanesque *Capilla de los Quiñones*, which has interesting capitals and frescos. The huge Romanesque tower, which is almost an integral part of the city wall, is 12C and stands on the W. side in front of the pantheon.

Panteón de los Reyes: The large crypt-like portico, which is groin-vaulted with sturdy columns, was built in 1054–66 to the W. of San Isidoro. The first monarchs to be buried in this royal mausoleum were King Alfonso V and the royal couple, Doña Sancha and Ferdinand I. Altogether the mausoleum houses the remains of 11 kings, 12 queens, 21 princes and many nobles. The mausoleum was initially a kind of portico to the W. of and on the same level as San Isidoro; it has a gallery for the royal family when they attended church services. The oldest monumental Romanesque interior in Spain, it measures 23 ft. by 30 ft. The groin vaulting is supported by two sturdy white marble pillars, from which wall arches project to the pilasters. The *capitals*

León, San Isidoro, Panteón de los Reyes, fresco

León, San Isidoro, cloister

León, San Isidoro, Panteón de los Reyes, capital

display Lombard influence and are among the earliest examples of genuine Romanesque sculpture in Spain. Some of the 30 capitals are entirely ornamental, with acanthus leaves, pineapples, gryphons, birds, and figures. Those by the original entrance depict the Raising of Lazarus and the Cleansing of the Lepers. Other capitals show Abraham sacrificing Isaac, Daniel in the lion's den, fighting dragons and mythical beasts including a unicorn. The Panteón de los Reyes is particularly well known for its *Romanesque frescos*, which have earned it the title of the *Sistine Chapel of Romanesque Art*. They date from Ferdinand II's reign (1157–88) and are preserved almost in their entirety; they cover the six rectangular vault sections and the E. and S. walls of the interior. The E. bay has Christ Pantocrator in the centre, with the Angel appearing to the Shepherds to the S. and the Apocalypse to the N. The W. side features the Last Supper in the centre, and to the S. the Massacre of the Innocents; that in the N. is unfortunately missing. The S. wall shows the Annunciation and Visitation, and nearby are the Epiphany, Flight into Egypt and Presentation in the Temple. The E. wall depicts the Lamb of God (in the tympanum), with a Crucifixion to the N. There are also some fine *friezes*, partly ornamental and partly illustrating Biblical scenes and the months. *Cloister:* The pantheon leads into a 16C cloister, which is surrounded by several chapels. Before reaching the cloister the visitor passes an 8C Visigoth font and the sarcophagi of princes and kings.

Tesoro: The way into the pantheon takes the visitor through the treasury and library, both of which contain some fine exhibits. The *library* contains a number of old manuscripts, including a Bible from 960 and a 15C breviary with ornate miniatures by Nicolas Francés. The *treasury* contains

León, cathedral, portal (detail)

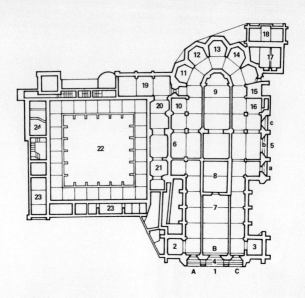

León, Cathedral 1 W. façade with portico and three portals (A,B,C) **2** Torre de las Campanas **3** Torre del Reloj **4** Nuestra Señora la Blanca **5** S. façade with portico and three portals **6** Puerta del Dado **7** Trascoro **8** Coro **9** Capilla Mayor **10** Capilla de Santa Teresa **11** Capilla del Nacimiento **12** Capilla del Rosario **13** Capilla del Salvador **14** Capilla de San Antonio **15** Capilla del Cristo **16** Capilla del Carmen **17** sacristy **18** oratory **19** Capilla de Santiago or Capilla de la Virgen del Camino **20** Capilla de San Andrés **21** Antigua Capilla de Santa Teresa **22** cloister **23** museum **24** chapterhouse

the precious *Reliquary of St. Isidore*, which dates from around 1063 and was presented to San Isidoro as a gift from King Ferdinand I and his wife Doña Sancha. 5 of the 6 embossed and gilded silver reliefs depict the Creation of Man, the Fall and the Expulsion from Paradise. Another fine piece is the *chalice*, which was left to San Isidoro by Doña Urraca on her death in 1101. It is made of agate, and has cameos picked out

in gold and precious stones. Of the *reliquary cross* of St. John the Baptist and St. Pelayo which dates from 1059 and which was a gift from the royal couple, the ivory panels with the figures of the 12 Apostles and 13 panels on the lid still survive. The 12C *enamel casket from Limoges* is also of interest; as are the 16C processional cross by Juan de Arfe, the 10C Moorish casket and numerous other pieces.

Cathedral of Santa María de Regla: In 1205 Bishop Manrique of Lara commissioned the building of the 'Pulchra Leonina', or Jewel of Léon. Work proceeded slowly at first, but was well under way by the middle of the century and continued until the beginning of the 14C. The cathedral's ground plan is based on that of Rheims, and the exterior is reminiscent of

León, cathedral

Amiens; it is built in purest Gothic style in yellow sandstone and appears as a symphony of stone and light. It has a Latin cross groundplan, a nave and two aisles and a tripartite transept. It is 295 ft. long, 131 ft. wide and 128 ft. high over the nave. The *W. façade*, which is grand and impressive is flanked by two huge towers, the Torre de las Campanas (213 ft. high) and the Torre del Reloj (a late Gothic clock tower, 223 ft. high). It has a massive rose window above the portico, which has three portals. The central column of the huge middle portal bears *Nuestra Señora la Blanca*, a splendid Madonna. The crowned Queen of Heaven is flanked by saints on each side of the doorway. The tympanum depicts Christ Pantocrator with angels and instruments of torture. The frieze below shows an angel with the scales of justice, with the damned on the left and the elect on the right. This theme is further elaborated in the archivolts. The left portal shows the Childhood of Jesus, and the right portal, which is named after St. Francis, has two fine sculptures of prophets. The decorations on all three doorways date from the second half of the 13C.

S. portal: This also has a tripartite portico with a huge rose-window above it. The ornate decoration of figures is reminiscent in places of the cathedral at Burgos. The *N. portal*, the Puerta del Dado, is at the opposite end of the transept where it opens into the cloisters. It is the oldest portal in the church and has some splendidly preserved paintwork and sculpture. There is a Virgin Mary on the central pillar under the tympanum.

Interior: Upon entering the church, the visitor is immediately struck by the light from the *stained-glass windows*. There are some 19,400 sq. ft. of coloured glass (some of which is 39 ft. high) with 57 openings as well as rose-windows such as the three huge ones above the portals. They date from the 13C to the 20C; the oldest are in the N. transept, the *Capilla Mayor* and the fine N. and W. rose-windows. The windows of the Santiago Chapel are Renaissance-influenced. The motifs depicted in this world of coloured glass include the trivium and the quadrivium, the Vices and Virtues, saints, earthly rulers, the mitre and staff, the sceptre and crown and plant decoration.

Trascoro: The gilded alabaster trascoro with its rich array of figures is a Renaissance piece dating from 1576. It was designed by Baltasar Gutiérrez and executed by Esteban Jordán. The central arch is framed by four reliefs and offers a view into the nave. Above the arch is a crucifix by Bautista Vázquez. The *coro* is one of Spain's oldest, dating from the second half of the 15C and constructed under the supervision of Flamen Jusquin; the *choir stalls* were completed between 1467–81 by Flemish carvers under the direction of Juan de Malina: his colleagues included Fadrique Alemán, Jorge Fernández and Diego Copin de Holanda, who also worked on parts of the high altar in Toledo. There is a fine Plateresque grille in front of the *Capilla Mayor*, whose winged altar was restored in 1724 by Narcisco and Simón Gavilán Tomé but still contains older parts from the first half of the 15C by Nicolás Francés (notably the Entombment on the left). The 16C silver shrine by Enrique de Arfe, which stands in front of the altar, contains the relics of St.Froilán. There is also a 16C silver monstrance, a Pietà by R. van der Weyden and a 15C bishop's throne.

ARITMETICA

GEOICA

León, cathedral, portal

The contents of the individual chapels (see ground plan) is also interesting: the most impressive items are the early-14C *tomb of King Ordoño II* (d. 924), which stands against the back wall of the Capilla Mayor, the tomb of Bishop *Rodrigo* (d. 1532), the Renaissance tomb of *St. Pelayo*, the tomb of Bishop *Manrique de Lara* (d. 1232), the church's founder, the 16C *Calvary* by Juan de Valmaseda in the Capilla del Cristo and *St. Theresa* by Gregorio Fernández. The most impressive of the chapels are the *Capilla de Santiago*, or *de la Virgen del Camino*, which has splendid stained-glass windows and carved ornament, and the *Capilla de San Andrés* with its 13C Gothic portal. The *cloisters* are 14C (altered in 1540) with frescos (1460–8) by Nicolás Francés, only some of which have survived. The Plateresque steps leading to the chapterhouse are by Juan de Badajoz. *Museum:* The cathedral museum, which is housed in a section of the cloisters, contains paintings, sculptures and manuscripts. There is a 10C Mozarabic *antiphonal*, a 6C *palimpsest*, an 11C *Lex Romana Visigothorum*, a 10C Visigoth Bible, a crucifix by Juan de Juni, a 13C Archangel Gabriel from the S. portal, a polychrome statue of King Ordoño II, Romanesque sculptures, a 16C Madonna and Child, an Adoration of the Magi, some 16C paintings by Pedro de Campaña, Gothic and Mudéjar caskets etc. Opposite the cathedral on the S. side is the *Seminario Mayor*, which houses the interesting *Diocesan Museum* (sculptures etc.).

San Marcos: Ferdinand and Isabella founded the Convento de San Marcos in

Léon, cathedral, high altar

León in the 16C in gratitude for the Knights of Santiago's help in wresting Spain back from the Moors. The site was previously occupied by a 12C hospital for pilgrims to Santiago, founded by the Order of Santiago. Work on the building we see today began in 1513, and the church was completed in 1541; it was finally completed under the supervision of Juan de Badajoz in 1549. Additions continued to be made to the complex until 1716. The most striking aspect of the exterior is the 328 ft. Plateresque *façade*, which is decorated with a richness of decorative elements, pilasters and medallions depicting famous individuals quite unprecedented in Spanish architecture. The E. wing, which is decorated with shell shapes, is joined to the unfinished cathedral, and on the other side is the monastery's 18C baroque main

portal. The old part of the monastery consists of the impressive *stairs*, the splendid 16C *cloisters*, the *chapterhouse* with its Mudéjar panelling and the Gothic *church*, of which the Renaissance choir and choir stalls are impressive works by Guillermo Doncel. The church also contains scenes from the Passion by Juan de Horoco and Juan de Juni. The monastery itself has been renovated, and now contains the luxury *San Marcos* hotel and the *Provincial Archaeological Museum*, where Celtic and Roman finds are among those on display. There is an impressive altar to Diana, an *ivory Christ by Carizzo*, a Byzantine-influenced 11C Romanesque carving and further sculptures and paintings.

Other Churches of Interest: The *Iglesia del Salvador del Nido* contains a 16C

León, San Marcos, façade

and rebuilt in the 11C. Part of the tower dates from this period, but the majority of the building we see today is by Juan del Rivero and Baltasar Gutiérrez. The high altar is 18C, with a crucifix by Gregorio Fernández. *San Martín* was originally 11C, but was altered in the 13&16C and largely rebuilt in the 18C. It has an interesting Pietà by Luis Salvador Carmona (1750) and sculptures in the style of Gregorio Fernánez. *Santa María del Mercado* (12C) has a nave and two aisles and combines Romanesque and Byzantine elements; it has a 15C Pietà. *Santa Marina de la Real* was built in 1571, and contains a Madonna and Child and St.John by Esteban Jordán and St.Ignatius Loyola by an artist from the school of Gregorio Fernández. Some 6 km. away is the *Santuario de la Virgen del Camino*, a fine example of contemporary religious architecture by Coello de Portugal. This pilgrimage church is dedicated to the patron saint of the area, and its bronze doors and statues (Descent of the Holy Spirit) on the façade by José María Subirach are worth mentioning.

Other interesting monasteries: The *Convento de Carvajal* was built in 1583, and has a fine 16C retable and a Pietà (1658) by Antonio Arias. The *Convento de la Concepción* has a 15C portal, and the *Convento de las Descalzas* was founded in 1606.

Also worth seeing: The *Consistorio (Antiguo)* on the Plaza Mayor was built in 1677; the *Ayuntamiento* on the Plaza de San Marcelo is an impressive Renaissance building, built in 1585 by Juan del Rivero. The *Casa de Botines,* a work by the contemporary architectural genius Antonio Gaudí, was built in neo-Gothic style at the end of the 19C. The *Palacio de los Guzmanes* was built in the second half of the 16C by Juan de Quiñones and Guzman. It has a remarkable Plateresque patio, a grand staircase and Renaissance sculpture. The *Palacio del Conde de Luna* has a 14C

Pietà by Bautista Vázquez; the *Iglesia del Salvador de Palaz de Rey* is regarded as León's oldest church: it was built in the 10C by Ramiro II and the remains of a Mozarabic chapel are still visible. There is a 16C polychrome wooden statue by Juan de Juni. *San Francisco* (originally 13C, but rebuilt in the 15&19C) has a baroque retable from the old church, built in 1721–4 by Simón Gavilán Tomé and Narcisco Tomé. *San Juan y San Pedro de Renaeva* has a portal from the Monasterio de Eslonza, begun by Juan de Badajoz in 1547 and finally completed by Juan del Rivero in 1719. *San Lorenzo* (originally 12C but later restored) has some 16C paintings of St.Lawrence and the Apostles. *San Marcelo* (1588 - 1627) is on the Plaza Marcelo and stands on the site of a 10C church which was destroyed by Almanzor

León, Casa de Botines

portal and 16C tower. The *Palacio de los Ponce de León* is 14C. The *Colegio de Teresianes* has remains of a 12C Romanesque building. Finally there are remains of the Roman *city walls*, which were dismantled by Almanzor in the 10C and rebuilt in the 11C, with their semicircular towers. 3 km. outside the city (towards Villaquilambre) are the ruins of the *Villa Romana de Navate-Jera* from the 3&4C with remains of mosaics and sculptures.

Lequeitio
Vizcaya/Basque Provinces   p.388☐H 1

This fishing village is situated on a charming bay, which is sheltered by the wooded island of San Nicolás.

Santa María de la Asunción: Consecrated in 1287. It was damaged by fire in 1442, as a result of which only the apse remained intact; rebuilt 1488–1508 as a late Gothic basilica with a nave and two aisles, which are separated by graceful arched buttresses. The *main portal* has some fine sculptures, and a gable with figures surmounted by splendid tabernacles. The nave has a five-bayed narthex with a triforium under the huge window. On the right are a sacristy and three chapels. The breathtaking *high altar* of 1508 comprises a number of free-standing sculptures with tabernacles and depicts scenes from the lives of Christ and the Virgin Mary. The statue of the Virgin, from the same period as the altar, is a copy of the *Virgen de la Antigua*, the patron saint of Lequeitio. The altarpiece in the *Capilla de Santa Ana* is

León, Santuario de la Virgen del Camino

late 15C, the work of a Flemish master, probably from one of the Brussels workshops. Another altar, baroque in style, bears a plain sculpture of the Virgin, *Nuestra Señora de la Antigua*, which is thought to be 12C.

Also worth seeing: The two towers, *Torre de Licona* and *Torre Turpín*, from the town's defences and the fortified hermitage *Ermita de Santa Catalina de Ansorz*. The caves of *Cumencha* have yielded several prehistoric discoveries.

Lérida

Lérida/Catalonia   p.390☐L 4

The northern part of the province of

Lérida borders on France and Andorra with the Pyrenees forming a natural frontier. The countryside is exceptionally beautiful, especially the Arán Valley, the Aigüe Tortes National Park with Lake San Mau ricio, and the valleys of Aneu, Cardós, Ferrera, Urgellet and Cerdaña. The main city Lérida, is on the Río Segre, in the south of the province. The Iberian Ilergeten clan founded their main settlement here and called it *Iltirda*. The two chiefs Indíbil and Mandonio defended it for years against the *Carthaginians* and the *Romans*, until it was eventually taken by the Romans and named *Ilerda*. Under Roman rule a bridge was built over the Segre and the city was enclosed by walls. It was, however, captured by the Visigoths and then shortly after by the *Moors*, who changed its name to *Lareda*. Hence its nickname 'Ciudad de lo

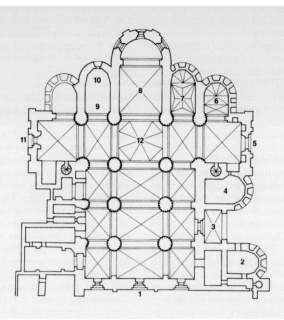

Nombres' (city of names). In 1149 Ramón Berenguer IV freed it from the Moors, and in 1300 James II founded a university: the Estudio General de Lérida. The city walls and much else besides were destroyed by fighting in 1464, and in 1810 it was besieged by the French.

Catedral Vieja: (The old cathedral; Seu Vella in Catalan.) Founded in 1203 and built to the plans of four architects (Pere Sa Coma, Berenguer de Coma and the Pennafreita brothers); consecrated in 1278. Building continued until the 16C, so its style encompasses Romanesque and Gothic. It has a nave, two aisles and transept on a Latin cross groundplan. The *interior*, Cistercian in its proportions, is not unlike the church of Santes Creus. The *nave*, which is wider than the aisles, is

divided from them by six pillars with attached columns, which support a rib vault. The aisles are Romanesque and have windows decorated with columns and capitals. There is a Romanesque dome over the *crossing*, which also has Gothic features. The *main apse* is round, and the four smaller ones are Gothic chapels (that on the extreme right was destroyed in 1812). The cathedral also has a number of interesting portals: three doorways lead from the main façade into the cloisters, of which the middle one (1210) has three columns on each side and decorated archivolts (1). The *Puerta de la Anunciata* (5), on the S. side, has superbly carved archivolts and capitals with flower and animal motifs. To the left and right of the portal there are some empty niches, which formerly contained two Romanesque figures of the Virgin Mary and angels, as a result of which it was known as the *Portal of the Annunciation*. The N. portal (11), known as the *Portal de San Berenguer*, is a plain doorway with round arches. The *Puerta del Fillols* (3) was once the church's main portal; similar to the others in style, its good proportions make it the foremost example of the Lérida school. Some of the church's capitals can be attributed to this school, which is itself influenced by the school of Toulouse. One of the cathedral's peculiarities is the positioning of the late-13C cloisters, which are in front of the main façade. The arcade on the façade opens out on to a garden; the opposite side has large windows affording a splendid view of the city. The *Puerta de los Apostoles*, which

leads from the cloisters to the outside, is 14C. The *bell tower* was built in the 14–15C by the architects Castalls and Carlí. It has an octagonal ground plan and a height of 198 ft. 10 in. but remains incomplete.

New Cathedral (Calle Carmelitas): Lérida's second cathedral was begun in 1761, with Francisco Sabatini directing the work according to the plans of M.Cermeño (permission originally having been granted by King Charles III). The Bourbon coats-of-arms are displayed on the façade. The *interior* consists of a nave, two aisles, transept, apse and ambulatory. The vaulting is supported by pillars; only some of the side chapels have altars. The choir stalls, which had 103 carved figures by Luis de Bonifás, were destroyed during the Civil War. The *high altar* has some fine paintings by Serrasanta. This leads through to the *sacristy*, which serves as an archive for thousands of important 12–17C documents, and then on to the *chapterhouse*, the site of the cathedral treasury which in-

Lérida, Catedral Vieja, cloister, capital

udes a valuable collection of paintings by
nton Raphael Mengs, Guido Reni, etc.

an Lorenzo (Plaza San José, on the cor-
er of the Plazoleta del Obispo): This
1urch has a nave and two aisles and was
uilt in transitional Romanesque-Gothic
yle. The *nave* has barrel vaulting sup-
orted by 13C false columns with simple
apitals; the *aisles* are 14–15C with ribbed
aulting and windows with pointed arches
i the small pentagonal apses. The *bell
wer* is built above a small aisle. The
1urch, which for many years was Lérida's
athedral, has two *portals*, the finest of
hich is the one facing out on to the Plaza
e San José, on which the coats-of-arms of
1e founder, Berenguer Gallart, are dis-
layed. The church treasures include a
aluable 14C retable and some Gothic
gures; the high altar has the superb *retable
f San Lorenzo* with twelve scenes from the
fe of the saint based on Jacobus de
'oragine's 'Legenda Aurea', and a life-size
gure of the saint in the tabernacle. The
isle contains Jaime Cascalls' *retable of*

Santa Úrsula, which depicts scenes from
the lives of the saint and her companions.
The *retable of San Pedro* is by Bartomeu
Robió.

Antiguo Hospital de Santa María
(Calle San Antonio Mayor): Built in the
15C to unite the seven earlier hospitals into
one complex, this building now houses
several museums, archives and the city library. It is square, with a plain façade, and
the city's coat-of-arms, together with a
figure of the Virgin Mary surmounted by
a Gothic tabernacle, stand over the entrance. Inside, there is a fine courtyard with
Gothic arcades and elegant columns on the
first storey. The chapel, which contains a
baroque retable by Escarpenter, is on the
ground floor.

San Martín (Calle Jaime el Conquistador): This small Romanesque
church with a 13C bell gable is situated
near the medieval fortifications. It was
built on the site of a mosque, which had
been converted for Christian worship in

érida, Catedral Vieja, cloister, capital

the 12C. Almost all the *capitals* in the single-aisled interior are foliate. The *apse* and *portal* are both interesting: they were brought from Tormillo (Huesca) when the church was renovated.

Castillo de la Zuda: This castle's name is derived from the Arabic *al-sudda*, which means castle. It was originally occupied by the Moors, and later by the kings of Catalonia. Catalonia and Aragon were united here by the marriage of Ramón Berenguer IV and Petronila of Aragon in 1150. It was blown up in 1812 and 1936.

Casa de la Pahería (Plaza de la Pahería): Lérida's Town Hall is situated on the Roman Via Augusta; it was built as the Sanahuya family residence in the 13C. The fine *façade* has a round-arched portal bearing the coats-of-arms of the city and province. To the left is a stone plaque in memory of the founding of the city's first bank, the Casa de la Moneda. The first floor has five Romanesque windows, each divided into three sections, with fine columns and carved capitals. Figures of men and animals are carved on the consoles of the first floor. To the right is a small square tower.

Memorial to Indíbil and Mandonio: This memorial is reached by crossing the Puente Mayor and passing through the Puerta de Lérida. It is dedicated to the two Ilergeten chiefs who defended the city against the Romans and the Carthaginians, and was erected by M.Sanmartín in 1882.

Museo Arqueológico Provincial: The archaeological museum is housed in the Antiguo Hospital de Santa María. It was founded in 1864 and contains some interesting early and late Stone Age and also Iron Age finds, Iberian and Roman collections, Visigoth and Jewish objects.

Museo Jaime Morera: Also housed in the hospital; It was opened in 1914 an houses 525 paintings by Catalan and foreign artists. It features works by Jaime Morera as well as ceramics and sculptures Also of interest in the same building is th *Coin Collection.*

Diocesan Museum (Seminario Co ciliar, Rambla de Aragón): Founded b Bishop Messeguer in 1893, this include departments of architecture, sculpture painting, iconography, furniture, numi matics, gold items, palaeography etc.

Also worth seeing: The *Castillo* Gardeny*, which is situated on the hill the same name and houses the Militar Museum. Near the castle, which was bui by the Knights Templar, is a simple chur (Santa María), with the remains of a 15 Gothic chapel.

Lerma
Burgos/Old Castile   p.388 □ G

The existence of Lerma is documente from the 10C onwards, but it seems to hav been founded as early as the 8C. It w originally settled because of its strateg position on a hill on the Arlanza. Durir the reigns of Ferdinand II and Alfonso ≻ it opposed the royal forces, but was eve tually taken by Alfonso XI after a bitt struggle. Much of the city was destroye in the course of its capture and its defe sive walls were razed to the ground on t king's instructions as a warning to the i habitants. The first Duke of Lerma, Dc Francisco Gómez de Sandoval y Rojas, w responsible for the numerous large buil ings erected during the first few years the 17C.

Ducal Palace: This was designed Francisco de Mora and built by Fr. Albe de la Madre de Dios. It stands on the si

Lérida, Catedral Vieja

Lérida, Catedral Vieja, cloister

f the old castle. The square courtyard, with its round arches, is especially fine.

Collegiate church of San Pedro: Built 1606–16, with a nave, two aisles and a fine choir. The bronze statue of Archbishop Don Cristóbal de Rojas in prayer is of particular interest. A masterpiece by Juan de Arce and his son-in-law Lesmes Fernández de Moral, it dates from 1603.

Also worth seeing: The monastery of *Santo Domingo* with a vaulted façade which ends in a flat tower; the monasteries of *San Blas*, *Santa Teresa* and *Santa Clara* are also interesting. The medieval *gateway*, which is flanked by two square towers, is all that remains of the medieval town; there are some picturesque streets and squares, including the *Calle de Reventón* and the old *marketplace*.

Environs: Castrillo de Solarana (*c.* 7 km. E.): The 12C Romanesque church of *San Pedro* has a Plateresque altarpiece; there are also a number of fine mansions nearby. **Villahoz** (*c.* 7 km. NE): The 14C Gothic *church* has a nave, two aisles and a hexagonal apse with a baroque altarpiece incorporating a large statue. **Mahamud** (*c.* 10 km. NW) is the site of the remains of some old *town walls*, a Romanesque *church* with a large altarpiece by Domingo de Amberes, a 15C *town hall* and a large palace and mansions from the 16&17C. **Santa María del Campo** (*c.* 18 km. NW): The 15C church of the *Asunción* has a high nave, two high aisles, fine Gothic choir stalls, some paintings by Pedro Berruguete and a number of tombs. The tower, by Diego de Siloé and Juan Salas, is of especial interest.

Leyre
Navarra/Navarra   p.388☐l 2

5 km. from the reservoir at Yesa is the *Leyre
monastery*, or *Monasterio de San Salvador*,
which is situated in craggy countryside on
the edge of the Sierra de Leyre. It was first
mentioned in 848, and its history is closely
tied in with the kingdom of Navarre. During the Moorish rule of the 9–10C, Leyre
was a refuge for the royal family and the
Bishops of Pamplona. The peak of its
historical importance came during the
reign of King Sancho el Mayor, his son
García de Nájera and his grandson Sancho
de Peñalén. After it was destroyed by
Almanzor, King Sancho el Mayor rebuilt
it in 1022; the Romanesque choir and
crypt were consecrated in 1057. The monastery was a Cluniac house, and a number
of inns and hospices were built along the
pilgrimage route to Santiago de Compostela. In 1307 it was handed over to the
Cistercians. It was uninhabited 1835–1954
but has since been taken over by the
Benedictines.

Monastery Church of San Salvador:
At the centre of the huge monastic complex, it marked a significant development
in Spanish Romanesque monasteries.
From the outside the most striking features
are the three semicircular apses. All the
same height they display a remarkable lin-
ear style. Containing the crypt and choir,
they lie at the end of the nave. The *choir
apse* is the oldest and most important part
of the church, being the first great example of Spanish Romanesque. The *crypt* has
a simple but unique entrance, which is
clearly Romanesque at its earliest stage.
The sturdy columns inside are impressive,
they are buried deep in the floor and
crowned with imposing but relatively plain
capitals. During the 9C, the crypt was the
royal pantheon. It contains the tombs of Iñigo Jiménez Arista, the first independent

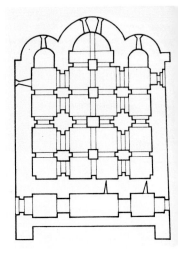

Leyre, crypt of the monastery church of San
Salvador

ruler of Navarre, Fortún Garcés, Sancho
Garcés and Sancho II Abarca. From the
crypt an interesting *portal* opens into the
large Gothic nave, which was completed
in the 14C and is an extension of the original nave and aisles. It is surrounded by a
Romanesque wall, which forms the S. side
of the nave. The influence of Jaca and Léon
is evident in the portal's design. It is decorated with a tympanum, on which the
Trinity is depicted. The nave leads out to
the very ornate *main portal*, which is
reminiscent of the Puerta de las Platerías
in Santiago de Compostela. The entrance
is divided by a column, and each group of
three columns at the side of the portal supports three arches. The columns have
decorated capitals, and the spaces between
the arches are filled with fine sculptures.
The ancient tympanum, the elegant S. portal and the capitals of the columns in the
choir all deserve special attention.

Leyre, monastery of San Salvador

Liébana
Santander/Old Castile   p.388□F 2

Monastery of Santo Toribio: This monastery was mentioned in the 8C, as being the sanctuary for the 'Lignum Crucis' which St.Toribius of Astorga brought back from Jerusalem in the 5C. Also from the 8C, is the 'Comentarios al Apocalipsis', which was written by the monk Beatus and illuminated with miniatures, and is often viewed as the beginning of Spanish medieval painting. The church is 13C in origin and consists of a nave, two aisles, groin vaulting and polygonal apses. In the 18C the baroque Chapel of the Lignum Crucis was built, with the statue of the founder, Francisco de Otero y Cissío in prayer.

Environs: Potes (*c.* 3 km. N.): The *Torre del Infantado* is a 15C fortress. **Piasca** (*c.* 6 km. E.): The Romanesque church of *Santa María la Real*, part of a Benedictine monastery in 930, was completely rebuilt and altered in 1172 and 1493. *Lebeña* (*c.* 8 km. N.): The church of *Santa María*, which dates from 930, includes examples of almost all pre-10C Spanish architectural styles: a Romanesque ground plan and apses, Mozarabic horseshoe arches and Gothic vaulting.

Liérganes
Santander/Old Castile   p.388□G 1

Palace of Rañada: This is a classical building with a façade decorated with arches.

Also worth seeing: The *house of the Pozas* has a Renaissance window built in the form of a retable; the *house of Cantolla* is 16C.

Environs: Pámanes (*c.* 5 km. N.): The *Palace of Elsedo* was built 1704–14 for the Counts of Torre-Hermosa. It is a fine example of local classical baroque architecture.

Linares
Jaén/Andalusia   p.394□G 9

Museo Arqueológico Municipal: The archaeological museum houses finds from the Carthaginian settlement of Cástulo, which was situated 7 km. N.; the site has yielded ruins and burial mounds, and also a Phoenician tomb and the remains of the walls of Roman houses.

Also worth seeing: The mining town of Linares has a number of interesting *palaces*; these include the Casa de la Cadena, the Casas Consistoriales and the Palace of the Marquis of Linares.

Environs: Bailén (13 km. W.): Late Gothic *parish church* with a baroque S. portal, which commemorates the defeat of the Napoleonic army in the battle of Bailén in 1809: the interior contains the tomb of the victorious Spanish general, Castaños y Aragori. The last side chapel on the left contains a fresco of a Madonna of the Rosary. **Baños de la Encina** (13 km. N.): The remains of a 10C Moorish *castle*. **La Carolina** (25 km. N.) has an 18C church, and a monument to the Spanish victory over the Almohades in 1212 at *Las Navas d' Tolosa* (2 km. N.). This victory was the turning point in the Reconquest of Moorish Spain. **Castellar de Santisteban** (5 km. NE): The *parish church* was built on the site of an old Moorish fortress: the bell tower stands on the site of the original tower. The Gothic structure was built in the 13C and extended in the 14C. The portal displays elements of Renaissance style. The collegiate church of *Santiago* contains 16–17C paintings. Nearby is an Iberian shrine (Cuevas del Biche) and many Ro man remains (burial sites, columns etc.) and early Stone Age ceramics.

Liria
Valencia / Valencia   p.396 □ K 6/7

This small town is some 25 km. NW of Valencia and well worth a visit. Situated in fertile countryside, it has a strong rural character. The town also has a rich history and important monuments. The Iberians knew it as *Edeta*, and their settlement survives in ruins on the Cerro de San Miguel, where painted ceramics have been found which tell us much about Iberian life. The predominant themes are hunting, warfare and dancing. There is a picture of a group of flute-players which is most life-like. These ceramics are currently housed in the Museo de Prehistoria in Valencia. It seems that this Iberian town flourished in the 3C BC. After this the troops of the Roman general Sertorius destroyed the town and settled the inhabitants elsewhere. The Romans themselves founded a new town on this plain, which they called *Lauro*. A splendid mosaic has been found here, depicting the labours of Hercules; it is now in the Museo Arqueológico Nacional in Madrid.

Iglesia de la Sangre: Liria's most important building. In a style transitional between Romanesque and Gothic, it is single-aisled with a timber ceiling and roof beams decorated with *paintings* depicting scenes of hunting and court life. There are also images of a dragon and a princess holding two large fish by the tail. The chapels have 13C wall paintings, one of which depicts a Dominican monk who is being attacked by two soldiers with lance and dagger.

Iglesia de la Asunción: This large 17C parish church has a splendid three-storeyed *façade*, with notable columns. The *interior* contains the tomb of a Duchess of Alba.

Iglesia del Buen Pastor (church of the Good Shepherd): This contains Gothic wall paintings, and Roman inscriptions and mosaics.

Ayuntamiento/Town Hall (Plaza Mayor): Housed in the Renaissance palace of the Dukes of Alba.

Environs: Benisanó (3 km. E.): A small fortress, whose Gothic structure has survived. Francis I of France, Charles V's enemy, was held prisoner here briefly after the battle of Pavia in 1525.

Llanes
Oviedo/Asturia   p.386 □ F 1

This small fishing port and seaside resort has some attractive old mansions, a massive town wall and a 17C castle with battlemented towers. The 15C Gothic church of Santa María has a fine altar of the Spanish-Flemish school.

Environs: San Antolín de Bedón: 11 km. W. of Llanes, in the direction of Ribadesella, lie the ruins of an 11C Benedictine monastery. The attached church is 13C. **Pena-Tu:** 6 km. from Llanes, in the direction of Pimiango, is the Pena-Tu cliff, with reliefs and rock paintings from the Bronze and Stone Ages. **Pimiango:** This village contains the ruins of the late-12C monastery of *Santa Ana de Tina*. It was a simple church with a nave, two aisles and three semicircular apses. **Cueva de Pindal:** Above Pimiango, on the slope of a steep rock, is the Cave of Pindal, where prehistoric drawings have been discovered.

Llansá
Gerona/Catalonia   p.390☐O 2

This small village has a fishing harbour (Port de Llansá), and is situated on the upper reaches of the Costa Brava. It has an 18C baroque *parish church*, and a shrine known as *La Mare de Deu del Port*, which dates from 1691.

Environs: San Pedro de Roda (15 km. drive inland, followed by 15 minutes on foot): Experts who have studied ruined monasteries are agreed that this is the cradle of the Catalan Romanesque style which, in contrast to the Lombard style, shows a synthesis of Visigoth and Mozarabic styles. The church was mentioned in 878 as belonging to the monastery of Banyola, and became independent in 927. It has a nave, two aisles, a transept and three apses; it was consecrated in 1023. The nave and aisles have tunnel vaulting, and the four connecting arches of the nave are supported by two rows of columns with a very high cornice, so that the impression given is one of a three-storeyed area. The columns are smooth, and the *capitals* are decorated in two different ways: the lower columns of the nave have Corinthian-style capitals with wolves' and dogs' heads, the others are decorated with loops. All the columns are said to be 11C. The monastery was expanded in 1022, with the addition of a surrounding wall and two *towers*: one, which serves as the bell tower, has four storeys, windows in a variety of styles and is decorated with the typical blind arcades which occur in all the later Romanesque churches in Catalonia. The other served as a defensive tower. The *cloister*, to the right of the church, has an irregular plan. The capitals of its columns are now housed in private collections. Only a few pieces survive of the sculptures in the main portal, which were by the Master of Cabestany: some are in the Museo Marés

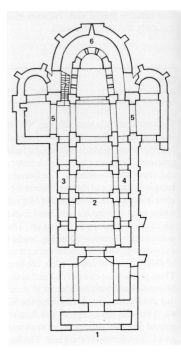

Monastery church of San Pedro de Roda The vaulting in this church is one of the earliest examples of Romanesque barrel vaulting — **1** main portal **2** nave **3** and **4** aisles **5** transept **6** ambulatory **7** staircase leading to the battlements over the ambulatory

in Barcelona and other collections. The celebrated four-volume 'Bible of Roda' (known as the 'Bible de Noailles' in the Bibliothèque Nationale in Paris), which was produced by hand during the 11C in the scriptorium here or in Ripoll, is a masterpiece of manuscript illumination.

Llerena
Badajoz/Estremadura   p.392☐D 8

This small fortified village still has some

of its surrounding walls, which were originally Moorish.

Plaza Mayor: This has Italianate double arcades on three sides. In 1618 Francisco de Zurbarán, who was staying here at the time, was commissioned to design the fountain.

Nuestra Señora de la Granada (Our Lady of the Pomegranate): This church (founded in the 13C) has two elegant arcaded galleries, which blend in with the square. The 18C brick tower is crowned by five small domed towers, rather like the Giralda in Seville. The granite foundation, with a Gothic portal, survives on the ground floor. The Plateresque main portal has a coat-of-arms incorporating a pomegranate.

Environs: The nearby village of **La Cardenchosa** has the church of *Nuestra Señora de la Paz*, which has a remarkable Gothic Mudéjar portal. **Azuaga** (35 km. E.): The parish church of *Nuestra Señora de la Consolación* is one of the province's most important churches. The tower has a splendid gateway, richly decorated with plant motifs; the interior of the church has a baroque retable. The baptistery, which dates from 1528, has a 16C glazed clay holy-water stoup. The monastery church of *Nuestra Señora de las Mercedes* has a gate with a horseshoe arch flanked by two round arched buttresses. Remnants still survive of the Moorish *castillo*, which was rebuilt in the late Middle Ages.

Llerena, Nuestra Señora de la Granada

of the Pyrenees of 1659, Llivia has been a Spanish exclave in France.

Santo Cristo: The parish church. Built on the site of an older church, which was mentioned in 835. In a transitional style between Romanesque and Gothic; it was fortified in the 16C.

Llivia
Gerona/Catalonia   p.390□N 2

This town is Iberian in origin; in Roman times it was known as *Iulia Lybica* and was the capital of the Roman province of Ceretania, now Cerdaña. Since the Treaty

Llusá
Barcelona/Catalonia   p.390□N 3

Monasterio de Santa María: Dates from the 12C. The new church was built in 1168. The cloister is very fine, with 22 capitals on simple columns. The frescos are 14C; they were originally beneath the choir but are now in the adjoining room.

A 13C panel painting on the altar frontal is now on display in the Museo Episcopal in Vich. There is some Byzantine influence in the figures, which are attributed to the so-called Master of Llusá.

Environs: The parish church of **Oristá** (10 km. S.) is 14C, and was built over a Romanesque crypt which still survives.

Loarre
Huesca/Aragon   p.388☐K 3

Castillo de Loarre: Spain's most important Romanesque fortress. It was built by King Sancho Ramírez of Aragon at the end of the 11C on the remains of a Roman castle called *Calagurris Fibularia*. The castle was used as a royal palace, and from the 12C onwards it was an Augustinian monastery. It has an irregular ground plan, two rings of walls with cylindrical towers, and two well-defended gateways. The *portal* in the façade has a beautiful relief of Christ Blessing. The Romanesque *church of Santa María* was completed in the 12C; it has a rectangular crypt with a semicircular apse, tunnel vaulting, a single aisle and a dome resting on double squinches. The capitals of the numerous columns supporting the tunnel vault are interesting and display flower decorations, small angels and animals.

Iglesia Parroquial: The parish church is 16C and has a slender, square tower. The *altarpiece* includes three 16C paintings depicting St.Peter, St.John and the Archangel Michael. The *church treasure* contains two splendid reliquaries, made of gold and dating from the 12C. One is reputed to contain the relics of St. Demetrius, who is revered mainly in the Eastern Orthodox church.

Also worth seeing: The *Ayuntamiento*

(town hall) is in a building dating from 1573, and is situated on the picturesque and typically Aragonese Plaza Mayor, Loarre's main square.

Logroño
Logroño/Old Castile   p.388☐H 3

Santa María la Redonda: A 15C church, which was extended in the 18C. It has three polygonal apses, and a nave and two aisles which are all of the same height. The many chapels include the outstanding *Capilla de Nuestra Señora de la Paz*, which has a Plateresque retable dating from 1541 and the tomb of the founder, Diego Ponce de León. The other chapels contain fine 16 – 18C baroque and Plateresque retables, and some tombs, notably those of Pedro González de Castillo (1627) and the mausoleum of General Espartero (1888). The 16C choir stalls are by Arnao de Bruselas, and the grille is from Elorrio. The dome was decorated by José Vexés in the 18C. The *portals* are all impressive, especially the one in the W. façade with the twin baroque towers dating from 1742. The portal is carved from stone like a retable and has numerous sculptures framed by a large niche.

Santa María del Palacio: This church was built on the site of the palace of the kings of Castile, which Alfonso VII gave to the Order of the Knights Templar. The founding of the monastery is attributed to the Emperor Constantine, but little remains of the old 11C building. The transept is 13C, and the portal, which is by Juan de Riba, and also the 148 ft. high tower with spire are 16C. The altarpiece of the high altar dates from 1561 and is by the sculptor Arnao de Bruselas and the painters Pero Ruiz and Francisco Hernández. The cloister is 15C. The Gothic

Loarre, Castillo de Loarre

chapel of *Nuestra Señora de la Antigua*, which contains the tomb of Juan de Vergara with its recumbent statue, and a baroque retable with a 13C image of Nuestra Señora de la Antigua, are especially interesting.

San Bartolomé: A church from the 13–14C and transitional between Romanesque and Gothic. The portal is the finest example of Gothic sculpture in the region.

Santiago: The church we see today is 15C in origin, and consists of a single aisle with six columns. The portal is by Juan de Raón (1662), and includes a sculpture of Santiago; the altarpiece of the high altar is Renaissance and dates from 1649.

Espartero Palace: An 18C building with an attractive façade. It now houses the *Provincial Museum*, which includes Bronze and Iron Age remains, and also some interesting paintings.

Environs: 10 km. E. is **Agoncillo**, which is the site of the remains of the old Roman settlement of *Egon*; there is also a Romanesque *church* with an impressive retable and a well-preserved square 13C *fortress* whose towers have arrow slits. **Alberite** (*c.* 10 km. S.): The *parish church* has a large 16C retable. **Albelda de Iregua** (*c.* 10 km. S.): The *parish church* has an interesting 16C retable; the Romanesque *Capilla de Santa Fe de Palazuelos* dates from the 12C. **Navarrete** (*c.* 10 km. SW): The Gothic *parish church* has a nave and two aisles, with stellar vaulting, a 16C Flemish triptych and a valuable collection of 16–18C

Logroño, Santa María la Redonda

Logroño, San Bartolomé

gold work. Note the cemetery portal in the Romanesque pilgrimage church. **Fuenmayor** (*c.* 8 km. W.): The 17C *parish church* has some fine altarpieces; 17C altarpiece by Juan Bascardo in the apse and another of interest in the Capilla de los Ruiz, both of which are Plateresque.

Lorca

Murcia/Murcia   p.396☐I 9

This town on the Río Guadalentín has some 72,000 inhabitants (if the farming communities are included); it lies on the southern slope of the Sierra del Caño, and the Romans knew it as *Ilorci* or *Heliocroca*. All the remains of the Roman settlement, however, were destroyed in the 17C by an earthquake. Lorca was a bishop's seat under the Visigoths, until the Moors took it in 780. They named it *Lurca*, and built a castle — part of which survives — on the higher ground, and also the original town ramparts, which have been frequently restored since. Lorca was finally freed from the Moors in 1266 by James I of Aragon. During the 17C it was the home of the well-known painting school of the kingdom of Valencia. The old town has much character, and is situated on the slope of the castle hill. In the hill there are some cave dwellings, and the lower town, some of which is baroque, contains numerous old buildings.

San Patricio: This 16C collegiate church is the only church in Spain which is dedicated to the Irish saint. The huge

Renaissance *main portal* has splendid baroque additions, and the mainly baroque *interior* has a nave, two aisles and seven apsidal chapels. The oldest parts are the nave and the transept; the huge four-storeyed *tower* was finished in 1772. The *Capilla de la Encarnación* has a massive *Annunciation* by Camacho. The *chapterhouse*, which is separate from the church, contains images of saints, some of which are attributed to Alonso Cano, Camacho and Ribera.

Monasterio de las Monjas de Abajo: This monastery has a fine 16C portal.

Iglesia de Santiago (on the plaza of the same name): This 16C church has a fine altar, and statues by Manuel Caro and Salzillo.

San Pedro: This 15C church has a fine Gothic portal, but was seriously damaged in the Civil War.

Santa María: This 15C late Gothic church was converted from a former mosque. The *portal* is from 1796, the *Resurrection of Christ* by Roque López is from 1701.

Capilla del Rosario (Calle de Santo Domingo): This has a dome painted by Manuel Martínez.

Castillo: The castle was restored in the 19C. It is situated on the highest point of the N. quarter, and dates from the reign of Alfonso the Wise (13C).

Ayuntamiento/Town Hall (Plaza de España): With two wings, the left one 17C and the right 18C. The building contains a number of historical memorabilia, such as Moorish banners from the battles of Cantoria and Salado, the city's own banner (Pendón), and six large battle paintings by Miguel Muñoz from 1723.

Casa de los Guevara (or *Casa de las Columnas*): The city's most interesting secular building. It dates from the 17C and has a splendid baroque portal of 1694 and a fine inner courtyard.

Casa de los Musso (Hotel Madrid): This has a 16C patio and tower.

Also worth seeing: Other impressive churches include the rococo *El Carmen* (1712), which has statues by Salzillo and Roque Lopez; *Santa María*, an early-15C building with a 16C portal; *Santiago* (17C); *San Mateo* (late-18C); *San Pedro* (18C portal); *San Francisco* (16/17C with a rococo chapel). In the W. of the town a Way of the Cross, 550 yards long, leads to the *Calvario*. The eight chapels have fine azulejos, including one with a wooden misericordia *crucifix* from 1689 and a Florentine painting of the *Annunciation* dating from 1560. The 13–15C towers are splendid and the following are of particular architectural interest: the 13C *Torre de l'Espolón*, the 14C *Torre Bélica* and the 15C keep or *Torre del Homenaje*.

Totana (*c.* 20 km. NE): The parish church of *Santiago* has a 233 ft. 16C tower, and a fine baroque portal. The interior contains a Mudéjar artesonado ceiling, and baroque and Renaissance altars. The *Ayuntamiento* is a splendid baroque building; the town hall square has a fountain with baroque sculptures by Juan de Uceta. 6 km. from Totana is the *Ermita de Santa Eulalia*, which has an artesonado ceiling and 17C wall paintings.

Los Arcos
Navarra/Navarra   p.388□H 2

Iglesia Parroquial de la Asunción (Plaza Mayor): It is hard to determine the period when this parish church was built, as new sections have repeatedly been added to it. The *bell tower* is 16C. A fine Plateresque *portal* leads through to the interior of the church, where there is a 17C *altar* with 15C paintings by an artist who is unknown, but whose work suggests that he was influenced by Pedro Díaz de Oviedo. The high altar has a 15C altarpiece and a fine Gothic statue of the Madonna. It is probable that this is 14C French in origin. The magnificent Gothic choir stalls are worthy of a cathedral. The *cloister* is 15C.

Also worth seeing: Just inside the boundary of Los Arcos are three *monoliths*, known to the locals as *Normas*.

Loyola
Guipúzcoa/Basque Provinces   p.388☐H 2

Iñigo López de Recalde—later to become St.Ignatius of Loyola, the founder of the Jesuit Order—was born here in *c*. 1491. The monumental Jesuit college and sanctuary were built in his honour. Parts of the house of the Loyola family were incorporated in this complex. Queen Marianne of Austria, Philip II's widow, enabled work to get under way by buying the Loyola property and presenting it to the Jesuits. The Order commissioned the celebrated Italian baroque architect Carlo Fontana to design the building. He created an edifice on a rectangular ground plan with annexes at the sides. This gave the impression of an eagle on the point of flight. The foundation stone was laid on 28 March 1689, and the work was supervised by the Ibero family. The building was consecrated in 1738.

Santuario de San Ignacio de Loyola: A magnificent *flight of steps* framed by balustrades leads up to the marble portal which is set in the semicircular *façade*.

This has huge columns and a pediment with the Spanish coat-of-arms in the middle of it. The visitor enters the extensive *ante-room* with statues of Jesuit saints: Francis Borgia, Aloysius Gonzaga, Stanislaus Kostka and Francis Xavier. The entrance to the church has a statue of St. Ignatius. The church is round and has a 184 ft. high *dome* (69 ft. across) which is supported by eight pillars and flanked by two smaller bell towers. The church *interior* contains a baroque high altar made of marble, and a silver altar by Zuloaga and Vicente Salmón. Space was left inside the complex for the *Loyola family's residential tower*, known as the Santa Casa, which has been preserved; and it was here that Ignatius was born. A bronze statue of the saint as a soldier stands before it; there is another which depicts a wounded Ignatius being supported by some soldiers. The *interior* of the tower, a remnant of the Loyola family's castle, has a white Carrara marble *ante-room*, from which two chapels lead, one dedicated to St.Joseph and the other to the Immaculate Conception. There is another chapel containing relics and memorabilia. On the *first floor* the former living rooms contain a display of further relics, 16C tapestries and also St.Francis Borgia's chasuble. In the former prayer room there is an altar of the Annunciation, which was a gift from Queen Isabella the Catholic to the saint's family. The second floor contains: the saint's sick-room, which has an altar and further memorabilia; a chapel with a valuable Damascus steel altar with gold inlay; and a sacristy with an ivory crucifix.

Lucena
Córdoba/Andalusia   p.394☐F 10

San Mateo: The Plateresque main portal leads into an interior with an artesonado ceiling. The high altar has a Renaissance

Lucena, San Mateo

Lucena, San Mateo

retable, and the *Capilla del Rosario* is in agitated 18C baroque style.

Alcázar: Two towers are still standing among the ruins: Boabdil, the last Moorish king of Granada, was once held prisoner in the octagonal *Torre del Moral*.

Also worth seeing: The *Hospital de San Juan de Dios* has a beautiful baroque portal, and a chapel with marble inlay. The high altar has a baroque retable.

Environs: Santuario de Araceli (6 km. S.): This is a sanctuary with a baroque altar. **Cabra** (9 km. NE): The ancient *Egabra;* the *Church of San Juan Bautista* is one of Andalusia's oldest churches. It has elements of Visigoth, Roman and Moorish styles.

Lugo

Lugo/Galicia   p.386□C 2

Lugo is a city with a long history: it was a Celtic religious site, as can be seen from the Celtic burial mounds which have been discovered, but it became famous after its capture by the Romans under Augustus, when it was given the name 'Lucus Augusti' and was enlarged into a city. Excavations have revealed a forum and a temple. Interesting remains of the well-built aqueduct and of the baths (Lugo has hot springs) can still be seen. The 2C AD Roman wall is in a remarkably fine state of preservation; a document from the time of Alfonso II tells us that it is the only such wall not to have been destroyed by the Moors. It is 1 mile 570 yards long, 32–49 ft. high and 14 ft. 9 in. thick. There are some 50 small watchtowers along this wall, which is interrupted by gates at ten points. The most interesting of these gates are: the Puerta Miña (or del Carmen), which is the oldest gate; the Puerta Nueva, which has a Roman relief; and the Puerta de San Pedro (or la Toledana), which opens the route to Astorga and León. The finest of the gates which were later expanded is the Puerta de Santiago, which was rebuilt in 1759 with a large coat-of-arms and equestrian statue, and leads to the cathedral.

The city was a bishop's seat even in Roman times, and in the 5&6C a number of major councils were held here. Lugo was later conquered by the Suevi, and then the Goths. In 714 it was raided by the Moors and set on fire, and was later rebuilt under Alfonso I. In 969 it was taken by the Normans, after which it had a more peaceful history until it was captured by the French in 1809.

Cathedral of Santa María: In 1129 Bishop Pedro Peregrino ordered Raimundo de Monforte to build a copy of the cathedral at Santiago on the site of Archbishop Odoario's pre-Romanesque church of Santa María. The cathedral took six centuries to build, and was eventually completed in 1768. Parts of the nave and of the narthex before the N. portal are from the original building, and there is an exceptionally fine Romanesque Christ in Majesty carved in stone in the tympanum over the Gothic portal. The pendent capital at Christ's feet depicts the Last Supper. The N. portal leads through into the left transept, on the S. side of which is a Plateresque altar (1534) by the Dutchman Cornelis de Holanda; it used to be the high altar. The 14C *Capilla Mayor* was altered by Charles de Lemaur in 1662; behind it is the remarkable *Capilla de Nuestra Señora de los Ojos Grandes*, which dates from 1726 and is by Casas Nóvoa, Miguel Romay and Garcia Bouzas. The figure of Nuestra Señora de los Ojos Grandes (Our Lady of the Large Eyes) is a celebrated 12C work in polychrome alabaster. The *Capilla de San Froilan* is among the most important chapels: it contains the relics of St.Froilan, who was born in Lugo and became Bishop of León and Lugo's patron saint. The right transept, which also contains an altar by Cornelis de Holanda, leads into the fine *cloister*, which was built by Fernando de las Casas Nóvoa in 1714. Behind the coro, which contains the richly carved choir stalls of 1624 by Francisco de Moure, is the beginning of the Romanesque section of the cathedral, with its nave and two aisles. The front section (ambulatory with coro) was originally 13C Gothic; the main portal with its classical façade dates from 1769.

San Francisco: The N. portal of the cathedral leads out into the Plaza del Campo, which has a fine 18C fountain, and down the Rua Nueva to the church of San Francisco, which is now the parish church of San Pedro. Originally 15&16C, it is a single-aisled Gothic church with tombs from the time of its foundation and a fine square cloister with double columns dating from 1452. Near the main portal of this church is the entrance to the *Museo Provincial*, which was destroyed in the 17C and rebuilt by Gómez Román. It is one of Spain's most important museums of cultural history, and includes prehistoric, Roman, Visigoth, pre-Romanesque and Romanesque inscriptions and architectural fragments, vessels, tools and sculptures. There is also a collection of paintings.

Santo Domingo: A short distance from the museum entrance is the church of Santo Domingo (on the Plaza de Santo Domingo). Today it serves as a chapel for Augustinian monks; it is a 14C building with a Romanesque portal and fine Romanesque capitals.

Lugo, Museo Provincial, cloister

Also worth seeing: *Santa María Nova* (now Santiago) and *Juan de Dios* (now the parish church of San Froilan), both baroque, have fine façades and altars. The *Palacio Episcopal* is an 18C building between the cathedral and the Plaza del Campo; it was commissioned by Bishop Gil de Taboada. The *Ayuntamiento* is E. of the cathedral, behind the Plaza de España, and was built in 1736 by Lucas Ferro Caaveiro; it has a beautiful façade, balconies and corner turrets, a coat-of-arms on top of the central projection and a baroque crown to the roof. The *Diocesan Museum* is housed in the Seminario, and it contains some remarkable religious works of art.

Lugo, Puerta de Santiago

Lugo, cathedral

Madrid
Madrid/New Castile   p.392☐G 5/6

Madrid, high on a plateau in New Castile, is the geographical centre of the Iberian peninsula. The city now has over 3.5 million inhabitants. The area of present-day Madrid was settled during prehistoric times, as numerous finds from the Stone Age bear witness. The Moors gave the then insignificant town the name 'Magerit', from which the name Madrid is derived. For centuries Madrid stood in the shadow of Toledo. In 1083 Madrid was captured by Alfonso VI and absorbed into the Christian kingdom. Under Henry II the town was totally destroyed by fire. It was later rebuilt by Henry III who had himself crowned in Madrid in 1390. Henry IV

Madrid, Prado, Francisco Rizi, 'Auto de fe in the Plaza Mayor in Madrid'

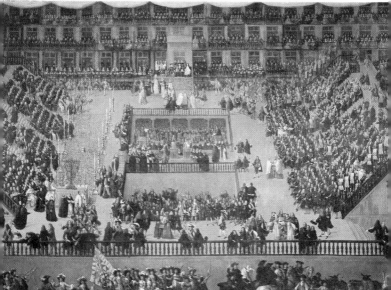

Madrid, panorama, painting by Antonio Joli

turned the Moorish alcázar into his favourite residence and granted the town market rights. In 1474 Ferdinand of Aragon and Isabella of Castile had the walls of Madrid destroyed. Nevertheless, the royal couple made their ceremonial entry here in 1477. In 1561 Philip II declared Madrid capital of the empire. Under Philip III monasteries, churches and hospitals were built and during the reign of Philip IV new buildings were constantly being constructed. The Bourbons demanded the further extension of the city, and this was continued under Charles III in particular. From 1860 the outer suburbs were developed and these are constantly being enlarged.

Cathedral of San Isidro (Calle de Toledo): Construction of the cathedral—originally the chapel of the Jesuit school

—began in 1626. The nave is spacious with a chapel at the side; there is a dome over the crossing. The magnificent portal is flanked by two bartizans. Inside there is an altar painting of the Holy Family by Herrera Barnuevo as well as another of his works. A few paintings by Rizi are also of interest. The cathedral contains the remains of the city's patron saint St.Isidore.

Catedral de la Almudena (Calle de Bailén): In 1883 work begun on the new cathedral; the crypt was consecrated three years later. Construction continued in Gothic style, but the cathedral is still unfinished.

Las Calatravas (Calle Alcalá): Built in 17C; the present façade dates from the 19C. Single-aisled interior with chapels,

galleries and a dome supported by bevelled columns. The altarpiece of the high altar is by José Churriguera.

Las Comendadoras de Santiago (Plaza de las Comendadoras): Construction of this monastery church began in 1668, although the monastery itself had already been founded by Iñigo de Zapata y Cárdenas in the early 16C. The church has an austere façade with two towers and a niche containing the figure of the patron saint. The interior has four vaulted chapels forming a Greek cross and a lavishly decorated dome. The sacristy was added in the 18C (c. 1746–53); it has a beautiful vault and richly decorated walls.

Montserrat (Calle San Bernardo): Built in 1720; crossing and the front are now missing. Of particular interest is the exterior, the work of the architect Pedro de Ribera. The baroque tower is also of interest.

Las Salesas Reales or Santa Bárbara (Calle de Bárbara de Braganza): This church dates from 1757. Built by Francisco Carlier, probably in collaboration with Francisco Moradillo. The façade is decorated with sculptures by Alfonso Vergaz. There is a dome over the crossing and the ground plan is in the form of a Latin cross. The dome is decorated with frescos by the brothers González Velázquez. In the crossing there is a rococo royal tribune, as well as the tomb of Ferdinand VI, designed by Sabatini and built by Francisco Gutiérrez.

San Andrés (Plaza de los Carros): San

Madrid, Iglesia de San Andrés, Capilla de San Isidro

Madrid, Las Salesas Reales

Andrés, one of the oldest churches in Madrid, was destroyed in 1936, leaving only the *Capilla de San Isidro* (built 1657 –69 by Pedro de la Torre). The brick building has corner pilasters and is crowned by a cornice ledge with a balustrade.

San Antón (Calle de Hortaleza): The church has a painting by Goya, *The Last Communion of St. Joseph of Calasanz,* dated 1820.

San Antonio de los Portugueses o Alemanes (Corredera de San Pablo): Founded by Philip II in 1606. It has an elliptical ground plan and is vaulted by a dome. The altars have portraits of Spanish monarchs and large paintings by Eugenio Cagés. The walls, decorated with frescos by Lucas Jordán, are of interest, as is the dome, which has frescos of scenes from the life of St. Anthony, by Carreño and Rizi.

Basilica of San Francisco el Grande (Plaza de San Francisco): This basilica was one of the most costly churches to be built in the 18C. It has a circular ground plan with a narthex, six chapels and an apse. Sabatini built the portal, the two towers and the enormous dome. The decoration of the interior was carried out by Goya and other artists in 1784. In the inner gallery there are oil paintings by Sánchez Coello, Pacheco, Ribalta, Zurbarán, Gaspar de Crayer, Carnicero and Bayeu.

San Ginés (Calle Arenal): One of the oldest foundations in Madrid; the present building dates from 1645 and was renovated in the 18C. The domed interior consists of a nave and two aisles. The Capilla del Cristo has an interesting collection of the paintings of El Greco.

Madrid, Goya, frescos in San Antonio de la Florida

San Jerónimo el Real (Calle de Alarcón): This church belongs to one of the monasteries founded by Ferdinand and Isabella in 1503–5. The building, originally Gothic with Mudéjar influences, was restored in the 19C. The interior consists of a spacious nave with rib vaulting, a crossing and polygonal apse.

San José (Calle Alcalá): Finished in 1742, with a façade of the same date, although it has been in the process of restoration for years. The interior is divided into a nave and two aisles. The nave is spanned by a lunette vault with frescos. Numerous altarpieces and paintings complete the baroque furnishing.

San Nicolás de los Servitas (Plaza de Herradores): A church, with a Mudéjar brick tower, probably dating back to the 12C. Although the church has undergone various alterations, the Gothic vault and panelling have survived.

San Pedro el Viejo (Calle del Nuncio): 14C church, built during the reign of Alfonso XI on the remains of a former mosque. It has a tower in the Mudéjar style of Toledo. The church interior has a nave and two aisles with a simple oval dome.

Capilla San Antonio de la Florida (Paseo de la Florida): The dome with frescos of 1798 by Goya is the most interesting feature. Since 1919 the church has housed the mortal remains of Francisco Goya.

Prayer Room del Caballero de Gracia (Calle del Caballero de Gracia): Small basilica with a large nave, a crossing and semicircular apse. Built 1786–95 in classical style by Juan de Villanueva.

Convento de las Descalzas Reales (Plaza de las Descalzas Reales): Founded in 1559 by the daughter of Charles V, Joanna of Austria. The building is a former palace of the kings of Castile. The interior houses an extraordinary collection of paint-

Madrid, San Jerónimo el Real

ings, tapestries, sculptures, objects in gold and liturgical items from the 16&17C. Among the paintings are works by Sánchez Coello, Pantoja, Titian, Breughel, Rubens, Zurbarán, Carreño, Rizi and Lucas Jordán, as well as works by Flemish painters. Of interest is the staircase, which is decorated with frescos by Antonio de Pereda, Ximénez Donoso, Claudio Coello and the Italians Mitelli and Colonna.

Royal Palace (Palacio Real): The palace, indisputedly the most important example of the classicism of Madrid, was built on the site of the old alcázar, which was destroyed by fire in 1734. Philip V entrusted the planning and execution of the building, firstly to F. Juvara (d. 1735) and then to the Italians Sacchetti and Ventura Rodríguez. Building began in 1738. Charles III moved into the palace in 1764. The building has a square ground plan. In the *courtyard* there are statues of the four Roman emperors born in Spain—Trajan, Hadrian, Theodosius and Honorius. The four-storeyed building is made of granite

from the nearby Guadarrama mountains and white limestone from Colmenar.

The monumental marble *Grand Staircase* was designed by Sabatini. The painted ceiling is by Conrado Giaquinto (1700–66); apart from this fresco, he also painted, the ceiling fresco 'Birth of the Sun' and 'Triumph of Bacchus' in the *Salón de Columnas* (Room of Columns). Tiepolo painted the fresco the 'Apotheosis of Aeneas', which graces the ceiling of the *Salón de Alabarderos* (the Guard Room), as well as the ceiling fresco in the *Salón del Trono* (Throne Room). In the *Saleta* (small room) there is a lovely fresco by Tiepolo on the theme of 'The Power and Magnitude of the Spanish Monarchy'. In the *Comedor de Gala* (State Dining Room) 'Aurora upon her Chariot' is by the German artist Anton Raffael Mengs. In the 30-odd rooms of the palace there are further frescos by Maella, González, Velázquez, Bayeu, Ribera, López and other great artists. The high point of the palace comes with the magnificently furnished rooms of Charles III: *Saleta, Antecámera de Gasparini* and

Madrid, Capilla del Obispo

Madrid, San Francisco el Grande

Madrid, Conv. de las Descalzas Reales: Sánchez Coello, 'Juana de Austria'; Pedro de Mena, 'Mater Dolorosa'

the *Salón de Gasparini*. These were named after the Italian painter and stucco worker Matías Gasparini. The walls and ceilings of these rooms are decorated with the finest stucco work. The adjoining *Sala de Porcelana* is a masterpiece. It is adorned with porcelain dishes from the 'Fábrica del Buen Retiro' of Madrid. Also of interest is the *Yellow Room (Sala Amarilla)*. The walls are hung with 16C Brussels tapestries. The *palace chapel* has a ground plan in the form of a Latin cross. The *Salón del Trono* (Throne Room), furnished under Charles III, is lined with red satin. The palace also has an interesting collection of tapestries. These include Flemish tapestries designed by Raphael and Giulio Romano as well as French tapestries from Beauvais and Aubusson. In order to better exhibit paintings from the many rooms, the *New Museums* were set up in 1962 (occupying 15 rooms in the NW wing). Room 3, for example, has tapestries based on designs by Goya. Room 5 is dedicated to Velázquez. Room 7 has 'St. Paul' by El Greco and two paintings by Watteau. Parts of the royal collection of porcelain are also displayed in this room, along with series from Meissen, Berlin, Vienna and Sèvres. The *Royal Library* occupies 24 rooms. There are *c.* 300,000 volumes, 4,000 manuscripts and 3,500 maps. Also worth seeing is the *Farmacía Real* (Royal Pharmacy) and the coach museum (Caballerizas), in the *Campo del Moro*. The *Armería Real* (Royal Armoury) is in the SW wing of the palace. It displays famous arms and armoury which belonged to the Spanish kings.

Palacio de las Cortes Españolas (the Spanish Parliament, Carrera de San Jerónimo): The palace was built in classical style in 1843–50. The interior is worth

Madrid, Prado, Velázquez, 'Don Baltasar Carlos on his Horse'

◁ *Palacio Real, sedan of Philip V*

Madrid, Palacio Real

seeing for its Isabelline decoration. In the tympanum there is an enormous relief of Spain with allegories of the fine arts, justice, industry, trade, etc.

Palacio de Liria (Calle Princesa): The palace was built for the family of the Duke of Alba by Ventura Rodríguez. The interior houses the best private art collection in Spain, with works by Fra Angélico, Perugino, Titian, Bassano, Ribera, Velázquez, Murillo, Rubens, Rembrandt, Goya and others.

Cárcel de Corte or Palacio de Santa Cruz (Plaza de Santa Cruz): This monumental red brick building used to house the royal administration. The Ministry of the Exterior occupies the former court prison, the façade of which is in the style of the Escorial. The rectangular courtyard is bounded by arcades supported by double columns. A magnificent staircase is worth seeing here, as are the statues *Elcano* by Bellver and *Columbus* by Samarti. The palace was built between 1629–34 by Juan Gómez de Mora and Alonso Carbonell. The portals and the towers are the work of Teodoro Ardemas in 1670. Originally a classical building, it was altered so that its present appearance is now distinctly baroque.

Hospiz San Fernando (Calle de Fuencarral): Philip V commissioned Pedro de Ribera to design the building in 1722. The wonderful portal and the fine, delicate or-

◁ *Madrid, Palacio Real, staircase*

Madrid, Palacio Real ▷

namentation are unique in the history of Spanish rococo. The building currently houses the history museum and the city library.

Royal Theatre (Plaza de Oriente): The Teatro Real is the work of López Aguado (1818–50). It was officially opened on behalf of Narváez in 1850. Here internationally famous opera stars, such as Adelina Patti and Gayarre sang.

Plaza de la Cibeles: The site of a fountain with the goddess Cybele, whose chariot is drawn by lions. The lions are by Roberto Michel (1720–86) and the goddess and her chariot are by the Spaniard Francisco Gutiérrez (1727 - 82). Buildings around the square include the War Office, the Bank of Spain and the *Palacio de Comunicaciones* (General Post Office), which was built by Antonio Palacios in 1904-18. A monumental building, it has elements of the Plateresque and features of architecture from the Habsburg period.

Plaza Mayor: A rectangular plaza built 1617-9 by Juan Gómez de Mora, who was strongly influenced by the master architect of the Escorial, Juan de Herrera. A number of three-storey houses have total of 114 arches. The *Casa de la Panadería*, by Claudio Coello, which is decorated with frescos, stands at the N. end of the square. Originally a bread shop, it is now used by the City authorities. In the middle of the square there is an equestrian monument of Philip III by the Italians Juan de Bolonia and Pietro Tacca.

Plaza de Oriente: This beautifully laid out square is the largest in the city centre. It dates from the time of Joseph Bonaparte and is adorned with 44 statues of Visigoth and Spanish kings. In the middle stands the equestrian statue of Philip IV, cast by Pietro Tacca following the model of Martínez Montañés, which was itself based on a painting by Velázquez. The old Augustine *Convento de la Encarnación* stands on the NE side of the square.

Madrid, Palacio Real, winged altar by Juan de Flandes

Madrid, Prado, El Greco, 'Gentleman with his hand on his chest'

◁ *Madrid, Plaza Mayor, Philip III*

Madrid, Plaza Mayor ▷

Puerta del Sol: Formerly the heart of Madrid but now a sprawling square of little architectural interest. The most important building is the *Palace of the Ministry of the Interior,* a monumental building by de Marquet from 1708, which was formerly the main post office. The main portal has a stone plaque displaying nil kilometres, as all official distances were formerly measured from this point.

Plaza de la Villa: The three-towered *Town Hall,* which was begun in 1640 by Villarreal stands on the square. The building has simple lines, its only decoration being gabled windows and two oriels. Inside there are a beautiful staircase, a room with columns in which there is a painting by Goya and a chapel with frescos by Palomino. The manuscripts of Calderón de la Barca are kept here. In the middle of the square stands the statue of Alvaro de Bazán, cast in bronze by Benlliure. Opposite the Town Hall stands a Gothic building, the *Antigua Casa de los Lujanes* from the early 16C; it has a massive tower and a beautiful Gothic portal. Francis I of France is thought to have been confined here after his defeat at Pavia. Nearby is the Plateresque *Casa de Cisneros.*

Puerta de Alcalá: Charles III commissioned Francisco Sabatini with the building of this elegant triumphal arch, which was completed in 1778. The decoration was the work of Roberto Michel and Francisco Gutiérrez.

Puerta de Toledo: This gate was built in

◁ *Madrid, Residencial Torres Blancas*

Madrid, Puerta de Alcalá ▷

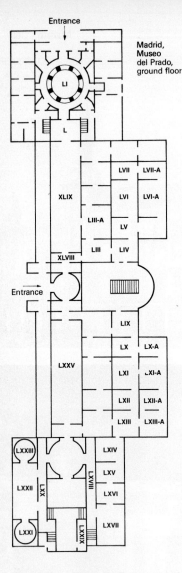

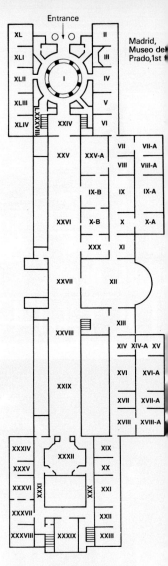

Madrid, Museo del Prado The present positions of the most important works are:
El Greco X, XI, XXX
Goya XXXII, LV-LVII, LV-A, LVI-A
Murillo XXVIII
Velázquez XII, XV
Dürer XLIV
Rembrandt XIX, XXIII
Rubens XVI, XVII, XVIII
Titian IX

Spanish baroque painters XXIV-XXIX
Italian school II-VI
Dutch masters XL-XLIV
Flemish school XIX
French school XXXV, XXXVI

Madrid, Prado, Dürer, self-portra

Madrid, Prado, Tintoretto, 'Christ Washing the Disciples' Feet'

1816–27 by Antonio Aguado. The sculptures are by Valerino Salvatierra and Ramón Barba.

Museo del Prado (or Museo Nacional de Pintura y Escultura): Built in 1785 under Charles III in classical style by Juan de Villanueva; originally intended as a natural history museum. Granite and brick were the building materials. Construction was completed in 1819 under Ferdinand VII, when it became a museum of painting. The Museo del Prado is one of the richest and most important museums in the world, containing some 3,000 paintings. The gallery's main treasure consists of its collection of paintings of the Spanish School, whose development stretches from the 15C to Goya. Major artists represented include J. Ribera with about 60 paintings

and El Greco with 34 (the large religious canvases are in Room XXX). The Prado has about 50 works by Diego Velázquez, including such famous paintings as *Las Meninas* (The Ladies of the Court) in Room XV, *Las Hilanderas* (The Spinners), *La Rendición de Breda* (The Surrender of Breda) and the *Equestrian portrait of Don Baltasar Carlos,* all to be found in Room XII. There are also numerous paintings by Murillo, including *La Immaculada Concepción de Soult* in Room XXVIII. The Prado has about 120 paintings by Goya, the best of his portraits being found in Room XXXII, including the *Maja Vestida,* the *Maja Desnuda* and the *Family of Charles IV.* Goya's well-known tapestry designs are housed on the ground floor in Rooms LV-LVII; Room LV-A has the famous painting *Tres de Mayo 1808* (Shoot-

ng of Insurgents). The *Pinturas Negras* (black paintings) can be seen in Room LVI; in two further rooms there is an extensive collection of drawings by the artist.

The main gallery (La Gran Galería, Rooms XXIV-XXIX) has Spanish baroque paintings by Murillo, Carreño, Ribera, Mayno, etc.

From the Italian School of the 15C there are paintings by Fra Angélico *(Annunciation)* in Room II, by Mantegna *(Death of the Virgin)* and by Antonello da Messina *(Body of Christ)* in Room IV. There are 8 paintings by Raphael, including the *Madonna with the Fish* and a portrait of a cardinal, both in Room II. The Venetian School is represented by Giorgione, Tintoretto, Paolo Veronese and both Tiepolos. There are about 40 paintings by Titian, including the *equestrian portrait of Charles*

V, the *portraits of Charles V and Philip II, Venus and Adonis* and *Danae,* all in Room IX. The early Dutch School is represented in Rooms XL-XLIV and includes Hieronymous Bosch's most famous work, the triptych *The Garden of Delights.*

The German School is represented by Albrecht Dürer's famous works *Self-portrait, Adam and Eve, Portrait of an Unknown Man* in Room XLIV and also by the paintings of Lucas Cranach and Hans Baldung. The Flemish School is represented by 86 paintings, including the work of Rubens, for example such beautiful later works as the *Three Graces* and the *Garden of Love* (Room XVIII-A) and *Peasant Dance* (Room XVII). Of the 20 paintings by Anton van Dyke two of his most beautiful, *Arrest of Christ* and *The Brazen Serpent* are to be seen in Room XVI-A. Jakob Jordaen's *Fa-*

mily Portrait in Room XVII is one of the artist's best works. Jan Breughel is also represented by several works. The Prado has one of Rembrandt's best-known pictures, *Queen Artemisia.*

The French School of the 17&18C is represented by paintings of Nicolas Poussin, Claude Lorrain, J.A. Watteau and others (Rooms XXXV and XXXVI).

Representing the English School, (in Room LXXXIV) are paintings by Thomas Lawrence, Gainsborough, Henry Raeburn and George Romney.

There is also a collection of Egyptian, Greek and Roman sculptures, as well as a collection of jewellery and *objets d'art,* the *Tresoro del Delfín* (Room LXXIII).

Museo de la Academia de San Fernando (Calle Alcalá, 13): The Academy of Art was founded by Ferdinand VI in 1774 and built by José Churriguera. It exhibits the work of Goya (e.g. *Burial of the Sardine*), Zurbarán, Murillo, Antonio Pereda, Ribera, Alonso Cano, Carreño, Callejo, Claudio Coello as well as other

notable artists. Of the foreign artists represented the most important are Rubens, Giovanni Bellini, Bassano, Tintoretto, Lucas Jordán and Mengs. There is also sculpture (e.g. *San Bruno* by Manuel Pereira) and a large crucifix by Leoni. The same building houses the 'Calcografia Nacional', where Goya's engravings were printed. Copper plates by artists from the 18–20C are kept here.

Museo Arqueológico Nacional (National Archaeological Museum, entrance on the Calle de Serrano, No.13): Occupies the E. section of the building in which the library and museum are housed. It contains prehistoric items and both ancient and modern works of art. There are Iberian antiquities, including the famous *Dama de Elche* from the 4 or 3C BC and the *Dama de Baza.* Further exhibits include *objets d'art* of Egyptian, Etruscan, Phoenician, Greek, Visigoth, Roman and Far Eastern origin, as well as a valuable collection of coins and medallions. The same building houses an exhibition of Modern Art. In the

Madrid, Prado, Hieronymus Bosch, 'The Garden of Delights'

garden there are good copies of the *cave paintings of Altamira.*

Museo de América (Avenida de los Reyes Católicos, 4): Devoted to documents, maps and sea charts related to the discovery of America and the development of the Spanish colonies. There is also a collection of Central and South American art (models of dwellings, fabrics, clothing, carved objects, etc.), as well as pre-Columbian art (e.g. the *Quimbaya Treasure*, which consists of 62 objects made of pure gold), and stone sculpture by the Aztecs, Incas and Mayas.

Museo de Cerralbo (Calle Ventura Rodríguez, 17): The museum was founded by the 17th Marqués de Cerralbo, who donated his three-storey palace (built around 1886) together with all his collections to the state. It houses an important *collection of weapons* and a valuable *porcelain collection.* The *collection of paintings* includes the work of Tintoretto, El Greco, Ribera, Zurbarán, Tiepolo, Mengs, Vicente López and other artists.

Museo del Ejército (Military Museum), Calle Méndez Núñez, 1: Founded by Godoy in 1803. It displays fine weapons and armour from various periods, as well as uniforms and medals.

Museo Lázaro Galdiano (Calle de Serrano, 122): This museum, housing one of the most important private collections in Spain, has recently been donated to the state. Apart from porcelain, ceramics, icons, objects in gold, weapons and armour, the museum also contains antique *carved ivory objects,* and *enamel and bronze items,* as well as *sculpture.* The upper floors have a valuable collection of paintings, including the work of Spanish, Flemish, Italian and, above all, English artists. The Spanish are represented by El Greco:, Velázquez, Zurbarán, Murillo and Goya, among others. Representing 15&16C Flemish painting are artists such as Isenbrandt, van Orley, Gossaert, Gerard David and Hieronymus Bosch. Dutch baroque painters are present in the form of Rembrandt and Hobbema. Representing Eng-

Prado, Raphael, 'Cardinal'

lish painting are works by Gainsborough, Reynolds and Lawrence. Italian art includes the work of Leonardo da Vinci, among others.

Museo Nacional de Arte del Siglo XIX (19C art), Paseo de Calvo Sotelo, 20: The 'Casón del Buen Retiro' has paintings and sculpture by 19C Spanish artists.

Museo Romántico (Calle de San Mateo, 13): This museum was founded by the Marquis of Vega-Inclán in 1924, in an old palace. The exhibition covers paintings from the period between 1814–60 (including Goya). The palace also contains furniture, clocks and other items from the Romantic Era.

Museo Sorolla (Paseo General Martínez Campos, 37): This museum was formerly the studio of the painter Sorolla (1863–1923). There are pictures by the artist, as well as antique furniture and sculpture.

National Library (Paseo Calvo Sotelo, 20): Occupies the W. section of the building housing the library and museum. Founded by Philip V in 1711. The library has one of the best collections of books in Europe with *c.* 2 million volumes, including 800 editions of Don Quixote, numerous manuscripts, documents, sketches and *c.* 2,500 early printed books. The extensive bibliography of the Spanish 'Siglo de Oro' (Golden Age) is of great interest.

Also worth seeing: The *Fuente de Neptuno* (Neptune Fountain), an interesting 18C fountain on the Plaza de Cánovas del Castillo, built by Juan Pascal de Mena. The *Fuente de Apolo* (Apollo Fountain), near the Museo del Prado; the statue of Apollo is by Giraldo de Bergaz and the four seasons are the work of Manuel Alvarez. The *Temple of Debod* (Parque de Rosales) is Egyptian from the 1C BC. Originally it

Madrid, Prado, Jusepe de Ribera, 'Martyrdom of St. Bartholemew'

Madrid, Prado, Rubens, 'Perseus and Andromeda'

stood S. of Aswan on the Nile; in 1972 the temple, a gift from the Egyptian president, was set up here. The temple has very beautiful columns and capitals. *Puente de Toledo* (*the Bridge of Toledo*), at the end of the Calle de Toledo): Built 1718 – 21 in Churrigueresque style by the Madrid architect Pedro de Ribera. The *Parque del Retiro*, one of Madrid's largest parks, once surrounded a summer residence laid out by

Left: Museo Lázaro Galdiano, 10C Byzantine gold enamel work

Below: National Archaeological Museum, relief from the cathedral at Astorga

Right: National Archaeological Museum, 4C Roman mosaic

Far right: National Archaeological Museum, Arabic vase

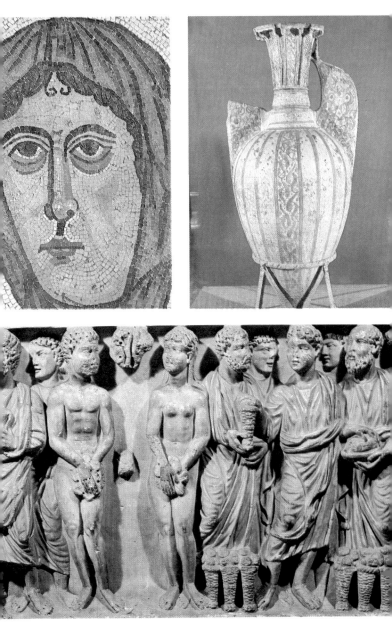

Philip II (destroyed by fire 1734). There are four main entrances with monumental gates: on the Plaza de la Independencia, the Calle de Alcalá, the Calle O'Donnell and the Calle de Alfonso XII. The last-mentioned, preceded by a semicircular flight of white stone steps, leads into a wide avenue inside the park, on either side of which are statues of Spanish kings. The avenue ends at the Paseo del Estanque Grande, the Great Lake Promenade. On the E. side of the lake stands the *Monument to King Alfonso XII.* If, on leaving the avenue, you turn right past the pond, you come to the *Alcachofa Fountain.* The *Museo Español de Arte Contemporáneo* (Museum of Contemporary Art) is in the S. of the park.

Environs: Alcobendas (some 15 km. N. of Madrid): The church of *San Pedro Mártir* is a landmark in contemporary religious architecture. Built in 1955 by Miguel Fisac, the church's interior decoration is pared down to essentials and there is a central altar. **Getafe** is 13 km. S. of Madrid.

Madrid, Museo de América

The town was settled as early as the Neolithic period and was later inhabited by Romans, as various finds in this area show. The *parish church of Santa María Magdalena* is one of the best Renaissance churches in the province. Built 1545-1645; the portal dates from 1770. The church has a nave and two aisles, with Tuscan columns supporting the vault and gallery. The sacristy contains pictures by Claudio Coello, Pereda and others. *c.* 3 km. E. of Getafe is **Cerro de los Angeles,** which is considered to be the geographical centre of Spain. Here stands the mighty monument, the *Sagrado Corazón de Jesús* (the Heart of Christ), which was consecrated in 1919 and built by Carlos Maura and Aniceto Marinas. (It was destroyed 1936 and rebuilt in 1939.)

Madrigal de las Altas Torres
Ávila/Old Castile   p.392 □ F 4/5

Madrigal de las Altas Torres was the birthplace of Isabella the Catholic, who lived here until her marriage to Ferdinand of Aragon. The great theologian Alfonso de Madrigal, Bishop of Ávila, was also born here.

Town Walls: These date from the 13C and are very like those of Ávila, although they are not so well preserved. They are laid out in a circle with tall, square towers. The Puerta de Cantalapiedra, with a sharply pointed arch and a tower, like the gates of Medina and of Arévalo, has survived in good condition.

San Nicolás de Bari: 12C Mudéjar church, in which the nave and two aisles are separated by pointed arches. There are

Madrid, Museo de América

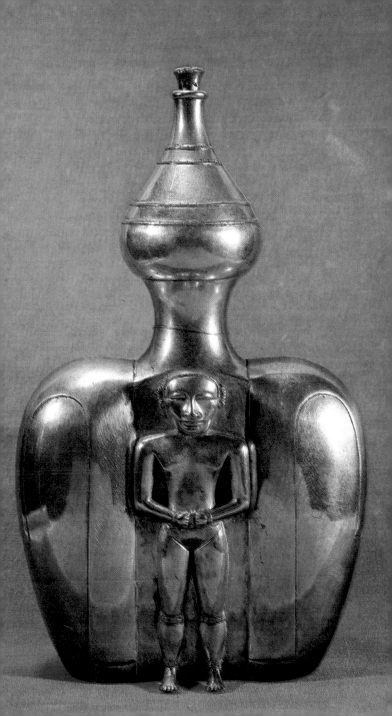

Madrigal de las Altas Torres, town walls

three apses, the middle one of which is decorated by three rows of arches on the outside. In the 16C the nave was covered by a Mudéjar ceiling. The main chapel has an 18C baroque altarpiece, as well as two 16C tombs. Also of interest is the 15C Capilla Dorada and the Renaissance Capilla de San Antonio, as well as the 17C choir.

Santa María del Castillo: 13C church, built on the remains of an old fortress. There is a Mudéjar apse and, in the main chapel, a baroque altarpiece. Also worth seeing are two valuable monstrances dated 1614 and 1757.

Convento de Madres Agustinas de Nuestra Señora de Gracia: Occupies the old palace of the kings of Castile, in which Isabella the Catholic was born. The building is a good example of a 15C Castilian palace. Charles V gave it to the sisters of the Order in 1527 and they then added a single-aisled church.

Monastery of San Agustín: In 1578 the façade was altered in the style of Herrera, which is also the style of the courtyard.

Hospital: Renaissance façade (with double arcades and escutcheons), stairs and the courtyard. The 16C church was converted in the 18C. The main chapel has an 18C altarpiece.

Environs: Mamblas (*c.* 20 km. S.): *Parish church* built in classical style in 1770. **Fontiveros** (*c.* 30 km. S.) was the birthplace of the great poet and mystic Juan de

Madrigal de las Altas Torres, monastery

Málaga, cathedral

la Cruz (John of the Cross). The *parish church* was built in two phases. Nave and two aisles, divided by pointed arches, are 12C; that part built by Rodrigo Gil de Hontanón, and the wooden ceiling over the nave and aisles are 16C. **Narros de Salﬂ dueña** (*c.* 40 km. S.): The interesting medieval *castle* is a good example of a Mudéjar fortified palace.

Málaga
Málaga/Andalusia   p.395☐F 11

A modern-looking provincial capital on the Costa del Sol. It dates back to a Phoenician foundation and has been an episcopal seat since the 4C. Málaga became culturally and economically important after its cap-

ture by the Moors in 711; they extended the town until it was retaken by Ferdinand and Isabella in 1487. Nevertheless, Arab influence continued until the final expulsion of the Islamic population by Philip III at the beginning of the 17C. Political unrest in 1931 and the Spanish Civil War of 1936–9 brought about the severe damage or total destruction of many historical buildings.

Cathedral: Construction began in 1528, following the plans of notable contemporary architects; building stopped in 1783. An imposing *marble stairway* leads up to the W. façade. Two towers–of which only the N. one was completed–flank the three portals; the other tower is called 'Manquita' in the local vernacular, which means 'the one without'. The middle por-

Málaga, view (Madrid)

tal has reliefs of the *Birth of Christ;* the side portals have Saints Paula and Cyriacus, the town's two patron saints. The interior (392 ft. long by 160 ft. high) has a nave and two aisles of equal height and a dome supported by compound pillars with Corinthian capitals. In the middle there are very beautiful *choir stalls* (100 seats) with 40 superb figures of saints, carved by Pedro de Mena (1658–60); further figures are by Luis Ortiz and José Micael. Some particularly fine vestments are on view. In the trascoro (retrochoir) there is a *Pietà* by Alonso Cano. The first chapel on the right of the ambulatory has *figures of Ferdinand and Isabella* in an attitude of prayer, probably by Pedro de Mena; there is also a gilded *statue of the Virgin,* which was reputedly carried during the battles of the Reconquista. The first side chapel on the

Málaga, cathedral 1 W. façade **2** N. tower **3** S. tower, 'Manquita' **4** choir **5** Capilla Nueva **6** Capilla del Rosario **7** Capilla de la Purísima Concepción **8** Capilla de Nuestra Señora de los Reyes **9** Capilla de Santa Bárbara **10** Sacristía Mayor

Málaga, alcazaba 1 entrance **2** Puerta de las Columnas **3** Torre de la Vela **4** Arco del Christo **5** Puerta de Granada **6** Cuartos de Granada, 11C **7** Sala del Siglo, 16C **8** Palacios Nazaries, 13/14C **9** cistern **10** baths **11** Torre del Homenaje **12** entrance to the Castillo del Gibralfaro

right has a 17C *crucifix* by Montañés. The third side chapel on the right has *the Virgin Mary with Saints* from the 17C by Alonso Cano, as well as two sculptures by Pedro de Mena. In the third chapel of the ambulatory *retable,* from the early 16C. The *Capilla del Sagrario* (in the E. of the ambulatory) was designed by Juan de Villanueva in the 18C.

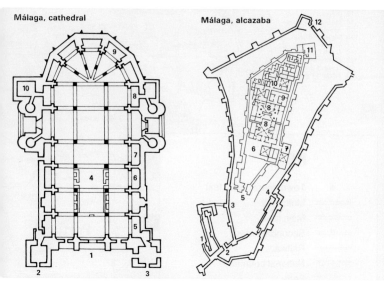

Málaga, cathedral

Málaga, alcazaba

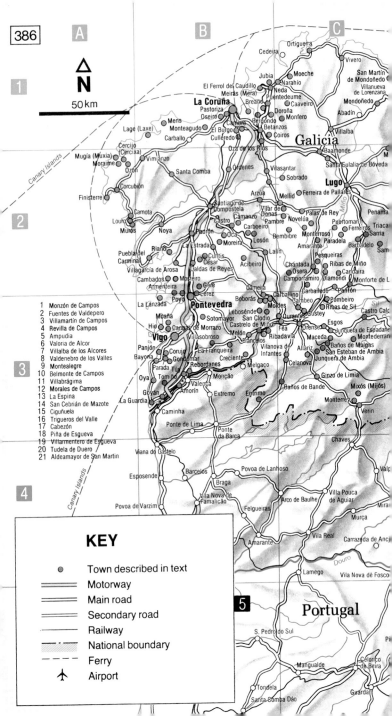

386

A   B   C

1

△
N
50 km

1 Monzón de Campos
2 Fuentes de Valdepero
3 Villamartín de Campos
4 Revilla de Campos
5 Ampudia
6 Valoria de Alcor
7 Villalba de los Alcores
8 Valdenebro de los Valles
9 Montealegre
10 Belmonte de Campos
11 Villabrágima
12 Morales de Campos
13 La Espina
14 San Cebrián de Mazote
15 Ciguñuela
16 Trigueros del Valle
17 Cabezón
18 Piña de Esgueva
19 Villarmentero de Esgueva
20 Tudela de Duero
21 Aldeamayor de San Martín

2

3

4

5

KEY

● Town described in text
═ Motorway
═ Main road
═ Secondary road
─ Railway
▨ National boundary
- - Ferry
✈ Airport

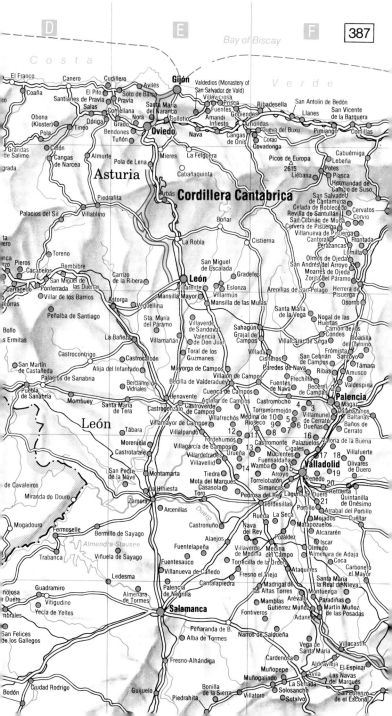

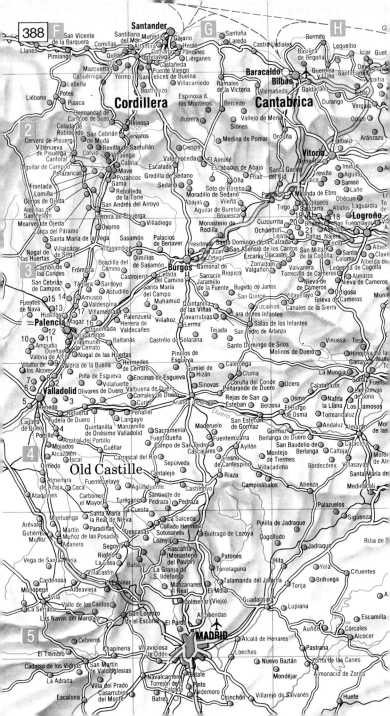

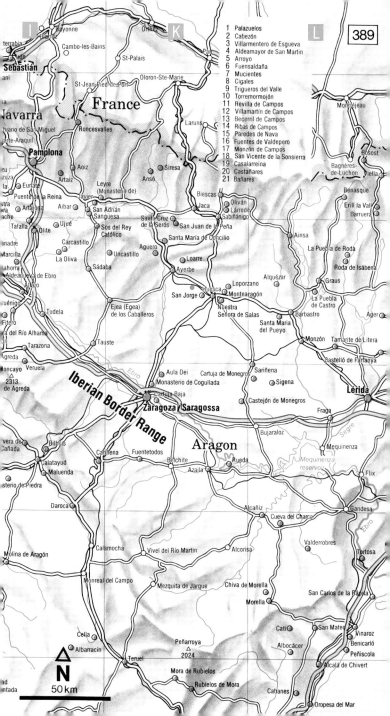

1 Palazuelos
2 Cabezón
3 Villarmentero de Esgueva
4 Aldeamayor de San Martin
5 Arroyo
6 Fuensaldaña
7 Mucientes
8 Cigales
9 Trigueros del Valle
10 Torremormojón
11 Revilla de Campos
12 Villamartín de Campos
13 Becerril de Campos
14 Ribas de Campos
15 Paredes de Nava
16 Fuentes de Valdepero
17 Monzón de Campos
18 San Vicente de la Sonsierra
19 Casalarreina
20 Castañares
21 Bañares

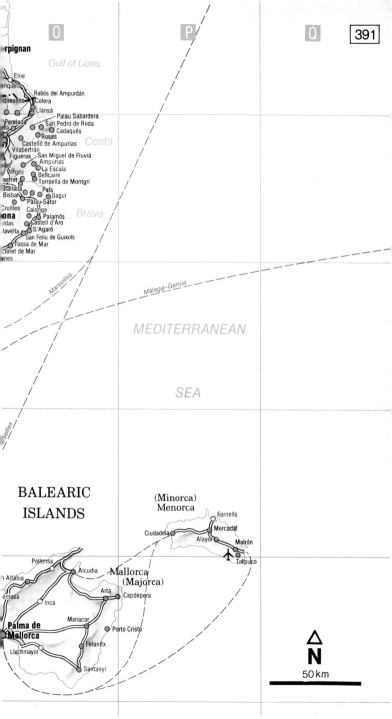

O   P   Q

rpignan

Gulf of Lions

Elne
nquera
quesens
Rabós del Ampurdán
Colera
Llansá
Palau Sabardera
San Pedro de Roda
Perelada
Cadaqués
Rosas
Castelló de Ampurias
Figueras
San Miguel de Fluviá
Vilabertrán
Ampurias
La Escala
Bellcaire
Torroella de Montgrí
Pals
Bagur
Palau-Sator
Calonge
Palamós
Castell d'Aro
S'Agaró
San Feliu de Guixols
Tossa de Mar
Loret de Mar
las
Vergés
astret
Bisbal
Cruilles
na
Idas
avella

Costa

Brava

Marseilles

Málaga–Genoa

MEDITERRANEAN

SEA

Marseilles

BALEARIC
ISLANDS

(Minorca)
Menorca
Fornells
Ciudadela
Mercadal
Alayor
Mahón
Trépuco

Pollensa
Alcudia
Mallorca
(Majorca)
Alfabia
Artá
Capdepera
mosa
Inca
Manacor
Porto Cristo
Palma de
Mallorca
Felanitx
Lluchmayor
Santanyí

△
N
50 km

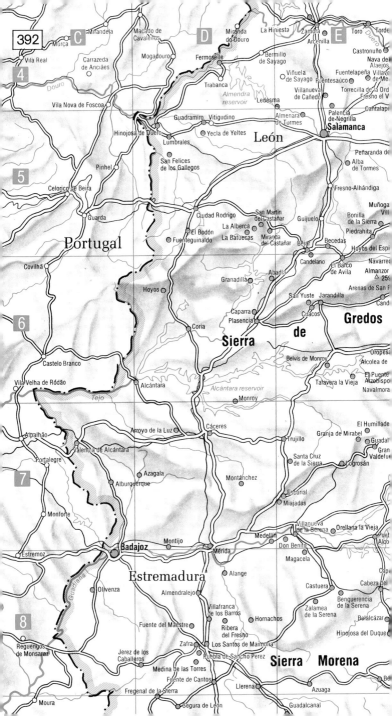

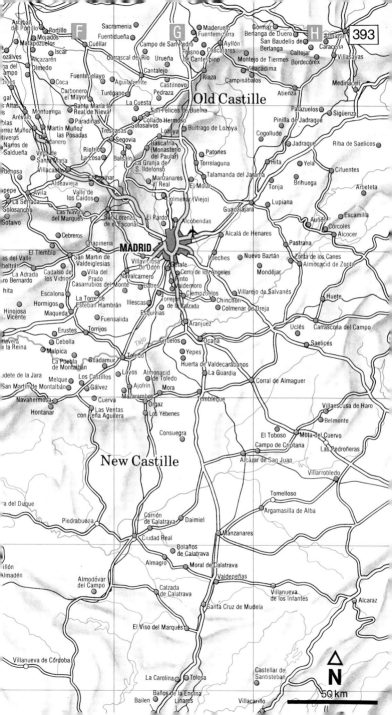

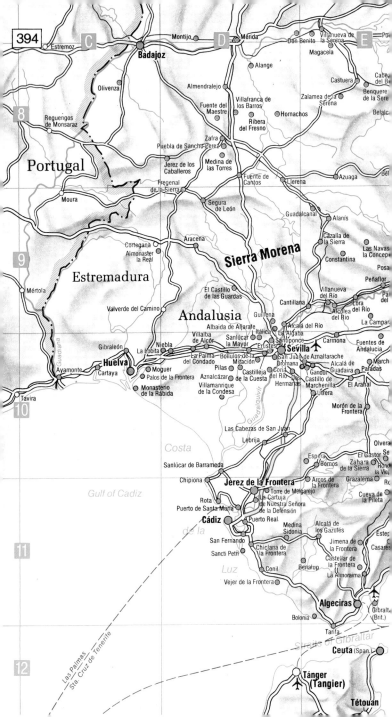

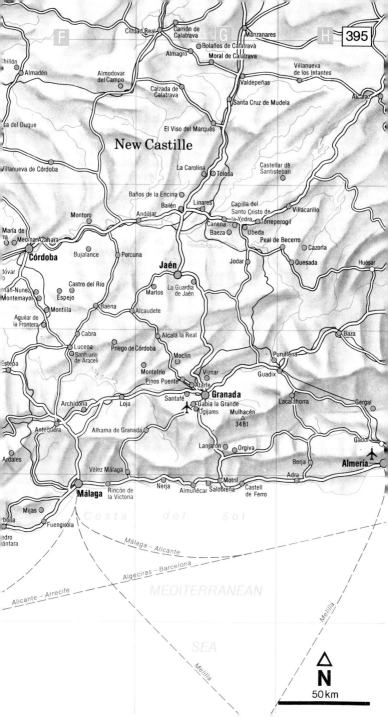

New Castille

Ciudad Real
Carrión de Calatrava
Manzanares
Bolaños de Calatrava
Almagro
Moral de Calatrava
Almadén
Almodóvar del Campo
Villanueva de los Infantes
Calzada de Calatrava
Valdepeñas
Alcara
sa del Duque
Santa Cruz de Mudela
El Viso del Marqués
Villanueva de Córdoba
La Carolina
Tolosa
Castellar de Santisteban
Baños de la Encina
Bailén
Linares
Capilla del Santo Cristo de la-Yedra
Villacarillo
Montoro
Andújar
Torreperogil
María de
Medina-Azahara
Canena
Baeza
Úbeda
Peal de Becerro
Córdoba
Bujalance
Porcuna
Cazorla
Jaén
Jodar
Quesada
Huésar
tóvar
Castro del Río
Martos
La Guardia de Jaén
mán-Nunez
Espejo
Montemayor
Montilla
Baena
Alcaudete
Aguilar de la Frontera
Cabra
Alcalá la Real
Baza
Lucena
Priego de Córdoba
Moclin
Purullena
Santuario de Araceli
Montefrío
Viznar
Guadix
Estepa
Pinos Puente
Atarfe
Granada
Archidona
Loja
Santafé
Lacalahorra
Gergal
Antequera
Gabia la Grande
Ugijares
Mulhacén
△ 3481
Ardales
Alhama de Granada
Lanjarón
Orgiva
Gador
Berja
Almería
Vélez Málaga
Motril
Adra
bella
Rincón de la Victoria
Nerja
Almuñécar
Salobreña
Castell de Ferro
Mijas
Málaga
Fuengirola
edro
ántara

Costa del Sol

MEDITERRANEAN

Málaga – Alicante

Algeciras – Barcelona

Alicante – Arrecife

SEA

Melilla

Melilla

N
50 km

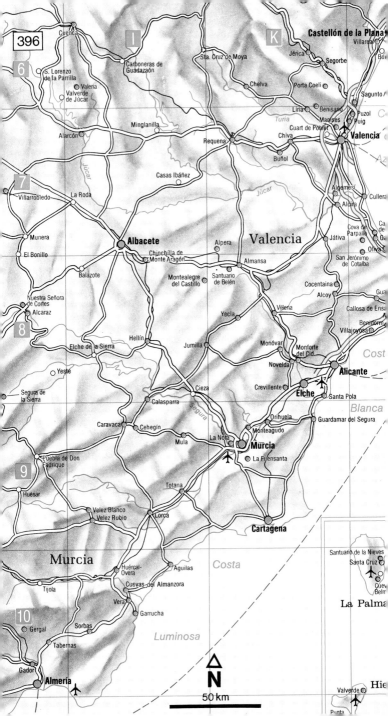

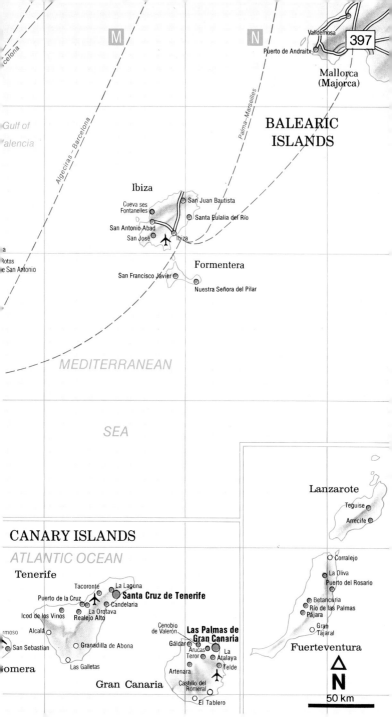

Parish church, El Sagrario (next to the cathedral): Dating from the 15C, it was founded by Ferdinand and Isabella on the site of a former mosque. The church has a particularly beautiful late Gothic portal with lavish decoration (including coats-of-arms) by Pedro López. The Plateresque high altar has statues and polychrome reliefs by Alonso Berruguete or Juan de Balmaseda.

Nuestra Señora de la Victoria (Calle de la Victoria): Built in 1487 by Ferdinand and Isabella, where their tent was pitched during the arduous siege of Málaga. Behind the altar is a *figure of the Virgin* in an over-ornately decorated *Camarín*.

Alcazaba: An Arab castle with particularly beautiful gardens and numerous courtyards. The fortress dates back to Roman origins. It was altered several times, especially under the Nasrite dynasty (14C) and extensively restored in 1933. An **Archaeological Museum** (Puerta de Granada) now occupies the buildings. On display there are Roman and pre-Roman finds, sculpture from Visigoth up to and including Arab times, Renaissance art, collections of coins and inscriptions and an important collection of Moorish ceramics from the 9–15C.

Roman Theatre (Calle de la Alcazabilla): Near the alcazaba. Built during the reign of the Emperor Augustus, making good use of the hillside. The ruins still have some of the marble furnishings.

Castillo de Gibralfaro (440 ft. above sea level): The castle's name comes from the Arab term for 'castle of the lighthouse'. The Arab fort was probably preceded by a Phoenician building. However, the building aquired its present form under the Nasrite ruler Yusuf I in the 14C. There is a beautiful Arab gate set into the wall. The former mosque lies within the castle area.

A double wall joins up with the alcazaba.

Museum of the History of Art (Museo Provincial de Bellas Artes, Calle San Agustín): This museum is housed in the beautiful 17C Palacio de Buenavista, which has two courtyards—one Mudéjar, the other Renaissance. The interesting collection is displayed on two floors.

The ground floor, mainly devoted to Spanish art from the 16–17C, has some superb paintings: for example, *Mater Dolorosa* and *Ecce Homo* by Luis de Morales; *St.Francis of Paola* by Murillo; the *Adoration of the Shepherds* by Antonio del Castillo, a pupil of Zurbarán; works by Zurbarán himself; paintings by Ribera, who is represented with the *Portrait of an Apostle, St.Francis of Assisi* and *St.John; John the Evangelist* by Alonso Cano; and sculptures by Pedro de Mena.

On the first floor, 19&20C paintings, etc., including sketches by the young Picasso, as well as pictures he painted at the ages of 10 and 14. Picasso was born in Málaga, on the Plaza de la Merced (memorial plaque on the house), in 1881. A small adjoining library contains information concerning the painter; one room is dedicated entirely to Picasso's teacher Muñoz Degrain.

Also worth seeing: The *church of Santiago el Mayor* (Calle de Granada): Mudéjar tower built in 1490. The round, domed 17C *church of Santo Cristo* (Calle Compañía) contains the tomb of the sculptor Pedro de Mena. The *Episcopal Palace* is 18C with a baroque façade. The beautiful *Fountain of Neptune* (*c.* 1560, Italian marble) is situated on the marble-paved Paseo del Parque. The entrance to the *Mercado* (main market, Calle Atarazanas), the *Puerta de Atarazanas*, is a (13C) white marble horseshoe gateway with inscrip-

Málaga, Nuestra Señora de la Victoria

Málaga, Alcazaba

Málaga, Alcazaba and Gibralfaro

tions. The gateway once stood on the fortified wharf near the Puente de Tetuán. *Casa del Consulado* (Plaza de José Antonio): Built in 1782, with an arcaded courtyard. The *Museum of Holy Week* (Plaza de San Pedro) belongs to the brotherhood, the 'Confradía del Santísimo Cristo de la Expiración'; it exhibits the figures carried in processions and their thrones.

Environs: Rincón de la Victoria (7 km. E.): A cave, the *Cueva del Tesoro*, in a park above the town, has drawings from the Palaeolithic age. It served as a burial chamber and also as a place of refuge for Christians and then Arabs. A small *museum* displays finds. **Fuengirola** (35 km. SW): Ruins of the 10C *Castle of San Isidoro*; renovated in the 16C. **Mijas** (9 km. N. of Fuengirola): Old *parish church* with

Romanesque features; Arab *fortress walls*; the *Plaza de Toros,* an ancient bull ring, with an unusual rectangular form; the 17C *Capilla de la Ermita de la Virgen de la Peña.* **Vélez-Málaga** (34 km. E.): This town was known in Roman times as 'Maenoba' and under the Arabs as 'Ballix'. The church of *Nuestra Señora de la Encarnación* was probably an early Christian foundation, although it later served as a mosque; Mudéjar wooden ceiling. The church of *San Juan Bautista* (Plaza de España is late Gothic; superb polychrome *sculpture* by Pedro de Mena and a valuable early 17C chalice, the 'Cáliz de las Esmeraldas'. The *pilgrimage church of Nuestra Señora de los Remedios* dates from 1640. The church of *San Francisco* has a domed chapel furnished in rococo style; cloister surrounded by two-storey arcades. Of historical interest

Málaga, monument to Picasso

s the *Chapel of San Sebastián,* in which King Ferdinand's equerry Sebastián Sánchez Pelao was laid to rest. He lost his life while protecting the king in battle in 1487. *Casa Consistorial* (1597) in Renaissance style. *Palacio de Veniel* (or Beniel); Arab Alcázar.

Mallorca/Majorca (I)

Balearic Islands   p.390☐N/O 6

With an area of 1,400 sq. miles Majorca is the largest of the Balearic islands. The 'Island of Tranquillity' has a very varied landscape. There are tall steep mountains on the N. coast, and idyllic valleys and wide plains. The coast is 250 miles long. In recent years numerous hotels and houses have been built. Majorca is visited by over 300,000 people annually. Apart from the tourist trade, Majorca is predominantly agrarian (almonds, carob, apricots). Stock breeding is also of importance. Industry is mainly confined to Palma, Manacor and Felanitx (production of leather goods, tiles, pottery, jewellery, woollen blankets and local fashions).

History: Numerous remains of megalithic buildings (talayots) show that there were settlements on the island as early as the Neolithic age. Later Phoenicians and Greeks left traces of their civilizations. In the 7C BC the Carthaginians took power. In 123 BC the Romans captured the islands and settled in several places (including in the region of Palma). After the fall of the Roman Empire the Vandals briefly

Palma de Mallorca, Arab bath

became lords of the Balearics. Majorca later became part of the Byzantine Empire. Towards the end of the 8C the Balearics were seized by the Arabs, who made their mark on the islands for five centuries. In 1229 the King of Aragon finally annexed the island and gave it the status of a kingdom. After brief independence the island was again annexed to Aragon (1345). From the 14C onwards the islands constantly fell prey to pirate raids. Majorca later became part of the kingdom of Spain and remains a Spanish province to this day.

Palma de Mallorca (pop. 265,000): Capital of Mallorca and of the province of the Balearics. It extends over 12 miles along the shore of a wide bay and offers the tourist numerous hotels, fine town planning and luxurious living quarters, apart from the totally preserved Old Town. The 17C *Consulado del Mar*, the former maritime trading centre, is graced with a five-arched Renaissance loggia. On the ground floor there is a *Maritime Museum* with numerous model ships, ship parts and documents. There is also an interesting late Gothic *chapel*. La Lonja is a beautiful Gothic building from the 15C by the Majorcan architect G. Sagrera. The four castle-like corner towers of the former exchange form a crown of battlements. Inside there is an interesting room with six columns. Housed here is the *Provincial Art Museum*. The *Almudaina Palace* was the seat of the Arab kings until the 13C. It later served as a residence of the Spanish kings. Interesting courtyard with Gothic ancestral chapel. *Cathedral (La Seo):* Built 1230–1600 and thus has parts which are Renaissance. The cathedral's proportions alone make an immediate impression on visitors. The *Puerta de la Mirador* with late Gothic carving and the N. portal, the *Puerta de la Almoina* are worth seeing. Within: there are pulpits on both sides of the choir; the Capilla Real and the Capilla de la Trinidad have tombs of Mallorcan kings; most of the 18 chapels have splendid baroque altars. *Monastery of San Francisco:* The single-aisled 14C Gothic monastery church is the town's most important building after the cathedral. There is a large baroque high altar and a very beautiful late Gothic cloister, which shows strong Moorish influence. *Town Hall:* Built in the 16&17C. Renaissance façade; roof with deep eaves. Inside is the *Historical Archive* of the Kingdom of Mallorca. Also worth seeing are the 17C *town walls*, *palaces* from the 16–18C (Casa Oleza and the Casa Vivot with a very beautiful courtyard) and the churches of *Santa Eulalia*, *San Nicolás* and *Santa Magdalena*. *Castillo Bellver:* A 13C Gothic castle which has served as a royal residence and a state prison. It now houses the *Archaeological Museum* of Palma. The *Baños Arabes* is the

Palma de Mallorca, cathedral, Puerta del Mirador

nly building to have survived from Moorh times.

Valldemosa: Famous for its Carthusian monastery (La Cartuja), which was converted into a castle by King James II round 1275. In 1399 it was repossessed y Carthusians. Interesting monastery church with beautiful frescos in the dome. Monastery pharmacy with old instruments; library with valuable documents. During the winter of 1838–9 the Polish composer Chopin and the French authors George Sand lived in the monastery. A w of their mementoes have been collected nd exhibited in a small museum.

Alcudia: Medieval town gates, remains of the town wall and a Roman theatre. The 3C *Santa Ana* is one of the oldest churches in Majorca. Also worth seeing is the harbour of Puerto de Alcudia on the site of the Roman town of *Pollentia*.

Porto Cristo: Little fishing village with a natural harbour. The main attractions of the area are the nearby stalactite caves of *Els Hams* (discovered in 1906; incomparable bizarre shapes; only 350 m. long) and *Drach* (2 km. long; known in ancient times; large subterranean lake).

Santanyi: Town walls from the 16&17C. Nearby there are prehistoric buildings from the Bronze Age. Also nearby: the natural rock arch of El Pontás and Cala d'Or, a lovely bay surrounded by cliffs.

Artá: The high-lying pilgrimage church of *San Lorenzo. Museum* with prehistoric finds. Talayot of Ses Pahisses (gateway made of huge stone blocks). 10 km. from Artá, at Cala Ratjada, are the *Artá Caves* (entrance via 100 ft. high crevice facing the sea!).

Capdepera: The largest *fortress* on the island. Built *c.* 1300 under James II, it has survived in good condition.

Puerto de Andraitx: Beautifully situated harbour. Nearby are the beaches of Camp del Mar, San Telmo and the Dragonera rock island.

Son Alfabia: Former summer seat of the Moorish Viziers of Majorca, now a country residence. The *Arab gardens* with subtropical vegetation and waterworks are particularly interesting.

Manacor: Second largest town on the island and important industrial and craft centre. *Parish church* with minaret-like bell tower; monastery of *San Domingo* (17/18C) with cloister. *Archaeological Museum* in the *Torre Ses Puntes*.

Felanitx: Majorca's wine-growing centre. Interesting 13C *parish church* with impressive baroque façade and wide flight of steps.

Maluenda
Zaragoza/Aragon

h3]p.388☐l 4

Santas Justa y Rufina: Begun 1413; Mudéjar style with ceramic plaques. The church has a very uniform style—even the pulpit with Moorish stucco is in keeping. Interesting altars: the high altarpiece is 15C and was probably made by the Aragonese artist Solives; there are also 15C winged altars; one altarpiece in particular worth mentioning was made by the artists Domingo Ram and Juan Ríus from 1475 -7.

Santa María: Mudéjar church with rec tangular ground plan and a groined vaul Some of the chapels were added in th 16&17C. The altarpieces (some of whic are now in the *Casa Rectoral*) date from th 15&16C.

Manresa
Barcelona/Catalonia   p.390☐N 3/

An ancient town, which had been settle in pre-Roman times. Historians are, how ever, undecided as to whether what you se today is the Roman settlement of Bocas or the ancient Minorisa.

Collegiata Santa María: Gothic, bui between 880–937 and consecrated in 94 The new church was designed by Bere guer de Montagut, who built the chur of Santa María del Mar in Barcelon Building continued 1328–1416; servic were held from 1371. The bell tower dat from 1592. There is a cloister. The *chur treasure* includes some valuable retable the Pentecost retable by Pere Serra (139 with an Entombment by Luis de Borrass on the predella (1411); the retable of Sa Marcos, which is probably by Arnau Bass (mid 14C); and the retable of San Nicol by Jaume Cabrera (1406). The Holy Vi gin, 'Mare de Deu de l'Alba', is by Pe Puig from the 14C. The church has bee a protected monument since 1931.

Bridges: Spanning the river Cardoner a two old bridges, the 12C *Pont Vell,* Romanesque construction, and the *Po Nou,* which is 14C Gothic.

Museum (Calle de Villadordis): Includ an archaeological collection, a section medieval ceramics and a collection of mo ern Catalan painting.

Also worth seeing: The hermitage

Santa Cueva, in which Ignatius Loyola wrote his 'Exercitia Spiritualia' in 1522. Nearby is the 18C church of *San Ignacio.*

Environs: San Fructuoso de Bages (4 km. NE on route 141): The *monastery of San Benito,* now private property, was consecrated in 972. The church, which is single-aisled with three apses, dates from the 12C. There is a beautiful cloister, also 12C, with round arches on double columns, the capitals of which have interesting, archaic-looking decorations. **Balsareny** (25 km. N.): The *fort* stands on a hill 1,400 ft. high. It is rectangular with an inner courtyard. The fort's church, *Mare de Deu de Balsareny,* is Gothic. The *parish church of Santa María* dates from the 11C, although the nave was not built until the 13C.

Mansilla de las Mulas
León/León   p.386□E 3

Defensive Walls: The best example of medieval defensive walls in the province of León. They were probably built in 1181, when Ferdinand II was helping to revitalize the town. Where the walls are not flanked by the Río Esla, they have defensive towers (134 ft. apart).

Also worth seeing: *San Martín:* 14C with simple Gothic portal; capitals with animal motifs. The *Convento de San Agustín:* founded by Fadrique Enríquez in 1500.

Environs: Between the rivers Esla and Porma in Castro de Villasabariego lies ancient **Lancia**, once the Asturians' most important town. Methodical excavation revealed many finds from Roman times. **Mansilla Mayor:** single-aisled Gothic *parish church* from the 15C, with some Mudéjar furnishings. Early 16C Gothic portal; 17C high altar. **Villarente** with the 16C parish church of *San Pelayo.* The church has a baroque altar and several Gothic panel paintings.

Manzanares el Real
Madrid/New Castile   p.392□G 5

Founded by citizens from Segovia in 1247; the town was a bone of contention between Madrid and Segovia during the Middle Ages.

Castle: Building began in 1435 under the Count of Santillana. The castle was built around an old 13C hermitage, which was used as a chapel. Square ground plan, with round towers at the corners; the Torre del Homenaje is larger and square. In 1473 the first Duke of Infantado made the castle more palatial. A few years later the second Duke commissioned Juan Guas with the construction of the lovely gallery—considered the most beautiful in Spain. Juan Guas equipped the towers with embrasures and decorated them with rings of round stones. The castle houses a *museum,* which displays models and documents relating to various castles.

Parish church of Nuestra Señora de las Nieves: Built at the beginning of the 16C. The S. façade has a beautiful portal and numerous memorial plaques with Maltese crosses. Nave and two aisles are separated by semicircular arches.

Environs: Colmenar, *c.* 25 km. SE of Manzanares el Real. The parish church, the *Iglesia de la Asunción,* built in the late 15C/early 16C, has three late Gothic portals, one of which shows Renaissance influence. The slender tower is crowned by a 16C spire. At the high altar are paintings by Sánchez Coello and sculptures by Francisco Giralte. An exceptionally beautiful Renaissance stairway leads to a gallery. El

Molar (E. of Manzanares el Real): The parish church, the *Iglesia de la Asunción,* now greatly altered, was initially 13C Gothic. The church has a portal of 1596 in Herrera style and a Gothic door from the late 15C.

Marbella
Málaga/Andalusia   p.394☐F 11

Fortifications: Well-known seaside resort. In the Old Town, parts of the *town walls* have survived, along with two battlemented *towers* near the parish church. The remains of the Moorish *alcazaba* have been restored. They date from the 10C, though the masonry shows signs of an older Roman structure. Keep and courtyard with armoury.

Town Hall: 16C building with very beautiful Mudéjar panelling and interesting 16C frescos of the Crucifixion (in good condition). In front of the town hall there is a charming 16C *fountain* and the *Cruz del Humilladero* which records the humble subjection of the Christian victors before the will of God at the time of the Reconquista.

Also worth seeing: *The monasteries of San Francisco and La Trinidad,* both 16C. *Hospital Bazan,* 16C, with archaeological *museum. Hospital San Juan de Dios.* Roman bridge over the Nagüeles.

Environs: Cave of Pecho Redondo: in which Palaeolithic finds were made (including ceramics, axes, arrowheads, jewellery etc.). At **San Pedro de Alcántara** (10 km. W.) are the ruins of *Silmiana,* a Roman town and harbour with an edifice with five arches, which was probably a water reservoir. Not far away are the remains of the early Christian *Basilica Vega del Mar,* which has nave, two aisles and two

apses (used as burial chambers in the 6C). A *pool* in the shape of a fish was used for baptism. **Estepona** (41 km. W.): Founded by the Romans and known in Arab times as Estebuna. 16C *Parish church.* Ruins of the *aqueduct* of Salduba. **Casares** (10 km. N. of Estepona): Ruins of an Arab alcázar. In nearby **Alarife** there are the remains of an old *Iberian settlement.* **Manilva,** also nearby, has traces of an old *complex of baths.*

Marchena
Sevilla/Andalusia   p.394☐E 10

San Juan: A 15C Gothic-Mudéjar church, which is surprisingly large. The inside, with nave and four aisles, contains an altar retable of 16C Flemish paintings, carved choir stalls, and a fine wrought-iron choir grille. In the sacristy there are pictures by Zurbarán ('Immaculate Conception', 'Crucifixion', 'John the Baptist' and 'St. James').

Environs: El Arahal (9 km. W.): church of *La Victoria* (16C; rebuilt in baroque style); *Iglesia de la Vera Cruz:* a round Byzantine building, with an interesting portal and carved sillería. *El Santo Cristo de la Misericordia:* 18C church with Plateresque tower. *Hospital de la Caridad* (15C). **Paradas** (3 km. W.): Church of *San Eutropio:* A beautiful church with an impressive Renaissance façade. **Gandul** (c. 25 km. W.): Arab *fortress ruins* with rectangular tower (12–13C). The church of *San Juan* is an old building (not restored since 19C). *Dolmen* on the Cerro de Bencarrón, from the Neolithic age. **Fuentes de Andalucia** (20 km. NW): *Hospital de San Sebastián:* The church has a beautiful 18C baroque portal; impressive *baroque house*

Manzanares el Real, castle

Marbella, Roman mosaic

fronts in the Calle de Fernando Llera, Nos. 7 & 8.

Martos
Jaén/Andalusia   p.394 ☐ G 9

Santa María de la Villa: This restored church was built in the 13C and underwent renovation in the 15C.

Santa Marta: A 15C church with a beautiful portal in late Gothic-Isabelline style.

Ayuntamiento/Town Hall: A former prison; interesting portal and finely nailed door.

Also worth seeing: Ruins of the Arab *fortress, La Peña.*

Environs: Alcaudete (23 km. SW): with two 16C churches, *Santa María* (with a Plateresque portal) and the Mudéjar *San Pedro.* A medieval *castle*, parts of which have survived (e.g. massive keep), stands high on a rocky hill. **Alcalá la Real** (50 km. S.): *Fortaleza de la Mota:* The large 14C fortress has undergone several conversions. 16C Gothic chapel, watch tower, bell tower of the razed church of Santa María de la Mota. *Santa María de las Angustias:* Church in which the painter Juan Martínez Montañés (born 1568) was baptized. *Fountain* for Emperor Charles V.

Mayorga de Campos
Valladolid/Old Castile   p.386 ☐ E 3

Picturesque village with Mudéjar features and baroque houses. In the main square there is an obelisk dating from the early 16C.

Santa María de Arbás: 15C Mudéjar church with two fine sculptures, one of the Virgin Mary from the 13C and another from the 15C.

Also worth seeing: The Mudéjar church of *Santa María* with a nave, two aisles, a baroque altarpiece by Pedro de Sierra and a beautiful 15C Gothic image of Christ. The church of *Santa Marina* is also Mudéjar, with a nave, two aisles, choir with openwork balustrade and an altarpiece by the Maestro de Palanquinos. The *Iglesia del Salvador* has a nave, two aisles and a massive tower. *San Pedro Mártir* is baroque. *Santo Toribio,* with a nave, two aisles, barrel vaulting, dome and altarpieces and paintings from the 16–18C is neo-Romanesque. The 18C *Hospital San Lazarus* has a reclining figure of Christ. 17C *Town Hall.* Remains of the old town walls.

Martos, view

Environs: Becilla de Valderaduey (*c.* 4 km. S.): A 16C Mudéjar church, *San Miguel*, has Mudéjar panelling and an altarpiece with fine carved figures of St. Anthony of Padua, St. Francis and St. Thomas Aquinas.

Medellín
Badajoz/Estremadura   p392☐D 7

Birthplace of Hernan Cortés, the conqueror of Mexico. Now an insignificant village at the foot of a mountain on the banks of the Río Guadiana. It was called Metellinum under the Romans, after the consul Quintus Caecilius Metellus, who was stationed here in 74 BC. After Arab occupation, Alfonso IX awarded Medellín to the

Order of St.James, who had seized the village from the infidels in 1229 under Ferdinand the Holy.

Castillo: Building began after the recapture of the town. It has a massive ring of walls. Most towers are 13C; one is 14C.

Also worth seeing: In the middle of the village square stands the *bronze monument to Cortés the conquistador* (1890). In his hand he holds a banner and at the foot of the monument, bronze plaques list his most important victories: 'Mejico', 'Tlascala', 'Otumba' and 'Tebasco'. The Gothic church, *San Martín*, (restored in the 17C) is situated half way up the cliff. Within is the font in which the conquistador was baptized. A stone bench with coat-of-arms marks the house in which he is supposed to have been born. There are interesting mansions, including the *Palace of the Dukes of Medinaceli*. The *Ayuntamiento* has a portrait of Cortés.

Environs: Don Benito (*c.* 8 km. E.): The late 16C parish church of *Santiago* has been altered many times. The main façade is crowned by a modern, pointed bell tower. There are two side portals, the *Portada de la Epístola* from 1570 and the *Portada del Evangelio* from 1598. Inside, (nave and two aisles), there are interesting chapels with tombs bearing coats-of-arms and inscriptions. The tower was rebuilt in the 19C. The façade of the *Iglesia de Santa María* is decorated with trefoils. There are numerous houses with noblemen's coats-of-arms and many have fine portals, e.g. the *Casa de los Anayas*, the *Casa Soto de Zaldívar*, the *Casa de Morales* and the *Ayuntamiento*, which has colonnades. **Villanueva de la Serena** (*c.* 16 km.): The *Iglesia Parroquial de la Asunción* is 16C Renaissance in Herrera style with 17C baroque features. Inside there are a nave, two aisles and several chapels in which there are two Gothic paintings by Luis de Morales *El Divino*. The *Convento de San Bartolomé* was founded at the end of the 16C. Part of the cloister has survived. The single-aisled church has tombs with coats-of-arms. The *Convento de la Concepción* dates from the early 17C. The *Ayuntamiento* was built in the 16C. Various *Residencias Solariegas* (noblemen's mansions) have survived. The *Palacio de los Priores de Magacela* was converted at the time of Charles III. A patio and a hermitage, which may have belonged to this residence have survived. **Magacela** (20 km. SE): Formerly the Roman *Contosolia* and the Arab *Um Gazala*, the town reached its peak in the 13C, when it was priory of the Order of Alcántara. The parish church of *Santa Ana*, within the walls of the castillo, has a Mudéjar portal. Inside the single-aisled church has a wooden ceiling and an

interesting font. The *Ermita de Nuestra Señora de los Remedios* has an interesting 16C tomb with the reclining figure of Don Cristóbal Bravo, a prior of the town and a canon of Seville. The building once adjoined the *Palacio de los Priores,* whose portal (1628) has survived. Numerous houses in the town have Gothic features and many of the façades have coats-of-arms. Only ruins of the *castillo* remain. The former Plaza de Armas has been incorporated into the cemetery. Remains of *cyclopean walls.* **Orellana la Vieja** (*c.* 38 km. E.): The *castillo* was a fortified palace, of which a beautiful Renaissance patio remains; this has stilted arches on the lower floor and flattened arches on the upper floor.

Medinaceli
Soria/Old Castile   p.388☐H 4

An old Celtic-Iberian settlement, which became the Roman *Ocilis* and later the Arab *Medina Salim* (Almanzor died here). After Alfonso I of Aragon seized the town from the Arabs and handed it over to the Kings of Castile, it became the medieval town of Medinaceli.

Roman Triumphal Arch: 2–3C; similar to the Arch of Constantine or that of Septimius Severus in Rome and the only one with three arches in the whole of Spain. The central arch is considerably larger than the two side arches.

Santa María: Gothic collegiate church built in the first part of the 16C by Pinilla and Pedro Jáuregui. It was a mausoleum for the Dukes of Medinaceli.

Also worth seeing: The *Monastery of Santa Isabel* dating from 1598. The *Beaterio San Ramón* ,a Beguine convent and now a Hieronymite monastery, was originally the old synagogue (minus apse

Médinaceli, Roman triumphal arch

and sanctuary). The *Chapel of Beato Julián of San Martín* has 16C paintings. The 16C *Alhóndiga*. The elegant 18C *Ducal Palace* forms an entire side of the Plaza Mayor.

Medina del Campo
Valladolid/Old Castile   p.386☐F 4

Historians put the foundation of the town at around 2000 BC. After recapture from the Arabs it was ruled by the lords of the town until 1407. The town steadily increased in importance and became the residence of the Kings of Castile, reaching its zenith under Isabella the Catholic, who spent the last years of her life here. During the 15&16C Medina del Campo's trade fairs and markets were the most important in Europe. In 1520 the town was set ablaze

for refusing to take part in the fight against the 'Comuneros'.

Castle: On a little hill. The castle's slender silhouette dominates the town and the surrounding landscape. It is a fine example of Gothic military architecture enriched by Mudéjar elements. Built on the foundations of an older castle by Fernando Carreño in 1440, on the orders of John II. It was restored and extended under Ferdinand and Isabella, who had their coat-of-arms added in 1482. The castle complex consists of an outer ring of walls and battlements, an armoury yard and a majestic keep, the vaults of which are particularly impressive (strong Spanish-Arab influence).

Collegiate church of San Antolín: An

early 16C Gothic church with nave, two aisles and stellar vaulting, dating from the early 16C. The high altarpiece has carved panels with paintings in Plateresque style by various notable artists. The *Capilla Quiñones* has a relief by Juan de Juni. The *Chapel of Tomás Coello* has two sculptures by Juan Picardo. Also worthy of attention are the portal and doors with iron doorknobs, as well as the spacious atrium and the unusual square tower.

Other interesting churches: The Mudéjar-Gothic *San Miguel* has a Renaissance portal by Martin de Répite. In the main chapel there is an altarpiece with figures by Leonardo Carrión from 1567, which shows the influence of Juan de Juni. The chapel on the Gospel side has a 'Deposition' by Juan Picardo. *Santiago*, (16C), was the first church built by the Jesuits in Castile and has numerous fine sculptures. *San Martín* contains a splendid Renaissance altarpiece with 16C sculptures and paintings. The Gothic *Santa María la Real*, founded by Ferdinand and Isabella, has baroque altarpieces. The *Capilla de San Juan de la Cruz* has paintings and sculptures by Alonso Berruguete.

The Monastery of La Magdalena: Founded by Rodrigo de Dueñas and built in the 16C by Juan de Astorga. The church has groin vaults and wall paintings attributed to Juan de Vélez. There is also a lovely altarpiece from 1571 by Estéban Jordán, who was one of the finest religious sculptors in Castile.

Other interesting monasteries etc: The Mudéjar-Gothic convent of *Santa Clara* has a 16C retable by Portillo, and 16C sculptures and paintings at the high altar. The 17C convent of the *Discalced Carmelite Nuns* has a beautiful portal, a good retable and the tombs of the founders. The 16C monastery of *San José* has a baroque church.

Palace of the Dueñas: A splendid residence with an austere façade and a large escutcheon on the portal. Of interest is the hall, which is panelled in Mudéjar style, and the Renaissance courtyard, in the corners of which are the Dueñas coat-of-arms. There are also medallions with the heads of the Kings of Castile.

Hospital: Founded and named after the banker Simón Ruiz. Built in the 16C in pure Herrera style by Juan de Tolosa. Large courtyard. In the patients' wards beds fit between the buttresses. Jesuit-style church with large altarpiece; sculptures by Pedro de la Cuadra, who is also responsible for the statues of the founders (their portraits are by Juan Pantoja de la Cruz).

Also worth seeing: *Plaza Mayor* with fine gardens. 17C *town hall* with large balconies and beautiful iron grilles. Remains of the old *Royal Palace*. Nearby, the *Casa Blanca*, which has a beautiful courtyard and polychrome panelling by Rodrigo de Dueñas.

Environs: Ataquines (*c.* 10 km. S.): The *parish church* has fine sculptures by Juan de Ávila and a 16C 'Immaculate Conception' by Gregorio Fernández. **Villaverde de Medina** (*c.* 5 km. W.): The 16C *parish church* has beautiful stellar vaulting and an interesting retable with sculptures by Gregorio Fernández and paintings by Alonso Berruguete. **Pozáldez** (*c.* 5 km. N.): Single-aisled church of *Santa María* from the 16C, with a good 17C altarpiece by Francisco Billota; the church of *San Boal* has a Mudéjar-Romanesque apse and several interesting retables.

Medina de Pomar
Burgos/Old Castile   p.388☐G 2

Convento de Santa Clara: Built in 1313

as a pantheon for the Velasco family and later extended —the large side chapel is by Fernández de Velasco. Apart from the *tombs* of the Constables of Castile, the single-aisled church has a 16C *altarpiece* by Diego de Siloé and Felipe Bigarny, a recumbent 'Christ' by Gregorio Fernández, fine grilles by Cristóbal de Andino, several 16C oil paintings and the ivory crucifix belonging to Don Juan of Austria. The museum has some splendid exhibits.

Castle: The austere façade is flanked by two tall towers. Inside: Mudéjar stucco with Arab and Gothic inscriptions.

Also worth seeing: The *parish church of Santa Cruz,* a 13C church with fine sculpture at the high altar. The *parish church of Nuestra Señora del Rosario,* a 13C parish church with a nave, two aisles and the altar of *Santo Cristo.* The *Hospital da la Vera Cruz* with a beautiful courtyard.

Environs: Valdenoceda (*c.* 8 km. S.): Romanesque *church* with a dome. **El Almiñé** (10 km. S.): Romanesque *church* with an unusual tower; the 11C Romanesque Abbey of Tejada has survived well.

Medina de Rioseco
Valladolid/Old Castile   p.386☐F 3

Medina de Rioseco, an important town under the Celts and Romans, enjoyed its heyday towards the late Middle Ages. The town still has numerous traces of its glorious past, such as the pergolas of the Calle de la Riva, old churches and palaces and the Gothic town gate of Ajújar, which has survived in fine condition.

Santa María de Mediavilla: Late 15C with a nave and two aisles and beautiful stellar vaulting. 18C tower. Inside, the main retable is a masterpiece by Juan de

Juni and Esteban Jordán. Of special interest is the *Capilla de los Benavente,* (built for the Benavente tombs) with polychrome stucco and paintings on the walls and the vault. The chapel's splendid altarpiece is by Juan de Juni (1557). Also of interest are the grilles by Cristóbal de Andino (Capilla de los Benavente and choir), a 14C Gothic image of Christ, a monstrance from 1585 by Antonio de Arfe and the processional cross by Pompeyo Leoni.

Iglesia de Santiago: A Renaissance church built by Rodrigo Gil de Hontañón in 1533. The lovely Plateresque *S. portal* of 1548 is by Miguel de Espinosa. The main façade is by Alonso de Tolosa. Inside: a 15C Gothic *Madonna* and the *altarpiece at the high altar* of 1703, which is by Joaquín de Churriguera.

Also worth seeing: The *Iglesia de la Santa Cruz* with a 17C altarpiece by Juan de Medina Argüelles, paintings by Diego Díez Ferreras and other good paintings and sculptures. The *Iglesia de San Francisco,* a single-aisled Gothic church was built in the late 15C as a burial place for the Enríquez family. Among the fine works of art are an altarpiece by Pedro de Correas, two Plateresque altarpieces of 1535 by Miguel de Espinosa with polychrome clay sculptures in niches by Juan de Juni (transept) and the founders' tombs with bronze statues by Cristóbal de Andino. The *Monastery of San José ,* in the style of Herrera, has statues by Gregorio Fernández. The baroque *pilgrimage chapel of Nuestra Señora de Castilviejo* has a 13C painting of the Virgin and Child and a 17C altarpiece by Joaquín de Churriguera.

Environs: Aguilar de Campos (*c.* 10 km. NW): The Gothic-Mudéjar 14C *parish church of San Andrés* has a main portal with archivolts and horseshoe arches. Preserved inside is a Gothic image of Christ and an 'Immaculate Conception' by

Gregorio Fernández. Opposite the church of San Andrés stands a *Rollo* (signpost) with most beautiful decoration. **Morales de Campos** (*c.* 3 km. SW): The 16C *Iglesia Parroquial* (parish church) has a retable by Juan de Medina Argüelles at the high altar and a baroque altarpiece by Juan Fernández. The baroque pilgrimage church, *Ermita de la Virgen de Arenales*, dates from the 18C. **Tordehumos** (*c.* 6 km. SW): *Santa María la Sagrada* has retables, including that at the high altar with reliefs by Felipe Bigarny and paintings by Cristóbal de Herrera. The Mudéjar *Iglesia de Santiago* (16C) has a lovely altarpiece, a fine choir and a beautiful Gothic-Mudéjar pulpit. Remains of the old 13C *castle* have survived. **Villabrágima** (*c.* 7 km. S.): The 16C Renaissance *church of Santa María* has a beautiful Plateresque portal. The 16C *church of San Ginés* has a Gothic font and alabaster reliefs. **Villagarcía de Campos** (*c.* 12 km. SW): The *Colegiata de San Luis*, a 16C Jesuit collegiate church, has a high altarpiece by Juan de Herrera with sculptures and alabaster reliefs by Juan Sanz de Torrecilla; in the chapel founded by Doña Inés de Salazar y Mendoza, there is an interesting collection of 17C altarpieces and sculpture. A small *museum* preserves various art treasures, such as 16&17C paintings, reliquaries and cult objects. Remains of an old *castle*. **Valdenebro de los Valles** (*c.* 6 km. E.): The 16C Gothic *church of San Vicente* has a baroque altarpiece and paintings by Antonio Vázquez. Remains of an old *castle*. **Montealegre** (*c.* 10 km. E.): The austere Gothic *castle* (14C) has enormous octagonal towers. The *church of San Pedro* has a Plateresque altarpiece with paintings in the style of Juan de Flandes. The *church of Santa María* (16C) has a classical altarpiece. **Villafrechós** (*c.* 6 km. W.): The *parish church of San Cristóbal* (15C) has groin vaulting in the main chapel and baroque and Renaissance altarpieces with paintings and sculptures. In the church of the

Monasterio de Santa Clara there is a 15C painting of the Virgin and Child; rococo choir stalls. The pilgrimage church of *Nuestra Señora de Cabo* has interesting carved figures of the Evangelists (16C).

Medina Sidonia
Cádiz/Andalusia   p.394□D 11

The old Phoenician foundation of *Assido* became *Medina Sidonia* (medina meaning town) in Arab times. It was settled by Greeks, Romans and then Visigoths, who made *Assidona* the seat of a bishop. Alfonso the Wise managed to drive the Moors from the town in 1264. The history of Medina Sidonia is closely linked with the family of Alonso Pérez de Guzmán, 'el Bueno', who had already been decorated under Sancho IV. This family became the Dukes of Medina Sidonia.

Parish church of Santa María la Coronada: A Gothic church situated high up. Inside: a very beautiful 16C Plateresque *retable* is attributed to Melchor Turín and Juan Bautista Vázquez (scenes from the Life of Christ).

Also worth seeing: *Ayuntamiento/Town Hall*, with an interesting tiled staircase. The *Arco de la Pastora*, a gateway with double Moorish horseshoe arches, formed part of the town fortifications. Towering above the ruins of the old *fortress* is the *Torre de Doña Blanca*, in which Blanche de Bourbon (wife of Peter the Cruel) was murdered. The *Iglesia de Santiago* and the *Convento de San Agustín* are both interesting.

Environs: Alcalá de los Gazules (25 km E.): Ruins of an Arab *castle*, given to the Knightly Order of Santa María de España after the Reconquest in the 13C. Of particular interest nearby are *caves* with prehistoric drawings and fragments of paintings, especially the *Laja de los Hierros*, a sandstone slab decorated with drawings. **Benalup** (25 km. SE): About 7 km. from the town are the *caves of El Tajo, El Arco, La Cimera, El Tesoro* and many others, all of which have prehistoric drawings. **Chiclana de la Frontera** (27 km. W.): The foundation of the town goes back to the time of Ferdinand IV (early 14C). *Parish church of San Juan Bautista:* This massive 18C building replaced a 16C church. **Sancti Petri** (7 km. towards the coast): Just off the island opposite, ashlars can be seen at low tide; these are thought to have belonged to a Phoenician *Temple of Hercules*, which was described by Arab writers. There are also the ruins of a 13C *castle.* **Conil de la Frontera** (40 km. SW): *Convento de la Victoria,* with a 16C church housing a miraculous painting which probably dates from the 12C and a painting of the Magi by Alonso Cano. The *Torre de Guzmán:* Part of the Arab fortress, which was built on Roman foundations and later became the property of the Dukes of Me-

dina Sidonia. *Arco de la Villa:* Gate in the town walls. **Vejer de la Frontera** (27 km. S.): An old town with an Arab townscape and an Arab fortress; recaptured under Sancho IV. *Iglesia Parroquial del Divino Salvador:* with Romanesque, Gothic and Mudéjar characteristics; built on the site of a mosque. Inside: *retable* with good sculptures and a tiled base. 5 km. away is the *pilgrimage church of Nuestra Señora de la Oliva,* built upon a Visigoth church.

Meira
Lugo/Galicia   p.386☐ C 1/2

The town of Meira, between Ribadeo (46 km. NE) and Lugo, is famous for its fairs and also for the Cistercian convent of Santa María, which was founded in 1154.
The Romanesque convent church has a nave and two aisles and dates from the late 12/early 13C. The interesting façade, transitional between Romanesque and Gothic, has a large rose window and a broad por-

Mellid, Santa María

tal with 13C metal-clad doors beneath a triumphal arch.

Mellid
La Coruña/Galicia   p.386□C 2

The Romanesque church of *Santa María* has interesting wall paintings. The church of *San Pedro* has a Romanesque portal and good sculptures. The church of *Sancti Spiritus,* which belonged to a former hospital for Santiago pilgrims, has old tombs. The town, which has kept its medieval appearance, has beautiful mansions, such as the *Palacio de los Segade.* The cross in the town is a typical feature in Galicia.

Environs: Villar de Donas: on a side road some 5 km. SE of Mellid and *c.* 10 km. W. of Palas de Rey. The little single-aisled church of *Santiago* originally belonged to a monastery built by the Order of Santiago in 1184. It was built by the Donas family in 1386, during the reign of King James I of Castile and the founders are portrayed in wall paintings in one of the church's three semicircular apses. The church's frescos are some of the most impressive in Galicia. The portal has survived in all its glory, with embellished archivolts and capitals, along with an ornate porch. Above a row of arches stand the statues of St.Michael, St.Bartholomew and the Virgin and Child. The little church also has a Gothic stone baldacchino. At **Pambre:** 5 km. S. of Villar de Donas, on the road leading from Mellid to Artoño, is the mighty, well-preserved 14C fortress. The fortress was built by Don Gonzalo Ozores de Ulloa on a rectangular ground plan. In each corner there is a tower and in the middle the keep. Within the two fortress walls there are various courtyards and a Romanesque chapel. **Palas de Rey** (SE of Mellid): The town's *parish church* has a beautiful Romanesque portal. **Ferreira de Pallarés:** Leaving Palas de Rey, via Guntin, you come to Ferreira de Pallarés with the 12C Romanesque parish church of *Santa María,* originally part of the old Benedictine monastery of Santa María de Ferreira, which was founded in 909. A massive cloister has survived. **Sobrado:** N. of Mellid lies *Sobrado de los Monjes* (reached via Corredoiras). This monastery was founded in the 10C and taken over by Cistercians in the 12C. The church, of which only the chapel of *San Juan* survived, dates from 1168. From this time also is a column in the chapterhouse and some capitals in the cloister. In 1498 the monastery submitted to the reforms of Ferdinand and Isabella and acquired great wealth. The present building dates from the beginning of the 18C. The high altar of 1771 is by Luis de Lorenzana. The lovely sacristy is Renaissance. The present *monastery* has beautiful courtyards and a cloister and in the main was built in the 17&18C. There is also an interesting 13C church. **Vilasantar:** Continuing N. on the road from Mellid to Corredoiras, you come to Vilasantar, a small town, near which once stood the monastery of *Santa María de Mezonzo,* of which only the Romanesque church remains.

Menorca/Minorca (I)
Balearics   p.390□P 5/6

Menorca is the second-largest of the Balearic islands both in size (669 sq. km.) and population (52,000). Despite the mild climate, bizarre shape (the coastline is 124 miles long, with a length of only 29 miles and a width of 6–12 miles) and excellent connections, Menorca is still on the whole undisturbed by tourism. The island bears numerous signs of its many past occupants, including megaliths from the Bronze Age. In the course of history the island has been ruled by Greeks, Car-

Trepucó (Mahón), Taula and Talayot

thaginians, Romans, Vandals, Byzantines, Arabs and Spaniards. By the treaty of Utrecht (1714) Menorca was handed over to the English. By the treaty of Amiens (1802) Menorca was finally reannexed to Spain.

Mahón (Pop. 20,000): The capital of the island, with one of the best and most beautiful natural harbours in the Mediterranean. On the right side of the harbour is the *San Antonio* estate (the Golden Farm), where Admiral Lord Nelson lived. The whole town has a definite English air. The *Iglesia Santa María la Mayor:* Work began on building this church as early as 1287, although it was not finished until the 18C, in neoclassical style. The cathedral boasts one of the finest organs in the world, built by the organ builders Otter and Kibuz in 1810. The two front side chapels are decorated with stucco. The *Palacio de la Casa de Cultura* (formerly the Casa Mercadal): Built in classical style in the 18C on the foundations of the former Castello de Maó. It now houses the Provincial Museum, a public library (over 20,000 volumes), the historical archives of Minorca and the *Archaeological Museum*, which has finds from the island's Talayot settlements. The church of *San Francisco* was part of the former monastery of the same name (built in 1459). The present building dates from 1717. There is a Spanish baroque cloister and the Capilla del Santísimo is baroque. Slender Gothic colonnade. The *Iglesia del Carmen:* Built 1726–1808 in neoclassical style. The main portal has a niche with a small Madonna; on the high altar there is a statue of the Virgin. The interesting cloister of the former monastery is now a co-vered market. In the *Trepucó prehistoric, megalithic settlement,* there are impressive talayot and taula.

Ciudadela (Pop. 15,000): The second largest town on the island and, until 1722, the capital; now the seat of a bishop. *Palacio de Squella:* façade with golden stucco, staircase with filigree work. Inside, the rooms have fine furnishings and paintings from the period of Anglo-French occupation. *Cathedral:* Single-aisled Gothic church, begun around 1300. Classical main portal dates from 1814. The following chapels are of interest: the Capilla de las Animas (Chapel of Souls), Capilla de la Purísma (Chapel of the Immaculate Conception) and the Capilla del Santísimo (Renaissance with elliptical vault). The *Naveta of Tudon,* the most important megalithic monument on the island, probably dates from the Minorcan Bronze Age. It is shaped like an upside-down ship. *Archaeological ruins of Ciudadela:* Many natural Stone Age caves; troglodytes in Cala Morell, Terreta Saura and Sant Juan Gran; wall paintings; cyclopean walls of Alfurinet, Torre Llafuda and Santa Rosa. Numerous Roman remains (tombs, burial niches) in Cala en Forcat; Moorish remains (minaret of a mosque).

Alayor, on a little hill, was probably founded in the 14C by James II. The parish church of *Santa Eulalia* is interesting. The town hall, *Cases Consistoriales,* built around 1612, has a good painting gallery and library. Nearby is the *Torre d'en Gaumes,* the island's largest megalithic settlement, which has three enormous talayots, the tallest of which is known as *S'Atalaya.*

Mercadal (Pop. 3000): Probably founded in the 14C. Interesting parish church of *San Martín* (1330).

Mérida
Badajoz/Estremadura   p.392□D 7/.

On the right bank of the Río Guadiana Mérida, also known as the *Spanish Rome* was a stage on the silver road from Salmantica (Salamanca) to Italica. The name of the town is derived from the Roman *Emerita Augusta,* for it was founded as a colony for veterans of the V and X legions in around 23 BC, during the reign of Augustus. It was soon promoted to capital of the province of Lusitania, which comprised great parts of Portugal and Estremadura. Towards the end of Augustus's reign it was one of the most important towns of the Roman Empire; many of its monuments were built by Agrippa, the Emperor's son-in-law. Under the Visigoths the town fell into decline, although Mérida was of some importance even under the Moors. Recaptured by Alfonso IX of León in 1228, the town came under the control of the Knights of Alcántara.

Puenta Romana: A granite Roman bridge across the Guadiana. Dating from the 1C BC, its 60 arches extend 2,650 ft

Alcázar (*Alcazaba/Conventual*): Standing on the opposite side of the river from the town, the castle was built in 835 by Abd ar Rahman II using materials from Roman and Visigoth buildings. A Roman wall some 20 ft. high, forms the foundations on the side next to the river. Inside, *well* with beautiful Visigoth frieze and staircase buil with Visigoth remains. Interesting Roman *mosaics* in the courtyard.

Teatro Romano: One of the most beautiful Roman complexes in Spain. Built by Agrippa in 18 BC. The wide semicircular terraced auditorium could seat up to 5,500 people. The stage is behind the semicircu

Mérida, Alcázar, Roman bat.

Mérida, Roman theatre

lar orchestra and the chorus area is some 60 ft. in diameter. The rear wall is a long two-storey façade with 32 marble columns with Corinthian capitals on tall bases. Behind these are actors' rooms with well-preserved marble floors, columns and statues.

Amphitheatre: Connected to the theatre by a 22 ft. wide passage, the amphitheatre had a seating capacity of some 14,000. It is an ellipse, *c.* 422 ft. long and *c.* 340 ft. wide. Fights with wild animals (venationes) and gladiator combats took place here. A tall podium, formerly clad in marble, protected the audience. The upper parts of the amphitheatre are in poor condition. In 1921 underground gladiator quarters *(spolaria)* and animal cages *(carceres)* were discovered.

Circus Maximus: The Roman circus lies a little further N. Of the race track (formerly 1,340 ft. long for two- and four-horse chariots) only traces remain e.g. the *spina,* a central wall with obelisks, around which the chariots raced.

Casa del Anfiteatro: A well-preserved Roman house near the amphitheatre, dating from the 2nd half of the 1C AD). It has a typical ground plan with a patio surrounded by galleries, off which lie rooms and baths. A lovely *mosaic floor* shows people squashing grapes with their feet. Various rooms are decorated with murals.

Iglesia de Santa Eulalia: This church on the N. edge of the town has an interesting little porch (added in 1612), which incorporates parts of an old temple dedicated

Mérida, Roman amphitheatre

Mars, the god of war, from the 1C AD. The architrave, supported by two Corinthian columns, bears an inscription stating that Vetila, the wife of Paulus, dedicated this temple to the god Mars. During the building of the portico a new inscription was added, 'Dedicated not to Mars, but to Jesus Christ and to the virgin martyr Eulalia, to whom this temple is now re-edicated.' Eulalia (Santa Olalla), a young girl during the rule of Diocletian, was ordered to renounce Christianity, whereupon she spat in the faces of the relevant officials and was burnt in an oven (horno) as a result. The chapel in front of her church is therefore called the *Horno de Santa Eulalia*. The church itself was founded in the 5C, enlarged in the 6C, but fully converted in the 13C, after the recapture of Mérida. Main and side portals are Romanesque.

The *interior* is late Romanesque and incorporates materials from Romanesque and Visigoth buildings (especially capitals). Churrigueresque *altar* dates from 1743.

Acueducto de los Milagros: An aqueduct on the road to Cacéres, which carried water to the town from Pantano de Proserpina, some 5 km. away. 37 pillars, 67–100 ft. high have survived. Of a second aqueduct, *San Lazaro*, there remain but three pillars.

Arco de Trajano (in the N. of the town): The superbly preserved triumphal arch of Trajan, some 50 ft high, consists of four rows of granite columns with capitals.

Museo Arqueológico: The Archaeological Museum, housed in the baroque church of the Convento de Santa Clara (founded in the 17C), has three rooms with exhibits from prehistoric times up to the 7C AD. *Room 1:* Finds from the town's former Roman temples, sculpture and architectural fragments, as well as inscriptions. *Room 2:* Inscriptions, particularly tomb stele, from the 1–4C AD. *Room 3:* Sculpture and architectural fragments from early Christian and Visigoth buildings.

Casa del Mithraeo (near the Plaza de Toros): A building from the 1C AD in which beautiful Roman *mosaics* have survived.

Also worth seeing: Remains of the former *Temple of Augustus* (incorrectly called the *Templo de Diana*) in the Calle Santa Catalina. Now standing on this site is a baroque palace, the *Casa del Conde de los Corbos,* which has five ancient fluted Corinthian columns.

Environs: Alange (18 km. SE): This town is dominated by an Arab *castle,* which

was taken over by the Templars. Well-preserved *Roman baths* in two circular, domed rooms, each of which had a swimming bath with marble steps. **Montijo** (24 km. W.): *Palace,* belonging to a descendant of Empress Eugénie, the Condes de Montijo; 16C Renaissance portal. The *Church of San Pedro* contains an unusual 17C painted altar.

Miranda de Ebro
Burgos/Old Castile   p.388 □ H 2

San Nicolás: Romanesque apse from the 12C; the pointed-arched portal and the groin-vaulted interior are later (14&15C)

Santa María: A church with a nave, two aisles and complex 15C vaulting. The *high altarpiece* has good sculptures and reliefs. the *Capilla de San Andrés* is a mausoleum with interesting statues of a lord and lady

Also worth seeing: *Convento de San*

Mérida, Roman aqueduct

gustín with a 16C church. The *Plaza Mayor,* with the town hall and two mansions.

Environs: Santa Gadea del Cid (*c.* 8 km. NW): The *Iglesia de San Pedro,* is Gothic with a nave and two aisles; it houses large collection of jewels and metalwork. The *Convento del Espino* is 15C with atrium, polygonal apse and complex groin vaults. Remains of a 15C *fortress.* **Pancorbo** (*c.* 10 km. S.): Picturesque village with ruins of two old castles.

Moguer
Huelva/Andalusia   p.394☐C 10

Convento de Santa Clara: Built in the 14C in Mudéjar-Gothic, of which it is the best example in the province. Columbus visited the church on his return from America. Inside Mudéjar choir stalls have base of azulejos. *Alabaster tombs* of the convent's founders in the Capilla Mayor.

There is a Sienese diptych (13/14C) and a 15C Gothic painting. The *chapterhouse* contains altars decorated with azulejos, and in the *refectory* a 'Last Supper' by Pedro de Córdoba.

Also worth seeing: *Nuestra Señora de la Granada,* a 16C church with a tower modelled on the Giralda in Seville. The 14/15C *Convento de Nuestra Señora de la Esperanza* with 16C azulejos inside. House and *museum* of the poet J.R.Jiménez.

Molina de Aragón
Guadalajara/New Castile   p.388☐I 5

On the right bank of the Río Gallo. Celtic originally and later Roman. It officially became part of the Moorish-ruled territories in 1009. In 1129 the town was captured by Alfonso I of Aragon.

Castillo: Consists of sparse crumbled brick walls and five towers — *Torre del*

Mérida, Roman theatre

Moguer, Nuestra Señora de la Granada

Homenaje, Torre de Armas, Torre de Vela-dores, Torre Cubierta, Torre de Aragón.

Convento de Santa Clara: 12C, transitional between Romanesque and Gothic.

San Martín: Three fine Romanesque windows have survived.

Convento de San Francisco: A mighty Gothic building with the lovely *'Giraldo'* tower.

Mombeltrán
Ávila/Old Castile   p.392☐F 6

Castle of the Dukes of Alburquerque: Built in 1393 and one of the most beauti-

ful buildings of its kind in Castile. Façades towers, courtyards and grand staircase are very fine.

Parish church: 15C Gothic; single-aisled with large vaults. Interesting altars and grilles.

Also worth seeing: The Renaissance *hospital* (16C). The town also has various *mansions* with escutcheons and crowns. The two monasteries, *San Andrés* and *Santa Rosa,* survive only as ruins.

Monasterio de Piedra
Zaragoza/Aragon   p.388☐I

A 12C Cistercian monastery in the village of Nuévalos, some 27 km. S. of Calatayud. In 1164 King Alfonso II of Aragon asked the monastery of Poblet to erect a new building on this chosen site. Construction duly started under the direction of Abbot Pedro de Poblet in an area of lush vegetation (which still surrounds the monastery and is now a national park). Surrounding the monastery there is a rough stone wall interrupted by square and round towers with battlements. Still standing are the apse of the old church and the chapter house, refectory, hostel and keep, all of which are 13C. In 1835 much of the monastery was destroyed by arson and pillaging, but it was later rebuilt. It is now a hotel, which is popular in the summer.

Church: The original Byzantine-influenced Romanesque can still be seen in the façade. The rest of the building shows Gothic and Renaissance elements with the addition of baroque features resulting from the 18C renovation. The church has a nave, two aisles and five apses. The main entrance is arched and has 16C frescos. There is a Gothic cloister with ibbed vault and a lovely 14C double staircase.

National Park: The monastery is situated in a picturesque park, which makes a delightful contrast to the barren landscape. The little Piedra river makes the park very attractive with waterfalls and pools. The individual cascades have names like *La Trinidad* or *Iris*, and at the *Cola de Caballo* (horse's tail) waterfall there is a lovely grotto.

Mondoñedo

Lugo/Galicia   p.386☐C 1

Cathedral (Plaza de España): Originally Romanesque; built in 1219 – 48 under Bishop Don Martin, and extended in Gothic style. It was extensively destroyed by fire in 1425 and rebuilt in the 16C. The baroque façade, flanked by two towers, was built in the early 18C by Master Augustin, who kept the Romanesque portal and the large 16C stained glass rose window. Inside, there are a nave and two aisles, and beautiful 15C frescos on both sides of the plateresque choir (16C), which is in the middle of the nave. On either side of the nave there are 18C *organs*. The *high altar* has a Madonna with angels (Nuestra Señora la Inglesa) in a large, carved, gilded baroque frame. This English (Tudor) sculpture was brought by English Catholics from St.Paul's Cathedral in order to save it during the Reformation. There are baroque frescos in the apse. The sacristy is 16C and houses the *Diocesan Museum*, which preserves many smaller works of art owned by the episcopate. These include a small St.Augustin by El Greco, St.Francis by Zurbarán, two pictures by Tiepolo, Roman corn mills, an 8C font, an urn from the Philippines, an 11C Madonna and a 13C St.John. The seminary was established in the 17C under the episcopacy of Losada y Quirogas. Of particular interest is the main façade with little towers and balconies.

Virgen de los Remedios: Founded in the 12C and rebuilt in 1558. The façade is baroque. Of interest inside are the baroque altars, particularly the high altar.

Hospital San Pablo: A battlemented hospital with a tower; the façade has a splendid coat-of-arms.

Also worth seeing: *Palacio de Luaces,* with unusual coats-of-arms. *Casas Consistoriales,* with the coat-of-arms of Charles V. The monastery of *Alcántara* was founded in 1741; the *old fountain* (1548) is interesting.

Environs: Near Mondoñedo are granaries *(Combarro)* typical of Galicia. In contrast to those in Asturia, these are long and narrow and raised on posts. They are often built entirely of stone with roofs of shingle or thatch. The roof ridges sometimes have small stone crosses and the granaries themselves are occasionally decorated with stone reliefs. **San Martín de Mondoñedo:** The ancient monastery of *San Martín de Mondoñedo* was formerly at **Foz,** N. of Mondoñedo. The 'Monasterium Maximi', built by King Silo in the 8C, was the oldest pre-Romanesque monastery in Spain. Some *pre-Romanesque tombs* still remain, and the now-restored Romanesque parish church of *San Martín de Mondoñedo* has a nave, two aisles and three apses. The simple portal has archivolts and, in the tympanum, a relief of the Holy Lamb with the Cross. The tower stands on the Epistle side. The capitals are decorated with historical and allegorical themes. There are Gothic frescos and 16C wall paintings. The entire mighty complex presents an interesting appearance, particularly from the E. (defensive walls, Romanesque windows, round arches and pilaster strips). **Villanueva de Lorenzana:** 9 km. NE of Mondoñedo, on the road to Ribadeo. A monumental 18C church, by Fernando de los Casas y Nóvoa, has an interesting façade and a beautiful dome over the crossing. It was part of the former monastery of San Salvador, which was founded in the 10C. In the chapel of Santa María de Valdeflores, to the left of the entrance, there is an early Christian sarcophagus of the Conde Santo (Count Gutierre Osorio, pilgrim and relative of the Kings of León and founder of the Benedictine monastery). In the sacristy there is a small *museum*. The *Palacio de los Tovar* in Santo Tomé was built in the 16C.

Monforte de Lemos

Lugo/Galicia   p.386□C 2

Monasterio de San Vicente del Pino: Originally a Benedictine monastery founded in the 10C. It stands near the ruins of a fortress. The late Gothic church has a nave and two aisles, beautiful stellar vaulting and a Renaissance portal from 1539. The high altar dates from the 18C, the altar on the epistle side from the 16C and that on the gospel side from the 18C, with a 15C panel depicting St.Anne with the Virgin and the Child. There is also a sarcophagus of 1334. The monastery was rebuilt in the 18C with a beautiful façade decorated with coats-of-arms.

El Colegio del Cardenal/Colegio de la Compañia: Built under Cardinal Rodrigo de Castro in 1593 in austere, typically Spanish, Renaissance style with a façade reminiscent of the Escorial. Interesting geometrical ground plan with two square patios to the sides of the church; that on the S. side is probably 17C by Simón de Monasterio and that on the N. side is 18C. The church is single-aisled, with transepts, chapels and beautiful domes. The high altar is by Francisco de Moure, a 17C French sculptor. On the right is the founder's tomb, by Juan de Bolonia. Inside

Villanueva de Lorenzana (Mondoñedo), monastery church of El Salvador

he convent there is a picture gallery with paintings by El Greco and five paintings by Andrea del Sarto. Relics and old books are also exhibited.

Also worth seeing: *Convento de Franciscanas Descalzas,* founded in 1622 by Don Pedro Fernández de Castro, Count of Lemos, and his wife. The convent houses one of the finest collections of relics in Spain.

Environs: Pantón: 12 km. W. of Monforte, with the *Monasterio de Ferreira,* an old Bernardine monastery, founded in the 10C by the Count of Amorante. The church has survived with an impressive 12C Romanesque apse. The existing monastery is baroque and has a beautiful portal of 1728. There are further interesting buildings in the vicinity e.g. *La Torre de Masid* (11C; restored in the 14C and repeatedly altered). There are also several Romanesque and Gothic monasteries, *San Miguel de Eiré, San Esteban de Atán, San Fiz des Cangas* and *San Vicente de Pombeiro.* **Pombeiro:** SE of Monforte, with a Romanesque *church* dating from *c.* 1200 formerly part of the monastery of San Vicente, which dates back to the 10C). **Ribas de Sil** (near Pombeiro) with the romantically situated monastery, *San Esteban,* founded in 550 and restored in the 10C. The existing church dates from 1184, and has a nave, two aisles, a beautiful Romanesque apse, 16C high altar and baroque façade. The monastery has three cloisters, one of which ('de los Obispos') is one of the most beautiful in Galicia. **Candaira:** (NW of Monforte; take the road to Bóveda and turn off towards Escairón), with the ruins of an old pre-Romanesque *fortress.* **Ribas de Miño:** with the Romanesque monastery of San Esteban, on the road to Chantada. **Pesqueiras:** The nearby monastery, *Benediktino de Santa María,* was restored in 1121 and has a beautiful Romanesque

Madonna. **Camporramiro:** (SE of Chantada) with a Romanesque church, which has a rose window and old frescos. **Diomondi:** (W. of Escairón) with the monastery of *San Pelagio,* (consecrated in 1170 and now a national monument). The church is single-aisled and has an interesting façade.

Montblanch

The town was founded on the bank of the Río Francolí under the name of *Vilasalva* in 1155. In 1162 King Alfonso I ordered the town to be resettled on the hill of Santa Bárbara on the other side of the river, where there had once been an Iberian settlement. The name Montblanch dates from this time. The town was walled from 1366 – 77. Many walls, towers and gates have survived and testify to the Montblanch's former importance.

Santa María la Mayor: A 14C Gothic building, with nave and two aisles, built on the site of a church mentioned in 1179. The baroque façade dates from 1688. Inside: a 16C polychrome wooden figure of the Virgin, a 14C retable of St.Bernard and St.Barnaby, reliquaries and one of the oldest organs in Catalonia, which dates from 1752.

Also worth seeing: The *Iglesia de San Miguel,* a Romanesque church inside the walls and more than once the meeting place of the Catalan Council. Until Santa María la Mayor was built, it was the parish church. *Casa Josa,* a museum with a collection of beautiful ceramics from the region. Equally interesting is the *Casa Desclergue* on the Plaza Mayor. Outside the town walls is the old Gothic *Hospital of Santa Magdalena* (14C) with a beautiful cloister. There is a medieval *bridge* over the Río Francolí.

Environs: Espluga de Francolí (*c.* 10 km. NW): The parish church of *San Miguel* is 19C and occupies the site of a Romanesque-Gothic church, which was destroyed in 1873.

Monteagudo de las Vicarías
Soria/Old Castile   p.388□H/I 4

Gothic **church** with 16C portico. 16C high altarpiece with sculptures from the Burgos school and an 18C picture of the Virgin. The baptistery has a retable of 1522.

Castle: Near the town. Rampart wall and 15C keep. The Las Eras gate and two large towers are particularly noteworthy.

Environs: Villasayas (*c.* 7 km. S.): The Romanesque *church* has a portal with interesting decoration.

Montearagón
Huesca/Aragon   p.388□K 3

A fortified monastery in the village of Quicena, not far from Huesca. Founded by King Sancho Ramírez I in 1085, the monastery was abandoned in 1835. Immediately afterwards it was destroyed by fire, so that now only ruins testify to the former size of the castle-abbey. The church was built in Churrigueresque style, but has an interesting Romanesque portal. The square tower was also the castle tower. Both the Gothic crypt and the cloister were destroyed in the 19C fire.

Environs: Loporzano: The Gothic *church of San Salvador* has a Plateresque

altar and tabernacle from the church of Monte Aragón. A side chapel has a painting of the 'Crucifixion' attributed to Rubens' circle.

Montederramo
Orense/Galicia   p.386□C

The convent of Santa María was founded in 1124 by Doña Teresa de Portugal, the daughter of Alfonso VI. It was taken over by the Cistercians in 1153. In the 16C the convent was rebuilt with the help of Juan Pedro de la Sierra and Juan de Tolosa. The church has a nave, two aisles, barrel vaulting and a dome over the crossing. The façade, with a wide portal and gabled roof, dates from 1607. There are beautiful choir stalls, which were probably made by Juan Martinez in the 17C.

Environs: Junquera de Espadañedo (Xunquera de Expadañedo): Between Montederramo and Orense lie Junquera de Espadañedo and Esgos and the ruins of the 12C Cistercian *Monasterio de Santa María* along with the church, which dates from 1607. The church has a nave, two aisles, a rose window in the baroque façade and a very beautiful, well-lit crossing. **Esgos:** The 12C church of *San Pedro de Rocas* whose three apses are carved out of the rock, originally belonged to an old monastery. **Castro Caldelas** (S. of Montederramo on the road from Orense to Ponterrada): The castle, which originally belonged to the Lemos family, stands in the middle of the town. It was rebuilt in the 14C. Three mighty towers have survived.

Monterrey
Orense/Galicia   p.386□C

The town occupies a hilltop site overlook-

Monterrey, fortress

ing the Támega valley. Within three rings of walls stands the *fortress* along with a church, hospital and palace. The site was originally occupied by the Castro de Baronceli, a Celtic settlement. The origins of the fortress date back to the 12C. It was rebuilt by Sancho López de Ulloa, Count of Monterrey, in the 15C. His coat-of-arms is to be found above the entrance gate. The massive 14C keep has survived, as has the Torre de la Damas, the Torre Nueva and the ruins of a beautiful courtyard with double rows of arcades. The castle hospital was built in the 14C and has a portal with a Romanesque-Gothic tympanum. The single-aisled church has a 13C wooden ceiling and a most interesting Gothic stone retable, which has scenes from the life of Christ (in the middle is Christ the Pantocrator beneath a large baldacchino). The portal is also beautiful, having a tympanum full of figures beneath richly decorated archivolts; there are also stone figures and reliefs with animals on either side of the entrance.

Environs: Verín (SE of Monterrey): Verín has a number of beautiful houses with coats-of-arms as well as mansions, such as the *Balneario de Cabreiroá*. Also worth seeing is the baroque *Iglesia de la Merced* and the crucifix by Gregorio Fernández in the church of *Santa María la Mayor*. **Mixós** (Mijós): (NE of Monterrey), with a pre-Romanesque church, *Santa María*, which is typical of Asturian churches from the 9&10C. Mozarabic influences are also visible. Behind the baroque altar there are interesting wall paintings. **Ginzo de Limia:** (some 30 km. NW of Monterrey) has a 12C *parish church* of Romanesque origins, beautiful old houses and the *Castillo de Peña,* which has a tower.

Monterroso
Lugo/Galicia   p.386☐C 2

A town with a long history, although many of its oldest buildings e.g. the castle, no longer exist. Some interesting monuments have, however, survived.

The Romanesque parish church, *San Miguel de Esporiz,* has a fine apse and portal. The *Pazo de Salgado* or *de la Laxe* is a granite palace built in 1550 by Don Alonso Gundín and his wife, Doña Beatriz Salgador. The façade is particularly interesting. In the 15C chapel there is a Madonna of 1450. The *Pazo de Lameiros* has a façade with coat-of-arms; next door there is an interesting chapel. **Novelúa** (on the road from Monterroso to Puertomarin), has a fine Romanesque church with interesting wall paintings. **Amarante:** The castle between Monterroso and Golada was of historic importance to Ferdinand and Isabella. **Bembibre:** (SE of Monterroso) has a single-aisled Romanesque church, San Pedro, which was built in 1171 and has richly decorated portals.

Montilla
Córdoba/Andalusia   p.394☐F 9

Near Montilla, at the ancient *Munda Baetica,* the famous battle of Munda, between Caesar and Pompey, took place in 45 BC. The town was the birthplace of Gonzalo de Córdoba, 'El Gran Capitán', who was Ferdinand and Isabella's famous general.

Convento de Santa Clara: Built in

Mudéjar style. The mystic John of God lived here for a time.

Casa de Garcilaso de la Vega (now the town's administrative offices and library): Small *museum* devoted to the Spanish historian, Garcilaso de la Vega (1539-1616), who had a Peruvian mother and became famous for his works on the history of the Incas. He was nicknamed 'El Inca'.

Environs: Montemayor (12 km. NE) with the imposing 14C *castle* of the Dukes of Frías and the *parish church of Nuestra Señora de la Asunción.* **Fernán Núñez** (14 km. NE) with the 18C *Palace of the Dukes of Fernán Núñez,* which houses an art collection. **Espejo** (15 km. NE) has the massive Mudéjar *castle* of the Dukes of Osuna. The 14C *church* has a retable by Pedro de Córdoba. **Castro del Río** (24 km. NE) has the ruins of a Moorish *castle* on the site of a former Roman fortress. *Town walls* and also Roman remains. *Ayuntamiento:* In 1592 Cervantes was imprisoned here for trying to levy taxes from the clergy, when he was a commissioner of Seville.

Montserrat
Barcelona/Catalonia   p.390☐N 4

The Benedictine monastery of Montserrat is some 2,400 ft. up in the Montserrat massif (4,140 ft.), an area of limestone conglomerate. In 875 the region was recaptured from the Muslims. Four hermitages were founded subsequently; two in the lower part of the massif (San Pedro and San Martín) and two in the upper part (San Iscle and Santa María). Oliva, Bishop of Vic and Abbot of Ripoll, converted the hermitage of Santa María into a monastery and, in 1082, he became the first Abbot. The monastery played an important role in the political and cultural life of Catalonia.

Since 1918 the monastery's own publishing company have published not only religious but also secular writings. The Escolanía, or the boys' choir from the monastery's boarding school, has produced quality Catalan musicians.

The monastery has a broad *façade*, by F. Folguera (1939) with reliefs by J. Rebull. On the right is the 'Abbot's Tower' and, on the left, are the remains of the Gothic *cloister*, which Giuliano della Rovere, Abbot of Montserrat and later Pope Julius II, had built in 1467. After the atrium comes the inner courtyard (19C), which has a Romanesque *portal* (12C) and 16C tombs. The marble façade was designed by D. Villar in the 19C, with sculptures by the Vallmitjana brothers. The *church* was consecrated in 1592 and has a central nave with round Gothic arches and six side chapels. The figures of the four prophets are by José Llimona. A small chapel in the apse, reached by a marble stair, contains the black Virgin of Montserrat (*La Moreneta*, the patron saint of Catalonia since 1881), a Romanesque carving from the 12C. The throne, which has reliefs in silver and gold by famous Catalan artists, was dedicated to the Virgin as a gift from the Catalan people in 1947.

Also worth seeing are the neo-Romanesque *cloister* and the monastery's 17C *refectory*. A large *library* contains 250,000 volumes, including 400 first editions and 2,000 manuscripts. Preserved in the archive are 6,000 parchments and 10,000 documents from the 18&19C. The *picture gallery* has paintings by El Greco (including one of *St. Francis*), Zurbarán, Rizi and Caravaggio. In the garden there is the Romanesque chapel of San Iscle (11C); at the end of the Via Crucis or the Via del Rosario is the the *Santa Cueva* (Holy Grotto), where, according to the legend, the Virgin appeared. Its chapel was built by Gaudí and Puig i Cadafalch (sculpture by Llimona and the Vallmitjana brothers). The other, smaller, chapels were built 1870–1916.

Montilla, Santa Clara, portal

Environs: Martorell (19 km. S.): Formerly the Roman *Tolobi*. The town's main attraction is the *Puente del Diablo* (Devil's Bridge) over the Llobregat and Noya rivers. In the middle of the bridge there is a medieval gateway. Nearby stands a Roman *triumphal arch*. The *Museo Municipal Vicente Ros*, occupying a former 11C monastery in the Calle Capuchinos, has modern Catalan painting, ceramics, and archaeological finds.

Monzón
Huesca/Aragon   p.388 □ L 3

This little town on the Río Cinca is dominated by a tall rock, around which the town was built.

Montserrat, view

Montserrat, black Madonna

Santa María: Built in the 12C and converted in the 16&17C. The tower is Mudéjar. Inside are several baroque altars and paintings from the school of Velázquez. The building is also of historical importance as the Cortes of Aragon assembled here many times up to the 16C.

San Juan: As early as the 12C a church occupied this site. The existing Gothic church is 15C. Inside there is a 16C altar by Jerónimo Vicente.

Castillo: Roman fortifications once occupied the site of this castle. Built in the 9C, it became a Templar castle in the 12C under Ramón Berenguer IV. The single-aisled *castle chapel* is interesting.

Also worth seeing: *Iglesia de San Fran-*

cisco: 13C Gothic church; only parts of the façade remain.

Mora
Toledo/New Castile   p.392□G 6

Iglesia Parroquial: This single-aisled Gothic church was built in the 15C and possibly rebuilt in the 16C after the Comuneros rebellion. The church interior is divided into four parts by arches and there are groin vaults. The *high altar* has a carved and gilded Plateresque retable (16C). The painting on wood shows scenes from the life of Christ and the Virgin Mary.

Castillo: The castle is just outside the town and dates from the 12C. It is in a dilapidated condition. Part of the square *Torre del Homenaje* remains. Ruins of the smaller towers have survived and these are connected by defence ramparts of masonry and underground vaults.

Environs: Ajofrín (*c.* 25 km. W.) has *mansions* with coats-of-arms on stone portals. The 16C *parish church* in Gothic-Renaissance transitional style underwent some renovations in the 18C. The church has some fine examples of the goldsmith's art in the form of a chalice and a 16C chased silver processional cross. **Almonacid de Toledo** (10 km. NW): with a *castillo*, now in ruins astride the saddle of a mountain S. of the village. Only the foundations of the walls and parts of towers, including parts of vaults remain. In the middle of a large courtyard stands the plain Torre del Homenaje on a base. The upper section has only survived in part. **Los Yébenes** (19 km. S.): *San Juan:*, the parish church has an early 16C main chapel built in a style transitional between Gothic and Renaissance. The 16C Mudéjar tower shows the influence of the Renaissance. *Castillo de Guadalerza:* Built by Christians after the area had been conquered by Alfonso VI. The keep (Torre del Homenaje) is surrounded by defensive ramparts with round towers at the corners. **Orgaz** (10 km. SW): The 18C *Iglesia Parroquial* is baroque and was built under the supervision of Alberto Churriguera, after an older church—of which the main chapel has survived—had been pulled down. The architect designed a building on a Latin cross ground plan, of which only the central part and a tower were built. The high altar of 1662 belongs to the older building. It is furnished with 17C paintings of the Madrid school of Francisco Rizi. There is also a copy of the famous painting *El Expolio (The Mocking of Christ)* by El Greco, the original of which hangs in the sacristy of Toledo Cathedral. The tower and apse project from the walls of the 14C *castle,*

which lies to the W. of the town. The castle interior is dilapidated. **Consuegra** (*c.* 30 km. SE): *Castillo:* with an irregular layout. It formerly belonged to the Knights of Malta. Only a few badly dilapidated towers remain. The castle has two fences and a defensive wall with three round towers. It was probably Roman in origin with later alterations by Visigoths, Arabs and Christians. **Mazarambroz** (*c.* 20 km. W.): The *parish church* has a 16C gilded monstrance. The square *castle* (S. of the town) looks more like a medieval tower. The three-storeyed structure dates from the late 14C/early 15C.

Mora de Rubielos
Teruel/Aragon   p.388 □ K 6

Iglesia Parroquial: A former collegiate church from the 15C, built in Gothic style. It has a nave with a ribbed vault and an interesting *portal.* The tower and the cloister are 17C. The numerous chapels, decorated with azulejos from Manises, date from the 18C. The church's *forecourt* is typically Aragonese, and similar to the forecourts of secular Renaissance buildings, having coats-of-arms and wrought-iron work. Interesting and valuable church treasure.

Castillo: Built in the 13&14C and almost totally rebuilt in the 15C. In 1614 a Franciscan monastery (later dissolved) was erected within the building. Today the castle is a protected monument.

Morella
Castellón de la Plana/Valencia   p.390 □ L 5

The town of Morella (3,350 ft. high and a pop. of 6,000) is 64 km. inland and reached by a winding road from the coastal

Morella, Puerta San Miguel

town of Vinaroz. Its commanding position amidst chains of hills was made use of in early times. Roman soldiers settled here, calling the place *Castra Aelia*. The Kingdom of Valencia later set up a border fortress here. Morella has kept its medieval appearance. The steeply-terraced streets are lined with picturesque houses, whose façades have projecting wooden balconies. But Morella is a silent town, whose alleys, arbours and buildings are visibly decaying. The town wall, which is 1.3 m. long with numerous towers, has survived in good condition. The fortress has cyclopean walls and affords a good view of the town and its surroundings.

Santa María la Mayor: The most beautiful Gothic church in Valencia. Fine pointed arches and sculpture on the *Puerta de los Apóstoles* and the *Puerta de las Vírgenes*. The latter, the most recently built, is most exquisitely decorated. The interior is also superb and has a nave, two aisles and three apses (but no transept). The *choir*, supported on four pillars (15C), is reached by a spiral staircase, decorated with bas-reliefs. The depiction of the Birth of Christ is particularly beautiful. The *trascoro* (choir screen) is Italian and has a Last Judgement with a host of relief figures. The *high altar* is a Churrigueresque masterpiece. In this church (in the presence of King Ferdinand of Aragon), the Antipope Benedict XIII, who was residing in Peñíscola, read the Mass at which St. Vincent Ferrer preached. A small *museum* has pictures by Ribalta, Espinosa, Titian and Juan de Juanes.

Aqueduct: Remains from the 14–5C survive outside the town.

Environs: Morella la Vella: At the Masía de Morella la Vella, a lonely farmstead a few km. from Morella, Stone Age rock paintings were discovered.

Moreruela

Zamora / León   p.386 ☐ E 4

Monasterio de Santa María: The oldest Cistercian Abbey in Spain but now just an imposing ruin exuding nobility and greatness. The first settlement established by St. Froilán and St. Atilano dates from the 9C.

 The existing Abbey complex was built in 1131 under Alfonso VII. Construction of the church began in 1168 and dragged on until the mid-13C. The church has a nave, two aisles and three apses with floral ornamentation.

Environs: The ruins of the deserted fortified village, **Castrotorafe,** are *c.* 12 km.

Morella, aqueduct

S. of Moreruela. It was destroyed under Alfonso VII in 1153 and rebuilt under Ferdinand in 1176. A fortress was built next to the fortification walls in the 14–15C. S. of Castrotorafe lies **Montamarta** with a 16C church, *Santa María del Castillo.* The church has a 17C high altar and a 16C Flemish Madonna and Child. **Tábara:** (N. of Moreruela), with the parish church of *Santa María* which was consecrated in 1132; apse and interior were restored in the 18C. The mighty tower is also striking.

Mota del Marqués
Valladolid/Old Castile   p. 386☐E 4

San Martín: A hall church with stellar vaulting and a Plateresque S. portal. Inside:

16C *retable* of St.Dominic, a 13C painting of Christ and a 16C Pietà.

Also worth seeing: The 16C Gothic-Mudéjar *pilgrimage chapel of Nuestra Señora de Castellanos*; the Renaissance *Palace of Count Viesca de la Sierra;* and the remains of a once-considerable old castle.

Environs: Pedrosa del Rey (*c.* 5 km. S.): The 16C *parish church* has a beautiful retable. **Casasola** (*c.* 4 km. S.) with 16C *parish church.* **Tiedra** (*c.* 5 km. W.): The Mudéjar parish church of *San Pedro* is 16C and has several altarpieces with sculptures and paintings. *El Salvador:* is a single-aisled Gothic church from the 16C. The *Santuario de la Virgen de Tiedra:* is a single-aisled baroque building with stucco and paintings inside. Mudéjar courtyard.

Moreruela, Monasterio de Santa María

grimage church with an early 18C stone retable by Miguel Romay at the high altar. In the atrium an enormous stone is on display; this is reputed to be part of the stone nave, in which St.James was visited by the Virgin Mary.

Environs: Moraime: (*c.* 5 km. S. of Mugía) with the 12C Romanesque church, *San Julian,* which has a nave and two aisles. The church originally belonged to an 11C monastery, which was destroyed by the Normans in the 12C. Inside the church frescos have survived. There are three portals of interest, especially the main portal which has figures in the tympanum, and double windows at the sides. The tower is also Romanesque. **Ozón:** (E. of Moraime) with the old church of *Santa María* and an enormous old stone *granary,* a typical Galician Hórreo on stone supporting legs. **Cereijo** /Cereixo (E. of Mugía) has a 12C Romanesque church with a beautiful portal and a 17C palace. **Vimianzo:** 15C fortress (restored in the 19C). In the middle of the town there is a magnificent Renaissance palace, the *Pazo de Trasariz.*

Castillo: Walls and keep have survived. **Villardefrades** (*c.* 7 km. NW): *San Cucufate,* a baroque church with a splendid façade, has a wooden figure of Christ by Diego de Siloé inside. **Villavellid** (*c.* 8 km. NW): *Santa María,* the parish church is baroque and has good sculptures and paintings from the 16&17C. Remains of the 14C *Fortaleza* (fortress).

Mugía (Muxia)
La Coruña/Galicia   p.386□A 2

A town in constant battle with the sea on the Atlantic coast. The Romanesque parish church dates from the 13&14C.

La Virgen de la Barca: A 17C pil-

Mula
Murcia/Murcia   p.396□I 9

A little town (pop. *c.* 15,000), 31 km. W. of Murcia, picturesquely situated in a fertile huerta watered by the Río Mula.

San Miguel: A church of 1618 with a baroque altar.

Convento de Descalzas Reales: A convent with beautiful statues by Salzillo, Roque López and La Roldana.

Murcia
Murcia/Murcia   p.396□K 9

Murcia (pop. *c.* 28,000) is capital of the

Moreruela, Monasterio de Santa María

province of the same name, the seat of a bishop and a university town. It is situated on the Río Segura in the middle of a fertile huerta. When the Moors first rose to power the town was a silk-producing centre, being rich in the mulberry trees necessary for silkworm breeding.

The town's name goes back to the Moorish *Medina Mursija*, which was founded in the early 8C by Abd ar Rahman II on the remains of a Roman settlement. It was subject to the Kingdom of Córdoba until becoming the capital of an independent kingdom in 1224. In 1243 it was conquered by Ferdinand the Holy and incorporated into Castile. The town's loyalty to the Crown was rewarded with the granting of a coat-of-arms with seven crowns. Subsequently the town prospered and flourished. In the War of the Spanish

Succession Murcia took the side of the French pretender. The town's capture by Archduke Charles was prevented by Bishop Luis de Belluga, who opened the dykes and flooded much of the huerta. In 1810 the town was occupied by the French. During the Spanish Civil War (1936) many buildings fell victim to sacking and looting. The Old Town, on the N. bank of the Río Segura, still has narrow and twisting streets and contains the most important sights. The Calle de Tomas leads NE from the Plaza de Martínez Tornel, by the Puente Viejo (Old Bridge), towards the cathedral on the Plaza del Cardinal Belluga, from which runs the town's most picturesque street, the *Calle de la Trapería*.

Cathedral (Santa María): Founded in 1394 above the remains of a mosque and consecrated in 1465. It was restored and extended in the 16C. In the 18C the large Gothic church was so badly damaged by the flooding of the Río Seguro that it was virtually rebuilt in baroque style (1737–92). The *façade* by Jaime Bort y Melía of Valencia is one of the finest architectural expressions of the Spanish baroque. Bort used a design which had been rejected for the church of Saint-Sulpice in Paris; to this he added a surfeit of ornamentation in accordance with the Spanish taste. The effect of the façade relies on strong light and shade. Pilasters were replaced by columns to form an aedicule, and from the customary concluding entablature an enormous round niche was created, which vaults the whole middle section. The carved decorations represent a piece of paradise. The exaggerated gestures of the saints (most of which are by Salzillo and his son Francisco, Juan de Egea, Martínez de Teina and others) standing in the aedicules or niches, give them the appearance of players in some eternal drama.

This animation is also reflected in the building itself, the architectural elements of which are contorted to varying degrees. Thus, for example, the customary side volutes have become slanting ovals and the Churrigueresque ledges have breaks in unusual places.

Also of interest are the side portals. On the S. front the 15C Gothic *Portada de los Apóstolos*, an imitation of the Apostle Gate in Valencia, is attributed to Antonio Gil. The *Capilla de los Junterones*, (1515–29) on the right side, has lavish Plateresque ornamentation. In the N. transept the octagonal *Capilla de los Vélez* is 15C and has late-Gothic architectural carving, in which Mudéjar influence is also apparent (late 15C). This chapel also has an excellent late Gothic stellar vault. The massive escutcheons on the exterior are reminiscent of the Capilla del Condestable in Burgos. The entrance, the 16C *Portade de las Cadenas* (cadenas = chains), is attributed to Fran-

cisco Florentín. Behind the Puerta del Pozo on the N. front stands the massive *bell tower*. Over 300 ft. high, it was begun in 1521 by Francesco l'Indaco of Florence and continued in the most varied of styles (Renaissance, Herrera, baroque); finally the tower was crowned with a classical steeple by Ventura Rodríguez. In spite of this mixture of building styles, the whole tower presents a harmonious unity. The Plateresque gate leading to the *sacristy* on the ground floor of the tower is reputed to be the work of Juan de Léon, but it was embellished with baroque decorations in the 18C. The vault in the sacristy is decorated with charming garlands of fruit, flowers and leaves.

The original Gothic style still dominates the domed interior. The fourth chapel in the right aisle—the previously mentioned Capilla de los Junterones—has a bas-relief of the *Nativity* from the early 16C by the brothers Francesco and Jacopo l'Indaco. In the Capilla de los Vélez, also mentioned above, the model for which was the sepulchral chapel of Alvaro de Luna in Toledo, there is an altar with a *Virgin* by Salzillo. In front of the *Capilla Mayor* is a 15C reja. The late Gothic *coro* has a Plateresque screen and stalls by Rafael de Léon (1567); above the lectern there is a figure of *Christ* by Salzillo.

The *Capilla de San Andrés,* in front of the ambulatory in the left aisle, leads to the Bishop's oratory (with a medallion of the Holy Family by Salzillo). Next to the N. transept there is a Plateresque door, through which you can get to the sacristy, which has beautiful 16C panelling. Here there is a monstrance by Pérez de Montalto from 1667.

The Gothic cloister dates from the 15C. The *Diocesan Museum,* housed here and in the chapterhouse, has a 14C altar with the portrait of the Infante Don Manuel and his wife, and other figures attributed to Francisco Salzillo, including the *Virgen de la Leche;* there are also Romanesque and

Murcia, Ermita de Jesús, crib

Murcia, cathedral

Gothic sculptures, among which a *Mater Dolorosa* deserves particular attention, as well as various reliefs by Rafael de Léon. Particularly good paintings include the work of Fernando de Llanos *(Adoration of the Shepherds)*, Pedro Orrente *(The Good Shepherd)* and a winged altar by Barnabas of Modena. Cathedral treasure also includes crosses, statuettes, chalices, monstrances, manuscripts, etc.

Palacio Episcopal (Bishop's Palace): Built in rococo style by Baltasar Canestro from 1748–77. The façade has shell-shaped gables (bolecón) reminiscent of the cathedral.

Santo Domingo: This church was gutted in 1936 but has since been restored. It has a Renaissance-baroque main façade (1543 –1742) and two interesting towers.

La Merced: Has a late 17C Churrigueresque portal lavishly adorned with figures. The domed baroque interior contains numerous paintings by local painters from the 17&18C.

San Bartolomé: Late 18C. In the right aisle, there is the *Virgen de las Angustias* by Salzillo, and an *Adoration of the Magi* by Juan Vincente Masip.

San Miguel: 17C. Houses Salzillo's processional figures (Pasos). There is a splendid high altarpiece with a statue of St. Michael by Roque Lopez.

San Esteban: Also known as *La Compañía*. Built by B. Bustamente for the Jesuits, 1557–69. It has a beautiful Renaissance façade.

San Nicolás de Bari (1736): The façade has carved medallions by Salzillo's school. The church houses sculptures by Salzillo, Pedro de Mena and Alonso Cano.

San Juan Bautista: 18C. The façade was created by Ventura Rodríguez. The (restored) interior contains beautiful sculptures and a jasper altar by R. Berenguer.

San Andrés: 1630–1762. Baroque church whose façade incorporates two columns of Roman origin. In a chapel there is the statue, the *Virgen de la Arrixaca* (a seated 13C figure of the Madonna); according to tradition she was also venerated by the Moors. Alfonso the Wise mentions her in his 'Cantigas'. The chapel also contains paintings of scenes from the life of the Virgin Mary by Senén Vila and figures of angels by Salzillo. There are further statues by Salzillo: *Purísima* and *Santa Monica* (right transept), *St.Andrew* (high altar) and *St.Augustine* (left transept).

Ermita de Jesús: With an elliptical chapel built 1777–92. The chapel has a large dome and is painted with frescos by Sistori. The *Salzillo Museum*, Murcia's largest art collection, is now housed here, along with Francisco Salzillo's famous and naturalistic passion figures or *Pasos*, which were formerly carried in processions during Holy Week. The *Oración en el Huerto* is one of Spain's most beautiful Pasos. Apart from the Pasos, there are the *c.* 1,500 painted clay statuettes of people and animals in the crib scene *(El Belén/Bethlehem)*. These occupy display cases 235 ft. long, and show many episodes in the Life of Christ, from the Nativity onwards. These figures give an excellent idea as to the manner of dress in Salzillo's time.

Museo Arqueológico Provincial: The regional museum houses finds from prehistoric, Punic, Roman, Visigoth and Iberian times and includes mosaics and fragments of carvings from the nearby Basilica of Algezares, as well as the treasure of Finca la Pita. There are also coins from Arab and Christian times.

Museo Provincial de Bellas Artes: This museum is housed in the new building (1910) of the former Trinity Monastery. The museum also contains several paintings by Nicolas Villacis (1616 - 94), a Murcia-born pupil of Velázquez *(Portrait of a Nobleman, Jesus in the Temple)*, as well as some of his frescos. Further paintings include the work Luca Giordano, Federico de Madrazo, Bartolomé Carducho, etc.

Santa Eulalia: This 18C church on the square of the same name contains sculptures by Salzillo and Roque López.

Santa Clara: A convent with an unusual façade, Mozarabic grilles, a domed church and a late Gothic cloister.

Santa Anna: The convent church dates from 1728 and houses sculptures by Salzillo.

Capilla de Santiago (or the Capilla del Apóstol): This 13C chapel is the town's oldest church.

Casino: (1852) With a patio in Pompeian style and another in Mudéjar style.

Also of interest: The baroque *Palacio del Marqués de Beniel*, the *Casa de los Celdranes* with a Plateresque balcony, and the *Casa Almodóvar*.

Environs: Monteagudo (4.5 km. NE): A little village of Roman origin at the foot of a steep crag. The finds excavated here (statues, coins, ceramics) are to be found

Murcia, Ermita de Jésus, the Garden of ▷
Gethsemane

in the Museo Arqueológico in Murcia. On the mountain there are the ruins of a fortress. Originally Roman, it was extended by the Arabs in the 12C and seized by Alfonso the Wise in 1243. At the highest point is a 50 ft. statue of *Christ Blessing (Corazón de Jesus).* **La Fuensanta** (6 km. E.): On the slopes of the Sierra de los Villanos lies the convent of *Nuestra Señora de la Luz.* The early baroque convent church of 1694 (restored) has a baroque façade flanked by towers and a central dome. Inside there is a miraculous picture of the Virgen de la Fuensanta (patroness of Murcia), sculptures in wood by Salzillo and Gonzáles Moreno and frescos by Pedro Flores. Lower down the slope is *Santa Catalina del Monte* (16C).

Nájera

Logroño/Old Castile   p.388☐H 3

Capital of Rioja. It was the seat of the court of the Kings of Navarre and the residence of the Kings of Castile. The first coinage of the Kingdom of Navarre was minted here.

Monastery of Santa María la Real: In 1032 King García Sánchez III found a Romanesque image of the Virgin in a grotto. He then had the monastery built and this became the pantheon of the Kings of Navarre and Castile. The Gothic church, built in 1422, has a nave and two aisles with stellar vaulting and a transept with groin vaulting. The baroque high altarpiece dates from the 17C and has a statue of the founder (kneeling in prayer) and a 12C Romanesque Madonna, the *Virgen de la Terraza*. The most interesting tombs are the tomb of Doña Blanca de Navarra, the top of which is covered entirely with Romanesque reliefs, and the 17C Renaissance tomb of the Dukes of Nájera by Juan Bascardo. A 14C wooden Madonna marks the spot where the image was found. The Gothic choir stalls in Isabelline style were made in 1495 by Nicolás and Andrés de Nájera. The splendid Gothic cloister was completed in 1528.

Environs: Cañas (8 km. W.): The *Monastery of Santa María* (1236) has the most beautiful stained-glass windows in the monastery church. **Santa Coloma** (*c.* 8 km. SE): 16C *parish church* and the remains of an 11C monastery. **Tricio** (*c.* 2 km. E.): This was the ancient Roman Tritium. The *Capilla de los Arcos* contains remains of an old Roman building. Built in the style associated with Ferdinand and

Nájera, Santa María la Real

Isabella, the church preserves a 17C retable and a 15C processional cross.

Nava del Rey
Valladolid/Old Castile   p.386☐E 4

Los Santos Juanes: A Romanesque church begun by Gil de Hontañón and completed in Gothic style in the 17C. The interior has a nave and two aisles divided by massive columns. The tall baroque tower was built by Juan Hernández; the fine sacristy with polychrome panelling is by Alberto de Churriguera. The high altarpiece (1605) has fine reliefs and carvings by Gregorio Fernández; there is a 15C relief in the chapel on the epistle side and there are paintings by Berruguete.

Also worth seeing: The church of the *Hospital of San Miguel*, with sculptures by Salvador Carmona and an altarpiece by Joaquín de Churriguera. In the *Augustine church* there are also beautiful sculptures by S. Carmona. The church of *Santa Cruz* has an altarpiece of 1600 by Juan de Muniátegui. The *town hall* is 18C.

Environs: Torrecilla de la Orden (*c.* 10 km. S.): The 17C Gothic *church* has a nave, two aisles, groin and barrel vaulting and an altarpiece with reliefs and sculptures by Francisco Giralte. The baroque pilgrimage chapel, *Virgen del Carmen* has a retable with a painting by Francisco de Zurbarán. **Fresno el Viejo** (*c.* 15 km. S.): The Romanesque-Mudéjar church (12C) has a Mudéjar roof. **Alaejos** (*c.* 5 km. W.): The Gothic church of *San Pedro* has a nave and two aisles and a tall baroque tower decorated with tiles. Inside there are interesting paintings and sculptures. The church of *Santa María* has a large tower and, in the main chapel, a gilded Mudéjar truss frame, one of the most beautiful in the province, as well as a retable of 1580 by Esteban Jordán with paintings by Francisco Martínez. In the sacristy there are several paintings, including works by Lucas Jordán. Also of interest is the typical *Plaza*

Nájera, Santa María la Real

Nerja, museum, clay pitcher

Mayor. **Castronuño** (8 km. NW): The 13C Gothic *Iglesia del Cristo* has a large rose window above the portal and a beautiful 14C image of Christ inside.

Navalcarnero
Madrid/New Castile   p.392☐G 6

Parish church, La Asunción: Begun *c.* 1520 in Renaissance style, but rebuilt several times since. The Mudéjar tower is crowned by a baroque spire. The interior has a nave, two aisles, and dome. The *Capilla de la Concepción* was built 1619–63. Philip IV and his wife were married here in 1649. The chapel has a baroque altar and a dome with frescos by Maella.

Plaza Mayor: An good example of an arcaded Castilian square.

Environs: Torrejón de Velasco (*c.* 30 km. SE): The *castle,* built at the start of the 14C, acquired its keep (Torre del Homenaje) in the 15C. There are only remnants of the *town walls,* which are as old as the castle. **Villaviciosa de Odón:** *Castillo:* 14 – 15C. Destroyed by the Comuneros in 1521 and rebuilt by Juan de Herrera.

Navalmoralejo
Toledo/New Castile   p.392☐E 6

Things of interest: The *Ciudad de Vascos,* a fortress outside the town. Its origin is unknown but it is thought to be Roman; later used by the Visigoths, Arabs and Christians.

Nerja
Málaga/Andalusia   p.394☐G 11

A town on the Costa del Sol with about

Villaviciosa de Odón (Navalcarnero), castillo

8,700 inhabitants. From the *Balcón de Europa* there is a beautiful view over the sea.

Cueva de Nerja: (4 km. E.) Also known as the Prehistoric Cathedral. This impressive stalactite cave is half a mile long and was discovered in 1959. Important prehistoric finds were made from the Neolithic (Late Stone Age: 4000–1800 BC). These can be seen in a small *museum* and include ceramics and parts of Cro-Magnon human skulls. The cave contains prehistoric paintings of goats, horses and fish (which are probably Mesolithic).

Niebla
Huelva/Andalusia   p.394 □ D 10

The Roman town Ilipula became the seat of a bishop in Visigoth times and later the centre of a small independent kingdom. Alfonso X of Castile, took the town after a 6-month siege.

Santa María de la Granada: The heavily-restored church has portals from the 10&11C. It was used by Christians even in Arab times, but the Almohades converted it into a mosque. It was altered in Gothic style in the 15C. The square *tower* has beautiful windows.

Town walls: Massive Moorish defensive walls; also a cyclopean wall from Iberian times. 46 defensive towers have survived, as have four old *gates:* the Puerta de Socorro and the Puerta del Buey with horseshoe arches, the Puerta de Sevilla from Roman times, and the Puerta de Agua. The alcázar was destroyed by French troops in 1813.

Also worth seeing: Ruins of the Moorish *church of San Martín;* inside, there is a 15C fresco of St.Martin. *Archaeological Museum.*

Environs: La Lobita (7 km. W.): Here there is a most interesting burial gallery, the *Dolmen del Zancarrón de Soto* dating from the Neolithic Age (*c.* 2000 BC). A passage 65 ft. long leads to the burial chamber, which is decorated with paintings. Nearby there are more *megalithic tombs*, which probably date from the Bronze Age. **La Palma del Condado** (12 km. E.): Church of *San Juan Bautista:* A 16C Plateresque domed building with a beautiful high altar and baroque chapels. **Villalba del Alcor** (21 km. E.): An interesting mixture of styles is apparent in the church of *San Bartolomé:* the façade has both a Gothic and a baroque portal; decoration, including azulejos and coats-of-arms, is late 15C. The tower comes from the former mosque. Mainly Gothic interior. The dome of the Capilla Mayor and the Capilla de Santa Ana (with horseshoe arches) date from the Almohaden period.

Noya
La Coruña/Galicia   p.386 □ B 2

Called Noega in Roman times. An important port, which later belonged to the diocese of Compostela. It flourished and became wealthy in the 15C, to which beautiful streets and houses still testify. It is not for nothing that Noya is nicknamed 'Little Florence'.

San Martín: Built by Archbishop Lope de Mendoza in 1434 on the site of an older church. It is single-aisled with pointed arches and has rib vaulting over the Capilla Mayor. The beautiful façade shows the influence of Santiago de Compostela, having a row of Apostles to the left and right of the portal, with biblical kings and angels in the archivolts above the tympanum. Above the portal there is a large rose window, which has fine tracery, is decorated with figures and surrounded by four angels

Niebla, view

La Palma del Condado (Niebla), San Juan Bautista

playing musical instruments. Also of interest are the N. portal's tympanum and the *Capilla de Valderrama*, which has stellar vaulting and an interesting altar. The stone pulpit by Salvador Araújo dates from 1570.

Santa María Nova/Nuestra Señora del Don: From the first half of the 14C. The 16C *Capilla de San Pedro* has a Gothic rose window, the Adoration of the Magi in the tympanum of the portal and two tombs within. The cemetery near the church is well worth seeing, having numerous tomb statues and a small temple with reliefs of burial scenes and burial symbolism. Also of interest are the Cruceros in the cemetery, one of which dates from the 13C.

San Francisco: A single-aisled 16C church belonging to the 14C monastery of San Francisco. The church has interesting rib vaulting. The Capilla de la Epístola has the tombs of the founders (Pedro Losada, Inés Yáñez Dacosta, and Francisco Bermúdez de Castro) with recumbent figures.

Also worth seeing: The Palace of *Peña de Oro* near the Romanesque cloister of the *Monasterio de Touxos Quitos*. The 15C *Palacio de Tapal*. There are also beautiful old mansions, such as the *Casa de los Churruchaos* with Gothic windows, the *Casa de Monroy* and the former *Colegio de Gramática*.

Environs: Muros: At the mouth of the Ría de Muros y Noya, N. along the coastal road (some 10 km. further along is Carnota and finally Finisterre, on the western tip of Spain.) Muros is an attractive old port with old houses, little alleys, arcades and beautiful churches. The town was fortified in the 16C and remains of these walls survive. Today Muros is split into La Cerca and Xesta. The collegiate church of *San Pedro* was built at the start of the 15C above an old Romanesque church, of which there are still some remains. The side chapels date from the 15&16C; the Capilla San Anton, with stellar vaulting, from the 17C. The façade has a beautiful portal and a Gothic rose-window. **Louro** (3 km. from Muros, on the road to Carnota) with a monastery, *San Francisco*. **Carnota:** Single-aisled church of *San Mamed* with a tall tower, and an altar retable by the sculptors Gambino and Ferreiro from the first half of the 18C. The church of *Santa Columba* has a low nave, two aisles and a very tall tower. Nearby is the enormous *Hórreo de Santa Columba,* the largest granary in Galicia. It stands on pillars and is built of granite blocks. **Corcubión:** Many houses here have small inner courtyards and there are interesting *Hórreos.* The single-aisled church of *San Marcos* dates from 1430. The Capilla Mayor has some structural elements from the 12&13C. The façade dates from 1885. The church was restored in 1967. Also worth seeing are the *Palacio de Altamira,* restored in the 18C, the 17C fortresses *El Cardenal* and *del Principe,* and the 13C church of *San Pedro de Redonda.* **Finisterre:** The most western and longest settled place in Galicia, where many old customs have survived. The narrow coastal road leading to it is very picturesque. *Santa María* is a single-aisled Romanesque church with a groin vault, which was renovated in the 15&16C. The chapels are of various ages and architectural styles. The main portal is Romanesque and the row of arches in front of the façade come from a former (baroque) portico. On the gospel side there is a beautiful Gothic door. The square tower has a 16C top.

Nuestra Señora de Irache
Navarra / Navarra   p.388 □ I 2

In the village of Ayegui (some 2 km. from Estella, on the road to Logroño), is one of the oldest monasteries in Navarre, Nuestra Señora de Irache. This Royal Monastery lies on the pilgrimage route to Santiago de Compostela, at the foot of Monte Jurra, and is one of the oldest hospices for Santiago pilgrims. It is now a national monument.

Church: Built in the 12–13C in a style transitional between Romanesque and Gothic and incorporating several architectural styles. The church has a Latin cross ground plan with a nave and three semicircular Romanesque apses. There is a beautiful dome over the crossing. The two portals are Romanesque. The arches of the W. portal are supported by four columns, whose capitals are lavishly carved with scenes from the life of St. Martin, scenes of chivalry and a group of wild animals. The capitals of the N. portal are decorated with carvings of flowers. The main apse is Romanesque and suggests the Cluniac style of building. Its seven arches are supported on columns with beautifully decorated capitals. The entrance to the main chapel has a triumphal arch, whose columns have richly carved capitals; the left column's capital has a battle scene; that of the column on the right has the Adoration of the Magi. The beautiful dome is supported by squinches, the pillars of which are decorated with pilgrim scallops. The Plateresque cloister (mid 16C) is lavishly decorated with carvings.

Nuestra Señora de Salas
Huesca / Aragon   p.388 □ K 3

Monastery and church: Doña Sancha of

Castile, the wife of King Alfonso II of Aragon, commissioned the building of this monastery in the 12C. It was almost totally rebuilt in 1722, but the Romanesque *façade*, with a blind rose-window and the late 12C tower have survived from the original building. At the high altar stands the famous *Romanesque statue* of the Virgin of Salas (13C). Near this is another statue, the Madonna of Huerta (15C), a wood carving partly clad in beaten silver. Interesting Mudéjar *guest rooms* in the N. part of the monastery.

Numancia

Soria/Old Castile   p.388□H 4

An old Celtic-Iberian fortified town, which achieved fame through the heroic resistance of its inhabitants against the onslaught of the Roman legions. Only after a siege of twenty years were the Roman troops able to force their way into the devastated town.

Pre-Roman or Celtic-Iberian ruins: Remains indicate that the town was a cultural centre up to the end of the Iron Age; the settlement is thought to have been at its zenith in the 2C BC.

Roman ruins: After the conquest in 133 BC the Romans rebuilt Numancia. Amongst the ruins the ground plan of a Roman town can be identified.

Environs: Garray (*c.* 3 km. NW): The Romanesque *Martyrs' Chapel* has a nave, two aisles and a semicircular apse. The side portal has archivolts and a beautiful tympanum. Inside there is a Romanesque altar table, an 11C Romanesque font and a small Gothic retable. **Hinojosa de la Sierra** (*c.* 15 km. NW): 16C *church* with a 17C retable; the *Palace of the Hurtado de Mendoza* dates from 1581. **Tera** (*c.* 15 km. Romanesque *church*, whose portal has archivolts; Romanesque font.

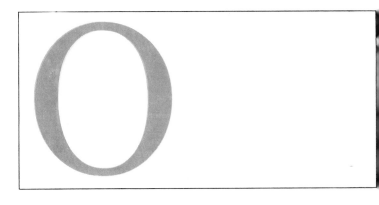

Ocaña

Toledo/New Castile   p.392□G 6

San Juan: Parish church from the 13–14C with a nave and two aisles in Gothic-Mudéjar style with later additions. The 15 - 16C *main chapel* is square, with a Gothic groin vault. On either side of the main chapel there is a *Gothic chapel*, one dedicated to the 'Virgen de los Dolores' and the other to the 'Concepción' or 'Chacón'. The latter houses the 15C tomb of Don Gonzalo Chacón and his wife; the Bujandas chapel houses the founder's tomb (early 17C).

Santa María: Parish church with a fine *Renaissance portal*. In a side chapel there is a beautiful reja and a 16C Plateresque tomb.

Monastery of Santo Domingo: The baroque monastery church is single-aisled with side chapels and a large dome over the crossing. The fine walnut *choir stalls* date from 1573.

Castle of the Dukes of Frías: A large late 15C Gothic building.

Marketplace (Plaza Mayor): Built in classical style towards the end of the 18C to the designs of the Madrid architect Francisco Sánchez. The symmetrical façades have arcades; semicircular brick arches.

Town Hall: Bearing the city's coat-of-arms; on one side of the market square.

Environs: Ciruelos (some 15 km. W.) The 16C *parish church* is late Gothic, with a nave, two aisles and groin vaulting. **Huerta de Valdecarábanos:** (*c.* 20 km. SW) The *fortress* was founded by the Order of Calatrava and occupies a hill above the village. The 12C fortress is built of irregular masonry held together by lime mortar. The inside has collapsed and the top of a tower in the SW wall has disappeared. *Loaysa Castle* was built in 1539 by Don Alvaro de Loaysa, the first Lord. The 16C Plateresque-Renaissance portal has survived unaltered. **Yepes:** The *city walls* are 13–14C; three of the four original gates, one of the towers and much of the walls themselves have survived. The mid-16C *parish church* is transitional between Gothic and Renaissance; there is a Gothic S. façade and a Renaissance entrance and W. façade. Inside there are a nave, two aisles, and two wings of side chapels—a later addition. The early 17C Renaissance altarpiece at the high altar comprises oil-paintings by Luis Tristán, signed and dated 1616.

Olite

Navarra / Navarra   p.388 □ I 3

A small country town, set in a fertile plain. It was originally founded by the Gothic King Swintila in 620 (gold coins with his image have been found in Navarre). Olite occupies a unique position in Navarre's history. The seat of the Kings of Navarre (until incorporated into Castile), it has a splendid castle from that time, which is now a national Parador (hotel). Olite was settled at a very early stage: Archbishop Don Rodrigo Ximénez de Rada mentions the name Ologitum. King García Ramírez gave it city status in 1147, and in a document dated 1266 Teobaldo II gives it the right to hold a market. There was a parliament here from 1276 onwards. Olite also has a number of Roman remains, on whose foundations many of the buildings visible today have been built.

Castillo (Palace of the Kings of Navarre): In 1406, when King Charles III moved his residence to Olite, he had the existing 13C castle converted into a palace by Saul de Arnedo. This was done in Gothic style with French influence. The pomp and majesty of the building finds expression in elegant towers and galleries, and the quasi-military style invites comparison with the Papal Palace of Avignon. The castle originally had some 15 towers, each with a different name e.g. 'Las Atalayas', 'Los Cuatro Vientos', 'Tres Coronas' and 'La Prisión'. The *keep* (Torre de Homenaje) is much larger than the other towers. Inside the castle there are Moorish tiles and pedestals, stuccoed walls and decorated and painted wooden ceilings. The castle has many rooms and galleries. There are also gardens built on rows of arches and a Leonera, where the Kings kept wild animals for amusement. But the royal family, despite living in the most delightful of surroundings, had tragic lives and internecine strife led to infighting and poisoning each other. The Parador Nacional was

Olite, Castillo

built in the oldest part of the castle, at the base of the 'Torre de las Cigüeñas'. The whole complex is a protected monument.

Santa María: The church, which is also the palace chapel, was built next to the castle in Gothic style at the end of the 13C. It is single-aisled with an apse and side galleries. The *main portal* is 14C Gothic and decorated with carvings. The *tympanum* has a Madonna and Child, and scenes from the life of the Holy Family (including the Massacre of the Innocents, Birth of Christ, Flight into Egypt, Dispute in the Temple and Baptism in the Jordan). To the side of the portal, under a blind arcade there is a relief with figures of the Apostles. The *inside* of the church is divided into four sections by diagonal arches. The *high altar* is decorated with scenes from the life of Christ, the Virgin Mary and sculptures of saints (all 16C); there is also a fine Madonna and an interesting 13C crucifix. The *cloisters* are also of interest.

San Pedro: Only the portal and parts of the façade remain of the original 12C Romanesque building; the rest is 12—13C Gothic. The cloisters are also 12C. The *tower* is unusual with a particularly graceful spire. The *façade* is a mixture of Romanesque and Gothic. The portal is highly ornate with columns and carvings of scenes from the life of St.Peter. The tympanum has figures of St.Peter, St.John and St.James. Also of interest on the portal are two eagles (each almost a metre long), symbolizing strength and humility.

Oliva

Valencia / Valencia   p.396☐L 7

A small town among olive and mulberry groves at the foot of the hill of Santa Ana. There was a settlement here in Roman times and in the Middle Ages it was the seat of a count.

Palace of the Dukes of Gandía: An interesting castle in transitional Gothic-Renaissance style.

Olite, Castillo

Santa María: With statues by Estere Bonet.

The Monastery of San Francisco: The church has a fine 13C Madonna, the *Virgen de Rebollet.*

Olivenza
Badajoz/Estremadura   p.392☐C 8

A border town on the frontier between Spain and Portugal and the scene of much fighting in the past. In 1298 the town was given to Beatrice of Castile by her brother on the occasion of her marriage to the Infante Don Alonso of Portugal. In 1607 it was occupied by the Spanish and then in 1801 snatched away during the course of the 'Orange War'. The *city walls* have three towers which are still standing and have been integrated into the modern town. There is a huge *castle* dating from 1306 with a 16C watchtower.

Santa María del Castillo: Near to the castle. It has groin vaulting, a Gothic winged altar with the family tree of the Virgin Mary, and a 16C Manueline altar in the apsidal chapel.

Santa María Magdalena: A 16C church in Manueline style. Baroque altar in the Capilla Mayor.

Hospital de la Caridad: Built in 1501 by the Portuguese King Manuel I. The chapel is rich in azulejos.

City Library: In an old 15C palace. The portal has blind finials decorated with crockets.

Environs: Risco de San Blas: (2 km. W. of Alburquerque) has impressive cave paintings.

Olmedo
Valladolid/Old Castile   p.386☐F 4

An old fortress-town, whose fame largely

Olite, Santa María, portal

Olivenza, Santa María Magdalena

Olivenza, town library, portal

of *San Andrés* has a Romanesque-Mudéjar apse from the 13C. The 15C remains of the *Convento de la Mejorada* are nearby.

Environs: Almenara de Adaja (*c.* 4 km S.) A Romanesque-Mudéjar church altered in the 17C. During the course of rebuilding, a *Roman villa* with impressive mosaic was discovered. **Iscar** (*c.* 7km. NE): Remains of the old city wall and a *castle*, with round towers and a keep; the church of *Santa María* is Romanesque-Mudéjar with an altarpiece of sculptures, paintings and an alabaster Pietà from the 16C. The Romanesque church of *San Miguel Arcángel* has a fine apse. **Alcazarén** (*c.* 5 km N.): The Romanesque—Mudéjar church of *Santiago* was renovated in the 17C.

Olot

Gerona / Catalonia   p.390 □ N

Mention was made of Olot as early as 872

San Esteban: Already standing in 977, rebuilt in 1750 in neoclassical style. The 'Capilla de los Dolores' has a remarkable *carved group* by Ramón Amadeu. The sacristy, which has 15 – 16C Gothic wood panelling, houses the church's *treasury*, including a picture by El Greco (Christ carrying the Cross).

Torre Castany: A palace built in 1845. It now houses the **Museum of Modern Art** and a collection of Catalan art from the Olot school (founded in the 19C by Joaquin Vayreda, it came to include a large number of Catalan artists, whose inspiration came from the countryside around Olot).

Environs: San Esteban de Bas (8 km S.): The 12C Romanesque parish church

came about because of the play 'Caballero de Olmedo' by Lope de Vega. The town saw the Mudéjar style flourish here in the 12–13C; the town walls, with their seven gates, and the main square with its arcades date from this period.

San Miguel: A fine example of 13C Mudéjar style. It has a nave, two aisles, tombs and Mudéjar stucco. The *Cripta de la Soterraña*, beneath the apse is unique, with baroque altarpieces and paintings by Luca Giordano.

Also worth seeing: The Gothic church of *Santa María* with a Romanesque portico, and an altarpiece, which is composed of fine 16C sculpture and painting. The church of *San Juan* has a sacristy and three stone graves by Juan de Guas. The church

Olivenza, Hospital de la Caridad

has one of the finest apses in the region. There are a number of 11–12C Romanesque churches in the areas around **Vall de Vianya** (15 km. N.) and **San Salvador de Vianya** (2 km. from Vall). The church of **San Joan de las Fonts** (5 km. away, in the direction of Castellfullit de la Roca) is Romanesque from the 12C, with a remarkable *portal* with three arches and unusual capitals. The interior is of marked Cistercian influence. There are a nave and two aisles and arches which are almost pointed; 12C carved font. The *Fortress of Juvinyá* is also 12C.

Oña
Burgos/Old Castile   p.388 □ G 2

Monastery of San Salvador: Founded in the 11C by Sancho de Castilla, and extended in 1033 by Sancho el Mayor. It has attractive 15C Gothic cloisters. The *church* contains a number of richly decorated tombs and 15C choir stalls. The portal is Gothic, but the façade betrays glimpses of the original Romanesque. The *Barcina Tower*, near the cloisters, is all that remains of a former fortress.

Also worth seeing: The church of *San Juan* with a huge tower and Gothic portal. There are also remains of old *mansions* and an old *synagogue*.

Environs: Frías (*c.* 8 km. N.): A picturesque village, whose old streets and squares have a medieval atmosphere. There is an impressive 12C *hill fortress* with elegant Romanesque windows and the 13C church of *San Nicolás*, which contains the founder's tomb (with a recumbent statue), a Plateresque altarpiece and interesting paintings. **Soto de Buerba** (*c.* 8 km. N.): Has one of the province's finest Romanesque churches. **Escobados de Abajo** (*c.* 10 km. W.): With the 12C Romanesque

chapel of *Nuestra Señora de Oliva*. **Abajas** (*c.* 18 km. S.): Has a 12C Romanesque church with barrel vaulting and finely decorated capitals.

Oñate
Guipúzcoa/Basque Provinces   p.388 □ H 2

A small town, at the foot of Mount Aloña (3,956 ft.) and one of the richest towns in Guipúzcoa. In earlier times, when it was the capital of a small republic, it was able to embellish itself with the title of 'Urbs magna' (great city); in antiquity it was called Goin-ate, which means 'high pass'. A university was founded here in 1542, and Don Carlos used it as his headquarters during the Carlist Wars of 1833–9. Oñate's remarkable architecture prompted the painter Zuloaga to call it 'the Basque Toledo'.

San Miguel: 15C parish church with nave, two aisles and a raised choir. In shape and appearance it resembles a cathedral. The baroque *bell tower* was built between 1779–83 by Manuel de Carrera. The *bishop's chapel* contains a fine Plateresque altarpiece behind a beautiful wrought-iron screen. Nearby is the tomb (by Diego de Siloé) of Don Rodrigo Sánchez de Mercado Zuazola, the founder of the university and Bishop of Ávila. The *choir* contains the 15C sarcophagus of the Count of Oñate. The church also has a fine Gothic-Plateresque cloister, beneath which run a number of small rivulets whose source is on Mount Aloña.

Universitas Sancti Spiritus: Founded in 1542 by the Bishop of Ávila, Don Rodrigo Sánchez de Mercado Zuazola, a friend of Cardinal Cisnero; it remained a seat of learning until 1901. The building

Oñate, university, façade (detail)

is highly decorated in Plateresque style with French influence. The 16C façade is decorated with coats-of-arms and carvings, and flanked by two fortress-like towers. The sculptures in front of the building are by a Frenchman, Pierre Picart. Two towers are attached to the grand staircase, which has a beautiful pannelled dome. The Plateresque altar in the *chapel* is also by Pierre Picart. The university *cloister* is worth seeing, having two galleries of rounded arches on columns decorated with simple capitals and medallions.

Also worth seeing: The baroque *Town Hall*, built by Manuel Carrera in the 18C. It contains a huge gold ciborium from the university chapel, which is decorated with the figures of the twelve apostles. The *Convento de Santa Ana*, on the other side of the river, has a *church* by Gregorio Fernández. Inside there are a fine altar and a statue of Santa Ana. The 16C Gothic *Convento de Bidaurreta* lies on the road to San Sebastián and has some important art.

Oncala
Soria/Old Castile   p.388☐H 3

San Millán: An 18C parish with a fine collection of ten Flemish tapestries based on Rubens cartoons.

Environs: Yanguas (*c.* 15 km. N.): A town defended by a Moorish fortress. It has a beautiful main square with arcades and some splendid mansions. **Cerbón** (*c.* 15 km. SW): Has a two-aisled 12C Romanesque church.

Orduña
Vizcaya/Basque Provinces   p.388☐H 2

An old town at the foot of the Peña de Orduña. It was Charles VII's headquarters during the Carlist Wars. The old city walls, with towers and six gates, have survived in good condition.

Santa María: A 15C church with a nave, two aisles and a transept; 17C baroque high altar. The side chapel, which is dedicated to St.Peter, has a 15C Gothic altarpiece. The Chapel of the Ortes family of Velasco has a fine Renaissance wrought-iron screen dating from 1584.

Santuario de la Virgen de la Antigua: A baroque sanctuary built 1750–82, whose façade has columns and arches. The church houses a 14C image of the Virgin Mary.

San Juan el Viejo: A former Jesuit college built by the Marquis of Villafuerte at the end of the 16C. The façade is decorated with three great arches and the college's coat-of-arms.

Also worth seeing: *Ayuntamiento*, the *Palace of the Marquis of Alameda* and the *Customs building*, (late 18C, classical).

Orense
Orense/Galicia   p.386☐C 3

The capital city of the province of the same name, situated in the fertile Valley of Miño. The town has had a colourful past. The Romans knew it as Aquae Urentes, which was famous for its hot water springs—to day these are still present in the area around Las Burgas, where Roman remains have been found. In the 4C the town was the seat of a bishop, and was known as Sedes Auriensis. During the 6 – 7C the town flourished under the Suevi, until it was destroyed by the Moors and after them the Normans. In the 11C it was rebuilt under Sancho II and his sister.

Orense, Roman bridge over the Río Miño

Cathedral: Built in the 12C on the site of an old Suevian church and dedicated to St.Martin of Tours. Apart from Santiago de Compostela, it is Galicia's finest and richest church. It has a nave, two aisles and a splendid tower over the crossing, which has a star-shaped dome within and was built by Rodrigo de Badajoz in 1499. The windows are beautiful, particularly on the W. side, which has three fine portals. The 13C *N. portal* has figures on either side, a variety of motifs on the archivolts, and a 15C Deposition of Christ in the tympanum. The *S. portal* has a richly decorated and carved 13C Romanesque door. The *main portal*, in a narthex, is the 13C Portal of Paradise, which has polychrome figures on the columns, capitals and in the archivolts in imitation of the Pórtico de la Gloria of Santiago de Compostela. Inside,

one can only marvel at the pointed arches above the pillars, the buttresses, clerestory, high ribbed vaulting and the unbelievably ornate high altar retable by Cornelis de Holanda, which is covered with reliefs and dates from 1521. To the right of the richly carved *choir stalls*, by Diego de Siloé and Juan de los Angeles, is a 15C bishop's tomb. The bronze pulpit and the screen, which is decorated with polychrome wooden figures, are both by Celma and date from the 16C. Above all, the chapels are of interest, with fine decorated screens and tombs. The most impressive is the chapel of *El Santo Cristo*, which was begun by Castro Canseco in 1567. The baldacchino is by Domingo de Andrade, and the altar crucifix dates from 1330. The Mater Dolorosa behind the altar is by Gregorio Fernández, and the Deposition opposite is 16C. The nave contains the *Capilla de la Reina de los Angeles*, with a 13C Byzantine Christ. The 16C sacristy has a 15C Gothic portal. The right aisle leads to the interesting *Diocesan Museum*, with the splendid church treasury, which is accommodated in the former cloister (Claustra Nova, 13–14C Gothic).

San Francisco: A 14C church, which has a beautiful apse with high Gothic windows. Inside there are fine Gothic sarcophagi and the door arches are decorated with carved figures. The cloisters have Gothic arches.

Santa Eufemia: An 18C church with a nave and two aisles, barrel vaulting and a dome over the crossing; altars date from the 17,18&19C. The beautifully balanced façade is decorated with coats-of-arms, columns, volutes, a large square window (in the centre above false windows) and a square portal.

Santa María la Madre: The church visible today was built in 1722 over the original 11C cathedral. The façade has huge overlapping double columns and two bell towers—from the steps leading to the main portal it makes a very attractive sight.

Santo Domingo: The church of a Dominican monastery. Built in 1641 it has barrel vaulting, a dome over the crossing and side chapels. The baroque high altar retable is the work of Castro Canseco.

Santa Trinidad: The façade is flanked by two towers and has a Gothic portal. The apse is 16C.

Also worth seeing: The chapel of *San Cosme y San Damian* dating from 1521, with a fine Renaissance portal. The chapel of *Nuestra Señora de los Remedios* dates from 1522. The *Archbishop's palace* dates

mainly from the 16–17C and part is Romanesque. It houses the *Regional Archaeological Museum,* which has Visigoth remains, Roman and prehistoric finds etc. The *Roman bridge,* which was rebuilt in 1230–1449, spans the Miño with seven arches. Modern Orense is not without its sights, e.g. the famous 'Paseo' with the tower block, 'La Torre', dating from 1968. However, some of the finest sights include the many old squares. The *Plaza de Fonte Nova,* bordering the cathedral, has arcades and old houses. The *Plaza Mayor* has arcades. The *Casino de Caballeros,* a 14C house, now houses a music conservatory and stage school. The *Town Hall* has a restored façade. The *Plaza de las Damas,* near the Fonte Nova, is also interesting. The *Plazuela del Hierro* has a fountain which originally belonged to a monastery in Oseira. The houses in these squares have coats-of-arms and attractive wrought-iron balconies. The *Plazuela de la Magdalena* has a 17C crucero.

Environs: Gustey (SW of Orense on the road to Cambio) with a Romanesque parish church with two splendid portals. **Feá:** (W. of Orense on the road to Ribadavia) has a single-aisled 13C Romanesque church with a most unusual portal. **Ourantes:** (near to Feá), with the 12C church of *San Juan* which was restored in the 18C. The old portal is interesting, and so is the baroque altar which has scenes of Heaven, Hell and Purgatory. **Carballino:** (NW of Orense) with the modern church, *Vera Cruz,* designed by Antonio Palacios. **Moldes:** with the church of *Santa Mamed,* which originally belonged to the Knights Templar. The most interesting parts are the apse, the portal and the Santiago sculptures on the side wall. At **Borborás** is the church of *San Julián de los Asturienses.* This was founded by the Knights Templar in the 12C, but since the 15C it has belonged to the Maltese Order (dedicated to St. John of Malta). The church is single-

Orense, cathedral, S. façade

Orense, cathedral

aisled with a semicircular apse, shell vaults and portals with decorated archivolts. **Cameija** with a late 12C Romanesque *church*, which has an interesting portal and richly decorated apse.

Orihuela
Alicante/Valencia   p.396□K 9

22 km. N. of Murcia, with a population of some 49,000 (including neighbouring areas). The town lies on the narrow strip between a mountain and the Río Segura, which is spanned by two bridges, the 'Puente de Poniente' and 'Puente del Levante'. The Romans knew it as *Aurariola* and the Moors as *Origuëla*. In the Middle Ages it was the capital of a region. It

has been the seat of a bishop since 1564. The irrigation system making Vega in the S. fertile dates from the time of Alfonso X (there are beautiful orange groves). The city's numerous monuments and buildings date from the Moorish period and the 14 -17C.

Cathedral: On the far side of the river. 14-16C Gothic with a fine *Renaissance portal*, the 'Puerta de la Anunciación' (on the N. side), which is attributed to Jeronimo Quijano (died 1564), the builder of Murcia Cathedral. The *interior* consists of a nave and two aisles with remarkable rib vaulting. One of the side chapels has a fine 16C winged altar; another altar, this time marble, is covered by a dome and has an embossed silver altarpiece; the *choir stalls* are by Mahagoni of Borja.

Orihuela, cathedral, cloister

Orihuela, Santiago, portal

Santiago: A late Gothic Isabelline church dating from the 15C. Built by Ferdinand and Isabella on the site of a mosque. The Gothic *façade*, with its fine portal, is 15C; one of the side portals is baroque. The tower is late 15C. Gothic nave and Renaissance choir and transept (1554–1609). The high altar is made of marble and jasper and has a painting, 'The Eucharist', by Juan de Juanes, and statues by Salzillo. The church's treasure includes a Christ attributed to Benvenuto Cellini.

Episcopal palace: Almost opposite the 18C cathedral. It has two fine staircases in marble and carved wood. The 13C Romanesque-Gothic *cloister* houses the **Diocesan Museum**, which has paintings by Velazquez ('Consolation of St. Thomas Aquinas', *c.* 1631), Ribera ('Mary Magda-

lene'), Rodrigo de Osona ('St. Michael'), and a number of other works by anonymous 16–17C masters. The church treasury contains Pope Calixtus III's missal (15C) with miniatures.

Monastery of Santo Domingo: The monastery's baroque church, built between 1654–9, has a pendentive dome and a fine portal. *Inside* there is a baroque high altar, and to the left of this a chapel with an altar by Juan Juanes. A passage with an artesonado ceiling leads from a large patio to a smaller Renaissance one, off which there is a 17C refectory decorated with azulejos.

Old University (now a high school): An impressive building to the right of Santo Domingo. It was begun in 1552 by Juan

Angeles and extended in the 17C by A.Bernardo.

City Museum: Houses the *Biblioteca Fernando de Loaces* (with a collection of early prints) and an archaeological collection of finds from around Orihuela; there are also paintings, especially the Paso, the 'Triumph of the Cross', also known as *La Diablesa*, by Nicolás de Busi.

Oropesa
Toledo/New Castile   p.392☐E 6

City Walls: Dating back to the 12C; some sections have survived intact.

Castle: Built in a strategic location in the 12-13C—very little remains from the original construction. The castle is surrounded by strong walls. When the Lords of Oropesa seized power and the 14C feudal wars began, the castle was completely renovated. The building you see today dates from 1402 and is the most interesting fortress in the province. Of the various towers, the E. tower is the most interesting.

The two Castles: These belong to the Lords of Oropesa. The *Old Castle* (15C) is a Gothic-Mudéjar construction, with some Plateresque features. The *New Castle* (16 -17C), added on to the Old, was built in Renaissance style to the designs of Herrera.

Parish Church: A 16-17C Renaissance church, with an early Renaissance-Plateresque main portal, in two parts. The tower of ashlars has a Renaissance balustrade and Gothic battlements.

Iglesia del Colegio de la Compañia de Jesús: Renaissance style; built in ashlars, 1590 - 1604 and based on the designs of Juan de Herrera. Latin cross groundplan.

Environs: Alcolea de Tajo: (*c.* 15 km. S.). The Chapel of *Nuestra Señora de Bienvenida* dates from the beginning of the 16C and has a nave and two aisles, a panelled ceiling and a main chapel with late Gothic groin vaulting and pointed arches. Columns separating nave and aisles are Renaissance. **El Puente del Arzobispo:** (18 km. S.) The *parish church* is 19C in origin. Nearby is the *18C church*—originally Gothic, it was damaged by an earthquake in 1755. The monks had it rebuilt in the style of the time, which was baroque. Single-aisled church with chapels along the sides, polygonal apses, a dome over the crossing and barrel vaulting with lunettes and intricate carvings. The alabaster *altarpiece* is a remarkable 15C late Gothic work, which is divided into numerous sections. The sections are separated by Renaissance columns, which have reliefs of scenes from the life of Christ and the Virgin. Behind the high altar is a *window* of 1719 by the architect Francisco Hurtado, the painters Palomino and Antonio Lanchares and the sculptor Cornejo. The highly colourful result is a fine example of high baroque.

Osera (Oseira)
Orense/Galicia   p.386☐C 2

Monasterio de Santa María: Osera lies in hilly countryside some 5 km. E. of Carballedo, and is the location of the most important monastery in Galicia. The monastery was founded by Alfonso VII in the first half of the 12C and later became Cistercian. It declined in importance in the 14C and doesn't seem to be mentioned again until the 16C when, after a fire in 1552, it was so lavishly renovated that it became known as the 'Escorial of Galicia'. The *church* has a nave and two aisles and is 12-13C, having survived the fire largely undamaged. There are flying buttresses, Romanesque-Gothic windows, a dome over the crossing and a groin-vaulted ambulatory. The façade is a fine example of Spanish baroque, dark and restrained but also grandiose; a high tower at either side of the façade frames the most impressive *portal*, which is surrounded by pillars and statues. Inside the church there are fine frescos on the walls and ceiling. The 16C *sacristy* is most unusual, having twisted columns and groin vaulting. The monastery's façade, at right angles to that of the church, is also a fine example of baroque. In front of it is an ornamental garden with clipped green shrubs typical of the 18C. Also of interest are three fine *cloisters*, the old *chapterhouse* which has curious pillars and rib vaulting in English Gothic style, a *library*, an old *kitchen* with a huge fireplace and numerous staircases, particularly a *spiral staircase*.

Environs: Carballedo: The church of *San Esteban de Chouzán* was originally part of a 12C Benedictine monastery; it was restored in the 14C and has 15C frescos in the apse. The church of *San Juan da Coba* is late 12C and was also originally part of a Benedictine monastery.

Osuna

Seville/Andalusia   p.394□E 10

Originally an ancient settlement by the name of Urso, Osuna reached its artistic and cultural peak during the 16C under the Dukes of Osuna.

Collegiate Church: An imposing building in the university complex on the hill above the town. Built 1534–9 in a highly ornamental Renaissance style. The W. façade has a *Plateresque portal*, the 'Puerta del Sol'. In the main chapel there is a baroque altar with four early *paintings by José de Ribera* — the Martyrdoms of St. Bartholomew, St.Jerome, St.Peter and St.

Sebastian. The *treasury* contains 16–18C gold objects. The *Renaissance patio* is very fine and is surrounded with two-storey galleries (with 16C Flemish paintings in the wall niches). From the patio you can get to the *burial chamber of the Dukes of Osuna* and the fine chapel, the *Capilla del Santo Sepulchro* (1540), which, along with the sacristy, the ante-room to the crypt and the Chapel of the Virgin of Granada, contains some splendid art e.g. an image of Christ by Luis de Morales, a terracotta St.Jerome by Pietro Torrigiani, Flemish paintings and a remarkably fine triptych.

University (today a school): Formerly famous for its theological faculty. Of artistic interest: some good Flemish paintings over the altar in the chapel and the Plateresque courtyard.

Santo Domingo: The church's treasures include a 'Crucifixion' by Ribera and a sculpture, 'Cristo de la Misericordia', by Juan de Mesa (16–17C).

Other things of interest: The 18C church of *Nuestra Señora de la Victoria* with a Pietà by José ·de Mora. The *Monasterio de la Encarnación* whose *patio* walls are covered with 18C polychrome tiles.

Oviedo

Oviedo/Asturia   p.386□E 1

The Benedictine monastery of San Vicente was founded on a hill in the middle of the fertile plains of Asturia in 761. The settlement of Ovetum developed quickly around the monastery. The Moors destroyed the town in 789 and Alfonso II (the Chaste) rebuilt it. In 792 the town became the seat

Oviedo, cathedral, miniature t

XEMENERGE   ALDEFONSIREX   GOMELREPS

MINISTRI EIVS

TESTAME HTVM

REX I VO

ARMIGERI EIVS

FADEFONSIREX ES XEMENER

of the Kings of Asturia. It was surrounded by mighty fortifications, the remains of which are still standing. During 810–924 Oviedo was the centre of the resistance of Christian Asturia against the Moors. In 1521 most of the city was destroyed by fire. In 1608 the university was opened by Bishop Fernando de Valdès y Salas. The coal and iron and steel industries, which began to develop around the beginning of the 20C, have given the city its present character. Many buildings were damaged first in the 1934 Worker's Revolt and then in the Civil War of 1936–7.

Cathedral/Sancta Ovetensis: The imposing Gothic cathedral is in the middle of the city, in the Plaza de Alfonso II. On the W. side stands a tower 270 ft. high; completed in 1539 it is one of Spain's most beautiful towers (it was restored in 1936 after the Civil War). Leopoldo Alas called it 'a poem in stone'. Originally the cathedral's site was occupied by a basilica erected by King Fruela I in the 8C. The Moors destroyed this basilica and it was rebuilt by Alfonso II. On the NE side of the cathedral there is an 11C tower with Roman windows. The church we see today was built 1328–1528. The W. portal is by the French architect Pierre Buyères. Stone carving over the main entrance into the three-aisled exonarthex is especially interesting. The church's interior (nave and two aisles) is well proportioned and not overbearingly large. The aisles have rib vaulting. The nave is 220 ft. long; the triforium has balustrades and Gothic window openings and the clerestory has stained glass windows with Gothic arches. The elevated sanctuary at the E. end is approached by steps and lies behind the choir screen. It has stained glass windows and a huge and highly decorated late Gothic-Renaissance retable illustrating the Passion; in the middle is Christ in Judgement, above it is an Annunciation by Giralte of Brussels and Juan de Balmaseda. This is one of the three most important reredos of its type in the whole of Spain. The aisles have a number of side chapels: from the W., on the right is the particularly impressive *Capilla Santa Barbara*, which is late 17C, and the connected *Chapel of St. Martin*, which has a fine 17C altar by Fernández de la Vega; the *Capilla San Roque* has a stone tomb from 1517. One of the pillars on the right hand side of the nave has a very interesting statue of Christ dating from the early 12C. The entrance to the *Cámara Santa* (or Capilla San Miguel, above the interesting Capilla Santa Leocadia, which consists of two rooms) is in the right arm of the transept. The larger is 12C and has six pilasters each with two fine statues of the apostles along the long sides. The smaller is 9C and houses the cathedral treasures and relics; most interesting is a cedar-wood *reliquary chest* with fine reliefs in silver dating from c. 1000, a much treasured *Cruz de los Angeles* (Angel's Cross) encrusted with precious stones (a gift from Alfonso II in 808), two Byzantine ivory diptychs from the 6C and 14C, and the highly ornamental *Cruz de la Victoria*, given to the church in 908 by King Alfonso III and which Prince Pelayo is said to have worn at the Battle of Covadonga. The right transept leads to the *cloisters*, which are early 14C Gothic in origin but were extensively renovated in 1934. Of the chapels on the left, the most interesting is the *Capilla del Rey Casto* (Chapel of Alfonso II, the Chaste), which is off the left arm of the transept. It is like a little church, with a nave, two aisles and its own tower; originally 9C it was redecorated in baroque style in the 18C. Outside the entrance to the Capilla del Rey Casto (late Gothic and decorated with figures), and also on the E. side of the N. arm of the transept, there is an imposing baroque altar with a beautiful Madonna with a halo of rays and supported by angels—by Juan de

Oviedo, cathedral, interior

Oviedo, cathedral

Oviedo, cathedral, Cámara Santa

Villanueva Barbales, dating from 1741. Inside the chapel and left of the entrance is a fine 16C statue of Nuestra Señora de la Luz, and in the NW corner is the *pantheon* of the Asturian kings, which still houses a 12C sarcophagus with a fine marble lid. The first chapel from the W. in the left aisle is the *Capilla de Santa Eulalia*; on the altar is a late 17C Churrigueresque shrine in gilded silver which contains the saint's mortal remains. Behind the choir in the E. there is an ambulatory with five chapels which are mostly decorated in baroque style.

Other churches of interest: To the NE of the cathedral lies the church of *Santa María La Real de la Corte*, which is 17C. To the SW of the cathedral is the church of *San Tirso*, which was originally built by

Alfonso II. From this time (9C) also date the great tripartite round-arched window, the conclusion of the choir and the remains of the foundations. The church was restored in the 17C and contains some fine pictures, e.g. Adoration of the Magi from the school of Hans Memling. The church of *San Isidoro*, on the Plaza Mayor, dates from the 16C and has a very beautiful carved wooden altar. Today a 12C portal from the original Romanesque church of San Isidoro stands in the Campo de San Francisco, a park.

San Julian de los Prados/Santullano: This basilica is the most important Asturian monument. It stands in a field away from the town and somewhat off the beaten track. It was built 812–42 under Alfonso II and has a nave, two aisles, a broad tran-

Oviedo, cathedral, Cámara Santa

Oviedo, cathedral, Cámara Santa

sept, apses with barrel vaulting and square columns between nave and aisles. The church is lit by three windows in the clerestory of the nave, and also by a semicircular window in both E. and W. ends. Sections have been added at both ends of the transept. This beautifully-proportioned building is above all interesting for the Christian murals on the walls inside. These paintings include a depiction of the construction of the church, along with paintings of plants (leaves and flowers) as well as pictures of men and animals. These accurate paintings, though restored in places but in general unfortunately badly damaged, are based on similar works of Byzantium, Ravenna and Rome, and are most unusual.

Also worth seeing: Near San Julian de los Prados is the 12C church of *Santa María de la Vega*. In the SW of the Plaza del Alfonso II, diagonally opposite the cathedral in the Cella del Rúa, is the 15C *Palacio de la Rúa*. This street opens on to the Plaza Mayor, with the *Ayuntamiento*, which is opposite San Isidoro. It was originally built in 1622 and rebuilt in 1939; the façade and the clock tower are original. Further to the SW is the 18C *Palais San Feliz*, which houses a good rt gallery, (with El Greco's 'Apostles'). The *University* (on the Calle di San Francisco), built 1534–1608 by Gonzales de Bracamonte and Juan del Ribero, was restored in 1934. It has a fine courtyard with a statue of the founder, Fernando Valdés. NE of the university is the 18C *Palacio de los Campos Sagrados*, which is now used as a court of law. Behind the latter lies the 18C *Palacio de Here-*

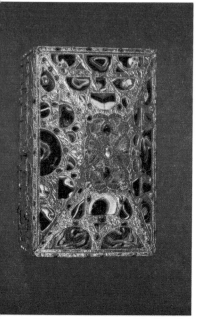

Oviedo, cathedral, Cámara Santa

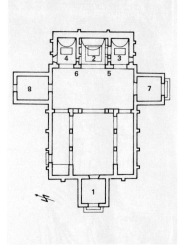

Oviedo, San Julian de los Prados 1 W. atrium **2** central apse with raised ceiling **3** and **4** side apses **5** and **6** pilasters at the entrance to the central apse covered in reliefs **7** and **8** ante-rooms added to the transept

dia; the baroque *Casa da Galazza* is nearby. The former Royal Palace, built during the 17C by Pedro Antonio Menéndez, has been converted into the elegant *Hotel Reconquista*. The monastery of *San Vicente* is to the E. of the cathedral, and was founded in 781, making it the city's oldest building; it was subsequently restored in the 9,11,14,15&16C, but some of the original building remains. It now serves as the *Provincial Museum*, and contains Romanesque and pre-Romanesque art. Behind the museum, and near the church of *Santa María de la Corte*, is the Benedictine monastery of *San Pelayo*, which was originally built by Alfonso II. Restored in the 18C it was seriously damaged in 1934. On the Plaza de San Domingo in the SE of the town is the *Monastery of Santo Domingo* from the 16&18C. Also of interest is the

very old *Foncalada* fountain, which was built by Alfonso III and has survived in good condition in the midst of modern houses. The *Teatro Campoamo*, a 19C building, is now used for operas.

Environs: Monte Naranco: (nearby, to the N. of Oviedo): The site of two of Spain's finest pre-Romanesque churches, Santa María del Naranco and San Miguel de Liño. **Santa María del Naranco**, originally the palace of King Ramiro (842–50), was converted into a church in the 13C and consecrated to the Virgin Mary. It was declared a national monument in 1881, and restored in 1931 and 1939. Today we can see this utterly beautiful and well-proportioned building in what must be very like its original form (at least as much of it as has survived). The

Oviedo, San Miguel de Liño, relief　　*Oviedo, San Miguel de Liño*

church, in the form of a long two-storey rectangle oriented E-W, with barrel vaulting and arches suppported on pilasters, is very like the great hall of a castle. Of paramount interest are the very beautifully decorated columns, arches and medallions, which are again reminiscent of the art of Ravenna and Byzantium. The ground floor is divided into three rooms, one of which was originally used as a chapel. When it was a palace it was probably part of a complex of royal buildings, another of which seems to have been the local church, **San Miguel de Liño** or Lillo. This is also 9C in origin, but was seriously damaged by an earthquake in the 13C; all that remains is the W. section with the original entrance. Its windows are particularly fine (e.g. the last on the S. side aisle). The apse visible today dates from the 13C. What was originally the hindmost bay of the nave now functions as a transept. The pillars have particularly fine reliefs and the pilaster decorations in the bay in the S. aisle echo Byzantine art. The alto-relievo on both sides of the entrance portal are particularly well executed. Remains of ancient wall paintings have survived. **San Pedro de Nora** (13 km. E. of Oviedo): A 9C church with barrel vaults and three square apses in the transept. **Santa María de Bendones** (5 km. S. of Nora): A 9C church with beautiful windows. **Tuñón** has a simple pre-Romanesque church, *San Adriano*, which was built under Alfonso III in 891 and restored in 1108. The church has a nave and two aisles and wall paintings from the time it was founded. Mozarabic influence is apparent. **Collotio** (on the route from Oviedo to San-

Santa María del Naranco (Oviedo), exterior

Santa María del Naranco (Oviedo)

tander): The site of a Roman bridge over the river Nora, and the 12C Romanesque church of *Santa Eulalia* which has beautiful columns and a triumphal arch. **Pola de Lena:** Near this village, which is en route to Puerto de Pajares, is the church of

Santa Cristina de Lena, a 9C building not unlike Santa María de Naranco, but with one storey and a Greek cross groundplan. The interior architecture is fine, especially the buttresses and the decoration on a balustrade slab in the sanctuary.

Santa María del Naranco (Oviedo) ▷

P Q

Padrón
La Coruña/Galicia   p.386☐B 2

Padrón was already known in Roman times by the name of Iria Flavia. There are still many finds from that period. The town, near the mouth of the Ría de Arosa, was also important during the Middle Ages and the baroque period, to which old villas and palaces in the vicinity of Padrón still testify. The church of *Santa María a Dina* (at the edge of the town) dates from the 11C. It was destroyed by the Normans and then rebuilt. It was the Archbishop's cathedral church, and was also a collegiate and pilgrimage church. It was again rebuilt in the 18C by Pedro García Cotobade, who retained the 12C portal and the 16C tower. Of interest are the grille in the sanctuary

Padrón, parish church

and the statue of San Pedro de Mezonzos (Archbishop of Compostela) by Ferreira.

Convento del Carmen: This monastery was founded by Dominicans in the 17C. In its church, with a nave and two aisles, 18C sculptures by Ferreira and Felipe de Castro can be admired.

Also worth seeing: The 18C *Ayuntamiento* and the *Palacio de Alonso Peña Montenegro.*

Environs: Rianjo (Riaño): SW of Padrón, just off the road to Puebla del Caramiñal, also on the Ría de Arosa is the coastal village of Rianjo, which has old *mansions* and the 15C church of *Santa Columba,* which has a beautiful 16C portal and a baroque tower. **Puebla del Caramiñal:** Some 30 km. SW of Padrón lies this old fishing port on the Ría de Arosa. It has a 17C *baroque church,* the 15C church of *Puebla del Déan* and the *Palacio de Xunqueiras,* as well as the *Torre de los Bermúdez* with beautiful Renaissance windows.

Palamós
Gerona/Catalonia　　　　　　p.390☐O 3

Santa María: Gothic parish church, built in 1371 and rebuilt in the 16C.

Environs: Calonge (6 km. inland): Interesting remains of the *castle of the Duke of Sesa,* e.g. the NW part and the S. side with four round towers and a rectangular one from the 12C. The main part of the fortress was added later (15C) and has Gothic windows. 18C chapel. On the façade are the coats-of-arms of the Cardone and Sesa families. **Castell d'Aro** (near Playa d'Aro, 2 km. inland): This site was originally a fortress called 'Benedormiens', little of whose walls have survived. In the vicinity are a few typical Catalonian *farm-*

houses with the characteristic defensive towers.

Palencia
Palencia/Old Castile　　　　　p.388☐F 3

The founding of this city goes back to the former 'Pallantia' of the Celtic-Iberian period, when it was the chief town of the Vaccaei. In the struggle against the Romans it was destroyed and captured, but later thhe Romans rebuilt it and made it capital of the region. In the 1C AD it became the seat of a bishop. During the Visigoth invasions it was destroyed by Theodoric, who later made it his headquarters. During this time it was, above all, the Bishops of Palencia who were important. In the Arab invasions the city was destroyed once again; twenty years later it was captured by Alfonso I and rebuilt under the rule of the Bishops. In the 13C Alfonso VIII of Castile founded Spain's first university here.

Padrón, family crest

Cathedral: This was built in the 14–15C on the remains of an old Visigoth church of the 7C, which was restored in Romanesque style in the 11C and now serves as the crypt. The cathedral remains in pure Gothic style with an unfinished tower, a very beautiful apse and richly decorated King's and Bishop's portals. It consists of a nave and two aisles with ambulatory and groin vaulting. Inside the church, behind the choir, there is a very beautiful wooden altarpiece in Plateresque style. It was made by Jan Joest de Harlem in 1505 and surrounded by stone carvings and bas-reliefs by Gil de Siloé. In front of the altar is a Plateresque staircase leading to the crypt of San Antolín. By the choir's right wall there are two fine Plateresque *altarpieces*. The *choir* has an excellent *grille* by Gaspar Rodríguez de Segovia and *choir stalls* with interesting reliefs from the 15C. The Renaissance pulpit by Juan de Ortiz also merits attention. Some of the chapels are particularly interesting. The *main chapel* has a monumental grille by Cristóbal de Andino (1520) and contains the cathedral's most valuable work of art, a Renaissance altarpiece with sculptures by Felipe Bigarny, paintings by Juan de Flandes and a sculpture by Juan de Balmaseda. The *old main chapel* contains the tombs of Doña Urraca (12C), Doña Inés de Osorio and Enríquez de Portillo (1492). *San Ildefonso* has Juan de Balmaseda's superb retable of the saint. *San Gregorio* has a Plateresque retable of St.Cosmas and St.Damian and the tomb of Juan de Arce. The *Capilla del Sagrario* has a Plateresque altarpiece with sculptures and paintings. Two Gothic doors on the right side lead to the 16C cloisters, which were built by Gil de Hontañón. The *museum* is housed in the sacristy and the chapterhouse. Its valuable treasures include *St.Sebastian* by El Greco, paintings by Nicolás Francés, Pedro Berruguete, Mateo Cerezo and Valdés Leal, Romanesque and Gothic sculptures, tapestries by Fonseca and wrought-iron pieces, including the monstrance of Benavente, as well as various religious objects.

San Pablo: This church, belonging to the

Palencia, statue of Cristo del Otero

Palencia, cathedral, trascoro

13C Dominican monastery, consists of a nave and two aisles with groin vaulting. The Capilla Mayor contains the fine marble tombs of the Marquises of Poza (attributed to Berruguete) and a Renaissance altarpiece and grille. In the chapel dedicated to Deacon Zapata there is a splendid Gothic altarpiece.

Other interesting churches: The 13C *San Miguel* has a graceful Gothic tower and a Romanesque portal. Inside, there are a nave and two aisles with three apses and a 13C Gothic cross. The Gothic *Santa Clara* has a beautiful 16C apse, a fine portal and, inside, an impressive recumbent Christ. *San Francisco,* belonging to an old Franciscan monastery, has a baroque sacristy with Mudéjar panelling. *San Bernardo* has a Plateresque façade. *Nuestra Señora de la Calle* contains baroque altarpieces. The Gothic *San Lázaro* dates from the time of El Cid and has a Romanesque tower and portal. Beside the pilgrimage chapel of *Cristo del Otero* stands an enormous statue by Victorio Macho, which dominates the whole countryside.

Provincial Archaeological Museum: This contains prehistoric finds, pre-Roman and Roman articles, a Gothic sarcophagus and other medieval tombs, 14C altarpieces and a large collection of coins.

Also worth seeing: *Plaza Mayor* with the 19C *Town Hall* and a *monument* in honour of the sculptor Alonso Berruguete by Victorio Macho. The *Hospital San Antolín* of 1183 with inner courtyard.

Environs: Some 2 km. N. lies **Fuentes de Valdepero** with a 14C *castle,* adorned with the Sarmiento coat-of-arms. **Husillos** (*c.* 3 km. N.): The 10C abbey of *Santa María* was used for national assemblies on several occasions; the present 12C Romanesque monastery has been declared a national monument. **Monzón de Campos** (*c.* 5 km. N.): The *fortress* was a royal residence in the Middle Ages; the *parish church* contains a Gothic altar with a superb sculpture of the Virgin and Child. **Valdespina** (*c.* 8 km. N.): The Romanesque *parish church,* with a beautiful portal and apse,

Palencia, cathedral

Pamplona, cathedral

has a Plateresque altarpiece with sculptures and reliefs. **Ribas de Campos** (*c.* 10 km. N.): The 12C church of *San Martín* contains valuable paintings, including that of St.Martin from the 13C and St.Francis by Zurbarán. The monastery of *Santa Cruz de la Zarza* dates from 1176 and has a two-aisled church with transept and three stellar-vaulted apses. **Amusco** (*c.* 12 km. N.): The 'Pajarón de Campos', as the baroque church of *San Pedro* is known, has two Romanesque portals; the pilgrimage chapel of *Nuestra Señora de las Fuentes*, from the Romanesque-Gothic transitional period, has a Plateresque pulpit and a 15C sculpture. **Villamediana** (*c.* 7 km. E.): The Romanesque *parish church* has a marvellous 15C altarpiece with reliefs by Juan de Balmaseda; there are also remains of the town walls and a medieval tower to be seen.

Torquemada (*c.* 10 km. E.): The 15C *parish church,* with a nave and two aisles, has an 18C baroque altarpiece and 16C choir stalls; the pilgrimage chapel of *Nuestra Señora de Valdesalle* contains elements from an old 13C church. **Herrera de Valdecañas** (*c.* 12 km. E.): The church of *Santa Cecilia,* with three apses and groin vaulting, has a portal, lavishly decorated with sculptures and, inside, an altarpiece with 15C paintings. **Palenzuela** (*c.* 20 km. E.): The church of *San Juan,* with 16C groin vaulting, nave and two aisles, contains valuable Renaissance altarpieces and Gothic tombs with recumbent statues; the retored church of *Santa Eulalia* dates from the 13C.

Pamplona
Navarra/Navarra   p.388☐I 2

Pamplona, the 2,000-year-old former capital of the kingdom of Navarre, stands on a hill in the Río Arga valley. Today it is the provincial capital of Navarra. The city dates back to a Roman foundation. In 75 BC Pompey built a settlement here called Pompaelo. Known to the Basques as Iruña, the city was occupied by the Visigoths under Euric in 466 and by the Franks under Childebert and Clothar in 542. It later came under the sway of Leovigild, until being seized by the Moors in 738. The Basques, with the help of Charlemagne, managed to drive out the Moors in 750. However, Charlemagne occupied Pamplona as part of his Spanish campaign and had the defensive walls destroyed. In revenge for this, the rearguard of Charlemagne's army, led by the legendary Roland, were annihilated by the Basques in the valley of Roncesvalles on 15 August 778. In 905 Sancho Abarca established the kingdom of Navarre and chose Pamplona for his residence. The kingdom existed until 1512, when Ferdinand and Isabella oc-

Pamplona, cathedral, cloister

cupied Pamplona and annexed Navarre to Castile. During the attempt to recapture the city of 1521, the young captain Iñigo López de Recalde, later St.Ignatius Loyola, was badly wounded. In the wars of the 19C Pamplona was again the target of many assaults and was occupied several times. Nowadays the city, with its picturesque medieval streets and interesting religious and secular buildings, is a popular place with tourists. Another attraction is the the well-known Fiesta of San Fermín on 7 July. The city and this festival provided the setting of Hemmingway's novel 'Fiesta', for which a monument was erected to him in front of the bullring.

Cathedral: A Roman capitol is supposed to have originally occupied this site, until a Romanesque church was built here in the 11C. This was replaced by another Romanesque building, consecrated in 1124, to which a new, larger church was added at the start of the 14C. In 1390 construction was started on the present Gothic cathedral. It was probably completed by 1527. This building with a nave and two aisles and a Latin cross ground plan, shows strong French influence. The church has numerous side chapels beneath the buttresses, as well as an apse with further chapels. It is roofed by a groin vault. The *classical façade* and the two 170 ft. towers date from 1783 and are the work of Ventura Rodríguez. In the right tower hangs the largest *bell* in Spain. It was cast at the end of the 16C and weighs 12 ton. The Capilla Mayor has choir stalls of 1540 by Esteban de Obray. A statue of the *Virgen del Sagrario,* also called Santa María la Real (the patroness of the church), was added to a Renaissance statue of the Infant Christ. In the *nave,* in front of the splendid wrought-iron Renaissance grille, stand the *sarcophagi* of King Charles III and his wife Leonor of Castile. This *alabaster tomb* (1416) is the work of the Flemish sculptor Janin de Lomme and has the recumbent figures of the couple and a relief with hooded men and lamenting women. The altarpieces in the *chapels* are of various dates. The altars of the chapels dedicated to San Blas, Santa Catalina, Christ and San Fermín, as well as the altars of St. Joseph and San Jerónimo in the transept, are all baroque. The chapels of San Juan Bautista, Santa Cristina and the Caparroso Chapel all have 15C altarpieces. A beautiful crucifix in the Capilla del Santo Cristo also dates from the 15C. From the S. transept you can get to the *cloister* via an interesting *portal,* which dates from the 14C and has a bas-relief of a scene from the life of the Virgin. The Gothic cloister has beautifully decorated capitals. It is divided into four parts, the oldest of which are the N. and E. walks. These date from the time of Bishop Barbazán. The S. and W. sides were presumably built under Charles III. In the NE of the cloister there is an Adoration of the Magi by Jaques Perut (early 14C). A 15C Madonna and Child is preserved in the chapel of Bishop Barbazán. The cloister has another beautiful portal, the *Puerta Preciosa* (14C). The tympanum of this door has carved scenes from the life of the Virgin. *Sarcophagi* of Prince Leonel of Navarre and his wife Elfa (15C). The tomb is adorned with a Calvary carved in stone. Tomb of the Conde de Gages by Robert Michel (late 18C). The *Diocesan Museum* is housed in the former refectory. The portal bears carvings of the church and the synagogue. In the tympanum is the Last Supper and the Entry of Jesus into Jerusalem. Apart from a large number of 13&14C sculptures, the Diocesan Museum also houses Gothic and Renaissance paintings,

sacred objects, as well as a splinter of the Cross, which is preserved in an finely-wrought reliquary of 1401.

San Nicolás: This 13C church with a nave and two aisles is still partly Romanesque and looks like a *fortified church.* Massive walls and watch towers, as well as beautiful vaulting. Interesting altars within.

San Ignacio: This basilica was built in Churrigueresque style above the former town fortifications, on the spot where St. Ignatius Loyola is supposed to have been wounded.

Santo Domingo: This Renaissance church dates from the 16C. Interesting altarpiece from the same period.

San Miguel: A modern church, with a 16C *altarpiece* (from the cathedral) by Pedro González de San Pedro, a pupil of Juan de Anchetas.

San Lorenzo: A classical church with medieval features. Within is the baroque chapel of San Fermín.

San Saturnino: This single-aisled church was built in the 13C as an extension of a 12C Romanesque church, and is thus a mixture of Romanesque and Gothic. Apart from several 13–17C *tombs*, the church also has a beautiful *main portal.* This is decorated with Gothic arches supported by columns, the capitals of which are embellished with scenes from the childhood of Christ and the Passion. The tympanum displays Christ in Judgement. The apse consists of three chapels; there are two more chapels in the two towers.

Museo de Navarra: This is housed in the

Pamplona, cathedral, 16C retable

former *Hospital de la Misericordia*, of which only the Plateresque portal of 1556 survives. The *museum* contains numerous objects from the Celtic-Iberian period, prehistoric finds from the Roman settlements, such as mosaic floors, and a collection of objects from the Stone Age up to the Roman period. The *sculptures* in the collection are of great interest, having come from various *religious buildings*. Amongst these are fragments of the mosque of Tudela and capitals of columns with lovely carvings from the cathedral of Pamplona and the monasteries of Leyre and Sangüesa. The *collection of paintings* covers works from the Romanesque up to the 18C, including the portrait of the Marqués de San Adrián (1804) by Goya. In the former *hospital chapel* is an *altarpiece* by Esteban de Obray. The *collection of wall paintings* includes excellent Gothic and 16C works. Wall paintings from the church of Gallipienzo (14&15C) alternate with ones from the church of Cerco de Artajona (mid 14C) and from San Pedro of Olite from the same period. In another room, wall paintings by Juan Olivier from the refectory of Pamplona Cathedral are exhibited (1330). One of the museum's most interesting objects is an *ivory casket*, which came from the Moorish workshops of Córdoba in 1005 and consists of 19 ivory plaques adorned with eight-lobed medallions depicting scenes from the lives of the Caliphs. The whole casket is embellished with decorations of plants, animals, fruit and human figures. The shrine came from the Monastery of Leyre, where it served as a reliquary.

Palacio de la Diputación: This provincial parliament building was built in the mid-19C by the architect José de Nagusía. There are beautiful tapestries and *paintings* by Joaquín Espalter. The portrait of King Ferdinand VII (1814) is by Goya, while the portrait of María Isabella de Braganza was painted by Federico de Madrazo.

El Archivo de Navarra: This archive is housed in a neoclassical building and contains various collections of manuscripts and a 14C 'Liber Regalis' from England.

Ayuntamiento/Town Hall: Baroque building (late 17C) with beautiful two-storeyed façade, columns and balconies.

Cámara de Comptos: The city's oldest secular building, dating from 1364.

Town fortifications: Little survives of the old Romanesque and medieval defences. The walls remaining today date from the 16C. Note the Puerta de Francia and la Taconera (17C) gates.

Also worth seeing: Numerous *palaces of noble families* still stand in the city (de los Antillón, Baron de Armendáriz, Ezpeleta, the Conde de Guendulain and Vesolla).

Paredes de Nava
Palencia/Old Castile   p.388☐F 3

Archaeological finds indicate that this town has an ancient past. It was the birthplace of the Medieval poet Jorge Manrique and of the painter Pedro Berruguete and his son, the sculptor Alonso Berruguete.

Santa Eulalia: This 11C Romanesque church with a splendid tower contains numerous *art treasures:* the 16C altarpiece on the high altar by Inocencio Berruguete and Esteban Jordán; the altarpiece with sculptures of St.Joachim and St.Anne, attributed to Gil de Siloé; a 16C Flemish triptych. Exhibited in the eight rooms of the **parish museum** are paintings by Pedro Berruguete, Juan de Flandes, Maestro Paredes, Nicolás Francés, Alonso Ber-

Pamplona, Palacio de la Diputación

Pamplona, town hall

Pamplona, Palacio de la Diputación

ruguete and Pantoja de la Cruz, as well as sculptures by Gil de Siloé, Juan de Balmaseda, Alonso Berruguete, Esteban Jordán, Gregorio Fernández, Rodrigo de León, Alonso Cano, Martínez Montañés and Pedro de Cuadra. There are also valuable items in various metals.

Environs: Becerril de Campos (*c.* 6 km. SE): The church of *Santa María* has a painting by Pedro Berruguete (15C), a Flemish triptych and a triptych from the Castilian school, as well as a Gothic-Mudéjar pulpit. The church of *Santa Eugenia* has a Gothic portico and several sculptures (15&16C). The Gothic church of *San Mario* has a Flemish triptych and the church of *San Martín* has several 16C paintings. **Cisneros** (*c.* 10 km. NW): The church of *San Pedro* has a tall portico and

beautiful Mudéjar panelling inside. 16C altarpiece by F. Giralte and the Gothic tomb of Don Toribio Ximénez de Cisneros (15C). The church of *San Facundo*, also has a portico and Mudéjar panelling, contains a Gothic altarpiece and the tomb of Don Antonio Rodríguez de Cisneros (16C). Near Cisneros is the *pilgrimage site of Santo Cristo del Amparo* with the Gothic *mausoleum* of Don Gonzalo Ximénez de Cisneros, one of the finest mausoleums from the 13C. **Frechilla** (*c.* 8 km. W.): Remains of the medieval *walls*. *Parish church* with altarpiece by Portillo and a 14C Stations of the Cross. **Fuentes de Nava** (*c.* 7 km. SW): The *parish church* has a nave, two aisles a massive tower and fine paintings and statues. The church of *Santa María* has lovely polychrome panelling. **Villada** (*c.* 15 km. SW): The baroque church of *San Fructuoso* contains a 15C Gothic image of Christ and the Renaissance tomb of Bishop Don Matías Moratino Santos.

Pastrana
Guadalajara/New Castile   p.388☐H 5

Pastrana is probably a Palatine foundation from 50 BC. The Romans gave the town the name 'Paterniana'; the present name is of Arab origin. The settlement belonged to the Knights of Calatrava until it was sold to the widow of Diego Hurtado de Mendoza by Charles V in 1541.

Santa María de la Asunción: This parish church, with a nave and two aisles, was built on the foundations of a smaller church of the Knights of Calatrava, dating from the 14C. Cardinal Pedro González de Mendoza decided to build a larger Renaissance church. However, as these plans could not be fulfilled, the old part was combined with the new. The doors date from the late 15C, the altarpiece from the 17C.

Parish museum: The sacristy houses a few highly interesting works, such as the parish cross of Martín de Covarrubias (1545), a 13C Gothic crucifix, a 13C casket with Limoges enamel work, a 17C Italian relief, various paintings from the same period, a painting by Carreño and a valuable collection of 15C Gothic tapestries from the workshop of Paschier Grenier in Tournai (Belgium) based on patterns by the Portuguese painter Nuño Gonçalves. Mementoes of St.Theresa of Ávila and of St.John of the Cross; note the embroidery on the priest's robes.

Convento de Concepcionistas: Founded in the 16C by St. Theresa of Ávila. A few relics of the Carmelite saint.

Franciscan monastery: Also a founded by St.Theresa. St.John of the Cross lived here. The building, which was abandoned by the Carmelites in the 19C, is very spacious and dates from the 16C. Important library.

Ducal castle: Built in the 16C by the first Duke of Pastrana, this is an extensive Renaissance building framed by two towers. The front has tall columns, roundels and a gabled roof. Remains of the former furnishings, such as panelling and tiled bases have survived.

El Albaicín district: Owes its origin to a colony of Moors, who came to the town because of the silk industry, which the Dukes of Pastrana had established.

Environs: Almonacid de Zorita (*c.* 15 km. S.): This town of Arab origin belonged to the Knights of Calatrava. *Parish church:* Built in decadent late Gothic style (late 15C). The interesting entrance portal with flame decoration dates from the time of Ferdinand and Isabella. The 13C *town walls* have to a large extent survived. There is also a 16C *tower* to be seen. **Zorita de los Canes** (near Almonacid): The *castle*, of Arab origin was already standing in the 9C. The ground plan is irregular, longer than it is wide. Towers from all periods survive, as do a part of the fortifications and the 12C Romanesque chapel with 13C atrium. Visigoth ruins of the town of **Recópolis** (on the Cerro de la Oliva). The *excavations,* which began in 1944 have uncovered traces of walls, a basilica, the ground plan of a palace, coins and other objects. A *Romanesque chapel* was built on the ruins in the 12C. A few arches remain. **Mondéjar** (*c.* 20 km. SW): *Santa Magdalena:* Work began on this parish church under the architect Cristóbal de Adonza in 1516. It has a nave, two aisles and a tall tower. Two doors, one Gothic, the other Renaissance, lead into the interior. The

columns and groin vaulting are Gothic.
The altarpiece was devastated in the last
Civil War, but still contains a few extraordinarily beautiful gold pieces, a 17C monstrance and a work by Damián Zurreño.
Ruins of the monastery of San Antonio: Lying just outside the town, this monastery
was the first to be built in Renaissance style
in Spain. Although the ground plan is
Gothic, the furnishings and decoration are
Renaissance. The architect Lorenzo Vázquez designed the building, which was
built in the late 15C/early 16C. Both
Gothic and Renaissance elements can be
discerned at the entrance doorway.

Pedraza
Segovia/Old Castile   p.388□G 4

Pedraza is said to be the birthplace of the
Emperor Trajan and is one of the towns in
this region with a highly individual
character.

Castle: This massive, austere castle stands
on an enormous outcrop of rock. It was
built in Gothic style and restored around
1430 by Don Pedro Fernández de Velasco.
There is a long row of embrasures in the
massive, bare outer walls. Inside are various sculptures, paintings and antique furniture, including a few works by Ignacio
Zuloaga.

San Juan: This church, with a tall
Romanesque tower, was rebuilt in the
17&18C and contains 17C sculptures.

Plaza Mayor: With its fine colonnades,
this is one of the most beautiful squares in
Castile. Other, smaller squares, streets,
mansions and palaces are also worth seeing, as are the well-preserved medieval
town walls.

Environs: Some 15 km. S. of Pedraza lies

La Salceda with a 17C baroque *parish
church,* containing a 14C Gothic sculpture
of the Virgin and a baroque altarpiece.
Santiuste de Pedraza (*c.* 17 km. W.):
The church of *Nuestra Señora de la Vega*
has a nave, two aisles and three apses. Built
in Romanesque style, it has a beautiful
tower and a portico.

Peñafiel
Valladolid/Old Castile   p.388□F 4

Castle: Founded in the 10C by Count
Laín Calvo. It is over 700 ft. long, only 77
ft. wide and looks like a beached ship. The
two side walls are defended by 12 cylindrical towers. The 13C *keep* has a square
ground plan with small towers at the
corners.

Monastery of San Pablo: This was built
in 1324 at the behest of the Infante Juan
Manuel. The interior of the Gothic-
Mudéjar *church* with blind arcades outside
the apse consists of a nave and two aisles.
The stellar vaulted Plateresque *chapel* of
Manuel is worth particular attention.

Also worth seeing: The Renaissance
church of *San Miguel* has an altarpiece in
the style of Bigarny, a painting of St.
Michael by the Maestro de Osma, a 13C
Gothic image of Christ and an altarpiece
from the church of El Salvador in the style
of Juan de Juni. The 14C church of *Santa
María* has a beautiful coro and a 16C
wooden altarpiece. The baroque church of
the convent of *Santa Clara* has a dome
decorated with painting and stucco.

Environs: Valbuena de Duero (*c.* 5 km.
W.): Unique 12C *Cistercian Abbey:* The

*Pastrana, Santa María de la Asunción,
parish museum*

Pedraza, Plaza Mayor

church, with a nave and two aisles, pointed arches and stellar vaulting, retains several baroque altarpieces and, in one chapel, stone coffins with frescos (13C). **Manzanillo** (*c.* 3 km. S.): The 16C *parish church* contains fine paintings, such as 'Entombment' by Maestro Manzanillo. **Langayo** (*c.* 4 km. S.): The parish church, with a nave, two aisles and 13C groin vaulting, contains a 14C Gothic image of Christ. **Corrales de Duero** (*c.* 6 km. N.): The Gothic *parish church* contains an altarpiece with sculptures in the style of Juan de Balmaseda and Francisco Giralte; another Plateresque altarpiece has paintings by Villoldo; there are also several paintings by the Maestro de Osma. **Curiel** (*c.* 3 km. N.): The Gothic-Mudéjar church of *Santa María* has a Romanesque portal and a 15C polychrome ceiling; the Capilla Mayor has

stellar vaulting and a good Renaissance altarpiece with sculptures and paintings. Of the famous *castle* only the façade and a gate survive. **Encinas de Esgueva** (*c.* 10 km. N.): The square *castle* has round towers; a 15C *Mudéjar church* preserves a fine altarpiece.

Peñaranda de Duero

Burgos/Old Castile   p.388□G 4

Miranda Palace (on the Plaza Mayor): This important Renaissance palace was built in the 16C. The coloured marble portal, decorated with angels and warriors, combines all the Renaissance characteristics. Square inner courtyard with elegant grand staircase. Numerous rooms, in

Peñíscola, view

which Gothic, Mudéjar and Plateresque friezes and panelling are worth special attention.

Also worth seeing: The *church* with classical portal; the 15C *castle;* a lovely old 15C *obelisk.*

Environs: Coruña del Conde (*c.* 10 km. N.): the 11C *Capilla del Santo Cristo* with a 17C altarpiece; *castle ruins.* **Clunia** (*c.* 12 km. N.) with the remains of the old Roman town, which served as Q. Sertorius's base during the rebellion in 75 BC.

Peñíscola

Castellón de la Plana/Valencia   p.390☐L 5

The old fortress of Peñíscola stands on a steep rocky promontory washed on three sides by the sea. The Phoenicians settled on this strategic site at an early date and they were later followed by the Carthaginians. James I of Aragon drove the Moors out of here during the Reconquista (in 1233) and handed Peñíscola over to the Knights Templar, who had broken away from the Montesa Order of Knights. From 1412–22 the Antipope Benedict XIII (Don Pedro de Luna) resided here, having fled from Avignon. Throughout his life he considered himself the rightful Pope. Peñíscola became Spanish under Philip II. Philip V granted the fortress municipal rights for remaining loyal to him throughout a 17-month siege during the War of the Spanish Succession. In 1814, the French held it against the attacks of the Spanish. The fortress walls date from the time of

Peñíscola, Virgen de la Ermitana

Cebrero (Piedrafíta), parish church

Philip II, whose coat-of-arms can be seen on them, as well as on the Puerta de Felipe. Steep and narrow alleys thread through the irregularly planned town.

Castle: Despite heavy damage in the War of the Spanish Succession and during the Napoleonic era, this Templar-built castle still retains beautifully vaulted rooms and Gothic windows. Benedict XIII had it converted to suit his small papal court. You can still see the chapel and the papal rooms.

Virgen de la Ermitana: This little church next to the castle has an ancient painting, traditionally believed to have been brought over by James the Great, the Apostle of Spain.

Parish church: Built in 1739; its treas-

ury contains mementoes from the time of Pope Benedict XIII.

Environs: A few km. N. of Peñíscola lies **Benicarló** (pop. 15,000), a Greek settlement. This terraced town with its white houses appears oriental. In the surrounding area, which produces good wines, one can still see the old 'norias' (cisterns with bucket-wheels), which irrigate the poor soil. *Parish church:* An 18C building, whose baroque façade, dome and tall tower are most interesting. Further to the N. lies **Vinaroz,** the northernmost town in the region of Valencia. It also marks the end of the *Costa del Azahar* (Orange Blossom Coast), which includes the coastline of the provinces of Castellón de la Plana and Valencia. Vinaroz (pop. 16,000) once belonged to the Templars, and was later a

Samos (Piedrafíta), San Julián

Commandery of the Knights of Montesa. The remains of *walls and old towers* bear witness to this era. *Parish church:* The tower and outer walls still have Romanesque features. For the rest, the church was altered in baroque style around 1700. Note the baroque main portal (several tiers) and a Renaissance side portal.

Piedrafita de Cebrero

Lugo/Galicia   p.386□ D 2

Piedrafita de Cebrero lies near the Puerto-de-Piedrafita Pass on the border between Galicia and León. To the N. are the Cebrero mountains with an ancient settlement of Celtic origin with thatched elliptical stone huts (Pallozas).

Cebrero, parish church: 560 yds N. of Piedrafita is Cebrero with a small pre-Romanesque parish church, which is all that remains of 9C monastery and hospital (under Benedictine monks up until 1486) built to accommodate pilgrims to Santiago. In the sacristy there is a famous 16C chalice, which is supposed to have given rise to a miracle in the 14C.

Environs: N. of Cebrero is **Doncos** with an ancient three-storeyed keep, which was originally part of a fortress. **Penamayor:** Further along the road from Piedrafita to Lugo is Becenera, 8 km. NW of which lies Penamayor, and the 12C Monastery of Santa María, which adopted the reforms of the Cistercians in 1225. The church, with a nave and two aisles, was built in 1164. The façade, altered in the 17C, re-

tains an interesting Romanesque portal.
Triacastela: Triacastela lies on the route
from France to Santiago, in a narrow valley W. of Piedrafita. Only the apse of the
Romanesque *parish church*, which is dedicated to St. James, is original. Tower and
façade were not added until the 18C. The
Hospital de la Condesa (or Casa Pedriña),
only fragments of which survive, was famous at the time of the pilgrimages.
Samos: In a narrow valley further to the
W., on the route to Santiago, is Samos with
the Benedictine Abbey of *San Julián*,
which existed as early as 655. Alfonso I,
the Catholic, of Oviedo spent his youth
here in the first part of the 8C. Nothing
remains from that time. The oldest surviving part is the *Capilla del Salvador* from
the 10C. The present church is an imposing building of 1604, the façade of which
is striking with its beautiful steps of 1779.
Also note the sacristy and the 18C high
altar by Antonio Domínguez de Estirada,
as well as the two cloisters, one from 1582,
the other modern, with monumental
frescos.

Plasencia, cathedral

Piedrahita
Avila/Old Castile   p.392☐E 5

Iglesia Parroquial de la Asunción:
Built in Gothic style in the 15C on the site
of the old palace of Doña Berenguela
Queen of Castile. 16C alterations almost
entirely eradicated its original character.
The portal, with five round arches, conceals the 15C Gothic entrance. The church
has a nave and two aisles. The Renaissance
cloister dates from the 16C.

Palace of the Dukes of Alba: The Duke
of Alba was born in this palace. Goya
worked on some of his paintings here. The
palace was built in the 18C by Jacques
Marquet on the site of the Valdecorneja
castle.

Monastery of Santo Domingo:
Founded in 1371 by Don Fernando Alvarez de Toledo, Lord of Villacorneja. The
grounds are now used as a cemetery and
only the Capilla Mayor remains of the old
church.

Convent of the Calced Carmelites:
Built in the 16C on the orders of the Duke
of Alba.

Environs: Some 10 km E. of Piedrahita
is **Bonilla de la Sierra.** Only ruins remain of the medieval *town walls* and *castle*. The 15C *parish church* has three Gothic
portals. The choir and the tower were added in the 16C. Inside is a barrel-vaulted
nave and a polygonal apse.

Plasencia
Cáceres/Estremadura   p.392☐D 6

This well-preserved little medieval town
is situated in a picturesque valley on the
right bank of the Río Jerte and surrounded

y steep hills. It was called *Dulcis Placida*
y the Romans was seized from the Moors
y Alfonso VI, but was so badly damaged
hat it had to be rebuilt under Alfonso
VIII. Dating from then are the massive
walls with 68 semicircular towers *(cubos)*
nd 6 gates *(puertas)*, only remains of
which, together with the citadel *(for-
alezza)*, survive.

Cathedral: The present building consists
of a part begun in the 13C (Capilla Mayor
and crossing), to which the incomplete
Catedral Nueva was added at the end of the
15C. Of the *old cathedral*, now the parish
church of *Santa María*, the Romanesque
Puerta del Perdón and the early Gothic
chapterhouse also survive. *Interior:* To the
right of the high altar there is the 13C polychrome 'miracle' picture of the 'Virgen del
Perdón'. The 13C *Capilla de San Pablo* has
a 13C statue, the Virgen de la Paloma. In
the *chapterhouse* there are two paintings by
Ribera and a small picture by Luis de
Morales, El Divino. The Romanesque-
Gothic *cloister* was started by the Arab

Asoyte in the 14C and completed by Juan
Martín in the 15C. A splendid staircase
with 125 steps, by Gil de Hontañón, leads
to the terrace, from which the 'Melón' type
dome of the sacristy can be seen. The master architects of the 16C collaborated on the
construction of the *new cathedral*, ('del En-
losado') and these included Juan de Álava,
Francisco de Colonia, Covarrubias, Diego
de Siloé and Rodrigo Gil de Hontañón.
The main portal is of interest, with four
tiers of columns one above of the other and
elegant carving (completed 1558). The *interior*, with a nave and two aisles, adjoining the old Romanesque cathedral, makes
an overwhelming impression with its tall
columns reaching right up into the ribs of
the stellar vault. *Choir stalls* by Rodrigo el
Alemán. The choir is enclosed by an iron
grille by Juan Bautista Celma (1598). In
the middle of the *high altar* of 1626 by
Gregorio Fernández, there is a dramatic
'Annunciation'. The mouldings bear splendid bas-reliefs. The four panels of paintings are the work of Francisco Rizi. The
crowning glory is a Calvary. In the *Capilla*

Plasencia, view

del Tránsito the retable of the Virgin Mary is by the brothers José, Joaquin and Alberto Churriguera.

San Nicolás: 13C Gothic church with a 14C apse in which there is a beautiful *rose-window*. Inside there is the *tomb* of Pedro González de Carjaval, Bishop of Coria.

San Martín: A fully-restored Gothic church with a Plateresque *winged altar* by Juan de Jaén with four paintings by Morales (1565)—one painting shows St. Martin sharing his coat with a beggar.

San Vicente (former monastery of Santo Domingo): Founded 1474. Splendid staircase by Juan Álvarez. A portal with 17C Corinthian columns leads from cloister to the sacristy, which is lavishly decorated with azulejos from Talavera.

San Pedro (Calle Alejandro Matias): This Romanesque church is the city's oldest, dating from the 13C.

Also worth seeing: To the N. are the churches of *Santa Ana* (1556) and *El Salvador* , whose underground vaults are the last resting place of the city's most distinguished families. The church of *San Ildefonso* (Calle de Sancho Polo) houses a *tomb* by Cristóbal de Villalba in the Capilla Mayor. Interesting *mansions,* such as the *Casa de los Torres.*

Environs: Granadilla (*c.* 25 km. N.): The 16C *Iglesia de la Asunción* has Gothic groin vaults. The village is surrounded by an irregular polygonal *wall* without towers. Two gates, one to the N., the other to the S., were built with Roman ashlars, which came from nearby ruins. The *castillo* (late 14C/early 15C) stands on the site of a former Arab alcázar. This beautiful building of granite ashlars is in good condition; it consists of a square tower with a semicircular tower on each face.

Monastery of Santa María: The founding of this monastery goes back to the time when Ramón Berenguer IV gave a plot of land to the French monastery of Fontfroide. The building was begun in Romanesque style in 1152 and is typically Cistercian Gothic; other parts were added later e.g. the *Golden Gate,* which was built in the 15C for the visit of Isabella and Ferdinand of Castile-Aragon. On the opposite side of the main square and behind the hospice, is the *church of Santa Catalina,* one of the monastery's few complete Romanesque buildings. It was originally dedicated to the Virgin Mary, but this was changed to St.Catherine in the 13C. The Puerta Real was built in 1379-97; the vestibule is 14C Gothic, like the locutory. The large *cloister,* which is on the left side rather than on the right, as is more usual, dates back to 1191. The Romanesque S. walk has been restored; its seven pointed arches are supported by pillars and columns in bundles; the ceilings, in contrast to the other sides, have typical Romanesque decoration with plant motifs (this is true of the chapel too). The features of the later wings are Gothic. On the N. side is the *Lavabo,* a hexagonal building with round arches and central columns (late 12C/early 13C), which blends well with the S. walk. Following this come the *refectory,* the kitchen and the 13C calefactory (heating room). A passage at the end of the gallery leads to the *scriptorium,* a rectangular room, serving as a library, with round windows (13C). A Romanesque gate leads into the *chapterhouse;* in front of this is the tombstone of Abbot Don Vicente Ferrer (d. 1411). The barrel-vaulted Romanesque locutory is next to the chapterhouse. The *church,* construction of which was started under Alfonso I (1162 - 96), was completed in Cistercian style in the 14C. It has a nave,

Poblet, monastery

two aisles, a transept, ambulatory and radiating chapels. Of outstanding interest are the Renaissance high altar, made of alabaster by Damián Forment (1480–1541) (4) and the kings' pantheon, which has two sarcophagi resting on columns, and which connects the nave and side aisle (2, 3). The *San Esteban cloister* is also Romanesque and is reached from the church via the *novices' dormitory*, a long narrow room (290 ft. x 34 ft.) with pointed arches and columns with unusually decorated bases. This cloister was used by the monastic community before the larger one was built and is rectangular with round arches supported on pillars. Some of the original columns, which were replaced by these pillars in the 15C, are to be found in other buildings of the monastery. In 1392 King Martin I, the Humane, of Aragon had a

residence built in the monastery, in order to spend his last years in peace and meditation. This pure Gothic *palace*, approached through the San Esteban cloister, has almost completely been restored. The monks' dormitory (Gothic, early-15C) houses a museum, which contains the monastery treasure with items of jewellery, sculptures and numerous relics. Next to the locutory is a further cloister with elements of the older cloister. The wine cellar can also be viewed.

Ponferrada

León/León   p.386 ☐ D 2

This town of some 50,000 inhabitants lies on a plateau overlooking the green land-

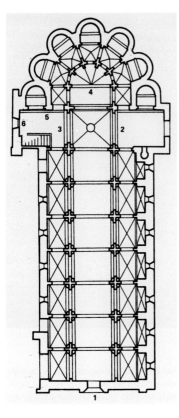

Poblet, monastery church 1 baroque façade and vestibule **2** tombs of Alfonso I (d.1196), Juan I (d.1396), Juan II (d.1479) and their wives **3** tombs of James I (d.1276), Pedro II (d.1285), Fernando I de Trastámara (d.1416) and their wives **4** tomb of Alfonso IV (d.1485) **5** Chapel of St. Benedict, with the tomb of Martin I

scape of the Bierzo. Ponferrada, nowadays a flourishing industrial town producing iron, looks back on a long history. It was known as Interamnium Flavium in ancient times.

Castillo de los Templarios/Templar Castle: This castle is one of the most important examples of medieval military architecture in Spain. The complex, dating principally from the 12&13C, was built to protect the way to Santiago. Laid out as an uneven rectangle, the castle is 543 ft. long and 305 ft. wide. In 1340 Alfonso XI handed the fortress over to the Count of Lemos, it later came into the hands of Ferdinand and Isabella.

Nuestra Señora de la Encina: Built in 1577 in transitional Gothic-Renaissance style. 17C tower. High altar by a pupil of Gregorio Fernández. There is a 15C Gothic statue of the Madonna with miraculous properties and a 17C retable by a pupil of Gaspar Becerra. The sacristy is 17–18C.

Also worth seeing: The 17C church of *San Andrés* with a baroque retable and a 13C Romanesque Christ (Cristo de las Maravillas). The suburb of Mascarón has the late-11C church of *Santa María de Vizbayo*, one of the oldest Romanesque structures of the Bierzo. It is single-aisled with a semicircular apse and a very simple portal with horseshoe arch. The *Iglesia del Carmen* was built in 1617. The *Hospital de la Reina* was built in 1498. Also of interest is the baroque *Ayuntamiento* (1692).

Environs: Just outside the town is its most important feature; the church of **Santo Tomás de las Ollas.** This small Mozarabic church, which belonged to the monastery of San Pedro de Montes, goes back to the 10C. It has nine round Moorish horseshoe arches and Visigoth elements. The church is single-aisled. The 10C *Capilla Mayor* has an oval ground plan, polygonal vaulting, a 12C *portal* (restored) and 16C wall paintings. **San Pedro de Montes** is the second foundation of St.Fructuosus in the Sierra de la Guiana. Rebuilt by St.Genadio and his companions in 895, it was consecrated in 919 when he was Bishop of Astorga. Only a few fragments of carving have survived from this

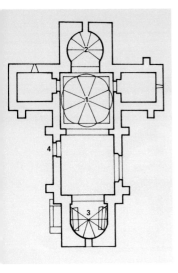

Santiago de Peñalba **1** dome over crossing **2** apse with horseshoe ground plan **3** domed vestibule in the form of an apse **4** double portal with Moorish horseshoe arches

Ponferrada, Castillo de los Templarios

time. The present building is 12C Romanesque with three apses and three chapels. **Villar de los Barrios** (S. of Ponferrada) has an 18C church, which has a 17C retable and Gothic sculptures. There are several interesting houses bearing coats-of-arms. The *Museo Yebra* has interesting regional exhibits (weapons, ceramics, coins, manuscripts, sculptures and paintings). **Peñalba de Santiago:** Some 20 km. S. of Ponferrada, at the foot of Monte Aguiana, stands the church of *Santiago de Peñalba,* a Mozarabic church run by Cordoban monks, which was consecrated in 931. The church, built under the rule of Ramiro, was commissioned by Salomon, a pupil of St. Genadio, the Bishop of Astorga. The ground plan is in the form of a Latin cross. Large, domed vault over the crossing. Apse with a Moorish horse-

shoe ground plan, opposite a domed, apse-like double portal with Moorish arches. **San Miguel de las Dueñas:** This convent, not far from Ponferrada, was founded by Gonzalo Bermúdez, Count of Bierzo, and restored in 1152 by Doña Sancha, sister of Alfonso VII, for the Cistercian nuns. A few beautiful fragments of buildings and decoration survive from this period, in particular an interesting Romanesque portal with plant motifs in the archivolt. The *monastery church* dates from 1625; there is a small *cloister* of 1683 and a larger *cloister* from the 18C.

Pontevedra
Pontevedra/Galicia   p.386□B 3

According to tradition this provincial capi-

Peñalba de Santiago (Ponferrada), Santiago de Peñalba

tal is supposed to have been founded by the Greeks. In the 12C it was called 'Pontis Vedris'. In the 'Zona antigua', or Old Town, many old mansions and town houses (Gothic, Renaissance and baroque) with coats-of-arms still stand.

Basilica of Santa María la Mayor: This church was built on the site of an old Romanesque church at the start of the 16C. The interior of this basilica, with a nave and two aisles, has decorated columns with beautiful capitals, a comparatively wide decorated arch in front of the crossing, a polygonal apse and rib vaulting. The altars are baroque. Wall reliefs, dating from the time of construction, survive in part. The side chapels are also of interest, particularly the *Capilla del Buen Jesús* of 1525. But the highlight of the church is its fa-

çade, richly adorned with sculptures by Cornelis de Holanda. Next to the portal stand the figures of Charles V and his wife. Over the portal, the Death of the Virgin Mary is depicted; above the rose-window is the Coronation of the Virgin and above this, the Holy Trinity. In the middle of the stone balustrade at the top of the façade there is a crucifix. On each side of the central projecting section there are six expressive figures—these are in tabernacles and flanked by columns with reliefs. Above the side portal of the basilica stand figures of saints, beside which and beneath a canopy there is an old crucifix, the famous *Cristo del Buen Viaje*.

San Francisco: On the large Plaza del Generalísimo and at the top of flights of steps, stand two important churches, Sa-

Pontevedra, ruins of Santo Domingo

Francisco and *La Peregrina*. The single-aisled, rib-vaulted Franciscan church belongs to an old monastery. Apse and crossing date from the late 14C. In front of the apse are various old tombs. The simple façade has a large rose- window and a portal with columns, pointed arches and archivolts.

La Peregrina: A shell-shaped church with two towers and a convex façade by Antonio Scouto. It was built in 1778 and has baroque and classical features. Inside the church is the much-revered statue, the Virgen Peregrina, the town's patroness.

San Bartolomé: A typical baroque church. It has a nave and two aisles. The second altar on the right has sculptures by Gregorio Fernández.

Santa Clara: This 15C convent church is single-aisled, with a polygonal apse and ribbed vault. The high altar is baroque.

Santo Domingo: Founded around 1282. All that now remains is the 14C apse, everything else is in ruins. The archaeological department of the regional museum is housed in the five polygonal apsidal chapels. It has prehistoric objects, Roman milestones, fragments of early Christian buildings, Romanesque capitals and Gothic tombs.

Also worth seeing: The *Plaza de la Herrería* with 18C fountains; the arcaded Plaza Mugartegui; the *Plaza de Teucro* with the baroque Casa Señoral and the *Plaza de Lena* with an old Crucero and houses, the fronts of which are supported by columns or arcades. The regional museum is housed here in two 18C mansions, the *Casa de Castro Monteagudo* and the *Casa García Flórez*. The prehistoric collections include finds from the Bronze Age up to the time of the Celts. There are important medieval and baroque sculptures (Bernini) and a collection of paintings. The latter includes: Dutch masters, such as Pieter Breughel the Elder, David Teniers the Younger and Snyders; Italian masters, such as Salvatore Rosa and Tiepolo; and Spanish masters like Morales, Ribera, Zurbarán and Goya.

Environs: Poyo (near Pontevedra, to the NW): with the monastery of San Juan, which was founded in the 7C by St. Fructuosus. The present monastery dates principally from the 16&17C. The church, with a massive façade adorned with columns and flanked by towers, was built by Melchor de Velasco. The large interior is subdivided by pillars, which support the arched vault. The high altar (1631) is baroque and is the work of Lucas Cabrera.

Pontevedra, La Peregrina

The 16C *cloister* encloses a beautiful fountain. The Claustro de los Naranjos dates from the 18C. **Armenteira** (W. of Poyo, 14 km. from Pontevedra): with the old Cistercian abbey of *Santa María*, which was established by St.Ero and occupied by the monks of Claraval in 1164. The sprawling church, built in 1168–1212, has a beautiful rose-window on the façade, a portal with numerous decorated columns and archivolts and a Mudéjar dome over the crossing. **Mosteiro,** near Meis, has a very beautiful, early Romanesque-Byzantine monument in the semi-dilapidated church of *San Pedro.* **Lérez** lies just NE of Pontevedra, on the little road to Lagoa. It has the monastery of *San Salvador,* founded as early as the 9C, under Ordono II. The present building dates from the 18C, but remains of the medieval structure have survived, e.g. part of the old cloister with a beautiful two-storeyed arcade. The baroque church has a façade from 1748. The retable of the high altar is by Juan Rodríguez de Barros and Juan Altamirano. **Sotomayor:** Near the road from Pontevedra to Vigo, at Puente Sampayo, is an 11C *castle,* which was extended in the 15C and recently restored. Of particular interest is the battlemented *Torre del Obispo.*

Portillo
Valladolid/Old Castile   p.388 ☐ F 4

Castle: Built in the 15C for the Counts of Benavente. It has a square ground plan with round towers at the corners and served as a state prison.

Santa María: This 16C Renaissance church with a nave and two aisles has a 14C Gothic altarpiece depicting the Virgin and baroque paintings in a niche.

San Juan: This 13C Mudéjar church has

Pontevedra, Santa María

a beautiful baroque grille and a cloister (1614).

Environs: Aldeamayor de San Martín (*c.* 2 km. N.): The Gothic *parish church* with a mighty tower contains numerous fine altarpieces (17C). **Arrabal del Portillo** (*c.* 2 km. S.): The *parish church* has a beautiful 16C Renaissance portal and a fine *altarpiece* with reliefs by Francisco Giralte, a *Pietá* by Pedro de Cuadra and a Plateresque altarpiece with Gothic sculptures. **Mojados** (*c.* 5 km. S.): 14C Mudéjar church of *Santa María* with splendid *paintings* by Alonso de Herrera, 16C sculptures and a Christ by Juan de Juni; the 13C Mudéjar church of *San Juan* has a portal with archivolts, an *altarpiece* by Pedro de Cuadra and the 17C baroque pilgrimage chapel of *Nuestra Señora de Luguillas.*

Priego de Córdoba
Córdoba/Andalusia   p.394□F 10

Santa María de la Asunción (near the

Priego de Córdoba, Fuente del Rey

castle): This church was built in 1771–86. The rococo interior culminates in the *Capilla del Sagrario* (1st chapel on the left) with a round altar and four large figures of Apostles mounted in gold. Beautiful retable at the high altar with paintings and carvings.

San Francisco: Fine 18C church façade. Inside there are several interesting *sculptures* by Martínez Montañés, in particular, 'Flagellation of Christ'.

Iglesia de la Aurora: High baroque façade and rococo interior decoration; large altarpiece.

Fuente del Rey: A most beautiful *18C fountain* with a figure of Neptune and 140 jets of water.

Also worth seeing: *Palace of the Dukes of Medinaceli.* Well-preserved *wall fortifications* (keep, horseshoe arches). Beautiful Spanish-Moorish *town quarter, 'Villa',* with beautiful façades on many *mansions.*

Environs: Baena (30 km. NW): The old upper town, the 'Almedina', is partly enclosed by the *Arab town walls.* The square tower, the *'Torre del Sol'* is domed. *Ruined fortress.* The Gothic church of *Santa María la Mayor* (restored) with its beautiful Isabelline portal contains the tombs of the Dukes of Sesa. Wrought-iron choir grille and pulpits. *Convent church of Madre de Dios:* Late Gothic portal. **Montefrío** (32 km. SE): *16C Renaissance church by Diego de Siloé.*

Puebla de Sanabria
Zamora/León   p.386□D 3

Parish church: This beautiful Romanesque church dates from the second half of the 12C, but has been altered several times.

The main portal is particularly beautiful and has round arches, a pointed arch door frame and, to either side, two columns, which support the arches and are decorated with figures. Inside, there is a 13C *font*. An interesting *baroque chapel* was added to the church.

Also worth seeing: The *castillo*, built around the middle of the 15C by Rodrigo Alonso de Pimentel, is still in good condition and dominates the little town (pop. *c.* 2,000) with its mighty tower. Also note the *Casa Consistorial*, the *Eremita de San Cayetano* and the 14C *walls*.

Environs: Some 17 km. N. of Puebla de Sanabria lies **San Martín de Castañeda** with the *Monasterio de San Martín*, beautifully situated just outside the town at 5,025 ft. above sea-level. The church, with a nave and two aisles, belonged to a former Benedictine monastery and was built in Romanesque style in the 12C. A Visigoth temple once stood on the site; it was destroyed by the Arabs and rebuilt after 921.

Inside are two interesting, recumbent wooden figures. **Mombuey** (some 25 km. E. of Puebla de Sanabria, in the direction of Benavente): has an interesting, single-aisled *parish church* from the 13C. The free-standing Romanesque-Gothic bell-tower is also 13C.

Puentedeume
La Coruña/Galicia   p.386□B 1

Puentedeume lies on the bay of Betanzos at the foot of the Breamo in one of the most beautiful spots in Galicia. Dating from Roman times and formerly known as Pontesdeume, it has impressive remains of its important history.

Church of Santiago: Dating from the 16C, it was rebuilt in the 18C. The 16C Capilla Mayor has a stellar vault. The Santuario de Nuestra Señora de las Virtudes (or El Soto) was built in 1675. The *Palacio-Fortalezza de los Andrade* of 1370 has a

Priego de Córdoba, Castillo

square keep, which testifies to the fact that the town once belonged to the powerful Andrade family, as do many other buildings in Puentedeume. The inner courtyard dates from the 15C. The famous *Torre de los Andrade* was built on the site of an older tower in the 13C. It has Gothic windows and an enormous coat-of-arms above the entrance. Equally famous is the old *bridge*, built in the 14C with many arches.

Also worth seeing: The *Ayuntamiento*, built under Archbishop Rajoy.

Environs: Breano: 2 km. S. of Puentedeume lies Breano with the Romanesque church of *San Miguel* (1187). **Noguerosa:** On the crag of Leboreira at Noguerosa, SE of Puentedeume, stands the 14C *Castillo de Andrade*. **Doroña:** Nearby, with a Romanesque church from 1162. **Caaveiro:** Near Capela, in wild countryside E. of Puentedeume, is the former monastery of *San Juan,* originally founded in the 10C. The single-aisled baroque church has a 12C apse. Near **Monfero** (SE of Puen-

tedeume) is the vast, isolated monastery of *San Félix,* which originally dates from the 12C and was rebuilt in the 17C. The single-aisled church has an imposing façade (1655) with enormous columns. It contains old stone tombs of the Andrade and Moscoso families. The cloister, with a beautiful fountain, was designed by Juan de Herrera (namesake of the famous Juan de Herrera) in the 16C and completed in 1733. **Mantaras** (2 km. from Monfero) Has a Romanesque *hermitage.*

Puente la Reina
Navarra / Navarra   p.388 □ I 2

This little town owes its importance to the veneration of St. James, for it is here that the pilgrimage routes from Central Europe to Santiago de Compostela converged, leaving the Pyrenees behind them at Roncesvalles and Jaca.

Santiago: The origins of this church go

Puente la Reina, bridge

ack to the 12C. In the 15C the old church was altered in Gothic style, and extended n the 18C. A *portal* with splendid sculptures survives from the old Romanesque church, as does the *arcade*, also richly decorated and with beautiful sculptures. *Interior:* altarpiece (18C) and statue of St. James as a pilgrim (14C). From the same period, a sculpture of St.Bartholomew. A beautifully carved Christ on the Cross is worth seeing.

Iglesia del Crucifijo: Founded in the 12C as a Romanesque church of the Knights Templar, to whom an adjacent monastery also belonged and which provided a hospice for pilgrims to Santiago. The present church was built in its place n the 15C. The Romanesque *portal* was retained. One of the arches above the portal is made of scallop shells, the emblem worn by the pilgrims. Inside is an interesting *crucifix* (14C), made in a German workshop and remarkable for its V-shape.

Bridge: The town took its name from this six-arched bridge, built in the 11C, on the order of the Queen, Doña Mayor, wife of Sancho the Great of Navarre, so that the pilgrims could cross the Río Arga.

Also worth seeing: The town still has numerous *Templar buildings*. 13C *walls* surround the town. *Parish church of San Pedro,* built in Romanesque style in the 13C. *Iglesia de la Trinidad* with beautiful Renaissance façade. Several *mansions* in the Calle Mayor.

Puente Viesgo
Santander/Old Castile   p.388□G 1

Cueva del Castillo: This cave contains numerous prehistoric rock paintings, including depictions of bison, bulls, horses and other animals, as well as of men's hands.

Cueva de la Pasiega: This neighbouring cave also contains rock paintings (in various shades) of bison, horses and deer.

Environs: San Felices de Buelna (*c.* 2 km. W.): *Cueva de Hornos de la Peña:* Cave with prehistoric paintings. **Bostronizo** (*c.* 10 km. SW): *San Román de Moroso* is a small 12C Mozarabic church. **Castañeda** (*c.* 5 km. N.): The church of *Santa Cruz* is an old 12C collegiate church. The tower, the portal and the apses are Romanesque. **Villacarriedo** (*c.* 25 km. NE): The *Palacio de Soñanes* or *Diaz de Arce* was built in 1718 to the plans of the Italian Cosimo Fontanelli and has a baroque façade.

Puerto de Santa María

Cádiz/Andalusia   p.394☐D 11

Founded as a Greek trading port, it was known as Portus Menesthei in Roman times. It was destroyed during the Arab invasion and rebuilt in the 13C by Alfonso the Wise. Famous discoverers and mariners lived here, notably Columbus, Juan de la Costa (helmsman on one of Columbus's ships), Amérigo Vespucci (from whom America took its name), Alonso de Ojeda and others.

Iglesia Mayor Prioral Nuestra Señora de los Milagros (Plaza de España): Originally 13C Gothic (façade), this priory and the parish church was altered on several occasions and acquired an extraordinarily beautiful Plateresque S. portal, the 'Puerta de la Madre del Sol', in the 17C. Inside is a domed, marble *high altar*. The 13C *figure of the Madonna* (right-hand chapel, next to the high altar) is revered as 'Nuestra Señora de los Milagros' and is the town's patroness. Altarpiece of Flemish paintings.

Castillo San Marcos: This medieval Moorish fortress (13C) with Gothic features (towers) is privately owned. A Mozarabic chapel and a patio are particularly beautiful. The mihrab of the former mosque has survived in good condition.

Also worth seeing: *Convent chapel (now prison chapel) of Santa María de la Victoria* (Paseo de la Victoria): 12C convent

Villacarriedo (Puente Viesgo), Palacio de Soñanes

foundation; very beautiful 15C Gothic chapel. *Church of Las Concepcionistas* (Calle de José Antonio): 18C, interesting altar. *Convent church of Las Capuchinas* (Calle Larga): 17C, dome, large retable; a 17C 'Crucifixion' reveals the distinctive Spanish feeling for realism. *Mansions: Casa de Bizarrón* (Plaza del Castillo), 17C; *Casa de Villa Real de Purullena*, rococo; *Casa de los Frailes* with imposing inner courtyard and others. One of the numerous bodegas *Bodega Terra* (Calle General Mola) has a 17C façade.

Environs: Puerto Real (10 km. S.): In the former Roman port of Portus Gaditanus is the 16C *Renaissance church of San Sebastián*. **Ruined castle of Santa Catalina** (3 km. W.). **Rota** (12 km. W.): Town walls and *castle* (14/16C.); *Church of Nuestra Señora de la Expectación*, 16C.

Puertomarín
Lugo/Galicia   p.386☐C 2

The former Portomarin was originally Ponte Miña, a bridge over the Miño, of which there now remains just one arch. It was probably built by Master Mateo, who was responsible for the famous Portico de la Gloria in Santiago. The pilgrim route to Santiago crossed this bridge and here the Order of the Brothers of St.John of Jerusalem had also settled and founded a monastery. The medieval village of Miño was flooded when a dam was built but the two churches of San Juan and San Pedro were saved. The present town of Puertomarin is near to the original village.

Church of San Juan: This church was removed after the dam was built and set up again on a different site. It belonged to the ancient, fortress-like monastery of San Juan, which had defensive towers linked by a passageway. The 12C single-aisled church has a pointed arch vault and a fine portal with sculptures on its main front. It also has rich side portals and old frescos in the apse.

San Pedro (near the Parador): This little church on the former pilgrimage route from France retains the main portal with archivolts and tympanum (1182) from the original Romanesque building.

Also worth seeing: The *Palacio de los Condes de la Maza* and the *Palacio de Berbetoros*.

Environs: Paradela: (On the road from Puertomarín to Sarria): The Romanesque church of *San Miguel* dates from around 1200. In spite of rebuilding the apse remains unaltered. **Ferreiros:** (N. of Paradela): With a single-aisled Romanesque *church*.

Puigcerdá
Gerona/Catalonia   p.390☐N 2/3

Walls were built around the original town centre and these have been continually extended in the course of the centuries.

Santa María: Built in Romanesque style in the 12C, with a nave, two aisles and an interesting portal. It was altered in the 14C, when Gothic features were added. In 1936 it was destroyed. Only the bell tower has survived. The rebuilt church contains a copy of the Romanesque Virgin, which was also destroyed.

Iglesia de la Gracia: This church contains three fine panels—the Annunciation, St.Stephen and St.John—, attributed to the Master of La Seo, originally known as the Master of Puigcerdá.

Quintanilla de las Viñas
Burgos/Old Castile   p.388 G 3

Santa María: Only the transept and the E. end survive from this 7C Visigoth church. Excellent 7C Visigoth stone friezes.

Environs: San Quirce (*c.* 8 km. N.): The 11C *collegiate church* belonged to an abbey and has been altered several times. **Lara de los Infantes** (*c.* 3 km. E.): Made famous by the Infantes of Lara, it was probably previously a Roman town, the remains of which can be seen in the museums of Burgos and Madrid. Romanesque *church.* Ruins of a *fortress.* **Jaramillo de la Fuente** (*c.* 4 km. E.): The 12C Romanesque *parish church* has a slender tower, arcaded portico and portal with columns and highly embellished capitals. **Salas de los Infantes** (*c.* 10 km. SE): The Romanesque *parish church* preserves a retable and a 12C Plateresque parish cross. **Vizcaínos** (*c.* 12 km. E.): 12C Romanesque *church of San Martín.* **San Pedro de Arlanza** (*c.* 20 km. SE): Only ruins remain of the monastery, which was begun in 912 and completed in the 12–13C. The outlines of the nave, two aisles and apses can, however, be discerned. Many parts of the monastery were used in other buildings. The Romanesque portal with archivolts and striped columns is now to be found in the Museo Arqueológico Nacional. The 12C tomb of the 'Mudarra' can be seen in Burgos Cathedral, while some of the paintings from the chapterhouse are to be found in the Metropolitan Museum of New York and in the Museo de Arte Románico in Barcelona.

San Pedro de Arlanza (Quintanilla de las Viñas), ruins of the choir

Reinosa

Julióbriga: On a small hill within the town are the remains of the capital of the Roman province of Cantabria. Excavations revealed masonry from buildings, a portico, mosaics and interesting ceramics, which are now preserved in the museum in Santander. The old Romanesque *church* of Reinosa was built with materials from Julióbriga.

Environs: Some 5 km. S. lies **Cervatos:** The 12C Romanesque church belonged to a 10C monastery. Most remarkable are the superb embellishments on the capitals, the portal and the apse. **Hermandad de Campoo de Suso** (NW): A 13C *castle* with two square towers and grand apartments.

Requena

This picturesque little town 72 km. W. of Valencia stands on two hills above the Magro valley and is an important agricultural centre. For a long time part of Castile Requena was not officially incorporated into the Province of Valencia until 1851. The local tongue is Castilian. Even the countryside is like Castile, with many poplars.

Castle ruins: These date from the 15C and dominate the Old Town, which has retained much of its medieval character. There are many mansions adorned with coats-of-arms. The *'Casa del Cid'* is 15C.

Santa María: This parish church has an interesting Gothic façade. The portal with its three large archivolts is richly decorated with sculptures: Madonna and Child on the door pillar, an Annunciation in the tympanum, the Apostles on the door frame and on the pilasters and small figures in tabernacles, between which there are reliefs with plant motifs. The wall above the portal has rows of blind arcades up to the roof. The interior was altered in baroque style in the 18C.

El Salvador: Dedicated to the Redeemer. It has an interesting late Isabelline-Gothic portal, which, like that of Santa María, is almost over-decorated with sculptures and may be by the same stonemason.

Ribadavia, arcaded square

Ribadavia

Orense/Galicia   p.386☐B 3

The ancient Abóbriga is now a delightfully situated old town with fine Romanesque and Gothic monuments. In the 11C it was the residence of King García I of Galicia. Remains of the old town walls survive.

Santiago: A 12C single-aisled church with a wooden ceiling, Gothic arches and a groin vault in the apse. The outside of the apse has windows with small columns and archivolts. The façade has a rose-window and a beautiful portal. Of particular interest are the decorated capitals and consoles. Inside, on the left of the entrance, there is a 13C statue of Christ.

Other interesting churches: The 14–15C Gothic *Santo Domingo* has a nave and two aisles and belongs to the 13C *Monastery of Santo Domingo.* The tall, richly ornamented church, with high Gothic windows in the apse, contains some old tombs of knights. The 12C single-aisled Romanesque church of *San Juan* has beautiful Romanesque windows. The façade was altered in baroque style. The 13C Gothic *Santa María de Oliveira* has a rose-window.

Castillo de los Condes de Ribadavia: The castillo is an old fortress built of ashlars.

Also worth seeing: Picturesque streets and a beautiful square with *arcades.*

Environs: Castrelo de Miño (Just SE of Ribadavia): The 18C church of *Santa*

María has an apse which survives from an earlier 12C church. The old bas-reliefs of figures still remain. The high altar dates from 1694. **Francelos** (SW of Ribadavia, near Melón): The pre-Romanesque church of *San Ginés* was built around 900. The façade is ornamented and the richly decorated, traceried windows are of particular interest, being similar to those found on old Asturian churches (e.g. San Miguel de Lillo) from the same period. **Melón:** The *Monastery of Santa María* was founded in 1142. The only original parts of its church, which has a nave and two aisles, are the apse, the cloister with two chapels and the very beautiful ambulatory. The rectangular bell tower is also old. **La Franqueira** (along the Ribadavia-Melón road you come to La Cañiza, SW of which is La Franqueira): The church of *Santa María* originally belonged to an 8C monastery. It has a beautiful portal and was completed in the 13C; it is now a pilgrimage destination. **Creciente** (on the Río Miño, SE of La Cañiza): The well-preserved keep was originally part of the medieval Castillo de Fornelos. **San Clodio** (NW of Razamonde): The ancient monastery of *Santa María* probably dates from the 6C. In 1151 the monastery adopted the Cistercian reforms. The 13C church has a nave, two aisles and stellar vaulting. The Gothic portal is 15C, the cloister is Renaissance. Nearby **Gomariz** has the 12C Romanesque church of *Santa María*. The coro within dates from the 18C. **Trasalba** (7 km. from Razamonde, in the direction of Amoeiro): The church of *San Pedro* is Romanesque. **Lebosénde** (SW of San Clodio): Has a 12C church, the sanctuary and side chapels of which were added in the 16C. The *portal* is Romanesque.

Ribadeo
Lugo/Galicia   p.386□D 1

Ribadeo is a seaside town, with old streets

and mansions recalling its rich past (18&19C). The 18C Colegiata de Santa María del Campo has a beautiful baroque altar. The 18C Ayuntamiento has a remarkable façade and is the old palace of Ibáñez, Marquis of Sargadelos, who wanted to make Ribadeo the most important port in northern Galicia and was murdered here during a rising.

Environs: Coaña: On a hill 5 km. from Coaña is the most important Celtic settlement in Spain. It is 4,000 years old and its original inhabitants built their close-knit network of dwellings on stone foundations, many of which have survived with some still standing up to head height. A number of the walls still contain hollowed-out stones, which were used either for crushing corn or as funerary urns. Remains of old pottery and Roman coins were also found here.

Riba de Saelices
Guadalajara/New Castile   p.388□H 5

Parish church: Built in the late 12C/early 13C in Romanesque-Gothic transitional style. The apse and main portal also date from this period. The Capilla Mayor has a 16C retable.

Also worth seing: Of the *castle* there remains only a tower. The *Cueva de los Casares* is a long, narrow prehistoric cave with drawings of men and animals on the stone walls.

Ribadesella
Oviedo/Asturia   p.386□F 1

The *parish church* contains an altar by the sculptor Gerardo Zaragoza and monumental wall paintings by the Uría brothers.

Ripoll, Santa María, cloister

Ripoll, Santa María, cloister

The beautiful *Palacio de Prieto-Cutre* dates from the Renaissance.

Environs: Cueva de Tito Bustillo: This stalactite cave is over half a mile long. Near the end of the cave are 20,000 year-old paintings of horses and smaller ones of deer, all of which have survived in splendid condition. The violet drawings were executed with a mineral found in the cave; a black horse's head is in charcoal. The cave was discovered in 1968 and is one of the few still open to the public. **Cueva de Les Pedroses:** In the village of El Carmen. The cave has pictures of horses and deer.

Ripoll
Gerona/Catalonia   p.390□N 3

Benedictine Abbey of Santa María: Founded as early as the 6C, it was later destroyed by the Arabs and rebuilt in the 9C. A new building was consecrated in 1032. The earthquake of 1428 and a fire in 1835 left only the famous 12C portal from the original building. The abbey was not restored until the 20C. Art historians disagree on the exact date of the portal, some date it 1032, at the time of Abbot Oliba, others as late as 1149. The *portal* opens at the back of a porch and measures 39 ft. wide, 25 ft. 7 in. high and 3 ft. 4 in. deep. Built in the classical form of the triumphal arch, it is considered the finest example of Catalan-Romanesque sculpture. The uppermost of the six rows shows a standing Christ Pantocrator, giving his blessing with a book in his left hand. Beside him are four angels and two Evangelistic symbols (a man and an eagle); the two others, the lion and ox, are in the second row. Beside them are the 24 Elders of the Apocalypse. In the third row, at the same height as the archivolts, are scenes from the Children of Israel's Exodus from Egypt (on the right) and scenes from the Book of Kings, showing the Ark of the Covenant and David and Solomon (on the left). Many of these scenes correspond to the Bible miniatures of Roda or Ripoll, although the historical order is slightly altered. In the next row there are King David and four musicians on the left, while on the right there are barely identifiable figures, which are believed to be King David and four representatives of the people. The last row has representations of two of David's visions of the end of the world. The bases are also decorated. The archivolts are also lavishly decorated. The outer one has plant motifs and the second has scenes from the lives and martyrdoms of Sts.Peter and Paul. The supporting columns have badly damaged statues of the two Apostles. The fourth archivolt is dedicated to the stories of Jonah and Daniel. In the middle of the inner archivolt is Christ Pantocrator again, flanked by scenes of Cain and Abel. On the pillars supporting this last archivolt are the 12 months of the year. The abbey has an interesting *cloister* from 12 – 15C. Various valuable *manuscripts* are preserved in the Archivo de la Corona de Aragón in Barcelona.

Environs: Vallfogona (9 km. E. on Route 150): Fine remains of Vallfogona *castle*, which has a six-storeyed tower built on to a wall. The castle has coats-of-arms below the windows. It was restored in the 20C. **Las Llosas** (10 km. SW on B road 149): In the vicinity are several Romanesque *churches*, e.g. *Santa María de las Llosas, San Sadurní de Sobellas* and others.

Roda de Isábena
Huesca/Aragón   p.388 □ L 3

Cathedral: Founded under King Sancho Ramírez and consecrated in 1067; construction work continued for centuries. The cathedral has a nave, two aisles and a barrel vault. The *interior* contains a *high altar*, which was decorated by Gabriel Yoly in 1533. The original sculptures and reliefs unfortunately no longer exist. Below the high altar is the *crypt* with a beautiful *sarcophagus*, in which St.Ramón, a bishop, was entombed in the 12C. It is lavishly decorated with reliefs of scenes from the New Testament. The walls of the crypt are adorned with 13C wall paintings. The *cloister* dates from the 12C.

Parish Museum: Housed in the former chapterhouse are numerous interesting objects, including St.Ramón's wooden chair and his 12C ivory crook. A further crook (13C) is considered to have belonged to St.Valero. It has beautiful enamelling and comes from the workshops of Limoges. Liturgical robes include those of St.Ramón and St.Valero.

Roncesvalles
Navarra/Navarra   p.388 □ I 2

The Pass of Roncesvalles was one of the most important N-S routes even in ancient times but it became famous as a consequence of Charlemagne's Spanish campaign. On 15 August 778, during the retreat following defeat at Saragossa, Charlemagne's rearguard, led by the hero Roland, was annihilated here by the Basques. Roland is supposed to have blown his magic horn Olifant to warn the rest of the army. Mortally wounded along with the twelve Paladins of Charlemagne, Roland is said to have thrown the sword Durandal into the water to prevent it from falling into the hands of the enemy. But Roncesvalles was also an important pilgrim station on the route from France to Santiago de Compostela. The village of Roncesvalles now consists of a few houses clustered around the massive Augustinian monastery.

Chapel of Sancti Spiritus: Roncesvalles' oldest building from the early 12C. *Crypt* with the bone of dead Santiago pilgrims.

Ermita de San Salvador de Ibañeta: This little church is reputed to stand on the site of the tomb Charlemagne had built for Roland and his retinue.

Real Colegiata: This collegiate church towers over the monastery founded by King Alfonso I, el Batallador, in 1130. The building of the church followed under King Sancho II, el Fuerte and it was consecrated in 1219. The monastery church has a nave and two aisles and is one of the most beautiful early-13C Gothic buildings in Spain. It is an example of the transition from the Romanesque to the Gothic in Spain. The church has a tall, square *tower*. *Interior:* Near the high altar, is the famous Gothic sculpture of the *Madonna of Roncesvalles*, which was carved in cedar by a master of the French school in the late 13C/early 14C. The statue, clad in silver and adorned with valuable jewels, has a silver tabernacle. A terracotta Mater Dolorosa is also famous and may be the work of Pedro de Mena; her tears are represented by diamonds. The monastery church also has a rich *treasury*, which includes the 12C *evangeliary* upon which the Kings of Navarre had to swear an oath. The book's cover consists of two silver plaques. On the front is Christ in Glory framed by the symbols of the four Evangelists. On the back is the Crucifixion flanked by the sun and the moon. Each image is framed by filigree and arabesque ornament. The collection also includes a late-14C *reliquary* with the Last Judgement in gold, silver and enamel. Two further caskets are of interest. The first is 12C and in silver with gold medallions; the second is Mudéjar and has the coats-of-arms of the Kings of Navarre. There is also a superb *painting* of the Holy Family by Luis de Morales and a triptych, a gift from the Duke of Orleans, which is attributed to the painter Hieronymus Bosch.

Monastery: The original monastery

Roncesvalles, Real Colegiata

Roncesvalles, Real Colegiata

buildings were destroyed by fire in 1400. The former chapterhouse, later the *chapel of San Agustín*, survived. It contains the 12C Gothic *sarcophagi* of King Sancho el Fuerte and his wife Doña Clemencia de Toulouse. The King's sarcophagus is adorned with a beautiful statue of the monarch.

Also worth seeing: *Church of Santiago:* 12C; built in Romanesque-Gothic style. Used by Santiago pilgrims. The *Hospital de Nuestra Señora de Roncesvalles* dates from the 12C, as does the *pilgrim's hostel.* There is a 14C *pilgrim cross* on the road out of the town.

Ronda

Málaga/Andalusia   p.394☐E 11

The Roman trading post of Arunda is one of the oldest towns in Spain. In the 8C Ronda became capital of a Moorish Emirate until falling to Ferdinand and Isabella during the Reconquista in 1485. Its capture by Napoleonic troops in 1808 resulted in the destruction of the Moorish alcazaba. The town's unique setting is most attractive.

Collegiate church of Santa María la Mayor (Plaza de la Ciudad, or Plaza de la Duquesa de Parcent): The *former mosque* has a minaret bell tower with an octagonal Gothic upper part. Its former function as a mosque can still be seen in the 15C Gothic interior (nave and two aisles) e.g. four Moorish domes, mihrab arches with stucco and mihrab. The Capilla Mayor is Plateresque. Renaissance sillería (choir stalls). Two baroque altars.

Bridges: The town has an extraordinary setting, on a high, fertile plateau some 2,580 ft. up, in the otherwise bleak region of the Serranía de Ronda. The plateau falls steeply away to the W. The town has several historically interesting bridges, which span the tremendous Gorge of the Guadalevin. The *Puente San Miguel,* or 'de los Cortadurias' is possibly of Roman origin. The *Puente Viejo* or Puente de la Mina was built on Arab foundations in 1616 and has horseshoe arches. The massive, three-arched stone *Puente Nuevo* (235 ft.) has beautiful wrought-iron parapet railings and spans a narrow part of the Tajo (gorge) de Ronda some 500 ft. above the river. Built in the 18C by the architect Martín Aldehuela it links two parts of the town—the northern new town *Mercadillo* (Merchant's quarter), dating from the time of Ferdinand and Isabella, and the walled Old Town, *or Ciudad,* south of the Gorge. On the gorge's rocky cliffs there are *molinos,* old Moorish mills.

Casa del Rey Moro (left of the Puente Nuevo, No. 17): This well-restored *Arab building* has beautiful *gardens,* with an octagonal marble fountain. A *stairway* of 365 steps descends to the bottom of the gorge.

Ronda, monastery of San Francisco, portal

Casa de Mondragón (just S. of the Plaza del Campillo): 16C. This former Moorish palace was converted into a residence for Ferdinand and Isabella. *Renaissance portal* and two inner courtyards.

Casa del Marqués de Salvatierra: The most striking feature of this 18C building is its Plateresque *portal*. The *patio* is also of interest.

Casa del Gigante (Calle del Teniente Gorgo): This Mudéjar *Moorish palace* dates from the 14C and has a beautiful *patio* with interesting capitals on the marble columns. Fine artesonado.

Puerta del Almocávar (Barrio de San Francisco): Historically interesting *gate* with horseshoe arch, which was the main entrance into the Moorish town. The Catholic King Ferdinand made his entry here in 1485. Another town gate to have survived is the *Arco del Cristo*.

Bullring: The Plaza de Toros (224 ft. diameter) was built in 1785 and has a baroque façade. It is the oldest bullring in Spain. Two storey arcades ring the arena. Bullfighting on foot (as opposed to the traditional long fight on horseback) was developed with special rules here as the 'estilo rondeño'. Pedro Romero, the most celebrated 18C Torero, has a *memorial* in the Alameda, the town park. Goya used this famous bullring for a series of works.

Also worth seeing: *Church of El Espíritu Santo* (near the ruins of the alcazaba): This Gothic church (15C) was built on the orders of the Catholic King Ferdinand to commemorate the Reconquista. The *church of San Sebastián* with *Alminar* (Calle de las Bóicas), a former minaret: also has a window with a horseshoe arch. *Monastery of San Francisco:* Plateresque portal. *Arab baths:* The ruins on the river bank reveal a large chamber divided by octagonal

columns with horseshoe arches and barrel vaulting. *Hotel Reina Victoria* (Calle de Jerez): Rainer Maria *Rilke* stayed here from Dec. 1912 to Feb. 1913 and there are mementoes of his stay. *Posada de las Ánimas* (near the Puente Viejo): Built *c*.1500. Cervantes was a guest at this inn, of which only the façade survives.

Environs: Ronda la Vieja (12 km. NW): The Roman foundation of Acinipio was built on a Phoenician settlement. *Amphitheatre.* **Cueva de la Pileta** (28 km. W., near Benaoján): This former subterranean river course is a 5,000 ft. long *cave*, whose red and yellow rock paintings date from the Palaeolithic age. Stylistically similar to the rock paintings of Altamira, they depict horses, goats, bulls, fish and cows. Also of interest are the black symbols, which are probably occult. **Grazalema** (30 km. NW): 'Lacidulo' in Roman times. The beautiful Gothic *church of La Encarnación* has a treasury, which houses 16C priests' robes and a silver monstrance. The *church of San Juan* has a Moorish arch. **Zahara de la Sierra** (40 km. NW): This town occupies a ridge and was a border stronghold against the kingdom of Granada. *Castle ruins* and *Arab bridge. The church of Santa María de Mesa* has 15C paintings, church treasure with 18C vestments, *urns* with wood carvings (of the 4 Evangelists; probably the work of Andrés Ocampo) and items in silver. **El Gastor** (35 km. NW): Remains of the '*Giant's Tomb*', a dolmen, 5,025 ft. up. **Setenil** (40 km. N.): Remains of castle wall and tower; 15C Gothic *church of La Encarnación; Ayuntamiento,* 16C with very beautiful artesonado; *chapel of San Sebastián del Carmen; chapel of San Benito.* **Olvera** (50 km. NW): Former *fortress* with keep and walls. Not far from the town is the beautiful 18C *pilgrimage church of Nuestra Señora de los Remedios* with a

Ronda, Moorish baths

Gothic image of the Virgin. **Ardales** (40 km. NE): Outside the town, by the Encantada hills, lie the *ruins of the old Arab town of Bobastro,* founded in the 9C to counter the Emirate of Córdoba. *Ermita de la Virgen de Villaverde:* The Mozarabic architecture can still be discerned amongst the ruins. *Alcázar:* Remains of walls and traces of cisterns. *Cueva de la Trinidad:* Palaeolithic rock paintings.

Rosas
Gerona/Catalonia   p.390☐O 3

In the present Gulf of Rosas, at the foot of the Roda mountains, the Romans built the town of Rhoda. Due to its strategic position the town was constantly refortified through the centuries.

Citadel: This fortress stood at the town's entrance. It was built in the form of an irregular pentagon. A few remains survive.

Romanesque church: Formerly part of a monastery. Construction of the present church began in 1543.

Environs: Palau Sabardera (5 km. inland, towards Vilajuiga to the N.): Two towers remain of the old *castle,* which was first mentioned in 882.

Rubielos de Mora
Teruel/Aragon   p.388☐K 6

This village in the lower Maestrazgo has 1,268 inhabitants. In the Middle Ages it was ringed with strong *defensive walls,* the only remains of which are two gates, the *Puerta del Carmen* and the *Puerta de San Antonio.* There are also medieval houses with coats-of-arms, such as the *Casa de los Villasegura.*

Parish church: Built in Renaissance style between 1604 and 1620. It has a square *tower* with an octagonal upper part. Con-

Ronda, Arco del Cristo

Ronda, San Sebastián, former minaret

tained within is a mid- to late- 15C Gothic altar.

Augustinian convent: This convent has an elegant late 14C *portal.* Inside the *church* is an interesting 15C altar by Juan Reixach, above which the Holy Trinity is depicted.

Rueda

Zaragoza/Aragon   p.388☐K 4

This abbey on the bank of the Ebro was established by Alfonso II at the start of the 13C in Romanesque-Gothic transitional style. It was abandoned in 1835. The church, with a nave and two aisles, contains interesting *tombs.* The columns of the Gothic cloister have fine capitals. The most beautiful parts of the abbey are the Gothic-Byzantine *chapterhouse,* from the second half of the 13C, and the Romanesque-Gothic *Refectory.* Also worth seeing is the Abbot's Palace, which was begun in 1610 and has a façade in the style of Herrara.

S

Sabiñánigo
Huesca/Aragon   p.388□K 2

The area of *Serrablo* is near the town of Sabiñánigo and above the Río Gállego. It contains over 20 churches from 10–12C. The oldest are *San Pedro* in **Lárrede**, *San Juan* in **Busa**, *San Bartolomé* in **Gavín**, and the churches in **Lasieso** and **Oliván**. All are Mozarabic.

Sádaba
Zaragoza/Aragon   p.388□I 3

Santa María: This 14C Gothic parish church is interesting and attractive in form. Its octagonal tower is a fine example of Spanish Gothic. The tympanum above the *portal* has a Madonna and Child. The stellar-vaulted *interior* consists of a nave, a transept and a number of side chapels. There is a large dome above the chapel in the transept. The late 16C *high altar* is from the school of Ancheta, and has fine reliefs and sculptures; the paintings on the early 15C *altar dedicated to the Virgin* are attributed to Pedro de Zuera. The Renaissance altar in the Chapel of St.James is early 16C; there are some fine statues from Gabriel Yoli's workshop. The pulpit is decked out most intricately, with reliefs of 1578 depicting the four Evangelists. The *choir* is furnished with late 16C wood panelling and choir stalls.

Castillo: The well-preserved 13C castle is square with nine square towers.

Environs: Just outside the town are the Roman remains of **Clarina**, which include a ruined temple, an aqueduct and baths. 3 km. along the road to Layana is the **Altar de los Moros**, the mausoleum of the Roman Atilia family, which dates from the 2C. The façade, with six pilasters and an attic, has survived. Niches contain busts of members of the family. Just inside the town limits of Sádaba is a 4C Roman building known as the *Sinagoga*, with two interior and two exterior apses. Presumably it was once used as a synagogue. Within 3 km. or so are the remains of two monasteries. The **Monasterio de Puilampa** has an attached Romanesque church which is still standing and is currently used as a barn; its portal is decorated with a Chi-Rho monogram with the sun, the moon and trees. The church has Gothic vaulting. The **Monasterio de Cambrón**, is now a farmstead; its portal, too, has a Chi-Rho monogram. The W. façade has a large 12C relief of the Virgin. The Romanesque nave is barrel vaulted.

Sagunto

Valencia/Valencia   p.396☐L 6

This town of medium size some 26 km. N. of Valencia on the right bank of the Río Palancia is surrounded by orange and lemon groves. It was founded by the Iberians. In 219BC it was the centre of dispute between Rome and Carthage and this led to the Second Punic War. Eventually, after an eight-month siege and despite the population's heroic resistance, it was captured by Hannibal. Livy, the Roman historian, writes that the Saguntines avoided capture by setting fire to the town and leaping, with their women and children, into the sea of flames. The Romans recaptured the town four years later and rebuilt it, but it was taken by the Vandals in the 5C and destroyed again, after which it lapsed into obscurity. The Roman 'Murusvetus' (old wall) survived as 'Murviedro', which fell to the Moors during their advance through the peninsula. Recaptured by El Cid, the national hero, it was retaken by the Moors four years later and only finally wrested from Islam in 1238. During the War of Independence it was occupied by Napoleon's French troops (1811 – 14). The town played one final historical role, when, after the abolition of the monarchy in 1873, Alfonso XII proclaimed himself king from inside its walls, and brought the Bourbons back to the throne. Since 1868 it has been known by its original name of Sagunto.

Castillo: This mighty ruined castle overlooks Sagunto from a 2,000 ft. long ridge, which is well protected with Iberian, Carthaginian, Roman and Moorish fortifications; various other buildings were added in the Middle Ages, when the whole fortress was separated into seven sections. The cyclopean walls are Iberian and contain the *Plaza de Armas* and also a medieval mill. A horseshoe gate leads through to the

Sagunto, Castillo

Moorish *Plaza de Almenara*. The *Plaza de San Fernando* is predominantly Roman, as is the *Plaza de Estudiantes*; the highest parts of the castle, the *Plaza Ciudadela* and the *Plaza del Dos de Mayo*, are largely medieval. The *Torre de Hércules*, destroyed by the French, was also situated here.

Roman Theatre: This is built on a slope with the sea as backdrop. Greek in origin, it was restored and extended by the Romans and could seat up to 6,000 people in a total of 33 rows. Unfortunately it was later used as a stone quarry, especially during the Napoleonic Wars, when stone was badly needed for fortifications. There has been some attempt at restoration in recent years.

Archaeological Museum: Next to the theatre. It contains finds from the neighbourhood of Castillo, which include an Iberian sculpture of a bull, a Bacchus and fragments of further Iberian and Roman sculptures, mosaics, ceramics, inscriptions and coins.

San Salvador: From the 13C, it is the older of Sagunto's two interesting churches. Mostly Gothic with a Romanesque portal.

Church of Santa María: Built on the site of an old mosque. Begun in the 14C but not completed until the 18C. The Gothic façade is interesting and there is a splendid 18C high altar.

Environs: A few km. to the S. of Sagunto is the small town of **Puzol**, which has a church with a fine baroque altar and 15–16C paintings. The *Palace of the Archbishop of Valencia* has some splendid paintings by Estéban March and Camarón from the 17C, and some 19C pieces by Vicente López. It is worth taking a detour via **Puig** nearby, which is the site of the ruins of the *Castillo de Entenza*. El Puig was important during the Reconquista, when it saw the first action which eventually led to the recapture of Valencia. James I of Aragon founded a *monastery* to commemorate the event. The monastery has a Romanesque-

Sagunto, Roman theatre

Sagunto, Castillo ↄ

Gothic portal. The church's interior contains a remarkable 15C *retable*.

Sahagún
León/León   p.386 □ F 3

This small town, known in antiquity as Cemala, has a number of old buildings which make it one of León's most interesting towns. During the 10C 'Repoblacion', when the Christians who had been driven out slowly began to move back into the empty spaces north of the river Duero, which formed the frontier, it was the site of several important monasteries. The original foundation stones were laid by Mozarab monks who had fled from Córdoba.

Monasterio de San Benito: This 12–13C monastery was once the most powerful Benedictine monastery in the kingdom of León. It was eventually destroyed in the 19C and today only parts of the E. section of the original Romanesque-Gothic structure survive. The *S. portal*, which dates from 1662, is also interesting, as are the *tombs* of Alfonso VI of León and Castile, Queen Isabella and Aben Omar, the daughter of the Emir of Seville. There is a fine 13C sarcophagus.

San Tirso: This 12C brick church is one of the finest examples of Romanesque-Mudéjar style. The huge square tower, three storeys high with arcades, is most remarkable. The three apses around the tower are of different heights. Splendid chancel.

San Lorenzo: This has a nave, two aisles, three apses, a transept and a dome, all 13C in origin; it is one of the finest examples of Romanesque Mudéjar brickwork. It has a huge Romanesque tower with four arcades of different heights. The interior contains a 16C sculpture by Jean d'Ángers, which is part of a baroque altar. The *Capilla de Jesús* contains 16C reliefs by Juan de Juni.

Santuario de la Peregrina/Franciscan monastery (just outside Sahagún, towards Palencia): The church dates from 1257 and was part of a Franciscan monastery. Its exterior has survived in good condition, especially the E. end, and it is yet another fine example of Romanesque-Mudéjar brickwork. Moorish stucco.

Ayuntamiento/Town Hall: The **museum** contains a splendid silver-gilt monstrance, which was made in the early 16C by Enrique de Arfe for the monastery of San Benito.

Salamanca
Salamanca/León   p.386 □ E 5

The Roman fortress of Salamantica was taken by Hannibal in 217 BC during the Second Punic War (218-201), then by the Romans, in the 6C by the Vandals, then by the Visigoths and in the 8C by the Moors. Alfonso VI of Castile and León won it back in 1085, and Alfonso IX founded modern Salamanca, establishing the university there in 1218; it soon became renowned, especially for its faculty of law. Salamanca became a bishop's seat and a cultural centre. In 1593, however, Valladolid was raised to a bishopric, and when the Mozarabs were thrown out in 1610 Salamanca lost much of its importance. It was built out of a pale sandstone, which in time acquired a golden hue and earned the city the name of 'La Dorada' ('the golden'). St. John of the Cross, Columbus, Calderón, Cervantes, Lope de Vega, Gongora, Ignatius Loyola and Un-

Salamanca, new cathedral, portal ▮

amuno y Jugo all lived in Salamanca and loved the atmosphere of magic and history of this city of many towers. The best view of the city, which is situated on a hill above the left bank of the Tormes, is obtained from the Plaza Mayor, which has numerous streets leading off it.

Plaza Mayor: This is one of Spain's most beautiful baroque squares. It measures 243 x 269 ft. and was laid out 1729–33 to the designs of Alberto de Churriguera. It was finally completed in 1755 with Andrés Garcia de Quiñones' baroque Ayuntamiento on the N. side. The whole square is surrounded by three-storeyed buildings above a series of arcades.

Catedral Nueva and Catedral Vieja: In the centre of the town is the initially confusing sight of two cathedrals in the same complex, together with cloisters, chapels and the Diocesan Museum. The original, 12C cathedral was linked to the new cathedral in 1513, but work continued until the 18C, which accounts for the unusual combination of architectural styles. The structure is visible in its entirety from the Plaza de Anaya, from which the new cathedral is entered.

New Cathedral: This was begun in late Gothic style under the supervision of Juan Gil de Hontañón; the work was carried on by Juan de Alava and Rodrigo Gil de Hontañón. The choir and façade by Joaquin and Alberto Churriguera, Juan de Sagarvinaga and Jerónimo Garcia de Quiñones date from the 17–18C. The interior consists of a nave, two aisles, side chapels and a dome over the crossing. The exterior is decorated with gables, cornices, balconies, coats-of-arms, carved figures and pinnacles. The *façade* is quite splendid, with three *portals* and Churrigueresque archivolts. It is richly provided with carved scenes, especially in the tympanum above the main portal, where there are depictions of the Adoration of the Shepherds and the Magi; there are also baroque statues in tabernacles. The *Portada de Ramos* is on the N. side, and has a relief by Juan

Salamanca, Plaza Mayor   *Salamanca, new cathedral* ▷

Salamanca, old and new cathedrals 1 main portal, Portada del Perdon **2** Portada del Obispo **3** Portada de San Clemente **4** Portada de Ramos **5** Coro **6** Capilla Mayor **7** Capillas de las Batallas **8** Capilla del Sagrario **9** Capilla de Santisimo or de San Nicolás de Bari **10** Antesacristia **11** Sacristia **12** Patio Chico **13** Capilla del Pilar **14** chapel leading through to the old cathedral **15** Capilla del Sudario **16** Capilla Dorada **17** Capilla San Lorenzo **18** Capilla San Antonio **19** tomb of Bishop Bobadillo **20** crossing dome **A** Torre del Gallo **B** high altar **C** Capilla San Martín **D** walled-over W. door **E** old tombs **F** Moorish-influenced Gothic tombs **G** Romanesque cloister door **H** Capilla Talavera **I** Capilla Santa Barbara **K** Capilla Santa Catalina **L** Capilla Anaya **M** ante-room to chapterhouse (now serves as museum) **N** chapterhouse (also museum) **O** cloister

Rodríguez depicting Christ's entry into Jerusalem. The stellar-vaulted cathedral itself is huge and has a domed crossing; the most striking area is the *coro*, which was designed by Joaquin and Alberto Churriguera in 1724. The upper *choir stalls* are by José Lara, the lower ones by Juan Mugica, and both date from 1725–30. Both the fine *organs* are by Pedro de Echivarría, and date from 1745. The area behind the coro

Old cathedral, high altar

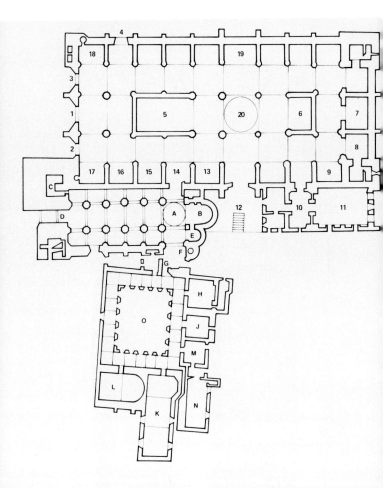

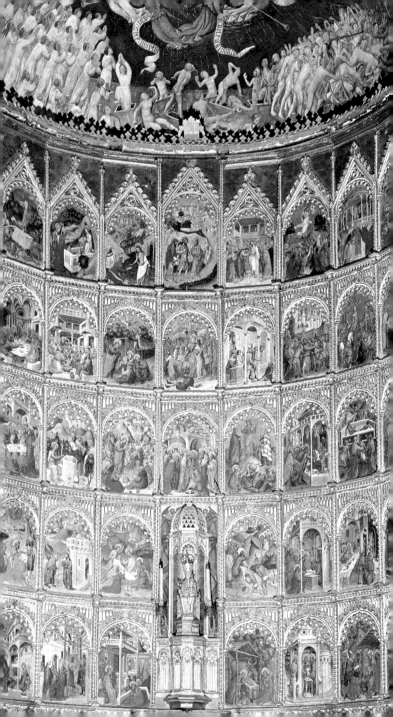

Salamanca, cathedrals

is the work of Joaquín and José Churriguera, and it contains a statue of St.Anne and a John the Baptist by Juan de Juni, which was originally in the Old Cathedral. The Virgin between the two is 16C. The *Capilla Mayor* has no retable, but in its place is a 17C Assumption of the Virgin surrounded by angels sculpted by Gregorio Fernández. The statues by Alberto Churriguera which originally adorned the altar have been separated and are now to be found in various of the chapels. Moving inwards from the W. end, the first two chapels on the left are by Juan Gil de Hontañón; the first three on the right, the oldest in the church, are by Juan de Alava. The following chapels are of interest. The *Capilla del Carmen* or *de las Batallas* is directly behind the altar and has a highly ornate altarpiece by Joaquín Churriguera,

which incorporates the famous 11C Romanesque crucifix, *Cristo de las Batallas*, which El Cid is said to have taken with him on his campaign. The *Capilla del Sagrario* has an altarpiece by José de Churriguera and a beautiful Pietà of 1763 by Salvador Carmona. The *Capilla Dorada* or *de Todos los Santos* has 110 figures by Juan de Alava and a grille by Juan de Buenamadre. The *Capilla del Sudario* has an Entombment by one of Titian's followers. The ante-room to the sacristy was designed by Manuel de Lara Churriguera and the sacristy itself is by Juan de Sagarvinaga.

Cathedral: When the New Cathedral was built, the old one was left standing and its N. transept was replaced by a chapel of the New Cathedral with a passage through to

Salamanca, new cathedral

the Old Cathedral. The original W. portal was walled up from the inside, but a 13C French Gothic Annunciation was retained. The Old Cathedral was built in the 12C on the site of another church; six architects were employed on it before its completion during the first quarter of the 13C. and the names of some of them, such as Maestro Pedro, who was taken on in 1213, and Petrus Petriz, who built the fine dome over the crossing in the celebrated *Torre de Gallo* (1163–4), are known. The tower has splendid Romanesque windows, arches, ornamentation, four turrets and a Byzantine-style *dome* supported on a large drum with columns and windows. The best view of the lovely exterior is from the Patio Chico. The church was begun in Romanesque style but as the work progressed it embraced elements of

French-Gothic and Byzantine styles. It has a nave, two aisles, three semicircular apses, cross vaulting and the dome over the crossing described above, all designed and constructed with elegance and harmony, in comparison to the New Cathedral which is decorated with fewer, but more splendid, pieces. The *vault of the choir* is frescoed with scenes from the Last Judgement by Nicolás Florentino, who was also responsible for the extraordinary 15C Gothic retable with its 53 panels, all framed by arches and depicting scenes from the lives of Jesus and the Virgin, each more beautiful than the last. At the bottom-middle of the retable, there is one of Spain's finest works of art, a statue of the the *Virgen de la Vega*, patron saint of Salamanca. It is early 13C and made of copper decorated with Limoges enamel. The crossing and

Salamanca, old cathedral

Salamanca, old cathedral, tomb

S. transept have *sarcophagi* from the 13–15C, of which the most interesting is a *Gothic tomb* of obvious Moorish influence. The sarcophagi are set in wall niches with pointed arches; they stand on lions, have recumbent figures on the top and polychrome reliefs. The arches are borne by columns and decorated with polychrome reliefs. The tympana contain either polychrome relief figures or frescos between polychrome ribs. At the end of the cathedral, N. of the original W. portal and beneath the tower, is the *Capilla San Martin* which has some fine, well-preserved wall paintings of 1262 by Anton Sánchez. Turning back to the crossing and passing through the right transept, there is a decorated 13C Romanesque door which leads through to the *cloisters* of 1162–78. They have been restored on numerous occasions

but still have original Romanesque capitals and tombs, such as the Tomb of Gutierre de Castro from the 16C, as well as some fine pieces such as the Pietà in relief by Juan de Juni or the 13C sculpture of Santa María de la Claustra. The following *chapels* are also of great interest. The *Capilla de Talavera* dates from around 1180 and contains original Gothic-Mudéjar stellar vaulting and, behind a rather unusual 16C grille, the tomb of Doctor Arias Maldonado (d. 1517). The altar has a fine 14C Gothic sculpture. Masses are held in this chapel today using the Mozarabic rite. The Gothic *Capilla de Santa Barbara* (1344) has interesting vaults. On the site where doctorates used to be examined is the sarcophagus of Bishop Juan Lucero surrounded by a plain wooden screen. The 16C Plateresque retable depicts scenes

Salamanca, old cathedral, vault, detail

from the life of St. Barbara. The *Capilla Santa Catalina* is mid 16C and consists of three sections with Gothic stellar vaulting and the coat-of-arms of Ferdinand and Isabella. The *Capilla de Anaya* or *San Bartolomé*, which dates from 1422, has a fine organ gallery and the *Anaya tombs*, notable among which is the late Gothic alabaster tomb of the founder of the chapel, Don Diego de Anaya Maldonado, which is surrounded by a wrought-iron grille by Francisco de Salamanca.

Museum: Between the Capilla Santa Barbara and the Capilla Santa Catalina is the entrance to the Diocesan Museum, which occupies the ante-room to the chapterhouse and the chapterhouse itself. It contains an important collection of 15C Spanish paintings, including work by Fernando Gallego

(notably a triptych). It also contains sculptures and reliefs from the 14–18C.

Other Religious Buildings:

San Benito: This 15C church is near La Clerecia and has an Isabelline-Gothic portal. The interior contains a number of Maldonado tombs.

San Cristóbal (now the **Colegio de San José**): This church is not far from Sancti Spiritus, and dates from 1145.

San Julián y Santa Basilisa: To the E. of the Plaza Mayor. Tower and portal date from 1107. It was extensively rebuilt in 1582. The interior contains the interesting *baroque tomb* of Don Francisco Ramos Manzano (1671). The high altar is by Joa-

Salamanca, Monterrey Palace

quin Churriguera, with a painting of the Immaculate Conception by José Antolinez. One of the side altars has a statue of St. Peter of Alcántara by Pedro de Mena.

San Juan de Barbalos on the Plaza San Juan Bautista was founded in 1139 and contains the 12C Romanesque statue of *El Cristo de la Zarza*.

San Marcos: In the NW of the old town is the Plaza San Marcos, on which stands a round Romanesque church of the same name dating from 1178. It has a bell tower with a Romanesque relief of St.Mark. The interior has early Gothic frescos by the Salamantine school on the walls of the central and right apses.

San Martín: On the S. side of the Plaza

Mayor. It was founded in 1103 and built during the 12C in Romanesque style. The Romanesque *N. portal* is of especial interest, with its unusual archivolt and exquisitely carved capitals with animals. The high altar is by Alberto Churriguera.

San Millán: Dates from 1480 and is situated near the Old Cathedral, next to the Capilla Vera Cruz; it has a baroque portal from 1635.

San Sebastián: To the left of the Colegio de Anaya. Built by Alberto Churriguera in 1731.

Sancti Spiritus: In the SE of the old town. Built in 1544 by Juan Gil de Hontañón (El Mozo) to the designs of Martin de Santiago. It occupies the site of an old

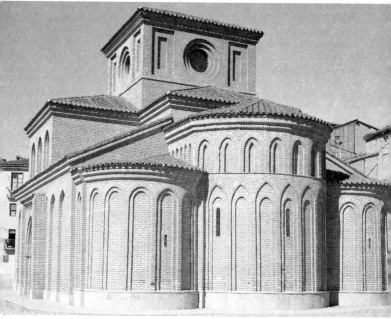

Salamanca, Santiago

parish church dating from 1190. The most interesting features are the Plateresque *façade*, the *high altar* of 1659, 13C *tombs* in the sanctuary, stellar vaulting over the single aisle, the highly carved Mudéjar *coffer ceiling* over the coro, 13C Madonna in the sacristy and, in particular, the 12C Romanesque *crucifix* in the nave.

Santa María de los Caballeros (near the Casa de las Muertes): Originally 12C but was rebuilt in the 16&18C. There are two interesting 15C tombs, and a fine 16C high altar. The sacristy has alabaster figures and 15–17C painted wooden sculptures.

Santiago: In the S. of the old town, on the Río Tormes near the Roman bridge. Romanesque-Mudéjar apses date from 1145.

Santo Tomás Cantuariense: Diagonally opposite the Colegio de Calatrava. Built in 1175 by two English architects. It is single-aisled with three apses and was the world's first church to be dedicated to St.Thomas Becket.

La Vera Cruz: A chapel near the Ursuline convent. It was rebuilt in 1713 by Joaquín de Churriguera and has a rich baroque interior. Only a portal remains from the original 16C structure.

Modern Religious Buildings: The most interesting are *La Nuestra Señora* de Fátima and the church of *El Arrabal*, which has an interesting fresco in the choir.

Convento de Agustinas de la Concepción (or **de Monterrey**): Opposite the

Monterrey Palace on the Plaza de Agustinas. It was founded by the Counts of Monterrey in the 17C and contains some interesting paintings and items in gold. Its church, *La Purísma*, was built in 1636 in Italianate style by Gómez de Mora, Baltasar López and Antonio de Carassa. It contains a Crucifixion by Francisco Barsano and depictions of St. Januarius, St. Augustine and the Adoration of the Shepherds by José de Ribera. The huge painting above the *high altar* is also by Ribera; it dates from 1635 and depicts the Immaculate Conception, or *Purísma*, and has been called 'the century's finest Virgin'. The *marble statues* of the Counts of Monterrey in prayer are also interesting. They are by the Italian sculptors Algardi and Finelli, who also fashioned the marble-faced *pulpit*.

Convento de las Bernardas de Jesús: A large complex of buildings in the E. of the city. Founded by Doña María de Anaya in 1552 it was designed and built by Rodrigo Gil de Hontañón. Its Plateresque façade was much copied in the rest of the province of Salamanca during the second half of the 16C.

Convento de Carmelitas Descalzas de San José/Casa de Santa Teresa: On the NE of the Plaza Mayor. According to the Carmelites St. Theresa stayed at a building on this spot when she came to Salamanca in 1570. The room in which she lived and in which she experienced her ecstacy in 1571 is now the Chapel of St. Joseph. The convent visible today dates from 1614.

Convento del Corpus Christi: Founded by Cristóbal Suárez in 1538. The Plateresque portal is interesting, as is the stellar vaulting in the interior and the 18C Athene.

Convento de las Dueñas: An interesting convent to the NE of the cathedral, near the Monastery of San Esteban. It was founded in 1419 by Doña Juana Rodriguez Maldonado as an addition to her palace. The Dominican convent visible today was built in 1533 and has a Plateresque façade, a late Gothic church and what must once have been an exceptionally fine *patio*, whose upper section has interesting capitals with mythical beasts and medallions.

Convento San Esteban: A Dominican monastery built by Juan de Ribero 1590 –9. It has arcades at ground level, wide windows and medallions on the first floor and Gothic windows and pinnacles on the second floor, all of which display Italian influence. The church is of particular interest. It was designed by Juan de Alava in 1524, and later extended by a number of architects including Martin de Santiago, Rodrigo Gil de Hontañón and Juan de Ribero. It is single-aisled with side chapels. The fine Plateresque façade is highly ornamented and beautifully proportioned. The relief over the portal depicts the Stoning of St. Stephen and was completed by Ceroni in 1610. The interior is also impressive. The high altar has gilded columns wound around with tendrils and is the work of José Churriguera. The middle section contains a painting by Claudio Coello. The *choir stalls* were made by Alfonso Balbás in 1651-8. The choir also contains a painting attributed to Rubens and a large fresco of the 'Triumph of the Church' (1505) by Palomino. The left transept contains the altar of St. Dominic by Joaquín Churriguera, which has a sculpture of the saint by Luis Salvador Carmona. The altar of the Rosary is also by Joaquín Churriguera, and the painting of the Coronation of the Virgin is by Villamor. The sacristy and the chapterhouse are 16C, by the architect Moreno. The 'Escalera de

Salamanca, new cathedral, Retablo de Cristo de las Batallas

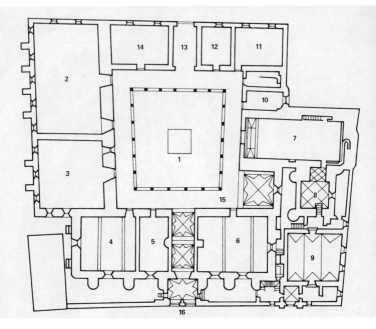

Salamanca, University 1 courtyard **2** Aula **3** Frater Luis de León lecture room or Theology lecture room **4** Miguel de Unamuno lecture room **5** Dorado Montero lecture room **6** Salinas music room (formerly Leyes) **7** chapel **8** sacristy **9** rectory **10** lecture room **11** lecture room with columns **12** lecture theatre **13** old chapel **14** Francisco de Vitoria lecture room **15** staircase **16** W. façade

Soto' (staircase) dates from 1533 and was designed by Martín de Santiago. The *Claustro de los Reyes* was built by Sardiña between the beginning of the 16C and 1591. It has two storeys of arcades; the lower level has English late Gothic vaulting. The late 15C *Claustro de Colón* also has a double row of arcades.

Convento de Santa Clara/de Corpus Christi: Near the Casa de Santa Teresa.

It was founded in 1220 but totally rebuilt in the 18C. The church's Plateresque portal dates from the 15C.

Convento Santa Isabel: Founded by Isabel Suárez de Solís in 1433. The church dates from the 16C and contains a Gothic painting of St.Elizabeth of Hungary by Nicolás Florentino and his workshop.

Convento de las Ursulas: To the W. of the Plaza Mayor. Founded in 1512; there are elements of Gothic and Renaissance in the church architecture. Both portals were rebuilt in the 18C. The most interesting feature is the *tomb of the founder*, Don Alonso de Fonseca in the middle of the church; it was carved by Diego de Siloé in 1529 and has a recumbent figure and a splendid relief.

Salamanca, Torre del Aire

Salamanca, House of the Shells

University — Estudios Menores:
Salamanca has been a university town for more than 700 years, ever since King Alfonso IX gave the charter for the institution in 1218 and Ferdinand III confirmed the privilege in 1243. The university was originally housed in the old cathedral. It flourished in the 16C, when it was known as one of the oldest and most distinguished of universities in the world; today it has lost much of its importance. The university buildings we see today, which are really a number of lecture rooms built round an interior courtyard, date from the 15C. The highly decorated façade is from the early 16C and is the most famous example of a Plateresque façade. The central section, which projects over the two gates, bears the medallion of Ferdinand and Isabella, with the coat-of-arms of Charles V above them,

and the Pope and cardinals at the very top. The whole relief is chiselled in the stone in quite extraordinarily fine detail. The university courtyard is arcaded and provides access to the separate lecture rooms. The Aula, now a museum, has baroque carpets and a painting of Charles IV in the style of Goya. One of the most interesting rooms is the *Frater Luis de Léon* lecture hall, which is furnished in its original style, with an old dais and primitive wooden desks for the students. The *Salinas Music Room* has two panel paintings by Juan de Flandes, and the *old chapel* has works by Fernando Gallego and Felipe Bigarny and a retable by Juan de Flandes. The *new chapel* has a baroque altar and paintings by Juan de Ribera. There is a fine, wide *staircase* (with reliefs and stellar vaulting) which leads through to the upper *cloisters*. A

Gothic door leads through to the old baroque-furnished *library*, which contains 50,000 old volumes, early printed works, miniature codices and Greek and Latin manuscripts bound in leather and parchment. Nearby is the *modern library*. Near the entrance to the university is the former *Hospital del Estudio*, now the Rector's residence, which was built in 1600, and the *Escuelas Menores*, which dates from 1533 and has a Plateresque façade, an arcaded courtyard, and a lecture room containing a huge fresco known as the *Ciclo de Salamanca*, a hunting picture by Fernando Gallego. There are paintings by Juan de Flandes in the same room.

La Clerecía/El Real Colegio del Espírito Santo: Salamanca in fact has three universities. That described above comprises the faculties of philosophy, philology, law, natural history and medicine. The Papal University, the Real Colegio del Espirito Santo, teaches theology, philosophy and canon law. The third university is that of the Dominican Fathers.
The building of the Jesuit college was commissioned in 1617 by Philip III and his wife Margaret of Austria to the plans of Juan Gómez de Mora. It was eventually completed in 1779 with the college portal. Various architects were involved in the design of the church, college and 'residencia de la Comunidad'. The church is single-aisled and is mostly the work of Gómez de Mora; the façade dates from 1657 and the large, gilded altar is 17–18C. The sacristy contains a retable by Andréz García de Quiñones, and there is a Flagellation of Christ by Luis Salvator Carmona. The college has a well-balanced façade and a baroque courtyard by García de Quiñones which must rank among the finest of its kind in Spain. He was also responsible for designing the staircases, which were built 1730–40.

Colegio de los Irlandeses /Arch-

bishop's College, formerly **Colegio Mayor de Santiago:** Dates from 1578 when it was commissioned by the Archbishop of Toledo, Alonso de Fonseca. It was designed by the architects Diego de Siloé, Juan de Alava and Pedro de Ibarra. The church portal was designed by Alonso de Covarrubias and the altar, which dates from 1529, by Alonso Berruguete.

Other colleges of interest: The *Colegio de Calatrava* was built by Joaquín and Alberto Churriguera in 1717. The *Colegio de Carvajal* dates from 1662; the founder's tomb is in the attached church. The *Colegio de Huérfanos* dates from 1549 and has a Renaissance portal by Alberto Mora and a baroque cloister with two galleries. The *Antiguo Colegio Mayor de San Bartolomé* or *Colegio Anaya* was founded by Diego de Anaya in 1411 but the building we see today was built in 1760–8. It includes the *Colegio Mayor*, the *Hospedería* (now the Escuela Normal), which was built by Joaquín Churriguera in the 18C, and the chapel of *San Sebastian*, which was built in 1731 by Alberto Churriguera. The *Antiguo Colegio Menor de San Millán* has a fine 15C portal and the *Colegio San Ambrosio* has a Churrigueresque façade.

Other secular buildings:

The House of the Shells/Casa de las Conchas: Dr.Talavera Maldonado, a Knight of Santiago and counsellor to Queen Isabella, had this built in 1514. The façade is decorated with shells, coats-of-arms and beautiful windows; the courtyard has a fine two-storeyed arcade and a staircase with decorated columns, lions and a coffered ceiling.

Other interesting houses: The *Casa de Doña María la Brava* is 16C; the *Casa de las Muertes* (House of the Dead) was built

Salamanca, old cathedral, tomb

in 1515 by Pedro de Ibarra and has an interesting façade. Other houses include the *Casa de la Concordia; Casa de los Abrantes; Casa de los Doctores; Casa de los Garcigrande; Casa de los Rodríguez de Figueroa; Casa de los Rodríguez de Manzano; Casa de los Rodríguez de las Vavillas*, and the *Casa de los Solís.*

The Casa los Abarca Maldonado, which belonged to Queen Isabella's physician, Dr.Ferná Alvarez Abarca, was built at the end of the 15C and has a fine façade by Francisco de Colonia and a splendid wood-panelled ceiling in one room. It now houses the *Provincial Museum of Fine Art,* which has some prehistoric and Roman finds as well as a collection of paintings which includes works by Morales and Caravaggio.

The *Casa Rectoral* has a baroque portal and houses a *museum* with works by the writer Miguel de Unamuno.

Palaces: The 16C *Palacio Arias Corvelle*; the 15C *Palacio de las Cuatro Torres,* only one tower of which survives; the impressive 16C *Palacio de Monterrey*; the 16C *Palacio de Orellana.* The *Palacio de la Salina* or *de Fonseca,* which was built in 1519, possesses an impressive front and courtyard with a first-floor arcade on huge pedestals with carved figures (built by Gil de Hontañón). It now houses the provincial government. Also of interest is the 16C *Palacio de San Boal.*

Also worth seeing: There is a massive Roman bridge over the Río Tormes; some 1,300 ft. long it rests on 26 arches, of which 15 are original. It is known to have been rebuilt as early as the 2C. The *Torre del Aire* has Gothic arched windows and is situated on the Plaza del Claudillo. It is all that remains from the 15C palace of the Fermoselle family. The baroque *Torre del Clavero* is surrounded by eight smaller towers, and was built in the 15C by Francisco Sotomayor.

Environs: Almenara de Tormes: The route from Salamanca to Ledesma leads past this village, which has a 12C parish church with a fine Romanesque portal, whose capitals are decorated with figures playing musical instruments. **Palencia de Negrilla** is to the N. of Salamanca and has the parish church of *Santa Cruz,* which is Romanesque in origin but was rebuilt in the 16C by Gil de Hontañón, who added the fine S. portal. The *Capilla Mayor* is Mudéjar and has a 13C Christ. The high altar has a number of paintings and reliefs and was completed in 1559. **Villanueva de Cañedo** is further N. of Salamanca and has a 15C Gothic palace, which is in good condition, with coats-of-arms, turrets, balconies and a courtyard with arcades on two storeys.

Salardú
Lérida/Catalonia   p.390□M 2

Salardú is the capital of the upper Arántales, known as Cap d'Arán. It is famous for its fine situation and has a view over the whole valley. During its history the inhabitants have frequently had to fight for their independence against feudal lords.

Parish Church: It has a nave and two aisles, apses and a small bellcote and is surrounded by blind arcades. The *main portal* has four archivolts, of which only the outer one is decorated. The capitals are simply carved. Near the main apse there is an elegant window with both pointed and rounded arches. The slender *tower* has its own entrance, which bears the coat-of-arms of Aragón in wrought-iron. The *high altar* has the celebrated 13C *Christ of Salardú,* which ranks with the Christ of Mig Arán in Viella as one of the most impressive of Romanesque woodcarvings.

Environs: Uña/Unya, in the direction of

the Valle de Unyola: the *Church of Santa Eulalia de Uña* is a 12–13C basilica with a nave and two aisles and decorated apses. The interior contains a Romanesque font. **Arties** (5 km. W., towards Viella): This is the site of the restored 13C church of *San Juan*. The three apses are polygonal rather than round, which is unusual for the area. Gothic windows. The small *chapel near the Hostería* is 17C. The *parish church* is to be found in the upper part of the village, along with the ruins of a 14C *castle*. The 13C *church* is a basilica with a nave, two aisles and three decorated apses. As well as the bell tower, it has a slender 16C tower. The *portal* opens on the N. side and has five decorated archivolts. The interior has low tunnel vaulting and the pillars are at a marked angle. It contains a good 15C wooden *altarpiece* by the Master d'Ax, two

fine wooden Virgins (13&16C), a Gothic-Mudéjar pulpit from 1622 and a Romanesque altar and font. **Tredós** (on the route to Puerto de la Bonaigua): The *church of Nuestra Señora de Cap d'Arán* has a 12C crypt.

San Baudelio de Berlanga
Soria/Old Castile   p.388☐H 4

San Baudelio: The chapel is 11C in origin and has a most unusual Mozarabic ground plan with a rectangular nave and square choir. The door is also Mozarabic and has horseshoe arches. The interior is exceptional, having a central pillar from which eight horseshoe arches radiate in the form of a palm tree to support the vault-

Arties, parish church 1 main portal (N. side) **2** 16C bell tower **3** 15C altarpiece by the Master d'Ax

Salardú, church 1 main portal **2** Romanesque window **3** high altar with the 13C 'Christ of Salardú'

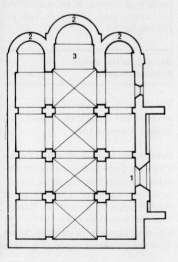

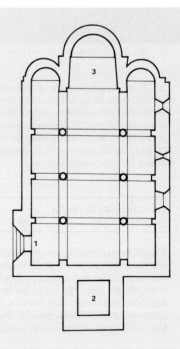

San Baudelio de Berlanga, central pillar

ing. There is a tribune running the entire width of the building on three small rows of columns with horseshoe arches. Most of the splendid 10–12C Romanesque wall paintings are in the Prado Museum in Madrid, the Museum of Fine Arts in Boston, or in private collections.

San Carlos de la Rápita
Tarragona/Catalonia   p.390□L 5

This picturesque fishing town is situated near the natural harbour at Los Alfaques, and was inhabited from antiquity through to the Middle Ages. The design and lay-out of the town visible today, however, is a clear example of 18C town planning. The large *main square*, which ends in a semi-

circle, is of interest, as are some of the buildings, such as the *Palacio del Gobernador*.

San Cugat del Vallés
Barcelona/Catalonia   p.390□N 4

Known to the Romans as Castrum Octavianum, and a small Visigoth basilica was recently dicovered here.

Benedictine Monastery of San Cugat: This dates from the 9C, and the remains of some cloisters from this period have recently been discovered. The cloisters and the three apses we see today are Romanesque, but everything else is Gothic. The 13C apses have delicate columns and are decorated with blind arcades. The lower part of the bell tower appears to have Romanesque elements, but the rest is 16C. The *façade* has a large portal and a fine 14C rose-window. The interior has a nave, two aisles, pointed arches supported by pillars and an octagonal ciborium. The *cloisters* are a fine example of 12–13C Catalan art; a number of sculptors worked on the *capitals*, one of whom — the monk Arnau Gatell — has left his signature. The monastery's *chapterhouse* has a *retable* by Pere Serra dating from *c.* 1375, which is a masterpiece of Catalan-Gothic painting.

Environs: Barbará del Vallés: The most interesting features of the 12C Romanesque church of *Santa María del Barbará* are the original *frescos*, which survived the fire of 1936. The main apse contains Christ Pantocrator, symbols of the Evangelists and tetramorphs. The side apses show St.Peter, St.Paul and the Holy Cross. The frescos demonstrate the narrative quality of Gothic painting.

San Esteban de Gormaz
Soria/Old Castile   p.388☐G 4

This is a very old fortified town with Roman inscriptions on the town walls and on the arch of an entrance gateway.

Nuestra Señora del Rivero: This 12C church has a portico with arches. The nave was rebuilt in Herrera style with pointed vaulting. The sanctuary is tunnel-vaulted. The church also contains a Renaissance burial niche with an inscription of an earlier date; the vault has 13C paintings.

San Miguel: This too is a Romanesque church with a single aisle, barrel vaulting and an apse. The splendid arched portico on the S. side dates from 1081.

Also worth seeing: The *main square* with

fine arcades, and the 17C *Town Hall.* The church of *San Esteban* has a 17C retable and a 14C cross. There is a medieval *bridge* over the Duero which has 16 arches and is 535 ft. long. A Moorish *castle* sits on a hill and dominates the town.

Environs: Near **Montejo de Tiermes** (*c.* 25 km. S.) are the *ruins of Termancia*, which contain elements from three separate cultures and periods, namely the Arevacos, the Celts and the Romans. Gateways, pathways cut out of the rock and rock-dwellings have been found side by side with Roman galleries, water-pipes and mosaic floors. During the Middle Ages this was the site of the Monastery of *Santa María de Termes*, the chapel of which is still standing. It has a single aisle, an apse, a portico and a portal with three archivolts. **Berzosa** (*c.* 6 km. N.): The Romanesque church has a portico with seven arches and a highly decorated portal. **Rejas de San Esteban** (*c.* 15 km. W.): The Romanesque churches of *San Martín* and *San Ginés* have porticoes and portals with archivolts.

San Felíu de Guixols
Gerona/Catalonia   p.390☐O 3

Monastery of San Felíu: This is referred to as early as 968; all that survives today is a *porch* known as the 'Porta Ferrada', which has three arches, simple Romanesque windows and blind arcades on the upper floor. The *parish church* is 14C.

Environs: S'Agaró (2 km. N. along the coast road): One of Catalonia's finest summer resorts and the venue of an international summer music festival. **Caldas de Malavella** (19 km. inland on Route 253): A spa known to the Romans as Aquae Vocontis. Prehistoric and Roman remains have been found on the Puig de las Ánimas and also the Puig de San Grau, which was

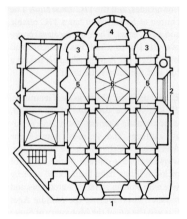

Sangüesa, Santa María la Real 1 portal 2 S. portal (richly carved) 3 side apse and 4 main apse, both with round-arched windows 5 transept (Gothic) 6 crossing with dome on squinches and octagonal tower over crossing

the site of a castle. There are ruins of another Romanesque castle near the hermitage of San Mauricio. The parish church of *San Esteban* is attached to the monastery of Breda and has three apses.

Sangüesa

Navarra/Navarra   p.388☐I 2

This city on the banks of the Río Aragón was at its zenith in the Middle Ages.

Santa María la Real: Begun in the 12C, it was consecrated upon completion in the 13C. A document dating from 1131 reveals that King Alfonso I, el Batallador, made his palace and the adjoining church of Santa María over to the Order of St.John. The chuch is transitional in style between Romanesque and Gothic and has a nave, two aisles and a transept in Cistercian style. The three *main apses* are from the first phase of building and have round arched

windows, columns and capitals. One of the more interesting capitals depicts the Flight into Egypt. The *S. portal* is interesting and is the work of two artists, one of whom was definitely Fransoze Leodegarius. The columns and carvings in the arches are his. The arrangement of this section is not unlike Chartres; the four arches of the portal rest on three columns on each side, and are decorated with figures of the saints. The tympanum also has some of Leodegarius's work. The second artist, who seems to be the master who built the Monastery of San Juan de la Peña, was responsible for the double row of *blind arcades*. Carvings on the archivolts seem to fall into groups: biblical figures on one side; craftsmen—cobblers, butchers and blacksmiths—on the other. There is a Last Judgement in the tympanum and the blind arcades are crowned by Christ in Glory and the symbols of the Evangelists. These scenes accompany statues of the Apostles. The spandrels and the sides of the portal are covered with a number of reliefs, including a depiction of the Norse *Sigurd's Saga* (on the right), the presence of which must be attributed to pilgrims travelling to Santiago de Compostela. Sigurd killed Fafner, the hero who had the dragon Regin as his mount. The *interior* has Romanesque capitals in the nave. The Gothic *transept* is surmounted by a large dome, which is supported by 13C squinches. The altarpiece of the *high altar* dates from 1554 and has sculptures by Jorge de Flandes. There is a 14C statue of the Virgin of Rocamador in one of the niches. The *tower* is octagonal and undecorated.

San Francisco: The most interesting part of this church is the 14C Gothic cloister.

San Salvador: The *portal* of this 14C Gothic church is decorated with scenes of

Sangüesa, Santa María, portal ▷

the Last Judgement and the Resurrection of the Dead. The interior contains a fine altarpiece of St.George and St.Damián, a 15C work by Juan de Berrueta.

Santiago: This is a 12C Romanesque church with a nave, two aisles and an impressive *portal* whose tympanum is decorated with a 13C figure of the Apostle St. James the Great.

Palacio de Valle-Sontoro: A splendid palace with an interesting baroque façade, whose entrance is flanked by columns and decorated with coats-of-arms; there is also a beautiful courtyard.

Ayuntamiento/Town Hall (Calle Mayor): Housed in a 12C building, which was built on the site of one of the wings of the palace of the Princes of Viana. It was rebuilt in the 14C.

Hospital: The hospital is housed in a 14C building, which includes cloisters and an interesting chapel of the same date.

Palacio del Duque de Granada (Calle Mayor): This 15C building was the Prince's palace and was also known as the Palace of the Counts of Guaqui and Guendalain. The façade has double windows and fine sculptures.

Palacio de Añues: Another secular building with interesting architectural features. It was once the residence of St.·Francis Xavier.

Environs: About 1 km. from Sangüesa along the route to Sos del Rey Católico, is the *church of San Adrián*. Today it is part of a farmstead and used for agricultural purposes. Sangüesa's oldest building, it is a single-aisled and has interesting consoles at the edge of the roof. The portal has three arches, the last of which is supported by rods. Capitals of the columns are decorated

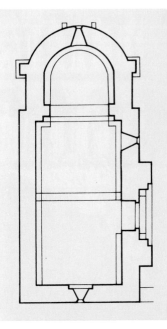

Church of San Adrián the Gothic portal is the most interesting feature of this old single-aisled church, whose ruins are now part of a farmstead

with plant and animal motifs. The tympanum has a Chi-Rho monogram above the middle of the entrance.

San Jorge
Huesca/Aragón   p.388☐K

Pilgrimage Church: There seems to have been a church here even before 1554 the year in which the sanctuary was built. It stands on the site of the Battle of Alcoraz, which was fought against the Moors in 1096. The church's architect was Domingo Almanzar. The site affords a fine view over the town.

San Juan de la Peña, cloister

San Juan de la Peña
Huesca/Aragón   p.388□K 3

Monastery: This Benedictine monastery is situated in the middle of a forest, beneath some overhanging, red cliffs. It is referred to as early as the 9C, and was for a long time the poltical centre of Aragon: it was here that the Reconquista was engineered. Several hundreds of towns paid taxes to the monastery and the kings of Aragon and Navarre were buried here. The monastery is not as large as might be expected. The *front courtyard* leads into the single-aisled *upper church* (consecrated in 1094). It is interesting to note that the three apses are partly carved into the cliff-side. Nearby is the best-preserved *Romanesque pantheon* in Spain, which contains the tombs of noble-men from the 11–14C. The Pantheon of Kings was restored under Charles III in the 18C. It contains 27 sarcophagi, including those of Ramiro I and Sancho Ramírez. Doña Jimena, wife of El Cid (see Burgos, may be buried here according to old sources. The 12C cloisters, for which the cliff provides a natural roof, can be reached past a late Gothic chapel and a Mozarabic horseshoe arch. The capitals of the columns depict Biblical scenes, along with animal and plant motifs, all the work of a local artist. The *lower church* is 10–11C and has two apses and the remains of some wall paintings. Adjoining this is the *chapter-house* of the old monastery. The *Capilla de San Voto* is 16C; the chapel dedicated to St. Victoria is 15C. The monastery was transferred to a new building in the 18C and this was itself destroyed by French

San Juan de la Peña, cloister, capital

San Juan de la Peña, pantheon

troops in 1809. The baroque façade and the two towers of the church, which was designed by Pedro Onofre, survived the blaze.

San Juan de las Abadesas
Gerona/Catalonia   p.390 □ N 3

Monastery: Founded by the Benedictines in 889. However, the building visible today dates from the 11C, when the monastery was taken over by the Augustinians. The *church* was consecrated in 1050 and has a groundplan in the form of a Greek cross and three apses. Some French influence is apparent in the main apse, which has three small, radiating apsidal chapels. There are two other chapels in the transept. The *pillars* have fine archaic carvings on the capitals. The church was seriously damaged in the Civil War, after which it was rebuilt. Parts of the Romanesque *cloisters* have survived but they were replaced by the 15C Gothic *Claustro Mayor*. The church contains a 12C tomb and a remarkable Descent from the Cross from 1250, which is known as the 'Misterio de San Juan de las Abadesas'. (The missing thief on the cross was burnt in 1936.) The 13C *abbot's house* has a small cloister. All that survives of the *church of San Pablo* is a Romanesque *portal* with a fine tympanum.

San Lorenzo del Escorial
Madrid/New Castile   p.392 □ F 5

El Escorial: The history of this town has always been connected with the 'Monasterio de San Lorenzo del Escorial', which was built under Philip II in thanks

El Escorial, Charles V and family ▷

for his victory over the French at St. Quentin in 1557. It was dedicated to St. Lawrence as the battle was won on his festival. In 1563 the commission was given to Juan Bautista de Toledo, who had worked under Michelangelo in Rome; after his death work continued under Juan de Herrera and the building was completed in 1584. The complex is built in a powerful, direct Renaissance style on a rectangular groundplan with four corner towers crowned by spires. The projecting central section of the E. façade contains the church's apse and the royal residence. The two bell towers and the high dome are a distinctive feature of the complex. Altogether it comprises 16 courtyards, 12 cloisters, 86 staircases, over 2,000 windows, 88 fountains and 13 chapels and oratories. The Escorial serves as church, monastery, palace, mausoleum, library and museum. It is constructed out of granite blocks from the nearby mountain range, the Sierra de Guadarrama.

Main façade: This is an imposing, un-

San Lorenzo del Escorial **1** Puerta Principal (main entrance) **2** Patio de los Reyes (Court of the Kings) **3** basilica **4** Panteón de los Reyes (Royal Pantheon) **5** sacristy **6** Patio de los Evangelistas (Court of the Evangelists) **7** Salas Capitulares (chapterhouse) **8** Escalera Principal (main staircase) **9** library **10** Palacio Real (royal palace) **11** museum

adorned granite front, 680 ft. long and 528 ft. wide, harmoniously articulated by pilasters. The only decorations are a statue of St.Lawrence by Juan Bautista Monegro and the Habsburg coat-of-arms.

Patio de los Reyes (Courtyard of the Kings): The main portal opens into this courtyard, on the other side of which stands the church. It is famous for the statues of the six Old Testament kings which grace the church façade.

Basilica: The church, on the E. side of the courtyard, has a Greek cross ground plan. The whole building is supported by four massive piers; there is a 295 ft. high *dome* over the four main arches. The apse, with its altarpiece, is the most highly deco-

San Lorenzo del Escorial

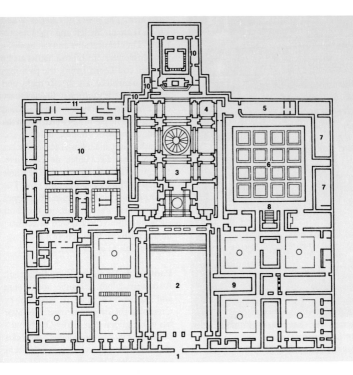

rated area. The *tombs* of Charles V and Philip II are on the left and right respectively. The classical altar and tombs are by Juan de Herrera, the bronze statues are by Pompeo and Leone Leoni, the paintings in the altarpiece are by Zuccaro and Tibaldi, and the vaulting in the sanctuary and coro was painted by Cambiaso and Giordano. The paintings which adorn the 43 side altars are by a number of Italian and Spanish artists, including Alfonso Sánchez Coello, Juan Fernández de Navarrete, Pellegrino, Tibaldi, Urbino etc. The whole church can be viewed from the *coro*. The ceiling painting is by Giordano, the frescos by Cambiaso and Cincinnato; the choir stalls are by José Flecha, who based them on designs by Herrera. There is a fine crucifix by Cellini at the back.

Panteón de los Reyes (Royal Pantheon): An octagonal domed chamber with bronze and marble decorations. It was built by Crescenzi, the Italian architect. The altar has a fine gilded crucifix by Guidi and a candlestick by Master Fanelli. The bodies of most of the Spanish kings and queens since Charles I lie here.

Panteón de los Infantes: Dating from the 19C, it is a burial chamber for princes and princesses who never reached the throne. The monument of Don Juan of Austria with a recumbent figure, by Ponzano, is especially interesting.

Sacristía: The next room is the *Antesacristía* (ante-room to the sacristy), a square room with vaulting frescoed by Castello and Granele; the sacristy itself is similarly frescoed. It also contains some 42 fine paintings, including: Ribera's 'Descent from the Cross', El Greco's 'St.Paul' and 'St.Eugene', Titian's 'Christ on the Cross'

San Lorenzo del Escorial, sacristy, Claudio Coello, 'The Holy Sacrament'

San Lorenzo del Escorial, basilica

San Lorenzo del Escorial, Philip II and ▷ family

and 'Christ on the Mount of Olives', and works by Zurbarán and others. The chapel at the end of the sacristy contains the celebrated 'Sagrada Forma' altarpiece by Claudio Coello.

Monastery and Patio de los Evangelistas (Court of the Evangelists): This is a large cloister which formed the centre of monastery life. It was built by Juan Bautista de Toledo under Philip II, and is Renaissance in style, with Doric and Ionic columns. Juan de Herrera added *fountains* in the centre and there is a temple with figures of the four Evangelists by Monegro. The lower walk of the cloisters has some fine frescos of scenes from the New Testament by Tibaldi.

Salas Capitulares (chapter rooms): These are where the monks used to meet. The Pompeian-style ceiling was painted by a number of artists including Granello, Castello and Urbino. The rooms contain biblical scenes by a number of artists including Navarrete, Ribera (the Nativity of Christ), Zuccaro, Carducho and Luca Giordano. The *Escalera Principal* (main staircase) is by Bergamasco, and on the vault is the Battle of St.Quentin by Giordano. There are expressive portraits of the architects Juan Bautista de Toledo, Juan de Herrera and Fray Antonio de Villacastín, and of the kings from Charles I to Charles II. The *Iglesia Antigua* contains Titian's Martrydom of St. Lawrence. One of the largest rooms houses the *library*; it has frescos by Peregrino, Bartolomeo Carducci, Tibaldi and Granello, and portraits including 'Philip II' by Pantoja de la Cruz, 'Charles II' by Carreño, and 'Herrera' and 'Pater Sigüenza' (the first librarian) by Coello. The simple lines of the wooden bookshelves are by Herrera. There are valuable collections of 10–11C *manuscripts*, such as 'Songs of Alfonso X, the Wise', missals which belonged to Charles V and his wife Isabella, Philip II, Philip III and a very old manuscript of the Bible in Hebrew. There are also a number of old Moorish manuscripts.

Palacio Real (Royal Palace): This palace was commissioned by the Bourbons Charles III and IV towards the end of the 18C. It opens with the highly decorated rococo 'Bourbon Room', with fine *tapestries* and paintings by artists such as Francisco and Ramón Bayeu, Maella, Castillo, Velázquez and Goya. The *staircase* by Villanueva is especially worthy of attention. The *Hall of Battles* has fine frescos of battles by Granello and Fabricio Castello, e.g. the Battle of Pavia, the Siege of St.Quentin and the naval battle of Lepanto in 1571. A steeply angled staircase leads up to the *Palace of Philip II*, which is furnished with 16C pieces and has paintings by Titian and Bosch. The *Throne Room* has various paintings and relics.

The *museum* is housed in Philip II's sum-

San Lorenzo del Escorial, courtyard

San Lorenzo del Escorial, library ▷

mer rooms and, since 1963, has contained a large collection of paintings. Works from the Flemish and German schools include paintings by Roger van der Weyden, Patinir, Hieronymus Bosch, Dürer and David; the Italians include Titian, Tintoretto, Veronese, Bassano and Reni; and the Spanish artists include Velázquez, Ribera, Valdés Leal, Mazo, Carreño and El Greco.

Casita del Principe (Prince's Pavilion): This is a small, two-storeyed T-shaped building situated in the middle of the park. It was built by Villanueva in classical style in 1772 by order of Charles III for his son and heir Charles IV. The ceilings are painted by Duque, Gómez, Gerroni, Maella, López and others, and the interior contains some 19 rooms with paintings by Caravaggio, Luca Giordano, Ribera and Domenichino, and panels by Altdorfer, Dürer and Goya. There is an interesting Buen Retiro porcelain collection.

Silla of Philip II: This 'chair', some 3 km. away from the palace, is carved out of a cliff and was the vantage point from which the king supervised the building.

Environs: Valle de los Caídos ('Valley of the Fallen', 13 km. N. of San Lorenzo del Escorial in the Sierra de Guadarrama): This is a memorial for those who died in the Civil War of 1936-9; it was built by Pedro Muguruza and Diego Méndez in 1948-58. José Antonio Primo de Rivera, the founder of the Falange, and General Franco are buried here. It consists of a *basilica*, the Basílica de Santa Cruz, which is cut out of the cliff face. The interior contains large *tapestries* depicting the Apocalypse of St.John. These were made in 1540 in Pannemaker's workshop in Brussels from threads of gold, silver, silk and wool and they were acquired by Philip II in 1553. The *dome* is 138 ft. high and has mosaics by Santiago Padrós. The *monument to those fallen in the Civil War* is in the transept. There is a cross (492 ft. high) on the hill and black limestone statues of the four Evangelists by Avalos at the cross's base.

San Martín de Valdeiglesias
Madrid/New Castile   p.392☐F 6

The village has a few very old buildings, such as the 'casa de las dos Puertas' and 'casa de la Santa', where St.Theresa of Ávila once stayed.

San Martín: A 16C parish church of which probably only a third is by Juan de Herrera; the tower is more recent. There is a splendid dome over the crossing, which spans the nave and the two aisles. The altarpiece on the high altar is baroque.

Castillo de Coracera: This castle was founded by Alvaro de Luna in the 15C; the outside walls form a rectangle, with round towers at the corners and a large central keep.

Environs: Cadalso de los Vidrios (S. of San Martín de Valdeiglesias): There are a number of fine old houses still standing; the finest the 'casa de Austria', has a Plateresque façade. The parish church, the *Iglesia de la Asunción*, was begun in 1498 but not completed until the 16C; it has highly complex cross vaulting. The *Palacio de Villena* belonged to Don Alvaro de Luna, who built the fortified castle (with corner towers). It was totally rebuilt in Italian style in the 15C, as can be seen from the arcades and other classical elements. **Chapinería** (*c.* 20 km. E.): The parish church of *La Purísima Concepción* was built in the 16C along the lines of the Escorial. The 16C *Palace of the Marquis de Villanueva de la Sagra* is built of ashlars and has a large courtyard with columns

San Millán de la Cogolla, Suso monastery

and a marble fountain in the centre. The **Villa del Prado** (*c.* 15 km. SE): The parish church of *Santiago Apóstol* is an important 15C building with two towers, one is 16C and has a slate spire. The interior has a single aisle and Gothic vaulting. There are various baroque altarpieces comprising sculptures and paintings.

San Martín Sarroca
Barcelona/Catalonia   p.390□M 4

Church: A 12C building which is unusually highly decorated for a Catalan-Romanesque church of the period; the exterior of the *apse* has seven columns with carved capitals and round arches. The *interior* has seven double arches on columns,

which are in turn decorated with thinner columns and ornamental capitals. The retable to the right of the altar is a 15C piece by Jaime Cabrera.

San Millán de la Cogolla
Logroño/Old Castile   p.388□H 3

The history of this village is intimately connected with the life of St. Millán, a shepherd who devoted his life to solitary prayer and penance in the countryside. He lived in a cave which became a focus for people who sought his help and advice. He died here in 574. Legend has it that he appeared to the Christians on a white horse to help them in their struggle against the Moors.

Monastery of Suso: This monastery contained the saint's tomb and was a place of pilgrimage throughout the Middle Ages. The oldest parts have kept their simplicity of design; the exterior has eaves with old Mozarabic rafters. The church was consecrated in 984. The forecourt contains the tombs of the seven Infantes of Lara, their tutors and three queens of Navarre. The portico opens into the church through a door with horseshoe arches. The interior is most unusual; the nave is built directly into the cliff behind and connected with it by caves, some of which serve as chapels. One of these caves contained St. Millán's tomb until it was transferred to the monastery of Yuso in 1053. There is now a recumbent Romanesque figure of the saint in its place. The splendid retable has Gothic paintings and is supported on pedestals. It depicts scenes from the saint's life (taken from a 13C text by Gonzalo de Berceo).

Monastery of Yuso: This monastery, also known as the 'Escorial de Rioja', was built in Romanesque style under King García Sánchez of Navarre in 1053 and rebuilt in Herrera style in the 16–18C. The entrance courtyard was closed off by stone walls with pyramids. The portal, with baroque reliefs of St. Millán on a horse, is surrounded by slender Corinthian columns. The interior has many interesting features. The *Salon de los Reyes* (Hall of the Kings) has some remarkable paintings by Fr. Juan Rizi. The *Claustro de San Augustín* has a neoclassical staircase with alabaster bannisters; the *Claustro de San Millán* by Andrea Rodi (1572) has 25 paintings by José Bexés from 1778–81. The *library* has valuable manuscripts and rare early printed books; the *archive* has over 400 parchments, codices and hymn-books illuminated with miniatures. The *church* was built by Tomás Rodi and has a nave and two aisles; the altarpiece on the high altar has eight paintings by Juan Rizi. The *sacristy* (1565) contains the tombs of St. Millán and St. Felice, which are decorated with magnificent 11C ivory-work. The *coro* has a desk, a grille and an organ; and the *lower*

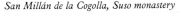

San Millán de la Cogolla, Suso monastery   *San Millán de la Cogolla, Suso monastery*

or *processional cloister* is in transitional Romanesque-Gothic style with highly decorated vaulting and a splendid Plateresque door which leads through to the church.

Environs: Ledesma de la Cogolla (*c.* 15 km. E.) has a single-aisled Romanesque church; **Valvanera** (*c.* 10 km. S.) has a 15C Gothic church which belongs to a Benedictine monastery and contains a 12C Romanesque painting of a seated Madonna and Child.

San Sebastián
Guipúzcoa / Basque Provinces   p.388☐ 1

This town is more than a thousand years old. It was known to the Basques as Donosti and its ancient name was Izurun. It is the capital of the province of Guipúzcoa and is also a bishop's seat. There was a hermitage on this site around 900 and this was part of the monastery of Leyre. However, the first mention of the town is in the writings of King Sancho el Mayor in 1014. Special rights were granted to it in about 1200 by Alfonso VIII of Castile but it was ravaged by a succession of fires in the 13&14C. Documents state that King Pedro removed its rights in 1366, so that he could collect a fishing tax. It was besieged by French troops in 1476 and 1512, and in 1622 Emperor Charles V gave it the title 'loyal and good' as a tribute to its spirited resistance. It regained its civic rights in 1662. The main source of income was traditionally fishing; its sailors had reached as far as Newfoundland and it had trading links with England and France. The mild climate and attractive location, on the finest Atlantic bay in northern Spain and surrounded by Mounts Igueldo, Ulía and Urgull have made it one of Europe's most popular holiday resorts. For these reasons San Sebastián became the royal summer residence in the middle of the 19C and Spain was ruled from here during the summer months.

Cathedral of the Good Shepherd: This

San Sebastián, Ayuntamiento

neo-Gothic building was erected by Manuel de Echave 1880–97. It has a nave, two aisles and a 246 ft. high bell tower which affords a splendid view over the town.

Church of Santa María (Calle Mayor): This is one of the city's oldest churches; it is baroque and was built 1743–64 by the architects Pedro Ignacio de Lizardi, Miguel de Salazar and Francisco de Ibero. The *rococo portal* in the Churrigueresque *façade* is flanked by two towers. The church itself has a nave and two aisles and its points of interest include a *gallery* named after St. Martha, which has a vaulted ceiling and a star-shaped skylight; an 18C *baroque altar* by Diego Villanueva and Ventura Rodríguez; and a *high altar* with fine paintings by Roberto Michel. The figure on the altar of St.Peter is by the sculptor Arizmendi, and the image of St. Catherine is by Juan Pascual de Mena.

San Vicente (Calle de Narrica): This is a 16C Gothic church with a nave and two aisles; it dates from 1570 and has a Churrigueresque *portal*. The Renaissance gilded wooden altar (1584) was the work of Antonio Bengoechea and Juan de Iriarte. Another Renaisance altar in the left aisle has a relief of the Holy Family by Felipe de Arizmendi.

Museo de San Telmo: This is housed in a former monastery, which was built (1531–51) to a design by the monk Martín de Santiago. It was founded by Alonso de Idiáquez, secretary to Emperor Charles V, and Doña Gracia de Olazábal and is in transitional Gothic-Renaissance style. There is an interesting *cloister* (in the Renaissance style of Herrera), which is now a protected monument. The original chapel is now the *aula*; it has Gothic vaulting supported by sturdy columns and *frescos* of the history of the Basque people by the Catalan painter José María Sert in black, red and gold. 16C *sarcophagi* with recumbent alabaster statues contain the remains of the monastery's two founders and are to be found at the entrance to the chapel. The monastery houses the *Basque Museum of the Province of Guipúzcoa*. This contains historical and *ethnographical* collections and includes old Basque agricultural implements, spinning wheels and looms, fishing tackle, Basque domestic furnishings and Basque women's headgear from the 15–17C. Near the extensive *library*, San Telmo houses a collection of *paintings* from a wide range of periods, including the work of El Greco (a Christ), Tintoretto, Goya, Beruete, Carducho, Carreño, Cerezo, Esquivel, Escalante, Lucas Jordán, Haes, Federico Madrazo, Santiago Morán, Sánchez Coello, Mayno, Regoyos, Rosales, Sorolla, Zubiaurre and Zuloaga. There is also a 'Venus and Cupid' sculpted by José Ginés (1768–1823). The collection of Basque graves and discoidal stele, as well as that of sculptures (which includes some 14C pieces), is also of especial archaeological interest. The sword of Boabdil, the last Moorish king, is among the other interesting exhibits.

Castillo de la Mota or **El Macho:** A 16C castle which dominates the town from Monte Urgull. The origins of the fortress go back to the time of the Norman raids on this part of the Spanish coast. The castle houses the *Museum of Military History*, which displays weapons from slings to the fire-arms of the late Middle Ages. The *Chapel of the Heart of Jesus* (1950) is crowned by a 40 ft. tall statue of Christ.

Ayuntamiento/Town Hall: This impressive building, which once housed the town's casino, was built by Adolfo Morales de los Ríos and Luis Aladrén.

Also worth seeing: The churches of *San Sebastián el Antiguo* and *San Ignacio* were built by the architect José Goicoa 1888–97. The *Plaza del 18 de Julio* was for-

San Sebastian, Provincial Diputación

merly a *bullring*. The square is surrounded by arcades and on one side has the *Town Hall*, which was built 1828–32 in classical style by Silvestre Pérez. To the side of the great staircase are paintings by Antonio Brugada of the sea battles of Admiral Oquendo, who was born in San Sebastián. The large reception room of the old Town Hall served as a throne room for the Spanish kings. Buildings in the *Plaza de Guipúzcoa* form an interesting group; the provincial *Diputación* was built by José Goicoa and Luis Aladrén 1883–5. The façade has busts of notable people from the province of Guipúzcoa. *Inside* there are paintings by Zuloaga and Salaverría, as well as tapestries (the battle of Cartagena and the discovery of Newfoundland) by Juan de Echaide. The square also has *tall houses* with arcades. In the middle of the

square there is a romantic little *park*, which was laid out to plans by Escoriaza in the 19C. A statue by Llimona of the local composer, José María Usandizaga, was erected in the park. The *Palacio Miramar* (Paseo de la Concha) is the former summer residence of the Spanish royal family. The palace dates from the time of Queen María Christina in the 19C, when Spain was ruled from San Sebastián in the summer. The Spanish royal family's current palace, the *Palacio de Ayete*, stands on higher ground in a park. Near the fishing harbour lies the *Parte Vieja*, or Old Town with narrow alleys, countless bars and good restaurants where the locals relax in the evenings. At the end of the harbour is the *Palacio del Mar*, which currently houses the Museum of Oceanography and a well-stocked aquarium.

Santa Coloma de Farnés
Gerona/Catalonia   p.390☐N 3

Farnés Fortress: The ruins of the 12C fortress stand on a very steep hill, which emphasizes its romantic appearance. Parts of the corner towers and the foundations of two other towers remain. Inside the fortress there is a battlemented keep.

Environs: Monastery of San Pedro Cercada (9 km. S.): 13C of fortress-like appearance; it has survived in good condition. Romanesque church. **Hostalrich** (24 km. S., on Road 253): The town occupies a strategic site and was fortified with walls and round towers. The walls were later partly converted into houses. On a hill to the S. are remains of the fortress of Hostalrich to which reference was made as early as the 12C.

Santa Coloma de Queralt
Tarragona/Catalonia   p.390☐M 4

This town owes its name to the Counts of Queralt, who had the castle built in the Middle Ages.

Santa María: A 14C Gothic church with Romanesque elements. It is single-aisled with chapels in the apse. *Inside* there is a fine *stone retable* of St.Lawrence by Jordi de Deu (1386). The church treasury contains several silver pieces, including a 14C processional cross.

Environs: Very near the town is the Romanesque church of *Santa María de Bell-Lloch,* which originally belonged to a monastery. The portal has five archivolts framed by a cornice (12C or 13C); in the tympanum there is an Adoration of the Magi. The single-aisled *interior* has a transept and houses the alabaster tombs of the Counts of Queralt, by Pedro Aguilar (1370).

Santa Cruz de la Serós
Huesca/Aragon   p.388☐K 2/3

Iglesia de San Caprasio: The Romanesque parish church (early-11C) near the monastery has an interesting façade with a blind arcade.

Monastery: The full name of this monastery was originally the *Monasterio de Santa María de las Sorores de Santa Cruz.* It is now known as *Santa Cruz de la Serós.* Sancho Garcés II of Navarre founded the monastery in 992 together with his wife Doña Urraca. Only the 11C church has survived. It has a nave, two aisles and transept on a Latin cross ground plan; semicircular apse. It is reminiscent of the cathedral in Jaca. The transept vault is supported by squinches. The church was rebuilt in the 12C. The *portal* dates from 1095 and has a Chi-Rho monogram flanked by two fabulous beasts in the tympanum. *Inside* there are beautiful capitals and an interesting holy-water stoup. The altarpiece on the high altar is 15C and has an alabaster Madonna and Child.

Santa Cruz de Mudela
Ciudad Real/New Castile   p.392☐G 8

Chapel of Nuestra Señora de las Virtudes: Begun in the 14C, the chapel has a few additions from later centuries. The Mudéjar roof has beautifully carved beams. The chapel is located right next to an ancient bullring, which is square and thought to be even older than the one in Ronda.

Environs: Viso del Marqués (22 km.

SW): The site of the *Castle of Santa Cruz,* a Renaissance building with vault *frescos* by Italian painters. It now houses the *National Archive of the Spanish Navy.*

Santa María de Concilio
Huesca/Aragon   p.388 □ K 3

Hermitage of Santa María de Concilio: In the village of Riglos, S. of the 'Mallos de Riglos' mountains. It dates from the 12C and has beautiful Romanesque wall paintings.

Santa María de Huerta
Soria/Old Castile   p.388 □ H/I 4

Santa María de Huerta: Surrounded by walls, the fortress-like monastery is one of the most beautiful in Spain. It was founded in 1162 by Alfonso VII. The church was begun in 1179. Abbot San Martin de Hinojosa (d. 1220) and his nephew Rodrigo Ximénez de Rada, Archbishop of Toledo, turned the building into one of the finest examples of Cistercian architecture. The original austere style of the outer walls with their arched buttresses is still visible. From the courtyard you can see the façade of the church, which has five archivolts and a rose-window. The church has a nave and two aisles and contains the tomb of Rodrigo Ximénez de Rada (with a recumbent figure). The *main chapel* has a large baroque retable of 1766. On the walls of the *sanctuary* there are frescos depicting events from the battle of Las Navas de Tolosa. The mid-16C walnut *choir stalls* are Plateresque in style. Next to the church is the *sacristy* (originally the chapterhouse). Behind the sacristy is a *funerary chapel,* which in earlier times was probably used as a library. The richly decorated 16C Gothic *cloister* contains a 13C sculpture of the Madonna and Child. The *refectory* of 1215 is very beautiful; this large room has a sexpartite vault, a large rose-window, six other windows and a lectern with a very

Santa Cruz de la Serós, monastery

beautiful staircase. The monastery grounds are very large and encompass other buildings, such as cellars and store houses, as well as extensive gardens and fields.

Santa María del Pueyo
Huesca/Aragon   p.388□L 3

Pilgrimage church: This 14C church was rebuilt in the 17C; a few minor Gothic traces remain. A much venerated 13C Romanesque Madonna stands in a niche, which has fine paintings by Francisco Bayeu, brother-in-law of the more famous Francisco Goya.

Santa María la Real de Nieva
Segovia/Old Castile   p.392□F 5

Parish church: The old Dominican monastery, to which the church belonged, was founded in 1393 by Don Enrique III and

Santander, cathedral, portal

his wife, Catherine of Lancaster. Building finished in 1432. The Gothic church, with a nave and two aisles, has a very beautiful main portal and a fine altarpiece in the main chapel. The church also contains a very beautiful gilded Renaissance altarpiece, painted by Antonio Vázquez in 1541, which is adorned with sculptures. Of particular interest is the 15&16C cloister, with its Romanesque and Gothic arches.

Environs: About 17 km. NE lies **Carbonero el Mayor,** with the parish church of *San Juan Bautista,* one of the most beautiful churches in the whole province. Gothic in style, its transept and the main chapel were rebuilt in the 17C. It has a lovely altarpiece of 1554 by Baltasar Grande and Diego Rosales. Another altarpiece is baroque and has a 14C Gothic cross. **Martín Muñoz de las Posadas** (*c.* 25 km. SW): Single-aisled Gothic *parish church* from the 16C with one portal from the 13C, one from the 15C and another in Renaissance style from the 16C. The altarpiece, made by the sculptor Antonio Martín and the painters Alonso and Pedro Herrera in 1584, has reliefs with scenes from the lives of Christ and the Virgin. The finest work of art in the church is the tomb of Cardinal Espinosa de los Monteros, which is adorned with a statue kneeling in prayer and was made of marble and alabaster by the sculptor Pompeyo Leoni 1577–82. The church also has a painting by El Greco. The *Palace of Don Diego de Espinosa* was completed in 1572 to plans by Juan Bautista de Toledo and is one of the best of its period. The façade has Doric towers and the escutcheon of the Cardinal. **Montuenga** (*c.* 20 km. W.): The church of *San Miguel* has a very unusual round aisle. **Paradiñas** (*c.* 7 km. S.): The *parish church* is single-aisled with groin vaulting; inside there are several baroque altarpieces, a 13C figure of the Virgin, a 16C silver reliquary and a Romanesque mosaic of marble and jasper with geometrical decoration.

Santander
Santander/Old Castile   p.388☐ G 1

This ancient town is referred to as *Puerto de San Emeterio* in a document relating to Sancho II from 1068. It was later extended as a fortress and in modern times it has developed into a trade and shipping centre. It was severely damaged by the explosion on board the 'Cabo Machichaco' in 1893 and a terrible fire destroyed most of the old town in 1941. It was rebuilt on modern lines and Santander now gives the impression of a lively, up-to-date town.

Cathedral: Originally built as the church of the abbey of San Emeterio in 791, it became a collegiate church in 1131 and a cathedral in 1752. In the last years of the 12C a Romanesque-Gothic crypt was built; this has three aisles and a nave with polygonal chapels. In the 17C the cathedral, with a nave, two aisles and groin vaulting, was built above the crypt, which had not been destroyed in the fire. Inside is the tomb of the writer Menéndez y Pelayo, made by Victorio Macho in 1956.

Museums: The *Fine Arts Museum* (in the Calle Rubio) has a collection of paintings from the 17–20C and includes work by Orrente, Zurbarán, Valdés Leal, Goya, as well as many more recent works by local artists. The *Museum of Prehistory* (in the provincial government building) has a large collection of finds from the province, such as a palaeolithic staff and the 'Venus del Pendo'.

Also worth seeing: The *Biblioteca Menéndez y Pelayo* (Calle Rubio), founded by the writer; it has an attractive façade—the statue of the writer is by Mariano Benlliure; the *Town Hall* and the 17C baroque church of the *Anunciación*.

Environs: About 5 km. S. is **Camargo** with the *Cave of El Pendo*, in which remains of rock paintings can be seen and from which many items in the *Museum of Prehistory* were taken. **Muriedas** (*c.* 3 km.

Santander, cathedral viewed from cloister

S.): The 17C *Casa Velarde,* in which the *Ethnological Museum of Cantabria* is housed and which has examples of folk art. **Gajano** (*c.* 10 km. S.): The *palace of the Riva Herrera.* **Heras** (*c.* 12 km. SE): The *tower* with its Plateresque portal is a good example of a building which has been converted from a fortress to a residential tower.

Santas Creus
Tarragona/Catalonia   p.390☐M 4

Abbey: Founded by the French abbey of Orand Selve (Languedoc) in 1169. Construction began in 1174. Dating from this first phase of building are the church, part of the cloister and the dormitory, which are in Cistercian style; the rest of the cloister, the Palacio Real and the fortifications are Gothic with Renaissance and baroque elements. The abbey is similar to that of Poblet but smaller; it became a protected monument in 1951, when essential restoration work also began. On the road is a 17C *cross* marking the way to the abbey. Single-arched bridge. The *complex* is arranged in three parts. The first is a courtyard with a locksmith's, rooms for the preparation of food and store houses. The *second ccourtyard,* which is to be found through a baroque portal is the main square and comprises the administrative buildings, 16C Abbot's Palace and guest house. The *third* part is made up of the *church* and other religious buildings. The church's façade (1174–1211) has windows from the late 13C; the church itself was completed in 1225 in pure, austere Cistercian style. The ground plan is in the form of a T, with five square chapels with groin vaulting and monochrome windows at the end. The beautiful façade windows and the ciborium are later. The Tower—Torre de las Horas—is 16C. There are tombs from the 13&14C; that of Pedro el Grande (1255) is by Bartomeu, that of James II and

Blanche of Anjou (1314) is the work of Pere de Bouhull. The *cloister* on the S. side of the church is rectangular. The oldest part is the small pavilion in the garden. The cloister walk is 14C hexagonal-Cistercian and has two kinds of arches—simple square ones and fine late Gothic ones by Reinard de Fonoll, which date from a time when this style was not yet known throughout Spain. The capitals are decorated and the walls have interesting sarcophagi. The 12C *chapterhouse* (to the E. of the cloister) has a nine-part groin vault supported by four columns; door and window are in austere Cistercian style. The *dormitory* on the upper floor (1191) has a wooden ceiling and Gothic arches. The *Palacio Real,* 1349–1402, has a courtyard which can be considered the masterpiece of civil architecture of the time — a slender porphyry column supports the arches of the first floor. Arches of the upper floor are supported upon fine columns. The Palacio Real originally served as the abbot's residence but it was later used by the Kings of Catalonia and Aragon, in order that they might withdraw to the abbey for rest and prayer. The *abbey prison* is also open to the public.

Santiago de Compostela
La Coruña/Galicia   p.386☐B 2

Santiago de Compostela, just 35 km. from the Atlantic in the extreme NW of Spain, was the former capital of the Kingdom of Galicia; it is now the seat of a bishop and has an old university. The town is dominated by Monte Pedro 2,470 ft. high. Excavations have revealed that there was a camp here in Roman times and there are the remains of a Roman mausoleum of the 1 or 2C. Sarcophagi from a Suevian necropolis have been shown to be 6C.

St. James's Way: The town became famous as a result of the great medieval pilgrimages to the tomb of the Apostle James the Great. Around the middle of the 9C a rumour spread through the West that the tomb of the apostle had been discovered on the Cantabrian coast in the distant kingdom of Galicia, which was not under Moorish rule. There were reports of miracles and soon great masses of people were flocking to the town to honour the relics of the saint, which had been carried here after his decapitation in Palestine. King Alfonso III, the Great of Asturia had a basilica built above the tomb in 896. Streams of pilgrims, from Germany, England, Italy and France journeyed westwards, from monastery to monastery, shrine to shrine, hostel to hostel, hospice to hospice. Under Alfonso VI of Castile and León (1072–1109) Santiago became the most important place of pilgrimage in medieval Christendom next to Rome and Jerusalem. Numerous Romanesque monuments still mark the pilgrim route. The mass pilgrimages inspired in this way had an important influence not only on art but also on philosophy, literature and social and economic life. The Way of St. James unrolled like a wide ribbon from the east over the Pyrenees to the north-west of Spain. Most of the pilgrims used the passes of Roncesvalles or Somport. The streams of pilgrims converged at Puente de la Reina and flowed on via Logroño, Santo Domingo de la Calzada, Belorado, Burgos, León, Astorga, Pontferrada, Villafranca and Mellid to Santiago.

Catedral de Santiago: The goal of the streams of pilgrims is the Plaza de España (or Plaza del Obradoiro, meaning the square of goldwork). This is surrounded by stately buildings, including the superb W. façade of the cathedral, one of the most beautiful churches on the Iberian peninsula.

History: As excavations have proved Alfonso II, the Chaste, had a church built

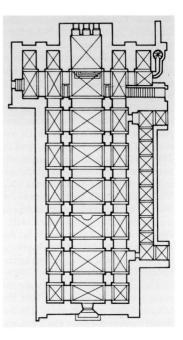

Santas Creus, abbey church The church has a ground plan in the form of a Latin cross. Note the dome over the crossing and the number of fine tombs in the transept and the side chapels.

here and Alfonso III, the Great, built a basilica on the same site in 899. In 997 the Moors stormed the city under Almanzor and destroyed the basilica. Reconstruction began in 1078 (during the reign of Alfonso VI) under San Pedro de Mezonzo. Bishop Diego Gelmírez consecrated part of the basilica in 1105, the choir and transept were completed in 1112 and the whole building was consecrated in 1211. In the following centuries various extensions and alterations were undertaken, e.g. the chapels, the clock tower (1325), the dome (1448), the bell tower and the cloister (around 1521) and finally the baroque façade.

W. façade: This splendid façade, also called Obradoiro, towers above the broad flight of steps of 1606. It was built in 1738–50 by the architect Fernando Casas y Novoa along with a monumental altarpiece, and is the most famous baroque façade in Spain. Within this three-dimensional structure the architect integrated the two towers. The bell tower, Torre de las Campanas (on the right) is partly 11C; it was reworked 1448–1675 and completed in 1725. The Torre de la Carraca (on the left) has the rattle, with which the faithful are called to prayer and dates from the 17C. The *tympanum* with the Adoration of the Magi is 14C; the wooden doors leading to the Pórtico de la Gloria are from 1610.

Pórtico de la Gloria: The portico, in fact the Romanesque fa[ce]ade of the church, is now screened (and also protected) by the baroque-Churrigueresque W. front. Maestro Mateo as master of the works was commissioned with the building in 1168. He completed work on the W. end in 1188 and created the three doorways which lead into the nave. The carving on the three doorways is among the finest of the entire Spanish Romanesque. A clustered column in the middle of the main doorway bears the tympanum. In front of this column and enthroned upon his own column (lavishly carved with the Tree of Jesse, the Virgin Mary and the Holy Trinity in the capital) is St.James the Great, the church's patron. The tympanum has Christ in Glory as Saviour of the World; he is surrounded by four angels with the symbols of the Evangelists, two angels wafting incense and eight angels carrying the symbols of the Passion in their hands. The angels are framed by 40 heavenly hosts and the righteous, those redeemed by Christ. In the archivolts, playing instruments, are the 24 Elders of the Apocalypse. The pillars on the left and right are surrounded by richly carved columns, upon which stand the Prophets and Apostles from the Old and New Testaments. On the right (working outwards) are

the Apostles Peter, Paul, James the Great and John and on the left (working outwards) Moses, Isaiah, Daniel and Jeremiah. On each of the columns to the left and right of the right side portal stand a pair of Apostles, while on each of those to the left and right of the left side portal stand a pair of minor Prophets. Both side portals are without tympana and have three archivolts. On the left these depict Christ with the Jews (the middle arch has 10 figures of rebellious Jews; on the inner arch are Adam, Abraham, Isaac, Jacob, Judah, Moses, Eve, Aaron, David and Solomon) and on the right these show Christ with the Heathens (on the keystones of both the inner and middle arches is Christ, with heathens pursued by monsters to his right and four angels to his left). In both of the angles between the arches of the main portal and those of the side portals there stands a tuba-blowing angel. Opposite the portico, on the inside of the Obradoiro, the Apostles Matthew, Luke and John the Baptist face the above-named eight apostles; opposite the eight figures of the Old Testament stand Job, Judith and Esther.

S. façade and Portico de las Platerías: The cathedral's oldest façade can be seen from the Plaza de las Platerías (Gold- and Silversmiths' Square) with its horse fountain and 18C flight of steps. On the left is the E. end of the cloister, a Plateresque work by Rodrigo Gil de Hontañón, and in the middle the splendid S. façade. To the right of the portal on the SE corner of the cathedral is the massive *clock tower*, started as early as 1316 and built in its present form 1676–80 by Domingo de Andrade. The two portals to the left of it were built with the S. transept and completed in 1103. The sculptures span several decades. Some of them were transferred here from the N. portal, which burned down in 1117

Santiago de Compostela, cathedral, W. façade

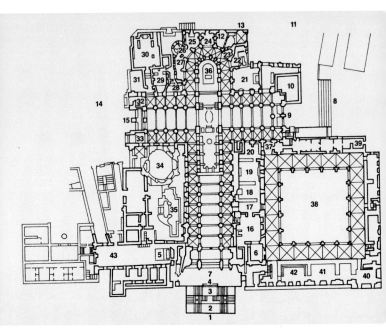

Santiago de Compostela, cathedral 1 Plaza de España or Plaza del Obradoiro **2** steps (1606) **3** Obradoiro **4** 14C tympanum and wooden doors **5** Torre de la Carraca **6** Torre de las Campanas **7** Pórtico de la Gloria (completed in 1188) **8** Plaza de las Platerías **9** Pórtico de las Platerías **10** clock tower or Torre de Reloj **11** Plaza de la Quintana **12** Puerta Santa (1611) **13** Puerta Real (1666) **14** Plaza de la Azabachería or Inmaculada **15** N. portal or Puerta de las Azabachería **16** Capilla de las Reliquias **17** ante-room (with entrance to 16 and 18) with equestrian statue **18** Capilla de San Fernando (treasury) **19** sacristy **21** Capilla del Pilar **22** Capilla de Mondragon **23** Capilla de San Pedro **24** Capilla del Salvador **25** Capilla de Nuestra Señora Blanca **26** Capilla de San Juan **27** Capilla de San Bartolomé **28** Capilla de la Concepción **29** Capilla del Espiritu Santo **30** Capilla de Corticella **31** Capilla de San Andrés **32** Capilla de San Fructuoso **33** Capilla de Santa Catalina **34** Capilla de la Comunion or del Corazon **35** Capilla del Cristo de Burgos **36** Capilla Mayor **37** entrance to cloister **38** cloister **39** Torre del Tesoro **40** Torre de la Corona **41** chapterhouse **42** library **Palace of Gelmírez**

The *tympanum* (on the right) shows scenes from the life of Christ, Flagellation and Crowning with Thorns, with the Adoration of the Magi in between. The left tympanum (W.) shows the Temptation of Christ and the Woman taken in Adultery. Both reliefs are by the same artist and date from *c.* 1103. Of an older date (probably from the N. portal) are the figures on the W. face of the door-posts: Christ Blessing (above); God the Father creating Adam and then below this King David with a stringed instrument. The figures above the tympana are by a different artist and added later (some after the fire of 1117). In the centre are Christ the Redeemer (around 1117), beside which, projecting prominently, is James the Great, the masterpiece of the creator of the Puerta de las Platerías. The relief at the feet of Christ

Santiago de Compostela, cathedral, Pórtico de la Gloria, tympanum

(Abraham rising from his tomb) is later than 1117.

Plaza de la Quintana/E. and N. façades: The Plaza de la Quintana is one of the most impressive squares in the world. It offers a view of the clock tower, the Royal Portico (designed by Vega and Verdugo and executed by José de la Peña del Toro in the mid-17C) and the Puerta Santa, the Holy Door (also called the Door of Pardon), which is only opened in jubilee years. The latter dates from 1611 and the 24 seated granite figures (apostles, patriarchs, prophets), which came from the Romanesque choir by Master Mateo have been restored several times, most recently in the 19C. To the left is the classical Puerta Real of 1666.

The *N. façade* or *Azabachería façade* is best seen from the Plaza de la Azabachería (or Plaza Inmaculada) or from the Paraiso (tradesmen's centre in the Middle Ages). The Romanesque N. portal of the late 11C, the *Puerta de la Azabachería* or *Parroquia,* was rebuilt by Ventura Rodríguez 1765–70. Luis Montenegro, Ferro Caaveiro and Fernández Savela also worked on the façade.

Interior: The cathedral has a nave and two aisles and a Latin cross ground plan. The nave and aisles are 325 ft. long, the transept 218 ft. The nave is 28 ft. 6 in. wide and 80 ft. high. The interior is a masterpiece of Romanesque architecture. The broad, very tall nave and aisles, with Romanesque round arches and gallery, and the transept make a superb impression. Around the nave and aisles there is a string of chapels, which are mostly Romanesque and have richly decorated altars, tombs and

Santiago de Compostela, cathedral, S. portal, King David

Azabachería façade

sculptures. The centrepiece is the baroque *Capilla Mayor* with the reliquary of the Apostle. *Capilla de las Reiliquias* (relic chapel): Built in 1527 as a chapel to the designs of Juan de Álava, it now serves as a relic chamber (valuable reliquaries, including one with the tooth of St.James). Next to this is a kind of ante-room with a 17C equestrian statue of St.James. Adjoining this is the Gothic *Capilla de San Fernando,* which is now a treasury. In particular note the monstrance by Antonio de Arfe (1539 –44), a triptych of the Flemish school (15C) and the candelabra (cornucopias) by the German J.Jäger (1683). The two adjoining rooms form the *sacristy* , which dates from the early 16C; Plateresque door and 17C paintings. To the right of the Capilla Mayor is the *Capilla del Pilar* from the early 18C, in Galician baroque style; altarpiece designed by Fernando Casas y Novoa and made by Miguel de Romay. A further series of chapels radiates off the apse (see the ground plan). First is the *Capilla de Mondragón.* This has a grille by the Frenchman Guillén Bourse and was itself built 1521 – 6 under the supervision of Jácome García; beautiful groin vault and the Gothic balcony and the altar with terracotta reliefs (1527) by Miguel Ramón are also fine. The 16C *Capilla de San Pedro* has the tomb of Doña Mencia de Andrade (J.B. de Celma, 1571). Next to the Holy Door is the *Capilla del Salvador* (directly behind the Capilla Mayor), which is also known as the chapel of the King of France, as it was endowed by Charles V of France in 1380. Construction of the Romanesque cathedral began with this chapel in 1085. The chapel contains a 16C Plateresque altar by Juan de Álava and sculptures of various dates including the tomb of Fr. Trevino from 1511. There follow the *Capilla de Nuestra Señora Blanca, Capilla*

Santiago de Compostela, cathedral, Pórtico de la Gloria

de San Juan and *Capilla de San Bartolomé,* which is 12C and in pure Romanesque style. In contrast are the Plateresque altarpiece and the lavishly decorated mausoleum of Diego de Castilla by the Flemish master Arnaud. The *Capilla de la Concepción* was formerly the Romanesque Chapel of Santa Cruz. It has rich Plateresque doors, a Churrigueresque altar, an Immaculate Conception and the tomb of Canon Rodríguez (attributed to the Dutchman Corniellis). The 13C *Capilla del Espíritu Santo,* by Pedro Vidal of Burgos, was extended in the 14C and rebuilt in the 16&17C. It contains tombs from the 14&17C, a choir by Domingo de Andrade and a 17C altarpiece. The *Capilla de Corticella,* originally the parish church, was not incorporated into the cathedral until later. The chapel, with two aisles and a groin-vaulted nave, has a very beautiful Romanesque portal with an Adoration of the Magi in the tympanum. The high altar dates from the 18C, the Agony in the Garden from the 15C. The *Capilla San Andrés* was built in 1674 and is dedicated to the Virgin of Fatima. The 16C tombs are by Juan Bautista Celma and the baroque altar by Fernández Espantoso. On either side of the Puerta de la Azabachería there are chapels: to the E. is the *Capilla de San Fructuoso* and to the W. is the *Capilla de Santa Catalina,* which is dedicated to the Virgin of Lourdes. The *Capilla de la Comunion* or *Capilla del Sagrado Corazón* was built in 1451 and altered in 1770. The marble and granite chapel is round with a classical dome and has the tombs of the archbishops Lope de Mendoza and Rajoy. The *Capilla del Cristo de Burgos* was commissioned by Archbishop Carillo y Acuña, whose tomb it contains. Churrigueresque altar. The *Capilla Mayor* with the high altar was built under the supervision of the Canon Vega y Verduga by the masters Francisco de Antas, Bernardo de Cabrera and Domingo de Andrade, along with the sculptors Mateo de Prado, Pedro del Valle,

Gutier and Brocos, who worked on the baroque remodelling of the chapel 1658–77. A beautiful bronze grille with two bronze pulpits by J.B. Celma (1585) encloses the sanctuary. On both sides there are 14C statues. The choir stalls are by Juan da Vila (1606). A striking feature is the outsize Churrigueresque gilded baldacchino, which is supported by iron girders, which are themselves concealed by eight massive angels. At the corners there are statues of the Virtues, which Pedro del Valle placed here; there is an equestrian statue of St. James by Mateo del Prado (1677) in the middle. The high altar itself is a late 17C work (reworked in 1890). Above the marble table is the baroque shrine with the seated statue of St.James holding the pilgrim's staff (a 13C polychrome stone sculpture, which was adorned with a diamond studded silver shawl in 1765). Above this is a group of statues of St.James and kings by Pedro del Valle (1657). Behind the altar pilgrims may kiss the robe of the illuminated statue of St.James, which is lit by a lamp bearing the coat-of-arms of Gonzalves de Córdoba, 1512. The crypt beneath the high altar, where the apostle is reputed to have been buried in a silver shrine (1896), has relics of the saint and his disciples, St.Theodore and St.Athanasius. Next to the above-mentioned bronze grille, in a metal column of the 12&13C are the pilgrim's staves of St.James and St.Francis On the column itself is a small 16C statue of St.James. In front of the Capilla Mayor is the octagonal lantern-tower (cimborio) which displays Romanesque, Gothic (drum) and Renaissance elements (attic dome and lantern); the lantern provides the cathedral with light in front of the high altar.

The *cloister,* one of the largest (inner court 100 ft. x 100 ft.) and most beautiful in

Santiago de Compostela, cathedral, St James on the Pórtico de la Gloria

Spain, was designed by a whole team of architects and built in a mixture of Castilian late Gothic and Renaissance styles in 1521–46 under the direction of Juan de Álava (d. 1537) and Rodrigo Gil de Hontañón (d. 1573), who were succeeded by Juan de Herrera and José de Arce (up to the end of the century). At the S. dolly of the cloister (near the entrance to the monastery) under a Romanesque arch in a 10C gable, is the tympanum with the Battle of Clavijo, the oldest representation of the apparition of St. James during the battle. From the cloister you proceed to the *museum section* with the *archive* and *library*, whose valuable treasures include the Tumbos Catedralicios and the Codex Calixtino with miniatures, incunabula, and also tapestries designed by David Teniers. The *Botafumeiro*, a vast silver censer, which is swung like a bell through the transept during services is also kept here. The *chapterhouse* contains Flemish tapestries by Jan Raës. The world-famous *Tapestry Museum*, which also contains the 'Pennant of Lepanto', was founded in 1571 by Don Juan of Austria. Of particular interest are the 8 tapestries of the Life of Achilles by Jan Raës (to designs by Rubens), the 12 made to Goya's designs and 25 carpets to the designs of David Teniers. The *Archaeological Museum* contains interesting sarcophagi, tombstones, capitals, reliefs and sculptures (12C seated Christ and Christ's Entry into Jerusalem, 13C).

Crypt/Old Cathedral: The entrance to the crypt-like lower church is on the Plaza de España. It lies with the apse below the W. bay of the cathedral nave; the rest extends in front of the cathedral. It is not clear whether the Old Cathedral was simply taken over in 1168 or whether it had been in existence for longer. The Romanesque building (with Gothic architectural elements) contains a 13C statue of the wife of Alfonso X and fragments of the former main portal and the Romanesque choir (both 12C).

Capilla de las Animas (Calle de las

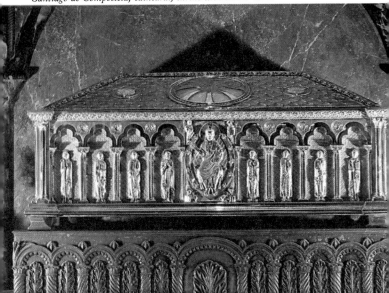

Santiago de Compostela, cathedral, shrine with saints' relics

Casas Reales): Built at the end of the 18C by Ferro Caaveiro and altered by Ventura Rodríguez and López Freire. The façade has massive columns and large classical window pediments. The wide nave inside is flanked by side chapels; the majestic Crucifixion is by Juan Pernas and the local artist Manuel de Prado, who also sculpted the terracotta reliefs in the side chapels.

Iglesia de las Angustias de Abajo: 18C; by Lucas Ferro Caaveiro with a dome and typical baroque façade. Inside there is an interesting 18C sculpture, Mater Dolorosa, by Antonio Fernández and a most beautiful 16C Crucifixion.

Santa María la Real del Sar (1 km. S. in the suburb Hórreo): Founded as a monastery in the 12C by Canon Munio Alfonso, the church was consecrated in 1136 by Archbishop Gelmírez. The present building dates from the time of Archbishop Pedro Gudesteiz (1168–72). Santa María has been a parish church since 1851. The Romanesque basilica, with a nave, two aisles and cylindrical vaulting is impressive for its sloping piers and walls. The massive buttresses date from the 18C. Inside there are interesting 13–16C tombs. The beautiful Romanesque cloister with interesting foliated capitals is attributed to the school of Maestro Mateo.

San Benito del Campo (Plaza de Cervantes): One of the town's oldest churches, dating from the 10C. The Romanesque tympanum (inside, to left of entrance) with the Adoration of the Magi, and a Gothic relief of the Visitation survive from the old church. The present building dates from the 18C; façade by Melchior de Prado.

San Fiz de Solovio/St. Felix (Plaza de San Felix): Originally 12C; the Romanesque portal dates from that period. The church was restored in the 18C and a baroque tower was added. Inside is the tomb of Cardinal Lope González (15C) and various 18C sculptures.

San Miguel dos Agros (Plaza de San

Santiago de Compostela, cathedral, Tesoro

Miguel): Destroyed by Almanzor and rebuilt in the 12,15&18C. The neoclassical façade is the work of Melchior de Prado and Mariño. 15C chapel.

Santa María del Camino (Calle de las Casas Reales): Rebuilt by Miguel Ferro Caaveiro in 1770. The Romanesque tympanum of the portal, with an Adoration of the Magi, comes from a former building.

Santa María Salomé (Rúa Nueva): Has parts of the 12C Romanesque façade. Baroque tower by José Crespo dates from 1743. There is an 18C retable by Miguel Romay and an 18C Calvary by Bartolomé Fernández.

Monastery of San Martín Pinario (opposite N. façade of cathedral): The monastery, which covers an area of 215,278 sq. ft., is closely linked to the history of the town. In 912 the prelate Sisnando built an oratory; this was extended in 1109 under Gelmírez and again on several occasions up to the 19C. For a time it governed 32 other

monasteries. The complex is built in several styles. The monastery façade (facing the N. side of the cathedral) in part dates from the start of the 16C and was completed in 1738. There are three cloisters (17&18C) and a baroque fountain. The adjoining church of the same name was built by Mateo López in 1590 and has a flight of steps of 1772. The impressive tripartite façade bears 15 statues in niches between columns. The foremost contemporary architects contributed to the design of the interior e.g. Peña de Toro, Melchor de Velasco and Domingo de Andrade. Note the large semi-cylindrical vault over the transept. Casas y Novoa and Miguel de Romay created the splendid high altar retable, which is a stunning example of Galician baroque. The aisles have fine Churrigueresque altars. Splendid choir stalls by Mateo de Prado 1644–7.

Monastery of San Payo/San Pelayo de Antealtares (E. of the cathedral): Founded by Alfonso II, the Chaste, the present building dates back to the 17&18C.

Santiago de Compostela, cathedral, tomb of Ferdinand II

The church façade of *c.* 1700) looks onto the Via Sacra. Churrigueresque altars. The Doric portal leading to the monastery is by Melchor de Velasco (1658).

Monastery of San Francisco de Valdedíos (Cuesta de San Francisco): In front of the monastery there is a statue of St. Francis by F.Asdrey (1926). Of the original Gothic building there remain just 5 door arches (N. façade of inner court) and parts of the chapterhouse, in which Charles V held court in 1520. The present church was built by Simón Rodríguez in 1742. The façade of 1779 has Ferreiro's St.Francis. Inside there are an interesting altar, a 16C reliquary cross by Ferreiro and the 14C tomb of Cotolay, a disciple of St. Francis and the founder of the monastery.

Monastery of Santa Clara (on the road to La Coruña): Probably founded by Queen Violande in 1260; the present building was built at the end of the 18C by Pedro de Aren. The beautiful 18C façade is by Simón Rodríguez. The high altar by Domingo de Andrade dates from *c.* 1700; 15C pulpits.

Monastery of Santo Domingo de Bonaval (Cuesta de St.Domingo): The 14C church, with a nave and two aisles, was built in a style transitional between Romanesque and Gothic. Inside there are 14&15C tombs; a dome in the Chapel of San Jacinto, a 16C pulpit and the stone statue of the Virgin of Bonaval, also 16C. The baroque façades of the monastery and the church are the work of Domingo de Andrade.

Other interesting religious buildings: The convent of the *Mercedarias Descalzas* (Mercedarians) was founded by Archbishop Andrés Giron in the 17C. The church was built by Diego Romay in 1673, the relief of the Annunciation in the façade is by Mateo de Prado (1674). The convent

of *Nuestra Señora de los Remedios* (Calle de las Huerfanas) was established in 1600 as a school for orphan girls. Baroque façade dates from 1671; beautiful bell tower. Inside there is a retable by Francisco de Siens. The monastery of *El Carmen* (1758) lies on the road to La Coruña. The Monastery of *San Agustín* and the church (Calle de José Antonio); monumental classical façade and 17C cloister.

Palacio de Gelmírez/Palacio Arzobispal/Archbishop's Palace (built onto the N. of the cathedral): The palace is the most important secular building of the Spanish Romanesque. Begun around 1120, it was not completed until 1253–66, long after the death of its founder, the first Archbishop of Santiago, Diego Gelmírez (d. 1149). The great hall on the ground floor is divided into two aisles by four pillars with rich capitals. The ceiling has 8 groin vaults. The banqueting hall on the upper floor is lower, but longer (107 ft. x 28 ft.). The gilded groin vaults date from the late 12C/early 13C. The consoles of the ribs, which are of great iconographic interest, are by the school of Maestro Mateo.

Hospital Real (now: **Hostal de los Reyes Católicos,** N. side of the Plaza del Obradoiro): Founded by Ferdinand and Isabella, this was for centuries a pilgrim hostel, before it became a luxury hotel owned by the state. The hostel, built more or less to the plans of Enrique de Egas, was begun in the 15C but not completed until the 17C. It contains elements of the late Gothic, Renaissance and baroque. The lovely portal with Plateresque features is the work of the French artists Martin de Blas and Guillén Colás. Elegant balcony from the late 17C. Of interest are the chapel (late Gothic and Renaissance), the two courtyards on either side of the chapel (from the time of Enrique de Egas), groin vault in the sacristy, the 18C rear inner courtyards and the staircase by Caaveiro.

University/Universidad (Calle de General Aranda): Founded in 1501, the present building was built 1769–1805 to the designs of Melchor de Prado (subsequently altered by Ventura Rodríguez and Pérez Machado.) The building itself was structurally altered and extended 1894–1904. 17C choir stalls in the rectory. The Great Hall has frescos by Fenollera and González; the late-18C library has incunabula and Ferdinand I's Book of Hours (a Mozarabic manuscript from 1055 with miniatures).

Other interesting secular buildings:
Colegium Mayor de Fonseca/Colegio Mayor de Santiago Alfeo (Plaza Fonseca): Founded in 1525 by Archbishop Alonso III and built in Plateresque and Renaissance style 1532–44. Of interest are the portal and the cloister. *Colegio San Jerónimo* (S. side of Plaza del Obradoiro): Also founded by Alonso III. Beautiful Romanesque portal; the rest of building is late-15C. Restored 1665. *Colegio de la Compania* (near the university): Founded 1576, with a church

of 1768; formerly a Jesuit college. Also note several palaces, e.g. on the Plaza de las Platerías there are the *Casa del Cabildo* (1758), the baroque *Casa del Deán* (opposite), the *Casa de la Parra* and the *Casa de la Conga o Canónica.*

Santillana del Mar
Santander/Old Castile   p.388□F/G 1

This picturesque town was once the capital of Asturia, to which its houses (barely more than 30) testify, since they all bear the escutcheons of the noble families of Castile.

Collegiate church: This originally belonged to a monastery dating from 870, which preserved the relics of St. Juliana. The monastery was converted to a collegiate church in the 11C. The Romanesque church consists of a nave and two aisles with barrel vaulting and it has a large portal. Inside there are several 11&12C tombs with Romanesque reliefs — the tomb of

Santiago de Compostela, cathedral, crypt, queen in prayer

Santiago de Compostela, cathedral, Capilla de las Reliquias

St. Juliana is outstanding. Three of the cloister's walks survive and they display a tendency towards Gothic naturalism.

Also worth seeing: The 16C *Monastery of Regina Coeli* , which houses the Diocesan Museum of religious art. There also some interesting mansions: *Torres del Merino* and *de Don Borja* from the 14&15C and the 15C *Palacio del Marqués de Santillana*.

Environs: Torrelavega (*c.* 3 km. S.): The neo-Gothic *church* contains an image of Christ by Alonso Cano, which is considered his masterpiece.

Santiponce
Sevilla/Andalusia   p.394☐D 10

Monastery of San Isidoro del Campo: Originally a Cistercian foundation under the protection of Guzmán the Good. It dates from 1298; in 1431 it was transferred to the Hieronymites. The monastery was dissolved in 1836. The buildings are fortress-like, their severity being particularly apparent in the heavy bracing of the apses. There are *two churches*, one of which is Gothic. It was restored in the 16C and contains the superb, polychrome *carved altar* of 1613 by Juan Martínez Montañés. In the middle of the altar is the figure of St.Jerome; to the left and right are carvings of the Adoration of the Magi. Montañés also produced the two statues of Guzmán the Good and his wife Doña María Coronel. The *second church*, is 14C and contains the tombs of Guzmán's son Juan Alonso Pérez de Guzmán and his wife Urraca Ossorio. Two Mudéjar *inner courtsyards* have 15C frescos and azulejos.

Santo Domingo de la Calzada
Logroño/Old Castile   p.388☐H 3

This town was founded in 1044 when St. Dominic the Hermit built a pilgrimage

Santiago de Compostela, Capilla de las Reliquias, 15C alabaster retable

Santiago de Compostela, Hostal de los Reyes Católicos, portal

Santillana del Mar, collegiate church, cloister

church and pilgrim hostel over the ruins of an abandoned building. He laid out a new road and built a bridge over the Oja. Pedro the Cruel of Castile fortified the town with walls.

Cathedral: This church was begun in Romanesque-Byzantine style by St. Domingo the Hermit and Alfonso VI in 1098. It was extended as early as 1158 in order to include the tomb of the saint and provide room for the growing circle of the faithful. It is a typical example of transitional style, having Romanesque elements in the apse and ambulatory and Gothic elements in the nave and aisles with their main pillars, columns, pointed arches and stellar vaulting. When the town became a bishop's seat in 1232 the church was elevated to a cathedral. Amongst the many interesting features the following are outstanding. The Plateresque *altarpiece* of 1537 at the high altar has reliefs by Damián Forment. The carvings in the *choir* date from 1521. The late Gothic *alabaster mausoleum* of St.Dominic the Hermit is by Juan de Rasines from 1513 and has a Romanesque tombstone and a recumbent figure. The *Chapel of St. Theresa* has a splendid Flemish altarpiece and the tombs of the Marquises of Ciriñuela. The *retrochoir* has three 13C reliefs. The *cloister* dates from 1384. In the *chapterhouse* and *sacristy* there is a collection of paintings, including a Spanish-Flemish triptych and beautiful gold items. The slender baroque tower was built alongside the church by Martin de Beratúa in 1762.

Also worth seeing: The old Romanesque

Santillana del Mar, collegiate church, high altar

chapel of *Nuestra Señora de la Plaza*. The church of *San Francisco*, which belongs to the old monastery of the same name, was built by Juan de Herrera in 1569 and is a perfect example of Herrera style, with stone sculptures at the high altar, the alabaster mausoleum of the founder Bernardo de Fresneda and the flattened-off pointed arch in the choir. The 17C *Convento de Bernardas* has a black marble baroque altarpiece with recumbent figures and the pantheon of the Manso de Zúñiga family. The old *pilgrim hospice* of St.Dominic. The 14C Gothic *Bishop's Palace*. The 18C *Town Hall*.

Environs: Bañares (*c.* 3 km. NE): The single-aisled, groin vaulted *parish church* is 16C and preserves a baroque altarpiece and the 12C wooden tomb of St.

Fromenius, which is covered with enamelled plaques. The Romanesque church of *Santa Cruz* has a Romanesque W. portal, as well as a tympanum and grille from an earlier epoch. **Cuzcurrita** (*c.* 10 km. N.): *Castle* keep and walls with corner towers. The *parish church* has a baroque portal and octagonal tower. **Leiva** (*c.* 5 km. N.) has a Gothic *church* and a 15C *castle*, with three octagonal towers and one with ten sides. **Ochánduri** (*c.* 8 km. N.): The 12C Romanesque *church* is single-aisled and has interesting groin vaulting.

Santo Domingo de Silos

Burgos/Old Castile   p.388 □ G 3

Monastery: A monastery dedicated to St.Sebastian existed in Silos from Visigoth

Santillana del Mar, collegiate church

S.Domingo de la C., cathedral

times, but was destroyed by the Arabs. In 919 Count Fernán González rebuilt the monastery after he had seized the area from the Emir of Cordoba. With the arrival of a monk from Navarre called Dominic, who came seeking refuge, life in the old monastery was given a new impetus and this led to it becominging a centre of spiritual and physical restoration, which has survived up to the present day. The monks of Silos named the monastery after the great saint and renovator in the 13C. Construction of the Romanesque *cloister* began in the late 11C during St.Dominic's lifetime and was completed around the mid 12C. The cloister has two storeys, the lower one of which is the more original. Each corner is decorated with two bas-reliefs. Lovely capitals have delicate, mysterious and symbolic plant and animal motifs, suggesting

Oriental, Byzantine or Persian influence. Mudéjar panelling in the lower cloister (14C) depicts a panorama of the social life of the period. A *museum* contains the most important items from the *monastery's archives*, including manuscripts, several codices of Mozarabic liturgy, a tympanum, a Romanesque altar frontal made of enamelled copper and the chalice and paten of St.Dominic. The *Pharmacy* of 1705 (for the monastery community and local inhabitants) has phials, glass vessels and earthenware mortars from Manises and Talavera. The *pharmacy library* consists of 387 books; the *monastery library* has over 40,000 books. The *monastery church*, built by Ventura Rodríguez on the site of the original Romanesque church in the 18C is built of ashlars and has the severe beauty of pure geometry.

Santo Domingo de Silos, cloister

Environs: Tejada (*c.* 4 km. W.):The Romanesque church of *San Pedro* has a tower in two sections, an interesting portal and fine capitals; Gothic altarpiece within. **Caleruega** (*c.* 10 km. S.): Has a *Dominican monastery,* standing on the site of the castle in which St. Dominic was born; also the church of *San Sebastián.*

the same height with stellar vaulting. The Chapel of San Antonio has a tomb (with recumbent statue) of the Corro family; a second tomb is Renaissance and by Bautista Vázquez.

Also worth seeing: The 16C *Hospicio de Corro,* which now serves as the Town Hall, and the ruins of the old 12C *castle.*

San Vicente de la Barquera

Santander/Old Castile   p.388□F 1

Nuestra Señora de los Angeles: This church, built 12–14C, is fortress-like in aspect with towers. The Romanesque portal dates from the 13C. The interior consists of a Gothic nave and two aisles of

---

San Yuste

Cáceres/Estremadura   p.392□E 6

Monastery of San Jerónimo de Yuste: This Hieronymite monastery, founded in 1408, became famous as Charles V's final retreat. He lived here after his abdication

Santo Domingo de Silos, cloister

Santo Domingo de Silos, cloister

in favour of Philip II on 3 February 1557 up to his death on 21 September 1558. In front of the monastery there is an old walnut tree, 'El Nogal del Emperador', beneath which the emperor liked to rest. The *entrance* to the monastery is over a ramp, which the Emperor (who suffered from gout) could mount on horseback. He did not spend his last years in the monastery itself, however, but in his own *building*, the inside of which is similar to the chambers of the Castle of Ghent. The entrance hall has columns and runs parallel to the adjacent monastery church. On the garden side there is a wide loggia with arches. The Emperor's desk still stands in the study. From his bedroom (where he died) he could follow the service in the church through a hatch. His rooms had carved 16C furnishings, dining room and kitchen. The church was built in 1508 in Gothic transitional style with Plateresque elements. *Inside:* Vaulting with Gothic ribs, which combine to form a tie-rib. Steps lead to the *high altar* which have Corinthian columns and a Titian 'Gloria'. Philip II took this painting to the Escorial after his father's death and replaced it by a copy; it is now in the Prado. *Crypt:* Oak sarcophagus, in which Charles V's body lay for 16 years, until Philip II had it transferred to the Escorial in 1574.

Two *cloisters:* one Gothic with tracery, the other Plateresque with a little 16C fountain. There are remains of the *refectory* of 1656 with Mudéjar azulejos, in which the Emperor occasionally dined with the monastic fraternity.

Environs: Castillo de Jarandilla (*c.* 18

Santo Domingo de Silos, cloister

Santo Domingo de Silos, cloister

km. away): Stands on top of a thickly wooded mountain slope. The former *castle of the Counts of Oropesa* (now a Parador) was the residence of *Charles V* until 3 February 1557, when his rooms in Yuste were ready. The fortress-like complex, dating from the late 14C onwards, has round corner towers and an inner courtyard with a Renaissance gallery. The open balustrade of the upper floor has Gothic quatrefoils. Four square towers at the sides of the gallery have baroque consoles. **Cuacos** (*c.* 2 km. away): A little town, with narrow alleys lined by overhanging houses. It includes the house in which *Don Juan of Austria*, later victor of Lepanto and illegitimate son of the Emperor lived as a child 1557–8. The *Iglesia Parroquial de Nuestra Señora de la Asunción* was completed in 1567 and altered in the 18C.

Sariñena
Huesca/Aragon   p.388 □ L 3/4

This little town lies on a hill in the middle of a fertile plain.

El Salvador: A 17C parish church, which formerly belonged to a Franciscan monastery.

Ermita de Santiago: A 13C Romanesque hermitage. The lovely *crucifix 'Cruz de Término'* was set up in front of the church at the end of the 15C; the relief has numerous beautiful figures.

Also worth seeing: A few beautiful *mansions*, ancestral seats of old noble families, with the roofs and balconies typical of Aragon.

Santo Domingo de Silos, cloister

Olmillos de Sasamón, Santa María

Environs: Cartuja de Monegros (*c.* 9 km. S.): A monastery of the closed Carthusian, which dates from 1731. Apart from the large baroque church with sacristy and chapels, there are several working quarters. Also preserved are the cloisters and the monks' cells. These rooms contain splendid frescos by Francisco Bayeu y Subías, brother-in-law of Goya.

Sarria

Lugo/Galicia   p.386□C 2

El Salvador: Sarria, with the late Romanesque Iglesia del Salvador, lies in the middle of a wide plain. The main portal has archivolts and the door has beautiful metal fittings. The tympanum of the N. portal has Christ Pantocrator.

Other churches worth seeing: *Santa Marína* is 13C, but has been restored several times. The impressive *Convento de la Magdalena* (Convento de Padres Mercedarios) was originally founded in the 13C. The façade is Renaissance. Inside there are various tombs and many coats-of-arms. The cloisters are transitional Romanesque-Gothic.

Castillo del Marqués de Sarria: The original castle was demolished in the 15C and rebuilt a little later. Now a semicircular bartizan alone remains.

Also worth seeing: One of the routes to Santiago de Compostela at one time passed through Sarria and a few old pilgrim hospices remain from that time, e.g. the 13C *Hospital de Magdalena* and the 16C *Hospital de San Antonio*.

Olmillos de Sasamón, Castillo

Environs: Barbadelo (SW of Sarria): A 9C monastery with a very beautiful Romanesque church.

Sasamón
Burgos/Old Castile   p.388□G 3

Of the old Roman town there are just a few remnants of the walls and a square tower with Gothic arches.

Church: 13C; the *main portal* is a copy of the 'Sarmental' portal in Burgos. There is a square *tower* with Gothic windows. The *interior* consists of a nave and two aisles of equal height and five chapels. Gothic *pulpit;* fine carpets. 15C Gothic cloister.

Environs: Olmillos de Sasamón (*c.* 3 km. E.): The beautiful *parish church* of 1504 has a nave and two aisles with groin vaulting and baroque altarpieces. The 16C *castle*, was both fortress and residence. **Villadiego** (*c.* 10 km. N.): The *church of San Lorenzo* has an 11C portal. *Santa María* is 13C and has a portal and a Renaissance retable. The *Augustinian convent of San Miguel* has a remarkable altarpiece in the style of Juan de Juni and a Spanish-Flemish polyptych. Several mansions. **Rebolledo de la Torre** (*c.* 30 km. NE): The inside of the church is Gothic; atrium and font are 11C Romanesque.

Sedano
Burgos/Old Castile   p.388□G 2

This town is at the centre of an area

Jérica (Segorbe), view

abounding in Romanesque monuments, many of which are under national protection. Of interest in the town itself are a superb *Renaissance church*, the *Bustillo Palace* and several *mansions*.

Environs: Moradillo de Sedano (very near by): With a 12C Romanesque *church*, a protected monument. The *portal's tympanum* has Christ Pantocrator with a book on his left knee. There is an atrium. **Gredilla de Sedano** (also very near): *12C Romanesque church* with an Annunciation and St. Peter and St. Paul in the *portal's tympanum*. **Escalada** (*c.* 10 km. N.): *Collegiate church:* The Romanesque portal has interesting capitals and archivolts. *The Palace of Gallo* is 17C and has twin towers and the Gallo coat-of-arms. A *pilgrimage chapel* has a triptych in the style of the Castilian school of the 15C. **Crespo** (*c.* 20 km. N.): The 12C *church* has a semicircular apse, barrel vaulting and a Romanesque font with unusual decoration.

Segorbe

Castellón de la Plana/Valencia   p.396☐K 6

A town with a pop. of 8,500, lying 31 km. NW of Sagunto in the Palencia valley. A Celtic-Iberian foundation, it was known as Segobriga under the Romans. There are still remains of fortifications dating from that period. Segorbe was the seat of a bishop as early as Visigoth times. In 1235 James I seized the town from the Moors. Lying between two hills crowned by castles, the town has preserved its medieval character through the centuries. The city

Segorbe, Diocesan Museum, 15C retable

walls and two massive 14C towers are still in good repair. A walk through the twisting alleys with their mansions adorned with coats-of-arms, gives an idea of Segorbe's former importance.

Cathedral: Built in the 15C and rebuilt or altered in the 16C and in the late-18C. There is a well-preserved Gothic *cloister* (14C) with simple pointed arches, flying buttresses and Renaissance gallery. Note the *tomb* of Gonzalo de Espejo and his wife, dating from around 1400. (The hound at their feet is a symbol of loyalty.) The cathedral's large *retable*, in warm colours and of masterful draughtsmanship, is one of Juan Vicente Macip's major works. Juan Vicente Macip (*c.* 1490–*c.* 1550) was the father of the painter Juan de Juanes, who introduced Raphael's style into

the art of Valencia and painted *panels* in the cathedral's side chapels. Apart from these painters, the following are also represented in the church and in the *Diocesan Museum*: Jacomart (15C), El Greco, Ribalta, Espinosa and others. Amongst the sculptures a *Madonna* by Donatello is of particular interest. The Bishop's Palace and other churches in Segorbe also house fine paintings by Spanish masters.

Also worth seeing: The *Plaza Mayor* with the *Palacio Medinaceli* (now Town Hall), the single-aisled Gothic *church of San Pedro* (1248), the timbers of which rest on cross beams like the church of S. Agueda in Barcelona. A walk of just over a mile to the ruins of the *Cartuja de Valdecristo,* founded in 1385, is also worthwhile.

Environs: Jérica: From Segorbe the road climbs up to this town (pop. 4,000) some 15 km. away. The town's old alleys and streets occupy the side of the hill, which is dominated by the ruins of the *Moorish castle*. There are also ruins of fortifications from Roman times. The *parish church* has an interesting brick *bell tower* in Aragonese-Mudéjar style, which is the only one of its kind in the province of Valencia. The *church of San Roque:* Of the original 14C Gothic church there remains only the *apse* with massive flying buttresses. There are important *panel paintings* from the Valencia school: a small retable by Lorenzo Zaragoza, dedicated to the Virgin Mary, St. Martin and St. Agatha and a uniquely realistic depiction of the Martyrdom of St. George.

Segovia
Segovia/Old Castile   p.392☐F/G 5

This city and capital of the province of the same name played an important role even in ancient times. Standing on a rocky outcrop between the two river valleys of the Eresma and Clamores it looks like a stranded ship. Segovia was the centre of Celtic-Iberian resistance against the Romans, before the latter first occupied and then destroyed the city in 80 BC. After rebuilding the city, the Romans made it one of the most important cities in colonized Spain, since it stood at the intersection of two major military roads. Under Visigoth rule it began to decline and this continued under the Arabs. Following the reconquest of Castile, Segovia acquired new importance, becoming the residence of several monarchs and reaching the peak of its importance towards the end of the Middle Ages through the Trastamara family. In 1474 Isabella the Catholic was proclaimed queen in the alcázar of Segovia; Ferdinand V of Aragon took the oath, the 'Fueros de Castilla', here. The city lost its position through the revolt of the Comuneros in 1520, which was initiated by the nobles of Segovia and

Segovia, cathedral

directed against the ever-growing might of Charles V. It did not regain its courtly splendour until the 18C, with the building of La Granja and the foundation of the Artillery Accademy by Charles III in 1762. Each period has left its mark on Segovia, making it one of the richest cities in Spain for monuments.

Roman aqueduct: The aqueduct, the city's landmark, is one of the finest structures from Roman times. The exact date of its construction is not known but it probably dates from between the 2nd half of the 1C and the start of the 2C AD, during the reigns of Vespasian and Trajan. The aqueduct carries water from the Riofrío, 17 km. away, to Segovia. Water collects in a water tower, 'El Caserón', whence it is conducted along a stone canal to a second tower, where cleaning takes place. From this second tower the aqueduct (119 arches, 2,446 ft. long) crosses Segovia's suburbs. This splendid structure is still in use today. The aqueduct is two-storeyed over a length of 927 ft. and is 97 ft. at its

highest—the Plaza del Azoguejo. It is built of granite blocks from the Guadarrama, so dressed that they could be laid one on top of the other without any kind of mortar. Many arches were destroyed during the Arabs' conquest of the city in the 11C, but these were rebuilt in the 15C.

Alcázar: The castle is one of Segovia's greatest sights and it has been the setting of important historical events. It was a royal residence until 1570. Isabella set out from here in 1474 to be crowned Queen of Castile. Philip II celebrated his marriage to Anne of Austria in the castle. In the 16C it was a state prison, where important persons were detained. The alcázar is strategically positioned at the confluence of the Eresma and the Clamores. Little is known of its origins, which are thought to go back to the post-Roman period. It was enlarged by Alfonso VII 1122–55. Alfonso X, the Wise, opened the Romanesque double-arched windows with Mudéjar paintings in the façade of the old palace. In the 15C the family of Trastamara made Segovia one

Segovia, view

Segovia, Alcázar, throne room

Segovia, Alcázar, throne room, ceiling

of its favourite cities. The alcázar was completely rebuilt under Juan II, who made splendid rooms, such as the N. hall (a large rectangular room), and La Galera, El Solio and Las Pinas, as well as the furnishing of these and the older rooms of Los Reyes, El Cordón, El Tocador de la Reina and the chapel. In the chapel the lovely glass windows were designed by the local artist Muñoz de Pablos, who also painted the enormous wall painting of the coronation of Isabella the Catholic in the Salón de la Galera. The lavishly decorated keep also dates from this time. Philip II had the slate roofs, the Herrera-style inner courtyard, the entrance portal and the enormous Habsburg escutcheon built. In the 18C Charles III installed the Artillery Academy here. In 1862 the alcázar was detroyed by fire. A.Bermejo's reconstruction of 1882 further enhanced the silhouette of the old palace. The fortress now serves as a military archive and houses an armaments museum with weapons from the 15–18C.

Cathedral: The old cathedral was totally destroyed in the revolt of the Comuneros. Charles V ordered a new cathedral with a different ground plan to be built on a higher site. Building of the late Gothic cathedral began in 1525. It is known as the 'Lady of the Spanish cathedrals' owing to its elegance, slender lines and restrained austerity. The ground plan was drawn up by Juan Gil de Hontañón, who was simultaneously building Salamanca Cathedral. After his death García de Cubillas took over, and after the latter's death Rodrigo Gil de Hontañón, son of the original architect, carried on the work in Gothic style.

Segovia, Roman aqueduct

The cathedral, with a nave and two aisles, was consecrated in 1768. The tower, the highest in Spain at its original height of 352 ft., was struck by lightning and had to be reduced to its current height of 295 ft. The dome over the crossing rises to a height of 225 ft. and is one of the most beautiful in Spain. The dome and tower were completed by Juan de Mugaguren in 1615 & 1620 respectively. With its beautiful windows, pinnacles and carvings, battlements, embrasures, flying buttresses and buttresses, the cathedral is a wonderful sight. The portal of San Frutos, on the N. side, was built in Hererra style by Pedro de Brizuela and has Doric columns and a classical frieze. The nave is 352 ft. long and 168 ft. wide, with beautiful, sturdy pillars which support the web of the vaulting some 110 ft. 6 in. up. The ambulatory has seven polygonal chapels. Above the arches of the nave, aisles and chapels are galleries with finely carved stone balustrades and these run the whole way around the building. The stained glass of the numerous great windows depicts Biblical scenes. The artists concerned include Pierre de Chiberry (1540), Francisco Herranz and Juan Danis (1680). The *Capilla Mayor* (main chapel), built by Diego Casado, Pedro Bustillo and Juan Garcia in 1614, has an apse, a balustraded gallery, large window and cornice. The chapel is groin vaulted with Doric pillars. The marble and bronze altarpiece, a gift from Charles III, is by Sabatini; it is decorated with large wooden sculptures of saints and an ivory and silver statue of the *Virgen de la Paz*. The chapel is enclosed by three large 18C grilles. The cathedral's other chapels also

Segovia, cathedral, crossing

Segovia, cathedral chapterhouse

contain a vast wealth of fine painting and sculpture. The *Capilla del Santo Entierro* has an impressive altarpiece by Juan de Juni (*Entombment* 1571) as well as a triptych by Ambrosio Benson from the early 16C and a painting by Sánchez Coello; the Gothic grille came from the old cathedral. The square ante-room of the Capilla del Sagrario, which is Plateresque and has three doors and groin vaulting, is by Rodrigo Gil de Hontañón (1562). The room serves as a sacristy and contains the *Cross of the Lozoyas* by Manuel Pereira (16C). The *Capilla del Sagrario* by José de Churriguera contains a ceramic altar with a *Dying Christ* by Daniel Zuloaga. The chapel of *Cristo Yacente* contains a recumbent Christ by Gregorio Fernández, a painting of the Descent from the Cross by Francisco Camino and a Plateresque grille.

The chapel of *San Blas* has a 16C grille and a 17C altarpiece. The chapel of *Santiago* has a marvellous grille by Juan de Salamanca (1596) and perhaps the finest altarpiece in the cathedral, made by Pedro de Bolduque 1580–91. In the chapel of *Santa Barbara* there is a 17C grille and a Gothic font with the arms of Henry IV from the old cathedral. The *Capilla de Nuestra Señora del Rosario* has a painting by Bayeu (1789) and interesting frescos. The chapel of *San José* contains an 18C altarpiece. In the chapel of *San Anton* is a grille (1755), a baroque altarpiece and the tomb of the bishop who founded the cathedral. The chapel of *San Pedro* has a 16C altarpiece and 18C paintings on the walls and in the vault. The *Chapel of Cristo del Consuelo* contains features from the old cathedral, such as a Gothic grille of 1515 and

Segovia, cathedral, font

Segovia, Vera Cruz

the outer portal to the cloister, designed by Juan Guas in the 15C. The *coro*, in the middle of the nave, is Gothic and it too is from the old cathedral. The choir stalls are by Martín Sánchez and the bishop's throne by the Madrid silversmiths González and Vergara (1658). The Plateresque choir stalls are by Vasco de la Zarzas, the coloured marble lectern is 17C and the baroque grilles are by Elora (1724) and others. The retrochoir was designed by Ventura Rodríguez (1784) in neoclassical style and has a marble and bronze altarpiece with sculptures by the Frenchmen Dumandré and Thierry, which was originally intended for the chapel of the royal palace in Riofrio.

The *cloister*, part of the old cathedral, was restored by José Campero in 1524 and rebuilt on a new site. It is almost square and the walks are groin vaulted. The chapterhouse and other rooms nearby house the interesting cathedral *museum*. The chapterhouse itself is a room of harmonious beauty and has a collection of tapestries; the panelling also is fine. The museum contains paintings by Pedro Berruguete, Alonso Cano, Morales, Van Eyck, a reliquary by Benvenuto Cellini, a 13C figure of the Madonna with the Infant Christ on her knee and the tomb of the Infante Don Pedro, Henry II' son. The museum also has a collection of incunabula from the second half of the 15C, which is one of the most valuable in Spain. Next to the chapterhouse are two paintings by Valdés Leal and Esquivel.

San Martín: The original 10C church was Mozarabic; the present church dates from the 12C. It has porticoes on three sides—typical of the region—with beautiful arcades and capitals. The three apses have Romanesque decorations; above one of the vaults rises a bold tower. The round-arched portal has four 12C Romanesque sculptures of St.Peter, St.Paul, Isaiah and Moses. Inside are a Gothic triptych with the *Descent from the Cross* by Maestro Rodrigo and a *recumbent Christ* by Gregorio Fernández. Also worth mentioning is the Herrera-style chapel with a portal by Juan Guas, which contains alabaster Gothic tombs and 15C paintings.

Vera Cruz: This church was founded by the Knights Templar in the 13C; building began in 1208. It is a unique religious building in late Romanesque style with 12 sides and was modelled on the Church of the Holy Sepulchre in Jerusalem. The *Chapel of Lignum Crucis* contains a carved wooden Christ from the 13C. The high altar has a small altarpiece with paintings of 1520. The church also contains remains of wall paintings from the 13&15C.

San Esteban: This 13C Romanesque church has a typical arcaded atrium and an extraordinary 13C tower, known as the 'reina de las torres españolas' (queen of Spanish towers). Inside the church is a 13C Stations of the Cross.

San Millán: Built in 1111–23 with a nave, two aisles, apses and transept. The 11C tower displays very strong Oriental influence. On the N. and S. side of the church are typical 13C arcaded courtyards.

San Justo: Dating from the 12&13C with Romanesque frescos—common in churches of the period in the region. The Chapel of the Gascones has an interesting figure of Christ.

Other interesting churches: *San Juan de los Caballeros*, with a nave and two aisles dates from the 12&13C. For centuries it was the burial place of Segovia's highest ranking families. It houses the *Zuloaga Museum,* which has work of the ceramic art-

Segovia, atrium of San Esteban

ist Daniel Zuloaga and the painter Ignacio Zuloaga. The 12C church of *La Trinidad* is single-aisled. Its interior has been most beautifully restored. Of particular interest is the Capilla del Campo with a portal by Juan Guas, groin vaulting and 16C stained-glass windows. The tower of *San Lorenzo* is a superb example of Mudéjar influence. *San Clemente* has a beautiful apse and Romanesque wall paintings. *San Andrés*, later altered, still preserves traces of the original Romanesque on the outside. *El Salvador* was originally Romanesque, has Gothic transept and vaulting and baroque decoration from the 17C. The church contains an *Inmaculada* by Gregorio Fernández. The coronation of Isabella the Catholic took place in the church of *San Miguel* in 1474. After its collapse in 1532 the church was rebuilt in Gothic style. It is single-aisled and has a baroque altarpiece by José de Ferreras (1672). The façade has a few Romanesque figures from the original building. *Corpus Christi* was a synagogue until the 15C and has retained its unusual style.

El Parral: This monastery was founded by Henry IV in 1447. Juan Gallego designed and built the church in 1494. After his death Juan Guas took charge of construction. The façade bears large escutcheons of the Villena family. The tower, built by Juan Campero in 1529, has Gothic carving and windows. The main chapel by Juan Bonifacio Gilás is an extraordinary example of the Plateresque style. Figures of the 12 Apostles by Sebastián Almonacid and the altarpiece adorned with numerous sculptures by Diego de Urbina (1553) are examples of late Gothic sculptural finesse and the decorative elements of the early Renaissance respectively. Tombs of the church's founders, Don Juan de Pacheco and Doña María de Portocarrero, masterpieces by Vasco de la Zarzas with alabaster carvings, are to be found on either side of the church. The cloister is Gothic. The refectory has wonderful panelling and paintings. The left gallery has a beautiful portal and serves as a pantheon for famous Segovians. The choir stalls, a masterpiece by Bartolomé

Segovia, San Justo, Romanesque frescos

Segovia, Alcázar, Henry IV

Segovia, Alcázar, Alfonso VIII

Fernández (1526), are now in Madrid (in the church of San Francisco el Grande and in the Archaeological Museum).

San Antonio el Real: This monastery was founded in 1455 by Henry IV on the site of an old palace. The hall, the main chapel with wonderful Mudéjar panelling by Xadel Alcalde, the nave and the choir are from the old building. Also worth seeing are a Flemish Stations of the Cross (15C) and several altarpieces from the same school.

Santa Cruz la Real: This monastery was founded by St.Dominic in 1218 and rebuilt by Ferdinand and Isabella in the 15C. The Plateresque portal by Juan Guas has several sculptures. The church is single-aisled with high groin vaults. The Gothic carv-

ing is reminiscent of 'San Juan de los Reyes' in Toledo.

Other interesting monasteries and convents: *Monjas Dominicas* (Dominican convent), with the 13C 'Hercules Tower'. *Carmelitas Descalzas* (Convent of the Discalced Carmelites): St.John of the Cross is buried here and there are numerous mementoes of the great mystic poet. *Santuario de la Fuencisla:* A place of pilgrimage. It was built in the 15&16C by Pedro de Brizuela. 15C figure of the Virgin. The *Seminary* (an old Jesuit college) has a beautiful façade in the style of the Escorial and a 16&17C inner courtyard by Juan de Mugaguren.

Town walls: These extended from the alcázar and were built after Segovia had been

Segovia, Alcázar, Henry III

Segovia, Alcázar, Henry II

seized from the Moors. Restored in parts, there are also later features. Of the seven gates, three still stand: *San Cebrián, Santiago* and *San Andrés*.

Mansions and palaces: The Romanesque houses in the Canonjía quarter still have their old portals with abutments and round arches. The fortress houses with their defensive towers, galleries, decorated façades, inner courtyards and Mudéjar roofs are later. The *Casa del Marqués de Lozoya*, built as a fortress to defend the town walls, has a battlemented tower and arrow slits. The 14C *Torreón de las Lozoya* has a round-arched door, double-arched windows and windows with embrasures. The tower of the *Casa de Arias Dávila* has wonderful patterns on the walls and a cornice with arrow slits, which is supported by figures of dogs. The *Casa de los Picos* is so-called because of the faceted stones in the façade, which produce charming effects. The house of *Don Alvaro de Luna* has Gothic windows and an inner courtyard. The *Casa de los Aspiroz* has Gothic windows. The 18C *Town Hall* was built by Pedro de Brizuela and has frescos by Antonio Garcia.

Fountains: The two monumental fountains *El Azoguejo* and *El Caño Seco* are 17C.

Museo Provincial de Bellas Artes: The provincial museum is in the House of the Hidalgo. It has an important collection of local paintings from the 15,16&17C, such as the *Conversion of St. Paul* by Francisco Camino. Also worth seeing are the Renaissance reliefs by Benito Giralde in the church of Santa Columba.

Environs: The altarpiece of the high altar of the *parish church* of **Trescasas** (*c.* 7 km. E.), which dates from the time of Charles III has an oil painting of the *Immaculate Conception* by Bayeu. Other altarpieces have paintings attributed to Bayeu or Maella. **Sotosalvos** (*c.* 8 km. N.): The Romanesque *parish church* has a very beautiful portico. Inside there are a 12C image of the Virgin and a baroque altarpiece. The church contains several paintings from the old altarpiece and these are in the style of Nicolás Francés. **La Cuesta** (*c.* 18 km. N.) has a Romanesque *parish church* with a nave, two aisles and three apses. Inside there are a 13C cross and several 15C Castilian paintings. **Collado Hermoso** (*c.* 18 km. NE) has the ruins of a 13C Cistercian monastery. Of the *church,* with a nave and two aisles, there remain pointed windows, Gothic arches and capitals.

Seo de Urgel
Lérida/Catalonia   p.390 □ M 3

Church of Santa María: A church of the same name was consecrated here as early as 839. At the start of the 11C there were three churches here, of which the church of Santa María was consecrated in 1041 and totally rebuilt in the 12C. In 1175 the Italian architect Raimondo Lombardo was engaged to complete the rebuilding. Consequently the little cathedral of *La Seo* is more typical of the Italian- than the Catalan-Romanesque. In 1195 the town was destroyed by Ramón Roger, Count of Foix. In the 18C the church was rebuilt in baroque style but the restoration of 1918 was carried out in the original Romanesque. The church *interior* on a basilican ground plan, consists of a nave and two aisles, five apses and a very long transept ending in square towers. Nave and transept are barrel vaulted; aisles are groin vaulted. There is a *dome* over the crossing. The

main apse encompasses the smaller apses and the two towers, as in the church of Santa María Maggiore in Bergamo. In the *main apse,* under the gallery, there are three beautiful windows with archivolts borne on columns. The *façade* has three doors, leading to the nave and aisles; at each side there is a tower, which is square at the base and octagonal above. The upper part of the façade has three *friezes* of geometrical motifs, three windows and a frieze of animals and men above the portal. The *portal* itself has archivolts, which are supported on double columns with decorated capitals. The two-storeyed bell tower has double- and triple-arched windows. A door on the S. side from the 12&13C leads to the *cloister.* The E. wing dates from 1603. The 50 simply decorated *capitals* show the influence of the Roussillon school. The *Diocesan Museum* contains valuable Beatus manuscripts, an 11C codex, a 12&13C retables and gold items.

Environs: Coll de Nargó (30 km. SW): This town on the Oliana reservoir has a Romanesque *church* with the original bell tower. At **Anserall** (3 km. NE) is the Benedictine abbey of *San Saturnino de Tabérnolas,* whose church was consecrated in 1040. The cloister had beautiful capitals, which are now to be found in Barcelona (Museo de Arte de Cataluña) and North America.

Sepúlveda
Segovia/Old Castile   p.388 □ G 4

This old town, known back in Roman times, still has remnants of the medieval town walls and castle, as well as numerous

Segovia, Cathedral Museum, Romanesque □
Madonna and Child

churches, palaces and mansions. The castle, built by Fernán González, was on several occasions the scene of violent battles, particularly during the war between Alfonso I and his wife Doña Urraca.

El Salvador: A pure Romanesque church of the 11C; the apse is very beautiful and has blind round-arched windows on the outside. The tower also has two round-arched windows. Preserved inside are a Gothic monstrance with Renaissance decoration and a cross with grotesques. On the S. side is a portico typical of the region.

Virgen de la Peña: 12C Romanesque church with apse, windows, round arch and cornice, portal, portico and three-storeyed tower, all in Romanesque style. The single-aisled interior has barrel vaulting, a 16C Gothic cross and several baroque altarpieces.

Other interesting churches: The Romanesque *San Justo* has a nave, two aisles, a crypt and two Romanesque statues (Virgin and Child and the figure of a bishop). The simple Romanesque *San Bertolomé* has a beautiful tower. *Santiago*, also built in simple Romanesque style, has a masonry tower and brick apse with two blind arcades with round arches.

Environs: Carrascal del Rio (*c.* 20 km. NW): The 12C Romanesque church of *San Frutos* was built by Maestro Miguel. It is decorated with blind arcades and has a portico on the W. side. **Castilnovo** (*c.* 10 km. S.): The *castle*, with its Moorish style towers, was built by Abd ar Rahman I. It later belonged to the Counts of Castile, who extended the original Arab fortress during the 12–15C. It is square with round and square towers. **Cantalejo** (*c.* 25 km. SW): The parish church of *San Andrés* has a nave and two aisles; it was built towards the end of the 17C and has a large altarpiece with marble columns and a figure of St.Andrew. The Romanesque church of *El Pinar* formerly belonged to the Knights Templar.

Seo de Urgel, Romanesque cloister

Seo de Urgel, Santa María 1 nave with barrel vaulting **2** aisles **3** entrance to cloister **4** small Italianate side apses, only apparent from inside

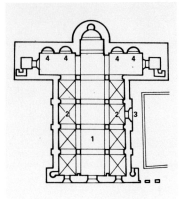

Sevilla

Sevilla/Andalusia   p.394 ☐ D 10

The capital of Andalusia is a busy city with an eventful history. This is apparent both from Seville's buildings, which are of great importance to the cultural tradition of Spain, and from its festivals. It is favourably situated in the fertile valley of the Guadalquivir, which curves gently past the city and is navigable for some 56 miles down to its mouth at Sanlúcar de Barrameda. From early times, this site was of great importance and frequently changed hands. The ancient 'Hispalis' was renamed 'Colonia Julia Romula' after Julius Caesar captured it in 45 BC. It became a Roman judicial district and was fortified —the remains of the wall can still be seen. Two Roman emperors, Hadrian and Trajan, were born in the area around Seville. In 411 the Vandals captured this much sought-after port and a little later, in 441, it was taken by the Visigoths, who made it the capital of their kingdom. Here Isidore, the celebrated Archbishop of Seville (d. 636), resisted the Arian heresy. When it was captured by the Moors in 712, it was again renamed and it is from the Moorish 'Ichbilija' that the name 'Sevilla' derives. Various dynasties ruled the city — the Omayads in the 10C, the Almoravides, the austere warrior order from the Islamic Sahara in the 11C, and in particular the Berber dynasty of the Almohades in the mid 12C. Most of the surviving Moorish monuments come from the building activities of the Almohades. These dynasties gave Seville a reputation which for a time rivalled that of the mighty city of Córdoba, the capital of the caliphate. Moorish influence waned during the Reconquista and Seville was taken in 1248 by Ferdinand III, the Holy, and his Castilian troops, after which he chose it as his private residence and moved Christians in from Castile. The Christians found that there was already a sophisticated culture and an intellectually active centre in Seville. But in the field of architecture, the Christians introduced Gothic and later Renaissance styles, thus

Sepúlveda, view

Castilnovo (Sepúlveda), castle

creating the mix of styles to be found all over the city. The history of the city up to this point is outlined by the proud inscription on one of Seville's gates: 'Hercules built me, Caesar surrounded me with walls and towers and the Holy King (Ferdinand III) occupied me'. After Alfonso X, the Wise (1252–84), and Pedro I, the Cruel (1350–69), Seville reached a new peak of worldwide political importance under Philip II following the discovery of America. It gained an overseas trade monopoly and became Spain's most important port, with a naval college and an exchange. Its importance diminished with Philip IV. However, the city came out of all the wars and battles relatively unscathed. Its vitality finds expression in numerous festivals. Some of the most important Spanish artists of the 17C were born in Seville: Velázquez, Murillo, Valdés Leal, Herrera the elder and Herrera the younger. Zurbarán worked here, as it was the birthplace of his teacher, Juan de las Roelas, and so did Spain's leading baroque sculptor, J.M. Montañéz, who was also known as the 'God of Wood'. Among the most important cultural events are the festival processions of Holy Week, with the 'pasos' — highly decorated statues and groups of figures—which are carried by 52 lay brotherhoods, the 'Confradías', who sing 'saetas' or short dirges with themes taken from the Passion. The members of the brotherhoods wear penitential robes (cowls and masks) and walk in procession through the streets as 'nazarenos', i.e. worshippers. After Holy Week, the six-day 'Feria de Abril' is held. This is another famous popular festival which began in the 19C and includes music, dancing (the Sevillana and the Seguidilla), horsemanship and bullfighting. The Feast of Corpus Christi is observed in the cathedral with Andalusian customs; a group of boys perform the 'Dance of the Seises' (dance of the six) in fine old 17C garments. At the feast of the city's patron saint, the 'Virgen de los Reyes' (on 15 August), the celebrated statue from the cathedral's Capilla Real accompanies the procession. Finally, there is the famous festive pilgrimage of the people of Seville to the sanctuary of El Rocío near Almonte (Huelva), which takes place during Whitsun week. All of western Andalusia, i.e. the provinces of Seville, Cádiz and Huelva, take part in this 'Romería del Rocío'.

Cathedral of Santa María: This huge building took a hundred years to complete (1402–1506), and is constructed on the foundations of a former Visigoth cathedral, on whose site the Almohades built an important mosque in 1172. This was reconverted to Christian worship in 1248, and continued as such, with interior redecoration, until the new building was begun in

1401. Such was the religious enthusiasm of the time that the cathedral which was built may be described as the largest Gothic cathedral in the world, and the third largest church in Christendom after St. Peter's in Rome and St. Paul's in London.

The cathedral has nine *portals*. The *Puerta Mayor*, in the main façade on the W. side, is partially 19C and is itself flanked by two fine portals, the *Puerta del Bautismo* and the *Puerta del Nacimiento*, which latter has some excellent 15C *sculptures* by Lorenzo Mercadante and Pedro Millán. The terracotta relief of the 'Birth of Jesus' is an unusually charming work by Mercadante. The *Puerta del Perdón* on the N. side is an impressive Mudéjar structure which stands at the top of steps and leads through to the *Patio de los Naranjos* or courtyard of oranges. The bronze panels on the door leaves are inscribed with 12C *Koranic texts* in vertical Kufic script. This portal and the Patio de los Naranjos both testify to their Moorish past. The octagonal *marble fountain* in the middle of the patio dates back to Visigoth times, and was used for ritual Islamic cleansing. Altogether, 19 horseshoe arches survive from this period. The battlemented wall on both sides of the Puerta del Perdón is from the Almohaden epoch. To the left of the *Puerta del Lagarto*, which has a horseshoe arch and a Mudéjar artesonado, is the *Capilla de la Granada*, which has some Visigoth fragments (capitals, reliefs on the arches, etc.), and was probably employed as an Islamic place of worship. On the E. side of the patio is the *Biblioteca Colombina*, which was established in the 13C and contains 13–15C manuscripts and books of hours, and also some works with notes by Columbus himself. Some of the contents of the library were a gift from Fernán Colón, Columbus's son. The W. of the patio is bordered by the 17C baroque single-aisled Sagrario, which is now the *parish church*. The *Giralda*, the bell tower which dominates

the city skyline and is about 318 ft. high overall, rises up between the *Puerta de Oriente* and the *Puerta de los Palos*. The tower takes its name from the crowning figure of Fides (Faith), 13 ft. high, which was made by Bartolomé Morel in 1564. Its banner serves as a weather vane or 'Giraldillo', after which the whole tower became known as the 'Giralda'. Originally a minaret attached to the mosque, it was built 1184–96. Seville has a further 12 minarets which were later altered. The sides of the tower are divided into three sections by divisions resembling pilaster strips. This articulation is broken up by twin windows (ajimez) with Visigoth and Moorish capitals. It was not until 1568 that Hernán Ruiz added the top five stages to the tower. There are 24 bells, and the platform affords a fine panoramic view of Seville. The *Puerta de los Palos* has a fine relief of the Adoration of the Magi (1520, by Miguel Perrin) in the tympanum; a relief of the Entry into Jerusalem' (1522) in the tympanum of the following portal, the *Puerta de las Campanillas*, is by the same artist. On the S. side, the neo-Gothic *Puerta de San Cristóbal*, also known as the *Puerta de la Lonja*, was built in the 19C. The *interior* of the cathedral is 249 ft. wide and has a nave, four aisles and a row of chapels along each N. and S. sides. The ground plan is based on that of the main Moorish mosque. The length is 384 ft. and the height of 131 ft. (184 ft. at the crossing) is emphasized by clusters of columns. There is an immense wealth of art treasures. The huge main area is illuminated by superb stained-glass windows, which date from 16–19C. Along the long axis there are three beautiful enclosures. The first, the *coro*, in the middle of the nave, is decorated with a splendid reja (grille, 1519) by the Carthusian Fray Francisco de Salamanca. This coro also contains exquisitely carved sillería (choir stalls, 1478) with 117 seats; the splendid carvings include a representation of the Giralda. The late Gothic and

Plateresque *alabaster chapels*, the *'Capillos de los Alabastros'*, are interesting for they are built against the outside walls of the coro and have fine wrought-iron grilles. The *Capilla de la Concepción chica* contains a wonderful wooden 'Immaculata' by M.Montañéz. The *Capilla Mayor* is surrounded on three sides by gilded 16C *rejas*. The central section, with the Entombment in the upper part of it, is by Fray Francisco de Salamanca, and the screens at the side are by Sancho Muñoz and Master Bartolemé of Jaén. The two wrought-iron *pulpits* with bas-reliefs are also of interest. The Capilla Mayor contains a huge late Gothic *retable* (75 ft. high, 66 ft. wide), which was designed by the Dutchman Pieter Dancart and built from 1482 onwards by Dancart and others. The side wings were added at a later date. There are around 1,000 figures grouped into 45 scenes from the life of Jesus and Mary; these include the figures of saints (including the patron saints of Seville) in the filigree work and tracery of the partitions between the niches. The altar surrounds were painted by Alejo Fernández and Andréz de Covarrubias. The 'Virgen de la Sede', a polychrome Virgin partly mounted in silver, is late 13C. The *Sacristía Alta* behind the altar contains a fine Plateresque artesonado and three paintings by Alejo Fernández. The third enclosure is the 16C *Capilla Real*, the royal burial chapel at the E. end of the cathedral. It is dedicated to Ferdinand the Holy, the conqueror of Seville, and the 18C *screen* depicts the scene of the handing over of the keys of the city. It is a domed Renaissance structure, and contains the *tombs* of Alfonso X, the Wise, and his mother Beatrice of Swabia. In front of the high altar there is an 18C silver shrine containing the remains of Ferdinand the Holy. In the centre is the ornate *'Virgen de los Reyes'*, a 13C Romanesque Virgin Mary which Ferdinand took into battle with him and Seville's patron saint. The *crypt* contains the remains of the rulers of Castile, includ-

ing Pedro I the Cruel and his mistress María de Padilla. There is also a 14C ivory figure of the 'Virgen de las Batallas', French work which Ferdinand is also said to have taken into battle as a talisman. The sacristy contains Murillo's painting 'Mater Dolorosa' and the chapterhouse has a painting of Ferdinand III attributed to Murillo. The elliptical *chapterhouse* is decorated by artists from Seville, and has an 'Immaculata' by Murillo among other works. The *Sacristía Mayor* is unusually fine and is decorated in Plateresque style. The rich *cathedral treasure* is housed here and includes: a reliquary shrine, the 'Tablas Alfonsinas', which is a triptych; large silver 16C processional monstrance by Juan de Arfe; a bronze candelabra over 20 ft. tall, Bartolomé Morel's mid-16C 'Tenebrario'; a fine 'Deposition' by Pedro de Campaña from 1548; Zurbarán's 'Our Lady of Mercy'; and 'Christ', an ivory carving by Alonso Cano. The 16C Gothic *Sacristía de los Calices* has *paintings* by Murillo ('Head of Christ' and the especially fine 'Holy Family'), Schongauer Goya ('St.Justina and St.Rufina', the martyrs and patron saints of Seville), Can Pacheco, Valdés Leal, Morales, Zurbarán Roelas, Titian, etc. There is also a wonderful, very realistically conceived crucifix by M.Montañés, the 17C 'Cristo de Clemencia'. Near the adjacent *Puerta de Lonja* is a large 16C *fresco* of St Christopher. The transept contains the *monument to Columbus* (1891), which was brought here from Havana in 1899. The *Capilla de la Concepción* or *de la Gamba* contains an exceptionally fine *altarpiece* by Luis de Vargas, which depicts Adam and Eve revering the Madonna and Child. The *Capilla de la Antigua* contains a fresco of the Virgin Mary and a *sacristy* with paintings by Zurbarán, Cano, and others. The *Capilla de San Hermenegildo* contains the

Seville, La Giral

outstanding late Gothic *alabaster tomb* of Archbishop Juan de Cervantes by Lorenzo Mercadante (1458). The *Capilla de San José* has *paintings* by Valdés Leal and Lucas Jordán. The *Capilla de Santa Ana* has a Gothic altar from around 1500. By the *Puerta del Nacimiento* is Luis de Vargas's *'Altar del Nacimiento'*. Near the *Puerta Mayor*, on the left- hand side, is the *'Altar del Santo Angel'*, with a fine image of the guardian angel by Murillo, who also painted the exceptionally fine late work, the 'Vision of St.Anthony of Padua' (1656), and the 'Baptism of Christ' in the *Capilla de San Antonio* or *del Bautisterio*. Opposite the Puerta Mayor is the *tombstone* of Fernán Colón, Columbus's son who died in 1540. The *Capilla de Escalas* contains some enamelled terracottas from the della Robbia workshop, and the *Capilla de Santiago* has Juan de Roelas's 'St.James the Great at the Battle of Clavijo' (1609), and paintings by Zurbarán ('Mary'), Simon de Vos, and Antonio Pérez ('Sibyls and Prophets', 16C). To the left of the *Puerta de los Naranjos* is the *Altar of the Virgen de Belén* (Bethlehem), with a Virgin Mary by Alonso Cano. At the bottom left of the altar in the *Capilla de los Evangelistas*, there is a depiction of the Giralda before its height was increased by the bell tower. The Virgin Mary on the altar of 'Nuestra Señora del Pilar' is by Pedro Millán and dates from around 1500. The *Capilla de San Pedro* has an early altarpiece by Zurbarán, with scenes from the life of St.Peter.

Church of Omnium Sanctorum (Calle de la Feria): This was restored after a fire in 1936. It has a fine Mudéjar *tower* with sebka ornamentation, Gothic *portals* in the Mudéjar façade and a Moorish chapel.

Church of El Salvador (Plaza del Salvador): This is a large and remarkable church which was built at the end of the 17C. It has a nave and two aisles and was constructed on the site of a former mosque.

Seville, Cathedral of Santa María 1 Puert Mayor **2** Puerta del Bautismo **3** Puerta del Naci miento or Puerta de San Miguel **4** Puerta del Per dón **5** Patio de los Naranjos **6** Puerta de Lagart **7** Capilla de la Granada **8** Biblioteca Colombin **9** Sagrario **10** Puerta de Oriente **11** Giralda 1 Puerta de los Palos **13** Puerta de las Campanilla **14** Puerta de San Cristóbal or Puerta de la Lonj **15** Coro **16** Capilla de la Concepción Chica 1 Capilla Mayor **18** Sacristía Alta **19** Capilla Real 2 chapterhouse **21** Sacristía Mayor **22** Sacristía d los Cálices **23** tomb of Christopher Columbus 2 Capilla de la Concepción or de la Gamba **2** Capilla de la Antigua **26** Capilla de San He menegildo **27** Capilla de San José **28** Capilla d Santa Ana **29** Capilla de San Laureano **30** Alt del Nacimiento **31** Altar del Santo Angel **32** tom of Fernán Colón **33** Capilla de San Antonio or d Bautisterio **34** Capilla de Escalas **35** Capilla d Santiago **36** Altar of the Virgen de Belén **3** Puerta de los Naranjos **38** Capilla de los Evar gelistas **39** Capilla de San Pedro

The Gothic *bell tower* has the substructur of an old Moorish minaret and a baroqu roof. The patio also comes from th mosque. The huge *Portal del Sagrario* an the *altarpiece* are of particular interest – both are Churrigueresque. The *interio* contains a fine 'Cristo del Amor' by Jua de Mesa and a splendid sculpture of 'St Christopher' by Juan de Mesa's teache Martínez Montañés, who was also respor sible for the outstanding sculpture of th Passion, 'Jesús del Pasión', in the sagrari

San Esteban (Calle de San Esteban): Thi church, near the Casa de Pilatos, is a cor verted mosque with 14C features rangin from Romanesque to Mudéjar. The *porta* are Gothic. The *interior* consists of a nav and two aisles with a fine Mudéjar coffere ceiling, a high altarpiece ('Peter and Paul by Zurbarán, and further paintings, whic are by Pacheco and Roelas.

San Gil (Calle de San Luis: very near th Puerta de la Macarena): Rebuilt in th 13,14&17C and gutted by fire in 1936. contained the celebrated 17C *'Virgen de Macarena'*, the patron saint of the poor ar bullfighters, by Pedro Roldán. This wor is now housed in the adjacent new churc of *La Macarena*, which also contains a

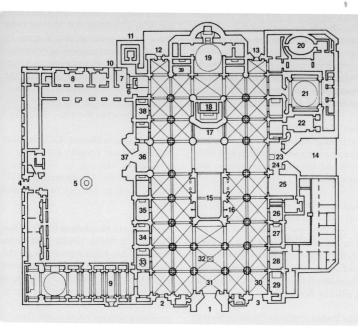

other Roldán sculpture, 'Christ before Pilate' (second chapel on the left). A *museum* houses the gorgeous garments of the figure of the Virgin Mary, and also the garments of famous matadors (Manolete, Sánchez Mejias, Joselito, etc.).

San Isidoro (Calle de San Isidoro): The Gothic S. portal of this church has zulejos. The *interior* contains a number of interesting *paintings* by the two Herreras, Luis de Morales, and others, including one of Juan de las Roelas's finest works, the 'Tránsito de San Isidoro' (in the sacristy), and a 'Deposition' by Alonso Cano.

San José (Calle de Jovellanos): This immensely charming 17C baroque church was built and decorated by order of the joiners' guild. Along with many of the city's other churches, it contains a work by

Roldán, in this case the 'Throne of Angels'.

San Juan de la Palma (Calle de San Juan de la Palma): A small church built on the site of a former mosque. It has a Gothic *portal* with a *Crucifixion* by Pedro de Campaña and an interesting *processional figure*, the 'Virgen de la Amargura' (Virgin of Bitterness), which is probably the work of 'la Roldana', Pedro Roldán's daughter.

San Lorenzo (Plaza de San Lorenzo): Originally a mosque, it was converted into a Gothic church with a nave and four aisles; redecorated in baroque style in the 17C. The superb *high altar* of 1638 is by M.Montañés and it has an image of St. Lawrence and four reliefs depicting scenes from his life. In a side chapel there is a life-sized *figure of Christ*, 'Nuestro Señor de Gran Poder', an outstanding work by Juan de Mesa.

San Luis (Calle de San Luis): This beautiful church was completed in 1731 by Leonardo de Figueroa and, along with the palace of San Telmo, is one of his finest works. Baroque *twin towers* rise above the Plateresque façade; the church has a square ground plan. There is a fine *fresco* by Lucas Valdés on the central dome.

San Marcos (Calle de San Luis): This 14C church was unfortunately devastated by fire; a fine *portal* decorated with sculptures and the *Almohaden minaret*, have both survived.

San Martín (Plaza de San Martín): In a *side chapel* on the right of this 14–15C church there are five *paintings* of scenes from the life of Christ, which are probably by Alonso Cano. At the *high altar* there are figures of Christ and various saints by Montañés; to the left of this a 'Deposition', a relief by Roldán.

San Pedro (Plaza del Cristo de Burgos): A tall 14C Gothic church with a *Mudéjar* tower similar to the Giralda. Diego Velázquez was baptized here in 1599. The interior contains a 16C *high altar* by Delgado, a fine altarpiece by Roelas showing 'Peter's release from prison' (first chapel on the right), and eight paintings by Pedro de Campaña.

Santa Ana (Calle de la Pureza; in a quarter of the city known as Triana): This church has a nave and two aisles. It is Gothic-Mudéjar in style and has been altered several times. It is probably the *oldest church in Seville*. The interior contains a Plateresque *high altar* with 17 paintings by Pieter de Kempeneer (also known as Pedro de Campaña); the *transept* contains an early-16C 'Virgen de la Rosa' by Alejo Fernández, and the right aisle has a *terracotta tomb* by Nicoloso Pisano.

Santa Catalina (Plaza Ponce de León):

Once a mosque, it has an Almohaden minaret with a battlemented *Mudéjar tower* above it; the apses are also Mudéjar in style. The *interior* contains an exceptionally fine *artesonado ceiling* and a Churrigueresque baroque *altar screen* from the 18C. There is a depiction of the 'Man of Sorrows' by Pieter de Kempeneer in the baroque chapel on the left.

Santa María la Blanca (Calle de Santa María la Blanca): *Formerly a synagogue*. It is possibly Moorish in origin, with Visigoth capitals. The decoration is 17C rococo. There are *paintings* by Vargas and Murillo.

Santa María Magdalena (Calle de San Pablo): The former Gothic Dominican church of San Pablo served as a ground plan for the large and impressive structure which L. de Figueroa built in the baroque style characteristic of Seville. The baptistery, by Murillo, dates from 1618. The *interior* has a nave and two aisles and contains *frescos* by Lucas Valdés which date from around 1600. The *Capilla de la Quinta Angustia* has an interesting Mudéjar dome, and the *Capilla Sacramental* has two fine *paintings* by Zurbarán. There are also works by P. Roldán (including a 'Deposition') and M. Montañés.

Santa Marina (Calle de San Luis): A former mosque with a Moorish *bell tower* and a 13C Gothic *portal* with figures in tabernacles. It was seriously damaged in the Civil War, but has since been restored.

University Church (Calle de Laraña) The university was founded in 1502 and became a Jesuit college in 1771. The old *university* (the new one is housed in the old tobacco factory) has a fine *manuscript room* which has *paintings* by Roelas, Valdés Leal

Seville, cathedral, high altar

and Herrera the younger, and sculptures by A.Cano. There is also a notable 16C *Renaissance church*, which was erected by the Jesuit Bartolomé de Bustamente. It contains the fine *tombs* of Don Pedro Enríquez and his wife, which are Genoese and date from 1520. The 'Holy Family' on the high altar *retable* is by Juan de las Roelas; 'John the Baptist' and 'John on Patmos' on the high altar itself are by A.Cano. 'St. Francis Borgia' and 'St.Ignatius Loyola' on the high altar are by M.Montañéz, as is the 'Altar of the Immaculate Conception'. Juan de Mesa's 'Santo Cristo de la Buena Muerte' is now housed in the chapel of the new university.

Monastery of San Clemente (Calle del Torneo): This 13C monastery replaced a palace from Abbadite times and was for many years a *royal burial place*. The 17C church contains a very beautiful *artesonado*, 16C azulejos and *frescos* by Valdés Leal. The *high altar* may be by Montañés.

Convento de Santa Clara (Calle de Santa Clara): A very beautiful *patio* precedes the entrance to the convent, which was founded in the 13C. The *Renaissance church* shows Mudéjar traces in the apse. There is a superb *artesonado;* 16C azulejo decoration. *Sculptures* by Montañés on the altar wall and on the side altars include a good 'St.Francis of Assisi' (right). Also of interest, is the three-storeyed *'Torre de Don Fadrique'* in the gardens. This is in Romanesque-Gothic transitional style from the mid 13C and was once a tower of the royal palace. (Don Fadrique was the eldest son of Alfonso X, the Wise).

Convento de Santa Paula (Calle de Santa Paula): Founded in the 15C. It has an unusually beautiful 16C *portal* in a mixture of Gothic, Mudéjar and Renaissance styles with polychrome medallions (coats-of-arms and saints) by Francisco Nicoloso Pisano and Pedro Millán. The single-aisled *interior* has an artesonado ceiling, a Gothic apse and three interesting *tombs* with wonderful *azulejos*.

Hospicio (or Asilo) de los Venerables Sacerdotes (Calle de Jamerdana): Built as a home for priests in 1657. It has a particularly beautiful *patio*. The richly decorated *chapel* contains *frescos* by Valdés Leal (dome) and Lucas Valdés (walls). The *high altar* has a *painting* by Roelas of the Last Supper. There are dome paintings by Rubens, an ivory figure of Christ by Alonso Cano, a beautiful Madonna and Child by Sassoferrato, 'St.Ferdinand' by Valdés Leal (high altar) and bas-reliefs of John the Baptist, John the Evangelist and St.Stephen by Montañés. The *Museum of Holy Week* displays the art treasures of the brotherhoods (Confradías) of Seville.

Hospital de la Caridad (Plaza de Jurado E. side): This beautiful baroque *hospital* (seat of a brotherhood) was commissioned by Don Miguel de Mañara 1661 – 4. Mañara is reputed to have been the model for the figure of Don Juan. He was, however, not the typical Don Juan figure for his thinking was deeply affected by the loss of his young wife. A bronze figure by Susillo (1902) depicts him as a charitable man with a dying beggar. The hospital aimed to take in the sick, the poor and the starving. The façade of the baroque church is adorned with beautiful azulejos depicting Faith, Hope, Love, St.George and St. Roch in shades of blue. The *interior* contains two impressive and realistic *paintings*, 'In Ictu Oculi' and 'Finis Gloriae Mundi' (1672) by Valdés Leal; their theme is death, the transitory nature of life and all aspects of decay. The six works by Murillo on the other hand (1660-74) are concerned with the depiction of Mercy; of particular in

Seville, Museo de Bellas Artes, El Greco, 'Portrait of a Painter'

terest are 'The Feeding of the 5,000', 'Moses Striking the Rock' and 'St. Elizabeth Nursing Lepers'. At the *high altar* there is a superb work by Pedro Roldán, the 'Burial of Christ' (1673). In the *chapterhouse* there is a portrait of the founder, Mañara, by Valdés Leal. Mañara, who died here in 1679, is also commemorated by a death mask and his sword.

Hospital de las Cinco Llagas (Hospital of the Five Wounds), or **Hospital de la Sangre** (Calle de Don Fadrique): An elegant 16C building with *marble façade*. The beautiful *church tower* was built by Hernán Ruiz (mid 16C). Paintings by Roelas and Al. Vázquez; the altar is by Diego López.

Alcázar: This *royal palace* has a long history. It is the most important piece of Mudéjar architecture. There are few remains from its fortress-like form of the Almohaden period in the 12C, e.g. the *Patio del Yeso* with its arches and stucco ornamentation. The influences of Toledo and the Alhambra, with its complicated stucco decoration, introduced by *Moorish artists* from Granada under Pedro the Cruel (14C) predominate. 15C alterations; enlargement under Charles V (1526) and restorations under Philip IV lasting into the 19C introduced a classical note. Passing beyond the Almohaden walls you come to the *Patio de los Leones*. On the right is the *Casa de Contratación* (founded 1503), which was the *administrative office* for traffic with the West Indies. It contains beautiful Flemish *tapestries* with mythological themes (17–18C). In the chapel there is a well-known painting by Alejo Fernández, which is known as the 'Madonna of Seafarers' (1530–5). On the left is the *Patio de la Montería*, which provides a view over the magnificent *palace façade*. The rectangular, strictly articulated façade is broken by one triple- and two double-arched windows, beneath which are sebka ornamentation and blind arcades. Above the windows an inscription refers to Pedro I and the building of this part of the alcázar in 1364. The blue and white *band of tiles* repeats, in Kufic characters, the verse from the Koran 'There is no victor but Allah'. The wings date from the 16&17C. The part of the *mexuar* which is open to the public, between a battlemented wall and the palace itself, leads to the *Patio de las Doncellas* (Court of the Maids of Honour), around which the official chambers are grouped. The arcades with their cusped arches rest upon 52 slender double marble columns. Of particular beauty are the 14C azulejos, the filigree-like stucco and the decorations on the wooden ceilings and doors. Around the courtyard are the *Salón del techo de Carlos Quinto* with its superb Renaissance coffered cedar ceiling (16C), the *Chambers of María de Padilla*, the *Dormitorio de los Reyes Moros* and, above all, the splendid *Salón de Embajadores (Ambassadors' Hall)* with its marvellous decoration from the reign of Pedro I. The high walls of the room were crowned by a massive *dome* (which was only built 1420) with geometric patterns, polychrome stucco, gilding and stalactite work. The room opens on three sides through horseshoe-arched entrances. The *frieze of portraits* of Spanish rulers dates from the time of Philip II. The *Salón del techo de Felipe II* leads to the third part of the palace, the *Patio de las Muñecas* ('Doll's Court', so named after the small, doll-like faces in the arch spandrels). This part contains the *harem* or *living quarters*. The capitals of the columns of the arcade are mostly from Cordoba and Medina Azahara. Here also the decoration is of high quality, if a little more modest. The first floor has rooms with valuable tapestries from the 17&18C, the royal chambers and the *Chapel of Queen Isabella* with an *altar*, the polychrome tiling of which was the work of Francisco Nicoloso Pisano in 1503. Behind the 18C *Patio de María de Padilla*, which has a few remaining Gothic arches and the 'Baths of María de Padilla',

Seville, Plaza de España

is the *Palace of Charles V* with the *Salón del Emperador*. This has an excellent series of 12 tapestries with scenes from the Emperor's Tunisian Campaign, 1535—woven by the Flemish artist Pannemaker in 1554. Beautiful 16C azulejos. This part of the building dates from the 18C, after the earthquake of 1755 had destroyed the older Gothic palace. The *chapel* contains a collection of paintings from the Granada school. The *gardens of the alcázar* are of extraordinary beauty, incorporating various stylistic elements: Moorish (the 'Galera' and 'Gruta' gardens), Renaissance (the 'Jardín Grande' and the 'Jardín del Naranjal'), and modern (such as the garden in the former 'Herta del Retiro'). A grotto wall divides the garden into two parts. There are orange trees, palms, tiled benches, fountains and, in the middle, the *Pavilion of*

Charles V (mid-16C) with its beautiful 10 ft. high azulejo covering.

Casa de Pilatos (Plaza de Pilatos): This splendidly planned and decorated palace (late 15C/early 16C) with its large courtyard and several small patios owes its name to a legend that it is a copy of Pilate's house. Each room takes its name from the an episode of the Passion. The palace was built in the style of a Roman villa by Fadrique de Ribera in 1519, on his return from Jerusalem. *Holy Week processions* started at the Casa de Pilatos and ended at the *Cruz del Campo* (on the other side of the city walls). The length of this Way of the Cross is the same distance as that from Pilate's Praetorium in Jerusalem to Golgotha. Gothic, Moorish and Renaissance styles are integrated here into a successful unity.

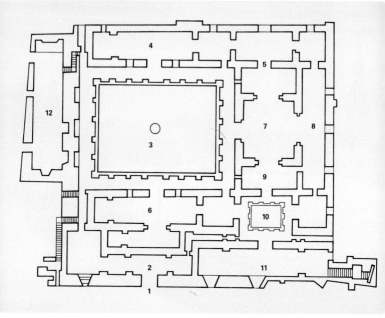

Seville, Alcázar **1** Puerta Principal or Puerta del León **2** Vestíbulo **3** Patio de las Doncellas **4** Salón del Techo de Carlos Quinto **5** chambers of María de Padilla **6** Dormitorio de los Reyes Moros **7** Salón de Embajadores **8** Salón del Techo(or Comedor) de Felipe II **9** Dormitorio de Felipe II **10** Patio de las Muñecas **11** Salón de Príncipe **12** Capilla

The decorated *marble portal,* in the form of a triumphal arch, is by Antonio María d'Aprile of Genoa (1533). The large *Renaissance courtyard* is surrounded by two-storeyed arcades on marble columns. The extravagant stucco surpasses even the splendour of the high azulejo bands on the walls (1538). Antique and Renaissance busts, four statues in the corners and an elegant *fountain,* crowned by a head of Janus, convey the strong empathy with the Graeco-Roman past. The *Salón del Pretorio* (Praetorium) has an excellent Mudéjar

coffered ceiling and fine Plateresque rejas. The *Gothic chapel* has heavy Mudéjar stucco and very beautiful azulejos. The interesting *Roman museum* contains antique statues and busts, including a Greek 'Athene' (possibly by Phidias, 5C bc), a Greek statue of Dionysus, Roman copies of Greek works and Roman portraits. The *staircase* is crowned by a 'media naranja' (half-orange) *dome.* On the upper floors are the *archives* of various Andalusian towns. On the left there is a room with a ceiling by Pacheco, which depicts mythological scenes (1645).

Casa Lonja (Plaza del Triunfo): This fine, well-balanced Renaissance building was designed as the *exchange* by Juan de Herrera and built in 1585 – 98. There is a charming *inner courtyard* with Doric and

Seville, Alcázar, Salón de Embajadores

Ionic columns. The *Academy of Arts* was founded here in 1660 at the instigation of Murillo, Valdés Leal, and Herrera the younger.

Palacio de San Telmo (Avenida de Roma): This fine 18C building was designed by L. de Figueroa in typical south Spanish baroque style with a large Churrigueresque *portal* (1734). It was once a school for sailors, but is now a priests' seminary attached to the church of San Luis. The palace is one of Figueroa's finest works.

Fábrica de Tabacos (Glorieta de San Diego): This enormous baroque building dates from 1757 and has four huge façades and over 100 inner courtyards and fortress-like extensions, such as ditches and sentry-boxes. It was the centre of the *tobacco monopoly*, and is the setting for Prosper Mérimée's book 'Carmen', which Georges Bizet set to music in his opera of the same name. Today it houses the *university*. This former tobacco factory has the largest dimensions of any building in Spain after the Escorial in Madrid.

Town Hall or Casa del Ayuntamiento (Plaza de la Falange Española): A Renaissance building from 1527–64. It has a magnificent Plateresque *façade*, which is highly decorated but nevertheless has a clear overall articulation. The façade was designed by Diego de Riaño. The *interior* mixes Gothic and Rennaissance stylistic elements. It houses the *city archive* and also the 15C city banner with a depiction of Ferdinand the Holy. The *picture gallery* contains works by Valdés Leal, Zurbarán and others.

Archbishop's Palace (Plaza de la Virgen de los Reyes): The beautiful *baroque portal* of 1704 is by Lorenzo Fernández de Iglesias; in structure it is very like a baroque retable. Inside there is a collection of *paintings*, including works by Velázquez, Murillo, and others.

Torre del Oro (Paseo de Cristóbal Colón): This twelve-sided *fortress tower* dates from 1220, the era of the Almohades, and was part of the alcázar. (It was formerly linked by a heavy chain to another tower on the other side of the Guadalquivir). It was reputedly once decorated with gilded tiles, which accounts for its name; the tower has an 18C lantern. Later it became a prison. Today it houses a small *Maritime Museum*. Together with the Giralda, it is one of the city's landmarks. Nearby, in the Calle de Santander, is the octagonal, battlemented *Torre de la Plata* (silver tower).

Puerta de la Macarena (Calle de San Luis): This gate bears the name of the daughter of a Moorish king and forms a section of the Almohaden wall. The wall itself is battlemented, defended by towers (7 rectangular and one octagonal) and extends for over 1,300 ft. as far as the Puerta de Córdoba.

Museo de Bellas Artes (Plaza del Museo): Formerly the *Convento de la Merced*, it dates from the 16–17C. The church is early 17C and was built by Juan de Oviedo. The museum has beautiful *inner courtyards* and a baroque *façade*. Since 1838 it has housed an excellent *picture collection* which occupies more than 20 rooms. Rooms 1 and 2 contain 13–16C paintings and sculptures, including work from the Seville school, e.g. Cristóbal de Morales' 'Entombment', and some Flemish painters. Room 3 is devoted to Renaissance works, with a particularly fine 'St.Jerome' by Pietro Torrigiani, whose 'Madonna of Bethlehem' is also of interest. Room 4 has paintings by Francisco Pacheco, and El Greco's 'Portrait of Jorge Manuel'. Room

Seville, Casa de Pilatos, courtyard

5 contains works by Ribera, Bocanegra, Alonso Cano, Herrera the elder, Juan de Roelas ('Martyrdom of St.Andrew', etc.), A.Vázquez, and others. Room 6 houses some exceptional work by Zurbarán: 'Apotheosis of St. Thomas Aquinas', 'St. Hugh of Lincoln', the celebrated 'Virgen de las Cuevas' (Virgin of the Caves), 'Pope Urban II', 'San Luis Beltrán' etc., and a sculpture of 'St.Dominic' by M.Montañés. Room 7 contains over 20 pictures by Murillo, including three on the popular theme of the 'Immaculata' ('Purísma', 'St. Justina and St.Rufina' and 'Madonna de la Servileta'). The painting of the 'Mercy of St. Thomas Villanueva' is among Murillo's finest works. Room 9, on the upper floor, contains some fine work by Juan de Valdés Leal, the great Spanish baroque painter: 'Flight of the Saracens from before the walls of Assisi', 'St.Jerome', 'Temptation of St. Jerome', 'Procession with a Monstrance', etc.. The upper floor displays a number of other interesting paintings, including some from the Romantic and Modern eras.

Provincial Archaeological Museum (Plaza de América): This collection is housed in a Renaissance pavilion and contains *prehistoric* finds (*c.* 2000 BC), some from nearby Itálica. There are also finds from the *Iberian* period, which is chiefly represented by objects from Andalusian burial areas. From *Roman* classical times we find a fine *mosaic floor* (3C AD), with a depiction of Bacchus. Amongst the collection of Roman works, which also includes copies of Greek originals, portrait busts, structural fragments such as columns, etc., note: a large statue of the Emperor Trajan, a Hermes (Mercury), the head of a goddess known as 'Hispania', and the finely worked torso of a Venus. There is also a collection of Roman glass. Another most interesting exhibit is the *'Treasure of El Carambolo'* (a hill near Seville), which was discovered in 1958 and consists of 21

pieces of gold jewellery: bracelets, brooches and a particularly fine chain. The origin of these finds is uncertain.

Gardens and Parks: Seville is justly famous for its splendid parks. For the *Gardens of the Alcázar* see alcázar. The *Jardínes de las Delicias* (Paseo de las Delicias) has pavilions, which are partly in the colonial style and which were built in 1929 on the occasion of the Spanish-American exhibition. The *Jardínes de Cristina* (Avenida de Roma) are particularly charming. The *Jardínes de Murillo* (Plaza de Santa Cruz) were formerly part of the alcázar and have arcades. The *Parque de María Luisa* (Plaza de España) was laid out by the French garden designer Forestier in the 19C. It was initially English in style, with splendid gardens featuring numerous fountains, avenues, azulejos, and a *monument* to the Romantic poet Gustavo Adolfo Bécquer of Seville. The *Plaza de España* is of interest. It is surrounded by a semicircular palace, the Palacio Español, which has arcades and was

Seville, Torre del Oro

built in 1929 for the Spanish-American exhibition. Inside the park is the *Plaza de América*, which has three pavilions: the Pabéllon Real, the Pabéllon Mudéjar, and the Palacio del Renacimento (see Archaeological Museum).

City Quarters: Apart from the individual buildings and monuments, some quarters of the city have a character of their own.

Barrio de Santa Cruz: Much of the atmosphere of Andalusia can be felt in the former *Jewish quarter*, with its innumerable alleyways, patios and whitewashed houses decorated with oriels, railings and flowers. The Calle de la Judería is covered over and leads directly into the quarter, as does the Callejon de Santa Marta near the cathedral and other access routes. Attractive *squares* include the Plaza de Doña Elvira (where theatrical performances formerly took place), the Plaza de las Cruces (which contains three crosses, including the fine 17C wrought-iron Cross of Cerrajería), and the Plaza de la Alianza.

Seville, Provincial Archaeological Museum, necklace

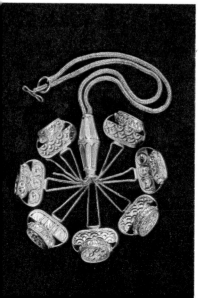

The most interesting of the many *alleyways* are the Calle de Susona, the Calle de Santa Teresa, the Callejón del Agua (with inner courtyards) and the Calle de Mármoles (with three Roman marble columns).

La Macarena Quarter: This quarter, on the outskirts of the city, is particularly *rich in folklore*. The famous 'Macarena' statue in the church beside San Gil is carried by the participants in the festival procession on Maundy Thursday.

Alameda de Hercules Quarter: This area was once a swamp, but was reclaimed as a *promenade* in the 16C; its N. and S. extremities are each bounded by two large *columns*. On the S. side there are two Roman-style granite *columns* with statues of Hercules and Caesar, the legendary founders of the city; the statues were carved by Diego de Pesquera in the 16C. The surrounding area contains numerous *churches and monasteries*, many of them worth visiting.

Triana: Formerly the Roman district of Trajana, it was once a centre for gypsies. It is linked to the centre of the city by the Puente Isabel II.

Calle de las Sierpes: A well-known, long, narrow and irregular *street*, which is now a pedestrian thoroughfare. It runs from the Campaña to the Plaza de San Francisco. Although commercial in character, it is used for the processions of *Holy Week*.

Also worth seeing: The *church of San Andrés* (Plaza de San Andrés) contains an 'Immaculata' by M.Montañés. *Church of San Benito* (Calle de Luis Montoto): 16C, with a 14C Virgin Mary inside. The *church of San Buenaventura* (Calle de Carlos Cañal) has paintings by Herrera the elder. In the *church of San Ildefonso* (near the Casa de Pilatos) there are paintings by Juan de

Roelas, including his 'Death of St. Ildefonso'. *San Jacinto* (Calle de San Jacinto) is a large baroque church of 1775, with a nave, two aisles, fine frescos in the dome, and some processional figures (pasos). The *church of San Nicolás* (Calle de Mármoles) is 18C. The *church of San Román* (Plaza de San Román) is 14C, with some sculptures by Montañés. The *church of San Vicente* (Calle de San Vicente) is a Gothic building with a 16C Renaissance portal; the interior contains fine baroque altars. The *church of Santa Isabel* (Plaza de Santa Isabel) is an early-16C Renaissance building. The *Capilla del Patrocinio* (Calle de Castilla) contains the famous 17C figure 'Cristo de la Expiración' or the 'Cachorro' by Francisco Antonio Gijón. The *Capilla del Seminario* (Plaza de Calvo Sotelo) is a Gothic chapel of 1506 with a fine portal, a single aisle with a fine artesonado, an attractive *retable* by Alejo Fernández, and Cuenca tiling. The *Cartuja de Las Cuevas* (Calle de Castilla) was founded in 1401 as a Carthusian monastery, but has been used as a *ceramics factory* since 1839. It has a fine Mudéjar-style church portal with Renaissance elements, and also a cloister. The *Monastery of la Madre de Dios* (near San Nicolás) is late 16C, with sculptures by M.Montañés and Jerónimo Hernández on the high altar. The *Monastery of Santa Inés* (Calle de Doña María) has a Gothic chapel which is most interesting because of the number of works which are attributed to M.Montañés: 'Madonna', 'St. Clare' and 'St.Ines' amongst others. The *Monastery of Santa María de Jesús* (Calle de Aguilas) was founded in the 16C and altered in the 17C; the portal includes a Madonna by Pietro Torrigiani. The *Palacio de las Dueñas* (Calle de Castellar) is a 15C Mudéjar palace. The *Palacio de la Condesa de Lebrija* (Calle de Cuna, 18) is a fine palace, with a 16–17C staircase with azulejo decorations and a 16C Mudéjar artesonado. There are Roman *mosaic floors* from Itálica on display and also busts and statues. The *Palacio de Santa Colóma* (Calle de Santa Clara) is 17C. The *Audiencia* (Plaza de la Falange Española) is a 16C law court with a 17C façade. The *Casa del*

Seville, Museo de Bellas Artes, Goya, 'Portrait of Canónigo Duaso'

Seville, Museo de Bellas Artes, Murillo, 'St. Justa and St. Rufina'

Duque de Alba (Calle de las Dueñas, 5) is a 15C palace. The *birthplace of Miguel de Mañara*, the founder of the Hospital de la Caridad, (Calle de Levies, 23) is another fine palace. The *Maestranza de Artillería* (Paseo de Cristóbal Colón) is a *artillery school* which was founded in 1587. The *Plaza de Toros de la Maestranza* is the site of the *bullring*, which was built in 1760; it is the largest such arena in Spain and holds around 14,000 spectators. The *Postigo de San Rafael* (Calle de Almirantazgo) is a *gate* which dates from 1573 and bears the coat-of-arms of Philip III. The *Acueducto de Carmona* (Calle de Luis Montoto) is the remains of a 12C Moorish aqueduct.

Environs: San Juan de Aznalfarache (4 km. W.): There are castle ruins, and a *church* containing paintings by Juan de Castillo. **Castilleja de la Cuesta** (6 km. W.) has a small *museum* in the Convento de las Irlandesas, where Hernán Cortés, who conquered Mexico and overthrew the Aztec kingdom, died in 1547. Nearby is the *Cueva de la Pastora*, a settlement and burial site during the third millennium BC. **Alcalá del Río** (14 km. N.) has the remains of a Roman settlement, which include baths and a necropolis. **Coria del Río** (15 km. S.) has the remains of the old Phoenician settlement of Caura. At **Sanlúcar del Mayor** (20 km. W.) the *church of Santa María* was originally an Almohaden mosque but was converted into a Gothic-Mudéjar church in the 13C (horseshoe arches, artesonado, Gothic choir). The *tower* was part of the mosque. The *church of San Pedro* is 12C, and its fortress-like aspect again betrays its Moorish origins. Remains of Roman walls are still visible. The *Puerta del Sol* is a Moorish gate. There are the remains of an *alcázar*. **Bollullos de la Mitación** (14 km. W.): Nearby is the *Ermita Cuatrovita*, which was formerly a mosque and contains a fine 12C minaret. **Pilas** (29 km. SW): Murillo

lived in a house here. **Villamanrique de la Condesa** (35 km. SW): The site of an unusually fine *castle* which belonged to the Infante *Don Carlos*; it has been altered many times since the 16C.
La Algaba (12 km. N.): The 15C *parish church of Nuestra Señora de las Nieves* was originally Mudéjar; rebuilt after the earthquake in 1755. The high altar and choirstalls are 18C. The Renaissance chapel has a fine altar and paintings; other altars are classical. **Torre de los Guzmanes:** This is the site of a marble slab bearing the Guzmanes' coat-of-arms. The irregular arrangement of the windows is most interesting. **Ares** has the *Ermita de la Concepción*, which has baroque and classical altars. **Guillena** (24 km. N.): The *church of Nuestra Señora de la Granada* is 15C Mudéjar. The interior contains baroque altars and a fine picture of the *Madonna of the Rosary* (1578) by Jerónimo Hernández. The entrance to the sacristy has 16C and baroque azulejos. There are remains of Gothic fortifications, including a *tower*. The surrounding area has *megalithic dolmens*, of which the most interesting is the *Llamado de las Canteras*, which has a round chamber reached by a corridor. *Bridges* over the Bureba include Roman fragments.
Albaida del Aljarafe (c. 25 km. NW): The *parish church* is late 18C, with classical elements on the façade. The interior contains a classical high altar, and some 17&18C paintings, including an 'Assumption of the Virgin' from the school of Murillo and a mid-18C Pietá on the Epistle side. The *Capilla de la Vera Cruz* has 17&18C paintings from the Seville school and an old inner courtyard with a Gothic portal. The *Torre Mocha* is a square tower which was built by Don Fadrique, the brother of Ferdinand III, the Holy. The only way to enter used to be by ladder, with ramps running up to the higher floors.

Seville, Museo de Bellas Artes, ceiling

Dos Hermanas (*c.* 19 km. S.): The *parish church of Santa María Magdalena* was in mixed Gothic and Mudéjar style before the fine 18C alterations. The interior contains baroque paintings (originally housed in the monastery of the Discalced Carmelites at Carmona). The altarpiece of the high altar depicts the Madonna and is by the school of Duque Cornejo. The Chapel of the Sacrament contains a 13C sculpture of the Virgin; the sacristy houses baroque and Renaissance gold pieces, including an 18C processional monstrance. The *monastery church of Santa Ana* has a single aisle and an artesonado; the altarpiece is a restored early-14C 'Madonna and Child' and a 'St.Roch' by the school of Bautista Vázquez 'el Viejo'. The single-aisled Mudéjar *hermitage of Nuestra Señora de Valme* has an 18C baroque altar. There is a Moorish *fortress tower*.

Las Cabezas de San Juan (53 km. S.): The *church of San Juan Bautista* (1762–77) is predominantly classical in style. The interior contains some fine baroque altars; the high altar has paintings by Francisco Augustín. The painting of 'Cristo de la Vera Cruz' on the Gospel side is attributed to Juan de Mesa. The sacristy contains a particularly valuable *treasure*. The *church of San Roque* has a remarkably fine figure of St.Anne, which is attributed to Montes de Oca. There are also some fine 18C *house fronts*, and a *ruined fortress*.

Aznalcázar (30 km. W.): The *parish church of San Pablo* is a fine Mudéjar building not unlike a number of churches in Seville, such as San Andrés or Omnium Sanctorum. The original interior was destroyed by fire in 1936. The *church of Nuestro Padre Jesús del Gran Poder* has a late-19C interior which contains a baroque high altar, a statue of St.Joseph from the school of M.Montañés, and a Mudéjar font. There are also a number of interesting and attractive houses, including the *Casa de los Camargo* and the *Casa Capitulares.*

Sigena
Huesca/Aragon   p.388 □ L 4

Some 16 km. SE of Sariñena is one of the most interesting convents in Spain, the Monasterio de Sigena. Founded in 1183 by Doña Sancha of Castile, daughter of Alfonso II, it was placed under the care of the Sisters of St.John of Jerusalem. The convent was partly destroyed during the Civil War.

Church: In spite of the above-mentioned damage, the Romanesque church of 1188 is worth seeing. It is laid out in the form of a Latin cross, with a nave and two aisles. The impressive Romanesque *portal* is distinguished by deep archivolts. In the transept is a 16C Plateresque *alabaster altar* . The prioresses of the convent used to be buried in the church and their tombs have remained. The *paintings* in the main apse, only parts of which survive, date from a later period. The *Capilla de San Juan* was built in 1720. The choir has pointed arches, the panelling may date from the 15C. The *Panteón Real* is to be found in the *Capilla de San Pedro* with the tombs of Pedro II of Aragon, his sister and the nobles who fell in the battle against Simon de Montfort in the 13C. The *treasury* contains, a 14C gold reliquary of French origin inlaid with enamel and mother-of-pearl.

Also worth seeing: In spite of their poor state of repair some of the rooms of the convent are of interest. The *chapterhouse,* which has survived several fires, still has part of its 14C groin vault. The walls of this room were decorated with Romanesque wall paintings, some of which are now preserved in the Museo de Arte de Cataluña in Barcelona. The *prioress's room* received a Mudéjar ceiling in the 13C and has beautiful frescos. The refectory leads to a Romanesque *cloister*.

Sigüenza

Guadalajara / New Castile   p.388□H 5

The seat of a bishop, Sigüenza lies at an altitude of 3,360 ft., above the Río Henares. It is a protected monument owing to numerous prehistoric finds. The old town, dominated by the battlements of its castle, clusters around the cathedral, which is also battlemented.

Cathedral: The 12C cathedral looks like a fortress. It has a nave and two aisles and is laid out in the form of a Latin cross. The building incorporates Romanesque with Gothic-Plateresque elements. *Inside* there are some splendid *statues,* in particular the 'Doncel', a most beautiful late Gothic sculpture. On both Gospel and Epistle sides there are Gothic *pulpits. Note* the Capilla de Santa Librada (patron saint of the town), the altar of St. Mark by Antonio Contreras and Mater Dolorosa and the Crucifixion, which are both by Pedro de Andrada. The retable dedicated to St. Catherine is by Juan de Sevilla. There is also an *Entombment of Christ* by Titian and an *Annunciation* by El Greco. The *sacristy,* the ceiling of which is adorned with many heads and rosettes of flowers, is by Covarrubias.

Also worth seeing: The picturesquely situated *Plaza Mayor* (with *Renaissance Town Hall*) is typical of Castile. The *castillo,* built by the Arabs in the 12C, is today a Parador. The *Casa del Doncel* (a young noble) stands in the Plaza San Vicente. Its *façade* is one of the finest examples the Gothic style. The *Chapel of the Humilladera,* a national monument, has a beautiful Renaissance portal. The *church of Santa María la Vieja* was probably the

Seville, Provincial Archaeological ▷
Museum, Aphrodite

town's *first cathedral* under the Visigoths and the Arabs. Up to the 15C the *atrium* served as a cemetery; today it is used as a *chapel* by the convent of the Poor Clares.

Environs: Palazuelos (just a few km. NW): The 15C *Town walls:* are extaordinarily well preserved; they were probably built on the initiative of the Princes of Santillana. The square towers were used for defence. The walls have three gates, one of which bears the coat-of-arms of the Mendoza family. *Castle:* Built on to the walls, it dates from the same time. Square ground plan, with round towers at the corners. *Parish church:* Late 15C, single-aisled.

Simancas
Valladolid/Old Castile   p.386☐F 4

Castle: The old Septimanca of the Romans. It is dominated by a castle, which once belonged to the Moors. The square interior was completely altered when Philip II designated it as the *General Archive of the Kingdom.* Over 30 million documents are preserved in 52 rooms.

El Salvador: The church, with a nave, two aisles and stellar vaulting (16C) contains fine *altarpieces* with sculptures by Inocencio Berruguete and paintings by Antonio Vázquez.

Environs: Arroyo (*c.* 2 km. N.): The church of *San Juan* is one of the best Romanesque buildings in the province.

Siresa
Huesca/Aragon   p.388☐K 2

Close to the hamlet of Siresa, near the mountain village of Hecho, is the *monas-*

tery of San Pedro, dating from Visigoth times. It was founded in 833, under the Aragonese Count Galindo Aznárez.

Church: Of the old monastery buildings there remains just this Romanesque church. Built in 1082 by Sancho Ramírez, it consists of a single aisle with an apse. The church contains interesting, painted winged altars (15C), a 13C image of the Virgin and a Gothic chalice.

Sitges
Barcelona/Catalonia   p.390☐N 4

The Iberians' Subur was mentioned by Pomponius Mela as early as the 1C BC. The village was adopted as a summer resort by the citizens of Barcelona back in the last century.

Cau-Ferrat Museum: This was founded by the painter and poet Santiago Rusiñol. Of most interest is the collection of Spanish *wrought-iron work,* whence the museum takes its name. Fine paintings by El Greco (St.Catherine and the Penitent Mary Magdalene), Zuloaga, Picasso, Utrillo, Ramón Casas and Rusiñol.

Maricel Museum: Old Gothic hospital (14C), consisting of two buildings connected by a bridge over the street. *Chapel* with frescos depicting the Life and Martyrdom of St.Bartholomew. Dating from around 1300, they are attributed to the Aragonese school. Also of interest are the collections of Romanesque *carvings* and the room with paintings of the First World War by José María Sert.

Environs: Olérdola: 15 km. NW of Sitges is the Roman settlement of *San Miguel de Olérdola,* with a cyclopean wall from the 3C. The early Romanesque church of *San Miguel* dates from the 10C.

Sigüenza, cathedral

Solsona
Lérida/Catalonia   p.390□M 3

Cathedral: Gothic building (14 – 15C) with Romanesque church front.

Palacio Episcopal: The 18C palace contains the *Museo Diocesano* , which has an important collection of prehistoric finds, Romanesque and Gothic painting and sculptures.

Environs: Olius (5 km. E.): 11C Romanesque *church* with beautiful capitals, interesting crypt and a wrought-iron staircase. **San Lorenzo de Morunys** (*c.* 25 km. N.): The *church* of the former monastery has survived. It contains fine Gothic altar panels by Serra.

Soria
Soria/Old Castile   p.388□H 4

The origins of the city are still unclear. Alfonso I of Aragon seized it from the Arabs and shortly thereafter it became part of Castile, whose king, Alfonso VIII, erected numerous Romanesque buildings. It reached the peak of its strategic and political importance with the assembly of the Cortes in 1350. There then followed centuries of medieval seclusion. Its charm was such that writers like Becquer, Unamuno, Arzorin, Gerardo Diego and, above all, Antonio Machado used the city in some of their best works.

Cathedral of San Pedro: Important parts still survive from the old building, such as the pure Romanesque windows and the cloister, which is one of the most beautiful examples of 12C Spanish Romanesque. In 1520 a large part of the building collapsed; the old structure was rebuilt as the present church; it was completed in 1573, with a very beautiful Plateresque portal. Inside there are two interesting altarpieces—Renaissance in the apse and Plateresque on the right. The Church's finest feature, in the Chapel of San Saturio, is a Flemish triptych of 1559. The chapterhouse serves as a museum.

San Juan de Duero: Only the church and the cloister remain of the former Templar monastery of the 12C. The 13C cloister is unique, symbolizing in its architecture the various cultures which Spain amalgamated in the Middle Ages; there are elements of Romanesque, Gothic, Mudéjar and Oriental styles. Inside the nave has a wooden ceiling and an apse with barrel vaulting.

San Juan de Rabanera: This 12C church shows the development of Castilian Romanesque architecture. Built in early Romanesque style, it shows Byzantine influences, as well as classical elements and pointed (Gothic) arches. The portal comes from the church of San Nicolás, as does the retable (1546–56), which is by the painter Juan de Baltanás and the sculptor Francisco de Agreda.

Santo Domingo: A 12C church with the most complete Romanesque façade in Soria. French influence is clearly apparent. Interesting sculptures.

Other interesting churches: In the old centre of Soria there is barely a street or plaza where a church façade cannot be seen. *Santa María la Mayor:* Of the old Romanesque building there remains just the tower and the portal; inside is a 12C tomb and, in the main chapel, a Gothic-Plateresque retable. *Nuestra Señora de la Merced* has paintings by Claudio Coello. *El Hospital* has a 16C altarpiece by Francisco de Pinedo. *El Salvador* has a 16C portico and a retable by Juan de Baltanás and

Siresa, San Pedro

Francisco de Agreda. The *Carmelite church* has a magnificent façade (1568) by Marcos de la Piedra and several baroque retables. The 18C baroque church of *Nuestra Señora del Mirón* has lavish decoration; the sacristy has Gothic vaults, which formerly belonged to an older church. The *Chapel of San Saturio* stands on a cliff on the right bank of the Duero; its ground plan is octagonal. The interior is adorned with paintings by Antonio Zapata (18C) and the altar is in baroque style. The *Capilla de la Soledad* contains one of the most impressive works of Spanish baroque sculpture, *El Cristo del Humilladero*.

Palace of the Counts of Gomara: Built in the last third of the 16C, it has an extensive façade and a tower, which dominates the whole city.

Other interesting buildings: The *Jesuit College* with a baroque façade; the Plateresque *Casa de los Castejones,* the *house of the Doce Linajes,* the present city hall, with a 17C façade.

Museo Numantino: The provincial museum contains archaeological finds from Celto-Iberian and Roman times, in particular from the ruins of the town of Numancia e.g. metal implements, bone and horn objects, clay statuettes, prehistoric remains, bronze objects, ceramics.

Environs: Almenar de Soria: The *castle* is square with round towers at the corners; the *Chapel of La Llana* dates from the 18C. **Fuensaúco** (*c.* 8 km. E.): Romanesque *parish church* with flying buttresses, battlements and semicircular apse. **La Mongía** (*c.* 8 km. W.): The Romanesque *parish church* belonged to an old monastery, of which only a few 15C windows are remain. Contained within are several oil paintings from the 15&16C. **Los Llamosos** (*c.* 12 km. S.): The little *church* shows interesting Mudéjar influence in the horseshoe-shaped apse and in the panelling. **Tozalmoro** (*c.* 15 km. E.): The single-aisled 12C *church*, has wooden panelling, a sanctuary with barrel vaulting and a semicircular apse. **Las Cuevas de Soria** (*c.* 10 km. SW): *Roman ruins* with the remains of a fortress are preserved here. There are still traces of a 2C AD settlement: rectangular rooms with polychrome geometrical mosaics on the floor. Many of the finds are displayed in the museum in Soria.

Sos del Rey Católico
Zaragoza/Aragon   p.388□I 3

This small, picturesque old town lies on the border with Navarre. It was formerly fortified and has preserved its medieval character well. It takes its name from the fact that Ferdinand the Catholic was born here in 1452.

San Esteban: The present church was

Soria, San Pedro, cloister

Soria, Santo Domingo

Soria, Count of Gomara's palace

preceded by one built in the 11–13C. The *crypt*, with a nave and two aisles, is a remnant of this earlier building. Two of its apses contain very well preserved *frescos* (13C). Also preserved here is a wooden *Virgin*, the Virgen del Perdón. The Romanesque church *portal* and the *capitals of the columns* inside are finely carved (12&13C). Beautiful font and two of the panels with depictions of Christ and the Virgen del Perdón (13C). Interesting choir stalls (16C) and treasury.

Palacio de los Sada: Remains of a 12C Romanesque chapel were discovered in this building with its fortress tower and beautiful inner courtyard. This old *mansion* was the birthplace of Ferdinand the Catholic, 'Rey Católico' in 1452. Recently

restored, the palace is a protected monument.

Ayuntamiento/Town Hall (Plaza Mayor): In a 16C Renaissance palace, whose façade is adorned with arches. The exchange was also housed here.

Also worth seeing: Numerous *palaces* and *mansions* from the 16&17C with splendid portals, wrought-iron grilles, balconies and beautiful coats-of-arms on the façades. *El Castillo*, the castle, has two beautiful, slender towers: the 'Torre del Homenaje' (keep) and the 'Torre del Reloj'. Of the town's *walls* there remain beautiful Gothic *gates. Outside the town* is the late Romanesque church of *Santa Lucía* and the 17C *Convento de Augustinos de Valentuñana*.

Tafalla
Navarra / Navarra   p.388 ☐ I 3

On the right bank of the Río Cidacos, this town is dominated by the castle of Santa Lucía.

Santa María: This Romanesque church has one of the most beautiful Renaissance altarpieces in Navarre. It was begun by Juan de Ancheta in the 16C and completed, following the death of the master, by his pupil Pedro González de San Pedro. It has more than 20 reliefs depicting the Passion and the Life of the Virgin Mary.

Convento de la Purísima Concepción: The church of this convent preserves a 16C altar, a lovely work, which originally stood in the Monasterio de la Oliva. The artists involved were Roland de Mois and Paul Ezchepers. These two Flemish painters worked in Spain for Prince Villahermosa. Work on the altar was started by Ezchepers in 1571 and completed by de Mois in 1579.

San Pedro: Construction of the nave began in the 16C but it was never completed. Contained within the church are several baroque altars and other pieces of artistic interest.

Convento de San Francisco: This convent was founded by Leanora de Foix and contains numerous works of art.

Castillo: Once the palace of the kings of Navarre. Charles III, the Noble ordered it to be built in the 15C. Building was abandoned on the orders of Cardinal Cisneros, however, so that only ruins of the Royal Palace remain.

Palacio del Marqués de Feria: Mudéjar and Plateresque decoration can be seen on the Marquis's palace.

Also worth seeing: Ruins of the church of *San Nicolás* with an interesting 11C portal.

Tahull
Lérida / Catalonia   p.390 ☐ M 2

San Clemente: This church in the San Clemente quarter is somewhat outside the town centre. Consecrated on 10 December 1123, it is a basilica with a nave, two aisles and arches supported on thick columns. The three apses, the central one of which is much the largest, have half columns and blind arcades, in keeping with Catalan-

Lombard tradition. Beside the S. apse stands the elegant six-storeyed *bell tower*, with double and triple windows. A wooden stair leads to the top storey of the renovated tower, affording a lovely view over the countryside of the Bohí and San Martín valley. The church became famous for its *wall paintings*, which are now in the Museo de Arte de Cataluña in Barcelona. The artist responsible for these—copies can be seen inside the church—became famous under the name of the Master of Tahull and was considered the most important painter on the peninsula. They show Christ Pantocrator, symbols of the Evangelists carried by angels, the Virgin with five Apostles and, in the vault, the Hand of God and the Lamb of the Apocalypse.

Santa María: This church was consecrated on the same day as San Clemente and originally had the same form. However, following rebuilding, its nave and two aisles were reduced to a single aisle. The five-storeyed bell tower and the S. wall are 12C. The church was recently renovated

and restored to its original form. Nave and aisles are of different size and are separated by thick columns. The *paintings* on view here are also copies, the originals being housed in the Museo de Arte de Cataluña in Barcelona. These paintings, in the typical Romanesque arrangement of three rows, are by two different artists. The Master of Santa María or Maderuelo painted the *Adoration of the Magi* on the wall of the apse and the so-called Master of the Last Judgement painted the N., S. and E. walls at a somewhat later date. (The latter artist takes his name from the paintings on the walls.) Also on display in the Barcelona museum are a 12C altar and a Christ on the Cross, part of a lost Descent from the Cross.

Talavera de la Reina
Toledo/New Castile   p.392□F 6

The former *Caesarobriga* of Roman times is famous for its porcelain.

Iglesia Parroquial de Santa María: This parish church, built in Gothic style in the 13–15C, has a rectangular ground plan, three apses and a nave and aisles without a crossing. Various chapels displaying Gothic elements were built on to the sides and contain interesting pieces from the 15&16C. Note the apse-shaped *Capilla de San Juan Bautista* with two 15C tombs. The cloister consists of four arcades with pointed arches and vaulting.

Iglesia Parroquial de Santiago: This 14C parish church was built in Mudéjar style and displays Gothic influence. The most interesting feature is the brick external decoration on the tower and façade.

Iglesia Parroquial de San Miguel: This Mudéjar church was probably founded in the 12C. It has a nave and two aisles with

Tahull, San Clemente

three semicircular apses in the E. end. The nave and aisles have a panelled ceiling and are divided by pointed arches on columns.

Iglesia Parroquial de San Pedro: This church was probably founded around the time of the reconquest of this region. It was almost entirely rebuilt in Mudéjar style in the 14C and there are few remains from that period. The Gothic Capilla de Cienfuegos was added to the right of the nave in the 15C. The church had a baroque extension in the 17C. The tower was altered in the 18C.

Iglesia Parroquial de San Clemente: This church, probably dating from the time of Alfonso VII (mid 12C), underwent various alterations in the 14–16C. It consists of a dilapidated nave and two aisles and three apses.

Iglesia Parroquial de Santa Leocadia y Santa Eugenia: This church has a rectangular ground plan and groin vaulting. The Gothic Capilla de la Saleta was added on to the right side in the 15C. The Capilla Mayor was altered in the following century, while much of the church was rebuilt at the turn of the 17&18C.

Monasterio Jerónimo de Santa Catalina: Founded in 1397, the monastery is now an Augustinian school. In 1469 a larger church was completed, which was needed because of the rapid growth of the monastery. In the 16C work began on a new building, the E. end and crossing of which (both Renaissance) survive.

Convento de Santo Domingo: Built 1520–36 and founded by Juan Hurtado de Mendoza. It was restored and altered in 1900. The Gothic church, with a Latin cross ground plan and a single aisle divided into seven bays has a buttressed vault dating from the late Gothic period. During the same period chapels were added to both sides of the aisle. The Capilla Mayor houses the Plateresque tombs of Pedro de Loaysa and his wife. The cloister has stone columns and flattened arches.

Santuario de la Virgen del Prado: A Gothic Madonna and Child (late 15C) is revered here. Talavera porcelain (16–19C) was used in the interior decoration.

Iglesia de Santiago de los Caballeros: This Mudéjar church dates from the 13C.

Also worth seeing: The *Casa de los Marqueses de Villatoya* and the *Casa de los Loaysa*, both Gothic, are particularly fine examples of secular architecture. Various houses in the town bear memorial stones with Roman inscriptions from the 1–3C.

Environs: Cebolla (*c.* 20 km. E.): The *Castillo de Villalba* (11&12C) is rectangular; some square towers have survived, as have entrance doorways with semicircular arches and parts of the outer wall. The interior of the fortress is totally destroyed.

Talavera de la Reina, vase

Hinojosa de San Vicente (16 km. NE): *Iglesia Parroquial:* This Gothic parish church (early 16C) consists of a nave and an apse. The whole building is supported by strong wall buttresses. The entrance arch is pointed and supported by columns with pearly decorations. The tower was built later than the church, probably at the end of the 16C. *Castillo de San Vicente:* This castle (12C or earlier) probably belonged to the Knights Templar. It has been in ruins since the 16C. Part of the walls and two towers survive. **Malpica** (*c.* 25 km. E.): *Iglesia Parroquial:* The *Virgen de Bernúy* is venerated in this parish church. Originally from the hermitage of the same name (now destroyed), it is a restored 13C statue of a seated Madonna and Child. *Castillo:* This medieval castle was probably built in the 14C on the remains of an Arab fortress. It stands on the left bank of the Tagus and is built of brick. The ground plan is rectangular. The castle has strong walls and massive square towers at the corners. The keep stands to the SW. The Marquises of Malpica almost completely rebuilt the interior in the 17C. Probably dating from this time are the Renaissance columns in the courtyard, as well as the brick arcades, the railings and balconies. **Alcaudete de la Jara** (20 km. S.): The *parish church* dates from 1530. The main façade is Plateresque with Gothic elements, while the tower is in Herrera style. The medieval tower, the *Torre del Cura* is the oldest structure in Alcaudete. Square ground plan. It has been altered considerably in the course of time.

Talavera la Vieja
Cáceres/Estremadura   p.392☐E 6

Talavera la Vieja: The Roman town of Augustobriga once stood by the Embalse de Valdecañas reservoir. Six Corinthian columns with an architrave and an arch survive.

Tamarite de Litera
Huesca/Aragon   p.388☐L 3

San Nicolás: This Romanesque parish church was built at the end of the 12C. Pope Pius V elevated it to a collegiate church. It consists of a nave, two aisles and a coro, which were rebuilt in the 13&14C. At the *high altar* stands an alabaster statue of the Virgin (1504) by the Flemish artist Jean Dusi. In the 16C the Romanesque S. portal was altered. The W. portal is baroque. The church treasure, preserved in the *sacristy,* includes 16 works by a painter of the Antwerp school, valuable liturgical vestments and beautiful reliquaries. The *bell tower* was built in the 14C.

San Miguel: This 12C church was originally Romanesque. It was altered in the 16C, from which period the Gothic vault also dates. The portals are also Roman-

Talavera de la Reina, view

esque. Contained within are interesting altarpieces with 15C paintings.

Tarazona
Zaragoza/Aragon   p.388 □ 3

This picturesque old town on the Río Queiles is also known as the 'Toledo of Aragon', due to its many Mudéjar buildings. In antiquity there was already an Iberian settlement here, called *Turiasso*. Tarazona rose to importance under the Romans, due to the discovery of iron ore in the Sierra de Moncayo. The town is the seat of a bishop, and the townscape is dominated by the bishop's palace, a former royal castle.

Cathedral: Construction of this building began outside the old town in 1162, after Alfonso I had recaptured the town from the Moors. There had previously been a Mozarabic church here. Its consecration was celebrated in 1235. However, by 1357 the church had been destroyed in the war between Peter I, the Cruel, of Castile and Peter IV. The rebuilding of the cathedral lasted until the 16C, though further parts were added into the 18C. As a result the church is principally Mudéjar and Gothic with baroque and Plateresque elements. The cathedral has a nave and two aisles. The domed vault, the brick tower — the *Torre del Reloj* — and the cloister were all built in pure Mudéjar style prior to the 16C. The tower and dome were influenced by the cathedral of *La Seo* in Saragossa. The N. portal was built by Juan de Talavera in 1588 and is lavishly adorned with sculptures. The *trascoro* dates from the 18C and contains a group of 17C polychrome sculptures consisting of a Christ flanked by John and the Virgin. The *coro* has 15C Gothic choir stalls and a baroque grille. The Capilla Mayor dates from 1560. The *altarpiece of the high altar* (1603) is decorated with reliefs and statues. Numerous works of art adorn the many side chapels. In the left aisle is the 16C *Capilla de la Visitación* with a Plateresque altarpiece. The *Capilla de Santiago* contains

Talavera de la Reina, view in tiles

Tarazona, cathedral, Capilla de los Calvillo

Spanish-Flemish style altarpieces from the workshop of Pedro Díaz de Oviedo in 1497. In the same aisle is the *Capilla de la Purificación* with an altarpiece (1493) by Martín Bernat. The chapels of the right aisle are equally interesting. The *Capilla de San Juan Bautista* contains a Plateresque altarpiece of 1542, and the *Capilla de San Pedro y San Pablo* has a retable in the same style. The *Capilla del Rosario* in the ambulatory has a 16C altarpiece, as well as a 13C sculpture of the Madonna. Also in the ambulatory is the Gothic *Capilla de los Calvillo*. Apart from the enormous altarpiece by the painter Jean Lévy, the chapel contains the Renaissance alabaster sacophagi of Bishop Pedro Calvillo and his brother Cardinal Calvillo. Next to the Renaissance portal of the cloister is a further sarcophagus, that

of Bishop Ximénez de Urrea, dating from 1317. The *cloister* is Mudéjar and dates from the 16C. It is decorated with beautiful stucco.

Convento de San Francisco: 13C. In the *sacristy* there is a 15C Gothic monstrance. The two-storeyed *cloister* is of interest.

Iglesia de la Magdalena: The town's oldest church; Romanesque apses. The tall tower is Mudéjar. Contained within are a few 16C altarpieces.

San Miguel: This church was referred to in documents as early as 1214 and was rebuilt in Gothic style in the 16C.

Convento de la Concepción: Mudéjar elements can still be discerned in this con-

Tarazona, Casa Consistorial

vent. The church contains a beautiful 16C high altar.

Convento de la Merced: 17C baroque.

Casa Consistorial: The town hall is housed in the former exchange building, which dates from the 16C and has a façade covered in reliefs. Next to the coats-of-arms of Aragon and Tarazona is that of Charles V.

Palacio Episcopal: The Bishop's Palace was built on top of a Moorish building. Dating from the 14C, it has beautiful wood panelling.

Palacio de los Condes de Alcira: The Count's family palace is a typical Aragonese building of the 17C and has a large inner court.

Also worth seeing: *Hospicio:* This former Jesuit monastery dates from the 17C. Remains of the 40 ft. thick *walls* in the Alfara district of town.

Tarifa

Cádiz/Andalusia   p.394 □ E 12

The situation of Spain's southernmost town (Roman *Julia Traducta*), at the narrowest point of the Straits of Gibraltar (some 8.5 miles between Europe and North Africa), meant that it was important to every wave of settlers, particularly the Arabs. The recapture of this town by the Christians was accompanied by the tragic story of the town's commander Alonso Pérez de Guzmán, who allowed his son to die

Tarragona, Forum Romanum

at the hands of the Arabs in order to hold the town.

San Mateo: This late Gothic church (16C) was built on the site of a mosque and the bell-tower was erected on the site of what was the minaret. Beautiful baroque façade.

Alcázar: This 10C Moorish fortress was rebuilt in the 13C during the Reconquista. The *town walls* , still in good condition, were fortified with further towers and ramparts. The octagonal tower, the *Torre de Guzmán* is historically important. Of the three original gates two survive: the *Puerta de Jerez* and the *Puerta del Mar*.

Also worth seeing: *Iglesia de Santa María* with a polychrome, carved wooden statue, the *Inmaculada* (16C).

Environs: Ruins of Bolonia (14 km. W.): The ruined Roman town of *Belonia Claudia* is known as the *Ruins of Baelo*. It was excavated by French experts around 1920 and shows the lay-out of a small Roman settlement (1C AD) with streets, forum, several temples, a semicircular fountain, theatre and baths. The form of its fortifications can be seen from a town wall (13 ft. high) with a gate.

Tarragona
Tarragona/Catalonia   p.390☐M 4

Tarragona is the capital of the southernmost province of Catalonia. Pliny, in his 'Naturalis Historia', refers to the town of *Tarraco* as being founded by the Scipios,

Tarragona, Roman amphitheatre

but the type of walls which surrounded the old town suggest that it must be earlier, probably from the 3C BC. The name does not seem to be of Roman origin, probably going back to a pre-Roman settlement on the hill within the town. When, in 197 BC, Roman *Hispania* was divided into two provinces, first Cartagena and later Tarraco became the capital of Hispania Citerior. In 45 BC Julius Caesar renamed the town *Colonia Julia Urbis Triumphalis Tarraco*. The town flourished thereafter: religious and political conferences took place here. The Emperors Augustus and Hadrian lived in the town, and Septimius Severus ruled the province before becoming Emperor. Redevelopment of the town began in 1117 after 400 years of Arab rule.

Cathedral: In 1194 work started on the cathedral and it was to last a whole century. The building was located beside an old church dating from 392. In Romanesque-Gothic transitional style, the church has a Greek cross ground plan, nave, two aisles, transept and four of the five apses planned originally. Pillars dividing nave and aisles are Romanesque; the rib vault is Gothic. This mixture of the two styles can be clearly seen in the *transept*. Over the Romanesque base of the crossing is a dome with pure Gothic windows. The two side doors on the façade are Romanesque, showing the *Adoration of the Magi* in the tympanum and the *Martyrdom of St. Bartholomew* on the capitals and a further *Adoration of the Magi* (2). The central portal (3) was started in 1278 by Master Bartoméu but was not completed until 1475 by J. Castails. In the *main apse* (11) is the

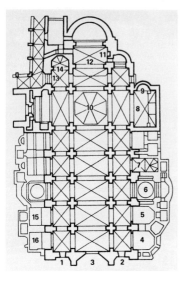

Tarragona, cathedral, 1, 2 Romanesque portals **3** main portal **4** Chapel of the 11,000 Virgins, now the baptistery (transitional style, 1341) **5** chapel of San Miguel (1360), Gothic, with an altar by Ramón de Mur (1432) **6** small murals opposite the chapel **7** Chapel of the Holy Family **8** 16C Gothic

chapel **9** Chapel of San Olegario **10** choir with late Gothic choir stalls (15C), organ figures by Juan Amiga (1561), panel paintings by Pere Serafi (16C), with the Papal banner from the Crusades against the Turks (1456) hanging on the right hand side **11** tomb of Archbishop Don Juan de Aragón **12** high altar by Pere Johan from 1426 **13** Romanesque door to cloisters **14** Chapel of Santa María or de los Sastres, late Gothic (1358–80) **15** Chapel of Montserrat, with the tomb of Archbishop Pedro de Cardona (d.1530), and a 14C altar **16** Chapel of Santo Tomás with a 16C altar

tomb of Don Juan de Aragón, son of James II, who was Bishop of Toledo at the age of 17 and Bishop of Tarragona at 28. He died in 1334 at the age of 33. The sculptures of the tomb are most impressive. The work is attributed to the French artist Pedro Ginés, but this is not entirely certain. There is a Romanesque altar table at the *high altar* (12) and a retable by Pere Johan, which was completed 1426–33 and shows St. Thecla, Christ Pantocrator, the Holy Ghost and the Hand of God. At the sides are four scenes from the life of St. Thecla, to whom the altar is consecrated. The door to the cloister (13), in white marble, dates from the 13C with the Pantocrator and the

Tarragona, cathedral, façade

Tarragona, cathedral, high altar

four symbols of the Evangelists in the tympanum. All the capitals of the columns display biblical scenes (e.g. *Adoration of the Magi, Nativity of Christ,* etc.). The cloister was probably started at the same time as the church (1171) and is similar to those of Vallbona and Poblet. It has pointed and round arches. The carved capitals show biblical themes, such as *Adam and Eve, Cain and Abel.* Others depict fables: *The cat and the cockerel, Burial of the cat by the rats* (3rd pillar in the S. walk) and *The fight of the cat and the dog.* Opening on to the cloister is the Gothic *Capilla del Corpus Christi* (1330), the first room of the *Diocesan Museum.* The museum contains a collection of Gothic paintings, including a retable by Jaime Huguet, Catalonia's most famous Gothic painter, woodcarvings from the 13–19C, a Renaissance retable and paintings from the 17&18C, copper items, ceramics, manuscripts and books from the 15–18C. Of particular interest is a collection of 54 tapestries from the 14–17C, catalogued in nine series, principally from the Brussels workshop. In the fourth apse of

the cathedral is the *Capilla de Santa María* or *de los Sastres* (the tailor), in a style quite different to the rest of the cathedral. It has a pentagonal ground plan and is lavishly decorated with sculptures. It was built in the 14C in fine late Gothic style, of which it is one of the earliest examples in Catalonia.

Capilla de Santa María la Vella: This was built behind the cathedral in the 18C on the site of a Romanesque church, which was a bishop's church in the 12C. This, in turn, was built over the ruins of a former Roman temple of Jupiter.

Paseo Arqueológico: This runs along the old town walls. Just over a half a mile of walls remain from the 2 miles that were originally built. The base is formed by a *cyclopean wall* with stones some 10 ft. thick and 13 ft. long. Five gates from this part of the wall survive. On top of the cyclopean wall there is a typically Roman construction of smaller ashlars, which was restored several times during the Middle Ages. At

Tarragona, cathedral

Tarragona, cathedral, façade

one corner stands the 14C archbishop's tower *(Torre del Arzobispo)*.

Palacio del Rey and **Museo Arqueológico:** This almost square building, which was part of a larger Roman structure, stands on the Plaza del Rey. Known locally as 'Pilate's Palace', archaeologists call it *El Pretorio.* In the Middle Ages it was renovated and used as a residence by the Catalonian-Aragonese kings. In 1813 it was set on fire by the French. A few walls, vaults and a façade with Doric elements survived. On the upper floor there is a 14C room, which serves as the museum's picture gallery. The adjacent archaeological museum has innumerable finds from Roman times.

Necrópolis Romano-Cristiana and **Museo Paleocristiano:** In 1923, during building of a tobacco factory, a Roman Christian cemetery was found, covering an area of 2,150 sq. ft., at a depth of 6 ft.—the largest of its kind in Spain. It contained 2,050 tombs from the 3–6C with all sorts of objects, e.g. an ivory puppet, which was found beside a little girl of six. Of particular interest are the beautiful mosaics. The ground plan of a basilica, built in the 4C over the tombs of the martyrs Fructuosus, Eulogius and Augurius, was also excavated. All these splendid finds can be seen in the museum.

Also worth seeing: Below the *Balcón de Mediterráneo* is the *Anfiteatro Romano* with the remains of a Visigoth basilica and the Romanesque church of *Santa María de Milagro.*

Environs: Centcelles (5 km. NW): The

Tarragona, cathedral, cloisters

remains of a 4C town were discovered here, the most important find being a tomb. Badly preserved mosaics have now been restored and depict biblical scenes. There are also remains of paintings. Restoration work was carried out by the German Archaeological Institute in Madrid. **Roman Aqueduct:** (4 km. NE): This was built by the Spanish-born Emperor Trajan. Known locally as the *Puente del Diablo (Devil's Bridge)*, it is 730 ft. long, 100 ft. high and has two tiers of arches, 11 below and 25 above. **Torre de los Escipiones** (6 km. towards Barcelona on the N 340): The remains of this Roman tomb date from the 1C AD. Two figures dressed as soldiers stand on tall plinths. There is no evidence of any connection between this tomb and the Scipios. **Tamarit** (*c.* 11 km. W., on the coast): The medieval castle, referred to as

early as the 11C, played an important role during the reconquest of the region. **Arco de Bará** (20 km. W.): This Roman triumphal arch, one of the most beautiful in Spain, was built in 107 under Trajan. It is 41 ft. high with Corinthian pillars. **Reus:** 13 km. from Tarragona and 8 km. from the sea, this little town is an important market centre specializing in dried fruit, wine and olive oil. The 15–16C *church of San Pedro* is worth seeing, as is the town's museum with archaeological collections, paintings and sculptures. There is also the Missal of Reus, an illuminated book by Ramón Destorrents (1363).

Tarrasa

Barcelona/Catalonia   p.390□N 4

In the suburb of Tarrasa, the ancient

Egara, three Visigoth churches, believed to have been built before the 9C, survive.

San Miguel: This church is a square building (rounded within) with a horseshoe-shaped apse. The apse was painted in the 11C with the *Ascension of Christ,* of which almost nothing remains. The church served as a baptistery. The dome is supported on four Byzantine columns.

San Pedro: Note the church's tripartite Byzantine apse. There is a stone retable within.

Santa María: This church has a Latin cross ground plan and a horseshoe-shaped apse. The frescos here are better preserved than in the other churches. A fresco in the apse depicts scenes from the life of the Virgin; another on the walls of the transept shows the *Martyrdom of St. Thomas Beckett* (1170). The Gothic panel paintings preserved in the church *museum* are worth seeing. One is by Luis Borrassá (1411) and

formerly belonged to the Iglesia de San Pedro, another is by Jaime Huguet (painted for the same church, 1459–60) and a third, the retable of San Miguel, was painted by Gabriel Talarn (1451).

Iglesia Parroquial: This parish church on the Plaza Mayor is a single-aisled 16C Gothic building. The crypt is more modern and houses an alabaster Entombment (1544) by Martín Díaz de Liatzasolo.

Also worth seeing: *Cartuja de Vallparadis* (Calle General Sanjurjo): This Carthusian monastery, built as a castle around 1110, was handed over to the Carthusians in 1344; Carthusian monks lived here until 1415. The best preserved feature is a 15C gallery of pointed arches. The monastery now houses the *Museo Municipal de Arte* (an art museum). In the adjacent building is the *Biosca Textile Museum* with collections of Egyptian, North African and oriental fabrics, as well as European and American examples from the time before Columbus.

Tarragona, Torre del Arzobispo

Tarragona, Museo Arqueológico

Environs: Sant Llorenç de Munt (8 km. NW): Situated at an altitude of 3,350 ft., this little church was consecrated as early as 1064. It is Romanesque with a nave, two aisles and three apses. The nave and aisles are barrel vaulted and over the crossing there is a beautiful dome. The exteriors of the apses bear typical Lombard decoration with blind arcades.

Tárrega

Lérida/Catalonia   p.390☐M 4

Iglesia Parroquial: The late Gothic style parish church dates from the 17C. It has a wide nave with a stellar vault.

Casa Sobiés: This 12C house is a beautiful example of Catalan-Romanesque architecture, with a wide gate, extensive living quarters and a chapel.

Environs: Verdú (6 km. S.): The Romanesque-Gothic *Iglesia de Santa María* (13&14C) was rebuilt in the 16C. The Romanesque portal, by the Lérida school, has a beautiful flying buttress. The church treasure includes gold items. The *castle*, of which there remains only a gateway, the keep and a room with Gothic windows, dates from the 14C. **Guimerá** (15 km. S.): Only a tower survives from the *fortress*. The portal of the *parish church of San Sebastián* is Gothic. Previously there was a wooden retable by Ramón de Mur (1402–12) here, but this is now housed in the Episcopal Museum in Vich.

Tauste

Zaragoza/Aragon   p.388☐I 3

Santa María: This Mudéjar parish church dates back to 1243. Its 240 ft. octagonal *tower* is of interest and inside the church the beautiful *retable* of the high altar is particularly worth seeing; this is a Plateresque work by Gabriel Yoly, Juan de Salas and Gil Morlanes (known as 'el

Tarragona, Torre de los Escipiones

Arco de Bará (Tarragona)

Joven') and it dates from 1520-24. The beautiful carved wooden figures were gilded in 1579. There are other 16C altars in the church and among the church's numerous paintings is a Flemish panel.

Also worth seeing: The most interesting of Tauste's secular buildings are the *Palacio de los Marqueses de Ayerbe,* known as the *Casa Grande,* and the former *house of the Antillón family.*

Tenerife

Santa Cruz de Tenerife/
Canary Islands   p.396☐M 10

Little is known of the early history of the Canary Islands. The question has often been raised as to whether, together with Madeira and the Azores, they might be the last remnants of the mythical continent of Atlantis. The Phoenicians, on their voyages along the W. coast of Africa, appear to have been the first to visit the Canary Islands in order to collect Orchilla lichens for the production of purple dye — hence the name *Purple Islands.* It appears that King Juba of Mauretania and Libya also sent ships to explore the islands in 25 BC. He is supposed to have received two dogs as a gift from the king and thus they came to be called the *Islas Canarias (Dog Islands,* from the Latin *canis,* a dog). The natives of the islands were called *Guanches.* They knew no metals, mummified their dead like the Egyptians and painted their bodies with colours made from burnt earth. Their system of government was monarchic, the kings *(Menceys)* being advised by a council of elders. Their weapons consisted of clubs, hardwood spears and arrows tipped with obsidian. They lived mainly in volcanic caves. A large role was played by a death cult. Mummified bodies are still preserved today, due to the dry air. The islands were discovered

in 1312 by the Genoese mariner Lanzarotto Malocello, after whom the island of Lanzarote was named. They were not colonized, however, until the Norman Jean de Béthencourt landed on Lanzarote from Cadiz in 1402 and went on to capture Fuerteventura, Gomera and Hierro by 1405. He received the title 'King of the Canary Islands' from Henry III of Castile, who financed the expedition. In 1491-6 Gran Canaria, La Palma and Tenerife were also seized from the Guanches, in the name of the Spanish Monarchy, by Fernández de Lugo. In the course of this most of the Guanches were killed; those who survived were converted to Christianity. Following the discovery of the New World the islands served as an intermediate station on the voyage and Columbus stopped off there several times. Other visitors included Alexander von Humboldt in 1799 and Emperor Maximilian on the way to Mexico in 1864. In the 17&18C there were constant attacks from Moorish, Dutch and English fleets (Nelson 1797), but none managed to land. Tenerife, covering 795 sq. miles and with some 450,000 inhabitants, is the largest of the Canaries, forming a rough triangle. Like all the other islands in the group it is of volcanic origin. In the centre, the summit of *Pico de Teide* (12,420 ft.) rises from the vast semicircular Cañada crater (6,700 ft. high and 8 miles wide). The *Cumbre,* the ridge which runs thence to the NE, divides the island into two totally different halves. The NW half of the island, with its rich sub-tropical vegetation, is one of the most fertile regions of the world, while the parched SE side is exposed to the hot desert winds of Africa.

Santa Cruz de Tenerife: The capital of the island and the province of Tenerife lies at the SW end of a bay some three miles wide. Diego de Herrera built a castle here as early as 1464, although this was later destroyed by the Guanches. After several attempts by the Spanish, Don Alonso

Fernández de Lugo finally managed to conquer the Guanches in 1494 and take Tenerife as a possession of the Spanish Crown. In the 16C work was begun to fortify the town, with the result that not only numerous pirate raids, but also three attacks by English fleets were repulsed. In 1723 the capital was moved here from La Laguna. *Iglesia de la Concepción:* The town's oldest church (1502) was rebuilt with the original low nave and four aisles following a fire in 1652. Square tower, attractive forecourt with balconies. Interior: richly carved baroque high altar, marble pulpit (1736), 17C choir stalls, as well as two flags seized from Nelson in 1797 and the *Conquest Cross,* which recalls Fernández de Lugo's victory over the Guanches. *San Francisco:* Founded on the square of the same name in 1680 as the church of the monastery of San Francisco de Alcántara, it was restored in 1777 and a tower with an azulejo-clad dome was added. Façade in the style of the Spanish colonial baroque. Interior: altarpieces of artistic interest and 17-18C ceiling frescos. The *Museo Municipal* behind the church has a picture gallery with works by Jusepe de Ribera, Jacob Jordaens and Guido Reni, among others, as well as a collection of old weapons. In the *Plaza de la Candelaria* in the middle of the docks stands the *Madonna de Candelaria* (Bringer of Light), by the Italian sculptor Canova (1778) on a pyramidal column of white Carrara marble, around which are grouped the figures of four Guanche princes. It commemorates an apparition of the Virgin. On the same plaza is the palace-like, mid-18C *Casino de Tenerife* with paintings by native artists (Nestor de la Torre, Aguiar and Bonnin). Also on the same square stands the *Palacio de la Carta* (18C), the former seat of the Civil Governor, with a beautiful patio and typical Canary-style balconies. The *Museo Arqueológico* on the Plaza de España in the Palacio Insular has extensive collections from the time of the Guanches (utensils, cult objects, mummies

La Lugana (Tenerife), Iglesia de la Concepción, font

and jewellery). In the old castle, the *Castillo de Paso Alto,* is the *Museo Militar,* in which, among other things, trophies of war, such as the 'El Tigre' cannon are displayed.

La Laguna: The former capital and now the second largest town on the island was founded in 1496 by Fernández de Lugo, who decisively defeated the Guanches here. It was the Captain-Generals' residence until 1723. With its palaces, grand town houses and chess board-style lay-out, La Laguna still has the aspect of an old Spanish town of the 16&17C.
Iglesia de la Concepción, one of the town's oldest churches (16C) with a beautiful tower (early 18C). Inside there are panelled ceilings, a baroque pulpit carved from a single piece of wood, cedarwood choir

stalls and a 15C Majolica font in the aisle. The *Dominican Monastery* in the Calle Santo Domingo is now a priests' seminary. The simple *Iglesia de Santo Domingo* contains the monumental fresco by a modern Spanish artist on the theme of the Mysteries of the Rosary. In the garden there is a 2000 year-old dracaena palm, the last of a whole forest which the Spanish conquerors had cut down. *Monastery of San Agustín* (17&18C) in the Calle San Agustín, together with the baroque *Episcopal Palace* (17C) with a beautiful patio, as well as other old palaces and the 18C *university*. The *cathedral* was begun in 1513 but has been altered several times since (most recently in 1908-9). Neoclassical façade. Inside: tomb of Fernández de Lugo, conqueror of Tenerife, baroque retable, beaten silver altar, baroque reredos and rich *church treasure*, consisting mostly of silver items.

Also worth seeing: Baroque *Palacio de Nava* (17C) on the Plaza del Adelanto, *Town Hall* (19C) with frescos of the island's history, *Santuario del Cristo* in the E. of the town, an early monastery church, containing the *Santísimo Cristo de la Laguna* (15C), a much revered image of Christ.

La Orotava: The former capital of a Guanche chief is now a picturesque little mountainside town with narrow cobbled alleys and numerous palaces adorned with coats-of-arms, ornately carved balconies and lintels.
Near the Plaza with its trees and flowers stands the *Iglesia de la Concepción* with two elegant towers and a dome; a masterpiece of rococo architecture. Inside: high altar of alabaster and marble by Giuseppe Gagini (18C), 17C baroque altarpiece, sculptures and carvings by local artists. Statue of St. John and a *Mater Dolorosa* by Lujón Pérez (18C) and rich treasury. The houses behind the Town Hall have the most beautifully carved balconies in the town.

Puerto de la Cruz: This town was founded at the start of the 17C. Originally inhabited by fishing folk, it only started to increase in importance when the English Yoeward Line enlarged the harbour with a mole, in order to export bananas.
The parish church of *Nuestra Señora de la Peña* (early 17C) contains several baroque works of art: high altar by Luis de la Cruz and 17C statues of saints, as well as wood carvings and gold pieces from the 17&18C. The fishing Chapel of *San Telmo*, built in 1629 and restored in 1968. It originally housed the statue of the patron saint of fishermen, St. Pedro Gonzáles Telmo, which was destroyed in a fire in 1788 (later replaced by a new one).

Tacoronte (20 km. W. of Santa Cruz): 17C baroque *parish church of Santa Catalina.* Inside: liturgical articles and a high altar of the pure Mexican silver brought here by the Mexican silver fleets. The *monastery church of San Agustín* (1662) is paved with black and white marble slabs in the Italian style. The ceiling is made of local pine wood, which is gradually darkening. The 17C wooden 'Martyred Christ' *(Cristo de los Dolores)* is probably the work of a Genoese artist.

Realejo Alto: It was here that the last Menceyes (kings) of the Guanches submitted to the Spanish conquerors and were baptized.
The *church of Santiago* is one of the oldest churches on the island and dates from 1498. The bells were a gift from King Ferdinand of Aragon.

Candelaria: A small fishing village and a most important place of pilgrimage on the island, 25 km. S. of Santa Cruz. 100 years before the conquest of the island the Guanches found a wooden statue of the Virgin Mary on the beach. This was set up in the grotto of San Blas and it was reputed—even before Christianity came to

La Orotava (Tenerife), Iglesia de la Concepción

the island—to have brought about a series of miracles. It was kept in a monastery until 1826, when it fell victim to a flood. Nevertheless, Nuestra Señora de Candelaria remained patron saint of the Canaries. The mighty *pilgrimage basilica* (completed 1958) is dedicated to her. It stands on the site of the original church, which was destroyed by fire at the end of the 18C, and contains a copy of the statue of the Virgin (made by Fernando Estévez, 1830). Also worth seeing is the parish church of *Santa Ana* (17&18C), containing a beautiful crucifix.

Icod de los Vinos (about 30 km. W. of Santa Cruz): The town is typical of Tenerife and also has the island's oldest dracaena palm (*c.* 3,000 years old). The Renaissance parish church of *San Marcos*

(16C) houses a baroque altarpiece (17C) and statues from the 17–19C. Rococo carvings in the *Capilla de los Dolores*.

Teruel

Teruel/Aragon   p.388□K 6

Teruel is a provincial capital and bishop's seat. The city was founded by the Iberians, who named it *Turba*. Surviving from that time are cave paintings, stone implements and ceramics. The city was destroyed by the Romans in 218 BC in retaliation for Hannibal's annihilation of Sagunto. The city later came under the sway of the Moors and was named *Teruel*, meaning *bull*. It was recaptured from the Moors by Alfonso II of Aragon in 1171. In 1176 the

Teruel, cathedral, Mudéjar ceiling

Teruel, cathedral, Mudéjar tower

Moors were granted generous special privileges, giving them the opportunity to lend their creative abilities to the developing Mudéjar style in particular. Teruel is the centre of this style. The last mosque was not closed until 1502.

In the 13C the city was scene of the tragic love affair between Diego de Marcilla and Isabella de Segura. The story became a theme of Spanish poets and sculptors and made the city the destination of many honeymoon couples. The two mummies are now contained in a mausoleum in the church of San Pedro.

Cathedral: Formally called Santa María de Mediavilla, it was built in the 12C, altered in the 13C and elevated to a cathedral in the 16C. The *tower*, built of gold-coloured bricks, with a prism-shaped top, reveals Romanesque influence and, with its ceramic decorations, is characteristic of the Mudéjar style. Inside the church the Gothic-Mudéjar style is discernible in the arrangement of both nave and transept. Pure Mudéjar style is revealed in the masterful vaulting (1314) in the nave and Capilla Mayor. The Plateresque altarpiece of the *high altar* (1536) is one of the most beautiful of Gabriel Yoli's works. Also of interest is the late-15C Gothic choir grille — a masterpiece of Teruel wrought-iron work. The *sacristy,* where the church treasure is kept, contains monstrances of the 15,17&18C, a 12C Romanesque processional cross and other valuable religious objects.

San Pedro (Calle de Harcembusch): The church was built in Gothic-Mudéjar style in the 13C. An interesting feature of the church is the ornamentation of the square brick tower (similar to that of the cathedral), the lovely apse and the beautiful cloister, all dating of which are 14C. Note

Teruel, San Pedro ▷

the carved wooden *Renaissance altar* from the mid 16C and, in the adjacent *Capilla de los Santos Medicos,* a carved gilded altar depicting the life of St.Peter by the French sculptor Gabriel Yoli. In a side building the famous Lovers of Teruel rest.

Iglesia de la Merced: This church has a 16C Mudéjar tower. Inside is a Plateresque altar dedicated to St.George.

San Martín: This church dates back to 1196 but received its present form in the late 17C. The oldest part of the building is the delicate, square, Gothic Mudéjar *tower* (1315), lavishly adorned with porcelain plaques, which are mainly green and white.

Convento de Santa Teresa: This baroque Carmelite convent has a lovely high altar, which is also baroque.

Convento de San Francisco: A Gothic monastery built 1391–1402. The single-aisled church has a groin-vaulted ceiling and a polygonal apse.

Acueducto de los Arcos: This aqueduct was begun in 1537 by the French engineer Quinto Pieres Vedel, following Roman models. The structure, which also serves as a viaduct, took the whole of the 16C to build.

Palacio Episcopal: The Bishop's palace was built in the 16–17C. It is a typically Aragonese building, with a gallery running below the eaves. Housed in the same building is the *Diocesan Museum,* in which numerous medieval paintings are preserved, including a work attributed to the Master of Teruel. This is Gothic from the second half of the 15C and depicts the Virgin sheltering supplicants under her cloak. Besides further works from the same period attributed to the circle of the painters Marçal de Sax and Pedro Nicolau,

the collection also has works from the 16C.

Museo Arqueológico Provincial: This is housed in the Casa de la Cultura and has a complete collection of traditional ceramics from the potteries of 13–15C Teruel, as well as large Roman mosaics.

Tineo
Oviedo/Asturia   p.386□D 1

This town, standing on the mountain of the same name, is surrounded by beautiful valleys. The labyrinthine old town with its narrow alleys and tiny streets has a particular charm.

Parish church: In the old town, it dates from the 13C. The Romanesque building reveals early suggestions of Gothic. The portal arch is adorned with geometrical motifs and the capitals are decorated with fantastical beasts and plants.

Also worth seeing: Both beautiful and interesting are the *Palacio de Maldonado y Campomanes* and the *Palacio de los Meras,* but above all the old *pilgrim hospital,* which has remains of medieval painting.

Environs: Obona: 7 km. W. of Tineo lies Obona Abbey, founded in 780. Little remains from that time. Much restored in the 17C. The Romanesque church has a nave two aisles and three apses and houses a Romanesque polychrome wooden figure of Christ, a silver-clad marble altar from the 11C and the tombs of the founders. **Celón** A further 27 km. on, not far from Cangas de Narcea, is Celón with the 11C church of *Santa María,* which has a Romanesque portal. The sanctuary is decorated with 15C frescos relating stories from the New

Teruel, San Pedro, retab.

Toledo, El Greco, 'View and plan of Toledo' (El Greco Museum)

Testament. On the *Castro San Luis* there are still traces of a pre-Roman settlement, where many items of archaeological interest were found. **Cangas de Narcea:** Once a Roman settlement. The *parish church* was built by Archbishop Valdés Llano in 1639 and his tomb now lies in front of the high altar. The *Ayuntamiento* is now in the old Palacio de Queipo de Llano, which was built around 1700 and has a remarkable portal and a particularly beautifully structured façade.

Toledo
Toledo/New Castile   p.392☐ G 6

This provincial capital has some 53,000 inhabitants and lies above the Tagus in the middle of the Meseta of Castile. One of the oldest cities in Spain, it was captured by the Romans in 192 BC and named *Tole tum*. The Visigoths occupied the city in 418. In 527 the 2nd Council of Toledo took place. From 569 Toledo was capital of the Spanish Visigoth empire. The city fell into the hands of the Moors in 711. Alfonso VI of Castile recaptured Toledo in 1085 and from then on Toledo became capital of the Kingdom and also the focal point of the Church in the whole of Spain. Ferdinand III, the Holy, founded the cathedral, and Alfonso X, the Wise, set up the famous school of translation, which made Toledo a centre of medieval knowledge. The city lost its political importance when Philip II moved his court to Madrid.

Cathedral: The foundation stone was laid

Toledo, panorama

under Ferdinand III, the Holy, and Rodrigo Ximénez de Rada, Archbishop of Toledo, in 1226. The first architect was Master Martín who was succeeded by Petrus Petri. Although the cathedral took two centuries and to build and was not completed until 1493, it is pure Gothic in structure, with Mudéjar elements discernible here and there. The *main façade* has three Gothic portals: *Puerta del Perdón*, *Puerta del Infierno* (left) and *Puerta del Juicio* (right), all lavishly decorated with figures. In the tympanum is a relief of *the Virgin giving St.Ildefonso a chasuble*, with the Last Supper above it. The tower (300 ft.) was built in pure Gothic style 1380–1440 by Rodrigo Alfonso and Alvar Gómez. In the top storey of the lower part hang the bells, the famous *campana gorda*, the great bell weighing some 17 tons and dating from 1753. The upper part is octagonal and ends in a spire with three crowns.

The S. façade has two portals, the *Puerta Llana*, built in classical style in the 18C, and the *Puerta de los Leones*, by Joaquín Egas with a row of columns at the entrance, adorned with lions.

On the north side is the *Puerta del Reloj*, also called *de la Chapinería*. This portal is lavishly adorned with Gothic pointed arches and ornaments from the early 14C, including figures of angels and scenes from the New Testament.

Leading to the cloister are the *Puerta de Santa Catalina*, which is Gothic with Mudéjar influence and the *Puerta de la Presentación*, which opens from inside the church. The cathedral has a large nave, four aisles (*c.* 340 ft. long, 200 ft. wide, nave

Toledo, cathedral

Toledo, cathedral, Puerta de los Leones

height *c.* 100 ft.) and 15 chapels. The aisles join up behind the altar. 88 massive pilasters support the vault. Many rosettes and lovely stained-glass windows from the 15&16C decorate the interior.

The *Capilla Mayor* is at the end of the nave behind a long, tall iron grille with an enormous crucifix by Francisco Villalpando. The late Gothic high altar has scenes from the Life of the Saviour and the Virgin Mary. It is the work of various artists; Diego Copín de Holanda, Sebastián de Almonacid, Peti Juan and others worked on the beautiful carving to drawings by Alonso Sánchez and Felipe Bigarny. Reliefs, statues, niches and coats-of-arms adorn the walls. Note the tomb of Cardinal Mendoza by Alonso de Covarrubias. The recumbent figure of the Cardinal is by Andrea the Florentine. On both sides of the altar are the tombs of the kings Alfonso VII, Sancho III and Sancho IV of Castile.

Behind the Capilla Mayor is the *Transparente*, a Churrigueresque altar (1732) by the architect Narciso Tomé. The vault above it was broken through to allow daylight to fall on the altar.

The *Capilla de Santiago* was built in late Gothic style in the 15C for its founder, Alvaro de Luna. The tomb of the Constable and his wife Juana Pimentel was made by Pablo Ortiz, the Gothic winged altar by Juan de Segovia, Pedro Gumiel and Sancho de Zamora.

The tomb of Cardinal Albornoz lies in the middle of the *Capilla de San Ildefonso*. In addition, the Renaissance tomb of Iñigo López Carrillo de Mendoza and the Gothic one of Juan de Contreras stand by the walls of the chapel.

The Plateresque *Capilla de los Reyes Nuevos* (16C), which is next to the sacristy, is the work of Alonso de Covarrubias. It was built for the burial of Henry II and

Toledo, cathedral, Gothic window

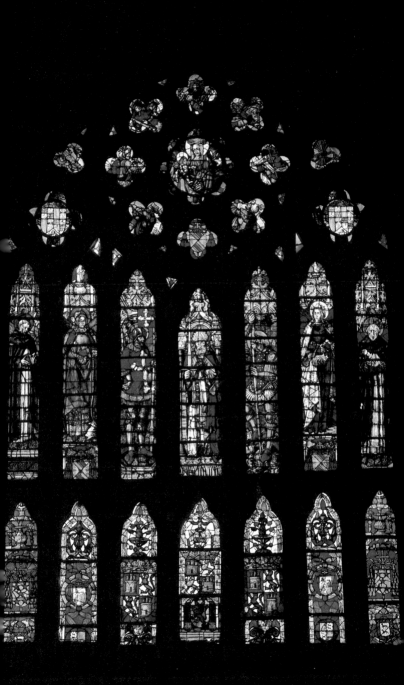

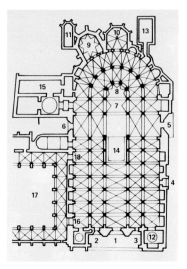

Toledo, Cathedral 1 Puerta del Perdón **2** Puerta del Infierno **3** Puerta del Juicio **4** Puerta Llana **5** Puerta de los Leones **6** Puerta del Reloj or de la Chapinería **7** Capilla Mayor **8** Transparente **9** Capilla de Santiago **10** Capilla de San Ildefonso **11** Capilla de los Reyes Nuevos **12** Capilla Mozárabe **13** chapterhouse **14** choir **15** sacristy **16** Puerta de la Presentación **17** cloister **18** Puerta de Santa Catalina

contains statues and splendid tombs of kings. The altars, designed by Ventura Rodríguez have paintings by Mariano Maella (Virgin Mary and St. Ildefonso). The **Capilla Mozárabe** was built by Enrique Egas under Cardinal Cisneros in 1504. Mass is held here daily using the old liturgy of the Christians living under the Arabs. Above the altar is a fresco by Juan de Borgoña of *the Madonna and Child.* The **Sala Capitular,** octagonal in form, was begun at the start of the 16C under Cardinal Cisneros with late Gothic, Plateresque and Mudéjar decoration. The wall frescos were painted by Juan de Borgoña. Beneath them is a long series of portraits of all the bishops of Toledo. The **coro** displays several styles. The elegant iron grille, which faces the main chapel, dates from

1547 and is the work of Domingo de Céspedes. The lower choir stalls were carved by Rodrigo Alemán in 1495 and depict the Conquest of Granada. The middle level on the gospel side is by Felipe Bigarny, the middle and top levels on the epistle side are by Alonso Berruguete. His work, which depicts scenes from the Old and New Testament, is one of the most beautiful pieces of Castilian carving. Behind the archbishop's throne is an alabaster *Transfiguration of Christ.* The two enormous iron and bronze reading desks are by Nicolás de Vergara and display altorelievo of *the Creation, David, Saul* and *Noah's Ark with the procession of animals.* *Sacristía:* This was built 1593–1616 by Nicolás de Vergara and contains paintings by famous masters. The ceiling fresco was painted by Lucas Jordán. On the altar is the painting *El Expolio (The Stripping of Christ)* and the Apostle cycle by El Greco. *The Arrest of Christ* by Goya and the Holy Family by Anthony van Dyck are also to be seen. On the right is the *Vestuario* (vestry) with a ceiling fresco by Claudio Coello and paintings by Giovanni Bellini *(Burial of Christ),* Peter Paul Rubens *(The Mystic Marriage of St. Catherine),* Anthony van Dyck *(Pope Clement VII),* Diego Velázquez *(Cardinal Borja),* Titian *(Pope Paul II),* Raphael *(Baptism of Christ),* to name but a few. Preserved in the adjoining rooms are tapestries and vestments, but above all the 13C Bible of St. Louis. The *cathedral treasure (Tesoro)* is kept right next to the *Puerta de la Presentación.* Apart from numerous gold and silver chalices, crucifixes and sculptures it includes Spain's most valuable monstrance (gold and silver, 10 ft. high, 380 lb.), made by the German goldsmith Enrique de Arfe (Heinrich von Harff), 1517–24.

The *cloister* was built under Archbishop Tenorio. The lower part dates from 1389,

Toledo, cathedral, door to chapterhouse ▷

Toledo, cathedral, high altar

Toledo, cathedral, choir stalls

the upper was added by Cardinal Cisneros. The sculpted decorations date almost exclusively from the 14C and were completed in the 15C. The frescos of the lower storey are by Francisco Bayeu and Maella. By the door leading to the upper storey is the *Capilla de San Blas* with Gothic sculptures and 14C frescos. Housed in the north gallery of the upper storey is the library with numerous manuscripts.

San Andrés (Plaza de San Andrés): The church and the two chapels at the crossing date from 1300. The crossing and the main chapel were commissioned in 1500 by Francisco de Rojas, Ferdinand and Isabella's envoy, who wanted these sections to be similar to those of San Juan de los Reyes. The three early-16C altarpieces at the end wall are the work of Juan de Bor-

goña and his colleague Antonio de Comontes.

Convento de la Concepción Francisca (behind the Hospital de Santa Cruz): This convent was given to the nuns by Isabella the Catholic in 1484. The church exterior dates from the 14C and is Mudéjar in style, as can clearly be seen from the tower. The interior is still in Renaissance style. The two chapels added on to the nave contain numerous Gothic and Plateresque tombs. The *Capilla de San Jerónimo*, built by Alfonso Fernández Soladio in 1422, has an octagonal dome and is furnished with azulejos from Valencia. Also preserved here is a mural depicting the Mass of St. Gregory.

Iglesia del Cristo de la Luz (Cuesta del

Toledo, San Salvador, Visigothic column

Toledo, Iglesia del Cristo de la Luz

Cristo de la Luz): The mosque of Bib-Al Mardón (built on to a Visigoth church in 999) was converted into a Christian church in the 12C. Inside are remains of Romanesque wall paintings.

Ermita del Cristo de la Vega (Vega del Tajo): This stands on the site of the Visigoth basilica of Santa Leocadia, in which many councils took place. It was rebuilt in 1166. The Mudéjar apse dates from that time.

Convento de Santa Clara la Real (Plaza de Santa Clara): This monastery has a Mudéjar patio with Arab horseshoe arches. Important remnants in this style are preserved in the church, such as the artesonado ceiling over the nave and the Gothic chapel.

Convento de Santo Domingo el Antiguo (Plaza Santo Domingo): The monastery contains many works of art, including the paintings in the lower ward and a 14C tomb. The church is of interest, built by Juan de Herrera and Nicolás de Vergara and for which El Greco painted his first works in Toledo. Most of these paintings were transferred to various museums, but *the Resurrection* and *John the Evangelist* can be admired in their original positions.

Convento de Santa Fé (Calle Santa Fé): This Mudéjar monastery takes its name from the *Capilla de Santa Fé* , which was built in 1226 by the Knights of Calatrava and has a polygonal apse. Next to it is the *Capilla de Nuestra Señora de Belén,* built at the time of the Caliphs, as one can see from the dome. Buried here are the Infante

666   **Toledo**

Don Fernando and the Infanta of León,
Doña Sancha Alonso, daughter of Alfonso
IX.

Convento de Santa Isabel de los Reyes
(Calle de Santa Isabel): This convent,
which takes in the Palacios de Casarrubios
and Arroyomolinos, was established in
1477. The two palaces were given as a gift
to the convent by Isabella the Catholic.
Preserved within are the *Patio del Laurel,*
which is modelled on the Alhambra, and
a few rooms, such as the *dormitorio de la
reina* (Queen's bedroom). The courtyard
of the sick-room, part of the Palacio Arroyomolinos, dates from a later period, but
is also in Mudéjar style. Integrated into the
church is the former *Parroquia de San Antolín,* the Mudéjar apse of which survives.
The interior consists of a nave with a
Gothic main chapel containing the tomb
of Doña Inés de Ayala. This was made of
black and white marble in the second half
of the 15C. There is also a large
Renaissance altarpiece of 1572.

Monasterio de San Juan de los Reyes
(Plaza de San Juan de los Reyes): The monastery was commissioned from the architect Juan Guas by Ferdinand and
Isabella, in thanks for the victory at Toro.
In just five years Guas created one of the
most beautiful examples of Spanish-
Flemish Gothic architecture. The church
consists of a single aisle with chapels along
the flank. The lavish interior is of interest.
The altarpiece of the *high altar* is by the
sculptor Felipe Bigarny and the painter
Francisco de Comontes. The *cloister* has
two storeys. The pillars display 15C figures
of saints. Note in particular the Mudéjar
ceiling of the upper storey.

Iglesia de los Santos Justo y Pastor
(Plaza de Santo Justo): Originally built in

Toledo, Santo Tomé, El Greco, 'Burial of ▷
the Count of Orgaz'

Toledo, Hospital Tavera

Toledo, Hospital de Santa Cruz

Mudéjar style, the church was converted to baroque. Inside is the 14C *Capilla del Corpus Christi*.

San Román (Calle San Román): This church is still Mudéjar in style, with the exception of the main chapel, which was altered in Plateresque style in the 16C. Of interest are the wall paintings (13C), in which Christian images are united with the geometrical and plant motifs of Arab decoration. The church now houses the *Museo de los Concilios y de la Cultura Visigoda,* in which various capitals, columns and reliefs from Visigoth times are to be seen.

Iglesia del Salvador (Plaza del Salvador): The church, founded at the end of the 15C by Alvarez de Toledo, was destroyed by fire in 1822. Only the *Capilla de Santa Cata-*

lina could be saved. The church and the altarpiece belong to the late Gothic style.

San Sebastián (Ronda de las Carreras): Rebuilt in Mudéjar style in the 13C, the church contains a few old Visigoth chapels. The high altar has a Renaissance altarpiece.

Santiago del Arrabal (Calle Real del Arrabal): This most important of Toledo's Mudéjar churches was built in the mid-13C. The oldest part, somewhat older than the church, is the 12C tower. Preserved inside are a Mudéjar pulpit, the 16C Plateresque altarpiece and a few tombstones.

Santo Tomé (Calle de Santo Tomé): This church dates from the 12C. It was rebuilt

Toledo, Monasterio de San Juan de los Reyes

in the 14C at the behest of Gonzalo Ruiz de Toledo, Lord of Orgaz. The main chapel and the Mudéjar tower date from this time. In the *Capilla de la Concepción* hangs the famous El Greco painting *The Burial of the Count of Orgaz*, 1586–8.

Sinagoga de Santa María la Blanca (Calle de los Reyes Católicos): This large synagogue stands almost in the middle of the Jewish quarter on the W. side of Toledo. Built at the end of the 12C, it was rebuilt after a fire in the 13C. The interior has five aisles, divided by horseshoe arches. The capitals are unusual, all being differently decorated with pine cones integrated into a geometrical arrangement. Around 1550 the synagogue was converted into a Christian church and three chapels were added on to the end wall. The retable of the high

altar by Bautista Vázquez and Vergara the Elder displays the Plateresque coat-of-arms of Cardinal Silíceo, who ordered the conversion.

Sinagoga del Tránsito (Paseo del Tránsito): This synagogue represents part of the splendid palace commissioned in 1366 by the Jew Samuel Leví, treasurer of Peter I of Castile. The interior of the building is richly decorated. Along the entire upper part is a stucco frieze with psalms in Hebrew script, interrupted by coats-of-arms from Castile and León. These point to the protection given by Peter I. The ceiling has octagonal wood panelling decorated with bows. Following the expulsion of the Jews in 1492, Ferdinand and Isabella gave the synagogue to the Knights of Calatrava. Now housed in the adjoining rooms is the *Museo Sefardí,* which houses items of interest relating to Jewish-Spanish culture e.g. religious objects, Torahs etc.

Palacio Arzobispal (Plaza de la Catedral): Surviving Mudéjar fragments include the panelling in the Salón de Concilios, a wide plaster frieze and a polychrome ceiling in a part of the tower.

Alcázar: This massive structure stands at the highest point in Toledo and was begun by the Romans. Following restoration by the Christians, particularly under Alfonso VI and Alfonso X, the Wise, the first alcázar developed with its square ground plan and four corner towers. In the 16C Charles V commissioned Alonso de Covarrubias with the building of the E. façade, with its Plateresque portal, and the N. façade. The S. façade was built to plans by Juan de Herrera. The alcázar burnt down in 1710 and the French set it ablaze once more in 1810. The fortress was rebuilt 1867–82, but in 1887 it burned down for the third time. At the outbreak of the Civil War the alcázar was occupied by the Military Academy. In 1936 it was almost totally destroyed and later rebuilt.
The arcaded court is two-storeyed with Corinthian columns. The main façade is of interest with its decorated main portal, windows and balustrade.

Ayuntamiento (opposite the cathedral): The City Hall was built to designs by Juan de Herrera in the early 17C. Building began in 1613 under the supervision of Jorge Manuel Theotocópoulos, El Greco's son. The *Salón de Sesiones* (conference hall) contains azulejos from Talavera de la Reina, depicting scenes from the war in Flanders. Hanging on the staircase are portraits of Charles II and his wife Marianne de Neuburg, painted by Carreño de Miranda.

Hospital de Santa Cruz (Calle de Cervantes): The hospital was founded by Cardinal Pedro González de Mendoza and built 1504–14. The plans were drawn up by Enrique Egas, architect to the Queen, who chose a Greek cross ground plan, formed by two intersecting, two-storeyed aisles. These have Mudéjar artesonado ceilings. The windows and, above all, the portal are Plateresque in style. The Renaissance courtyard was created by Alonso de Covarrubias. Of particular interest here is the Plateresque staircase leading to the second storey. A *museum* is now housed in the hospital and consists of three departments. The archaeological section has prehistoric, Roman, Arab and Visigoth finds, amongst which are interesting Roman mosaics. The painting and sculpture departments have a collection of paintings, principally from the Toledo School, with various works by El Greco (18 paintings, including an *Assumption of the Virgin*). The most important work in the sculpture collection is the altarpiece of the *Visitation* by Alonso Berruguete. The third department, the crafts section, has exibits of porcelain, glass, iron and gold.

Hospital Tavera: This building stands outside the city walls, N. of the *Puerta de Bisagra,* and is also called *Hospital de Afuera.* Founded by Cardinal Tavera, it was built 1541 – 1626 by Bartolomé Bustamante, Hernán González de Lara and the Vergaras (father and son). The large *inner courtyard* is surrounded by beautiful arcades; its 96 arches and 112 columns make it one of the most beautiful patios in Spain. The church is in the courtyard and has an octagonal dome framed by four obelisks. The tomb of Cardinal Tavera inside is by Alonso Berruguete. The painting at the high altar is by El Greco, as are the portrait of Cardinal Tavera, *the Baptism of Christ, Virgin Mary, the Holy Family* and others.

Toledo, cathedral, Mozarabic chapel, ▷
painting by Juan de Borgona

Toledo, Palacio Galiana

The hospital also has paintings by Titian, Tintoretto, Carreño, Zurburán, Ribera and others. In the left wing is the *Museo Tavera,* a private museum of the Duquesa de Lerma, containing works of art, furniture and paintings from the 16&17C.

Casa del Greco (Calle de San Juan de Dios): This house was one of the 'Casas de Villena'. The famous master lived in this quarter in 1585, then from 1604 up to his death in 1614. However, whether or not he lived in the present *Casa del Greco* has not been proved. The tiny courtyard with a well-laid-out garden has remained Mudéjar in style. The rooms are very low-ceilinged and the windows adorned with grilles. The walls of the kitchen are decorated with tiles from Talavera. The house is restored and furnished in the style contemporary with El Greco. On the upper floor there is a collection of photographs of El Greco's large output. Next to this is the *Museo del Greco,* whose most important possessions are El Greco's *12 Apostles.* Some of the works are unfinished and show the painter's method of working. *St. Bernardino of Siena* (1603) and the *View and Plan of Toledo,* which incorporates the scene in which the Virgin Mary hands the chasuble to St.Ildefonso are also on display.

Taller del Moro (Moorish Workshop, Calle Taller del Moro): Built in the 14C, the building has only partly survived. There is a large rectangular room, at both ends of which are the bedchambers or *al-hamías,* on the Moorish-Granadan model. Combined in the lavish stucco decoration are geometrical-plant patterns and Arab

Toledo, Castillo de San Servando

and Christian inscriptions. A museum of Mudéjar crafts was set up here in 1963.

Casa de Mesa (Calle Esteban Illán): This 14C Mudéjar castle was given to Esteban de Illán of Toledo, a noble, as a gift from Alfonso VIII. Presently housed here is the *Real Academia de Bellas Artes y Ciencias Históricas*.

Palacio de Fuensalida (Plaza del Conde): This palace was built at the start of the 15C by the first Conde de Fuensalida. Next to the door are columns crowned with lions, as dictated by the classical model for 15C Toledo palaces. Inside there are still a few Mudéjar stucco works to admire. The courtyard is in the same style and has brick pillars; the old staircase has a 16C Plateresque artesonado ceiling. Empress Isabella of Portugal died in this palace in 1539.

Posada de la Santa Hermandad (Inn of the Holy Brotherhood, Calle de la Tripería): This served simultaneously as prison and barracks and has in part preserved its original late-15C form, e.g. the façade, which is adorned with the coat-of-arms of Ferdinand and Isabella.

City Walls: These existed as early as Roman times and were rebuilt by the Visigoth King Wamba in 674. Even today there are remnants from that time. The current walls date from the Arabs and were completed by Alfonso VI.

Puerta de Alcántara: The Mudéjar gate and the Roman bridge of the same name were restored by the Arabs and extended under Alfonso the Wise. On the W. side there is a tower with a statue of St.Ildefonso and the coat-of-arms of Ferdinand and Isabella.

Puerta del Sol: This gate dates from the 14C and is built in Mudéjar style. It consists of three main parts, a square tower, a central arch supported by columns and a large semicircular tower.

Puerta de Bib-Al Mardón: In spite of several alterations, its Mudéjar character is still discernible.

Puerta Antigua de Bisagra: The city gate is flanked by a projecting square tower.

Puerta Nueva de Bisagra: Charles V had this gate built to plans by Covarrubias in 1550. Semicircular towers surround the main gate.

Puerta del Cambrón: An interesting structure with a square ground plan, begun in Renaissance style under Philip II.

Puerta de San Martín: This has an octagonal tower and dates from the 14C.

Puente de San Martín: This bridge from the time of Alfonso the Wise was restored in the 14C.

Also worth seeing: *Castillo de San Servando*, a medieval castle, it served to protect the *Puente de Alcántara*. It was restored under Alfonso VI and extended in the 14C by Archbishop Tenorio. Ruins of the *Circo Romano* (Paseo del Cristo de la Vega): The only remains of a Roman building. Note in particular the *Espina* and the triumphal arch.

Environs: Los Palacios de Galiana (1 km. NE in the *Huerta del Rey*): These Mudéjar palaces form a structural unity

and were built on the site of an 11C Moslem building. The ground plan is rectangular with two towers on the flanks.

Tolosa

Guipúzcoa / Basque Provinces   p.388☐I 2

Parroquia de Santa María: This 16C parish church is the town's most important monument. The *bell gable*, consisting of a single wall with free-hanging bells, dates from the 18C. The church façade is adorned with a monumental statue of John the Baptist. A baroque portal leads into the splendidly furnished interior which includes large *wall paintings* of scenes from the Bible, and bas-reliefs on the altars of John the Baptist and St. Ignatius. The splendid *altarpiece* in classical style is a work by Silvestre Pérez.

San Francisco: This 16C Herrera style Renaissance church has a beautiful retable at the high altar by Ambrosio de Bengoechea.

Also worth seeing: The 16C *Armería* (armoury), with interesting weapons. The provincial archive is also kept in Tolosa. Much Roman material has survived in the town and there are remains of Templar buildings.

Tordesillas

Valladolid / Old Castile   p.386☐F4

This old town above the Duero was rebuilt and enclosed by walls after being recaptured from the Moors and the kings of Castile made Tordesillas their residence

Toledo, 'Charles II' by Carreño ▷

Toledo, Puerta Vieja de Bisagra

once more. The Treaty of Tordesillas between Spain and Portugal was signed here in 1494, in which it was agreed that the newly discovered and all yet-to-be-discovered overseas territories would be divided by a line drawn from pole to pole.

Real Monasterio de Santa Clara: This convent, built as a palace at the behest of Alfonso XI in 1340, served as residence to Peter I, the Cruel and was converted into a convent of the Poor Clares after his death. Built in pure Mudéjar style, it has a very beautiful *inner court* with horseshoe arches. In the ante-rooms numerous art treasures are preserved. From the inner court one comes to the *Salón Dorado* (gilded room), with horseshoe arches along the walls and richly decorated capitals and dome, with 16C frescos, a 13C altar front, a clavichord

with Flemish paintings and the organ of Joanna the Mad. The Arab baths with lavish wall decorations are also preserved. The *church* was built in 1430 and has a stellar-vaulted nave. Of particular interest are the *Capilla Mayor* with a most beautiful wooden ceiling and the 15C Gothic *Capilla del Contador Saldaña* , with the tombs of the Saldaña family, a triptych by Nicolás Francés and paintings by the Maestro de Portillo.

San Antolín: This single-aisled Gothic church dates from the 16C. Of particular interest is the *Capilla de los Alderete* with a wonderful grille, a Renaissance altarpiece by Gaspar de Tordesillas with sculptures (1569) by Juan de Juni and the tomb of the founder, Alderete, by Gaspar de Tordesillas. The church is now a *museum* housing valuable art treasures, such as the *Immaculada* by Pedro de Mena and several altarpieces.

Also worth seeing: The 16C *Iglesia de San Pedro* has a nave and two aisles, with valuable altarpieces and tombs in the Capilla de los Gaitán; the single-aisled *Iglesia de Santa María* with a beautiful apse. Also of interest are the baroque churches of *San Juan Bautista* and *Santiago*, the medieval *bridge* over the Duero and the *main square* with 17C wooden arcades.

Environs: Rueda (*c.* 5 km. S.): The baroque *Iglesia Parroquial de Santa María* has two round towers with sculpted decorations by Pedro de Sierra. Inside are valuable gold items. The *Ermita de San José* contains sculptures and paintings from the 16 – 18C. **La Seca** (*c.* 7 km. S.): The Renaissance *Iglesia Parroquial,* contains a beautiful altarpiece by Joaquín Churriguera and 16C paintings attributed to the Maestro de Portillo. The baroque *Iglesia de San Francisco* with altarpieces and sculptures from the 16–18C. **Matapozuelos** (*c.* 15 km. SE): The hall church of *Santa*

María Magdalena, with graceful columns dividing the nave and two aisles, has a splendid tower, completed by Matías Machuca, and an 18C façade. Of interest within is the altarpiece of the high altar with sculptures by Petro de la Cuadra.

Toro
Zamora/León   p.386☐E 4

Toro is picturesquely situated in fertile countryside above the Duero, famous for its wines. This was probably the pre-Roman settlement of 'Arbocala', which Hannibal captured in 221 BC.

Colegiata Santa María la Mayor: This collegiate church, starkly reminiscent of Zamora Cathedral, was founded by Alfonso VII and begun in 1160, but could not be completed until 1240. The church, with a nave, two aisles and three apses, has only three bays in the nave and the aisles are only slightly narrower than the wide nave. The transept arms, on the other hand, project only slightly beyond the aisles. Nave and transept have half-barrel vaults but the aisles are groin-vaulted. Most interesting of all is the *dome over the crossing*, with lantern and drum. Two rows of columns and arches on top of each other allow light to stream into the crossing. The late-12C *N. portal* displays excellent carving. Clusters of lavishly carved columns support archivolts with rich sculptural decoration. Outside, next to Christ with John and the Virgin, are the 24 Elders of the Apocalypse, inside are 14 angels playing musical instruments. The *S. portal,* also Romanesque, with three archivolts is not of the same standard. The *W. portal,* 13C the Puerta de la Majestad (painted in 1774), which already shows Gothic elements and is reminiscent of the Portico de la Gloria in Santiago, is one of the church's most important works of art. The middle

Tolosa, panorama with the Río Oria

column is a Virgin and Child, in the tympanum is the Coronation of the Virgin, on top of the arches are the Heavenly Hosts and on the outer archivolt is the Last Judgement. The *bell tower* dates from the Renaissance. Inside, on both sides of the sanctuary, are the 15C *tombs* of the Fonseca and Ulloa families. The high altar is baroque. Beside it are various other Renaissance and baroque retables. In the sacristy is a fine alabaster work (Magi), a reliquary bust of St.Teresa from the school of Gregorio Fernández and a 'Calvary' (Italian School, ivory, 17C). The painting *'The Virgin with the Fly'* (La Virgen de la Mosca) is famous, because the princess pictured on it is considered to be a portrait of Isabella the Catholic.

San Lorenzo: This is the best-preserved

Romanesque church in Toro. It was built with a single aisle in the 12C and displays heavy Mudéjar influence (in the base, the blind arcades and the saw-tooth frieze; brick building). The retable of the high altar (15C) was created by Fernando Gallego and his pupils. At the sides of the altars are Plateresque tombs (Pedro of Castile and his wife, 15C).

Other interesting churches: *El Salvador* is a Mudéjar church from the early-13C with a nave, two aisles and three apses. Inside is a beautiful Virgin and Child (15C). *San Julián de los Caballeros* still shows relics of a simple Mozarabic temple. The present church, with a nave and two aisles was built by Rodrigo Gil de Hontañón. The retable is a 16C work (in the style of Esteban Jordán). 15C pulpit. 16C Plateresque retable in the sacristy. *San Pedro del Olmo,* brick building from the first half of the 13C, rebuilt in the 14C. Mudéjar apse. 14C Gothic portal. Interesting wall paintings inside. The church of *San Sebastian,* founded in 1294, rebuilt in the 16C, has a Renaissance altar. *Santa María de la Vega* or *del Cristo de las Batallas,* Mudéjar in style, lies 14 km. outside the town on the other bank of the Duero. It was built in 1208 and the apse contains remains of 15C frescos. *Santíssima Trinidad* (16C; Mudéjar), 16C high altar. *El Santo Sepulcro* (Mudéjar), with nave, two aisles and three apses, has several notable 13C crucifixes, including one from the school of Gregorio Fernández. Also of interest is the Gothic church of *San Tomás Cantuariense* with a high altar from the first half of the 16C.

Interesting monasteries and convents: The *Convento de Santi Spiritus* was founded in 1307. The church, built in 1316, remains in Mudéjar style. 16C cloister. Interesting alabaster tomb of Queen Beatrice of Portugal, wife of John I of

Toro, Colegiata Santa María la Mayor The ground plan is strongly reminiscent of Zamora cathedral. The most interesting features are **1** the cimborrio with drum **2** N. portal **3** S. portal **4** W. portal, Puerta de la Majestad **5** bell tower

Toro, S.María la Mayor, W. portal

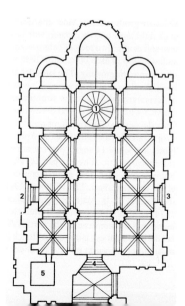

Castile. *Convento de Santa Clara*, restored in the 16C, has two 13C Calvaries and a 16C retable. Early-14C painting in the Coro. The *Convento de Mercedarias Descalzas* with a beautiful 15C palace. The church contains various paintings from the 16&17C. The *Convento de Santa Sofía* from the 14C, with an interesting 14C Crucifixion.

Also worth seeing: The *fortification walls* were restored in the 18&19C. The *Ayuntamiento* was built to plans by Ventura Rodríguez in 1778. The *Torre del Reloj* (clock tower) dates from 1733. The *Palacio del Marqués de Santa Cruz de Aguirre* from the first half of the 14C. The *Hospital de la Cruz* was founded by Juan Rodríguez de Fonseca in 1522.

Torrecilla en Cameros
Logroño/Old Castile   p.388 □ H 3

Church: 16C, nave and two aisles. Inside there are a Plateresque altarpiece at the high altar and another altarpiece with a 13C Gothic Virgin on the right. The sacristy has a 16C Flemish triptych and a fine 18C baldacchino.

Environs: The *parish church* of **Almarza** (*c.* 3 km. E.) has a 12C Romanesque font. **Nieva de Cameros** (*c.* 4 km. S.): The church of *San Martín* with a lovely Gothic portal preserves a Romanesque Virgin and two Plateresque altarpieces. **Ortigosa** (*c.* 10 km. S.): The church of *San Martín*, completed by Juan de la Mazueca and Pedro García Gariego in 1580, consists of two aisles of equal height with stellar vaulting; baroque altarpiece. The single-aisled church of *San Miguel* is 16C, the *Brieva House* was built in 1550. The **Brieva de Cameros** (*c.* 20 km. SW): The *parish church* contains a 12C font decorated with reliefs.

Torrelobatón
Valladolid/Old Castile   p.386 □ F 4

Castillo: This 15C castle is square with round towers at the corners and a massive keep.

Santa María y San Pedro: This church, built in Mudéjar style in the 16C, consists of a nave and two aisles divided by three large arches; 18C baroque stucco ceilings. Inside there are beautiful altarpieces with sculptures, which show the influences of Isaac de Juni, Alonso Berruguete and Gregorio Fernández.

Environs: Castromonte (*c.* 5 km. N.): The 16C *Iglesia Parroquial*, with a nave, two aisles and stellar vaulting, has a Stations of the Cross and an Assumption on the high altarpiece. **Wamba** (or *Bamba*, *c.* 8 km. NE): The 13C Romanesque *Iglesia de Santa María* has a Mozarabic part from the 10C. **Ciguñuela** (*c.* 7 km. NE): *Iglesia Parroquial* from the 16C.

Torremormojón
Palencia/Old Castile   p.386 □ F 3

Church: Contains a fine altarpiece attributed to Juan de Flandes.

Castillo: Remains of a 12C castle.

Environs: Revilla de Campos (*c.* 4 km. NE): The baroque *Iglesia Parroquial* contains a Renaissance altarpiece, a polychrome seated Virgin and several paintings. **Villamartín de Campos** (*c.* 6 km. NE): The single-aisled Renaissance church has a 16C tower adorned with a coat-of-arms. The altarpiece at the high altar depicts St.Francis in the style of Pedro de Mena. Baroque *Palacio de Jerónimo*

Ovejero. **Castromocho** (*c.* 5 km. N.): *Iglesia de Santa María* with a beautiful Plateresque portico and Gothic panelling inside. *Iglesia de San Esteban* with the tomb of the cleric Gudivero from the 16C. Near the village is *Los Cenizales* with prehistoric finds. **Belmonte de Campos** (*c.* 12 km. W.): Of the *castillo* there remains the façade with Plateresque balcony, the four-storeyed keep and parts of walls.

Torres del Río
Navarra/Navarra   p.388☐H 2/3

There is a Romanesque *chapel* here, which was mentioned for the first time in 1192 but was, however, much earlier. The chapel is an octagonal building surmounted by a funeral lantern. It has been suggested that it was a Templar church, built in the style of the Church of the Holy Sepulchre in Jerusalem. Each side of the church is divided into three storeys, each flanked by columns. The round-arched windows in the uppermost storey are adorned with columns, the capitals of which have plant motifs. The building is crowned by a beautiful dome, supported inside by crossed ribs.

Torroella de Montgrí
Gerona/Catalonia   p.390☐O 3

Iglesia Parroquial: The parish church is 14C Gothic. However, the vault and the façade date from the 16C.

Casa Solterra: This mansion, built in Plateresque Renaissance style, has a beautiful courtyard.

Castillo: King James II of Catalonia had this castle built in 1294, and it later became a palace of the Aragonese kings. It is a simple square building with round towers at the corners.

Also worth seeing: *Torre de les Bruixes* and *Torre de Santa Catalina,* two gates in the town walls. *Ayuntamiento,* 14C, on the Plaza Mayor.

Environs: Vergés (8 km. E.): Remains of the former surrounding walls. The whole town has a strong medieval character. Every Maundy Thursday a traditional procession takes place with a Dance of Death, which is unique in Catalonia. **Bellcaire** (9 km. N.): The two churches and the *castillo* of Bellcaire are protected monuments. The parish church of *Santa María* dates from the 13C, the church of *San Juan* is a Visigoth building. The paintings in the latter date from the 12C and are housed in the Museum of Gerona. **Ullestret** (8 km. S.): *Ciudad Ibérica:* This Iberian settlement stood upon an island in the middle of a lake, which has now dried up. The perfection of this important settlement suggests Greek involvement. The town flourished in the 6–3C BC and stood on the site of a prehistoric settlement, as finds from the Hallstatt period testify. It traded briskly with Emporion (now Ampurias), which lies only a few miles away. Judging by the quantity of Ionic and Phocaean finds, it would seem quite probable that there was actually a Greek colony in the town. The *museum,* housed in a 5C chapel, has most of the items excavated here.

Tortosa
Tarragona/Catalonia   p.390☐L 5

This town on the bank of the Ebro was already inhabited by the Iberians and in Roman times acquired the name *Colonia Julia Augusta Dertosa.* Tortosa was liberated from the Arabs by Ramón Berenguer IV in 1148.

Cathedral: Building began in 1347, but the cathedral was not completed until the 18C. The plans were by Benito Dalguavre. It stands on the site of a Romanesque church. The classical façade dates from the 18C. Most impressive inside is a feeling of weightlessness, created by the columns and pointed arches. The nave and aisles are of varying heights and the choir is one of the finest in Catalonia. The *Almudena tower* is probably of Moorish origin. Church treasure includes a valuable *retable* with three carved and painted wings (1351). Another retable (Retablo de la Transfiguración) may have originated in the workshop of Jaime Huguet. The treasury also contains a very interesting, but unfortunately badly preserved enamel triptych. A baroque door (1705) leads to the 13C *cloister*. The ground plan is irregular and the vault made of wood. The pointed arches may be of a later date.

Archivo Municipal: The archive is housed in the former church of the Convento de Santo Domingo (16C) and contains 1500 valuable documents, from the 16&17C in particular, including the town charter of 1148 and the book of customs of Tortosa (Llibre de les Costums) from the mid 13C.

Colegio de San Luis Gonzaga: The old Real Colegio San Matías was founded by Charles V in 1544 and served to educate young baptized Moors (Moriscos). The building is Renaissance. The three-storeyed inner courtyard has busts of the kings of Aragon.

Palacio Episcopal: The Bishop's Palace is a well preserved 14C building with a Catalonian courtyard, galleries and a beautiful staircase. On the first floor there is a square chapel with stellar vaulting.

Lonja: The covered market was built 1368–73 and is unusual in having a rectangular ground plan and large arcades. It served as a meeting place for traders and is now a market hall.

Also worth seeing: *Castillo de la Zuda,* a remnant of the town's defences, in the upper part of the town. The Gothic façade of the *Casa Consistorial/Town Hall* dates from 1545, that of the *Casa Oliver de Boteller* from the 15C. The *Convento de Santa Clara* has a beautiful Gothic cloister.

Tossa de Mar
Gerona/Catalonia   p.390☐O 3

Vila Vella: In the old quarter of Tossa are remains of the old fortification system, which was built in 1387. The towers, however, belong to a fortress of the 12C.

Treviño
Burgos/Old Castile   p.388☐H 2

San Pedro: The church has a beautiful 13C portal and an elegant baroque tower (18C). Inside are a large baroque altarpiece, a 13C Gothic image of the Virgin, the *Virgen Blanca,* and a Gothic picture of Christ from 1400.

Environs: Saraso (*c.* 4 km. E.): Romanesque church of *San Andrés from the 13C.* **Aguillo** (*c.* 5 km. E.): 13C Romanesque church of *San Pedro* the main body of which is pentagonal. 12C *Ermita de San Pedro.* **Imiruri** (*c.* 5 km. NE): The 15C *Iglesia de San Román* contains a copper crucifix (13C). **Arana** (*c.* 25 km. E.): The 13C Romanesque *Iglesia de Nuestra Señora de la Asunción* contains Gothic paintings from the 15&16C. **Laño** (*c.* 15 km. SE): 13C *Iglesia de Nuestra Señora de la Asunción.* **Obécuri** (*c.* 20 km. SE): 13C Romanesque church of *San Juan* with fine Plateresque

Trujillo, Plaza Mayor

altarpiece. **Araico** (*c.* 2 km. S.): 13C *Ermita de Nuestra Señora de Uralde* with a beautiful Flemish sculpture of the Virgin.

Trujillo
Cáceres/Estremadura   p.392 □ E 7

This picturesque town lies on a granite hill and is the birthplace of Fráncisco Pizarro (1475–1541), conqueror of Peru.
Trujillo, the Roman *Turgalium*, was fortified under the Arabs (town walls have survived in part) and given the name *Torgiela* or *Truxillo*. After the town was recaptured under Ferdinand III in 1232 it became the seat of the Trujillo Order of Knights.

Santa María la Mayor: This church was built in Romanesque style on the foundations of a mosque in the 13C and altered in Gothic style in the 15&16C. It stands at the NW edge of the old ring of walls and has a beautiful portal in transitional style and late 15C vaulting. Inside are numerous sarcophagi, some Roman. To the left of the choir the tomb of Juana Pizarro, sister-in-law of Francisco Pizarro. The choir contains a lovely Gothic *winged altar* by Fernando Gallego, which was painted in the late 15C or early 16C. One of the chapels has the tomb of Diego García de Paredes, one of Ferdinand and Isabella's generals, who acquired the nickname the 'Spanish Samson', because of his great physical strength.

San Martín: This church on the Plaza Mayor dates from the 15&16C. It is single-aisled with Gothic vaulting and Renaissance portal.

San Francisco: In the crypt are the tombs of Hernando Pizarro and his wife Francisca, the daughter of the Conquistador and an Inca princess.

Santiago: The formerly Romanesque church of the 12C was altered in the 17C.

Castillo: The massive square towers are of Moorish origin. The semi-cylindrical towers were added after the Reconquista. On the keep (Torre del Homenaje) stands the 16C statue of the Virgen de la Victoria, patron saint of the city. Four of the seven gates are preserved.

Plaza Mayor: One of the most impressive squares in Spain with arcades and beautiful mansions. The bronze equestrian statue of Francisco Pizarro, conqueror of Peru (born in Trujillo in 1475), is by the North American sculptors Carlos Rumsey and Maria Harriman (1927).

Trujillo, Palacio del Marqués de la Conquista

Palacio del Marqués de la Conquista: This palace was built by Hernando Pizarro, son-in-law of the Conquistador. It has a Plateresque façade with a coat-of-arms, window grilles and twelve statues on the cornice, which depict the months of the year. The medallions on the corner balconies depict Pizarro and his wife, the Indian princess Inés Yupanqui, as well as the builder Hernando Pizarro and his wife Francisca.

Casa Piedras Albas: The house displays Gothic ornament and a double, Italianate gallery.

Palacio de los Vargas-Carvaial: This early baroque building dates from the 17C. All over the walls and the staircase is the coat-of-arms with the double-headed eagle, which was given to the family for services in the discovery of the New World.

Palacio de Mirabel (or Almaraz y Zúñiga). The palace was formerly a fortress. Beneath the roof of the broad façade runs a dwarf gallery. The Renaissance inner courtyard has of two storeys. The palace was built by the enemies of the Monroy family, the Almaraz.

Palacio de los Orellana-Pizarro: This 16C palace is one of the most beautiful in Trujillo. It has a Renaissance façade and a charming Plateresque patio.

Palacio de Quintanilla: The gate of the palace is flanked by twisted columns. Late Gothic-Isabelline windows.

Trujillo, Pizarro monument in the Plaza Mayor

Ayuntamiento Viejo: The old City Hall (1686) has a salon by Tibaldi adorned with wall paintings.

Palacio de los Escobar: This 15C building has Gothic pointed windows.

Palacio de los Altamiros: This palace was once a fortress, of which there remain two towers.

Also worth seeing: *Casa del Deán* (deacon's house) on the Plaza Santo Domingo with corner balconies and coats-of-arms (16C). *Casa del Doctor Trujillo* (14C) with late medieval residential tower. **Casa de las Bóvedas** with an interesting patio and *Palacio de Paniagua* with beautiful corner balconies.

Environs: Belvís de Monroy (*c*. 60 km. N.): Town and *castillo* date from the 13C. The castle is one of the most important in the province. *Parroquia de Santiago:* 15C parish church with 16C portal. Baroque retable inside. **Escurial** (*c*. 38 km. S.): 16C Gothic *parish church of Nuestra Señora de la Asunción* with additions from later periods. The tower is crowned by a crooked spire. The single-aisled interior is cross-vaulted. Note the 16C *high altar*, adorned with gilded polychrome carvings, and the altar front adorned with azulejos from the same time. There are further baroque altars and interesting sculptures, including the *Cristo del Desamparo*, also called *del Perdón* or *de la Agonía*, a superb, painted, life-size carving from 17C. **Miajadas** (*c*. 44 km. S.): *Parroquia de Santiago* in Escorial style (late 16C), with interesting windows and portals, the most important of which, to the S., dates back to the 17C. Of the 13C *castillo* there remains a round tower. Remains of the *town walls*. In the vicinity there are *dolmen*. **Montánchez** (*c.* 35 km. SW): 16C Gothic parish church of *San Mateo*, altered in the 17C. Nave with four bays and barrel vaulting. The tower, also 16C, stands apart from the church in the middle of the square. The *Ermita de Nuestra Señora de la Consolación* (17C), within the fortress walls, has a *camarín*, furnished with azulejos. Here the Virgen del Castillo, patroness of the town (traditionally, but erroneously, considered to be a Visigoth work) was honoured. The irregularly planned *castillo* has two walls. The former Roman fortress was converted into an alcázar by the Arabs. The cisterns also date from that time. Lining the streets of Montánchez are numerous mansions, including the *Casona Gómez de Trezo*, the *Casona Orozco* and the *Casona Carvajal y Gil*. **Santa Cruz de la Sierra** (*c.* 15 km. S.): The church of *La Santa Vera Cruz* reveals elements of Gothic and Renaissance style. The single-aisled interior contains Gothic altars with 16C azulejos from Talavera, a 17C high altar and an 18C pulpit supported by Visigoth pillars.

Tudela, cathedral, Puerta de Juicio

Tudela
Navarra/Navarra   p.388 □ I 3

The second largest city in Navarra, on a tributary of the Ebro, the Queiles. Former capital of the *Merindad de la Ribera*, a federation of the villages on the banks of the river. It was founded at the start of the 9C by Amrús, a vassal of Al-Hakam I, Emir of Córdoba. The city had its own Moorish kings and Moors continued to live in their quarter here into the 16C. In 1119 Tudela was recaptured by Alfonso I of Aragon. Taking part in the fighting were the Norman Rotrón, the Counts of Bearne and Bigorre, the Bishop of Lescar and other nobles from the French part of Navarre. The city resisted the Inquisition and did not submit to Ferdinand the Catholic until 1512. Apart from the Moorish quarter, one of the most heavily populated was the Jewish quarter. The geographer Benjamín de Tudela came from the Jewish quarter. He was the leader of the Jewish community for many years and travelled through Arab lands in 1160–73.

Cathedral: This is the city's most important building and was built over the remains of a mosque dating from the 9C. Sancho VII, the Strong, ordered the building of the church, which was started in 1194. It was completed in 1234 and the cathedral is thus a good example of Romanesque-Gothic transitional style.

The ground plan is a Latin cross with a nave, two aisles and transept; Cistercian influence is discernible. The Romanesque part of the church comprises the E. end and the supporting elements; the Gothic part is visible in the vaulting, the proportions and the windows. On the main façade the portal, *Puerta de Juicio (Door of the Last Judgement)*, dates from around 1200. This splendid work consists of a somewhat pointed arch, with eight archivolts supported by columns, and a tympanum. Clear French influence is apparent here. Inside the cathedral there are some superb works of art. The altarpiece (1487–94) of the *high altar* is by Pedro Díaz de Oviedo and Diego de Águila. The twelve large altar panels, by Juan Bascardo of 1606, depict the Assumption of the Virgin. Also to be seen on the altar is a piece of a chain bequeathed by King Sancho the Strong, who brought it from the battle of Las Navas de Tolosa. On the triumphal arch is a 12C Virgin and Child. The cathedral's most beautiful work of art, in the *Capilla de Nuestra Señora de la Esperanza,* is the double tomb of the chancellor of Navarre, Mosén Francés de Villaespesa, and his wife Doña Isabel de Ujué. This is a Burgundian-style Gothic tomb with polychrome masonry. Also worth seeing is the Gothic altarpiece with paintings by Bonanat Zaortiga (15C). The same chapel has the Gothic sarcophagus of Bishop Sancho Sánchez de Oteiza. Also of interest, apart from the three other apsidal chapels are the baroque chapels of Espíritu Santo and Santa Ana. In the latter the sculptures are worthy of note, as is the medieval statue of St.Anne, who is patron saint of the city. The Plateresque *choir stalls,* the work of Esteban de Obray, were begun in 1519. In a side room there are several tombs, including the sarcophagus of the Infante Don Fernando, son of Sancho the Strong. The Romanesque *cloister* dates from the 12C. Excavations here recently revealed the remains of an 11C mosque.

Palacio Episcopal: Built next to the cathedral in the 16C. It was commissioned by the chamberlain Don Pedro Villalón de Calcena, a favourite of Pope Julius II. Over the Plateresque portal is Don Pedro's coat-of-arms. The newly elected Pope Hadrian VI resided in this palace on his way to Rome.

Diocesan Museum: The museum is housed in rooms next to the cloister.

La Magdalena: This church was built on the remains of an old Mozarabic building in the 13–15C. Its portal is older than that of the cathedral. French in style, it is 12C and has a round arch and four archivolts, all richly adorned with figures. The altarpiece of the high altar dates from 1551.

San Jorge: One of the church's retables, as well as a statue of San Esteban, were made by the sculptor Gabriel Yoli in 1537.

San Nicolás: This Mozarabic church already existed in the 12C. A few remains survive from that time, including the tympanum over the portal, an interesting Romanesque work. To prevent impending collapse the church was restored and altered in baroque style in the 18C.

Ayuntamiento: Near the cathedral is the City Hall from the second half of the 18C. In the entrance is a splendid coach with rich fabrics and beautiful painting.

Also worth seeing: Tudela still boasts numerous old buildings and palaces, including the *Palacio del Marqués de San Adrián,* a Renaissance building with beautifully carved eaves. On the *Rúa* stands the *Casa del Almirante,* adorned with beautiful reliefs. Further along are Renaissance

Tudela, cathedral

buildings such as the palaces in the Calle Villanueva of the Marqués de Huarte and of Count Heredia Spinola, which have fine staircases. The 1,275 ft. long *bridge* over the Ebro is the emblem of the city. Some of its 17 arches are from the old Roman bridge; the others are 13C Gothic. The *city archive* has an important collection of old seals. Outside the city, in the *Soto del Ramalete,* a 4C Roman villa with mosaics was discovered during excavations.

Parish church: This old Romanesque building has a beautiful apse with a blind, round-arched window.

Environs: The Morisco-style *parish church* of **Aguilafuente** (*c.* 10 km. NW) has an interesting Gothic portal. A polychrome Roman mosaic of marble and jasper and Roman stone plaques were discovered in the town. **Fuentepelayo** (*c.* 20 km. NW): The Romanesque church of *Santa María la Mayor* has a beautiful apse.

Turégano
Segovia/Old Castille   p.392□G 4

Castle: The imposing castle and the Romanesque church within its walls were built in the 15C, or possibly the 13C, and belonged for many years to the diocese of Segovia. The castle has a double ring of walls, dominated by the splendid silhouette of the keep. On the S. side is the church façade, above which rises the tower (added later).

Túy
Pontevedra/Galicia   p.392□B 3

The city was known as Tude under the Iberians. Under the Suevi and Visigoths it was the seat of the kingdom of Galicia. It was destroyed by the Moors and in 1012 came under the sway of the Viking King Olof. Alonso V recaptured the city and fortified it. It was captured several times by the Portuguese in the 11–16C.

Turégano, castle

Cathedral: The cathedral, construction of which was begun in 1120 and completed in 1287, is one of Galicia's most interesting monuments. From the outside it offers a fortress-like aspect with battlements and towers which look like defensive towers and were originally used as such. The cathedral, the apse of which, as well as the chapel of Santiago el Mayor and the Capilla San Pedro, date from the 15C, was badly damaged by an earthquake in 1761, resulting in extensive restoration. In the 18C a flight of steps was added in front of the main façade leading up to the atrium. The main portal (15C) has numerous decorated archivolts and the Adoration of the Shepherds and the Magi in the tympanum. On both sides of the portal stand four figures in tabernacles on columns. Of interest are a beautiful side portal with a rose-window and the Romanesque bell tower, built in the 12,13&18C. The clock tower dates from the 15C. The interior, with a nave and two aisles, has a high groin vault. In the crossing are Gothic tombs. The choir stalls date from the 18C. Note the large 13&15C *cloister* with twin columns, double arches and some richly decorated capitals. *Museum.*

Santo Domingo: This church originally dates from the 14C, but was extended in the 18C. The single-aisled groin-vaulted interior has a classical façade and a Gothic portal in the S. transept. The *cloister* contains Romanesque and Gothic bas-reliefs.

Also worth seeing: *San Bartolomé* was rebuilt in the 10C in early Romanesque style. The capitals are of interest. The church of *San Francisco* with Gothic elements. The church of *San Pedro Telmo* from the 18C.

Environs: Amorín: SW of Túy, on the road to La Guardia, lies Amorín with the ruins of a fortress built under Philip IV. **La Guardia:** This fishing port, charmingly set in the Río Miño estuary, has a 16C *church* and is dominated by **Monte Santa Tecla,** the summit of which affords a splendid view over the Río Miño valley,

Túy, cathedral, cloister

Túy, cathedral

Túy, cathedral

the sea and, on the other side of the river Portugal. On the way up to the summit there is a *Celtic settlement,* founded around 500 BC. This poblado consists of about 1,000 round stone houses, which are preserved as ruins. All the finds have been collected together in the *Casa Celta* and include tools, vessels etc., which to all appearances seem to date from an even earlier time, around 700 BC.

Monte Santa Tecla, Celtic settlement ▷

U

Úbeda
Jaén/Andalusia   p.394☐G 9

Úbeda, the old Moorish fortress town of Obdah, is remarkable for its wealth of 16C Renaissance buildings.

Iglesia del Salvador or Sacra Capilla del Salvador (Plaza de Vázquez de Molina): This church dates back to a foundation of Francisco de los Cobos y Molina (secretary of Emperor Charles V). The plans for this massive church (1540–56) were drawn up by Diego de Siloé and were executed by Andrés de Vandaelvira. Interesting *main front* with lavish Renaissance decoration. The interior contains a superb *carved altar* by Alonso Berruguete with figures from the 'Transfiguration of Christ' and a beautiful *choir grille* (1557) by Villalpando; the choir stalls are Renaissance. Amongst the treasures in the sacristy are a triptych of the Flemish school and a chalice.

Santa María de los Reales Alcázares (Plaza de Vázquez de Molina): On the site of this 13C church there once stood a mosque. Remnants of the old castle, as well as of the town walls can be seen at the church. The Renaissance façade is of in-terest. The little Gothic *cloister* forms what was once the patio of the Arab place of worship. The interior, with a nave and two aisles, contains a beautiful grille by Master Bartolomé in the Gothic *Capilla de la Yedra*; this depicts the Tree of Jesse and the story of Joachim.

San Nicolás (Plaza de San Nicolás): Although the church was founded in the 13C, the building dates from the 14C. The Renaissance portal (1576) is by Andrés de Vandaelvira; the S. portal (1509) remains Gothic in style. Most interesting of all is the beautiful *Capilla del Deán* in ornamental Plateresque style, with a fine reja (grille).

San Pablo (Plaza del Generalísimo): This 13C church has strikingly beautiful *Gothic façade* on the S. side. The central pillar of the portal has a statue of St.Paul; the tympanum above it depicts the Coronation of the Virgin. To the left of the portal is a deep niche, braced by a column, for the reading out of town decrees (early 17C). Above the architrave there is a late-17C balcony (there is another to the right of the portal). The apse dates from 1380 with a fountain from the mid 16C. The main portal is Romanesque. Inside there are numerous capitals with Romanesque figures. The *Capilla del*

Camarero is a Plateresque funerary chapel (by the N. portal). Interesting rejas.

Hospital de Santiago (Carrera del Obispo Cobos): This impressive 16C Renaissance building is one of the most beautiful monuments in the town. It was built by Vandaelvira and praised as the 'little Andalusian Escorial'. A flight of steps flanked by lions leads up to the entrance door, the enormous vault blocks of which are particularly striking. Monumental staircase in the inner courtyard, which has two storeys of arcades.

Mansions: Grouped around the Plaza de Vázquez de Molina are various interesting buildings: *Palacio de los Ortegas* (now Parador Nacional del Condestable Dávalos), whose simple two-storey façade with grilles and balconies remains in classical Renaissance style (16C). *Palacio de las Cadenas* (now Town Hall): Severe classical Renaissance façade by Vandaelvira. Archive room with artesonado ceiling. *Palacio del Marqués de Mancera*, late-16C. The

Carcel del Obispo is a monastery dating back to the 16C.

Other palaces: *Casa de las Torres* (near the Puerta de Granada), also called *Palacio Dávalos*. Over-decorated Plateresque façade (16C) with columns, niches, coats-of-arms, heraldic figures, medallions etc. *Palacio del Conde de Guadiana* (Calle de José Antonio): early 17C with corner balconies on the four-storey tower. *Palacio Vela de los Cobos* (Calle Montilla): corner balconies and galleries under the roof. *Palacio los Cobos* (Calle los Cobos, near the church of El Salvador). *Palacio la Rambla* (Calle de Jaén): 16C with patio. *Palacio de los Busianos* (Calle de A. Pasquado): Renaissance building of 1580, attributed to Vandaelvira. *'Casa Mudéjar'* (Calle de Cervantes).

Torre del Reloj (Plaza del General Saro): This square 13C clock tower was part of the town fortifications and is adorned with the town's coat-of-arms.

Úbeda, view, Plaza de Vázquez de Molina

Puerta de Losal: Mudéjar gate of the 13C with a double horseshoe arch.

Also worth seeing: The church of *Santo Domingo:* Plateresque portal, artesonado. Church of *La Santísima Trinidad* (near the Plaza del General Saro): early-18C baroque building. *Oratorio de San Juan de la Cruz* (Calle de San Juan de la Cruz): this 17C memorial stands on the site where the mystic died. *Convent of the Carmelitas Descalzas* (near the Puerta de Losal): containing mementoes of St. Theresa of Ávila.

Environs: Capilla del Santo Cristo de la Yedra (5 km. W.): Beautifully situated chapel in Churrigueresque style. **Canena** (9 km. W.): The *castle* was altered by Vandaelvira in the 16C; Renaissance patio. **Torreperogil** (9 km. E.): Church of *Santa María*: mixture of Gothic and Renaissance styles. Ceiling fresco over the altar. Two towers of the former castle have survived. **Jodar** (24 km. S.): Massive ruins of the *Carvajales fortress.* **Cazorla** (50 km. SE):

remains of Moorish *castle,* ruins of the Renaissance church of *Santa María. Puente de los Herrerías,* 15C. **Quesada** (40 km. SE): *Zabaleta Museum* with interesting works by the painter (1907–60). **Peal de Becerro** (30 km. SE): Nearby is the old Roman town of Tugia, now *Toya,* with an *Iberian necropolis* (7–6C BC). **Villacarillo** (32 km. NE): Church of *La Asunción:* Monumental building, probably by Vandaelvira.

Uclés
Cuenca/New Castile   p.392☐H 6

Monastery: This was built in the 16–18C. The church, in the style of the Escorial, consists of one very spacious aisle. Francisco de Mora was involved in the building, creating the 17C N. and W. façades. Main gate with beautiful baroque portal; the patio has an interesting baroque fountain.

Uclés, monastery

Uclés, monastery, portal

Castillo de Albar Llana: This castle dates from the Middle Ages and is surrounded by thick walls. It has two towers, linked by an arch.

Environs: Carrascosa del Campo (*c.* 15 km. NE): The 15C *parish church* contains a few altarpieces from the 16C. **Huete** (30 km. NE): Remains of the town walls survive. The church of *Santa María de Castejón*, built in the 16C, has a beautiful portal on the main façade with Ionic columns and statues of St.Peter and St.Paul. The church of *Santo Domingo* houses a 15C sculpture. Parish church of *San Esteban,* the churches of *San Nicolás* and *San Pedro* and the *Benedictine monastery.* The *Town Hall* dates from the 17C. A few *mansions* dating from the same century also remain. **Saelices** (12 km. S.): Roman and Visigoth remains were found here. Roman features include the enclosure of the settlement, the theatre, amphitheatre and temple. Dating from Visigoth times there is a 6C basilica, discovered in 1793, as well as numerous capitals.

Ujué
Navarra / Navarra   p.388 ☐ I 3

From 1076 the town stood under the protection of Sancho Ramírez, first king of Navarre and Aragon. A deed of gift (1089) ascribes the building of the church of Ujué to the king.

Santa María: This church has a large Gothic nave and a Romanesque choir. It is surrounded by fortifications. There are three Romanesque apses, the central one of which is badly damaged, but its interesting arches are still preserved. Also of interest are the two side apses with columns bearing strange capitals and windows with round arches. The Gothic part of the church dates from the second half of the 14C, during the reign of Charles II of Navarre, who was called 'the Wicked', whose heart is preserved in the church. Inside note a Byzantine Madonna and several Renaissance altars.

Saelices (Uclés), amphitheatre

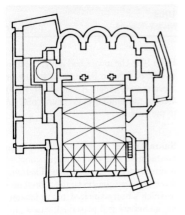

Ujué, ground plan of the fortified church of Santa María

survives from the original building. It contains beautiful sculptures and interesting capitals (1217). The Renaissance choir was added later. Inside the church is an interesting 15C high altar.

Also worth seeing: The church of *San Miguel,* built in the 12C, is a typical example of the Romanesque-Gothic transitional style. From the same century are the churches of *San Felices* and *San Lorenzo.* Also of interest is the church of *San Andrés* with interesting 16C wall paintings. The *Plaza Mayor* is enclosed by beautiful arcades. Also worth seeing are the numerous *mansions* with their coats-of-arms. The remains of an *Iberian settlement* were discovered just outside the town. Not far away from that excavations revealed the remains of a *Roman town* with baths, aqueduct and a forum.

Uncastillo

Zaragoza/Aragon   p.388 □ K 3

On a rocky crag above the town stands a massive 12C castle, from which Uncastillo (un castillo, meaning a castle) takes its name. The town has officially been declared to be of cultural interest owing to its medieval character with its pretty little alleyways.

Santa María la Mayor: This beautiful Romanesque church is a protected monument. Of particular interest are the portal, one of the most beautiful examples of the Romanesque, and the Gothic fortified bell tower.

San Juan: This church was built above a cemetery, carved out of the rock face in the 7C. Inside are fine Romanesque-Byzantine paintings from the 12C.

San Martín: This church dates from the 12&13C, but only the Romanesque apse

Utrera

Sevilla/Andalusia   p.394 □ E 10

Santiago: This 15C Gothic church has a beautiful W. portal in late Gothic Flamboyant style.

Santa María de la Asunción (or Santa María de la Mesa): 14C Gothic church with interesting Renaissance portal.

Nuestra Señora de la Consolación (on the edge of town): This pilgrimage church dates from the early 17C. It has a baroque façade, high-baroque altars and a particularly beautiful Mudéjar artesonado over the single-aisled interior. Interesting Plateresque choir grille.

Environs: Morón de la Frontera (36 km. E.): The church of *San Miguel* contains a superb Renaissance *grille* in front of the Capilla Mayor. Ruins of a Moorish *castle.*

Valderrobres

Teruel/Aragon   p.388 ☐ L 5

This old village is overlooked by a massive ruined castle which was built by the Knights of Calatrava in the late 14C.

Santa María: This beautiful church has a magnificent Gothic portal with a rose-window in Catalan-Gothic style.

Ayuntamiento/Town Hall: 16C Renaissance building with a fine cornice.

Valencia

Valencia/Valencia   p.396 ☐ K/L 7

Valencia, which is the capital of the province of the same name and the third largest city in Spain, is situated on the Río Turia in the middle of an extensive and fertile plain, the Huerta of Valencia. It is a university town and the seat of an archbishop. Various annual festivals are held in this cheerful, lively city. Of these, the 'Fallas' deserves particular mention. This festival, dating from the 18C, is held on the 19 & 20 March each year in honour of St.Joseph. Life-size carnival figures and objects of wood, fabric or cardboard are set up all over the city, and personalities in the public eye are made the target of mockery.

The city was founded by the Greeks under the name of 'Thuris'. The Greeks had settled in many places on the E. coast of Spain. It is not quite certain whether the Cathaginians also built a military base here. In 138 BC the town was founded anew under the Roman consul Decimus Julius Brutus, who colonized the site with the legionaries who had fought against the Lusitanians. The city, which had previously been devastated because it took the side of Sertorius the insurgent, began to flourish under Augustus, and was now called 'Valentia'. The Visigoths ended the Roman domination in 413. In the early 8C, Valencia attained great political and cultural importance under the Moors and finally became the capital of a flourishing Moorish kingdom, which stretched from Ebro in the N. to Segura in the S. The irrigation systems which cover this area are the work of the Moors. In 1096 the city was taken by Rodrigo Díaz, known as the 'Cid'. After his death in 1099, his wife Jimena was only able to hold the city for another few years. But James I of Aragon later succeeded in finally liberating Valencia, and the city once again experienced a major economic upswing. The Moors were initially allowed to remain in the area of Valencia, whereas they were expelled from Castile in 1492. They retained their religion, their language and their own laws until 1609, when they too were ordered to leave the country. As a result, Valencia fell into economic decline. It was at about this time that the importance of the harbour of Valencia also declined. The city was on the side of the Habsburgs in the War of the Spanish Succession, and this meant that it lost some privileges after the victory of the Bourbon king Philip V. It was obliged to take in some Napoleonic troops in 1812–13. In the Spanish Civil War (1936–9), Valencia was for a long time the seat of the Republican government. Many churches were plundered and devastated at that time. The city is today the economic and cultural centre of the coastal region.

Cathedral: After James I of Aragon had taken Valencia in 1238, Gothic churches and monasteries were built in Valencia and all along the coast. Almost all these build-

Valencia, Torres de Serranos

ings were later altered in the baroque style and thereby frequently disfigured. This also applies in part to Valencia cathedral. In 1262 the foundation stone was laid for the building, on whose site there had previously stood a Roman temple of Diana, a Visigoth church and a mosque. Of the three portals, the late Romanesque *Puerta de Palau* in the E. transept is the oldest (13C). With its beautiful archivolts and delicate ornaments, it belongs to the first phase of building and clearly shows Catalan influence. The *Puerta de los Apóstoles* in the W. transept is part of the Gothic phase of construction, which ended in the 15C. The portal is decorated with numerous statues, including six Apostles under tabernacles and, in the tympanum, the Virgin with musicians and angels. Above the portal there is a rose-window with magnificent tracery. In accordance with an old custom, which is said to go back to the time of the Moors, the Tribunal de las Aguas ('Tribunal of the Waters') meets each Thursday at noon in front of this portal. The tribunal settles disputes arising from the distribution of water in the Huerta. No appeal is possible against the decision reached by the judges, who are themselves peasants. The main entrance, an 18C baroque portal, is on the S. side of the cathedral. It is also called the *Puerta de Hierros,* because of the grille which closes the portal forecourt. It is actually a three-storeyed façade and portal. Narrow and concave in form, it is the work of the German artist Konrad Rudolf, a pupil of Bernini, and was completed by Ignacio Vergara, who was also responsible for the statues. The top storey of the magnificent façade bears an Assumption of the Virgin. The cathedral's free-standing octagonal *bell tower,* known as Miguelete or Micalet, stands beside and to the left of the baroque portal. This sturdy tower, 223 ft. high (built 1380–1420), is the landmark of Valencia. Above the three undecorated storeys of red brick is a fourth storey with

8 windows, crowned with Gothic ornament. The bell, hung in the bellcote (a later addition), formerly regulated the irrigation of the Huerta. From here there is a fine view of Valencia, the Huerta and the sea. The *Cimborrio*, the octagonal tower above the crossing, is in Flamboyant style. The eight tracery windows are incomparably beautiful.

The cathedral displays Renaissance elements in addition to the Gothic and the baroque. The two-storeyed round gallery surrounding the choir apse is in Renaissance style. The *interior* of the cathedral was altered in baroque style and is somewhat excessive. The length of the nave is 322 ft. and that of the transept is 177 ft. The crossing contains the monumental *high altar* with its pillars and baldacchino. The twelve panel paintings on the enormous altar wings date from the early 16C and show scenes from the life of the Virgin Mary. They are the work of Hernando Yáñez de la Almedina and Hernando Llanos, who were both influenced by Leonardo da Vinci. The cimborrio has retained its Gothic structure, and is much more impressive when seen from inside the church. The *Capilla del Santo Cáliz* (Chapel of the Holy Chalice) is also Gothic. Tradition has it that Christ's chalice at the Last Supper is preserved here. After being brought to Rome by St.Peter, it is said to have come to Huesca two and a half centuries later during the persecution of the Christians under Emperor Valerius. During the period of Moorish rule, the chalice was in the monastery of San Juan de la Peña and finally, after some further travels, came into the possession of the cathedral of Valencia. The chalice, a green agate bowl set with precious stones and pearls, is borne through the streets of Valencia in a solemn procession on Maundy Thursday. The chapel where the Holy Chalice is preserved dates from the 14C and has a splendid stellar vault and twelve alabaster reliefs showing scenes from the Old and New Testaments by the Florentine master Giuliano (early 15C). This church is by no means uniform in style. However, the cathedral itself and its

Valencia, Torres de Serranos

various associated buildings contain a number of important works of art, including some by famous painters e.g. Ribera (*Adoration of the Shepherds*), Ribalta, Macip (*Baptism of Christ*), Nicolás Florentino (*Adoration of the Magi*, 1469) and Goya (2 paintings with episodes from the life of St. Francis Borgia).

Nuestra Señora de los Desamparados (Our Lady of the Forsaken): This baroque church is joined to the cathedral by an arch. It was formerly the church of a lay brotherhood which cared for foundlings and lunatics. The inside is in the form of a large oval, surmounted by a massive dome on which there is a fresco of the Virgin with Saints. The 14C statue of the 'Virgin of the Forsaken' is revered as the city's patron saint. It is draped with sumptuous garments and has a valuable crown. When people who had been executed or abandoned were buried, this statue was borne on the coffins.

Santa Catalina: The hexagonal baroque

Valencia, cathedral, El Miguelete

tower of the church of Santa Catalina is Gothic in its basic conception but was altered later. Its slender tower is described as the finest in the region around Valencia. The richly decorated portal and the church itself have both remained Gothic in style.

Santo Domingo: This church has a Gothic choir apse; the interior was rebuilt in neoclassical style. It contains works by the sculptors Salvador Gómez and Vergara and a high altar in the Plateresque style. On the right side is the 15C *Capilla de los Reyes* with its fine pointed arch vaults. The Gothic cloister, with traceried windows, is worth visiting. The chapterhouse has splendid columns and ribbed vaults and is known as the *Sala de las Palmeras* (palm room). The Burgundian style monument to the founders of the chapterhouse is fine and has mourners.

San Agustín: From the architectural point of view, this church has the purest style, and is the most beautiful, of any church in the city. Dating from the 14C, it is single-aisled; chapels are inserted between the buttresses. Models for this type of construction occur in Catalonia.

San Martín: A church with a simple, undecorated façade. A niche shows St. Martin on horseback dividing his cloak in order to give half of it to the beggar. This bronze statue is by a Flemish artist. The church interior was altered in the baroque style; there is a fine portrait of an archbishop by Goya.

San Nicolás: Built on the site of a mosque. The church dates from the 13C but was rebuilt in the 14C and later overloaded with baroque decoration. Inside there are many works of art, including an altar with enamel inlay (a 16C work from Limoges) and numerous 16C paintings. The dome was painted by Juan Vicente Macip, his son Juan de Juanes, and other artists of this school. There is a Calvary by Rodrigo de Osona (1476); the painting of the landscape in the background and the group of Pharisees in the foreground is masterly.

Colegio del Patriarca: This priests' seminary was founded by Juan de Ribera, the archbishop and later viceroy of Naples. The name 'Patriarca' derives from the fact that he also held the title of Patriarch of Antioch. The palace is in the purest Renaissance style and dates from the mid 16C. The double row of arcades in the inner courtyard consists of 56 marble columns; in the middle of the courtyard is the monument to the founder. This inner courtyard is rightly thought to be among the finest of the Spanish Renaissance. Also note the staircase with fine tiles. The church of *Corpus Christi*, which belongs to the college, betrays the influence of the church of the Escorial. Its interior is frescoed throughout by Bartolomé Matarana. Above the high altar there is the famous Last Supper by Francisco Ribalta. Every Friday during the service, it is made to disappear by the action of a mechanical device and is replaced by a Cross.

The Colegio itself houses a small *museum*, which contains works by Italian and Flemish artists in addition to local and native artists. There is a Descent from the Cross by Dirk Bouts, a Calvary triptych attributed to Roger van der Weyden, three paintings by El Greco (including an Adoration of the Shepherds) and pictures by Juanes, Ribalta, Ribera, Murillo and Zurbarán.

Apart from the numerous examples of religious architecture, most of which have been altered to baroque style, Valencia also has some important secular buildings:

Lonja de la Seda (silk exchange): A Moorish castle formerly stood on the site of this building, which is one of the finest Gothic secular buildings in Spain. The merchants of Valencia had their exchange here for a long time, and it was also the seat of the Consulado del Mar, an institution

Valencia, cathedral, Puerta de Palau

Valencia, tower of Santa Catalina

Valencia, Colegio de Patriarca

which watched over shipping. Pedro Compte designed the late Gothic building (1483–98). A square tower, whose severity is lightened by its variety of windows, divides the whole complex into two parts. Large Gothic windows with fine tracery are to be seen in the right wing. There is a teeming abundance of small, grotesque figures, both animal and human, between the Gothic arches of the portal. Angels situated half way up on the right and left sides hold the coats-of-arms of Aragon, to which Valencia belonged for some time. The left wing was only added in the 16C. The Renaissance influence becomes noticeable in the upper windowed gallery and also in the frieze above this, which has medallions with portraits of the kings of Aragon. The large *Sala de la Contratación* (exchange hall) in the right wing of the building is 118 ft. long and 69 ft. wide, with 24 spirally twisting columns supporting a magnificent stellar vault.

Mention should also be made of the *grand hall* on the main floor of the Consulado del Mar. It has a splendid coffer-work ceiling. The church also contains Espinosa's 'Virgin with the Conspirators of Valencia'.

Palacio de la Generalidad (palace of the assembly of the representatives of the estates): A beautiful 15&16C Gothic building; the tower shows Renaissance influence. The patio with its arcades is one of the finest in Spain. The interior of the palace has several spectacular halls: the *Salón de Reyes* with portraits of the Aragonese and Spanish kings, the *Salón de Cortes* with large wall paintings by Zariñena (17C) and the *Sala Dorada*, which has a gilded and polychrome coffer-work ceiling, as does the Salón de Cortes.

Palacio del Marqués de Dos Aguas: This palace, built in *c*. 1740, is the culmination of the baroque in Valencia. Unusual, winged façade. It is in Ignacio Vergara's *alabaster portal* that the ultra-fanciful taste of the baroque is most apparent. The Enthroned Madonna and Child, surrounded by angels and rays of light, crowns the portal; underneath there are two cowering slaves, which are evidently personifications of the two rivers of Valencia, the Turia and the Júcar, whose waters (dos aguas = two waters) flow from the overturned jugs. A profusion of flowers, climbing plants, palms, etc. clusters around the whole group, which is also enlivened by colour. This decorative effect extends from the portal to the whole façade and, in particular, to the richly adorned windows with their vaulted balconies and the grilles of the ground floor.

Today the palace houses the most important *ceramics museum* in Spain. There are 16 rooms containing splendid tiles (azulejos) and ceramics of all kinds, from the Iberian period up to the present. Many of the exhibits come from the towns of Paterna, Manises and Alcora, situated near Valencia.

Museo Provincial de Bellas Artes (provincial museum of fine arts): One of the most important museums in Spain. It has some 2,000 paintings and is housed in the rooms of a former monastery, the Colegio San Pío. The painting of Valencia, especially the 'primitive' variety (14&15C), features strongly here, representatives being Fray Bonifacio Ferrer (retable of the charterhouse of Porta-Coeli) and Marçal de Sax (*Doubting Thomas*), who was from Saxony. Of the local Renaissance painters, Juan de Juanes is particularly well represented. Two pictures by Francisco Ribalta, *St. Bruno*, who is holding his finger to his mouth to indicate the Carthusians' injunction to be silent and the *Mystical Embrace of St.Francis and the Crucified Christ*, bear witness to mystical empathy. However, Jusepe de Ribera, Valencia's greatest painter, is insufficiently represented in this museum — works attributed to him are probably not actually by him. The most famous of the numerous modern painters from Valencia on show here is Joaquín Sorolla (1863-1923). The following should be mentioned among the other Spanish painters represented in the museum: El Greco, Murillo, Zurbarán, Velázquez (self-portrait) and Goya (Doña Joaquina Candado and the portrait of his brother-in-law Francisco Bayeu). Works by non-Spanish painters are also to be found here. These include Hieronymus Bosch, van Dyck, Pinturicchio, and Andrea del Sarto. The museum also contains works by contemporary sculptors, finds from classical times, and remnants of buildings from various periods.

City gates: All the city walls and gates in Valencia were torn down in 1865, with the

Palacio del Marqués de Dos Aguas

exception of the *Puerta de Serranos* (1238) and the *Puerta de Cuarte* (1441–60). The first of these two gates is a fine Gothic structure with polygonal towers and is more like a triumphal arch in appearance. On the city side it comprises rows of pointed arches. For a long time the gate served as a prison. The other gate, the Puerta de Cuarte, has semicircular towers and makes a more rugged and ponderous impression; it was modelled on the Castel Nuovo of Naples.

Also worth seeing: Before leaving Valencia, the visitor should also go to the Jardín Botánico, one of the best botanic gardens in Europe. It contains not only the local flora but also a wealth of exotic plants and trees. It is also worthwhile paying a visit to the *Mercado Central*, probably one of the largest markets in Europe, which is full of activity, particularly in the mornings. The *Palaeontological Museum,* which is housed in an 15C granary and the *Museum of Prehistory,* accommodated in a Gothic palace, should also be noted.

Environs: Manises: A village on the Huerta, 8 km. W. of Valencia on the right bank of the Turia. There has been an important faience industry here since the 14C. The numerous workshops can be visited. **Chiva** (40 km. W. of Valencia): Overlooked by the ruins of a *Moorish fortress.* Features of interest in the castle chapel are a Madonna, sculptures and paintings. The remains of a *Romanesque church,* and the 18C *parish church* with sculptures by I.Vergara and frescos by J.Vergara, are also worth seeing. The adjoining town of **Buñol,** a thermal spa, lies in a very picturesque and fertile valley. The ruins of a Moorish *castle,* where Francis I of France was held captive for some time, are also to be seen. The town's church has some fine paintings and sculptures by Ignacio Vergara (18C). There are numerous caves and waterfalls in this region. On the road from Valencia to Játiva is the town of **Algemesí:** Its *church* has three large paintings by Francisco Ribalta; a small picture gallery in the sacristy deserves attention. The same road to Játiva leads to the picturesquely situated town of **Alcira:** The *Casa Consistorial/Town Hall* displays Gothic and Renaissance features and houses an important archive. The parish church of *Santa Catalina,* with a baroque façade, has some paintings by Ribera. There are also interesting *mansions.* Some 30 km. N. of Valencia is the magnificently located charterhouse of **Porta Coeli** (also known as Porta-Celi). Surrounded by pine woods, it was founded in the early Middle Ages. The large complex of buildings from the 18C is less interesting than the church and cloisters. The single-aisled, originally 14C Gothic *church* was enlarged

and altered in the 18C. A marble portal with Doric columns leads into the interior, which has a large amount of marble decoration. The magnificent retable by Bonifacio Ferrer, a masterpiece of 14C Valencian painting, formerly adorned the high altar; it is now in the Museo Provincial de Bellas Artes in Valencia.

Further items of interest are: the 14C Gothic cloister, with 18C azulejos (tiles); the small cemetery cloister; the Renaissance inner courtyard; and the chapterhouse and refectory, which are also decorated with azulejos.

Valencia de Don Juan
León/León   p.386 □ E 3

Castillo: The massive 14C castle of the Counts of Oñate was rebuilt by the Acuñas in the 15C. It has a double enclosure and a moat. The walls are defended by battlements and towers. There is an enormous keep, with six attached round towers at the corners.

Iglesia de Nuestra Señora del Castillo Viejo: This 16C church has a notable 13C statue of the Virgin Mary, the local patron saint. The monuments to the Counts of Valencia de Don Juan have been in the *Capilla Mayor* since the 16C. The altar is in the style of Gaspar Becerra.

Other churches worth seeing: The parish church of *San Pedro* was built in the 19C by Sánchez Puelles and Sánchez Ibáñez, two architects from León. The high altar retable is the chief item of interest here. Originally in the former church of San Salvador, it is by Guillén Doncel (1543). Gold and silver objects are also to be seen, especially a Flemish processional cross. *San Juan* dates originally from the 12C but in its present form it is 14C, as are the two portals. Inside there are two 15C

Valencia de Don Juan, Castillo

Valladolid, Colegio de San Gregorio

altars from the school of Fernando Gallego.

Environs: To the S. of Valencia de Don Juan, on route 630, is **Toral de los Guzmanes** with the *Palacio de los Guzmanes,* a massive square building with corner towers. This building has a façade decorated with coats-of-arms and was built by Juan Ramírez de Guzmán in the 14C. The inner courtyard is 16C. The parish church of *Santa María,* in the Mudéjar style with Gothic influence, has a nave, two aisles, and a fine 16C *Capilla Mayor.* There are sculptures from the school of Gaspar Becerra. *San Juan,* which has much in common with Santa María, has an interesting Mudéjar ceiling. **Villaverde de Sandoval,** with the *Monasterio Benedictino de Santa Maria,* is to the N. of Valencia de Don Juan. The monastery was founded in

1167. The late-12C church, which has a nave, two aisles and three apses, is strongly reminiscent of Gradefes. Inside, note the three recumbent statues of the founders (13C) and Diego Ramírez de Cifuentes (14C). The monastery and cloister are originally 13C but were rebuilt in the 17C.

Valladolid

Valladolid/Old Castile   p.388 ☐ F 4

The origins of this city date from the time of the colonization of the Duero basin, although Count Ansúrez has been recorded in the annals of history as the city's founder. It is first mentioned, under the name of 'Belad Walid', in a document dating from the time of King Alfonso VI. After being captured from the Moors in 1074, it constantly increased in importance until it finally became the seat of the Counts of Castile. Towards the end of the Middle Ages it even became the residence of the Kings of Castile. Some important events in Spanish history occurred in Valladolid: Ferdinand III was proclaimed king; the Catholic Monarchs Ferdinand and Isabella were married; Christopher Columbus died; and Philip II was born. It became the capital of Spain for a short period under Philip III, and Napoleon established his headquarters here in 1809. As a result of this rich history Valladolid boasts a plethora of monuments.

Cathedral: It was at the behest of Charles I that Francisco de Colonia and Rodrigo Gil de Hontañon began building the cathedral on the foundations of an old 11C collegiate church. In 1585 Philip II commissioned Herrera, the builder of the Escorial, to redesign the cathedral. Herrera continued the building in his own style. Alberto Churriguera later undertook to continue the work and completed the façade in 1729. The cathedral nonetheless remained unfinished and only one of the two towers was completed. The main façade consists of two sections with Doric columns and, in the middle, the main portal set in an arch. The inside of the church consists of a nave, two aisles and side chapels. The tunnel vaults are borne by Doric columns. A magnificent retable, executed by Juan de Juni in 1572 for the church of Santa María la Antigua, adorns the high altar. The 17C choir stalls are by Francisco Velázquez. The apsidal chapels contain the tombs of Juan de Velarde and Count Pedro Ansúrez; an oil painting attributed to Goya may be seen in the chapel of San Pedro Regalado. The *Diocesan Museum* contains valuable sculptures and gold items, including a polychrome wooden retable dedicated to John the Baptist, a silver monstrance by the goldsmith Juan de

Arfe, a polychrome clay Pietà by Juan de Juni, a 13C Christ and Gothic tombs.

Santa María la Antígua (Calle de Marqués del Duero): The Romanesque church was built by Count Ansúrez. The magnificent tower and the 13C portico survive from the old building, while the remainder dates from the 14C and is Gothic. Inside, the nave and two aisles have groin vaults; in the sanctuary there is a Plateresque grille by Cristóbal de Andino.

Las Angustias (Calle de Angustias): This 16C church has a façade by Juan de Nates. The high altar has sculptures and reliefs by Francisco del Rincón and there are also fine sculptures of Mary Magdalene and St.John by Gregorio Fernández and the famous 'Virgen del Cuchillo', one of Juan de Juni's most important works.

San Pablo (Plaza de San Pablo): This church, which formerly belonged to the Dominican monastery, was built in the 15C by Simon de Colonia. It has a splendid dome and two very fine small portals. The façade is Isabelline-Gothic. Inside there are a statue of St. Dominic by Gregorio Fernández, a recumbent Christ by one of his pupils, and a 17C marble retable with a painting by Bartolomé de Cárdenas.

Other churches worth seeing: The church of *Santa Magdalena* was built by Gil de Hontañón in the 16C by order of Bishop Pedro de Lagasca. On the façade is the Bishop's resplendent, monumental coat-of-arms and inside, his tomb with a recumbent statue and a retable, both by Esteban Jordán. The Chapel of Los Corrales has a Renaissance retable dating from 1537 with reliefs and rich decoration by Fran-

Valladolid, National Museum of ▷
Sculpture

cisco Giralte. Inside the baroque church of
the *Vera Cruz,* which has a splendid portal by Diego de Prades, there are several
Stations of the Cross, including an Ecce
Homo by Gregorio Fernández. The interior of the 16C church of *San Miguel* has
a splendid retable by Adrián Alvarez with
sculptures by Gregorio Fernández, the
monuments to the Vivero family with praying statues by Francisco de Prades (1611)
and several statues by Gregorio Fernández
and Pompeo Leoni. The 14C church of
San Benito is in the Gothic style and has
an impressive portico by Gil de Hontañón.
The single-aisled church, *El Salvador,* was
built on the foundation walls of a 12C
chapel and contains a fine Flemish retable
by Quintin de Metsys. The church of *Santiago* is single-aisled in Renaissance style
with tunnel vaulting. It contains a retable
by Alonso Berruguete of the Adoration of
the the Magi. In the nave there is a baroque
retable by Alonso Manzano with statues by
Juan de Avila; there is an interesting statue
of Christ by Francisco de la Mata in the
Chapel of Siete Palabras. The single-aisled
baroque church of *San Martín,* with its
13C Romanesque tower, has an impressive
Pietà by Gregorio Fernández. The retable
at the high altar of the church of *El Carmen* has 17C sculptures and 18C paintings;
in one of this church's chapels there are a
Christ and a Virgin Mary by Gregorio Fernández and, in the nave, Santa Ana by Juan
de Juni. The single-aisled church of *Descalzas Reales* has a retable (1612) by Juan
de Muniátegui with paintings by Vicente
Carducho and Matías Blasco.

Convent of Las Huelgas Reales (Paseo
de Ramón y Cajal): This convent was
founded in 1282 by Doña María de Molina, the wife of Sancho IV. The church is
single-aisled and tunnel-vaulted and has a
retable (1613) by Francisco de Prades with
sculptures and reliefs by Gregorio Fernández and paintings by Tomás de Prado. In
the middle of the transept is the monument

to the foundress, with a recumbent alabaster figure and some works by Juan de Juni.

Convent of Santa Ana (Plaza de Santa
Ana): This convent founded by Philip II
was rebuilt by Sabatini in neoclassical style
in 1780 at the behest of Charles III. The
retable at the high altar is 17C. Three
paintings by Goya may be admired on the
epistle side and three by Ramón Bayeu on
the gospel side. In addition, there are also
some beautiful sculptures to be, including
the work of Gregorio Fernández and Pedro
de Mena.

**Other interesting monasteries and
convents:** *Porta Coeli* with a 17C single-
aisled and tunnel-vaulted church. Inside
there is a retable by Juan de Muniátegui
with paintings by Horacio Borgianni and
also the tombs of Don Rodrigo Calderón,
his wife and her parents. These are
adorned with statues in prayer. *Santa Catalina:* The retable of this single-aisled
church has paintings by Diego Valentín
Díaz and various sculptures, including a
16C Christ by Juan de Juni and a tomb
with a praying statue. *Augustinian monastery:* In the sacristy of the church there is
an interesting collection relating to the
Philippines, including some ivory statues.
Santa Clara: The 13C church was altered
in the 18C. It has several retables, including one at the high altar, which is an 18C
work by Pedro de Correas. *Santa Isabel:*
This Gothic church contains a retable by
Juan de Juni dedicated to St. Francis of
Assisi.

Colegio Santa Cruz (Plaza de Santa
Cruz): This college was founded by Cardinal González de Mendoza in 1474; the
building was completed by Lorenzo Vázquez in 1491. In the church there is a
depiction of Christ by Gregorio Fernández. The library has over 50,000 books.

National Museum of Sculpture: This

museum is housed in the *Colegio San Gregorio*, a lovely building in which Gothic, Mudéjar and Plateresque influences mingle in splendid harmony. The magnificent, richly adorned façade, which is a masterpiece of the Isabelline style, the inner colonnaded courtyard surrounded by a magnificent Plateresque gallery, the majestic staircase with its Gothic balustrade, and the Mudéjar panelling, are all outstanding examples of the Spanish early Renaissance. Juan de Gúas and Diego de Siloé are thought to be responsible for this building. Inside is the most extensive collection of Spanish sculpture of the 13–18C and it is also regarded as the most important European collection of polychrome sculpture. There are three rooms devoted to Alonso Berruguete, whose masterpieces, namely the retable of San Benito el Real, St.Jerome, and St.Sebastian, are to be seen here. In other rooms there are works by Juan de Juni and Gregorio Fernández, the greatest Spanish artists of the 16C. Baroque sculpture is well represented, with works by Pedro de Mena, José de Mora, Salvador Carmona, Francisco Salzillo and others. There are also works by Inocencio Berruguete, Pompeo Leoni, Pedro de Cuadra and Jorge Inglés. One section of the museum is devoted to painting. Paintings by Gregorio Martínez, Vicente Carducho, Felipe Gil de Mena, Lucas Jordán, Juan Rizi, Francisco Bayeu and others are to be found here.

Other museums: The *Provincial Archaeological Museum* is housed in the 16C palace of Fabio Nelli. 20 chronologically arranged rooms display interesting finds from prehistory, the Bronze Age, and the Roman, Visigoth, Arab and Mozarabic periods; there are also some fine frescos dating from the 13–15C. A *picture gallery* with works from the 16–18C has been established in the church of la Pasión. The *Casa de Cervantes* has been turned into a museum, with furniture, carpets and tapestries of the time. Cervantes spent the last years of his life here.

Also worth seeing: The former *royal palace* with its monumental staircase. The *palace of the Pimentel family*, where Philip II was born in 1527, with a tower and a Plateresque window. The *Archbishop's Palace*, the former house of Count Villasante, has a retable by Portillo in its chapel. The *fortified palace of the Counts of Benavente* dates from 1518. The 15C *palace of the Vivero*, where Ferdinand and Isabella were married, was rebuilt in neoclassical style but the staircase and an inner courtyard survive from the old building. Today, the archive of the Royal Chancellery is housed here. The *Plaza Mayor*, framed by galleries and arcades, was laid out to a 16C design. In its centre is the statue of Count Ansúrez of Carretero; on the N. side is the Town Hall. The gardens of the *Campo Grande* are also worth seeing.

Environs: Laguna de Duero (about 5 km. to the S.): In the parish church of *La Asunción*, note the retable of the high altar, and some fine 16C paintings. The pilgrimage chapel of the *Virgen del Vilar*, with a baroque high altar retable and two Gothic sculptures. **Renedo** (about 2 km. NE): The baroque *parish church* has some beautiful 17&18C sculptures. **Villarmentero de Esgueva** (some 5 km. NE): The 13C *parish church* in Gothic-Mudéjar style contains two fine retables with paintings. **Piña de Esgueva** (10 km. NE), with a Romanesque *parish church;* Visigoth remains were discovered here in the course of excavation work. **Villafuerte** (about 12 km. NE): *Castle* with keep and inner courtyard. **Tudela de Duero** (14 km. to the SE): The 16C Gothic *parish church* contains a retable attributed to Gregorio Fernández and a statue of Archbishop Alonso Vázquez in prayer by Esteban Jordán. The pilgrimage chapels of *Quinta Angustia* and *Santo Cristo*, dating from the 16&17C, are also worth seeing. **Retuerta** (about 18 km. SE): 12C *Premonstratensian monastery* in Cistercian style. **Quintanilla de Onésimo** (about 21 km. SE): This *parish church* (one nave, two aisles) has a retable with paintings by Jerónimo Vázquez dating from 1571 and sculptures by Francisco Giralte. The crypt of the 13C *monastery of Santa María de la Armedilla* is also worth seeing. **Olivares de Duero** (22 km. SE): The Gothic *parish church* has a Renaissance retable with sculptures by Guillén de Holanda and a wooden sculpture of Christ by Juan de Juni.

Vallbona de las Monjas
Lérida/Catalonia   p.390 □ M 4

Convent: This convent dating from the mid-12C is from the same period as the monasteries of Poblet and Santas Creus. Like these two, it is in Cistercian style. The nuns of this Order lived in the convent from 1176 until the Order was dissolved after the Council of Trent. The convent, which is now occupied by Bernardine monks, was surrounded by a wall and had three entrance gates. The single-aisled *church* is in plain Cistercian style. There are three rectangular chapels off the ambulatory and arcades. Above the crossing there is a large dome with a groin vault. The octagonal Gothic tower (12C or 13C) is the only one surviving in this form in the whole of Catalonia. The church was renovated in the 14C, which explains why some parts of it are in pure Gothic style. The originally Romanesque cloister has Gothic arches. There are two fine tombs. Church treasure.

Valls
Tarragona/Catalonia   p.390 □ M 4

San Juan Bautista: This single-aisled late Gothic parish church dating from the 16C has fourteen side chapels. It was built on the site of a Romanesque church. The *Chapel of St.Alejos* is the most interesting, having the recumbent statue of the Saint and two reliefs by Luis Bonifàs (18C). Parts of the 17C high altar, some gold pieces and paintings by Jaime Pons (17–18C), have survived. The 17C *Chapel of Nuestra Señora del Rosario* has a fine series of typically Catalonian tiles (azulejos), which depict scenes from the naval battle of Lepanto.

Vendrell
Tarragona/Catalonia   p.390 □ M 4

Vendrell was the birthplace of the world-famous cellist Pau (Pablo) Casals (1876–1973). The 18C parish church of *San Salvador* has a baroque façade and a bell tower dating from 1769. The town *museum* has fine prehistoric, Roman and medieval collections. In addition, there are some mansions (16–18C) in Catalonian style which are worth seeing.

Vera
Almeria/Andalusia   p.396 □ I 10

Vera is a small town with some 5,000 inhabitants. The chief item of interest is the *Real Hospital de San Agustín* (1521), which has a *church* with a fine high altar.

Environs: Cuevas de Almanzora (6 km. N.): Arab *castle*, rebuilt in Gothic style. **Garrucha** (9 km. S.): a fine *fortress.* **Huércal Overa** (21 km. NW): *Parish church of La Asunción* with a fine high altar in the baroque style dating from the 18C. **Vélez Rubio** (65 km. NW): The fine 18C neoclassical *church* is a monumental building with two baroque towers and a dome.

Valladolid, Colegio de San Gregorio

Valladolid, cathedral, monstrance

Vélez Blanco (70 km. NW): After the conquest of the town by Ferdinand and Isabella in 1488 the magnificent, gorgeously decorated *castle* was built in Italian Renaissance style; it is guarded by battlemented bastions. The patio, with columns and marble staircases, was especially splendid (it has been rebuilt in its original form and is now in the Metropolitan Museum, New York). Nearby (1 km. to the S. of Vélez Blanco) is the *Cueva de los Letreros*, with prehistoric drawings depicting astronomical and other symbols as well as men (including a magician).

Vergara

Guipúzcoa / Basque Provinces   p.388☐H 2

This small industrial town lies at the con-

fluence of Anzuola and Deva. It was here, in 1839, that the Generals Espartero and Maroto signed the treaty which brought the first Carlist war to an end.

San Pedro de Ariznoa: The present building, in late Gothic style, dates from the first half of the 17C and is the result of the rebuilding of a Gothic church which existed before 1348. It contains the famous *Christ Dying* (1622), a masterpiece by the sculptor Juan de Mesa. A beautiful Plateresque high altar and a Flemish winged altar in the sacristy, are also worth looking at.

Santa Marina de Oxirondo: This church was built in Gothic style in the 14C and rebuilt in 1542. It has a nave, two aisles, and a rib vault supported by Ionic

Vergara, San Pedro de Ariznoa

Veruela, monastery, portal

columns. The baroque bell tower was added in 1701. This church is regarded as one of the most typical examples of the Basque Gothic style in Guipúzcoa.

Real Seminario: In 1775 the Royal Basque Society of the Friends of the Country built the royal seminary for the nobility, the first of its kind in Spain. It was like a university and was under the supervision of the Dominicans. A sculpture by Gregorio Fernández depicts St. Ignatius Loyola.

Casa Consistorial/Town Hall: On the Plaza Mayor. It was built in Herrara style in 1620. The façade is decorated with a fine coat-of-arms and the top storey is supported by arcades.

Also worth seeing: There are also numer-

ous old mansions with their typical overhanging eaves and corner balconies. The 16C *Casa de Jáuregui* has a unique façade and is classified as a historical monument. Also note the houses of the *Gaviria, Ozaeta, Olaso* and *Arrese* families. The Treaty of Vergara was signed in the house of the *Irízar* family.

Veruela

Zaragoza/Aragon   p.388☐ I 3/4

The village of Vera de Moncayo lies at the foot of Mount Moncayo. From here the traveller continues to the Monasterio de Nuestra Señora, which was formerly the most important monastery in Spain. It is now classified as a historical monument.

Veruela, monastery, apses

Monasterio de Nuestra Señora: This monastery was founded in 1146, probably by Pedro de Atarés, the ancestor of the Borgia family. It was occupied by Cistercians who impressed their own style on the church. Today the monastery is a Jesuit college. It is surrounded by a massive, battlemented wall flanked by two round towers. The church was built in transitional style between Romanesque and Gothic and was not consecrated until the 13C. The simple Romanesque *portal* dates from the same period. Modelled on the church of Poblet, it has a nave, two aisles, a transept and five apsidal chapels. The interior decoration is late Romanesque in the manner of Clairvaux. The visitor enters the sacristy through a baroque portal. The chapterhouse and the refectory are 14C, as is the Gothic *cloister* with its square ground plan and groin vault. Here there are several Romanesque and Gothic *tombs*. Mementoes of the poet Gustavo Adolfo Bécquer are preserved in the monastery.

Viana

Navarra/Navarra   p.388☐H 3

This picturesque little town was founded in 1219 by King Sancho VII in order to protect the southern border of Navarre. In 1423 King Charles III made the town the capital of a principality, which was given in fee to the crown prince of the day. Don Carlos, the nephew of Charles III, was the first to hold the title.

Santa María (Plaza de los Fueros): Old

Veruela, monastery, chapterhouse

documents show that the present church was preceded by another which dated from the 14C. Built in Gothic style, the present church was rebuilt and extended several times during the 15–17C. The Chapel of San Juan Bautista was added in the 18C. The church has a fine Renaissance portal with interesting reliefs. It was built by Juan de Goyaz 1549–67. In front of the portal is the tomb of Cesare Borgia. The retable of the high altar is 17C and shows Plateresque and baroque influences. There are notable wall paintings in the Chapel of San Juan Bautista, the dome of which was painted by Luis Paret y Alcázar in 1787. The church treasure, with its numerous 16C religious objects, is kept in the sacristy.

San Pedro: The church was built in the 14C but is in a state of considerable dilapidation today. The apse and the 18C baroque portal have survived reasonably well.

Also worth seeing: Parts of the old *walls* have survived. The *Town Hall* and the *Tower of San Pedro* are also of interest.

Vich
Barcelona/Catalonia   p.390☐N 3

Vich, the Roman Ausa, is on the site of an Iberian settlement. In the Visigoth period the town was known as Ausona. After being devastated by the Arabs it remained uninhabited for almost a century before it was colonized once more under Wilfredo el Velloso in 878.

Vich, cathedral

Vich, Roman temple

Cathedral: Built in 1038. However, only the crypt, a six-storeyed Romanesque tower and Gothic cloister have survived from the original building. The cathedral was rebuilt in 1871 but had to be restored again after the Civil War. The wall paintings by José Maria Sert cover all the walls of the church and are its most notable feature. The frescos to be seen here today are the third cycle he painted—the first was not to his liking and the second was destroyed in the Civil War. After his death in 1945 the paintings were completed by his pupil M.Massot to the original designs. They depict various scenes from the Old and New Testaments: Adam and Eve, Paradise Lost, Christ's Passion and the Crucifixion, the Entombment and the Resurrection. The severity of these dramatically depicted scenes is muted by the restraint of the

colours employed (only sepia and metallic grey). The silver sarcophagus of Bishop Bernardo Calvo in the sixth chapel on the left is by Juan de Matons (1728); the marvellous alabaster retable is by Pedro Oller (1427) as is the tomb of Canon Despujol (1434). A silver processional cross (1394) completes the church treasure, which was looted when the church was devastated in the Civil War (1936).

Museo Episcopal: Owing to its collections of Romanesque, Gothic and Catalan art, the Episcopal Museum of Vich is the best of its kind after the Romanesque Museum of Barcelona. Room 1: Romanesque *frescos* from various churches in the region (San Saturnino in Osormort, San Martín de Sescorts, El Brull), and the *Baldacchino of Ribas,* which is attributed to the school of Ripoll; there is also the 12C *Deposition* from Erill la Vall. The fine *alabaster altar* by Bernardo Saulet (1341), consisting of twenty carved panels, is in the Sala de los Amigos del Museo (room of the friends of the museum). Outstanding amongst the winged altars is that taken from the church of Santa Clara in Vich. It is a masterpiece by Luis Borrassa (1414) and depicts scenes from the life of St.Dominic. The altar by Rubió (*c.* 1350) in room 3 and that by Guimerá (1450) in room 4, are also worth seeing. Gothic painting is also represented by the paintings of Ramon de Mur, Bernardo Martorell, Jaime Huguet (small winged altar with Madonna, 15C) and Ferrer Bassa, among others. The museum also has furniture, ceiling panels, ceramics, etc.

Also worth seeing: The restored *Roman temple* from the 3C AD, which was discovered near the museum in 1882. The 18C *Monastery of Santo Domingo* in Plateresque style with a fine cloister. The Gothic church of *San Justo.* The *Iglesia de la Piedad*, with a fine baroque façade and *Santa Teresa* (1646). The 16C *Hospital de la Santa Cruz* has a baroque church consecrated in 1753.

Environs: Tabérnolas (7 km. to the NE): The village church dates from the 11C and has a crypt. **Santa Eugenia de Berga** (6 km. S.): The parish church, consecrated in 1173, is one of the best in this region. The transept and bell tower were added in the 12C.

Viella
Lérida/Catalonia   p.390 □ L 2

This little town is situated in the centre of the Arán valley, in Migarán, where the rivers Nere and Garona join. Viella is regarded as the main town of the valley. Founded by the Romans under the name of Vetula, the old part of town has retained its appeal to the present day.

Parish church of San Miguel: This 12&13C Romanesque church, with its cross arch and nave dating from the 18C, is the most conspicuous building in this little town. Below the octagonal tower, which is built on a square base, there is an original portal with four archivolts (13C), whose reliefs depict the Last Judgement; St.Michael, the Creation and the Flagellation of Christ can be seen in the tympanum. On the right wall of the church is a 13C Romanesque relief depicting the Crucified Christ. The interior of the church is not very well preserved but there are fine works of art to be admired: a Romanesque font with floral decoration; a 15C Gothic altarpiece painted on wood and depicting scenes from the life of Christ and the Apostles; and, best of all the *Christ from Migarán* in the N. side chapel, a marvellous bust which was once part of a Deposition. This work is attributed to the school of Erill la Vall-Tahull (12C). The Virgin Mary at the high altar is a copy of a Romanesque carving destroyed in the Civil War.

Also worth seeing: The old 17C mansions of *Burgarol, Rodes* and *Fedusa.* The *Tower of Martignon* has a slate spire; today it houses the *Ethnological Museum.* The annex containing the archive dates from the 16C and displays typical Renaissance windows.

Environs: Betrén: The church of *San Esteban* is single-aisled, dates from the 12–13C and possesses Gothic windows, which are of a later date. The portal, with its five archivolts and decorated capitals, is one of the finest in the whole valley. The decoration in the tympanum includes a relief of a (seated) Madonna and Child. **Escuñau** (2.5 km. W. of Viella): Old Renaissance houses, e.g. the *house of Pere Joan.* The *church* has a 12C Romanesque portal. Near **Casarill** are the ruins of the Romanesque church of *Santa María de Migarán,* which was destroyed in the Civil War.

Vigo
Pontevedra/Galicia   p.386□B 3

The Roman Vicus was always a major port but it is only since the second half of the 19C that it has become the most important transatlantic port in Spain and also a centre of sardine fishing. The economic impetus which the town received in the 19C was so strong that most of its old buildings and fortifications fell victim to modernization. Thus, the present *collegiate church* is a neoclassical work built by Melchor de Prado in 1816. On the castle hill are two more fortresses, the *Castillo de Castro* and the *Castillo San Sebastián,* which originally date from the 10C but have been rebuilt several times, especially in the 17C. Old houses with arcades belonging to the no-

bility and the gentry still survive, particularly in the old harbour district of Berbés.

Also worth seeing: The two squares, the Plaza Mayor and the Plaza Almeida, with the *Casa de los Pazos y Figueroa* with its Plateresque decorations. The *Pazo de Castrelos,* dating from 1670, is in a lovely park at the edge of the town. It houses not only the *town museum* with its Roman stele, but also a collection of furniture and sculpture and a good picture gallery.

Environs: Moaña: On the Ría del Vigo, immediately opposite Vigo, it has a Romanesque *parish church* with a fine portal decorated with figures. **Cangas de Morrazo:** Cangas de Morrazo and Hio are just to the W. of Moaña, again on the Ría del Vigo. Cangas has a 16C *collegiate church,* which has a good portal decorated with columns and a large rose-window. There are also some interesting old sculptures inside the church. In the town there are old mansions and some picturesque corners. **Hio:** Hio has the Romanesque

Vigo, view

Vigo, city museum

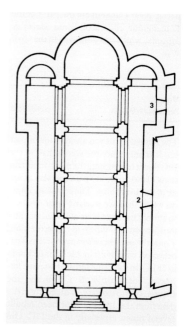

Vilabertrán, Santa María 1 main portal **2** entrance to cloister **3** entrance to monastery

church of *San Andrés* with a noteworthy portal. The atrium has a cross and Deposition; this famous and expressive cross with figures that are hewn from granite with unbelievable delicacy, is one of the most beautiful in the whole of Galicia. **Villasobroso:** A side road to Mondariz branches off the road to Orense, to the E. of Vigo. Shortly before Mondariz is Villasobroso, with a well-preserved 11C *Romanesque fortress* standing on Monte Landin.

Vilabertrán

Gerona/Catalonia   p.390 □ O 3

Santa María de Vilabertrán: Collegiate church. This former Romanesque

monastery in the vicinity of Figueras is worth visiting. The church was consecrated on 11 November 1100. The Gothic Capilla de Rocabertí was added later; there were further additions in the 18C. The three-storeyed tower has Catalan-Lombard decoration with blind arcades and double round windows. The cloister is from the original building. The irregular arrangement of the beautiful Gothic windows is a conspicuous feature of the rather plain 15C abbey.

Environs: Perelada is mentioned under the name of Castro Tolón as early as the 9C. The *castle* was built in the 14C and later rebuilt several times. The main façade

Villacastín, parish church

Villafranca del Bierzo, Santa María

is Renaissance; the E. façade has two monumental battlemented towers. There are a *museum* and a *library* on the first floor. The *monastery of Santo Domingo* has a fine 11C Romanesque cloister.

Villacastín
Segovia/Old Castille   p.392☐F 5

Parish church: This church, with a Gothic interior, is the work of Fray Antonio de Villacastín, an assistant to the architect Juan de Herrera. The church's external façade and the tower were both built in purest Herrera style. The main chapel has a Renaissance altarpiece; in the aisles there are several altarpieces with oil paintings by Alonso de Herrera from 1596.

Environs: El Espinar (some 15 km. SE): The parish church of *San Eutropio* was rebuilt by Juan de Mijares after a fire in 1542. The altarpiece (1563–73) is by the sculptor Francisco Giralte; the pulpit also dates from the 16C. In the church there are several paintings by Sánchez Coello.

Villafranca del Bierzo
León/León   p.386☐D 2

Villafranca, the main town of the fertile Bierzo, stands some 1,600 ft. above sea level at the confluence of the Río Burbia and the Río Valcárcel. It has some 6,500 inhabitants. The town owes its foundation to French pilgrims on their way to Santiago in the 11C. Indulgences were granted to the pilgrims even at this stage, if they fell ill on the way.

San Juan en San Fiz: The little church at the edge of this town is a well-preserved plain Romanesque building.

Santiago: This single-aisled church, in which indulgences were granted to pilgrims to Santiago, is a typical example of Romanesque architecture (12C). The N. portal with its sculptures is regarded as one of the best in the province.

Convento de San Francisco: The church has a 13C Romanesque portal. The vaulted nave is 15C Mudéjar.

San Nicolás: Built in Jesuit style by Gabriel de Robles in the 17C, this church was part of a Jesuit college. The rich sculptural decoration includes a Christ which the founder had probably brought with him from America.

Santa María de Cluniaco: Originally built by Cluniac monks in the 12C. The present building was erected in the 16–18C. Its style is reminiscent of Rodrigo Gil de Hontañón. The ground plan is in the form of a Latin cross.

Convento de la Anunciada: Founded in the early 17C by Pedro de Toledo y Osorio, the 5th Marquis of Villafranca. This single-aisled church has a spacious choir in the E., and a gallery and family tomb to the W. The large Italianate portal has a wide arch and Tuscan columns. The tabernacle at the high altar is an Italian work.

Also worth seeing: *Palacio de los Marquéses/Palace of the Marquises of Villafranca:* A massive rectangular building with round towers at the corners, probably built by the 1st Marquis in the early 16C. There are also splendid mansions with escutcheons.

Environs: A short way to the E. of Villafranca is **Pieros** with the *Castro de la Ventosa,* the ancient Bergidum (origin of the

Villafranca del Bierzo, Santiago, portal

Villafranca del Bierzo, Santiago, portal

name 'Bierzo'), an Asturian fortress, parts of the walls and towers of which still stand. On the other side of the road is **Cacabelos,** with a museum in which numerous finds from the above-mentioned site are on display. The *parish church*, which has a nave, two aisles, and a 16C transept, is also worth looking at. The E. of this church, which dates originally from the 12C, has a Romanesque apse. To the S. is **Carracedo del Monasterio:** The *Monasterio de Benedictinos de Santa María*, as it is also known, was founded by King Bermudo II in 990. In 1138 Alfonso VII of León rebuilt it for his sister Doña Sancha. The present church is 18C but incorporates older parts and decorative features. The most notable features are the 12C chapterhouse and the 13C royal palace, which is an early work from the transitional period between Romanesque and Gothic (rebuilt in the 18C). The *cloister*, *sacristy* and *refectory* all date from the first half of the 16C. The *tower* is from 1602.

Villafranca del Panadés
Barcelona/Catalonia   p.390☐M/N 4

Villafranca, situated in the centre of the vine-growing area of Panadés, is regarded as the richest and most famous vine-growing town in the region. The famous 'llivre vert'—the green book dating from the 16C—is preserved in the archive in the Town Hall.

Monastery of San Francisco: This monastery, which today houses a hospital, dates from the 13C. The Catalan parliament (Cortes) met here several times. The Gothic *church* belonging to the monastery has some fine medieval tombs and a fine retable by Luis Borrassá.

Santa María: This church too is 13C and was built in pure Catalan-Gothic style. It is single-aisled, with side chapels and a polygonal apse. In the crypt there is a group by the sculptor José Llimona.

Chapel of San Juan de los Hospitaleros: This single-aisled Gothic chapel built in 1307 is unusual in structure and has a wooden vault.

Regional museum: Beside the church of Santa María there are two palaces of the kings of Aragon, which date from the 13&14C. One of these houses the regional museum (Museo Comercal), which is divided into two sections. On the first floor is the *Town Museum*, where the exhibits include a Gothic retable (1459) and some others from the 16&17C. The *Wine Museum* is housed on the ground floor.

Villajoyosa
Alicante/Valencia   p.396☐L 8

Villajoyosa is some 40 km. N. of Alicante.

Villafranca del Bierzo, Santiago, apse

Fruit plantations and olive groves surround this harbour town, which lives largely on its fishing industry. Here there are numerous remains from the Roman period. Two sturdy towers survive from the medieval *fortifications*. The old *town wall* has a Gothic *church* built into it, and the church takes on a fortified aspect as a result. Its tower has a horseshoe arch suggesting a Visigoth model.

Environs: A few kilometres N. of Villajoyosa is **Benidorm**. The name of the town is Moorish in origin: Beni-Darhim. A few decades ago Benidorm was still an unknown farming and fishing village but today this seaside resort is a major tourist centre. The old fishing village still has some picturesque corners.

Villalba

Lugo/Galicia   p.386 ☐ C 1

This small town is especially famous for the large markets held there each month, particularly the capon fair held on 19 December at which the Christmas capons are offered for sale in accordance with the old tradition.

Fortress: The 14C fortress was destroyed in the 15C and then rebuilt. The keep is octagonal, which is rare in Spain. The wall dating from 1480 still survives. The imposing fortress tower (Castillo de Andrade) is today used by the Counts of Villalba as a hotel.

Environs: 17 km. SW of Villalba is **Baamonde** with Santiago, a fine single-aisled Romanesque church with a rectangular apse and interesting portals. **Santa Eulalia de Bóveda:** Some 7 km. to the SE of Baamonde is the church of Santa Eulalia underneath which a room was discovered which must be from the 4/5C AD. On the walls of this underground vault (where there is the source of a stream), there are some well-preserved frescos with geometric and animal motifs. These im-

Carracedo del Monasterio (Villafranca del Bierzo)

ply Byzantine or early Christian ideas and probably symbolize the depiction of Paradise as seen in the Roman catacombs and other early Christian images. Shrubs, garlands and birds are depicted. Some researchers suggest that there was originally a Roman nymphaeum here which did not acquire its Christian significance until later.

Villalón de Campos
Valladolid/Old Castile   p.386☐F 3

San Miguel: This 14C Gothic-Mudéjar church has a portal with Isabelline decoration; the tower is Mudéjar in the lower section and 17C in the upper section. Inside there are an altarpiece with a 15C Spanish-Flemish sculpture of the Madonna and Child, the tomb of González del Barco (1536) by Juan de Juni, and paintings, grilles and two Renaissance pulpits.

San Juan Bautista: This 15C Mudéjar church has a nave, two aisles and a 16C altarpiece (by Maestro de Palanquinos).

Also worth seeing: The 18C baroque church of *San Pedro* contains an altarpiece with fine sculptures and also several paintings. The magnificent *hospital* was built in Gothic-Plateresque style. The *rollo* (obelisk) with its Gothic and Renaissance elements dates from the 16C and has been declared a national monument.

Environs: Cuenca de Campos (about 3 km. S.): The interior of the 16C Mudéjar church of *San Justo y Pastor* contains some outstanding gilded panelling, an altarpiece with sculptures, and a Stations of the Cross dating from the 16C. The Gothic-Mudéjar church of *Santa María del Castillo* has a horseshoe arch portal. The 17C church of

San Mamés has a 16C Plateresque altarpiece. The *monastery of San Bernardino de Siena* contains the notable 16C tombs of its foundress Doña María Fernández de Velasco and the cleric Diego de Guevara.

Villanueva de los Infantes
Ciudad Real/New Castile   p.392☐H 8

This town contains a large number of interesting, historical buildings; the numerous portals decorated with the coats-of-arms of the nobility are particularly striking.

Parish church of San Andrés: This church was built in the 15&17C in late Gothic style. The gate is of wrought-iron; the tower dates fom the late 17C. Inside there are a baroque altarpiece with frescos at the high altar and a marble choir. The church is adjoined by the 16C Renaissance *rectory.*

Villalba, fortress

Also worth seeing: The 15C *monastery of San Francisco*. The 16C *Franciscan nuns' convent*. The *monastery of la Trinidad* with baroque portal and altarpiece. The *monastery of Santo Domingo* dating from the early 16C.

Environs: Manzanares: (about 50 km. to the NW): The late-14C/early-15C *parish church* was rebuilt in Renaissance style after a fire in the 16C. It consists of a nave with a crossing and dome, five side chapels and a portal. A tower completes the exterior. The retable at the high altar has paintings in the style of Ribera and dates from the 16–17C. Two further retables date from the 16C and 17C respectively; the choir stalls are 16C. The sacristy was built in the late 17C. The castle, Arab in origin, belonged to the Orders of Santiago and Calatrava. It was restored by the latter. **Valdepeñas** (35 km. W.): The late-15C *parish church,* built in late Gothic style, has a portal showing Plateresque influence. The bell tower is 16C. The interior is divided into two aisles.

Villanueva y Geltrú
Barcelona/Catalonia   p.390 □ N 4

Victor Balaguer Museum: Designed by the architect J.Graell, the museum was founded in 1882 by Victor Balaguer, poet, historian and politician. The museum contains a well-stocked library, an archaeological collection and collections of pictures and sculptures, including work by well-known Catalan artists.

La Geltrú Castle: The finest works of art, however, are to be seen in the castle, a 12C building rebuilt several times up until the 17C. Only the keep and the castle wall are Romanesque. There are works by Carrecío and Escalante, an 'Annunciation' by El Greco and an 'Adoration of the Shepherds' by J.B. Mayno (1568 – 1649).

San Salvador de Valdedios basilica with a nave and two aisles but no transept **1** atrium **2** and **3** arcades **4** main apse **5** and **6** side apses **7** portico **8** chapel

Villanueva de los Infantes, San Andrés

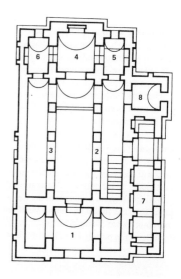

Also worth seeing: In the *Joaquín Mir Museum,* there is a fine collection of coloured azulejos, which show the various trades of the 17&18C. Some landscape paintings by the Catalan painter Joaquín Mir (1873–1940) are also on display. The church of *Santa María* has a fine 17C Renaissance retable.

Villarejo de Salvanés
Madrid/New Castile   p.392□G 6

Fortress: Today only the imposing square keep survives. The fortress formerly belonged to various military orders from the Middle Ages onwards.

Villarrobledo
Albacete/Murcia   p.392□H 7

San Blas: Built in Renaissance style with some Gothic and baroque structural elements. The portals on the S. side are reminiscent of Renaissance works by Andrés de Vandelvira. The entrances and the tower are Gothic. The high altar is baroque. The church of *Santa María* has a Mudéjar tower with tiled decoration. The *Ayuntamiento,* with its double arcaded gallery, dates from the late 16C. Some houses with good portals survive from the 17&18C. The neoclassical *Casa de los Diezmos* belongs to Marquis of Villena.

Villaviciosa
Oviedo/Asturia   p.386□E 1

Villaviciosa, a charming little town of winding streets and old houses decorated with coats-of-arms, dates from the Roman period and was first mentioned by name in the 13C. Most of it was destroyed in a fire in the 15C, but it was subsequently rebuilt.

Santa María: This 15C church has a

San Salvador de Valdedios (Villaviciosa)

richly decorated 12C Romanesque portal decorated with figures. At the E. end there is a small Romanesque window with richly decorated capitals and arches. A projecting annexe with a wooden roof (characteristic of this region) is attached to the S. of this church.

Also worth seeing: A former Franciscan monastery (16C), which today functions as a parish church.

Environs: The *granaries* (hórreo) typical of the whole of Asturia are to be found around Villaviciosa. They are raised off the ground on four posts, are built of wood or stone and often are surrounded by a balcony; the roof is tiled. Some of them, particularly the wooden ones, have decorated cross-ribs and cornices. **Priesca** (11 km. NE of Villaviciosa) has the fine pre-Romanesque church of *San Salvador*, which was consecrated in 921. **Gobiendes** (12 km. further towards Ribadesella on the side road to Ariondas) contains the church of *Santiago de Gobiendes*, built under Alfonso II in the late 9C. In **Fuentes,** 2 km. from Villaviciosa, in the direction of Coro, the visitor will find *San Salvador de Fuentes*, a national monument. Decorated with columns and arches, it was consecrated in 1023. The bell tower was added later. **Amandi:** 1 km. from Villaviciosa, in a remote location on a hill, is the beautifully proportioned church of *San Juan*, originally 12C. The two main features surviving from the original church, even though they have been partly renovated, are the beamed ceiling and the apse which is rounded in Romanesque style and has columns and richly decorated arches and capitals. The choir windows with their capitals decorated with figures and their ornamented arches can be seen to particular advantage from the outside. The church's fine baroque façade dates from 1755 and it has a portico with a flight of steps. The bell tower was rebuilt in

1832. **San Salvador de Valdedios:** 9 km. SW of Villaviciosa, in a wooded valley, is the *monastery of Santa María*, which is surrounded by hills. The Romanesque church and cloister were built during the 13–17C. To the left of the entrance to the monastery, in an enclosure, is the church of *San Salvador (El Conventin)*, which was built in 893 under King Alfonso III, the Great. This tunnel-vaulted basilica with a nave and two aisles, but no transept, has three rectangular apses. On the epistle side, parallel with the aisle, there is also a side portico. The church's notable features are the fine windows, the capitals of the columns inside and the remains of wall paintings, which probably formerly adorned all the interior walls and which are reminiscent of San Julian de los Prados in Oviedo and of San Miguel de Liño in Monte Naranco.

Villena
Alicante/Valencia   p.396☐K 8

Villena (1,644 ft.) stands in an extensive and well-watered huerta. James I, the Conqueror, liberated the town from the Moors in the 13C, but then ceded it to Castile. Today, Villena, which was only incorporated into the province of Alicante in 1836, has the air of a small town of the Mancha.

Castillo: The castle was originally a Moorish alcázar but its present form is 15C. The walls, round towers, a massive keep with six turrets and a vault within have stood the test of time well. Enrique de Villena, the famous 15C Spanish literary figure and the first to translate Dante's 'Divine Comedy' into Spanish, lived in the castle.

Santiago: This late Gothic church was begun in 1492 and completed in the 16C. Inside the most striking feature is the powerful spirally-fluted columns of the kind occurring in the lonjas of Barcelona and Palma de Mallorca. The capitals are richly decorated with leaves, fish and angels. Also note the retable of the high altar, which is by Jerónimo Quijano, the architect and sculptor from Murcia (1540).

Also worth seeing: It is also worth paying a visit to the *Archaeological Museum*, where there are splendid prehistoric, Iberian, Roman and medieval collections. The visitor taking a walk through the town will also find here and there sober, severe 18C mansions, a particularly prominent feature of which are the proudly displayed coats-of-arms.

Vinuesa
Soria/Old Castile   p.388☐H 3

Church: Built in the 16C, it has a nave and two aisles. The altarpiece at the high altar is 17C; the baroque organ dates from the 18C.

Also worth seeing: The *Casa Concejo* and the *Arca de Misericordia* from the 16C. The *palace of Don Pedro de Neyla* and other mansions.

Environs: Los Molinos de Duero (about 5 km. W.), with fine buildings in vernacular style.

Vitoria
Alava/Basque Provinces   p.388☐H 2

This city is the capital of the Basque provinces and is also the seat of a bishop. It consists of two parts, namely the old city with its Gothic quarter, standing on a hill, and the new city in the plain. The city was originally founded by the Visigoths, who gave it the name of 'Gasteiz'. It derives its present name from the victory of Sancho VI, King of Navarre, over the rebellious Basques in 1181. The name 'Vitoria' is a corruption of the word 'Victoria', meaning victory. When it was occupied by Napoleon's troops, the city became a centre of guerrilla warfare. It was liberated on 21 June 1813, when English, Spanish and Portuguese troops led by Wellington decisively defeated the French.

Cathedral of Santa María: This Gothic church built in the 14C on the site of a Romanesque chapel became a collegiate church in 1496, and a cathedral in 1862. The impression made by the exterior is rather that of a fortified church, particularly in the N. section. The magnificent 14C main doorway has a portico of three arches from the second half of the 14C. The sculptured decoration depicts scenes from the life of the Virgin Mary. The portal was renovated in the 19C. The church has a nave and two aisles, and takes the form of a Latin cross. The transept and aisles have large arcades and galleries. In the

Vitoria, monastery of San Antonio

Chapel of Santiago there are a Mater Dolorosa and an 18C Judas. Some further notable works in the cathedral are a painting of Christ by Rubens, a Virgin of the Rosary in the Dutch Gothic style, a Romanesque Virgin, and a Renaissance sarcophagus of Don Cristóbal Martínez de Alegría. An Immaculate Conception (1666) by Carreño de Miranda is also worth seeing. The sacristy contains a Deposition by van Dyck and a processional cross by Benvenuto Cellini.

New Cathedral: This notable neo-Gothic church with its nave and four aisles was built 1907–69.

San Miguel: This church has a nave and two aisles and was built in the late 14C on the site of a Romanesque place of worship. The statue of the *Virgen Blanca* (White Virgin), the city's patron saint, was installed in the main portal, which dates from the late 14C. Gregorio Fernández made the altarpiece at the high altar in 1632.

San Pedro: This 14C church has a richly decorated Gothic main portal. Inside there is a Platereesque high altar, and the Chapel of the Tabernacle has a Mater Dolorosa attributed to Gregorio Fernández. Splendid Renaissance bronze statues are to be found by the tombs of Bishop Diego de Álava y Esquibel and his father Pedro Martínez de Álava.

San Vicente: This church was begun 14C and not completed until the late 15C. The tower is 19C. Inside the church is a large baroque high altar. The Chapel of the Holy Cross, with its 16C decoration, is worth seeing.

Museo de Arqueología y Armas (Museum of Archaeology and Arms): Housed in a 16C palace, this archaeological collection has finds from the Roman period (including sculptures and tomb furnishings)

and also items from primitive settlements in the province of Álava. The arms museum has interesting German, Spanish and Italian armaments from the 15&16C and also a collection of weapons from prehistoric times up to the 19C.

Museo Provincial (Provincial Museum): This museum (housed in the Casa de Álava, built 1916) has a noteworthy collection of paintings and sculptures. Items from the Flemish school include a triptych which dates from *c.* 1500 (from the church of Salinas de Añana), a Deposition and two 16C triptychs. Paintings by Ribera, the 'Immaculate Conception' by Alonso Cano, and works by the painters Arocena, Arraiz, Carnicero, Díaz de Olano, Dublang, Iturrino, Madrazo, Martínez, Cubells, Benjamín Palencia, Pichot, Rosales, Salaverría, Suárez Alba, Vicente López and others, are all to be seen here. The museum also houses liturgical garments and religious objects from the 16C. The sculptures include a notable 12C Deposition, which consists of four figures by an unknown artist from Álava.

Also worth seeing: *Monastery of San Antonio,* founded in 1604 by the widow of Don Carlos de Álava. The church is early 17C and has two portraits of San Antonio and San Francisco, painted by Gregorio Fernández. Inside the church are the tombs of the monastery's founders and the Romanesque painting, the *Virgen de los Remedios.* The *monastery of San Prudencio* is today used as a hospice. Founded in the late 16C, it has a neoclassical arcade with Tuscan columns. On the façade of the 16C *monastery of Santa Cruz* are the coats-of-arms of Charles V and the Aguire and Esquibel families. The church has a Gothic nave. The *Casa del Cordón* was built in the Gothic style in the late 15C, around an old 13C tower. On the façade are the coats-of-arms of Ferdinand and Isabella and the cord of the Franciscans. The *Pala-*

cio de Bendana, also built in the late 15C, has a fine inner courtyard and is Plateresque in style. The *Palacio de los Álava—Esquibel* was built in the 16C. A small cloister, and a portal from the Berruguete school, are both worth seeing. The *Palacio de los Escoriaza—Esquibel,* with a Plateresque portal and an inner courtyard with three galleries and a Renaissance staircase. The *Palacio Episcopal* (bishop's palace) was built in *c.* 1500. It has interesting Renaissance windows and was the headquarters of Joseph Bonaparte during the Peninsular War. The *Paseo de los Arquillos,* with its long 18C arcade, is unique in Spain. *El Portalón,* the medieval house of a merchant's family, was built in the 15&16C and was also used as a rest-house for travellers. It contains a *Bullfighting Museum* and the *Museum of the battle of Vitoria. Palacio de la Diputación:* Built in the mid 19C, it is the seat of the provincial parliament. There is a painting by José de Ribera, dating from 1643 and depicting the Crucifixion, in the parliament chamber.

Vivero
Lugo/Galicia   p.386□C 1

A picturesque town on the N. Atlantic coast of Galicia. Parts of the old town wall still survive. Note in particular the Puerta del Castillo (or Puerta de Carlos V), with its coats-of-arms, projections and turrets. The Romanesque church of *Santa María del Campo,* a national monument, has a beautiful façade. In the church of *San Francisco,* with its fine Gothic apse, is the tomb of Doña Constanza de Castro, the daughter of Pardo de Cela. The Gothic church of the *Convento de Valdeflores* has pointed arch windows in the lower part of its façade. The monastery of *El Colegio de la Natividad,* founded in 1563, was a cultural centre in its day. Among the secular buildings, special mention should be made of the 16C *Customs House (Aduana).* In the outskirts of Vivero: the *Iglesia de San Pedro* and the *Pazo de Grallal* (pazo = ancestral mansion). The picturesque houses in the Malecón district are worth seeing.

Vitoria, new cathedral, apse

Yecla de Yeltes

Salamanca/León   p.386☐D 5

Yecla de Yeltes or Yecla de Vieja, 7 km. S. of Vitigudino, has the remains of an Iberian *castillo*, which was captured as early as the 1C AD by the Romans who colonized the area up to the end of the 5C. Numerous inscriptions have survived. Close by is the *Ermita de Nuestra Señora del Castillo*, a hermitage founded by Ferdinand and Isabella. The parish church of *San Sebastián* is 16C.

Environs: Guadramíro: (about 4 km. W. of Vitigudino) with a 15C *parish church*, and the domed 16C *Ermita del Arbol* which has a massive late-16C statue of San Cristóbal. Also of interest is a *palace* dating from the time of the Ferdinand and Isabella. Following Route 517 for a good 20 km. you come to **Lumbrales** with the Herrera-style parish church, *Santa María del Castillo* (late 16C), and pre-Romanesque defensive walls with three gates. NW of Lumbrales is **Hinojosa de Duero** with an *old parish church* from the 15C and a *new parish church* from the 16C (crucifix, also 16C). About 10 km. S. of Lumbrales is **San Felices de los Gallegos,** which has a 15C *castle* and old *church* (originally Romanesque, simple portal; 16C conversion).

Zafra

Badajoz/Estremadura   p.392☐D 8

This charming little provincial town is also known as *Sevilla la Chica* (Little Seville), owing to its Andalusian character. The two old squares with their delicate arcades and balconies have an old-world character. Zafra—*Segida* of the Iberians, *Julia Restituta* of the Romans and *Zafar* of the Moors—had its town walls, two gates of which survive, built by the Moors.

Alcázar: The fort has high battlemented walls with towers at the corners and at the front. It was extended in 1437 by Lorenzo Suárez de Figueroa and partly modernized in the 16C. The two-storey, white marble patio dates from the same time and is attributed to Juan de Herrera. The *Salón Dorado,* in the main tower, contains paintings and has an artesonado ceiling. Gothic-Mudéjar chapel.

Nuestra Señora de la Candelaria: This collegiate church from the 14–16C is a large single-aisled building with a short transept, stellar vaulting and a Herrera-style portal. Inside there is a retable with ten paintings by Zurbarán.

Convento de Santa Clara: Founded in the 15C and altered in the 17C, apart from the 16C Capilla Mayor. Of interest inside are the 17C high altar and sarcophagi from the 11&17C, in particular that of Lorenzo Suárez de Figueroa, who founded the new alcázar, and his wife.

Hospital de Santiago: This building has an interesting Gothic portal. Inside there is an *Annunciation* in Italian Renaissance style.

Environs: Los Santos de Maimona (*c.* 7 km. E.): the Roman *Segeda-Angurina*, it has remains of a fortress from the time of Trajan; beautiful patio in the Casa de la Encomienda. The church of *Nuestra Señora de los Angeles,* is a Gothic building with a nave, two aisles and Renaissance portal. Inside there is a painting from the school of Murillo. **Medina de las Torres** (9 km. S.) with the ruins of a Moorish castle and 17C mansions. **Fuente de Cantos** (*c.* 25 km. SE): A little town near the Sierra Morena and the birthplace of the painter Francisco de Zurbarán. The parish church of *Nuestra Señora de la Granada* is 16C with a 17C main portal. At the side there is an interesting doorway, whose portico is in the form of a two-storeyed gallery. Inside there is a nave, Capilla Mayor, a gilded and painted baroque high altar and a Renaissance font. The *Convento de Nuestra Señora del Carmen* is a single-aisled building with barrel vaults, lunettes, a dome, baroque altars and a polychrome stone Pietà from the early 19C. The *Ermita de Nuestra Señora de la Hermosa* is 18C. The single-aisled interior has a dome and barrel vaulting. *Capilla Mayor* and *Camarín* are lavishly stuccoed. The baroque high altar has twisted columns; other altars are mostly baroque. An image of the Virgin, *Nuestra Señora la Aparecida,* dates from the late 13/early 14C. Nearby are *Roman ruins.* **Puebla de Sancho Pérez** (10 km. S.): The parish church of *Santa Lu-*

Zafra, Plaza Chica

Zafra, Alcázar courtyard

cía has remains of the original Gothic building. The 18C *Ermita del Belén* is decorated with stucco. A large patio occupies one side of the church. In the *camarín* a polychrome alabaster image from the late 15C is revered. An interesting mid-18C stone 'Way of the Cross' leads to the hermitage. **Segura de León** (*c.* 35 km. S.): This town was subject to the Commandery of Santiago and the Priory of San Marcos de León. The parish church of *Nuestra Señora de la Asunción* is predominantly Gothic but has some baroque and Renaissance features. The portal on the gospel side still has Romanesque features. Inside: nave, two aisles, tombs, holy-water stoups, a Plateresque grille and several baroque altars. The **Ermita del Santo Cristo de la Reja** was the church of a Franciscan monastery, of which part of the cloister survives. In the single-aisled interior the choir is separated off by a grille, over which there is a 15C crucifix. Azulejo-clad altars and tombs are preserved. The *Ayuntamiento*, originally built in the 16C, was rebuilt in the 18C and displays the marble coat-of-arms with the double-headed eagle of Charles V. The ruins of the medieval *castillo* (13C), with an elongated ground plan, are still battlemented.

Zalamea de la Serena
Badajoz / Estremadura   p.392☐E 8

Iglesia Parroquial: The parish church, built in the 13&14C, was rebuilt in the 16C, but still has Gothic parts. Set into the tower are Roman pilasters and columns, which probably came from a pagan temple.

Capilla del Cristo: This early-17C chapel has an interesting door. Inside is the 17C image of Christ, 'Cristo de Zalamea', and in the *sacristía* are beautiful azulejos.

Castillo: The castle, in the middle of the town, dates from the end of the Middle Ages.

Environs: Castuera (*c.* 13 km. NE): The birthplace of Pedro de Valdivia, conqueror of Chile. The *Parroquia de la Magdalena:* An 18C church with an interesting portal with the cross of the Knightly Order of Alcántara. *Ermita de San Benito:* This hermitage dates from the 17C and has baroque retables. *Ermita de San Juan:* A small baroque building from the 16C whose portal has a large keystone. **Puebla de Alcocer** (*c.* 62 km. NE): 15C parish church of *Santiago*, Mudéjar, with a granite Plateresque portal and inscriptions. The interior, with a nave and two aisles, contains Mudéjar azulejos. Remains survive of the *Convento de San Francisco*, built in the 16C and restored in the 17C. The interesting *castillo* belonged to Gutierre de Sotomayor, Grand Master of the Knightly Order of Alcántara. Irregular ground plan, walls from various periods. **Benquerencia de la Serena** (*c.* 10 km. NE): The *castillo*, once an Arab alcazába, served as Commandery for the Order of Alcántara. Preserved in the 16C Gothic *parish church* are some Mudéjar azulejos. **Cabeza del Buey** (*c.* 45 km. NE): The parish church of *Nuestra Señora de la Armentera* is 16C. *Convento de la Purísima Concepción*, founded in the 16C, has an interesting Gothic portal. *Escuela del Cristo de la Misericordia:* Housed in a flagstoned chapel is a baroque image of the 'Merciful Christ'. In the present *Hospital de Santa Elena* one can see the remains of the original foundation walls, which date back to the 15C. The *Ermita de San Mateo*, now dedicated to San Marcos, dates from the 16C. The nearby *Ermita de Nuestra Señora de Belén* used to belong to the Knights Templar. Baroque furnishing. Most interesting of the mansions is the *Casa de la Audiencia*. Numerous Gothic and Renaissance buildings. **Capilla** (*c.* 58 km. NE): The *castillo*, built by the Knights Templar, has an ir-

Zamora, Cathedral 1 N. portal **2** S. portal **3** dome over crossing **4** pulpit **5** pulpit **6** grille **7** grille **8** grille **9** high altar **10** altar with a Christ Crucified from the Berruguete school **11** altar with the 'Nuestra Señora la Calva' **12** altar with early-16C paintings **13** Coro **14** door to sacristy **15** door to cloister **16** Capilla San Juan Evangelista with tomb of Dr.Juan de Grado **17** Capilla de San Bernardo **18** Capilla de San Ildefonso or del Cardenal **19** tower

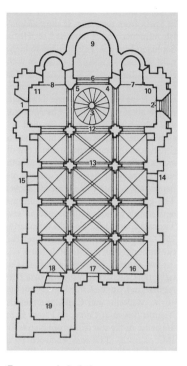

regular, octagonal ground plan and round towers. There are remains of the *Monasterio de la Encarnación,* which also dates back to the Knights Templar.

Zamora
Zamora/León   p.386☐E 4

This provincial capital and diocesan town on the Duero lies on the site of an area of ancient settlements. In Roman times the place was called Ocellum Duri. Under the Visigoths and the Moors it was a constant theatre of war. Ferdinand I handed the fortified city over to his daughter Urraca. Sancho II, Urraca's brother, who wanted to make himself lord of Spain and to wrest Zamora from his sister, died during a lengthy siege of the city. Zamora played an important role in the heroic epic of El Cid. The numerous monuments from the city's heyday in the Middle Ages have earned Zamora the title of the 'Museum of the Romanesque'.

Cathedral: The cathedral, with its nave and two aisles, massive tower and Byzantine-influenced dome over the crossing, lies above the Duero at the furthest end of the old town. Work began under Alfonso VII in 1135 and was completed in 1171. Despite several restorations and extensions it has, on the whole, retained its original character. The tower dates from 1200. The *dome,* along with that of the Torre del Gallo of the Old Cathedral in Salamanca and the dome of Toro cathedral,

Zamora, cathedral, dome

is one of the three most beautiful domes in Spain from that time. It shows Moorish influence and is modelled on Hagia Sophia in Istanbul. The nave has 16 high, narrow windows and 4 small domes with ridges in between. Scale-like stone tiles cover the roof up to the top of the dome, which is crowned by a sphere. The main portals are to the N. and S. The *N. portal* was rebuilt in 1591 after a fire had destroyed the original door. The *S. portal* (Puerta del Obispo) stands under a row of arches at the top of a flight of steps; on both sides it has relief figures, scenes and ornamentation, with a blind arcade above. The groin-vaulted interior has columns with simple capitals and attached pillars. The *high altar* is 18C. Note the three early-16C Gothic *grilles* in front of the apses; the two wrought-iron *pulpits;* and, above all, the two *altars* in the crossing with, on the right, the Crucifixion by the school of Berruguete and, on the left, a late-13C statue of the Madonna and Child, the famous *Nuestra Señora la Calva,* or *Virgen de la Majestad.* At the rear of the coro is an early 16C painting. The *coro,* enclosed by a beautiful 16C wrought-iron grille, is remarkable for its incredibly richly carved *choir stalls* (1502–10) in the style of Rodrigo Alemán. The 13C *Capilla de San Juan Evangelista* contains the late Gothic (early 16C), stone tomb of Dr. Juan de Grado. The *Capilla de San Bernardo* is 16C. The *Capilla de San Ildefonso* or *del Cardenal* (1466) contains various tombs from the 15&16C, as well as an altar by Fernando Gallego (1465). The Gothic *Capilla de San Pablo* has a 17C altar and the *Capilla del Cristo de las Injurias* has a monumental 16C Crucifixion by Gaspar Becerra. The old *cloister* was destroyed by the fire of 1591 and rebuilt in 1621 by Francisco de Mora. Housed in the S. side of the cloister is the *cathedral museum,* which contains the church treasure and above all a series of a fine Flemish tapestries from the 15&16C, as well as a particularly beautiful marble

statue of the Virgin Mary by Bartolomé de Ordóñez (16C).

Iglesia de la Magdalena: On the old Rua de los Notarios stands this single-aisled Romanesque church, built around 1200, with a semicircular apse, robust buttresses, rose-windows and windows with columns. Of particular interest is the beautiful *S. portal* with wide stone archivolts decorated with leaf and flower patterns, masks and heads. Inside is an extremely interesting 12C *tomb* with a recumbent figure; Romanesque angels watch over the dead. The tomb is covered by a stone tabernacle with reliefs of buildings and fabulous beasts and rests upon partly twisted columns, the capitals of which have animals and acanthus motifs.

Zamora has many more beautiful old churches, the most important of which are briefly described below:

Iglesia del Espiritu Santo: This early-13C church has a beautiful rose-window.

San Andrés: This single-aisled church (1550) with a Mudéjar coffered ceiling and beautiful groin vaulting in the apses contains the interesting Renaissance tomb of its founder, Antonio de Sotelo, which was made of alabaster by Pompeo Leoni in 1592.

San Cipriano/San Cebrián: This church was built within the city walls in 1025, during the reign of Alfonso V, and has an unusual grille in the apse window. The church has been altered several times, but has kept the three rectangular apses of the original buildings. Of interest inside are a 15C Madonna and a 16C retable.

San Claudio de Olivares: This church on the bank of the Duero was probably built at the start of the 12C. The single-aisled church with a semicircular apse has

retained interesting archivolts on the N.
portal and, inside, very beautiful early
Romanesque capitals with figures.

San Pedro/San Ildefonso: This 11C
church still contains the semicircular apse
and the portal with archivolts from the old
building. The interior was groin vaulted
in the 15C. The tower was built by Joaquín
Churriguera in 1719. Inside, note the 14
–16C tombs and a 16C triptych.

Santa María de Orta (de Horta): This
beautiful, single-aisled 12C church, with
chapels, tower and semicircular apse, has
two interesting portals. Preserved inside
are the old altar, columns with Romanesque capitals and a 13C San Juan.

Santa María la Nueva: This church
probably originally dates from the 7C. Remaining from the 12C building are the
apse—beautiful from the outside too, with
blind arcades—the S. façade and the S. portal with horseshoe arches. Inside is a
recumbent figure of Christ by Gregorio
Fernández.

Santiago del Burgo: This church with
a nave and two aisles was built at the same
time as the cathedral. Note the Byzantine-
influenced Romanesque *S. portal,* whose
tympanum has a pendent keystone, and the
N. portal with archivolts superimposed like
rows of teeth. Above both portals are rose-
windows. The harmoniously arranged interior is most beautiful.

**Santiago el Viejo/Santiago de los
Caballeros:** According to tradition, El
Cid was knighted in this single-aisled 12C
church which has interesting capitals with
figures.

Iglesia del Santo Sepulcro: This
church, which belonged to the Templars,
originally dates from the late 12C.

Santo Tomé: This single-aisled 12C
church has three square apses.

Other interesting churches: The
church of *San Esteban* of 1186 was rebuilt
in the 18C. The church of *San Frontis* is
originally 13C, while that of *San Isidoro,*

Zamora, Santa María de Orta

Zamora, San Ildefonso

also 12C Romanesque, underwent various alterations in the 16C. The church of *San Juan*, originally with a nave and two aisles (single-aisled since the 16C), was built around 1200. The S. portal is still original with partly twisted columns, acanthus capitals and flowers in the archivolts. The tower dates from the 16C. The 13C church of *San Lazaro* has a Mudjar timber roof. The church of *San Torcuato* is baroque and was built in 1673. Inside are various paintings from the 16&17C. The church of *San Vicente* (12&13C) still has the old tower and an old main portal. The church of *Santa Lucia* is Romanesque.

Convento de las Dueñas: This 16C convent was built on the site of an older building of 1258. Note the church and cloister from the 16C, as well as 13C sculptures,

and paintings from the 15&16C in the monastery.

Colegio de Nuestra Señora Transito: The college is housed in the buildings of the former Hospital de la Encarnación, which was built in 1629-62. The *portal* with Doric columns, and the *patio* are interesting. The chapel has a beautiful altar, supposedly by Gregorio Fernández.

Monasteries: The old monasteries of *San Francisco, San Jerónimo* and *Corpus Christi* are in ruins.

Secular buildings: Zamora's secular buildings of course also testify to its great medieval past, particularly the *city walls,* originally built under Alfonso III in 893. They were rebuilt in the 11&12C and also again later. In the upper part of the city there used to be three *castles;* the ruins of that of Ferdinand I—deep moats, patio and the keep—survive. Also of interest are the *Puerta de Doña Urraca,* the old gate between two massive towers, through which one approached the palace of Doña Urraca; the *Portillo de la Traicíon,* the traitor's gate, where Sancho II is supposed to have been murdered; the *Puerta de Olivares* or *del Obispo de Olivares,* an old round arch near the Bishop's Palace; the *Puerta del Mercadillo* and the *Puerta de Santa María.*

Also worth seeing: The former *Ayuntamiento* (1622), the *Casa del Cid* by the Puerta de Olivares, the 16C *Casa de los Momos* with a beautiful façade, the *Casa del Conde de Alba y Aliste* from around 1600 with four towers and inner court (now a Parador) and the *Hospital del Sotelo* with a Renaissance façade (1526). Two old *bridges* cross the Duero, the Puente Viejo (Old Bridge) from the 11 or 12C and the Puente Nuevo from the 13C, which was rebuilt in the 16&17C.

Museums: *Museo Provincial de Bellas*

Artes: The regional museum, housed in the 17C church of las Marinas, which displays the Roman, Visigoth and medieval treasures of the city and the *Museum of the Holy Week* (Museo de la Semana Santa), which has a collection of pasos (pictures of saints, which are carried in processions). The *processions* of Zamora are famous. Hooded individuals carry figures of saints, such as the Cristo Yacente, through the streets, often accompanied by drumming. These processions take place principally during Holy Week.

Environs: La Hiniesta: Some 7 km. NW of Zamora is La Hiniesta with a superb *parish church* from the first half of the 14C. The *Capilla Mayor* is from an even earlier building, which Sancho IV, the Brave, had built in commemoration of the vision of the Virgin Mary in a broom bush (hiniesta). The most interesting feature of the present church is the *S. portal,* with a Gothic vault and four pointed archivolts decorated with figures and plants, a broad door and tympanum. The latter has a Christ Pantocrator, St.John, the Virgin and, below, an Adoration of the Magi. Left and right of the portal are rows of Gothic blind arcades, above which, standing, kneeling or enthroned, are some most expressive, animated figures in tabernacles. Inside the church there are, among other things, a large painting of John the Baptist by Antonio de Villamon (1706) and Gothic sculptures—a Madonna and Child and an Annunciation. **San Pedro de la Nave:** 20 km. NW of Zamora in the village of El Campillo stands this ancient Visigoth church, built in 691. The church originally stood in the Esla valley but its site was flooded to form a reservoir and the church was moved to a raised, rocky platform in 1934. The church, with a simple exterior, a nave, two aisles and a rectangular apse, is subdivided inside by columns and arches and shows Byzantine influence, particularly in the very well-preserved

Zamora, Iglesia de la Magdalena

partly relief friezes, bases and *capitals.* Especially worthy of attention is a capital at the NW corner of the crossing, which depicts Daniel in the Lions' Den, and one at the SW corner, depicting the Sacrifice of Isaac. The triple windows on the N. and S. wall of the sanctuary and the Moorish arch in the apse are harmoniously arranged. **Arcenillas:** SE of Zamora is Arcenillas. Of the Gothic church there remains just a window and an arch. Inside, note the 15 fine *panel paintings* by Fernando Gallego, which originally came from Zamora cathedral. These pictures with scenes from the Life of Christ were painted by Gallego and his pupils in 1490 – 5. **Fermoselle:** 61 km. SW of Zamora, via Bermillo, is Fermoselle with a *parish church* from around 1200, which was converted in the 16C with beautiful

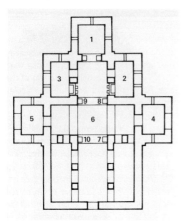

San Pedro de la Nave: The groundplan is based on the form of a Latin cross with chapels extending to the E. of the transept and chapels attached to both the transept's ends. The sanctuary can only be reached through doors and windows in the aisles. **1** Sanctuary with Moorish arches in the choir **2** and **3** chapels **4** and **5** chapels extending from the transept **6** crossing **7** column to the SW (capital depicting Abraham's sacrifice) **8** column to the SE (capital with bird-motifs) **9** column to the NE (capital with bird-motifs) **10** column to the NW (capital with Daniel in the Lions' Den)

groin vaults and a tower. Its museum contains interesting sculptures from the 14–16C. The *Convento de San Francisco* was founded in 1730. Its 12C church, extensively restored in the 18C, contains 'El Crucificado de Santa Colomba' from the 13C. The *Ermita de la Soledad* is originally 13C. The *Ermita del Santo Cristo del Pino* has an interesting little window with two arches from an earlier Mozarabic or Visigoth building. The *castillo* is an old fortress, which belonged to Bishop Don Antonio Acuña.

Zaragoza/Saragossa

Zaragoza/Aragon   p.388☐K 4

The old royal residence of Aragon lies in the fertile plain of the Ebro valley. The city is the capital of Aragon, a spiritual centre with one of Spain's best-known universities and the seat of an archbishop. In Iberian times it was called *Salduba*. Roman soldiers settled here around 23 BC and Au-

'View over Zaragoza', painting by Velázquez

gustus had a military camp built here and called it *Caesar-Augusta*. Around AD 40 the Apostle James the Great arrived in the city and successfully converted it to Christianity. This had manifold consequences, particularly in the 4C, when St.Engracia and her companions were martyred under Diocletian. The city was captured in 452 by the Suevi, who were followed by the Visigoths in 476. In 537 the city successfully withstood a siege by the Franks under Childebert. Even Charlemagne had to withdraw empty-handed. The Moors, however, had already taken over the city by 716, under Musa ibn Nusair. From then on it was known as *Medinat Saracusta* and was subject to the Caliph of Cordoba. During Moorish rule many splendid buildings were built and made their mark on the city. In the course of the Reconquista, Alfonso I of Aragon managed to drive the Moors from the city in 1118. Now Christian, it became capital of the important medieval kingdom of Aragon. The city remained the royal residence until Ferdinand II, the Catholic, combined his kingdom with Castile, through his marriage to Isabella of Castile. During the Christian epoch Saragossa enjoyed the heyday of Romanesque and Mudéjar styles, to which many monuments testify. During various wars of the 14,17&19C, such as the War of the Spanish Succession and the Peninsular War, the inhabitants of Saragossa distinguished themselves by their heroism. When the city was besieged by the French in 1808 and 1809, the inhabitants offered such heroic resistance that, following their defeat, the French granted them an honourable surrender. The besiegers admitted that they had never encountered such resistance. In the Carlist Wars too the inhabitants of Saragossa distinguished themselves gloriously, since which time the city has had the honorary title *siempre heroica* (ever heroic).

Cathedral of Nuestra Señora del Pilar (Plaza Nuestra Señora del Pilar): A striking feature of this church are its numerous domes and four tall corner towers. The domes are covered with polychrome cer-

Zaragoza, La Seo, Mudéjar ceiling

Zaragoza, La Aljafería, portal

amic tiles (azulejos) and are dominated by the central dome. The cathedral was built on the site at which the Virgin Mary appeared to James the Apostle in AD 40. To commemorate this miracle a simple chapel was built, a marble column marking the spot of the vision. A Romanesque church was later built, the predecessor of the present cathedral, of which there remains a tympanum in the cathedral façade. Nuestra Señora del Pilar (pilar = column), in its present form, was begun in 1515 at the instance of Archbishop Hernando de Aragón as a single-aisled Gothic church. The work was continued in baroque style in 1677 by Francisco de Herrera the younger, son of the builder of the Escorial in Madrid. Large parts of the cathedral were built in classical style by Ventura Rodríguez in 1753. Today the cathedral has

a nave and two aisles and a rectangular ground plan. At the corners stand the four towers. There are numerous side chapels between the buttresses. The paintings on each of the cathedral's vaults are interesting works. That of the *Santa Capilla* was painted by Antonio González Velázquez with scenes of the apparition of the Virgin. Francisco Bayeu was commissioned with the decoration of the chapel's four vaults. The church's main dome was painted in the 19C to designs by Bernardino Montañés. The decoration of the choir vault was entrusted to Goya in 1772. He created a superb allegorical fresco. Entering the cathedral from the plaza, one first comes to the Santa Capilla. This was altered in baroque style by Ventura Rodríguez and is richly adorned with marble and silver. In the centre of the chapel, allegedly on the

Zaragoza, Nuestra Señora del Pilar, fresco by Goya

spot where St.James set up his statue of the Virgin, stands the Gothic alabaster statue of the Virgen del Pilar. This is probably 14C and by a French master. The statue stands on a silver-clad marble column and is dressed every day in a different splendid coat. The miraculous image is framed by the right altar. Above the central altar is an 18C relief by Carlos Salas, showing the Assumption of the Virgin. The left altar has a work by Ramírez, which depicts St.James with his disciples. In the W. part of the cathedral stands the alabaster *high altar* (1509), in which Gothic and Renaissance elements are combined. It is by Damián Forment. The choir ends in a beautiful grille made by Juan Celma in 1574. The choir stalls (1544–6) are of interest, consisting of 150 seats arranged in three rows. They are the work of Nicolás Lobato, Es-

teban de Obray and Juan de Moreto. The *Capilla de San Lorenzo* contains a St. Lawrence by Jusepe Ribera and a bronze and marble altarpiece by Ventura Rodríguez. Other interesting chapels are the *Capilla de la Virgen del Rosario* with a Gothic altarpiece and works by Alejo Fernández, the *Capilla de Santa Ana* with a mausoleum, adorned with statues by Ponziano Ponzano and the *Capilla de San Juan Bautista*, which has a retable and painting by Mariano Salvador de Maella. Numerous votive gifts to the miraculous image are displayed in the *Sacristía de la Virgen*. Amongst these are valuable crowns and items of clothing, as well as busts of saints. The *Sacristía Mayor* contains a Flemish tapestry, silver statues and paintings.

Cathedral of La Seo or **San Salvador**

Zaragoza, Nuestra Señora del Pilar

(Plaza de la Seo): The titular church of the archbishop, it took 400 years to build. Originally the site was occupied by an early Christian church, which was converted into a mosque under the Moors. Construction of the Gothic cathedral was begun at the start of the 14C and completed at the start of the 15C. Further additions and alterations were made subsequently. During the first phase of construction the nave, two aisles and the coro were built. At the end of the 15C the cathedral acquired two more aisles and in the 16C the cathedral was lengthened. It now has a nave and four aisles, separated by pillars, three apses and and numerous side chapels. The *main façade* was built in classical style at the end of the 17C by Julián Yarza, a pupil of Ventura Rodríguez. The octagonal tower goes back to a design by the Italian Giovanni

Battista Contini. It was built in baroque style in the 17C. The façade opposite the Archbishop's Palace was built of brick in Mudéjar style and is decorated with azulejos. The octagonal Mudéjar dome was completed in 1412 and is the work of Juan de Barbastro and Domingo Serrano. The dome was altered in Plateresque style by Enríquez Egas in 1520. The groin vault of the church is matched by the pattern of the yellow, black and white marble pavement. The *trascoro* is one of the most beautiful Renaissance works in Spain and was begun by Arnao de Bruselas. In the middle is the beautiful *Capilla del Santo Cristo,* a large baroque baldacchino with four twisted black marble columns, which was designed by Juan Zabalo and built by Gregorio Mesa. The Gothic figure of Christ in the gilt dome of the baldacchino

Zaragoza, La Seo, dome

Zaragoza, La Seo

dates from the 15C, while those of the Virgin and of St.John are 16C. The *coro*, in the middle of the nave, is enclosed by a beautiful grille, and has elegant choir stalls dating from the mid 15C. The lovely lectern was a gift from the Antipope Benedict XIII. The *Capilla Mayor* contains a lovely alabaster altar, begun by Pere Johan and completed by Hans de Suabia. The altarpiece is decorated with scenes from the Life of Christ. On both sides of the chapel are tombs of nobles. On the gospel side the sarcophagus of Archbishop Don Juan de Aragón is of interest, dating from the late 15C. The *Capilla de San Pedro y San Pablo* is baroque and contains 16C sculptures on the baroque altar. In the *Capilla de la Virgen Blanca* there is a Plateresque portal and a 15C sculpture of the Virgin. This chapel is in the old Romanesque apse of the ca-

thedral. The sarcophagus of Archbishop Lope Fernández de Luna, made by Pedro Moragues in 1382, is in the *Capilla de San Martín*, or *Parroquieta*. Here there are remnants of the walls of the old mosque and a splendid Mudéjar dome. The chapels on the E. side of the church also have interesting works of art. The 16C *Capilla de Santa Elena* has a stuccoed dome. The *Capilla de San Miguel* contains a beautiful altarpiece by Juan de Ancheta (early 16C) and a pretty bronze grille. The altarpiece (1520) in the *Capilla de San Agustín* is by Gil Morlanes and Gabriel Yoli. The chapel of San Pedro de Arbués was dedicated to the inquisitor of the same name, who was murdered in the cathedral transept. His sarcophagus, placed in this chapel, is by Juan de Salazar. The chapel has a lovely vault. The S. side of the cathedral contains the

Capilla de la Virgen de las Nieves with a retable, adorned with 16C paintings, and a marble sculpture by Ramírez, representing the Virgin Mary. A pretty baroque portal of the 18C leads into the *Capilla de San Valero*, vaulted by a baroque dome. Also of interest is the *Capilla de San Bernardo*. The altarpiece is adorned with a marble bas-relief by Pedro Moreto from the 16C, depicting the appearance of the Virgin to St.Bernard. To the right and left of the altar are the Plateresque sarcophagi of Archbishop Don Ernando de Aragón and his mother. The *sacristía* contains interesting works of art, including a collection of busts, most notable of which is one of San Valero, a gift from the Antipope Benedict XIII. There is also a silver processional tabernacle, which was made in the workshop of the French master Pedro de la Maisson in 1537. In addition, the collection has beautiful chalices and valuable gold and silver items from the 15–18C. The *Museo Diocesano* is housed in the former chapterhouse and has a beautiful collection of Flemish and French tapestries of the 14–16C.

Santa María Magdalena (Plaza de la Magdalena): This parish church, originally built in Mudéjar style in the 14C, was altered in baroque style in the first half of the 18C. The Mudéjar tower and apse were preserved. The beautiful *baroque portal* dates from 1730. The main chapel contains a classical altarpiece by Ramírez. The *sacristía* houses a 16C figure of Christ by Juan de Salazar.

San Miguel de los Navarros (Plaza San Miguel): This Mudéjar church dates from the 14C and was rebuilt by Gil Morlanes in 1520. The massive tower, originally built in Mudéjar style, was altered in the 16C. The *main portal* is baroque. It bears a sculpture of the Archangel Michael by Gregorio Mesa. The *high altar* (1519) is by Damián Forment. On the altarpiece are beautiful sculptures with scenes from the Passion of Christ and a figure of St. Michael by Gabriel Yoli. The beautiful baroque choir stalls are of interest. The church contains the tomb of the painter Jusepe Martínez. Two works by the artist, depicting St.Philip Neri and St.Jerome, hang in the *Capilla de la Virgen del Pilar*. A teacher of Goya, José Luzán, frescoed the walls of the *Capilla de Nuestra Señora la Vieja*.

San Gil: This parish church was built in Mudéjar style in the 14C and rebuilt at the start of the 18C. The Mudéjar bell tower, with intricate arches, remains. The walls of the *sacristía* were frescoed by Bayeu. A bust of St. Andrew, decorated with engraved silver is also kept here.

Santa Cruz: This baroque church was built in 1780. Its main architects were pupils of Ventura Rodríguez. The decoration of the church with *wall paintings*, particularly the apse with a painting of the battle of Navas de Tolosa, was carried out by the brothers Francisco and Manuel Bayeu.

San Felipe y Santiago: This parish church was built in 1691. It consists of a nave and side chapels under the buttresses. The splendid portal with twisted black marble columns is adorned with sculptures. Inside is a 16C *Ecce Homo* and a Renaissance Madonna. The altar table of the *Capilla del Carmen* was painted by Francisco Bayeu.

San Pablo Apóstol (Calle San Pablo): This Gothic parish church was built in the 13C and originally had a nave with side chapels between the buttresses. The church underwent numerous alterations up into the 18C. The tall, octagonal Mudéjar tower was adorned with green and

Zaragoza, La Seo, San Valero ▷

Zaragoza, Santa María Magdalena

church dates from the second half of the 17C and was built by Domingo Zapata. The simple façade is flanked by two towers. The church has a nave and side chapels. The crossing is crowned by a dome. The side chapels are also domed and the vaults are embellished with decoration recalling the Mudéjar style. The altarpiece in the transept contains a 15C Gothic figure of the Virgen del Pilar. The baroque sarcophagus of Cardinal Xavierre is also housed here. The sculptures on the classical *high altar* are the work of Ignacio Ferrant.

Santa Engracia (Plaza de Santa Engracia): This old monastery church was totally destroyed by the French in 1808. It was rebuilt at the end of the 19C. The tower displays Mudéjar elements, while of the original church there remains just the Plateresque alabaster *portal*. This is by Gil Morlanes and is decorated with sculptures of Ferdinand and Isabella. The church's patron saint, who was martyred during the persecution of the Christians under Diocletian, is buried in the crypt. Two beautiful early Christian sarcophagi were discovered here. They probably date from the 4C and are decorated with scenes from the Old and New Testaments.

San Juan de los Panetes (Paseo de Echegaray): San Juan was built on the foundations of an early Romanesque church. It has a nave and two aisles with barrel vaulting. The striking octagonal tower, a baroque work with Mudéjar features, is crooked. The portal is decorated in Churrigueresque style.

Nuestra Señora del Portillo: The present church is the result of the alteration of a 16C church. The church was renovated in baroque style in the 18C and restored in the 19C. It has a nave and two aisles with a dome over the transept and barrel vaulting. The high altar was taken from the Convento de Santo Domingo.

white glazed bricks. Today San Pablo has a nave and two aisles divided by pillars. Of interest are the two *portals* on the N. and S. façades. One has a large arch and niches separated by Corinthian columns. The second portal is adorned with a beautiful tympanum. The nave contains the choir, dating from 1572, with choir stalls and organ. The gilded wooden altarpiece (1529) of the *high altar* is by Damián Forment and his pupils. The *Capilla de la Virgen del Rosario* is in the left aisle and contains the 17C sarcophagus of the Bishop of Huesca, Diego de Monreal. The altar paintings date from the 15&16C. The rich church treasure is displayed in the sacristy and includes a collection of Flemish tapestries, woven to designs by Raphael.

San Ildefonso (Plaza de Salamero): This

Zaragoza, La Seo, tomb of Archbishop Lope Fernández de Luna, detail

San Fernando: This round building with a large dome was built in classical style. The façade is flanked by two towers and has Corinthian columns.

San Juan y San Pedro: This single-aisled brick building has a square tower and a baroque portal. The side chapels were added in the 16&17C. The church contains a 16C Plateresque altar by Gil Morlanes, sculptures by Gabriel Yoli and a 15C Christ.

Real Seminario de San Carlos Borromeo: The Jesuit seminary was built over the remains of a synagogue in 1570. The church of San Carlos is single-aisled with side chapels. At the start of the 18C it acquired over-elaborate baroque decoration and several altars are baroque. Note the *sacristía*, the vault of which is frescoed.

The mid-18C *library* contains a book of the Bishop of Palencia, made in Bruges in the 16C and manuscripts by Petrarch.

Convento del Santo Sepulcro: This monastery was founded in 1300. The oldest part of the building is the church of San Nicolás, which has been rebuilt several times and contains a Churrigueresque chapel.

Convento de las Escolapias or **La Mantería:** This building, belonging to the Order of the Escuelas Pías, was built 1663–6. Façade and portal are baroque. Inside are interesting altars and paintings by Claudio Coello and Sebastián Muñoz.

Convento de Santo Domingo: This building used to be the City Hall. Only the refectory (15C) remains of the original structure.

Convento de Santa Lucía: This 16C building has a Mudéjar façade. The church is single-aisled and has an interesting vault.

Convento de Santa Inés: This classical building was built in the 19C on the remains of the old monastery, which was founded in 1295.

Convento de Franciscanas de Altabás: This convent was founded in 1527. Its old church was destroyed during the wars with the French and the present building dates from 1833.

La Aljafería (Avenida de Madrid): This square building was built as a pleasure palace for the Moorish kings in 864, under Aben-Alfage. The palace reached its maximum size in 1030–81. Following the expulsion of the Moors from the city, the palace was taken over by the Benedictines who made it into a monastery. In the 14&15C it was the residence of the kings of Aragon and later served as the court of the Inquisition. It was partly destroyed during the siege of the city by the French in 1809. Inside the palace there are numerous courts and living quarters. A vault next to the entrance leads to a small 11C *mosque.* This is in good repair, has a dome and is decorated with beautiful stucco and ornament. St.Elizabeth, later Queen of Portugal, was born in the *Sala de Santa Isabel,* which has a richly decorated ceiling. The gold used here is supposed to have been brought back by Christopher Colombus from his first voyage. In the N. part of the palace is the prison cell made famous in Verdi's opera 'Il Trovatore'.

Muralla Romana: In the Convento del Sepulcro and next to the church of San Juan de los Panetes there are remains of the old Roman walls from the 2C.

La Zuda (Plaza de César Augusto): This Mudéjar brick tower is a relic of the former Moorish palace, which the Arab Governor had built in 918.

La Audiencia (Coso): The former palace of the Condes de Luna was built in 1551 –4. The façade is flanked by two towers with blind arcades. There are two atlantes on either side of the portal, which support the door arch. The upper part is adorned with a bas-relief depicting the arrival of the Antipope Benedict XIII in Rome—Benedict XIII was a member of the Luna family. Inside the palace is an *inner court* with blue and green azulejos. The rooms are decorated with lovely artesonado ceilings. A beautiful polychrome wooden Christ is housed in the palace chapel. The palace is now used as a Court of Justice.

La Lonja (Calle Fernando el Católico): The exchange was installed in this Renaissance building, built 1541–51 by the architects, Gil Morlanes and Juan de Sariñena. The inside of the exchange consists of a large room, subdivided by Ionic columns, which support a beautiful vault.

Palacio de los Condes de Argillo: This palace is a typical example of 17C Aragonese architecture. IT has blind arcades and a roof projecting well beyond the building, the eaves of which are decorated with plant motifs. The inner courtyard is two-storeyed and the beautiful staircase is crowned by a dome.

Palacio Arzobispal: The Archbishop's Palace is right next to the cathedral of La Seo. This classical building (1787) has two inner courtyards, in which a few capitals of late-12C columns are preserved. These come from the destroyed church of Santiago. Several beautiful paintings are dis-

Zaragoza, La Aljafería ▷

played in the palace, including a work by Goya and Gothic panel paintings.

Palacio de la Real Maestranza: This palace dates from the first half of the 16C. The façade has a typical Aragonese roof and gallery. Inside is a Plateresque courtyard and beautiful wood panelling on the stairs and in various of the rooms.

Museo Provincial de Bellas Artes (Plaza José Antonio): The provincial museum is housed in a building which recalls the style of Renaissance Aragon. The archaeological collection occupies several rooms. Apart from finds from the Bronze and Iron Age, it includes Iberian ceramic vessels, Roman mosaics and sculptures, as well as remains from the time of the Moors. The sculpture collection includes Romanesque and Gothic works, such as the *Entombment of Christ* by Damián Forment, the sarcophagus of Isabel de Castro from the Rueda convent and other works by Pere Johan, Alonso Berruguete and Gil Morlanes. The picture gallery includes 15C altar paintings from the church of Santa Cruz de Blesa, as well as paintings by Francisco Bayeu, Fray Manuel Bayeu, Ramón Bayeu, Beruete, Martín Bernat, Claudio Coello, Corrado Giaquinto, Dióscoro Puebla, Goya, Carlos Haës, Eugenio Hermoso, Jaime Huguet, Isenbrandt, Lucas Jordán, Vicente López, Mengs, Rolan de Mois, Jusepe Martínez, Meléndez, Moreno Carbonero and Ribera.

Also worth seeing: *Palacio de Azara:* A typical Aragonese building with a Renaissance inner courtyard. *Palacio del Duque de Villahermosa:* Renaissance, with beautiful portal and inner court. *Palacio del Conde de Fuenclara:* Beautiful inner court and rooms with artesonado ceilings. *Palacio de Pardo:* 16C Plateresque inner court. *Baños Árabes:* Ruins of Jewish baths (13C) in the Calle Coso.

Environs: Monasterio de Cogullada: This monastery lies 3 km. outside Zaragoza. It was founded by St.Braulio in 1637. Of the old buildings only the church survives.

Zarauz
Guipúzcoa/Basque Provinces   p.388☐H 1

This town of 10,800 inhabitants lies at the foot of Monte Santa Bárbara and is a popular seaside resort. For many years it was the rendezvous of the Spanish upper classes. In the 16C the town was particularly famous for its shipyard. One of the first ships to circumnavigate the world, Juan Sebastián Cano's *Victoria*, was built here. Cano, who was part of Magellan's expedition, was the first to achieve this feat 1519–22.

Santa María (Plazuela de la Marquesa de Narros): This church was built in Gothic style and restored in the late 18C. The beautiful baroque altar is of interest. The church's bell tower (14C) is fortified.

Palacio de Narros: The palace of the Marquis of Narros dates from the 15C and dominates the beach. It was here that Isabella II learned of her deposition.

Ayuntamiento: The Town Hall (late 18C) has a sober façade with four Ionic columns.

Torre Lucea: This is one of the most important towers in the Basque Provinces and an interesting Gothic building. It probably dates from the early 15C.

Zumaya
Guipúzcoa/Basque Provinces   p.388☐H 1

San Pedro: Built in Gothic style, the church has an interesting triptych with

Renaissance sculptures, completed in the 16C by Juan de Ancheta and Blas de Arbizu. The work is the only completely intact altarpiece by the sculptor Ancheta in the province of Guipúzcoa. Preserved in the church is an interesting votive picture, painted in 1475. It depicts the battle of Gibraltar between the squadrons of Portugal and Castile.

Villa Zuloaga: The painter Ignacio Zuloaga established a museum in his beachside house. It contains, apart from his own works, paintings by El Greco and Zurbarán and the portrait of General Pala-
fox by Goya, as well as interesting ceramics.

Also worth seeing: The old mansions *Casa de Olazábal* and *Casa de Uriarte*, as well as the towers *Torre de Arriba* and *Torre de Abajo*. Pilgrimage chapels of *San Telmo* and *Nuestra Señora de Arritokieta*.

Environs: Iciar (10 km. towards Deva): Famous 12C pilgrimage church of *Santuario de Nuestra Señora de Itziar*. The Plateresque altar may be by Andrés de Araoz. The statue of the Madonna of Seafarers is 12C.

Index of towns and places of interest mentioned in the Environs sections
The → symbol indicates the entry under which they can be found.

Ullastret → Torroella de Montgrí
Uña (Unya) → Salardú
Urueña (Yrueña) → Ciudad Rodrigo
Urueña → La Espina

Valbuena de Duero → Peñafiel
Valdedios → Villaviciosa
Valdemoro → Aranjuez
Valdenebro de los Valles → Medina de Rioseco
Valdenoceda → Medina de Pomar
Valdepeñas → Villanueva de los Infantes
Valdespina → Palencia
Valencia de Alcántara → Alburquerque
Valería → Alarcón
Valgañon → Ezcaray
Valldemosa → Mallorca
Vall de Uxó → Castellón de la Plana
Vall de Vianya → Olot
Valle de los Caídos → San Lorenzo de El Escorial
Vallejo de Mena → Espinosa de los Monteros
Vallfogona → Ripoll
Valmaseda → Bilbao
Valoria de Alcor → Ampudia
Valoria la Buena → Fuensaldaña
Valvanera → San Millán de la Cogolla
Valverde → Hierro
Vega de Santa María → Ávila
Veguellina → Astorga
Vejer de la Frontera → Medina Sidonia
Vélez Blanco → Vera
Vélez Málaga → Málaga
Vélez Rubio → Vera
Verdú → Tárrega
Vergés → Torroella de Montgrí
Verín → Monterrey
Vilanova → Celanova dos Infantes

Vilasantar → Mellid
Vileña → Briviesca
Villabrágima → Medina de Rioseco
Villacadima → Atienza
Villacarillo → Úbeda
Villacarriedo → Puente Viesgo
Villada → Paredes de Nava
Villa del Prado → San Martín de Valdeiglesias
Villadiego → Sasamón
Villaescusa de Haro → Belmonte
Villa Fortunati → Fraga
Villafranca de los Barros → Almendralejo
Villafrechós → Medina de Rioseco
Villafuerte → Valladolid
Villagarcía de Arosa → Cambados
Villagarcía de Campos → Medina de Rioseco
Villahoz → Lerma
Villalba del Alcor → Niebla
Villalba de los Alcores → Fuensaldaña
Villalcázar de Sirga → Frómista
Villalpando → Benavente
Villamanrique de la Condesa → Sevilla
Villamartín de Campos → Torremormojón
Villamayor de Campos → Benavente
Villamediana → Palencia
Villamuriel de Cerrato → Baños de Cerrato
Villanueva de Cañedo → Salamanca
Villanueva de la Serena → Medellín
Villanueva de Lorenzana → Mondoñedo
Villanueva del Río → Carmona
Villanueva de Pisuerga → Cervera de Pisuerga
Villar de Donas → Mellid
Villardefrades → Mota del Marqués

Villar de los Barrios → Ponferrada
Villareal de los Infantes → Castellón de la Plana
Villarente → Mansilla de las Mulas
Villarmentero de Esgueva → Valladolid
Villarmún → Gradefes
Villasandino → Castrojeriz
Villasayas → Monteagudo de las Vicarías
Villasobroso → Vigo
Villatoro → Ávila
Villavega → Aguilar de Campóo
Villavelayo → Canales de la Sierra
Villavellid → Mota del Marqués
Villaverde de Medina → Medina del Campo
Villaverde de Sandoval → Valencia de Don Juan
Villaviciosa de Odón → Navalcarnero
Vimianzo → Mugía
Vinaroz → Peñíscola
Virgen de la Montaña → Cáceres
Viso del Marqués → Santa Cruz de Mudela
Viznar → Granada

Wamba (Bamba) → Torrelobatón

Yanguas → Oncala
Yecla → Jumilla
Yela → Cifuentes
Yepes → Ocaña
Yermo → Altamira
Yrueña → Urueña

Zahara de la Sierra → Ronda
Zorita de los Canes → Pastrana
Zorita del Páramo → Herrera de Pisuerga
Zorraquín → Ezcaray

Glossary of the most important Spanish terms

Ajimez: Moorish window, divided by a column.
Alcázaba: Moorish citadel.
Alcázar: Moorish fortified castle/palace.
Alfiz: Moulding, especially around a horseshoe arch.
Artesonado: Coffered wooden ceiling.
Ayuntamiento: Town Hall.
Azulejos: Glazed tiles (originally blue).
Camarín: Shrine with an image.
Capilla Mayor: Main chapel with high altar.
Casa Consistorial: Town Hall.
Castillo: Castle, stronghold.
Churrigueresque: Extremely ornate Spanish baroque style named after José Churriguera (1665-1725).
Cimborio: Lantern light over crossing.
Claustro: Cloister.
Convento: Monastery, convent.
Coro: Choir, usually in the middle of the nave and surrounded by screens or grilles.
Crucero: Crossing of the church; transept.
Custodia: Monstrance.
Ermita: Hermitage.
Herrera style: Spanish Renaissance style characterized by geometrical severity; named after Juan de Herrera (c. 1530-97).
Hórreo: Raised granary.
Iglesia: Church.
Lonja: Market, exchange.
Mezquita: Mosque.
Mihrab: Prayer niche in a mosque facing towards Mecca.
Morisca: Baptized Moor.
Mozarabic style: Spanish style evolved by Christians under the Arabs in Spain, characterized by Moorish and Romanesque elements.
Mudéjar style: A composite style containing Moorish and Gothic elements; named after the Mudéjar Moors, who remained in Spain after the Christian reconquest.
Parroquia: Parish church.
Paso: Holy picture, figure etc. carried in processions.
Patio: Inner courtyard.
Plateresque: Lavishly ornate Spanish architectural style practised during the 16C. Characterized by intricate decorative motifs, like those used by silversmiths.
Reconquista: Christian reconquest of Moorish-occupied Spain.
Reja: Iron grille, usually in front of a chapel.
Retable: Large altarpiece covering the back wall behind the altar; it may be painted, carved, or both.
Seo: Cathedral.
Sillería: Choir stalls.
Talayot: Megalithic monument (stone tower).
Taula: Megalithic construction (T-shaped stone table).
Trascoro: Outer wall of choir.

Index of major artists whose works are mentioned in this guide